Keep this book. You will need it and use it throughout your career.

QUALITY
SANITATION
MANAGEMENT

Educational Institute Courses

Introductory

INTRODUCTION TO THE HOSPITALITY INDUSTRY
Third Edition
Gerald W. Lattin

AN INTRODUCTION TO HOSPITALITY TODAY
Second Edition
Rocco M. Angelo, Andrew N. Vladimir

TOURISM AND THE HOSPITALITY INDUSTRY
Joseph D. Fridgen

Rooms Division

FRONT OFFICE PROCEDURES
Fourth Edition
Michael L. Kasavana, Richard M. Brooks

HOUSEKEEPING MANAGEMENT
Second Edition
Margaret M. Kappa, Aleta Nitschke, Patricia B. Schappert

Human Resources

HOSPITALITY SUPERVISION
Second Edition
Raphael R. Kavanaugh, Jack D. Ninemeier

HOSPITALITY INDUSTRY TRAINING
Second Edition
Lewis C. Forrest, Jr.

HUMAN RESOURCES MANAGEMENT
Second Edition
Robert H. Woods

Marketing and Sales

MARKETING OF HOSPITALITY SERVICES
William Lazer, Roger Layton

HOSPITALITY SALES AND MARKETING
Second Edition
James R. Abbey

CONVENTION MANAGEMENT AND SERVICE
Leonard H. Hoyle, David C. Dorf, Thomas J. A. Jones

MARKETING IN THE HOSPITALITY INDUSTRY
Third Edition
Ronald A. Nykiel

Accounting

UNDERSTANDING HOSPITALITY ACCOUNTING I
Fourth Edition
Raymond Cote

UNDERSTANDING HOSPITALITY ACCOUNTING II
Third Edition
Raymond Cote

BASIC FINANCIAL ACCOUNTING FOR THE HOSPITALITY INDUSTRY
Raymond S. Schmidgall, James W. Damitio

MANAGERIAL ACCOUNTING FOR THE HOSPITALITY INDUSTRY
Fourth Edition
Raymond S. Schmidgall

Food and Beverage

FOOD AND BEVERAGE MANAGEMENT
Second Edition
Jack D. Ninemeier

QUALITY SANITATION MANAGEMENT
Ronald F. Cichy

FOOD PRODUCTION PRINCIPLES
Jerald W. Chesser

FOOD AND BEVERAGE SERVICE
Anthony M. Rey, Ferdinand Wieland

HOSPITALITY PURCHASING MANAGEMENT
William P. Virts

BAR AND BEVERAGE MANAGEMENT
Lendal H. Kotschevar, Mary L. Tanke

FOOD AND BEVERAGE CONTROLS
Third Edition
Jack D. Ninemeier

General Hospitality Management

HOTEL/MOTEL SECURITY MANAGEMENT
Raymond C. Ellis, Jr., Security Committee of AH&MA

HOSPITALITY LAW
Third Edition
Jack P. Jefferies

RESORT MANAGEMENT
Second Edition
Chuck Y. Gee

INTERNATIONAL HOTEL MANAGEMENT
Chuck Y. Gee

HOSPITALITY INDUSTRY COMPUTER SYSTEMS
Third Edition
Michael L. Kasavana, John J. Cahill

MANAGING FOR QUALITY IN THE HOSPITALITY INDUSTRY
Robert H. Woods, Judy Z. King

CONTEMPORARY CLUB MANAGEMENT
Edited by Joe Perdue for the Club Managers Association of America

Engineering and Facilities Management

FACILITIES MANAGEMENT
David M. Stipanuk, Harold Roffman

HOSPITALITY INDUSTRY ENGINEERING SYSTEMS
Michael H. Redlin, David M. Stipanuk

HOSPITALITY ENERGY AND WATER MANAGEMENT
Robert E. Aulbach

QUALITY SANITATION MANAGEMENT

Ronald F. Cichy, Ph.D., CHA

EDUCATIONAL INSTITUTE
of the American Hotel & Motel Association

Sponsored by

Diversey

Disclaimer

...rate and authoritative information in regard to the subject matter ...at the publisher is not engaged in rendering legal, accounting, or ...professional service. If legal advice or other expert assistance is required, the services of a competent professional person should be sought.

> —*From the Declaration of Principles jointly adopted by the American Bar Association and a Committee of Publishers and Associations.*

The author, Ronald F. Cichy, is solely responsible for the contents of this publication. All views expressed herein are solely those of the author and do not necessarily reflect the views of the Educational Institute of the American Hotel & Motel Association (the Institute) or the American Hotel & Motel Association (AH&MA).

Nothing contained in this publication shall constitute a standard, an endorsement, or a recommendation of the Institute or AH&MA. The Institute and AH&MA disclaim any liability with respect to the use of any information, procedure, or product, or reliance thereon by any member of the hospitality industry.

©Copyright 1994
By the EDUCATIONAL INSTITUTE of the
AMERICAN HOTEL & MOTEL ASSOCIATION
1407 South Harrison Road
P.O. Box 1240
East Lansing, Michigan 48826

The Educational Institute of the American
Hotel & Motel Association is a nonprofit
educational foundation.

Printed in the United States of America
   5 6 7 8 9 10 98 97

Library of Congress Cataloging-in-Publication Data
Cichy, Ronald F.
    Quality sanitation management / Ronald F. Cichy.
      p. cm.
    Includes bibliographical references and index.
    ISBN 0-86612-084-X
    1. Food Service—Sanitation. 2. Food service management—United
States. 3. Restaurants—Sanitation. 4. Risk management. I. Title.
TX911.3.S3C52   1994
647.95'0289—dc20   94-16272
                                                      CIP

Editors: Priscilla J. Wood
         Marj Harless
         Lisa Kloack

A Message From Diversey Corp.
Sponsor of *Quality Sanitation Management*

Donald N. Gray, President
Diversey Corp.

Diversey Corp., a global supplier of cleaning chemicals and systems to the institutional market, is committed to food sanitation and safety. It is our pleasure to sponsor *Quality Sanitation Management*, with its focus on a systems approach—an approach enabling food service owners, managers, and staff members to minimize or eliminate sanitation risks while promoting guest satisfaction. In a world of concern for and litigation involving food safety, *Quality Sanitation Management* is a must. It comprehensively covers the 1993 Food Code and relates it to a food establishment's ten control points or operating activities in which the points and procedures apply.

Quality Sanitation Management was designed by food service professionals who understand sanitation essentials and realize their importance. The knowledge and tools presented have been developed and tested over several years in real operations.

Effective training in food service sanitation enhances the quality and safety of food while providing a more desirable workplace. Diversey stands behind the Educational Institute's *Quality Sanitation Management* program and strongly believes it will be an asset to your operation.

Contents

Congratulations. . .

You have a running start on a fast-track career!

Developed through the input of industry and academic experts, this course gives you the know-how hospitality employers demand. Upon course completion, you will earn the respected American Hotel & Motel Association certificate that ensures instant recognition worldwide. It is your link with the global hospitality industry.

You can use your AH&MA certificate to show that your learning experiences have bridged the gap between industry and academia. You will have proof that you have met industry-driven learning objectives and that you know how to apply your knowledge to actual hospitality work situations.

By earning your course certificate, you also take a step toward completing the highly respected learning programs—Certificates of Specialization, the Hospitality Operations Certificate, and the Hospitality Management Diploma—that raise your professional development to a higher level. Certificates from these programs greatly enhance your credentials, and a permanent record of your course and program completion is maintained by the Educational Institute.

We commend you for taking this important step. Turn to the Educational Institute for additional resources that will help you stay ahead of your competition.

Preface

Quality Sanitation Management presents a systems approach to answering public health concerns, reducing risks, and ensuring satisfaction for guests, staff members, and owners. This systems concept provides a framework for viewing a food establishment as a series of interrelated control points or basic operating activities. The knowledge and tools presented have been developed and tested over several years in real operations. The systems approach to sanitation risk management helps you define and implement quality, cost control, and risk reduction standards in your place of hospitality. As such, the SRM program goes beyond the Hazard Analysis Critical Control Point (HACCP) Program.

It is critical that a food establishment comply with local, state, and federal regulatory agency requirements. The establishment and its systems must minimize or eliminate sanitation risks while at the same time promoting the satisfaction of guests, staff members, and owners. To that end, *Quality Sanitation Management* was developed utilizing the Food and Drug Administration's 1993 Food Code. The Food Code is designed to safeguard public health and provide to consumers food that is safe, unadulterated, and honestly presented. The 1993 Food Code publishes definitions, sets standards for management and personnel, food operations, and equipment and facilities, and provides for food establishment plan review, permit issuance, inspection, staff member restriction, and permit suspension. In all cases, individual food establishments must comply with their local and state regulations, which may differ from federal codes.

After an overview of the sanitation risk management (SRM) program and HACCP, an explanation of regulatory and professional organizations is presented. Included are sanitarian and management responsibilities, along with a system for self-inspection.

Information about food contamination, food spoilage, and food preservation provides the underpinning for the SRM program. A system for handling a suspected food-borne illness outbreak is presented and will help managers be proactive, not reactive.

An in-depth treatment of each of the ten control points and four resources under a manager's control helps the reader see the operation from a big picture perspective. After each control point is subdivided and analyzed, an explanation of how the basic operating activity fits into the overall SRM program is provided. A practical example for implementing the principles of the SRM program is provided at each control point. Additionally, an ongoing case study further reinforces the systems thinking behind the SRM program.

The objectives of the book are (1) to present the opportunities and challenges facing managers and staff members as they strive toward guest, staff member, and owner satisfaction; (2) to help staff members and managers establish a sanitation risk management program utilizing HACCP and systems thinking; and (3) to reduce risks while improving the operation's bottom line. Sanitation risk management must be a strategic partnership among staff members, guests, public health officials, owners, and suppliers. The end result will be a safer and more financially sound food service industry.

The author wishes to acknowledge the contributions of many individuals and organizations in the preparation of this book. Students in Michigan State University's

School of Hotel, Restaurant and Institutional Management provided valuable immediate feedback as they completed the course. Students at other hospitality institutions, both four-year and two-year, as well as hospitality industry executives participating in independent learning, group study, and Educational Institute chapter courses, were honest and forthright with their suggestions for improvement. Instructors of the earlier course from four-year and two-year hospitality institutions, as well as from industry settings, furnished key ideas to enhance this book. It is literally impossible to individually recognize the contributions, and their significance, made by each person.

The author would also like to acknowledge several industry professionals who reviewed the proposed outline and completed manuscript for *Quality Sanitation Management:* Mike Farnsworth, former Chief of the Food Service Sanitation Section of the Michigan Department of Public Health; Tom Gable, Executive Vice President of the National Sanitation Foundation; D. J. Inman, Regional Food Specialist for the Food and Drug Administration; D. L. Lancaster, Manager of Educational Program Services for the National Sanitation Foundation; Herb Rafetto, Executive Assistant Manager and Food and Beverage Director for the Hyatt Regency Hotel-Dearborn; Keith Schaffner, Director of Food and Beverage for the Westin Renaissance Center Hotel-Detroit; B. J. Stone, Regional Director for Bennigan's Restaurants; and Betty Wernette, Sanitation Safety Officer for the Department of Public Safety at Michigan State University. These individuals helped make this book "real."

The author conveys his heartfelt thanks and deep appreciation to Phil Kirkwood, Chief of the Food Service Sanitation Section of the Michigan Department of Public Health. Mr. Kirkwood provided an untiring review of this book from beginning to end. His years of experience and real-world expertise contributed greatly to this book.

The author also wishes to thank the EI editorial and production team for their commitment, tenacity, and fortitude in taking this project from manuscript to completed form.

Quality Sanitation Management is dedicated to Dr. Lewis J. and Mrs. Ruth E. Minor, founders of the L. J. Minor Corporation. Dr. Minor is Professor Emeritus of the School of Hotel, Restaurant and Institutional Management at Michigan State University. He taught the author and thousands of today's hospitality industry and education leaders the value of high standards with his classic statement: "Aim for the eagle, don't shoot for the rat."

Ronald F. Cichy
Okemos, Michigan

About the Author

Ronald F. Cichy is the Director of and a Professor in the School of Hotel, Restaurant and Institutional Management at Michigan State University. Previously, he was the Director of Educational Services for the Educational Institute of the American Hotel & Motel Association. Dr. Cichy has also served on the faculties of the University of Denver and Lansing Community College. He holds a Ph.D. from MSU's Department of Food Science and Human Nutrition, and an MBA and a BA from the University's School of Hotel, Restaurant and Institutional Management.

Dr. Cichy earned the designations of Certified Food and Beverage Executive (CFBE) and Certified Hotel Administrator (CHA) from the Educational Institute in 1983 and the Certified Hospitality Educator (CHE) in 1992. In 1981, the National Institutional Food Distributors Association (NIFDA) named him Outstanding Educator of the Year. His industry experience includes positions in lodging and food service operations as a hotel manager, food and beverage manager, banquet chef, and sales representative.

Dr. Cichy has written more than 100 articles for food service and lodging audiences. He is the author of *The Spirit of Hospitality*, in addition to *Sanitation Management*, and is the co-author, with Dr. Lewis J. Minor, of *Foodservice Systems Management*. He developed the *Nutrition Certification Correspondence Course* on cassette tapes for the American Culinary Federation.

Active professionally, Dr. Cichy is Vice President–Academia of the Educational Institute's Board of Trustees, Chairman of the Institute's Certification Commission, a member of the Board of Directors of the Michigan Travel and Tourism Association, and a member of the Educational Institute's Executive Committee. He has served as a consultant for commercial and non-commercial lodging and food service operations, and has traveled extensively throughout the United States, Australia, Canada, Europe, and Japan to conduct training programs, present seminars, and participate in conferences.

Study Tips for Users of
Educational Institute Courses

Learning is a skill, like many other activities. Although you may be familiar with many of the following study tips, we want to reinforce their usefulness.

Your Attitude Makes a Difference

If you want to learn, you will: it's as simple as that. Your attitude will go a long way in determining whether or not you do well in this course. We want to help you succeed.

Plan and Organize to Learn

• Set up a regular time and place for study. Make sure you won't be disturbed or distracted.

• Decide ahead of time how much you want to accomplish during each study session. Remember to keep your study sessions brief; don't try to do too much at one time.

Read the Course Text to Learn

• *Before* you read each chapter, read the chapter outline and the learning objectives. Notice that each learning objective has page numbers that indicate where you can find the concepts and issues related to the objective. If there is a summary at the end of the chapter, you also want to read it to get a feel for what the chapter is about.

• Then, go back to the beginning of the chapter and *carefully* read, focusing on the material included in the learning objectives and asking yourself such questions as:

  —Do I understand the material?

  —How can I use this information now or in the future?

• Make notes in margins and highlight or underline important sections to help you as you study. Read a section first, then go back over it to mark important points.

• Keep a dictionary handy. If you come across an unfamiliar word that is not included in the textbook glossary, look it up in the dictionary.

• Read as much as you can. The more you read, the better you read.

Testing Your Knowledge

• Test questions developed by the Educational Institute for this course are designed to reliably and validly measure a student's ability to meet a standard of knowledge expressed by the industry-driven learning objectives.

• End-of-the-chapter Review Quizzes help you find out how well you have studied the material. They indicate where additional study may be needed. Review Quizzes are also helpful in studying for other tests.

• Prepare for tests by reviewing:

  —learning objectives

—notes

—outlines

—questions at the end of each assignment

- As you begin to take any test, read the test instructions *carefully* and look over the questions.

We hope your experiences in this course will prompt you to undertake other training and educational activities in a planned, career-long program of professional growth and development.

Chapter Outline

Learning Objectives

1. Define the term *control points,* and identify the ten control points in the food service system. (pp. 2-4)

2. Explain the focus of the sanitation risk management (SRM) program discussed in this chapter. (pp. 4-7)

3. Describe the various food safety ordinances and codes leading to and including the FDA 1993 Food Code. (p. 7)

4. Describe the responsibilities of executive managers, mid-level managers, staff members, and regulatory authorities with respect to a food establishment's SRM program. (p. 8)

5. Identify the benefits of an SRM program. (pp. 8-9)

6. Describe the Hazard Analysis Critical Control Point (HACCP) system and how it relates to the SRM program. (pp. 9-11)

7. Briefly describe the seven HACCP principles, and demonstrate how they are used to establish a HACCP plan. (pp. 11-21)

8. Identify the purposes of food establishment inspections, define the types of inspections, and describe how a HACCP inspection should be conducted. (pp. 21-25)

9. Describe HACCP inspection documentation and reports. (pp. 25-31)

10. Define *imminent health hazard.* (pp. 27-28)

1

The SRM Program and the HACCP System

Serving safe food to the public is a major responsibility of food service owners and staff members. Food establishments that do not have effective sanitation programs run the risk of initiating an outbreak of foodborne illness—one that could have dire consequences for the business as well as its guests, staff members, and owners. Consider the following newspaper and magazine excerpts:

Fatal Salmonella Outbreak Probed

> State officials are interviewing kitchen workers and reviewing health charts at a nursing home in hopes of tracing an outbreak of salmonellosis that killed five residents and sickened 20 others.
>
> *Lansing State Journal*

Feeling Low? Probably Something You Ate

> The average person's probability of getting ill from an improperly run restaurant is far greater than from a leaking underground storage tank.
>
> *The Detroit News*

3rd Salmonella Outbreak Here After Fund-Raiser Chicken Sale

> State Health Department officials said yesterday they have uncovered a third outbreak of salmonellosis involving the sale of fund-raiser chicken from the same barbecue chicken operation. . . . The manager said his business is suffering. "I need a tourniquet to stop the bleeding, man."
>
> *The Honolulu Advertiser*

Botulism Feared in Illness

> Seven people were in [area] hospitals yesterday with suspected botulism poisoning after dining at a posh restaurant featuring French cuisine at the upscale [name] Hotel. . . . The restaurant kitchen has been closed until further notice.
>
> *Winnipeg Free Press*

Typhoid Outbreak Hits 7

> A total of seven people, including two children, have come down with typhoid fever in an outbreak that was related to a [location and name] restaurant. Four of the victims had eaten shrimp salad. . . . Although none of the recent cases have been fatal, four people have been hospitalized.
>
> *Restaurant Business*

1

When the Unthinkable Happens

> Until early 1987, the [name] group in [location] was a thriving company consisting of five casual dining restaurants. . . . Now, there are two. In early February 1987, catastrophe struck at one of the restaurants in the form of a salmonella outbreak. The company is still staggering from the blow and owner [name] is still assessing the damages. . . . Some 200 cases of salmonellosis were reported.
>
> *Restaurant Business*

When Foodborne Illness Strikes!

> A hepatitis epidemic had been linked to the family's restaurant. . . . After discussing the situation, the [name] decided reluctantly to close the restaurant. Newspaper headlines blared, "Deadly Disease Attacks Restaurant Customers," and "[name] to Face Lawsuits." . . . The media and the public seemed to view the prospect of a meal at [name] restaurant as only slightly less risky than a game of Russian roulette.
>
> *Restaurants & Institutions*

Guests and potential guests of the food establishments named in these articles read the reports. How do you think they reacted? What effects do you think these reports had on staff members?

The operation of a food establishment is an inherently risky business. As you read this book, you will learn that sanitation hazards are among the most critical risks food service managers must control. Failing to understand and manage these risks can quickly ruin a business. A comprehensive sanitation risk management (SRM) program is thus essential to the long-term success of a food service operation.

Making Risks Manageable:
The Sanitation Risk Management Program

A food service organization can be thought of as a system of basic operating activities or **control points.** Each control point is a miniature system with its own recognizable structure and functions (see Exhibit 1.1). The overall success of the operation depends upon the success of each of these interrelated activities.

The SRM program described in this book focuses on managing risks at each of the ten control points. This approach systematizes the otherwise overwhelming task of managing the sanitation risks of the entire food establishment. The SRM program involves identifying the risks at each control point and implementing procedures for reducing those risks in the course of daily operations. By thus reducing risks at each control point, managers can successfully reduce the overall risks of operating a food establishment. The end result is satisfaction for guests, staff members, and owners.

The Control Points

Menu planning is the initial control point in the food service system. Because the menu influences the remaining control points, managers must understand all the control points before developing the menu. For example, the menu affects purchasing, receiving, storing, issuing, preparing, cooking, and serving procedures because these procedures vary with the food product in question. The menu also affects and, in some cases,

Exhibit 1.1 Flowchart of Basic Operating Activities or Control Points in a Food and Beverage Operation

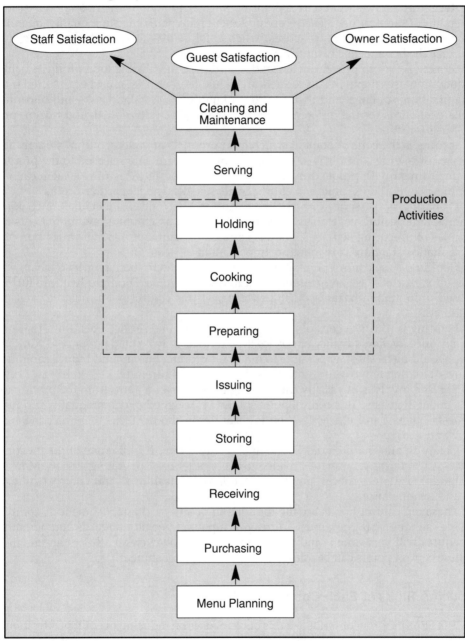

may be affected by the facility's design and layout, equipment requirements, and labor needs. A properly designed SRM program must begin with the menu.

Purchasing is important for maintaining the value and quality of products, minimizing the investment in inventory, and strengthening the operation's competitive position.

Sound purchasing techniques can protect profits, control costs, and reduce risks. A sound purchasing system is essential to the operation's SRM program.

Receiving is a critical control point because at this point the operation assumes ownership of the products. The receiving function involves checking quality, quantity, and price. Proper receiving practices, when combined with skillful purchasing, can maximize the benefits of a carefully planned menu.

Storing serves to prevent deterioration and theft of valuable food products before the operation uses them. Food products are valuable assets that must be protected from contamination, spoilage, and theft in order to minimize costs and risks and maximize profits. Standards for the different types of storage (dry, refrigerated, and frozen) provide this protection.

Issuing is the control point at which food products are released from storage. The objective of issuing controls is to ensure that products are only released to the production department with proper authorization. A poorly designed issuing system can undermine an operation's sanitation efforts, increase risks, and jeopardize profits.

Preparing is the series of activities performed on food products before cooking. Cleaning and peeling vegetables, trimming meat, and assembling raw ingredients are examples of preparing activities. Food is exposed to sanitation hazards during preparing; sanitation standards are therefore important at this control point.

Cooking is the control point at which heat is applied to food in order to change its color, odor, texture, taste, appearance, and nutritional value. Food products are further exposed to sanitation hazards during cooking, so this control point must be carefully monitored.

Holding is a critical control point, particularly in food service operations that prepare products well in advance of service. Menu items may be held hot or cold. Holding times should be as short as possible to maintain product quality and reduce sanitation hazards. Holding temperatures must also be monitored carefully.

Serving involves physically transferring finished menu items from the production department to guests. This control point should be designed to deliver quality products to guests quickly and efficiently. Serving standards should focus on protecting food safety and quality.

Cleaning and maintenance is the final control point; it is also one of the most important. Cleanliness is intimately related to every other basic operating activity. Many of the standards at other control points are standards of cleanliness and relate to sanitization and maintenance.

These ten control points are the foundation of any food establishment. A comprehensive sanitation program must address each point. Specific standards and operating procedures will vary among individual operations. However, an SRM program based on these control points can be adapted to any food establishment.

Reducing Risks at Each Control Point

The SRM program described in this book focuses on reducing overall risks by identifying the risks at each control point in a food service operation. This approach is a modified version of the Hazard Analysis Critical Control Point (HACCP) approach developed jointly by the Pillsbury Company, the United States Natick Laboratories, and the National Aeronautics and Space Administration in 1974. The HACCP approach seeks to eliminate safety risks—primarily microbiological—in food processing by identifying the specific hazards (hazard analysis) at each important point (critical control point) in a food production system. A **hazard** is a biological, chemical, or physical property that may cause an unacceptable consumer health risk. A **critical control point** is a point or procedure in a specific food system where loss of control may result in an unacceptable health risk. A **HACCP plan** is a written document that delineates the formal procedures for following HACCP principles.

The FDA states:

"Hazard" means a biological, chemical, or physical property that may cause an unacceptable consumer health risk.

"Critical control point" means a point or procedure in a specific food system where loss of control may result in an unacceptable health risk.

"HACCP Plan" means a written document that delineates the formal procedures for following the Hazard Analysis Critical Control Point principles developed by The National Advisory Committee on Microbiological Criteria for Foods.

Critical Item.

(a) **"Critical Item"** means a provision of this Code that, if in noncompliance, is more likely than other violations to contribute to food contamination, illness, or environmental degradation.

(b) **"Critical item"** is an item that is denoted in this Code with an asterisk (*).

"Critical limit" means the maximum or minimum value to which a physical, biological, or chemical parameter must be controlled at a critical control point to minimize the risk that the identified food safety hazard may occur.

Source: FDA 1993 *Food Code.*

The Food and Drug Administration's regulatory activities are conducted using the HACCP approach; for example, the FDA first applied HACCP to the low-acid canned food industry. Individual hospitality organizations, including Marriott, Red Lobster, and Dobbs International Services, have also instituted successful HACCP programs. More detail about HACCP is provided later in this chapter.

The SRM program presented here is a HACCP-based approach which focuses on essentials: the ten control points common to most food establishments. Standards and procedures for each control point are presented as they relate to the four resources under a manager's control: inventory, people, equipment, and facilities. A resource evaluation is necessary for each of the ten control points. The result is a systematic approach to managing risks. Exhibit 1.2 presents an SRM diagram for baked chicken. The left side of the diagram indicates the ingredients that are added to the chicken as it passes the control points. The right side of the diagram indicates the appropriate SRM actions that reduce risks at each control point.

Inventory is an essential management resource because it is converted into revenue and, ultimately, into profits. Inventory in a food service operation normally consists of food products, beverages, and non-food items such as linens and cleaning chemicals. Inventory control is a vital link in an operation's cost and quality control systems. Inventory

Exhibit 1.2 SRM Diagram for Baked Chicken

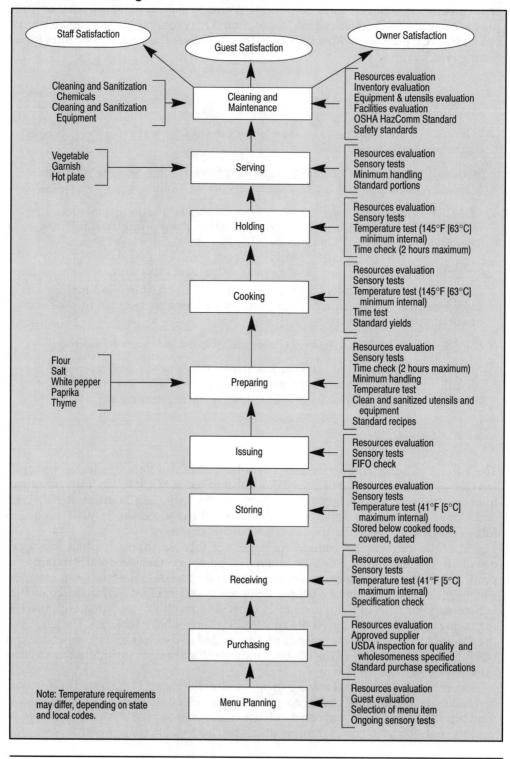

items are assets which must be protected from spoilage, contamination, pilferage, and waste.

Because the hospitality industry is labor-intensive—that is, it relies on large staffs—people are an important resource. It is management's responsibility to train staff members in proper sanitation practices. Failing to control this important resource undermines the SRM program and jeopardizes the establishment's bottom line.

The food establishment's equipment represents a substantial investment. Equipment selection is important to the SRM program, as is the proper cleaning and maintenance of each piece of equipment. A food service operation's facilities also represent a sizable investment, and their design and layout have a great impact on the success of the SRM program.

The FDA's Food Code—the Foundation of the SRM Program

In 1940, the Public Health Service of the United States (which oversees the Food and Drug Administration in the Department of Health and Human Services, formerly the Department of Health, Education, and Welfare) published the *Ordinance and Code Regulating Eating and Drinking Establishments* for the sanitary control of food prepared and served to the public. The ordinance and code were designed to guide state and local health authorities in protecting the public food supply. These guidelines were developed with the assistance of experts in the public health field and the food service industry.

In 1976, the Food and Drug Administration released the *Model Food Service Sanitation Ordinance* as a single set of recommended standards to guide both public health agencies and food service operations. The 1976 ordinance also addressed the need, purpose, and scope of a food protection program, and suggested ways by which effective programs could be implemented. The Public Health Service released another code in 1978, *The Vending of Food and Beverages, Including a Model Sanitation Ordinance.* A third code, the *Retail Food Store Sanitation Code,* was jointly published by the FDA and the Association of Food and Drug Officials in 1982. These three codes were adopted by various national, state, and local regulatory authorities.

In 1986, food protection officials attending the Conference for Food Protection endorsed the development of a single code to eliminate the confusion stemming from the existence of the three codes. This code was envisioned as a single document that would include sanitation requirements for all establishments in the retail segment of the food industry. (This segment includes commercial and institutional food service operations, food vending machines, and most retail food stores.) The project was started in April of 1987 and released in draft form in March of 1988. It was developed under the leadership of the Food and Drug Administration with substantial input from a task force made up of health officials and executives from the hospitality industry.

In 1993, the **Food Code** was published. It represents the FDA's best advice for a uniform system of regulations to ensure that food at retail is safe and properly protected and presented. The Food Code provides a system of prevention and overlapping safeguards designed to minimize foodborne illness, and to ensure staff member health, industry manager knowledge, safe food, nontoxic and cleanable equipment, and acceptable levels of sanitation on food establishment premises. The Food Code also promotes fair dealings with consumers.

Responsibility for the SRM Program

The responsibility for the SRM program should be accepted throughout a food service operation, shared alike by top management/owners, mid-level managers, and staff members. Regulatory authorities also share this responsibility by virtue of their positions.

The SRM program must start at the top of a food service organization. Owners, chief executive officers, presidents, and corporate executives must be genuinely committed to making sanitation a top priority. The SRM program should be addressed in the mission statement, corporate policies, and operating philosophies. It should be clearly documented with written comprehensive sanitation standards and procedures. Top management is responsible for enforcing these standards and ensuring regulatory compliance, as well as for developing and implementing training materials for use at lower levels.

Mid-level managers include individual operation managers and supervisors. These managers must also accept responsibility for the SRM program at their levels. Like top managers and owners, mid-level managers must provide leadership by demonstrating their commitment to sanitation risk management.

Mid-level managers are responsible for planning and conducting staff member training programs and for monitoring the SRM program on a day-to-day basis. Mid-level managers must make many decisions in the course of daily operations; the SRM program helps them make these decisions by providing guidelines at each control point.

Staff members share the responsibility for the SRM program; in some ways, they are most important to its success. Making every staff member in a food service operation aware of his or her role in the SRM program helps ensure the program's effectiveness and build staff member commitment to the program. An overview of the SRM program should be part of every staff member's orientation. The overview should cover the objectives and major components of the program. SRM training should address concepts, procedures, and policies that help reduce risks. Follow-up during training should review each individual's role in the overall program.

Staff members should participate in the development of sanitation standards. This participation will reinforce the importance of the SRM program and encourage stronger commitment to it. Staff members should also be expected to report sanitation risks and guest complaints to management.

Regulatory authorities, by the very nature of their profession, are committed to reducing risks in food service operations. They are therefore an important resource for food service managers and share the responsibility for the success of the SRM program. Their primary role is to protect the safety of the food supply by enforcing regulations. Their inspections serve to identify risks to the public health. Regulatory authorities can also help train staff members and managers and provide suggestions for reducing risks.

Benefits of the SRM Program

A formalized SRM program ensures a continuous effort toward better sanitation. It guarantees that important points are not overlooked or forgotten in the course of daily operations and personnel changes. Naturally, a comprehensive SRM program costs money. However, it provides an immediate payback to the business by performing the following functions:

- Meeting guest expectations, upon which the establishment's success (and everyone's job) depends

- Protecting guest and staff health, thereby reducing staff member absences
- Reducing the operation's liability for accidents, injuries, or deaths
- Increasing the useful life of the operation's facilities and equipment
- Increasing the effectiveness and reducing the cost of cleaning and sanitization procedures with the proper use of chemicals
- Reducing the risks associated with the storage and application of toxic chemicals by standardizing products and procedures
- Simplifying supervision with the use of checklists
- Eliminating product waste and simplifying work methods through the use of written cleaning procedures
- Establishing management objectives which can be used to measure the progress of the business toward reducing risks
- Providing an acceptable return on investment for the owners of the business
- Reducing the risks of operating a food establishment

As this list of benefits indicates, a comprehensive SRM program does not cost as much as it pays. However, the return on this investment depends on how well management communicates the SRM standards and how well everyone performs to uphold these standards. Management must make sanitation part of daily operations and make all staff members aware of its importance.

Introduction to the HACCP System

The remainder of this chapter addresses two key issues: the HACCP system and the food establishment inspection. They are integrated and interrelated.

Recall that the SRM program is a HACCP-based system that goes beyond issues of food safety. The SRM program uniquely presents not only safety but also quality and cost control concerns. The SRM program has as its very core HACCP and the reduction of risks. Risks not only apply to food safety hazards, they also affect cost control and quality implications. The SRM program goal is achieved when the unique blend of safety, quality, and cost issues is integrated, resulting in staff member, guest, and owner satisfaction. It is possible to control risks and maximize satisfaction at the same time. Each complements the other, resulting in a system that works.

Consider poker, a game of chance played according to specific rules. It is a game of chance because players are not guaranteed to win or lose. Whether a player wins or loses depends on the cards he or she is dealt, on the cards dealt to other players in the game, and on each player's skill level in playing each hand. While it is possible to define the probability of winning given a particular poker hand, it may not be possible to entirely prevent oneself from losing.

Consider managing a food establishment. It is somewhat like playing a poker game in that there are rules, and managers are not guaranteed to win or lose. The manager's skill level and the skill of the other players (employees, for example) directly affect the success or failure of the food establishment. It is possible to control the risks of losing through the implementation of a food safety program. HACCP is the program that helps control such risks.

The HACCP system is prevention-based. It is designed to prevent potential food safety problems. Risks are reduced by, first, assessing the risks of a product or food production process, and, second, determining the steps that must be taken to control these risks. The reader must fully understand the following definitions before reading the discussion of the HACCP system:

(1) *Acceptable level* means the presence of a hazard that does not pose an unacceptable health risk.

(2) *Control point* means any point in a specific food system at which loss of control does not lead to an unacceptable health risk.

(3) *Critical control point,* as defined in the Food Code, means a point at which loss of control may result in an unacceptable health risk.

(4) *Critical limit,* as defined in the Food Code, means the maximum or minimum value to which a physical, biological, or chemical parameter must be controlled at a critical control point to minimize the risk that the identified food safety hazard may occur.

(5) *Deviation* means failure to meet a required critical limit for a critical control point.

(6) *HACCP plan,* as defined in the Food Code, is a written document that delineates the formal procedures for following the HACCP principles developed by the National Advisory Committee on Microbiological Criteria for Foods (NACMCF).

(7) *Hazard,* as defined in the Food Code, means a biological, chemical, or physical property that may cause an unacceptable consumer health risk.

(8) *Monitoring* means a planned sequence of observations or measurements of critical limits designed to produce an accurate record and intended to ensure that the critical limit maintains product safety. Continuous monitoring means an uninterrupted record of data.

(9) *Preventive measure* means an action to exclude, destroy, eliminate, or reduce a hazard and prevent recontamination through effective means.

(10) *Risk* means an estimate of the likely occurrence of a hazard.

(11) *Sensitive ingredient* means any ingredient historically associated with a known microbiological hazard that causes or contributes to production of a potentially hazardous food as defined in the Food Code.

(12) *Verification* means methods, procedures, and tests used to determine if the HACCP system in use is in compliance with the HACCP plan.

The HACCP system identifies and monitors specific foodborne hazards. The hazard analysis establishes critical control points (CCPs), which identify those points in the process that must be controlled to ensure food safety. In addition, critical limits are established that document the appropriate parameters that must be met at each CCP. CCPs are monitored and verified in subsequent steps to ensure that risks are controlled. All of this information is specified in the HACCP plan.

The HACCP plans mandated by the Food Code must include flow diagrams, product formulations, training plans, a corrective action plan, and a verification plan. The HACCP plans developed under the Food Code enable food managers and staff members to assess whether the food establishment has a system of controls that will sufficiently ensure safety of the products. The plan must include enough detail to facilitate staff member and management understanding of the operation and the intended controls.

When used properly, HACCP is an important food protection tool. The key to success is staff member training. Staff members must know which control points are critical and what the critical limits are at these points—for each preparation step they perform.

Exhibit 1.3 The Seven HACCP Principles

1. Hazard Analysis
2. Identify the Critical Control Points (CCPs) in the Food Process
3. Establish Critical Limits for Preventive Measures Associated with Each Identified CCP
4. Establish Procedures to Monitor CCPs
5. Establish the Corrective Action to Be Taken When Monitoring Shows that a Critical Limit Has Been Exceeded
6. Establish Effective Recordkeeping Systems that Document the HACCP System
7. Establish Procedures to Verify that the HACCP System Is Working

Adapted from FDA 1993 *Food Code.*

Management must routinely follow up to verify that all staff members are controlling the process by complying with the critical limits.

HACCP is a system of preventive controls that effectively and efficiently ensures that food products are safe in a food establishment. It emphasizes the food service industry's role in continuous improvement: rather than relying only on periodic facility inspections by regulatory agencies to point out deficiencies, food service operations should engage in ongoing problem-solving and prevention. HACCP clearly identifies the food establishment as the final party responsible for ensuring the safety of the food it sells. It requires the food establishment to analyze its preparation methods in a rational, scientific manner to identify CCPs and to establish critical limits and monitoring procedures. The establishment is responsible for maintaining records that document adherence to the critical limits that relate to the identified critical control points; this results in continuous self-inspection. The HACCP system also helps managers and staff members to determine the establishment's level of compliance with the Food Code.

A food establishment's use of HACCP requires development of a plan to prepare safe food. The plan must be shared with the regulatory agency, which must have access to CCP monitoring records and other data necessary to verify that the HACCP plan is working. With conventional inspection techniques, a regulatory agency can only determine conditions that exist during the time of the inspection. However, both current and past conditions can be determined when a HACCP approach is used. Therefore, the regulatory agency can more effectively ensure that processes are under control. The HACCP approach to ensuring food safety is preventive, while traditional inspection is reactive.

The Seven HACCP Principles

The National Advisory Committee on Microbiological Criteria for Foods (NACMCF) consists of regulatory officials, academicians, consumer groups, state government, and the food industry. NACMCF has developed seven widely accepted HACCP principles. They are listed in Exhibit 1.3 and discussed in the following section of the chapter.

Principle #1: Hazard Analysis

The hazard analysis process identifies significant hazards, estimates the likelihood that these hazards will occur and their severity if they do occur, and develops preventive measures for a process or product to ensure or improve food safety. HACCP's focus is high-risk hazards that are likely to occur. HACCP includes an analysis of ingredients, processing, distribution, and the intended use of the product. Such an analysis would state that sensitive ingredients (such as raw eggs) can create microbiological, chemical, and/or physical hazards in food.

Hazard analysis includes a flow diagram that depicts the control points or basic operating activities (see Exhibits 1.1 and 1.2). The significant hazards associated with each control point are listed, but, more important, preventive measures to control the hazards should be highlighted by management and staff members. In Exhibit 1.2, for example, preventive SRM actions are listed to the right of the control points. SRM is more comprehensive than HACCP, since its results transcend food safety and ultimately integrate quality and cost control with safety concerns to achieve staff, guest, and owner satisfaction. Each flow diagram should be constructed by a HACCP team that has knowledge about all control points on the product, the process, and likely hazards.

Hazards. Hazards can be categorized as biological, chemical, and physical. Biological hazards include bacterial, viral, and parasitic organisms. (More detail about these hazards is found in Chapter 3.) Refer to Exhibit 1.4 for a summary of hazardous microorganisms and parasites grouped on the basis of risk severity. Chemical hazards may be naturally occurring or may be added during food processing. (Chemicals are discussed in detail in Chapters 3 and 4.) Exhibit 1.5 lists types of chemical hazards and examples. Physical hazards are hard foreign objects found in food; sources are presented in Exhibit 1.6. (Physical hazards are discussed in Chapter 3.)

Level of Risk. An assessment of the risk of each hazard must consider the likelihood of occurrences and severity. The estimate is based on experience, epidemiological data, and technical information. When hazard identification and risk estimation are combined, significant hazards can be highlighted and addressed in the HACCP plan.

Hazard Analysis Process. In this step, management must ask and answer a series of questions for each control point in the flow diagram. The questions are listed in Exhibit 1.7. Once these questions are answered, preventive measures (which may be physical or chemical) can be taken to control hazards. For example, cooking sufficiently to kill pathogens is a physical preventive measure that can eliminate enteric pathogens.

Principle #2: Identify the CCPs in the Food Process

Recall that a CCP is a step or procedure at which control can be applied and a food safety hazard prevented, eliminated, or reduced to acceptable levels. Some CCPs are cooking, chilling, sanitation procedures, product formulation (recipe) control, prevention of cross-contamination, and certain aspects of environmental and staff member hygiene. While there may be many control points in a food process (as shown in Exhibits 1.1 and 1.2), few may be *critical* control points.

CCPs differ with the layout of a facility as well as the equipment, ingredients, and processes used. They vary with the staff members, too. Exhibit 1.8 presents a CCP decision tree used to help identify CCPs.

Principle #3: Establish Critical Limits for Preventive Measures Associated with Each Identified CCP

A critical limit is a boundary of safety. Some preventive measures have upper and lower critical limits. For example, the temperature danger zone (TDZ) is 41°F (5°C) to

Exhibit 1.4 Hazardous Microorganisms and Parasites Grouped on the Basis of Risk Severity[1]

Severe Hazards

Clostridium botulinum types A, B, E, and F
Shigella dysenteriae
Salmonella typhi; paratyphi A, B
Hepatitis A and E
Brucella abortis; B. suis
Vibrio cholerae 01
Vibrio vulnificus
Taenia solium
Trichinella spiralis

Moderate Hazards: Potentially Extensive Spread[2]

Listeria monocytogenes
Salmonella spp.
Shigella spp.
Enterovirulent *Escherichia coli* **(EEC)**
Streptococcus pyogenes
Rotavirus
Norwalk virus group
Entamoeba histolytica
Diphyllobothrium latum
Ascaris lumbricoides
Cryptosporidium parvum

Moderate Hazards: Limited Spread

Bacillus cereus
Campylobacter jejuni
Clostridium perfringens
Staphylococcus aureus
Vibrio cholerae, non-01
Vibrio parahaemolyticus
Yersinia enterocolitica
Giardia lamblia
Taenia saginata

---

[1]Adapted from International Commission on Microbiological Specifications for Food (ICMSF), 1986. Used with permission, "HACCP Principles and Applications," Pierson and Corlett, eds. 1992. Chapman & Hall, New York, NY.

[2]Although classified as moderate hazards, complications and sequelae may be severe in certain susceptible populations.

Adapted from FDA 1993 *Food Code.*

140°F (60°C); potentially hazardous foods should not be held within this range of temperatures. Both critical limits must be met for this preventive measure.

Consider the cooking of freshly ground beef patties. Critical limit criteria in this instance would include temperature, time, and patty thickness. Each patty should be cooked to a minimum internal temperature of 155°F (68°C) for a minimum of 15 seconds if a broiler set at 400°F (207°C) is used. Patty thickness should not exceed $1/2$ inch (2.6 cm). These three critical limit criteria—temperature, time, and patty thickness—must be evaluated and monitored regularly. Other critical limit criteria include humidity, water activity (a_w), pH, preservatives, salt concentration, available chlorine, and viscosity.

Exhibit 1.5 Types of Chemical Hazards and Examples[1]

Naturally Occurring Chemicals

Mycotoxins (e.g., aflatoxin) from mold
Scombrotoxin (histamine) from protein decomposition
Ciguatoxin from marine dinoflagellates
Toxic mushroom species
Shellfish toxins (from marine dinoflagellates)
    Paralytic shellfish poisoning (PSP)
    Diarrhetic shellfish poisoning (DSP)
    Neurotoxic shellfish poisoning (NSP)
    Amnesic shellfish poisoning (ASP)
Plant toxins
Pyrrolizidine alkaloids
Phytohemagglutinin

Added Chemicals

Agricultural chemicals: pesticides, fungicides, fertilizers, insecticides,
    antibiotics, and growth hormones
Polychlorinated biphenyls (PCBs)
Industrial chemicals
Prohibited substances (21 CFR 189)
    Direct
    Indirect
Toxic elements and compounds: lead, zinc, arsenic, mercury, and cyanide
Food additives:
    Direct—allowable limits under GMPs
        Preservatives (nitrite and sulfiting agents)
        Flavor enhancers (monosodium glutamate)
        Nutritional additives (niacin)
        Color additives
    Secondary direct and indirect
        Chemicals used in establishments (e.g., lubricants, cleaners,
        sanitizers, cleaning compounds, coatings, and paints)
Poisonous or toxic chemicals intentionally added (sabotage)

[1]Used with permission, "HACCP Principles and Applications," Pierson and Corlett, eds. 1992. Chapman & Hall, New York, NY and adapted.

Adapted from FDA 1993 *Food Code.*

Principle #4: Establish Procedures to Monitor CCPs

Monitoring comprises a planned sequence of measurements or observations taken to ascertain whether a CCP is under control. Monitoring procedures establish an accurate record for future verification. Monitoring procedures should: (1) track the system's operation so that a trend toward a loss of control can be identified and corrective action taken to bring the process back into control before a deviation occurs; (2) indicate when a loss of control and a deviation have actually occurred, and corrective action must be taken; and (3) provide written documentation for use in verification of the HACCP plan. Examples of measurements for monitoring include sensory observations (such as sight, smell, touch), temperature, time, pH, and a_w.

Monitoring procedures must be effective to avoid unsafe food. Continuous monitoring is always preferable when feasible. Instruments used for measuring critical limits must be carefully calibrated and used accurately, and calibration records must be

Exhibit 1.6 Main Materials of Concern as Physical Hazards and Common Sources[1,2]

Material	Injury Potential	Sources
Glass fixtures	Cuts, bleeding; may require surgery to find or remove	Bottles, jars, lights, utensils, gauge covers
Wood	Cuts, infection, choking; may require surgery to remove	Fields, pallets, boxes, buildings
Stones, metal fragments	Choking, broken teeth, cuts, infection; may require surgery to remove	Fields, buildings, machinery, wire, staff members
Insulation	Choking; long-term if asbestos	Building materials
Bone	Choking, trauma	Fields, improper plant processing
Plastic	Choking, cuts, infection; may require surgery to remove	Fields, plant packaging materials, pallets, staff members
Personal effects	Choking, cuts, broken teeth; may require surgery to remove	Staff members

[1]Adapted from Corlett (1991).

[2]Used with permission, "HACCP Principles and Applications," Pierson and Corlett, eds. 1992. Chapman & Hall, New York, NY.

Adapted from FDA 1993 *Food Code.*

maintained as part of HACCP plan documentation. When it is not possible to monitor continuously, sampling systems or statistically designed data collection should be used. The most appropriate staff member should be assigned responsibility for monitoring each CCP, and must be trained to be accurate. If an operation or product does not meet critical limits, immediate corrective action should be taken. All records used for monitoring must be initialed or signed and dated by the person doing the monitoring.

Principle #5: Establish the Corrective Action to Be Taken When Monitoring Shows that a Critical Limit Has Been Exceeded

Although some say that practice makes perfect, perfection is rarely achieved. A corrective action plan determines the disposition of any food produced while a deviation is occurring, corrects the cause of the deviation and ensures that the CCP is under control, and maintains records of corrective actions.

Specific corrective action plans are required for each CCP. Corrective action procedures should be well documented in the HACCP plan. When a deviation occurs, more frequent monitoring may be temporarily required to ensure that it is brought under control.

Principle #6: Establish Effective Recordkeeping Systems that Document the HACCP System

The preparation and maintenance of the written HACCP plan is the responsibility of the food establishment management. The plan must detail hazards, identify CCPs

Exhibit 1.7 Hazard Analysis Food Process Questions

1. **Ingredients**
   - Does the food contain any sensitive ingredients that are likely to present microbiological hazards (e.g., *Salmonella, Staphylococcus aureus*), chemical hazards (e.g., aflatoxin, antibiotic, or pesticide residues), or physical hazards (stones, glass, bone, metal)?

2. **Intrinsic factors of food**

   Physical characteristics and composition (e.g., pH, type of acids, fermentable carbohydrate, a_w, preservatives) of the food during and after the process can cause or prevent a hazard.
   - Which intrinsic factors of the food must be controlled to ensure food safety?
   - Does the food allow survival or multiplication of pathogens and/or toxin formation before or during the process?
   - Will the food allow survival or multiplication of pathogens and/or toxin formation during subsequent control points, including storage or consumer possession?
   - Are there similar products in the marketplace? What has been the safety record for these products?

3. **Procedures used for the process**
   - Does the procedure or process include a controllable step that destroys pathogens or their toxins? Consider both vegetative cells and spores.
   - Is the product subject to recontamination between production (e.g., cooking) and packaging?

4. **Microbial content of the food**
   - Is the food commercially sterile (i.e., low acid canned food)?
   - Is it likely that the food will contain viable sporeforming or nonsporeforming pathogens?
   - What is the normal microbial content of the food stored under proper conditions?
   - Does the microbial population change during the time the food is stored before consumption?
   - Does that change in microbial population alter the safety of the food?

5. **Facility design**
   - Does the layout of the facility provide an adequate separation of raw materials from ready-to-eat foods?
   - Is positive air pressure maintained in product packaging areas? Is this essential for product safety?
   - Is the traffic pattern for people and moving equipment a potentially significant source of contamination?

6. **Equipment design**
   - Will the equipment provide the time/temperature control that is necessary for safe food?
   - Is the equipment properly sized for the volume of food that will be prepared?
   - Can the equipment be sufficiently controlled so that the variation in performance will be within the tolerances required to produce a safe food?
   - Is the equipment reliable or is it prone to frequent breakdowns?
   - Is the equipment designed so that it can be cleaned and sanitized?
   - Is there a chance for product contamination with hazardous substances, e.g., glass?
   - What product safety devices such as time/temperature integrators are used to enhance consumer safety?

7. **Packaging**
   - Does the method of packaging affect the multiplication of microbial pathogens and/or the formation of toxins?
   - Is the packaging material resistant to damage, thereby preventing the entrance of microbial contamination?
   - Is the package clearly labeled "Keep Refrigerated" if this is required for safety?
   - Does the package include instructions for the safe handling and preparation of the food by the consumer?
   - Are tamper-evident packaging features used?
   - Is each package legibly and accurately coded to indicate production lot?
   - Does each package contain the proper label?

8. **Sanitation**
   - Can the sanitation practices that are employed adversely affect the safety of the food that is being produced?
   - Can the facility be cleaned and sanitized to permit the safe handling of food?
   - Is it possible to provide sanitary conditions consistently and adequately to ensure safe foods?

9. **Staff member health, hygiene, and education**
   - Can staff member health or personal hygiene practices adversely affect the safety of the food being produced?
   - Does the staff understand the food production process and the factors they must control to ensure safe foods?
   - Will the staff inform management of a problem that could negatively affect food safety?

10. **Conditions of storage between packaging and the consumer**
    - What is the likelihood that the food will be improperly stored at the wrong temperature?
    - Would storage at improper temperatures lead to a microbiologically unsafe food?

11. **Intended use**
    - Will the food be heated by the consumer?
    - Will there likely be leftovers?

12. **Intended consumer**
    - Is the food intended for the general public, i.e., a population that does not have an increased risk of becoming ill?
    - Is the food intended for consumption by a population with increased susceptibility to illness (e.g., infants, the elderly, the infirm, and immunocompromised individuals)?

Adapted from FDA 1993 *Food Code.*

and critical limits, specify CCP monitoring and recordkeeping procedures, and outline the implementation strategy.

Recordkeeping makes the system work. The level of sophistication of recordkeeping depends on the complexity of the food establishment. The simplest effective recordkeeping system is the best.

The approved HACCP plan and associated records must be on file at the food establishment. Documents to include are the following:

- List of the HACCP team and assigned responsibilities
- Description of the product and its intended use
- Flow diagram indicating CCPs
- Hazards associated with each CCP and preventive measures
- Critical limits
- Monitoring system
- Corrective action plans for deviations from critical limits
- Recordkeeping procedures
- Procedures for verification of HACCP system

Other information in the HACCP plan can be tabulated using the format shown in Exhibit 1.9. Some examples of records obtained during the operation of the HACCP plan are described in Exhibit 1.10.

Exhibit 1.8 Critical Control Point Decision Tree

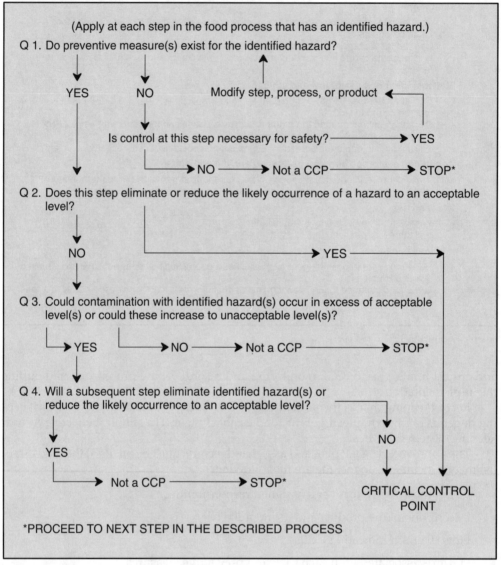

(Apply at each step in the food process that has an identified hazard.)

Q 1. Do preventive measure(s) exist for the identified hazard?

YES   NO   Modify step, process, or product ◄

Is control at this step necessary for safety? ───────► YES

NO ───► Not a CCP ───────► STOP*

Q 2. Does this step eliminate or reduce the likely occurrence of a hazard to an acceptable level?

NO ───────────────────► YES ───────►

Q 3. Could contamination with identified hazard(s) occur in excess of acceptable level(s) or could these increase to unacceptable level(s)?

YES   NO ───► Not a CCP ───────► STOP*

Q 4. Will a subsequent step eliminate identified hazard(s) or reduce the likely occurrence to an acceptable level?

YES   NO

Not a CCP ───────► STOP*   CRITICAL CONTROL POINT

*PROCEED TO NEXT STEP IN THE DESCRIBED PROCESS

Adapted from FDA 1993 *Food Code*.

Principle #7: Establish Procedures to Verify that the HACCP System Is Working

The first phase of the verification process involves the scientific or technical verification that critical limits at CCPs are satisfactory. This can be complex and may require outside expert help. The second phase of verification ensures that the HACCP plan is functioning effectively. This involves frequent reviews of the HACCP plan, verification that the plan is correctly followed, review of CCP records, and determination that appropriate risk management decisions and product dispositions are made when production deviations occur. The third phase comprises documented periodic revalidations,

Exhibit 1.9 HACCP Information Reporting Form

Process Step	CCP	Chemical/ Physical/ Biological Hazards	Critical Limit	Monitoring Procedures/ Frequency/ Person(s) Responsible	Corrective Action(s)/ Person(s) Responsible	HACCP Records	Verification Procedures/ Person(s) Responsible

Adapted from FDA 1993 *Food Code.*

independent of audits. The revalidations are performed by the HACCP team. The fourth phase is verification by the regulatory authority.

HACCP plan verification procedures may include the following:

- Establishment of appropriate verification inspection schedules
- Review of the HACCP plan
- Review of CCP records
- Review of deviations and their resolutions, including the disposition of food
- Visual inspections of operations to observe if CCPs are under control
- Random sample collection and analysis
- Review of critical limits to verify that they can adequately control hazards
- Review of written record of verification inspections that certifies compliance with the HACCP plan or deviations from the plan and the corrective actions taken
- Validation of HACCP plan, including on-site review and verification of flow diagrams and CCPs
- Review of modifications of the HACCP plan

HACCP verification inspections should be conducted:

- Routinely or on an unannounced basis, to ensure that selected CCPs are under control

Exhibit 1.10 Examples of Records Obtained During the Operation of the HACCP Plan

---

1. **Ingredients**
   - Supplier certification documenting compliance with establishment's specifications.
   - Establishment audit records verifying supplier compliance.
   - Storage temperature record for temperature-sensitive ingredients.
   - Storage time records of limited shelf-life ingredients.

2. **Processing**
   - Records from all monitored CCPs.
   - Records verifying the continued adequacy of the food processing procedures.

3. **Packaging**
   - Records indicating compliance with specifications of packaging materials.
   - Records indicating compliance with sealing specifications.

4. **Finished product**
   - Sufficient data and records to establish the efficacy of barriers in maintaining product safety.
   - Sufficient data and records establishing the safe shelf life of the product, if age of product can affect safety.
   - Documentation of the adequacy of the HACCP procedures from an authority with knowledge of the hazards involved and necessary controls.

5. **Storage and distribution**
   - Temperature records.
   - Records showing no product shipped after shelf-life date on temperature-sensitive products.

6. **Deviation and corrective action**
   - Validation records and modification to the HACCP plan indicating approved revisions and changes in ingredients, formulations, preparation, packaging, and distribution control, as needed.

7. **Staff member training**
   - Records indicating that food staff responsible for implementation of the HACCP plan understand the hazards, controls, and procedures.

Adapted from FDA 1993 *Food Code.*

- When it is determined that intensive coverage of a specific food is necessary because of new information concerning food safety

- When foods prepared at the establishment have been implicated as a vehicle of foodborne disease

- When requested on a consultative basis and resources allow accommodating the request

- When established criteria have not been met

- To verify that changes have been implemented correctly after a HACCP plan has been modified

  HACCP verification reports should include information about:

- The existence of a HACCP plan and the person(s) responsible for administering and updating the plan

- The status of records associated with CCP monitoring

- Direct monitoring data of the CCP while in operation

- Certification that monitoring equipment is properly calibrated and in working order
- Deviations and corrective actions
- Any samples analyzed to verify that CCPs are under control; analyses may involve physical, chemical, microbiological, or sensory methods
- Modifications to the HACCP plan
- The training and knowledge of individuals responsible for monitoring CCPs

Staff member training is a very important element in the success of HACCP in a food establishment. HACCP works best when it is integrated into each staff member's duties and not seen as an "add-on." The fundamental training goal should be to make staff members and managers proficient in the specific tasks that the HACCP plan requires them to perform. Managers need a deeper understanding of HACCP than staff members do. The training plan should be specific to the establishment. Training may be reinforced through the Educational Institute's *Fast Track Food Safety* program (which includes videotape training for line employees in four different job areas: receiving and storage, food production, service, and warewashing), HACCP training videos, changing reminders about HACCP critical limits such as "HANDWASHING PAYS BIG DIVIDENDS" printed on employee time cards or checks, and work station reminders such as pictorials on how and when to take food temperatures. Remember that, each time the menu changes, the HACCP plan should be reevaluated. The HACCP plan should include a feedback loop for employees to suggest what additional training is required.

Food Establishment Inspections

The overall desired result of **food establishment inspections** is to prevent foodborne illness. Inspections are the primary means by which food establishment management and staff members and the regulatory authority detect procedures and practices that may be hazardous. Once deficiencies are found, management and staff members can take action to correct them.

Food establishment inspections serve as educational sessions regarding specific Food Code requirements as they apply to a particular establishment. Inspections also convey new food safety information and provide opportunities to ask questions. In addition, inspections provide a written report to the permit-holder or person in charge, so that the responsible person can bring the establishment into compliance with the Food Code. Using the HACCP system to refocus inspections is nothing new. Some jurisdictions have done so since the early 1980s.

Even though this discussion of food establishment inspections will focus at times on the role of the regulatory authority, it can be applied directly to managers, staff members, and owners. For example, jurisdictions must consider the number of hours required to perform inspections when allocating resources. So must a food establishment's management team consider resources (i.e., people, food, equipment, facilities, time, and money) and the worth of activities in relation to the amount of resources used. The FDA recommends that approximately eight to ten hours be allocated per establishment per year for regulatory inspections. Other factors affecting resources are inspection frequency for each category of establishment, any variations over time in inspection violations or scores, and training provided to inspection staff.

Inspectors must have the correct equipment, including necessary forms, thermocouple or thermistor, alcohol swabs, flashlight, sanitizer test kit, 160°F (73°C) maximum registering indicators for verifying mechanical warewasher sanitization, pressure

Exhibit 1.11 Risk Categorization of Food Establishments

RISK TYPE	RISK TYPE CATEGORY DESCRIPTION	FREQUENCY #/YR
1	Pre-packaged nonpotentially hazardous foods only. Limited preparation of nonpotentially hazardous foods only.	1
2	Limited menu (1 or 2 main items). Pre-packaged raw ingredients are cooked or prepared to order. Retail food operations exclude deli or seafood departments. Raw ingredients require minimal assembly. Most products are cooked/prepared and served immediately. Hot and cold holding of potentially hazardous foods is restricted to single meal service. Preparation processes requiring cooking, cooling, and reheating are limited to 1 or 2 potentially hazardous foods.	2
3	Extensive handling of raw ingredients. Preparation process includes the cooking, cooling, and reheating of potentially hazardous foods. A variety of processes require hot and cold holding of potentially hazardous food. Advance preparation for next-day service is limited to 2 or 3 items. Retail food operations include deli and seafood departments. Establishments doing food processing at retail.	3
4	Extensive handling of raw ingredients. Preparation processes include the cooking, cooling, and reheating of potentially hazardous foods. A variety of processes require hot and cold holding of potentially hazardous foods. Food processes include advanced preparation for next-day service. Category would also include those facilities whose primary service population is immunocompromised.	4
5	Extensive handling of raw ingredients. Food processing at the retail level, e.g., smoking and curing; reduced oxygen packaging for extended shelf-life.	4

gauge, and light meter. If the food process flow is complicated, the inspector may also need a pH meter, a_w meter, and time-temperature data loggers.

Risk Categorization of Food Establishments. The establishments with the highest risks are targeted for inspection by regulatory authorities, based on the types of food served, the process flow the foods require, the volume of food produced and served, the population served, and the establishment's previous compliance history. All of these variables can affect the probability of a foodborne illness outbreak in a food establishment. Exhibit 1.11 presents the risk categorization of food establishments.

Types of Inspections. The Food Code specifies that access to a retail establishment for inspection is a condition of the acceptance and retention of the food establishment permit. (More information about permits is covered in Chapter 2.) Inspections are generally unannounced to obtain a more accurate assessment of normal operating conditions and practices. Inspections determine compliance with the Food Code, and are of five types: preoperational, routine, follow-up, HACCP, and complaint.

Preoperational inspections are conducted to ensure that the establishment is built or remodeled in accordance with the plans and specifications approved by the regulatory authority. *Routine* inspections are full reviews of operations and facilities and their impact on food safety. *Follow-up* inspections concentrate on correction of critical violations within ten days of the routine inspection. *HACCP* inspections review critical limits, required records, and corrective actions outlined in the establishment's HACCP plan. *Complaint* inspections follow consumer complaints and may involve the regulatory agency's medical staff.

Staff Training

Staff training is the key to reducing risks and increasing staff, management, guest, and owner satisfaction. Food establishments should begin with a well-defined training process and use the resources of local, state, and national regulatory agencies.

The first phase of staff training should provide information on program history and structure, and should emphasize specific goals and objectives. The study of the epidemiology of foodborne illness—including organisms, foods, contributing factors, case studies, and all aspects of basic microbiology—is critical for both the inspector as well as the inspected. The second phase of training is on-site training conducted by trainers familiar with HACCP inspecting. The trainees should demonstrate expertise in data gathering and analysis before moving to the third phase of training, which is standardization. In this phase, points of violation are fully discussed and differentiated from similar conditions that are not violations. The final phase of training—lifelong or continuing education—is ongoing. Managers and staff members must remain current in this rapidly changing world through seminars and workshops offered by colleges and universities, professional associations, regulatory agencies, and private companies. Food service training programs offer excellent opportunities for acquiring, reinforcing, and retaining food safety knowledge (see Appendix D for more information).

Conducting the Inspection

The HACCP inspection views a food establishment and its operations as a total process by identifying CCPs in an attempt to prevent food safety hazards. Regulatory agencies take individual program, personnel, establishment, and jurisdiction differences into account when establishing procedures for assigning food establishments and preparing for and conducting inspections.

The menu and food product flow are the place to start the review for the inspection. Full food flow diagrams should be reviewed by the regulatory authorities even though only a portion of the steps will take place during the inspection. The focus during the inspection must be, first and foremost, the food.

The sources of food, storage practices, and process flow steps all should be noted. Risk assessment data guide the allocation of time and focus during the inspection. Complex, higher-risk food processes that involve multiple ingredients, potentially hazardous foods, long holding times, foods to be cooled, and reheating steps should be given a high priority. Foods that have been implicated in foodborne illness should receive high priority, too. Other high risk indicators are foods prepared in large volumes and those requiring manual assembly and manipulation during preparation or portioning.

Accurate measurements during inspections are essential. Accuracy of measurements depends on at least two variables: calibration of the equipment and procedures followed by the person making the measurements. Critical limits to be measured include temperature, pH, a_w, food additive concentrations, warewashing processes, wash/rinse/heat sanitization, sanitizer concentrations, pressure and time measurements, light distribution, and insect and rodent infestations.

Temperature measurements. Food product internal temperatures should be taken in the geometric center of the product. Additional measurements (taken at points farthest from the heat source) may be necessary when foods are held hot on steam tables. Ambient temperature monitoring devices should be used as indicators of where further temperature investigations are warranted. Temperatures monitored between packages of food, such as milk cartons or packages of meat, also indicate the need for further examination. However, the temperature of a potentially hazardous food itself, rather than the temperature between packages, is necessary for regulatory citations.

The three dimensions of bacterial load, temperature, and time must be considered when inspecting the cooking process. Temperature measurement should take into account post-cooking heat rise (which allows the temperature to reach equilibrium throughout the food), particularly for foods cooked in a microwave oven. Product cooking temperatures and times should be carefully evaluated during inspections.

Modern thermometers that measure temperature electrically, rather than bimetal types that rely on thermal expansion of two different metals, are recommended by regulatory authorities. Such modern thermometers yield faster responses and provide greater overall accuracy. Before internal food temperatures are taken, the probe must be cleaned and sanitized. Boiling water, alcohol swabs, or sanitizers can destroy pathogens on the probe. When a series of temperatures is taken, it is important that the probe be thoroughly cleaned and sanitized between uses to prevent cross-contamination.

pH measurements. The pH measurement is important in determining if a food is potentially hazardous. The closer the food approaches the critical limit of 4.6, the more precise the measurement should be. (Chapter 3 discusses pH in more detail.)

Water activity measurements. Water activity (a_w) is another factor used to determine if a food is considered potentially hazardous. (A discussion of a_w can be found in Chapter 3.) The a_w is measured with a laboratory or field a_w meter.

Food additive concentrations. Samples of food are sometimes collected and sent to a laboratory for analysis (Chapter 3 presents this subject in more detail).

Warewashing process evaluation. Because proper cleaning and sanitization of food-contact surfaces are important safeguards of public health, the washing, rinsing, and sanitizing processes must be verified to ensure that they meet Food Code provisions.

The FDA states:

"Food-contact surface" means:

(a) A surface of equipment or a utensil with which food normally comes into contact; or

(b) A surface of equipment or a utensil from which food may drain, drip, or splash:

    (i) Into a food, or

    (ii) Onto a surface normally in contact with food.

Source: FDA 1993 *Food Code.*

Mechanical warewashers are required to have data plates that indicate acceptable parameters for temperatures and cycle times for particular machines. (More on mechanical and manual warewashing is presented in Chapter 9.)

Wash/rinse/heat sanitization measurement. Devices used for measuring food product temperature can also be used for determining the critical limits of washing, rinsing, and sanitization. Both a three-compartment sink and many mechanical warewashers have vats for water that can be checked with a probe thermometer and compared to the installed thermometer readings.

Sanitizer concentration. Sanitizer test kits are used. (See Chapter 9 for more information about sanitization.)

Pressure measurements. The hot water sanitizing rinse pressure of mechanical warewashing machines is an important factor.

Time measurements. Time is significant in the evaluation of warewashing operations, as are temperature and concentration. Time should be measured with a watch that has a second hand or readout.

Light distribution. Portable light meters are used to take measurements of the amount of light. The measurements should be taken 30 inches (76 cm) above the floor. (Chapter 10 presents more information about lighting.)

Insect and rodent infestation. Physical evidence of insect and rodent infestation can take the form of dead vermin, droppings, nesting, gnawings, and grease marks on the walls. A bright flashlight, a magnifying lens, and an ultraviolet light to detect rodent urine stains can reveal infestations.

Inspection Documentation

It is essential that accurate notes be taken during a HACCP inspection. One acceptable format is the HACCP Inspection Data form shown in Exhibit 1.12. This form consists of an administrative section, a food flow section, a section for recording temperatures that are spot-checked, and categorical sections to record other data.

Note that the administrative section identifies the date and time of the inspection. The food flow section is used to record detailed information regarding as many as four food items identified as having the most potential for presenting problems. Additional sheets can be used if more than four food items are tracked. The foods are listed horizontally across the top, and steps from source to reheat are listed down the left side of the form. Under each food identified, space is provided for recording information observed such as time and temperature for each of the steps. A shaded column is provided for each of the foods to identify any critical limits that exist for each of the steps.

The entire production and service cycle might not take place while the food establishment is being inspected. Therefore, it should be clearly delineated on the form at which point the observations began and ended.

The food temperature recording section can list both acceptable and violative temperatures.

The back of the form asks for data relating to other areas of the operation.

Many violations found during inspection can be corrected immediately if the permit-holder or person in charge accompanies the inspector. Immediate correction does not negate the original violation, but should be recognized as part of the inspection documentation. The inspector will note violations and corrections on the official inspection report.

Inspection Report

The inspection report is the official regulatory agency document. It is completed for routine, follow-up, and complaint inspections. A copy should be kept in the food establishment's files.

The inspection report can be prepared using either the Food Establishment Inspection Report or the FDA Electronic Inspection System. The report is usually completed at

Exhibit 1.12 HACCP Inspection Data

<table>
<tr><td colspan="2">FDA</td><td colspan="2">DEPARTMENT OF HEALTH AND HUMAN SERVICES
PUBLIC HEALTH SERVICE
FOOD AND DRUG ADMINISTRATION</td></tr>
</table>

HACCP INSPECTION DATA

EST. NAME:	PERMIT NO.	INSPECTOR:	
DATE:	TIME IN:	:AM / PM TIME OUT:	:AM/ PM

Record all observations below - transfer violations to Inspection Report

FOOD TEMPERATURES / TIMES / OTHER CRITICAL LIMITS
Use Additional Forms If Necessary

FOOD / STEP	1.	CRITICAL LIMIT	2	CRITICAL LIMIT	3	CRITICAL LIMIT	4	CRITICAL LIMIT
A. SOURCE								
B. STORAGE								
C. PREP BEFORE COOK								
D. COOK								
E. PREP AFTER COOK								
F. HOT/COLD HOLD								
G. DISPLAY/ SERVICE								
H. COOL								
I. REHEAT								

OTHER FOOD TEMPERATURES OBSERVED						Use steps from above for location					
FOOD	TEMP. °C/°F	STEP	FOOD	TEMP. °C/°F	STEP	FOOD	TEMP. °C/°F	STEP			

Page 1 of 2

the end of the inspection. Not every item recorded on the HACCP Inspection Data form is included in the inspection report. The HACCP Inspection Data form may include some information, such as documentation of acceptable holding temperatures, that is not necessary for the final report.

Exhibit 1.12 *(continued)*

MANAGEMENT / PERSONNEL OBSERVATIONS	
OTHER FOOD OBSERVATIONS	
EQUIPMENT, UTENSILS, AND LINEN OBSERVATIONS	
WATER, PLUMBING, AND WASTE OBSERVATIONS	
PHYSICAL FACILITIES	
POISONOUS OR TOXIC MATERIALS OBSERVATIONS	

HACCP Inspection Data Page 2 of 2

Source: FDA 1993 *Food Code.*

The final score indicates how well an establishment is complying with the regulatory agency's food safety rules. Compliance with provisions of the Food Code is the basis for retaining the permit to operate the food establishment. Certain Food Code violations are called **imminent health hazards** and require immediate action or closure of the affected part of the food establishment. Sewage backing up in a food preparation area is an example of an imminent health hazard.

The FDA states:

"Imminent health hazard" means a significant threat or danger to health that is considered to exist when there is evidence sufficient to show that a product, practice, circumstance, or event creates a situation that requires immediate correction or cessation of operation to prevent injury based on:

(a)   The number of potential injuries, and

(b)   The nature, severity, and duration of the anticipated injury.

Source: FDA 1993 *Food Code.*

Critical items are Food Code violations that may contribute to food contamination, illness, or environmental degradation and represent substantial public health hazards. The Food Code delineates critical items by the use of an asterisk (*) after the tag line. A bold superscripted N (^{N}) means an item is noncritical; a bold superscripted S (^{S}) designates an item that may or may not be critical, depending on the circumstances. In previous codes, violations have always been designated as critical or noncritical. Under the Food Code, the inspector can use professional judgment regarding some of the violations to determine how serious the violations are—that is, how critical or noncritical— based on the likelihood of food contamination, illness, or environmental degradation.

The Food Code is based on citing violations in two categories: critical and noncritical. The final score, which is the number of items in violation, is significant as an indicator of the food establishment's overall control of hazards; however, there is no defined point at which a score translates into a significant health hazard. A jurisdiction can choose the method it will use to score its food establishments, including total quality management (TQM), fixed categorization, or fixed without categorization methods.

The *TQM method* employs statistical process control to focus on continuous quality improvement. The method uses percentile rank to judge compliance against a range of compliance levels of similar establishments within the category. The *fixed categorization method* uses a fixed number of critical violations selected for each category of establishment. The *fixed without categorization method* is the simplest method. It sets a single level of compliance for all types and complexities of establishments.

Food Establishment Inspection Report

Exhibit 1.13 shows the Food Establishment Inspection Report. The introduction and administrative data clearly ask for key information, including inspection type and time.

It is essential that regulatory officials standardize the inspection process within an agency. Inspectors mark violations on the inspection report when they clearly exist in the food establishment. A violation represents a deviation from a Food Code provision. Each violation is recorded as a separate item on the report.

Critical violations are indicated with an X in the first column. Critical violations are always listed first for emphasis. Repeat items are those that were in violation on the previous inspection and are indicated in the second column, Repeat, with an X. Specific Food Code section references are recorded in the third column, Code References. Inspectors use

Exhibit 1.13 Food Establishment Inspection Report

DEPARTMENT OF HEALTH AND HUMAN SERVICES
PUBLIC HEALTH SERVICE
FOOD AND DRUG ADMINISTRATION

FOOD ESTABLISHMENT INSPECTION REPORT

Violations cited in this report shall be corrected within the time frames specified below, but within a period not to exceed 10 calendar days for critical items (§ 8-405.11) or 90 days for noncritical items (§ 8-406.11).

VIOLATIONS: CRITICAL _____   NONCRITICAL_____

ESTABLISHMENT:	PERMIT NUMBER:	DATE:

ADDRESS: CITY: STATE: ZIP:

PERSON IN CHARGE / TITLE: TELEPHONE:

INSPECTOR / TITLE:

INSPECTION TYPE: ROUTINE   FOLLOW-UP   COMPLAINT   OTHER: TIME:

Critical (X)	Repeat (X)	Code Reference	Violation Description / Remarks / Corrections

Food Establishment Inspection Report Page __ of __

(continued)

Exhibit 1.13 *(continued)*

FOOD ESTABLISHMENT INSPECTION REPORT

ESTABLISHMENT:		PERMIT NUMBER:	DATE:

Critical (X)	Repeat (X)	Code Reference	Violation Description / Remarks / Corrections

Food Establishment Inspection Report Page __ of __

Source: FDA 1993 *Food Code.*

the fourth column, Violation Description/Remarks/Corrections, to briefly record the specifics of the observed violation. Any additional information or explanation should be recorded here, including, if appropriate, that the establishment permit-holder or person in charge corrected a violation during the inspection.

Once the inspection form has been completed, a closing conference is held to give the inspector the opportunity to clearly and firmly convey the compliance status to the permit-holder or person in charge. It may be beneficial to include other members of the food establishment management team in the closing conference. The written report is the focus of the closing conference. The listing of the results with the critical violations listed first helps focus the discussion on violations that could directly lead to a food-borne illness.

The closing conference gives establishment management the opportunity to ask questions of the inspector. A detailed discussion of the establishment's plans for correcting violations revealed during the inspection must be included in the closing conference. Timely follow-ups are mandated under the Food Code. Some jurisdictions require establishments to return a notice to the agency that violations cited during the inspection have been corrected.

The FDA Electronic Inspection System (FDA EIS) is an alternative to the inspection form. It is a powerful tool for regulatory agencies to use in managing important program data. FDA EIS software is provided to state and local regulatory agencies. It can be used to integrate data management between existing agency database management systems and the food protection program. It can also consolidate inspection data collection and reporting between different levels of food protection programs within a state.

Record Maintenance System

A detailed record maintenance system supports the HACCP program and tracks potential compliance actions. The following documents should be included in the food establishment's active files: records related to initial plan review, permit application and issuance, inspection reports, complaints, investigations, management training and certification, correspondence, and compliance actions.

Summary

This chapter introduced the Sanitation Risk Management (SRM) program and the Hazard Analysis Critical Control Point (HACCP) system.

The SRM program makes risks more manageable. It positively affects quality, cost, and food safety risks. The FDA's 1993 Food Code is the foundation for the SRM program. While responsibilities for SRM are shared by managers, staff members, and regulatory agents, the benefits affect all, including guests.

The seven HACCP principles are presented and applied to the HACCP plan. The chapter reviews the HACCP Inspection Data form.

The chapter also presents the planning and training requirements for a food establishment inspection. Even though the discussion focuses, at times, on the role of the regulatory authority, it also applies directly to the permit-holder and person in charge as well as to staff members in a food establishment. A sample inspection report is presented and reviewed.

HACCP is one of the foundations of the SRM program. SRM goes beyond HACCP and its focus on food safety to include issues related to both food quality and food cost control. HACCP is one of the core beliefs and foundations upon which the SRM program is built.

Key Terms

cleaning and maintenance • control point • cooking • critical control point
• critical limit • Food Code • food establishment inspection • HACCP
plan • hazard • holding • imminent health hazard • issuing • menu
planning • preparing • purchasing • receiving • serving • storing

Discussion Questions

1. What are control points? What are the ten control points in the food service system?

2. Why is menu planning of special importance?

3. What is an SRM program and how does it work?

4. What is the relationship of FDA food service sanitation codes to the SRM program described in this text?

5. How should responsibility for the SRM program be handled?

6. What are the benefits of an SRM program?

7. What are the definitions of *critical control point, critical limit, hazard, risk,* and *sensitive ingredient*? How does an understanding of these terms affect the HACCP plan?

8. What are the seven HACCP principles? How are they used to establish a HACCP plan?

9. How does a HACCP inspection differ from a food establishment inspection? What are the similarities?

10. What are critical violations? How can they be reduced?

References

"Botulism Feared in Illness." *Winnipeg Free Press,* Friday, February 20, 1987, p. 1A.

Burris, Jerry. "3rd Salmonella Outbreak Here After Fund-Raiser Chicken Sale." *The Honolulu Advertiser,* Thursday, December 3, 1987, p. A1.

Cichy, Ronald F. "HACCP as a Quality Assurance Tool in a Commissary Food-Service System." *International Journal of Hospitality Management,* 1982, pp. 103–106.

———. "Sensory Evaluation as a Quality Assurance Tool in a Commissary Foodservice System." *Dairy and Food Sanitation,* August 1983, pp. 288–292.

Cichy, Ronald F., Richard C. Nicholas, and Mary E. Zabik. "An Application of the Pareto Principle to a Critical Control Point in a Commissary Foodservice System." *Food Technology,* September 1982, pp. 89–92.

Evans, Dean. "FDA Proposes Food 'Unicode'." *Nation's Restaurant News,* June 27, 1988, p. 74.

Feltenstein, Tom. "Quality: An Issue of Survival." *Nation's Restaurant News,* March 9, 1987, p. F48.

Food Code—1993 Recommendations of the United States Public Health Service/Food and Drug Administration.

Kochak, Jacque White. "When the Unthinkable Happens." *Restaurant Business,* March 1, 1988, p. 102.

Lydecker, Toni. "When Foodborne Illness Strikes!" *Restaurants and Institutions,* September 30, 1987, pp. 34–37, 40–41, 46, 52.

McGrath, Anne. "Fatal Salmonella Outbreak Probed." *Lansing State Journal,* November 30, 1986, p. 3A.

Minor, Lewis J., and Ronald F. Cichy. *Foodservice Systems Management.* Westport, Conn.: AVI, 1984.

Stiles, Edward. "Feeling Low? Probably Something You Ate." *The Detroit News,* Thursday, October 20, 1988, p. 1F.

"Typhoid Outbreak Hits 7." *Restaurant Business,* November 1, 1986, p. 36.

REVIEW QUIZ

When you feel you have covered all of the material in this chapter, answer these questions. Choose the *best* answer. Check your answers with the correct ones found on the Review Quiz Answer Key at the end of this book.

1. Which of the following is one of the functions of the issuing control point?

    a. to minimize investment in inventory
    b. to release inventory to properly authorized employees
    c. to maintain the quality and safety of finished menu items
    d. to transfer products from the production department to guests

2. A sanitation risk management program based on a HACCP approach focuses on reducing overall risks by:

    a. identifying risks at each control point.
    b. controlling potentially hazardous employee behavior.
    c. educating top management about the importance of sanitation.
    d. streamlining operational procedures.

3. The FDA's *Model Food Service Sanitation Ordinance* was released in 1976 as a single set of recommended standards for:

    a. retail food outlets and vending operations.
    b. food service operations and public health agencies.
    c. vending operations and food service operations.
    d. all of the above.

4. Staff member participation in the development of sanitation standards will tend to:

    a. cause confusion and tension among the staff.
    b. reduce the need to monitor critical limits.
    c. help staff members pass health code tests.
    d. encourage a stronger commitment to the sanitation risk management program.

5. Which of the following is *not* one of the functions of a comprehensive sanitation risk management program?

    a. eliminating the risks of using toxic chemicals
    b. meeting guest expectations
    c. reducing the operation's liability for accidents
    d. simplifying supervision

6. Besides food safety, the sanitation risk management program is concerned with:

   a. guest relations and revenue enhancement.
   b. guest relations and cost control.
   c. revenue enhancement and quality issues.
   d. cost control and quality issues.

7. Which of the following HACCP principles dictates the development of a process to identify tendencies toward a loss of control at a critical control point?

   a. hazard analysis
   b. establish critical limits for preventive measures
   c. establish procedures to monitor critical control points
   d. establish procedures to verify that the HACCP system is working

8. The primary focus during an inspection must be:

   a. the food.
   b. holding procedures.
   c. the personal hygiene of employees who handle food.
   d. the sanitary condition of kitchen equipment and facilities.

9. Which of the following is noted on the FDA's Food Establishment Inspection Report, but *not* on the HACCP Inspection Data form?

   a. code references
   b. acceptable holding temperatures
   c. food establishment permit number
   d. noncritical violations

10. Which of the following is an example of an imminent health hazard?

    a. spoiled beef stored in a freezer
    b. frozen chicken thawing at room temperature
    c. sewage backing up in a food preparation area
    d. all of the above

Chapter Outline

Learning Objectives

1. Briefly describe the major federal laws regulating food safety, and explain the significance of government regulation for the food service industry. (pp. 35–37)

2. Explain the functions of the regulatory agencies within the U.S. Department of Health and Human Services. (pp. 37–38)

3. Identify and briefly describe the agencies within the U.S. Department of Agriculture (USDA) relevant to the food service industry. (pp. 38–40)

4. Explain the significance of the National Marine Fisheries Service (NMFS) and the Environmental Protection Agency (EPA) to the food service industry. (p. 41)

5. Describe the role of state and local regulatory agencies in sanitation training and certification. (pp. 42–44)

6. Identify and describe the industry and trade organizations important to the food service industry. (pp. 44–46)

7. Describe the permit requirements for a food establishment. (pp. 46–57)

8. Identify the frequency of regulatory authority inspections, and describe important aspects of the inspection procedure. (pp. 57–62)

9. Explain management responsibilities before, during, and after an inspection. (pp. 62–63)

10. Describe permit suspension and revocation, identify when administrative remedies may be applied, and list the types of possible judicial remedies that may be applied. (p. 63)

2

Regulatory and Professional Organizations

The food industry is one of the most heavily regulated industries in the United States. A number of laws cover the land on which food is grown and the oceans from which it is harvested. The pesticides and chemicals used in agriculture are also regulated by law. Once processing of raw food products begins, other laws enter the picture. The preparation and service of food in food establishments are also regulated. The objective of all of this control is to protect the consumer's health and safety. At the same time, this control helps reduce risks to the food service industry and its guests.

> The FDA states:
>
> **"Food"** means a raw, cooked, or processed edible substance, ice, beverage, or ingredient used or intended for use or for sale in whole or in part for human consumption, or chewing gum.
>
> **"Law"** means applicable local, state, and federal statutes, regulations, and ordinances.

Source: FDA 1993 *Food Code.*

Food Laws in the United States: A Brief History

The first food law in the United States was enacted in 1649 in Massachusetts Bay Colony: the governor of the colony specified how much a loaf of bread should weigh to be sold for a penny. In 1785, Massachusetts passed the state's first general food law. It was titled An Act Against Selling Unwholesome Provisions. The Food and Drugs Act of 1906 was the first federal food and drug law in the United States. This act was the forerunner of the 1938 Food, Drug, and Cosmetic Act.

The 1938 **Food, Drug, and Cosmetic Act** provided increased consumer protection. The 1938 act covered labeling requirements, standards of identity and fill, sanitary manufacturing techniques, and misbranding and mislabeling of food products. The Pesticide Chemicals Amendment (1954), the Food Additives Amendment (1958), and the Color Additives Amendment (1960) brought the 1938 act up to date with technological advances in food production. This act with its amendments continues to be the most all-encompassing law related to the food industry in the United States.

A few other laws are historically significant to the food service industry. The 1906 Meat Inspection Act made mandatory the inspection of meat and meat products shipped across state lines. The 1930 Perishable Agricultural Commodities Act required the licensing of dealers, commission agents, and brokers of fresh fruits and vegetables. The 1946 Agricultural Marketing Act defined the functions of the United States Department of Agriculture (USDA). The Poultry Products Inspection Act, passed in 1957, covers wholesomeness and package labeling. The 1967 Wholesome Meat Act amended the 1906 Federal Meat Inspection Act, extending the inspection program to meat shipped within a state. The Egg Products Inspection Act of 1970 improved the safety and wholesomeness of eggs and egg products.

These federal food laws continue to be enforced by the United States government. Several states, counties, and cities have additional food laws that are more rigorous than the federal requirements. Government regulations at all levels are designed to protect the individual consumer and the food processing and food service industries. It has been estimated that more than 3,000 federal, state, and local regulatory agencies are responsible for monitoring the multi-billion dollar food service industry and ensuring food protection.[1]

In recent years, however, the lack of uniformity in food regulations has raised concern. One estimate states that industry expenditures resulting from regulatory variations average between $5.25 million and $15.75 million annually.[2] By the same estimate, it is not unusual for an operation to invest $25,000 to satisfy the peculiarities of the local jurisdiction's code. Some industry executives have proposed a nationwide series of codes and ordinances applicable to the design, construction, and operation of food establishments. Such codes could result in enormous savings for the industry. The FDA's Food Code, which covers health and sanitation, is such a nationwide code. It provides guidance on food safety, sanitation, and fair dealing that can be uniformly adopted for the retail segment of the food industry. This model code is useful to business in that it provides accepted standards that can be applied in training and total quality management programs. The Food Code is also helpful to local, state, and federal governmental organizations that are developing or updating their own codes. Other proposed codes would cover building construction, fire safety, plumbing, electrical, and HVAC systems. Savings for the food service industry could be enormous.

Of course, some argue that too much government involvement is undesirable and unnecessary. Critics say some government regulations are too broad and thus require interpretation by the individual regulatory official or inspector. On the other hand, they say other regulations are too specific and leave no room for the official to consider variables or unique conditions. Worst of all, some regulations are said to contradict or overlap with others so that compliance with one necessitates non-compliance with another.

Some companies complain that careful compliance with government regulations puts a strain on productivity. Regulations are often complex and confusing. Some laws require a great deal of paperwork and recordkeeping. Opponents of more regulation often argue that it costs taxpayers too much to enforce some food laws. Other critics point out that some regulations are outdated and impractical because of rapid technological advances in recent years.

It would be wrong to infer from the criticisms just cited that most people are opposed to current food regulations. In fact, many Americans feel fortunate to live in a country with so many laws governing food safety. Those who have visited countries where there is little or no government regulation of food safety often comment about the difficulty of adjusting to the relatively low level of sanitation.

Advocates of food regulations point to the fact that our country has relatively few food-related health problems on a per capita basis. They also argue that written standards in the form of federal, state, and local food laws make the immense job of running a food service business more manageable. Finally, the defenders of food regulations

Exhibit 2.1 The Government of the United States

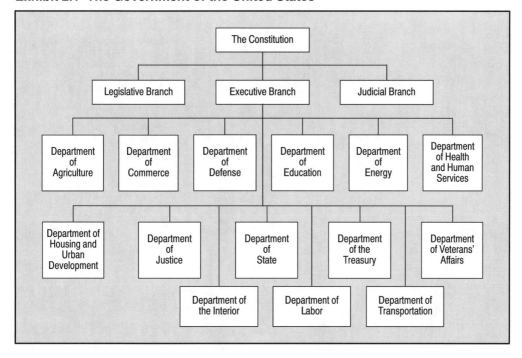

argue that guests expect food service businesses to maintain high levels of safety and sanitation in their operations.

Federal Regulatory Agencies

Most of the federal agencies that regulate the food supply are in the executive branch of the government, which is divided into a number of departments. Of these, the Department of Agriculture, the Department of Health and Human Services, the Department of the Treasury, and the Department of Commerce are most important to the food service industry. Exhibit 2.1 illustrates the general organization of the executive branch.

The Food and Drug Administration (FDA) is a division of the Public Health Service within the Department of Health and Human Services. The FDA is responsible for ensuring that foods are safe, wholesome, and sanitary. The FDA is also responsible for ensuring that regulated products are honestly, accurately, and informatively represented and that these products are in compliance with the law and FDA regulations. Noncompliance is identified and corrected and any unsafe or unlawful products are removed from the marketplace.

The FDA states:

"Regulatory authority" means the local, state, or federal enforcement body or authorized representative having jurisdiction over the food establishment.

Source: FDA 1993 *Food Code.*

Exhibit 2.2 The FDA's Role in Improving Food Sanitation

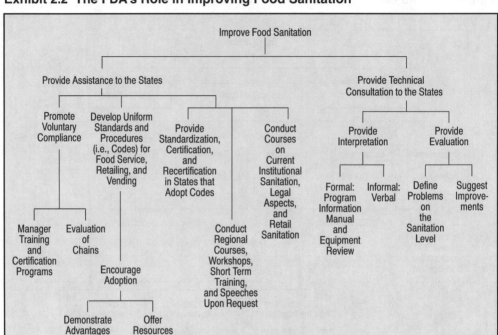

The FDA endeavors to assist the approximately 85 state and territorial agencies and more than 3,000 local departments that have primary responsibility for preventing foodborne illness. Among other duties, the FDA develops and interprets surveillance and compliance programs, model ordinances, codes and regulations, and good manufacturing practices. The many ways in which the FDA improves food service sanitation are presented in Exhibit 2.2.

The FDA also administers the Center for Food Safety and Applied Nutrition. This Center generates policies covering the safety, composition, quality, and labeling of foods and food additives. The Center also assists other federal, state, and local agencies in ensuring a safe and wholesome food supply for the consuming public. This assistance is provided through the Center's Retail Food Protection Branch. Traditionally, the FDA conducts its activities at the wholesale level, while retailers are regulated through state and local public health agencies. The organization and functions of the Center for Food Safety and Applied Nutrition, its Retail Food Protection Branch, and one of its regions are shown in conjunction with state and local agencies in Exhibit 2.3.

The U.S. Centers for Disease Control and Prevention (CDC) are another part of the Public Health Service in the U.S. Department of Health and Human Services. The CDC investigate foodborne disease outbreaks, analyze surveillance data, and publish the results of their data analyses. The CDC also provide training materials and services on the topic of food service sanitation. The CDC perform a variety of valuable field services, such as compiling foodborne illness statistics for the Public Health Service.

The United States Department of Agriculture (USDA) is another major department in the federal government's executive branch. The USDA consists of four broad divisions: Food and Consumer Services, Marketing Services, Economic Policy Analysis and

Exhibit 2.3 Organization and Function of Federal, State, and Local Food Service Sanitation Regulatory Agencies

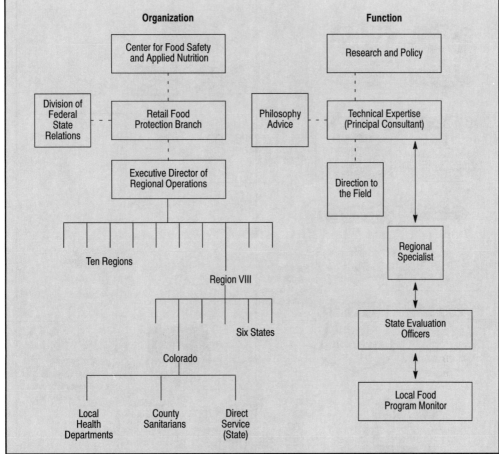

Budget, and Conservation Research and Education. The first two divisions are of interest to the food service industry.

The Food and Consumer Services division contains two agencies. The first agency, the Food Safety and Inspection Service (FSIS), provides continual in-plant inspections of all manufacturers processing meat, poultry, and egg products. The FSIS also reviews inspection procedures in foreign plants shipping meat and poultry products to the United States. The FSIS establishes and maintains uniform quality standards for food commodities and provides inspection and grading services (see Exhibit 2.4).

The FSIS inspects all interstate-shipped meat, poultry, and egg products for wholesomeness and sanitation. The USDA mark of wholesomeness (see Exhibit 2.5) means that the food is fit for human consumption. The FSIS also provides commodity purchase services which remove surplus quantities of food from market channels.

The other agency of the USDA's Food and Consumer Services division is the Food and Nutrition Service (FNS). The FNS administers the food stamp program, the national school lunch program, and the child nutrition program.

Exhibit 2.4 Sample USDA Quality and Yield Grade Stamps

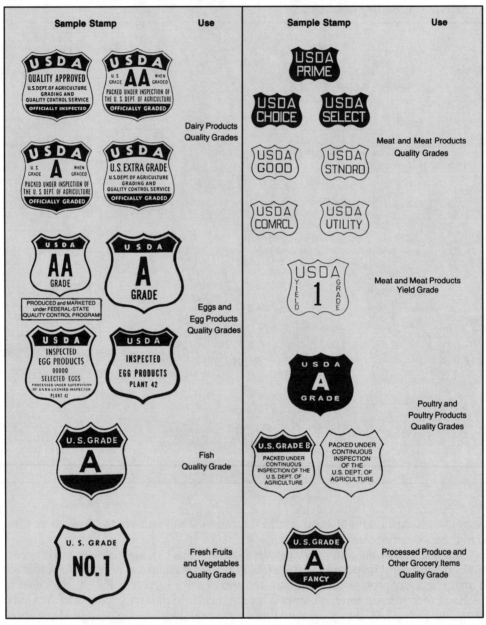

The Marketing Services division of the USDA comprises the Agricultural Marketing Service (AMS), the Animal and Plant Health Inspection Service (APHIS), and the
Federal Grain Inspection Service (FGIS). AMS provides market news, guidelines for fair
business practices, and freight rate services. APHIS prevents the introduction of animal
and plant diseases and pests at ports of entry into the United States. FGIS monitors the
marketing of grains for animal, human, and industrial uses.

Exhibit 2.5 Sample USDA Wholesomeness Inspection Stamps

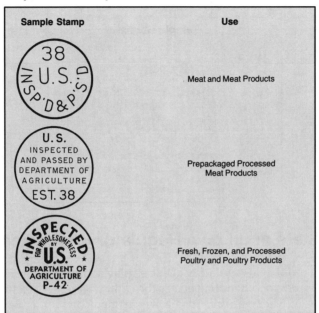

Sample Stamp	Use
	Meat and Meat Products
	Prepackaged Processed Meat Products
	Fresh, Frozen, and Processed Poultry and Poultry Products

The United States Department of the Treasury is important to food service businesses because it includes the Bureau of Alcohol, Tobacco, and Firearms. This bureau enforces laws and regulations pertaining to the production and sale of distilled spirits, beer, and wine.

The United States Department of Commerce includes the National Marine Fisheries Service (NMFS). This service monitors the quality, safety, and identity of fish and shellfish products. NMFS provides a voluntary inspection and grading service for the fishing industry. Inspected products bear a Department of Commerce stamp (see Exhibit 2.6). The stamp is used on products, packages, and in advertising to indicate that the products are clean, safe, and wholesome.

The Environmental Protection Agency (EPA) is an independent agency in the executive branch of the government. The major mission of the EPA is to control and minimize pollution of water, air, and the environment in general. The EPA monitors and enforces regulations related to toxic substances (pesticides, sanitizers, germicides, and other chemicals), waste management, noise control, radiation, and environmental pollution.

The Federal Trade Commission (FTC) is another independent agency in the executive branch. The FTC monitors and eliminates unfair methods of competition and deceptive trade practices. The FTC helps protect American consumers from false advertising claims. The FTC also enforces the Clayton Act, which prohibits monopolies in commerce.

The Occupational Safety and Health Administration (OSHA) was developed as a result of the 1970 Occupational Safety and Health Act. OSHA is charged with developing and monitoring regulations and standards of occupational safety and health. OSHA also conducts inspections and investigations and may issue citations for non-compliance.

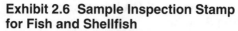

Exhibit 2.6 Sample Inspection Stamp for Fish and Shellfish

State and Local Regulatory Agencies

State, county, and municipal regulatory agencies play an important role in guaranteeing food safety and proper food handling across the United States. For example, the government of the State of Michigan includes a Department of Public Health. Within this department is the Division of Environmental Health, Food Service Sanitation Section. This division enforces Michigan's Food Service Sanitation Statute, contained in Michigan's Public Health Code. The statute is based on the FDA's *Model Food Service Sanitation Ordinance.*

Some states have launched food service sanitation management certification programs. Ohio's program, initiated in 1973, was the first comprehensive program at the state level. Managers must attend a minimum of four day-long sessions on various aspects of food service sanitation. They must also be recertified every two years. Other states have adopted Ohio's certification program or a similar training program.

Local regulations may differ within states, but the FDA's sanitation codes are usually adopted statewide. Some county and municipal health departments have adopted the Food Code even though their states have not yet done so.

For an example of local regulation, consider Ingham County in Michigan. The local health authority, called the Ingham County Health Department, includes a Bureau of Environmental Health. This regulatory authority monitors food establishments throughout the county. It uses the Ingham County Sanitary Code, which is based on the State of Michigan's and the Food and Drug Administration's codes. Food establishment operators in Ingham County must have a system in place which complies with the county code.

Besides the assistance available through regional offices, state and local regulatory agencies can be very helpful in sanitation training. These agencies have several other roles in improving food service sanitation (see Exhibit 2.7). State and local agencies can be invited to monitor training programs to ensure that they are satisfactory and complete. Whenever possible, sanitation training programs should be jointly sponsored by industry associations and regulatory agencies. Certification of managers and staff members is a desirable and attainable goal of interest to both groups. Certification success rates are usually higher if the exams are preceded by well-designed training programs.

Exhibit 2.7 The Roles of State and Local Regulatory Agencies in Improving Food Sanitation

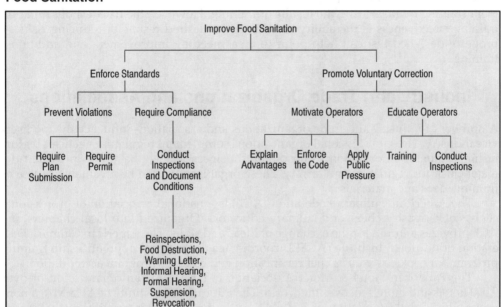

Reciprocal recognition for state-approved training programs is also desirable. Uniformity in the enforcement of rules and regulations covering food service not only benefits the industry as a whole but may reduce enforcement costs for regulatory agencies. Multi-unit chains operating in more than one state can also function more efficiently under similar regulations. Furthermore, considering mobility and turnover in the food service industry, reciprocal recognition would allow previously certified managers and staff members to be recognized as such when they move from one state to another.

In an attempt to promote reciprocity along with certification, the FDA, state and local regulatory agencies, educators and trainers, and representatives from a number of food service industry segments worked with the Educational Testing Service (ETS) to develop a food protection certification program. The Food Protection Certification Program test focuses on generally recognized standards, procedures, and practices in the following three areas:

- Purchasing, receiving, and storing food (approximately 20%)

- Processing, serving, and dispensing food (approximately 50%)

- Employees, facilities, and equipment (approximately 30%)

The test consists of multiple choice questions and is based on the FDA's Food Code. Upon successfully completing the test, a candidate receives a certificate and a wallet card from ETS. The decision of whether to endorse or require the test is left to the individual states.

Training prior to testing presents the critical knowledge that is necessary to understand the "whys" behind the "how-tos." Training, not testing, is the key to effectively managing the sanitation risks in a food establishment. Training helps develop the skills, knowledge, and behaviors that are necessary in managing risks. Testing can complement training by measuring the results of training. However, the true test of sanitation training effectiveness is the ability to achieve the desired results of reducing risks. A properly designed test can help point to areas needing improvement and additional training.

Industry and Trade Organizations and Associations

A number of industry and trade organizations and associations influence the food service industry. These professional organizations complement regulatory agencies by furnishing valuable information to hospitality businesses. They have also provided the major push for regulatory uniformity. These organizations can be a valuable source of training ideas and materials.

The American Culinary Federation (ACF) is a national association of professional chefs, cooks, pastry chefs, and culinary educators. Organized into local chapters, the ACF provides a forum for the exchange of ideas and skills. The American Culinary Federation Educational Institute (ACFEI) coordinates the national apprenticeship training program for cooks, as well as chef certification and culinary program accreditation.

The American Hotel & Motel Association (AH&MA) is an organization of over 9,000 hotels and motels all over the world. The Educational Institute of AH&MA, a nonprofit educational foundation of AH&MA, is the forerunner in providing educational materials for hotel, motel, restaurant, and institutional managers and staff members. The Educational Institute develops textbooks (such as this one), video training tapes, seminars, software, interactive video programs, how-to manuals, professional certification, and hospitality training programs. The Institute offers courses through independent learning, team learning, EI chapters, and many colleges and universities worldwide.

The American Public Health Association (APHA) is one of this nation's oldest professional societies for doctors, nurses, and sanitarians. APHA's Food Protection Committee focuses on public health and periodically recommends standards and policies pertaining to food protection.

The Food Research Institute (FRI) generates research data in the areas of food contamination and the prevention of foodborne diseases. FRI works closely with food processing establishments and the food service industry.

The Foodservice Consultants Society International (FCSI) is a non-profit professional society of consultants in design, equipment, engineering, and management of the food service industry. FCSI furthers research, development, and education in the food service field and was established to promote professionalism in food service and hospitality consulting. FCSI has developed a code of ethics for the profession it represents.

The International Association of Milk, Food, and Environmental Sanitarians (IAMFES) is a professional organization for people in the fields of food research and technology and food protection. IAMFES publishes two journals featuring articles on the topic of food protection.

The International Food Service Executives Association (IFSEA) is a professional organization dedicated to raising food service industry standards, educating members and future industry leaders, and recognizing members' achievements. Active members include personnel in all aspects of food service: executive chefs; operators; dietitians; consultants; and managers and owners of catering firms, restaurants, hotels, clubs, institutions, armed forces dining facilities, and other organizations with food service operations.

Exhibit 2.8 NSF Seal of Approval for Equipment and Utensils

Source: National Sanitation Foundation, Ann Arbor, Michigan.

The National Environmental Health Association (NEHA) is a society for environmental health officials at various levels of government. NEHA provides educational services, publishes a journal, and conducts research and programs in the field of environmental health.

The National Restaurant Association (NRA) is a trade organization for food service industry professionals in the United States. The NRA adopts policies and publishes position statements on issues of concern to commercial and non-commercial food service owners and managers. The NRA's Health and Safety Committee addresses issues of public health as they relate to the food service industry. NRA also maintains a strong lobbying force in the nation's capital. The Educational Foundation of the National Restaurant Association is responsible for educational materials and certification courses.

The National Sanitation Foundation (NSF) is a not-for-profit corporation that develops and administers programs relating to public health and environment in areas of service, research, and education. NSF develops and adopts voluntary consensus standards, and evaluates and tests products (equipment and utensils) against these standards, other standards, and government regulations. The standards are agreed upon by public health officials and industry representatives alike. Their purpose is to assist manufacturers in the production of equipment that meets minimum health code requirements. If NSF determines that equipment and utensils meet its minimum acceptance levels, the manufacturer can display the NSF seal on the tested equipment. This seal (see Exhibit 2.8) indicates that the equipment or utensil will normally meet regulatory requirements as they relate to public health. (In some areas, the NSF standards *are* the regulatory requirements.) Thus, NSF standards also make it easier for equipment buyers and regulatory agencies to determine if equipment meets the code requirements.

NSF also provides a certification service program for products or services which conform to standards other than official NSF regulations or specifications. NSF's assessment service is an additional program that covers such areas as consulting, testing, and inspections, research or studies, pre-market evaluations, demonstration projects, and performance studies.

The Society for the Advancement of Foodservice Research (SAFSR) is a national professional organization which provides a network for the exchange of ideas, as well as for the presentation of the current status of evolving technology and its applications for the food service industry. SAFSR is the only association that presents an annual industry position regarding the status of research and development in the food service industry.

The Society for Foodservice Management (SFM) is the only national professional organization serving the needs and interests of people in business and industry (non-commercial) food service. SFM sponsors a number of regional conferences and a national conference annually for members.

Several of these trade, industry, and professional organizations also operate at the state and local levels. Both AH&MA and NRA have state groups that are affiliated with the national organizations. Food service owners, managers, and staff members are encouraged to join and become active in local and national associations and professional organizations. Aside from the usual advantages of informal contacts with other professionals, these groups offer two clear benefits to their members: (1) they are valuable sources of training materials, and (2) industry-sponsored educational programs help reduce the need for governmental regulations and mandatory inspections.

Obtaining Permission to Operate a Food Establishment

The FDA's Food Code sets forth minimum requirements for the operation of a food service establishment. As mentioned earlier, most states and localities have used the FDA's Food Code in formulating their regulations. Some have adopted it verbatim; others have made minor changes to fit local conditions. Since it would be impossible to cover all of these variations and adaptations, this book focuses on the federal compliance procedures. You should obtain a copy of the regulations used by your state and county or city. Ask the appropriate health authorities if these codes are based on the FDA's Food Code and, if so, what changes (if any) have been made. This way, you will know how closely the recommendations given here match those in your area.

The FDA states:

Food Establishment.

(a) **"Food establishment"** means an operation that stores, prepares, packages, serves, vends, or otherwise provides food for human consumption:

   (i)   Such as a restaurant; satellite or catered feeding location; catering operation if the operation provides food directly to a consumer or to a conveyance used to transport people; market; vending location; conveyance used to transport people; institution; or food bank; and

(ii)   That relinquishes possession of food to a consumer directly, or indirectly through a delivery service such as home delivery of grocery orders or restaurant takeout orders, or delivery service that is provided by common carriers.

(b) **"Food establishment"** includes:

(i)   An element of the operation such as a transportation vehicle or a central preparation facility that supplies a vending location or satellite feeding location *unless the vending or feeding location is permitted by the regulatory authority;* and

(ii)   An operation that is conducted in a mobile, stationary, temporary, or permanent facility or location; where consumption is on or off the premises; and regardless of whether there is a charge for the food.

(c) *"Food establishment" does not include:*

(i)   *An establishment that offers only prepackaged foods that are not potentially hazardous;*

(ii)   *A produce stand that only offers whole, uncut fresh fruits and vegetables;*

(iii)   *A food processing plant;*

(iv)   *A kitchen in a private home if only food that is not potentially hazardous is prepared for sale or service at a function such as a religious or charitable organization's bake sale if allowed by law and if the consumer is informed by a clearly visible placard at the sales or service location that the food is prepared in a kitchen that is not subject to regulation and inspection by the regulatory authority;*

(v)   *An area where food that is prepared as specified in Subparagraph (c)(iv) of this definition is sold or offered for human consumption;*

(vi)   *A kitchen in a private home, such as a small family day-care provider; or a bed-and-breakfast operation that prepares and offers food to guests if the home is owner occupied, the number of available guest bedrooms does not exceed 6, breakfast is the only meal offered, the number of guests served does not exceed 18, and the consumer is informed by statements contained in published advertisements, mailed brochures, or placards posted at the registration area that the food is prepared in a kitchen that is not regulated and inspected by the regulatory authority; or*

(vii)   *A private home that receives catered or home-delivered food.*

Source: FDA 1993 *Food Code.*

In the United States, a food establishment cannot operate without the required permits. (These documents are also called certificates or licenses, depending on the jurisdiction; the three terms are used interchangeably in this text.) Permits are usually issued by local or state regulatory authorities, and they are generally non-transferable. The valid documents must be posted in a conspicuous place in the food establishment. Permits can be issued only to businesses that comply with the requirements of the state or local regulatory agency which issues such documents. Establishments serving beer, wine, and alcoholic spirits must obtain additional documents from the state liquor control commission. A sample license is presented in Exhibit 2.9.

Exhibit 2.9 Sample License Form for a Food Service Establishment

LICENSE NO.	STATE of MICHIGAN LICENSE	EXPIRES
ISSUED BY THE MICHIGAN DEPARTMENT OF PUBLIC HEALTH TO OPERATE UNDER THE PROVISIONS OF PART 129 ACT 368, PUBLIC ACTS OF 1978 AT:		THIS LICENSE IS NOT TRANSFERABLE AS TO PERSON OR PLACE. NOTIFY THE LOCAL HEALTH DEPARTMENT PRIOR TO CHANGE OF OWNERSHIP [SECTION 12904(6)]
IS GRANTED TO: +	SAMPLE +	RESTRICTIONS OR CONDITIONS:
+ DIRECT INQUIRIES TO:	+	

Source: State of Michigan.

The FDA states:

8-101.10   Public Health Protection.

(A) The regulatory authority shall apply this Code to promote its underlying purpose, as specified in § 1-102.10, of safeguarding public health and assuring that food is safe, unadulterated, and honestly presented when offered to the consumer.

(B) In enforcing the provisions of this Code, the regulatory authority shall assess existing facilities or equipment that were in use before the effective date of this Code based on the following considerations:

(1)   Whether the facilities or equipment are in good repair and capable of being maintained in a sanitary condition;

(2)   Whether food-contact surfaces comply with Subpart 4-101; and

(3)   The existence of a documented agreement of the permit holder that the facilities or equipment will be replaced as specified under ¶ 8-304.11(G).

8-102.10   Preventing Health Hazards, Provision for Conditions Not Addressed.

(A) If necessary to protect against public health hazards, the regulatory authority may impose specific requirements in addition to the requirements contained in this Code that are authorized by law.

(B) The regulatory authority shall document the conditions that necessitate the imposition of additional requirements and the underlying public health rationale. The documentation shall be provided to the permit applicant or permit holder and a copy shall be maintained in the regulatory authority's file for the food establishment.

8-103.10   Modifications and Waivers.

The regulatory authority may grant a variance by modifying or waiving the requirements of this Code if in the opinion of the regulatory authority a health hazard will not result from the variance. If a variance is granted, the regulatory authority shall retain the information specified in § 8-103.11 in its records for the food establishment.

8-103.11   Documentation of Proposed Variance and Justification.

Before a variance from a requirement of this Code is approved by the regulatory authority, the information that shall be provided by the person requesting the variance and retained in the regulatory authority's file on the food establishment includes:

(A)   A statement of the proposed variance of the Code requirement citing relevant Code section numbers;

(B)   An analysis of the rationale for how the potential public health hazards addressed by the relevant Code sections will be alternatively addressed by the proposal; and

(C)   A HACCP plan if required as specified in § 8-201.13(A) that includes the information specified in § 8-201.14 as it is relevant to the variance requested.

8-103.12   Conformance with Approved Procedures.*

If the regulatory authority grants a variance as specified in § 8-103.10, or a HACCP plan is otherwise required as specified in § 8-201.13, the permit holder shall:

(A)   Comply with the HACCP plans and procedures that are submitted and approved as specified in § 8-201.14 as a basis for the modification or waiver; and

(B)   Maintain and provide to the regulatory authority, upon request, records specified in ¶¶ 8-201.14(D) and (E) that demonstrate that the following are routinely employed:

(1)   Procedures for monitoring critical control points,

(2)   Monitoring of the critical control points,

(3)   Verification of the effectiveness of an operation or process, and

(4)   Necessary corrective actions if there is failure at a critical control point.

8-201.11   When Plans Are Required.

A permit applicant or permit holder shall submit to the regulatory authority properly prepared plans and specifications for review and approval before:

(A)   The construction of a food establishment;

(B)   The conversion of an existing structure for use as a food establishment; or

(C)   The remodeling of a food establishment or a change of type of food establishment or food operation as specified in ¶ 8-302.14(C) if the regulatory authority determines that plans and specifications are necessary to assure compliance with this Code.

8-201.12   Contents of the Plans and Specifications.

The plans and specifications for a food establishment, including a food establishment specified in § 8-201.14, shall include, as required by the regulatory authority based on the type of operation, type of food preparation, and foods prepared, the following information to demonstrate conformance with Code provisions:

(A)   Intended menu;

(B)   Anticipated volume of food to be stored, prepared, and sold or served;

(C)   Proposed layout, mechanical schematics, construction materials, and finish schedules;

(D)   Proposed equipment types, manufacturers, model numbers, locations, dimensions, performance capacities, and installation specifications;

(E)   Written standard operating procedures that reflect the knowledge specified in § 2-102.11 and implement the requirements of this Code, including indication of how practices assure that:

(1)   The transmission of foodborne disease is prevented by managing job applicants and food employees as specified in Subpart 2-201,

(2)   Food is received from approved sources as specified in § 3-201.11,

(3)   Food is managed so that the safety and integrity of the food from the time of delivery to the establishment throughout its storage, preparation, and transportation to the point of sale or service to the consumer is protected,

(4)   Potentially hazardous food is maintained, including freezing, cold holding, cooking, hot holding, cooling, reheating, and serving in conformance with the temperature and time requirements specified in Parts 3-4 and 3-5,

(5)   Warewashing is effective, including assurance that the chemical solutions and exposure times necessary for cleaning and sanitizing utensils and food-contact surfaces of equipment are provided as specified in Parts 4-6 and 4-7, and

(6)   Records that are specified in §§ 3-203.11 and 5-205.13 are retained for inspection;

(F)   Proposed program of training for the persons in charge and food employees pertaining to protecting public health and the safety and integrity of food; and

(G)   Other information that may be required by the regulatory authority for the proper review of the proposed construction, conversion or modification, and procedures for operating a food establishment.

8-201.13   When a HACCP Plan Is Required.

(A) Before engaging in an activity that requires a HACCP plan, a permit applicant or permit holder shall submit to the regulatory authority for approval a properly prepared HACCP plan as specified under § 8-201.14 and the relevant provisions of this Code if:

(1)   Submission of a HACCP plan is required according to law;

(2)   A variance is required as specified under § 3-502.11, ¶ 4-204.110(B), or Subparagraphs 3-201.14(A)(2)(b), 3-203.12(B)(2), or 3-401.11(B)(2); or

(3)   The regulatory authority determines that a food preparation or processing method requires a variance based on a plan submittal specified under § 8-201.12, an inspectional finding, or a variance request.

(B)   A permit applicant or permit holder shall have a properly prepared HACCP plan as specified under § 3-502.12.

8-201.14   Contents of a HACCP Plan.

For a food establishment that is required under § 8-201.13 to have a HACCP plan, the plan and specifications shall indicate:

(A)   A categorization of the types of potentially hazardous foods that are specified in the menu such as soups and sauces, salads, and bulk, solid foods such as meat roasts, or of other foods that are specified by the regulatory authority;

(B)   A flow diagram by specific food or category type identifying critical control points and providing information on the following:

(1)   Ingredients, materials, and equipment used in the preparation of that food, and

(2)   Formulations or recipes that delineate methods and procedural control measures that address the food safety concerns involved;

(C)   Food employee and supervisory training plan specified in ¶ 8-201.12(F) that addresses the food safety issues of concern;

(D)   A statement of standard operating procedures for the plan under consideration including clearly identifying:

(1)   Each critical control point,

(2)   The critical limits for each critical control point,

(3)   The method and frequency for monitoring and controlling each critical control point by the food employee designated by the person in charge,

(4)   The method and frequency for the person in charge to routinely verify that the food employee is following standard operating procedures and monitoring critical control points,

(5)   Action to be taken by the person in charge if the critical limits for each critical control point are not met, and

(6)   Records to be maintained by the person in charge to demonstrate that the HACCP plan is properly operated and managed; and

(E)   Additional scientific data or other information, as required by the regulatory authority, supporting the determination that food safety is not compromised by the proposal.

8-202.10   Trade Secrets.

The regulatory authority shall treat as confidential in accordance with law, information that meets the criteria under law for a trade secret and is contained on inspection report forms and in the plans and specifications submitted as specified in §§ 8-201.12 and 8-201.14.

8-203.10   Preoperational Inspections.

The regulatory authority shall conduct one or more preoperational inspections to verify that the food establishment is constructed and equipped in accordance with the approved plans and approved modifications of those plans and is in compliance with [the] law and this Code.

Source: FDA 1993 *Food Code.*

The process for obtaining a valid permit may appear long and complicated. However, the objective of the paperwork is to make it possible for the government to protect the public health. Application must be made in writing to the appropriate regulatory agency. Required information includes the name and address of each applicant, the signature of each applicant, the type and location of the proposed food service business and the HACCP plan. Additionally, the intended menu, anticipated volume of food, proposed layout and schedules, proposed equipment specifications, written standard operating procedures, proposed training program for both managers and staff members, and other information may be required. Check with your local regulatory agency for the specific details in your area.

The FDA states:

"Permit" means the document issued by the regulatory authority that authorizes a person to operate a food establishment.

"Permit holder" means the entity that:

(a)   Is legally responsible for the operation of the food establishment such as the owner, the owner's agent, or other person; and

(b)   Possesses a valid permit to operate a food establishment.

8-301.11   Prerequisite for Operation.

A person may not operate a food establishment without a valid permit to operate issued by the regulatory authority.

8-302.11   Submission 30 Calendar Days Before Proposed Opening.

An applicant shall submit an application for a permit at least 30 calendar days before the date planned for opening a food establishment or the expiration date of the current permit for an existing facility.

8-302.12   Form of Submission.

A person desiring to operate a food establishment shall submit to the regulatory authority a written application for a permit on a form provided by the regulatory authority.

8-302.13   Qualifications and Responsibilities of Applicants.

To qualify for a permit, an applicant shall:

(A)   Be an owner of the establishment or an officer of the legal ownership;

(B)   Comply with the requirements of this Code;

(C)   As specified under § 8-402.11, agree to permit access to the food establishment and to provide required information; and

(D)   Pay the applicable permit fees at the time the application is submitted.

8-302.14   Contents of the Application.

The application shall include:

(A)   The name, birth date, mailing address, telephone number, and signature of the person applying for the permit and the name, mailing address, and location of the food establishment;

(B)   Information specifying whether the food establishment is owned by an association, corporation, individual, partnership, or other legal entity;

(C)   A statement specifying whether the food establishment:

(1)   Is mobile or stationary and temporary or permanent, and

(2)   Is an operation that includes one or more of the following:

(a)   Prepares, offers for sale, or serves potentially hazardous food:

(i)   Only to order upon a consumer's request,

(ii)   In advance in quantities based on projected consumer demand and discards food that is not sold or served at a frequency approved by the regulatory authority, or

(iii)   Using time as the public health control as specified in § 3-501.19,

(b)   Prepares potentially hazardous food in advance using a food preparation method that involves two or more steps which may include combining potentially hazardous ingredients; cooking; cooling; reheating; hot or cold holding; freezing; or thawing,

(c)   Prepares food as specified in Subparagraph (C)(2)(b) of this section for delivery to and consumption at a location off the premises of the food establishment where it is prepared,

(d)   Prepares food as specified in Subparagraph (C)(2)(b) of this section for service to a highly susceptible population,

(e)   Prepares only food that is not potentially hazardous, or

(f)   Does not prepare, but offers for sale only prepackaged food that is not potentially hazardous;

(D)   The name, title, address, and telephone number of the person directly responsible for the food establishment;

(E)   The name, title, address, and telephone number of the person who functions as the immediate supervisor of the person specified in ¶ (D) of this section such as the zone, district, or regional supervisor;

(F)   The names, titles, and addresses of:

(1)   The persons comprising the legal ownership as specified under ¶ (B) of this section including the owners and officers, and

(2)   The local resident agent if one is required based on the type of legal ownership;

(G)   A statement signed by the applicant that:

(1)   Attests to the accuracy of the information provided in the application, and

(2)   Affirms that the applicant will:

(a)   Comply with this Code, and

(b)   Allow the regulatory authority access to the establishment as specified under § 8-402.11 and to the records specified under §§ 3-203.12 and 5-205.13 and Subparagraph 8-201.14(D)(6); and

(H)   Other information required by the regulatory authority.

8-303.10   New, Converted, or Remodeled Establishments.

For food establishments that are required to submit plans as specified in § 8-201.11 the regulatory authority shall issue a permit to the applicant after:

(A)   A properly completed application is submitted;

(B)   The required fee is submitted;

(C)   The required plans, specifications, and information are reviewed and approved; and

(D)   A preoperational inspection shows that the establishment is built or remodeled in accordance with the approved plans and specifications and that the establishment is in compliance with this Code.

8-303.20   Existing Establishments, Permit Renewal, and Change of Ownership.

The regulatory authority may renew a permit for an existing food establishment or may issue a permit to a new owner of an existing food establishment after a properly completed application is submitted, reviewed, and approved, the fees are paid, and an inspection shows that the establishment is in compliance with this Code.

8-303.30   Denial of Application for Permit, Notice.

If an application for a permit to operate is denied, the regulatory authority shall provide the applicant with a notice that includes:

(A)   The specific reasons and Code citations for the permit denial;

(B)   The actions, if any, that the applicant must take to qualify for a permit; and

(C)   Advisement of the applicant's right of appeal and the process and time frames for appeal that are provided under law.

8-304.10   Responsibilities of the Regulatory Authority.

(A) At the time a permit is first issued, the regulatory authority shall provide to the permit holder a copy of this Code so that the permit holder is notified of the compliance requirements and the conditions of retention, as specified under § 8-304.11, that are applicable to the permit.

(B) *Failure to provide the information specified in ¶ (A) of this section does not prevent the regulatory authority from taking authorized action or seeking remedies if the permit holder fails to comply with this Code or an order, warning, or directive of the regulatory authority.*

8-304.11   Responsibilities of the Permit Holder.

Upon acceptance of the permit issued by the regulatory authority, the permit holder in order to retain the permit shall:

(A)   Post the permit in a location in the food establishment that is conspicuous to consumers;

(B)   Comply with the provisions of this Code including the conditions of a granted variance as specified under § 8-103.12, and approved plans as specified under § 8-201.12;

(C)   If a food establishment is required under § 8-201.13 to operate under a HACCP plan, comply with the plan as specified under § 8-103.12;

(D)   Immediately contact the regulatory authority to report an illness of an applicant or employee as specified under § 2-201.15;

(E)   Immediately discontinue operations and notify the regulatory authority if an imminent health hazard may exist as specified under § 8-404.11;

(F)   Allow representatives of the regulatory authority access to the food establishment as specified under § 8-402.11;

(G)   Replace existing facilities and equipment allowed in § 8-101.10 with facilities and equipment that comply with this Code if:

> (1)   The regulatory authority directs the replacement because the facilities and equipment constitute a public health hazard or no longer comply with the criteria upon which the facilities and equipment were accepted,

> (2)   The regulatory authority directs the replacement of the facilities and equipment because of a change of ownership, or

> (3)   The facilities and equipment are replaced in the normal course of operation;

(H)   Comply with directives of the regulatory authority including time frames for corrective actions specified in inspection reports, notices, orders, warnings, and other directives issued by the regulatory authority in regard to the permit holder's food establishment or in response to community emergencies;

(I)   Accept notices issued and served by the regulatory authority according to law; and

(J)   Be subject to the administrative, civil, injunctive, and criminal remedies authorized under law for failure to comply with this Code or a directive of the regulatory authority, including time frames for corrective actions specified in inspection reports, notices, orders, warnings, and other directives.

8-304.20   Permits Not Transferable.

A permit may not be transferred from one person to another person, from one food establishment to another, or from one type of operation to another if the food operation changes from the type of operation specified in the application as specified in ¶ 8-302.14(C) and the change in operation is not approved by the regulatory authority.

Source: FDA 1993 *Food Code.*

Approval is also required whenever any of the following activities takes place:

1. Construction of a food establishment
2. Conversion of an existing structure for use as a food establishment
3. Remodeling of a food establishment or change of type of food establishment or operation

All of these situations require a submission of plans for review by the appropriate regulatory authority. Plans and specifications must contain the proposed layout, arrangement, mechanical plans, and construction materials of work areas, as well as the type and model of proposed fixed equipment and facilities. Approval is based on whether the new, remodeled, or converted facility meets the minimum specifications of the Food Code. After plan approval and prior to the opening of the establishment, the regulatory authority must inspect the completed construction to ensure that it has been built according to the approved plans.

When an existing food establishment is purchased, the procedures vary. Some jurisdictions do not automatically issue a license to the new owner simply because the previous owner was once granted permission to operate. The regulatory authority may reserve the right to inspect the premises. If any problems are discovered, the new owner may be required to bring the operation into substantial compliance with the jurisdiction's code. Anyone who plans to purchase an existing food establishment should: (1) check the inspection history with the local health department; (2) try to obtain a commitment (preferably in writing) from the health department stating that the existing operation has no problems requiring correction to achieve compliance; (3) consider hiring a facility consultant; and (4) make the purchase contingent upon the seller's correction of all health code violations.

Inspections by Regulatory Agencies

Regardless of how a food establishment is acquired or remodeled, regulatory officials must inspect it prior to issuing a permit. The inspectors determine whether the facilities comply with the jurisdiction's sanitation requirements. If the application has been properly filed and the facilities pass the inspection, the agency's approval will be forthcoming.

The FDA states that food establishment inspections should be performed at least once every six months. State and local jurisdictions may perform inspections more or less frequently, depending on budgets, available personnel, philosophy, past performance (either for nonconformance with Code or HACCP plan requirements that are critical or numerous or repeat violations of Code or HACCP plan requirements that are noncritical), hazards associated with the particular foods, type of operation, number of people served, and whether the population served is highly susceptible. Generally, facilities which regularly receive low sanitation scores, and thus have higher risks, are inspected more frequently.

The FDA states:

8-401.10   Establishing (Frequency).

(A) Except as specified in ¶ ¶ (B) and (C) of this section, the regulatory authority shall inspect a food establishment at least once every 6 months.

(B) *The regulatory authority may increase the interval between inspections beyond 6 months if:*

(1) *The food establishment is fully operating under an approved and validated HACCP plan as specified under § 8-201.14 and ¶¶ 8-103.12(A) and (B);*

(2) *The food establishment is assigned a less frequent inspection frequency based on a risk-based inspection schedule that is formally adopted and is being uniformly applied throughout the jurisdiction and at least once every 6 months the establishment is contacted by telephone or other means by the regulatory authority to assure that the establishment manager and the nature of food operation are not changed; or*

(3) *The establishment's operation involves only coffee service and other unpackaged or prepackaged food that is not potentially hazardous such as carbonated beverages and snack food such as chips, nuts, popcorn, and pretzels.*

(C) The regulatory authority shall periodically inspect throughout its permit period a temporary food establishment that prepares, sells, or serves unpackaged potentially hazardous food and that:

(1) Has improvised rather than permanent facilities or equipment for accomplishing functions such as handwashing, food preparation and protection, food temperature control, warewashing, providing drinking water, waste retention and disposal, and insect and rodent control; or

(2) Has inexperienced food employees.

8-401.20   Performance- and Risk-Based.

Within the parameters specified in § 8-401.10, the regulatory authority shall prioritize, and conduct more frequent inspections based upon its assessment of a food establishment's history of compliance with this Code and the establishment's potential as a vector of foodborne illness by evaluating:

(A) Past performance, for nonconformance with Code or HACCP plan requirements that are critical;

(B) Past performance, for numerous or repeat violations of Code or HACCP plan requirements that are noncritical;

(C) The hazards associated with the particular foods that are prepared, stored, or served;

(D) The type of operation including the methods and extent of food storage, preparation, and service;

(E) The number of people served; and

(F) Whether the population served is a highly susceptible population.

8-402.11   (Access) Allowed at Reasonable Times after Due Notice.

After the regulatory authority presents official credentials and provides notice of the purpose of, and an intent to conduct, an inspection, the person in charge shall allow the regulatory authority to determine if the food establishment is in compliance with this Code by allowing access to the establishment, allowing inspection, and providing information and records specified in this Code and to which the regulatory authority is entitled according to law, during the food establishment's hours of operation and other reasonable times.

8-402.20   Refusal, Notification of Right to Access, and Final Request for Access.

If a person denies access to the regulatory authority, the regulatory authority shall:

(A)   Inform the person that:

(1)   The permit holder is required to allow access to the regulatory authority as specified under § 8-402.11 of this Code;

(2)   Access is a condition of the acceptance and retention of a food establishment permit to operate as specified under § 8-304.11(F); and

(3)   If access is denied, an order issued by the appropriate authority allowing access, hereinafter referred to as an inspection order, may be obtained according to law; and

(B)   Make a final request for access.

8-402.30   Refusal, Reporting.

If after the regulatory authority presents credentials and provides notice as specified under § 8-402.11, explains the authority upon which access is requested, and makes a final request for access as specified in § 8-402.20, the person in charge continues to refuse access, the regulatory authority shall provide details of the denial of access on an inspection report form.

8-402.40   Inspection Order to Gain Access.

If denied access to a food establishment for an authorized purpose and after complying with § 8-402.20, the regulatory authority may issue, or apply for the issuance of, an inspection order to gain access as provided under law.

8-403.10   Documenting Information and Observations.

The regulatory authority shall document on an inspection report form:

(A)   Administrative information about the establishment's legal identity, street and mailing addresses, type of establishment and operation as specified in ¶ 8-302.14(C), inspection date, and other information such as type of water supply and sewage disposal, status of the permit, and personnel certificates that may be required; and

(B)   Specific factual observations of violative conditions or other deviations from this Code that require correction by the permit holder including:

(1)   Failure of the person in charge to demonstrate the knowledge of foodborne illness prevention, application of HACCP principles, and the requirements of this Code specified under § 2-102.11,

(2)   Failure of food employees and the person in charge to demonstrate their knowledge of their responsibility to report a disease or medical condition as specified under §§ 2-201.14 and 2-201.15,

(3)   Nonconformance with critical items of this Code,

(4)   Failure of the appropriate food employees to demonstrate their knowledge of, and ability to perform in accordance with, the procedural, monitoring, verification, and corrective action practices required by the regulatory authority as specified under ¶ 8-304.11(C),

(5)   Failure of the person in charge to provide records required by the regulatory authority for determining conformance with a HACCP plan as specified under Subparagraph 8-201.14(D)(6), and

(6)   Nonconformance with critical limits of a HACCP plan.

8-403.20   Specifying Time Frame for Corrections.

The regulatory authority shall specify on the inspection report form the time frame for correction of the violations as specified under §§ 8-404.11, 8-405.11, and 8-406.11.

8-403.30   Issuing Report and Obtaining Acknowledgment of Receipt.

At the conclusion of the inspection and according to law, the regulatory authority shall provide a copy of the completed inspection report and the notice to correct violations to the permit holder or to the person in charge, and request a signed acknowledgment of receipt.

8-403.40   Refusal to Sign Acknowledgment.

The regulatory authority shall:

(A)   Inform a person who declines to sign an acknowledgment of receipt of inspectional findings as specified in § 8-403.30 that:

(1)   An acknowledgment of receipt is not an agreement with findings,

(2)   Refusal to sign an acknowledgment of receipt will not affect the permit holder's obligation to correct the violations noted in the inspection report within the time frames specified, and

(3)   A refusal to sign an acknowledgment of receipt is noted in the inspection report and conveyed to the regulatory authority's historical record for the food establishment; and

(B)   Make a final request that the person in charge sign an acknowledgment of receipt of inspectional findings.

8-403.50   Public Information.

Except as specified in § 8-202.10, the regulatory authority shall treat the inspection report as a public document and shall make it available for disclosure to a person who requests it under law.

8-404.11   Ceasing Operations and Reporting.

(A) Except as specified in ¶ (B) of this section, a permit holder shall immediately discontinue operations and notify the regulatory authority if an imminent health hazard may exist because of an emergency such as a fire, flood, extended interruption of electrical or water service, sewage backup, misuse of poisonous or toxic materials, onset of an apparent foodborne illness outbreak, gross insanitary occurrence or condition, or other circumstance that may endanger public health;

(B) *A permit holder need not discontinue operations in an area of an establishment that is unaffected by the imminent health hazard.*

8-404.12   Resumption of Operations.

If operations are discontinued as specified under § 8-404.11 or otherwise according to law, the permit holder shall obtain approval from the regulatory authority before resuming operations.

8-405.11   Timely Correction.

(A) Except as specified in ¶ (B) of this section, a permit holder shall at the time of inspection correct a critical violation of this Code and implement corrective actions for a HACCP plan provision that is not in compliance with its critical limit.

(B) *Considering the nature of the potential hazard involved and the complexity of the corrective action needed, the regulatory authority may agree to or specify a longer time frame, not to exceed 10 calendar days after the inspection, for the permit holder to correct critical Code violations or HACCP plan deviations.*

8-405.20   Verification and Documentation of Correction.

(A) After observing at the time of inspection a correction of a critical violation or deviation, the regulatory authority shall enter the violation and information about the corrective action on the inspection report.

(B) As specified under ¶ 8-405.11(B), after receiving notification that the permit holder has corrected a critical violation or HACCP plan deviation, or at the end of the specified period of time, the regulatory authority shall verify correction of the violation, document the information on an inspection report, and enter the report in the regulatory authority's records.

Source: FDA 1993 *Food Code.*

When a **sanitarian** (often called a health inspector) enters a food establishment, the sanitarian, the manager, and the staff members have a number of responsibilities to ensure a professional approach to the inspection.

The Sanitarian's Responsibilities

As a representative of the regulatory agency, the sanitarian has the responsibility to carry out his or her duties in a professional manner. The sanitarian may inspect all areas of the facility and may even examine the records of the business to obtain information on the purchase, receipt, and use of food supplies. The sanitarian must record all inspection findings on an inspection report form such as the FDA's **Food Establishment Inspection Report** (see Chapter 1).

The inspector may examine or sample food products. Using a written notice to the owner or person in charge, the sanitarian may place a **hold order** on food products that, for reasons specified in the notice, cannot be served. The manager, also known as the "person in charge" is the individual present at the food establishment who is responsible for the operation at the time of inspection. In extreme cases, immediate destruction of the food may be ordered. The manager should voluntarily destroy food of questionable quality or safety.

At the conclusion of any inspection, the sanitarian is required to present the written final report to the manager or person in charge. Inspectors are often willing to discuss the findings.

Inspections often help operators identify areas for improvement. Sanitarians can provide food service owners and managers with professional advice on how to correct sanitation problems. Sanitarians may also provide training upon request. However, the primary responsibilities of a sanitarian are determining the compliance of food establishments and requiring the correction of deficiencies.

Management Responsibilities

Food service managers and staff members also have a set of responsibilities with respect to inspections. They too must act professionally. If an adversarial relationship has been established between the operation and the regulatory officials, it was probably initiated by an overly defensive or unreasonable manager or staff member. Professionals recognize the roles of inspectors, managers, and staff members and strive for a spirit of cooperation. The responsibilities of the manager or licensee are to be in substantial compliance at all times and to correct any deficiencies as required by the health authority. No one gains by non-compliance or by perpetuating an adversarial relationship.

Managers should instruct staff members to allow properly identified sanitarians to enter the food establishment at any reasonable time for the purpose of making an inspection. Managers are obligated to furnish any relevant records the sanitarian may request. The manager or a designated staff member of the food establishment should accompany the sanitarian on the inspection. This allows the establishment's representative to observe any violations firsthand, to answer any questions, and to correct problems immediately, if possible. When the sanitarian presents the inspection report, the manager should review it for accuracy; he or she may request corrections and additions to, or deletions from, the report. Any deficiencies corrected at the time of the inspection should be so noted.

Since the completed inspection form is a public document, it may be made available to people who legally request it. In addition, most courts have ruled that inspection records must be accessible to the public. Reporters and other news media personnel may review health department records. Some newspapers publish inspection scores, along with the names of the businesses, on a regular basis. Food service managers can protect the reputation of their establishments by improving their sanitation scores.

Food service managers should feel free to ask questions of the health inspector. The objective is to set up a two-way communication flow between the sanitarian and the operation's management. Such cooperation has an added benefit: the operation's history of compliance could be important if complaints or allegations of injuries or foodborne illness outbreaks are made. Regulatory officials and food service managers share the responsibilities for achieving a common goal—the safe and sanitary operation of a food establishment.

Suspensions

A food establishment's permit to operate may be suspended if either the operator or permit holder does not comply with relevant food service regulations or if there is an imminent health hazard. The regulatory agency may suspend the permit with a summary suspension notice. Once the suspension takes place, all food service operations must stop. The permit holder is entitled to a hearing by the regulatory agency within 5 days of the agency's receipt of a request for a hearing.

Permits may be revoked if the operation has a number of serious or repeated violations. Revocation can also take place if the manager or employees interfere with the regulatory agent's performance of duties. However, prior to revocation, the regulatory agency must notify the permit holder in writing. Notices are usually sent by certified or registered mail. If a permit is revoked, a written application for new documents must be filed. Obviously, the regulatory authorities will not approve the new application until previous deficiencies have been corrected.

A regulatory authority may use a number of remedies to achieve compliance with the provisions of the code. Administrative remedies, such as summary permit suspension, restriction of infected or diseased employees, or the examination, holding, and destruction of contaminated food, may be used when the food establishment:

- Fails to have a valid permit to operate;

- Violates any term or condition of the permit;

- Allows serious or repeated code violations to remain uncorrected beyond time frames for correction approved, directed, or ordered by the regulatory authority;

- Fails to comply with a regulatory authority order issued concerning an employee suspected of having a disease transmissable through food by infected persons;

- Fails to comply with a summary suspension order;

- Fails to comply with a hold order; or

- Fails to comply with an order issued as a result of a hearing for an administrative remedy.

Judicial remedies may take the form of judicial inspection orders, civil proceedings, injunctive proceedings, or criminal proceedings. For example, if a manager or staff member denies access to the premises, food, or records, the regulatory authority may seek a judicial remedy.

Partners in Success

Managers have a valuable associate who can help ensure the success of the business—the sanitarian. Managers should see the health department sanitarian as an ally and should maintain a spotless establishment not only because the sanitarian expects it but because it makes good business sense. In the long run, cleanliness will cut food and labor costs and make the operation more prosperous and productive. Furthermore, the sanitarian can offer professional assistance and advice on how to improve the operation's level of sanitation and safety. Professional sanitarians are partners in the success of your business.

Self-Inspection

In addition to depending on training, the success of a sanitation risk management program depends to a great extent on enforcement of the operation's standards. Routine self-inspections allow the staff to monitor the general sanitation levels throughout the organization. Any deficiencies that are discovered can be corrected. Thus, the result of the self-inspection should be a higher level of sanitation in the facility.

A number of sanitation self-inspection forms have been developed for use in food establishments. The best form is one that highlights the same inspection items that are checked by the state and/or local health inspectors. At the very least, the points covered on the form used by your local regulatory authority should be covered by self-inspections. Use of this form for self-inspections permits the operator to anticipate the items the health inspector is likely to check during regularly scheduled inspections. State and local health departments and professional organizations also provide sanitation self-inspection forms.

A regular program of in-house inspections contributes to the overall positive image of the business. Basically, both the dedication of staff members and the integrity of management contribute to the overall level of sanitation in the operation. Ideally, self-inspections should not be performed exclusively by management. Staff member involvement is highly desirable. When staff members are intimately involved in the sanitation risk management program, they think of workable ideas for improvement. They become committed to the operation's program as if it were their own. Staff member commitment can be achieved through the team approach.

The team approach to sanitation self-inspection has the potential to improve the establishment's level of sanitation. Inspection teams of three to five people, made up of both managers and staff members, work together to identify deficiencies, take corrective action, and increase the awareness of the operation's personnel. A four-team system is probably sufficient to meet the inspection needs of most food service and lodging operations. The inspection duties should be divided evenly among the four teams.

Team one is responsible for facilities inspection. This group monitors housekeeping and maintenance of facilities, including floors, walls, ceilings, lighting, storage areas, ventilation, garbage and refuse disposal, dressing rooms, plumbing, water supply sewage disposal, handwashing and toilet facilities, and insect and rodent control.

Team two is charged with food and food handling inspection. This group monitors raw and cooked products as they flow through each of the operation's control points from receiving through serving. Team two closely checks product time and temperature combinations along with quality standards.

Team three is held accountable for personnel sanitation training and performance. This group establishes and audits staff member training programs covering elementary bacteriology, foodborne diseases, food infection, food intoxication, personal hygiene, staff member health habits, safety, and standards for production service.

Team four is responsible for equipment and utensil sanitation and safety. This team regularly inspects food-contact surfaces and non-food-contact surfaces, looking at design, construction, maintenance, installation, and location. Team four audits warewashing equipment and procedures and the use of cleaners and sanitizers.

All teams must make routine sanitation and safety inspections and file written reports with top management. These written reports are prepared, reviewed, discussed, and acted upon. Later, the teams conduct follow-up inspections to ensure the effectiveness of the corrective action. This team concept provides a rational and objective way to implement and monitor a sanitation risk management program. It also intensifies the operation's commitment to high sanitation standards by means of group involvement.

To prevent boredom, staff members and managers may be periodically rotated from team to team. This cross-training builds sensitivity to and an appreciation for the responsibilities of others by giving the staff members or supervisors an opportunity to carry out new tasks.

Summary

As the population of the United States has grown, so have the food laws which are designed to protect the public health. Several federal regulatory agencies oversee a considerable number of food handlers to ensure the safety of products as they move through the channels of production, processing, and distribution. State and local regulatory agencies promote food safety in retail food establishments.

Industry and trade organizations and associations exert a positive influence on the food service industry through the voluntary cooperation of their members. A number of educational materials and a variety of training programs are available at both the national and state levels from these organizations and associations. These groups work with regulatory agencies to improve food safety in this country.

Regulatory agencies are empowered to enforce current requirements for the operation of a food establishment. Permits are issued if an operation complies with relevant rules, regulations, and ordinances. Managers, staff members, owners, and regulatory officials all have responsibilities during sanitation inspections. Managers should strive for a cooperative relationship with the regulatory authority.

It is important that a food establishment operate in compliance with the sanitation rules and regulations governing its jurisdiction for several reasons. Guest satisfaction will increase, as will repeat business. The reputations of the business, the owner, and the manager will be enhanced. Staff members will feel proud to work in an operation that takes a professional approach to sanitation. The operation will be able to reduce its risks, and the business will enjoy a stronger financial position.

Endnotes

1. Shelley Wolson, "Food Regulations: No Uniformity," *Restaurant & Institutions*, November 12, 1986, p. 203.
2. National Restaurant Association, "Non-Uniformity in the Food Service Industry," June 1986.

Key Terms

Food, Drug, and Cosmetic Act (1938) • food establishment • sanitarian

Discussion Questions

1. Which early federal laws continue to have an impact on the food industry in the United States?

2. What are the responsibilities of the Food and Drug Administration (FDA)?

3. What are the responsibilities of the U.S. Department of Agriculture (USDA)?

4. What other agencies are involved in regulating, maintaining, or improving food quality and sanitation?

5. How are the Federal Trade Commission (FTC) and the Occupational Health and Safety Administration (OSHA) involved in food service industry concerns?

6. What functions do state and local regulatory agencies typically perform with regard to food service?

7. How do food-related industry and trade organizations and associations influence and serve the food service industry?

8. What is the process for obtaining a permit to operate a food establishment?

9. What are the responsibilities of sanitarians, management, and staff members during an official inspection?

10. What is the team approach to self-inspection? How does it work?

References

Andrews, Edmund. "Industry Shouts Stop." *Restaurant Business,* April 10, 1988, pp. 153–157, 166–167.

Baker, K. J. "Foodservice Sanitation Training and Reciprocity in the 80s." *Journal of Food Protection,* October 1980, pp. 805–807.

Bernstein, Charles. "Operators' Sanitation Responsibilities." *Nation's Restaurant News,* April 18, 1988, p. F3.

Bryan, F. L. "Foodborne Disease Risk Assessment of Foodservice Establishments in a Community." *Journal of Food Protection,* January 1982, pp. 93–100.

Centers for Disease Control. *Guide for Investigating Foodborne Disease Outbreaks and Analyzing Surveillance Data.* Atlanta, Ga.: Public Health Service, U.S. Department of Health, Education, and Welfare, 1973.

Cichy, R. F. "Proper Procedures for Complaints." *Restaurant Business,* November 20, 1984, pp. 114, 116.

Ebert, H. "Government Involvement in the Food Industry." *Dairy and Food Sanitation,* November 1981, pp. 458–459.

Facts About NSF. Ann Arbor, Mich: National Sanitation Foundation, June, 1986.

"FDA Plans to Recommend Food-Service Operator Certification." *Nation's Restaurant News,* November 17, 1986, p. 77.

Ingham County Sanitary Code. Lansing, Mich.: Ingham County Health Department, Bureau of Environmental Health, 1988.

Kaplan, O.B., and A. El-Ahraf. "Relative Risk Ratios of Foodborne Illness in Foodservice Establishments: An Aid in Deployment of Environmental Health Manpower." *Journal of Food Protection,* May 1979, pp. 446–447.

Kochak, Jacque W. "When the Unthinkable Happens." *Restaurant Business,* March 1, 1988, p. 102.

Kolb, P. M. "Focus on Sanitation." *Restaurant Business,* December 15, 1978, p. 100.

Lydecker, Toni. "When Foodborne Illness Strikes!" *Restaurant & Institutions,* September 30, 1987, pp. 34–37, 40, 41, 46, 52.

Michigan's Food Service Sanitation Regulations. Lansing, Mich.: Food Service Sanitation Section, Division of Environmental Health, Bureau of Environmental and Occupational Health, Michigan Department of Public Health, June 1988.

Mutkoski, S. A., and M. L. Schurer. *Meat and Fish Management.* North Scituate, Mass.: Breton, 1981.

National Institute for the Foodservice Industry. *Applied Foodservice Sanitation,* 2d ed. Chicago, Ill.: D.C. Heath, 1978.

Nickel, C. Russell. "A Call for a National Ordinance." *Nation's Restaurant News,* March 9, 1987, p. F55.

Procedures to Investigate Foodborne Illness, 3d ed. Ames, Iowa: International Association of Milk, Food, and Environmental Sanitarians, 1976.

Rankin, Ken. "Debate Over FDA Performance Grows on Capitol Hill." *Nation's Restaurant News,* March 30, 1987, p. 31.

Reedy, L. "Safety and Health—No Betting Matter." *Food Service Marketing,* December 1980, pp. 43–46.

Rules and Regulations Governing Restaurants in the City and County of Denver. Denver, Colo.: Denver Department of Health and Hospitals, Environmental Health Services, 1980.

"Safe Food a Growing Concern." *Lansing State Journal,* May 27, 1988, p. B5.

Sanitation Operations Manual. Chicago, IL: Public Health and Safety Department, National Restaurant Association, 1979.

Schultz, H. W. *Food Law Handbook.* Westport, Conn.: AVI, 1981.

Semling, H. V. "Forecast for Food Safety Legislative Changes." *Food Processing,* July 1981, pp. 8–9.

———. "New Food Policy Lines Begin to Sharpen, Reinforce Industry's Hopeful Mood." *Food Processing,* August 1981, pp. 10–12.

Stefanelli, J. M. *Purchasing: Selection and Procurement for the Hospitality Industry.* New York: Wiley, 1981.

Stevens, William D. "Turn Complaints Into Gold." *Restaurants USA,* May 1989, p. 17.

Weinstein, Jeff. "USDA Proposes New Food Inspection System." *Restaurants & Institutions,* February 20, 1989, pp. 28–29.

Weckel, K. G. "Professionalism: What It Should Mean to You." *Journal of Food Protection,* March 1979, pp. 273–276.

Whitmarsh, J. "Is Your Kitchen Clean Enough for Uncle Sam?" *Institutions/Volume Feeding,* 1 March 1976, pp. 50–51.

Wolson, Shelley. "Food Regulations: No Uniformity." *Restaurants & Institutions,* November 12, 1986, p. 203.

REVIEW QUIZ

When you feel you have covered all of the material in this chapter, answer these questions. Choose the *best* answer. Check your answers with the correct ones found on the Review Quiz Answer Key at the end of this book.

1. The 1946 Agricultural Marketing Act defined:

    a. standards for wholesomeness in poultry and meat products.
    b. the functions of the U.S. Department of Agriculture.
    c. labeling requirements for food products.
    d. licensing criteria for dealers and brokers of fresh fruits and vegetables.

2. The Food and Drug Administration develops and interprets which of the following?

    a. guidelines for the marketing of grains for animal, human, and industrial uses
    b. agricultural commodity purchase policies and services
    c. food service surveillance and compliance programs
    d. all of the above

3. Which federal department conducts continual in-plant inspections of all processors of meat, poultry, and egg products?

    a. U.S. Department of Commerce
    b. Food and Drug Administration
    c. Centers for Disease Control and Prevention
    d. U.S. Department of Agriculture

4. Regulations related to the use of toxic substances, such as sanitizers and pesticides, are enforced by the:

    a. Environmental Protection Agency.
    b. Agricultural Marketing Service.
    c. Department of Commerce.
    d. Animal and Plant Health Inspection Service.

5. Uniformity in the enforcement of rules and regulations covering food service may reduce:

    a. the effectiveness of the regulations.
    b. the willingness of food service managers to cooperate with sanitarians.
    c. mobility and turnover in the food service industry.
    d. regulatory agencies' enforcement costs.

6. Which of the following organizations develops standards to assist manufacturers in the production of food service equipment that meets minimum health code requirements?

   a. National Environmental Health Association
   b. National Sanitation Foundation
   c. Society for the Advancement of Foodservice Research
   d. Society for Foodservice Management

7. Which of the following is usually *not* required information on a food establishment permit application?

   a. type of proposed food service business
   b. the HACCP plan
   c. names of the top manager and executive chef
   d. address of each applicant

8. One of the *primary* responsibilities of a sanitarian is to:

   a. offer advice on how to correct sanitation problems.
   b. provide sanitation training.
   c. identify areas for operational improvement.
   d. determine food establishments' compliance with regulatory requirements.

9. When completed by a regulatory agency, the Food Establishment Inspection Report is:

   a. a public document.
   b. made public only if the food establishment's license is revoked.
   c. available only to local health department sanitarians for their reference before subsequent inspections.
   d. completely confidential.

10. If a food establishment's permit is suspended, the permit holder is entitled to a hearing by the regulatory agency within _____ days of the agency's receipt of a request for a hearing.

    a. 5
    b. 7
    c. 10
    d. 14

Chapter Outline

Learning Objectives

1. Distinguish between pathogens and spoilage organisms, and list the four types of microorganisms responsible for most food contamination. (pp. 69–70)

2. Explain the four factors affecting bacterial reproduction. (pp. 73–80)

3. Briefly describe food infections and intoxications. (pp. 83–84)

4. Identify and briefly describe the seven most important agents of foodborne infection, their sources, and their manifestations. (pp. 84–88)

5. List common chemical poisons and foodborne physical hazards, and briefly describe control measures. (pp. 92–94)

6. Describe the personal health and hygiene practices necessary in a food establishment. (pp. 94–111)

7. Explain the conditions leading to an outbreak of foodborne illness. (pp. 111–114)

8. List the 11 steps in handling a foodborne illness complaint. (pp. 114–119)

9. Explain what food service managers should know about AIDS and HSV. (pp. 119–120)

3

Food Contamination

Food service managers and staff members are responsible for serving safe food to the public. Moreover, guests *expect* food service businesses to provide them with safe, wholesome food. The publicity generated by an outbreak of foodborne illness (when two or more people become sick from eating the same food)[1] can be disastrous for a business.

It is estimated that 24 to 81 million people become ill from microorganisms in food every year, resulting in an estimated 10,000 deaths. For most victims, foodborne illness results only in discomfort or lost time from work. However, foodborne illness is more serious and may be deadly for preschool-age children, those with impaired immune systems, and the elderly in health care facilities. The annual cost of foodborne illness is estimated to be between $7.7 billion and $23 billion.[2]

The FDA states:

Foodborne Disease Outbreak.

(a) **"Foodborne Disease Outbreak"** means an incident, except as specified in Subparagraph (b) of this definition, in which:

(i)   2 or more persons experience a similar illness after ingestion of a common food; and

(ii)   Epidemiological analysis implicates the food as the source of the illness.

(b) *"Foodborne Disease Outbreak" includes a single case of illness such as 1 person ill from botulism or chemical poisoning.*

"Confirmed disease outbreak" means a foodborne disease outbreak in which laboratory analysis of appropriate specimens identifies a causative organism and epidemiological analysis implicates the food as the source of the illness.

Source: FDA 1993 *Food Code.*

Managers of food service businesses can protect the public health, as well as the establishment's reputation and profits, by making sure that all staff members understand the fundamentals of food contamination and foodborne illness and how to prevent them. This chapter covers food contaminants, the diseases they cause, and preventive measures.

Microorganisms Responsible for Food Contamination

A microorganism (or microbe) is a small living organism. Most microorganisms consist of a single cell. Microorganisms are ubiquitous in our environment: they are found in

Exhibit 3.1 Beneficial Uses and Behaviors of Microorganisms

Dairy Product Production	Vinegar Production
Sausage Production	Vegetable Fermentation
Baked Goods Production (Leavening)	Coffee and Tea Production
Cheese Production and Ripening	Soy Sauce Production
Bakery Product Production	Animal Feed Production
Alcoholic Beverage Production	Vitamin Production
Toxic Chemical Breakdown	Antibiotic Production
Enzyme Production	Decay of Organic Matter

and on humans, animals, plants, water, air, and soil. Most microorganisms need organic matter (matter containing carbon) to survive and often obtain this "food" from our own food supply.

The majority of microorganisms are beneficial. Some serve as food for humans or animals, while others provide or help produce special nutrients and enzymes. Microbes are used to produce fermentation in food products such as beer and pickles. They also play a role in the decay of organic matter, in which the complex organic compounds present in dead plants and animals are broken down into simple inorganic compounds necessary for new plant growth. Recently, genetically altered hybrid bacteria have been used to break down the toxic chlorinated-aromatic compounds (potential cancer-causing agents) found in waste from industrial and chemical production. Exhibit 3.1 presents a summary of the beneficial uses and behaviors of microorganisms.

There are, however, many harmful microorganisms. These can be divided into two broad categories: pathogens and spoilage organisms. **Pathogens** are disease-causing agents; they are the source of the foodborne diseases described later in this chapter. Spoilage organisms do not cause disease, but they make food products unusable. These microbes render food products unfit for human consumption by altering their color, odor, texture, taste, and appearance. This chapter will focus on pathogens; food spoilage is discussed more fully in Chapter 4. Appendix B at the back of this book presents a summary of pathogenic microorganisms and a pronunciation guide.

Four types of microorganisms are responsible for most food contamination: bacteria, parasitic worms, fungi, and viruses. Food service managers and staff members should understand these four groups and their characteristics, factors affecting their reproduction, common food sources, incubation periods, symptoms produced when they are ingested by humans, and methods of control. In describing these microorganisms, special emphasis will be placed on the largest group: bacteria.

Bacteria

Bacteria are single-celled organisms. They have Latin names; the first name, which is always capitalized, represents the genus (plural *genera*), and the second name represents the species. A genus name followed by the abbreviation "spp." indicates more than one (or all) of the species in that genus. A single bacterium is extremely small. If 60 *Escherichia coli* cells (an abundant species found in the intestines of animals and people)

Exhibit 3.2 Microscopic Appearance of Bacterial Cells

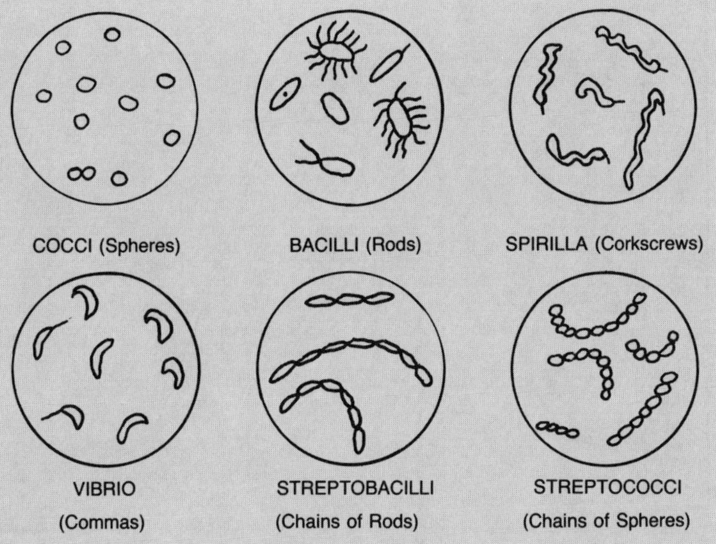

COCCI (Spheres)   BACILLI (Rods)   SPIRILLA (Corkscrews)

VIBRIO   STREPTOBACILLI   STREPTOCOCCI
(Commas)   (Chains of Rods)   (Chains of Spheres)

(Note that the name indicates the shape.)

could be lined up end-to-end, their total length would be approximately equal to the diameter of a human hair. Individual bacterial cells can only be viewed through a microscope. A bacterial **colony**—a large number of isolated cells which have developed from a single cell—can be seen with the naked eye. A colony can contain more than 10 million cells.

Most bacteria possess cell walls which give them their characteristic shape. Bacteria take in nutrients and expel waste products through their cell walls. Exhibit 3.2 shows the four basic bacterial shapes individually and/or in chains.

Bacterial cells contain all the genetic material necessary for reproduction. Most are able to reproduce asexually through a process called binary fission, in which a single cell divides itself into two equal-sized cells. Only **vegetative** (actively growing) **bacterial cells** can reproduce. The time it takes for one cell to undergo fission is called the **generation time.**

Some bacilli (see Exhibit 3.2) can assume dormant forms called **spores.** Spores are vegetative cells subjected to environmental conditions which are unfavorable for reproduction. Bacterial spores are more resistant than vegetative cells to temperature extremes, low humidity, and chemicals.

Bacterial growth refers to an increase in the number, not the size, of bacterial cells. (Throughout this text, the terms "growth" and "reproduction" will be used interchangeably.) A normal bacterial growth curve has four phases: the lag phase, the log phase, the stationary phase, and the death phase (see Exhibit 3.3). In the **lag phase,** living bacteria are present, but there is no increase in the number of cells. In fact, if some organisms fail to adjust to the new environment, the total number of bacteria may decline during this phase. The lag phase can be as short as a few minutes or as long as several months. The

Exhibit 3.3 Normal Bacterial Growth Curve

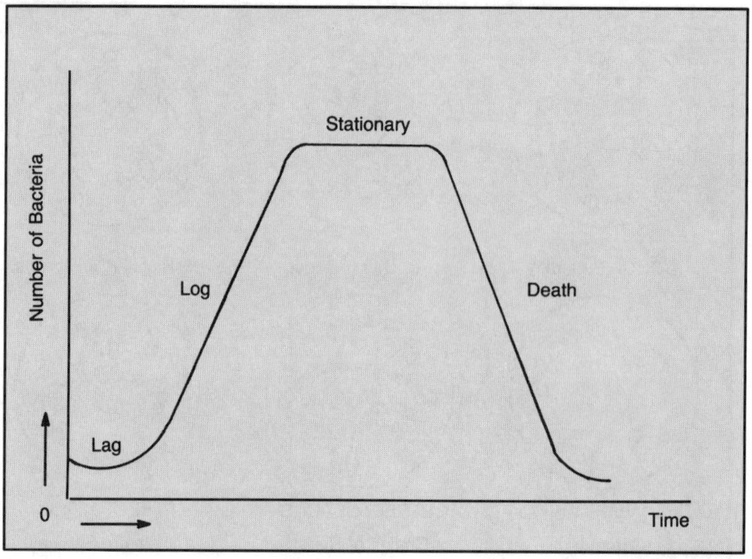

objective of low-temperature food preservation (refrigeration and freezing) is to lengthen the lag phase. Adding preservatives to food also extends the lag phase.

The lag phase is followed by the **log phase,** during which the bacteria, having adjusted to their new environment, reproduce rapidly. Bacterial generation time is shortest during this stage. The number of cells increases exponentially; that is, because each cell produces two cells capable of reproduction, the bacterial population grows at a constantly increasing rate. Most new cell reproduction takes place during the log phase, which can last 15 to 40 minutes and is dependent on the organism and environmental conditions. Time periods vary also with the size of the initial population and the age of the cells.

The third stage of bacterial growth is called the **stationary phase.** In this stage, the number of new bacterial cells equals the number of dying cells so the total number of cells remains constant; there is no *net* increase in the bacterial population. The length of the stationary phase depends on the reduction in nutrients available to the microbes, the amount of accumulated waste products, and the type of microorganisms present. Once bacterial growth in food products reaches this stage, the food is generally unacceptable in terms of appearance, odor, taste, texture, and color. One exception is fermented food (such as olives and pickles) which is made palatable by bacterial action.

The **death phase** is signaled by a reduction in the total number of living bacteria present. During this stage the population falls at a rapid rate. When no effort is made to completely destroy the bacteria, the death rate eventually levels off and a number of organisms survive to begin the cycle again.

To illustrate what can happen when bacteria are not properly destroyed, let's assume a bacterial cell has a generation time of 30 minutes under ideal conditions. Starting with one cell at time zero, over 280 trillion cells would be present at the end of 24 hours. Exhibit 3.4 shows this phenomenal growth. In reality, it would be unusual to find one cell existing alone; so, increases would normally occur at a much faster rate. To put it another way, assume you could work for an employer at the rate of $1.00 for the first

Exhibit 3.4 Growth Rate of Bacteria with a Generation Time of 30 Minutes Under Ideal Conditions

Number of Organisms	Time	
	In Minutes	In Hours
1	0	0
2	30	0.5
4	60	1
8	90	1.5
16	120	2
64	180	3
256	240	4
1,024	300	5
4,096	360	6
65,536	480	8
1,048,576	600	10
1,073,741,824	900	15
1,099,511,627,776	1,200	20
281,474,976,710,656	1,440	24

day, $2.00 for the second, $4.00 for the third, $8.00 for the fourth, and so on. You might be amazed to find that on the twenty-first working day, you would have accumulated earnings of $1,048,576!

Exhibits 3.3 and 3.4 are idealized illustrations of normal bacterial growth; under actual conditions, growth rates vary. (Some factors affecting bacterial reproduction are presented in the next section.) Nevertheless, these exhibits help us understand events which we are unable to observe directly. By understanding how bacterial reproduction occurs in theory, we can apply these principles to the construction of a program for controlling bacteria. It is important to remember that any method used to destroy bacteria will not accomplish the destruction instantaneously. Just as it takes time for bacteria to reproduce, it also takes time to kill bacteria or reduce their numbers.

Factors Affecting Bacterial Reproduction. Environmental conditions influence the rate of bacterial reproduction. Bacteria differ in the environmental conditions they require, and food products also differ in the degree to which they provide favorable conditions for bacterial growth. The most important conditions affecting bacterial reproduction are moisture, oxygen, the level of acidity, time, and temperature.

    Moisture. All bacteria need moisture in a usable form to grow and reproduce. The amount of water available to microorganisms in an environment is expressed as its **water activity** value or a_w. The water activity value is the measure of the free moisture in a food and is simply the ratio of the water vapor pressure in the food to the vapor pressure of pure water at the same temperature. The a_w of pure water is 1.0. In general, bacteria prefer an a_w greater than .85, although the minimum value necessary for growth

Exhibit 3.5 Approximate Minimum a_w Values Permitting the Growth of Microorganisms in Food

Microorganism	Minimum a_w
Bacillus cereus	.92
Clostridium botulinum	.93
Escherichia coli	.94
Pseudomonas aeruginosa	.96
Salmonella spp.	.93
Staphylococcus aureus	.86
Vibrio parahaemolyticus	.93
Most spoilage bacteria	.90

Source: Food and Drug Administration, *Interpretation: Definitions— Potentially Hazardous Food,* May 9, 1986, p. 4.

varies with the microorganism (see Exhibit 3.5). Exhibit 3.6 lists the a_w values of a number of common foods. Notice that fresh animal and plant products have an a_w ranging from .97 to .99+.

The amount of water in a food product can be reduced in several ways. Water can be removed by drying. Because they have a reduced a_w, food products which have been dried generally have a longer shelf life than do food products in their original moist state (see Exhibit 3.6). Food may be frozen, making the water unavailable (bacteria cannot use water unless it is in liquid form). Sugar or salt added to food also binds water and reduces the a_w.

When water is added to dried or reconstituted foods, the rehydrated foods can again support bacterial growth. Some microorganisms are hardy enough to survive the drying process, so the food may not need to be recontaminated before microbial growth occurs.

Oxygen. The availability of oxygen also greatly influences microbial growth rates. Oxygen requirements of bacteria vary with the species; all bacteria are aerobic, anaerobic, or facultatively anaerobic. **Aerobic** organisms require free oxygen. **Anaerobic** microbes grow best in the absence of oxygen. **Facultatively anaerobic** organisms reproduce either with or without free oxygen; included in this group are microaerophilic organisms, which need oxygen but can tolerate only very small amounts.

Acidity or alkalinity. The acidity or alkalinity of the environment is an important influence on bacterial activity. The standard measure of acidity or alkalinity is the hydrogen ion concentration, also known as **pH.** As Exhibit 3.7 shows, the pH scale ranges from 0 to 14. Food products with pH values less than 7 are acidic; those with pH values greater than 7 are basic or alkaline. A pH of 7 is considered neutral. Exhibit 3.8 shows the pH values of several common foods.

In general, microorganisms reproduce best in food products with a pH between 6.6 and 7.5. Each microorganism has a minimum, optimum, and maximum pH at which it will reproduce. Exhibit 3.9 lists this information for a selected group of microorganisms. Many bacteria can survive at pH values above or below those illustrated in Exhibit 3.9.

Exhibit 3.6 Approximate a$_w$ Values of Selected Foods

Animal Products	a$_w$
Fresh meat, poultry, fish	.99 to .99+
Most cheeses	.95 to .99+
Cured meats	.87 to .95
Parmesan cheese	.68 to .76
Dried whole milk	.20
Plant Products	
Fresh fruits, vegetables	.97 to .99+
Jams, jellies	.75 to .94
Uncooked rice	.80 to .87
Dried fruits	.55 to .80
Cereal	.10 to .20
Sugar	.19

Source: Food and Drug Administration, *Interpretation: Definitions— Potentially Hazardous Food,* May 9, 1986, p. 5.

Exhibit 3.7 The pH Scale and Some Representative Foods

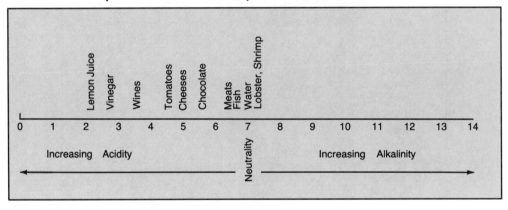

In higher or lower pH environments, there is little reproduction; but, once the environment again becomes favorable, reproduction can resume. The lowest pH value at which a foodborne pathogen will reproduce is 4.0; however, pathogens reproduce extremely slowly at a pH below 4.8. *Clostridium botulinum,* the microorganism which causes botulism poisoning, produces its toxins at pH values of 4.7 and higher. This fact, coupled with information about a$_w$, led the USDA and FDA to establish a definition for **potentially hazardous foods.**

Exhibit 3.8 Approximate pH Values of Some Common Foods

Food	pH Range
Apples	2.9–3.3
Asparagus	5.0–6.1
Bananas	4.5–5.2
Beans, lima and string	4.6–6.5
Beers	4.0–5.0
Bread	5.3–5.7
Broccoli	6.5
Cabbage	5.2–6.3
Carrots	4.9–6.3
Celery	5.7–6.0
Cheese, Cheddar and American	4.9–5.0
Chocolate	5.2–6.0
Cocoa, Dutch process	6.0–8.8
Corn, sweet	5.9–7.3
Eggs	
Whole	7.5–8.2
White	8.6–9.0
Yolk	6.4–6.9
Fish, cooked	6.0–6.9
Grapefruit	2.9–4.0
Grapes	3.3–4.5
Lemon Juice	2.2–2.4
Lettuce	6.0–6.4
Limes	1.8–2.0
Lobster or Shrimp, cooked	7.1–7.3
Meat, cooked	5.6–7.0
Melons, honeydew	6.3–6.7
Milk	6.3–6.8
Olives	3.6–8.0
Onions	5.3–5.8
Oranges	2.8–4.0
Peaches	3.1–4.2
Pears	3.4–4.7
Pickles, dill	3.2–3.5
Pineapple	3.2–4.1
Potatoes	5.3–6.3
Sauerkraut, cooked	3.3–3.5
Spinach	5.1–6.8
Strawberries	3.1–3.5
Tomatoes	3.7–4.9
Vinegar	2.4–3.4
Water, distilled	6.8–7.0
Watermelons	5.2–5.6
Wines	2.8–3.8

Exhibit 3.9 Approximate pH Values Permitting the Growth of Microorganisms in Food

Microorganism	pH		
	Minimum	Optimum	Maximum
Clostridium botulinum	4.8	—	—
Clostridium perfringens	—	6.8	8.5
Escherichia coli	4.4	7.0	9.0
Pseudomonas spp.	5.6	6.8	8.0
Salmonella spp.	4.0	6.8	9.0
Staphylococcus aureus	4.0	—	9.8

Source: Food and Drug Administration, *Interpretation: Definitions—Potentially Hazardous Food,* May 9, 1986, p. 6.

The FDA states:

Potentially Hazardous Food.

(a) **"Potentially hazardous food"** means a food that is natural or synthetic and is in a form capable of supporting:

 (i) The rapid and progressive growth of infectious or toxigenic microorganisms; or

 (ii) The growth and toxin production of *Clostridium botulinum*.

(b) **"Potentially hazardous food"** includes an animal food (a food of animal origin) that is raw or heat-treated; a food of plant origin that is heat-treated or consists of raw seed sprouts; cut melons; and garlic and oil mixtures.

(c) *"Potentially hazardous food" does not include:*

 (i) *An air-cooled hard-boiled egg with shell intact;*

 (ii) *A food with a water activity (a_w) value of 0.85 or less;*

 (iii) *A food with a hydrogen ion concentration (pH) level of 4.6 or below when measured at 24°C (75°F);*

 (iv) *A food, in an unopened hermetically sealed container, that is commercially processed to achieve and maintain commercial sterility under conditions of nonrefrigerated storage and distribution; and*

 (v) *A food for which laboratory evidence that is the basis of a variance granted by the regulatory authority demonstrates that rapid and progressive growth of infectious and toxigenic microorganisms or the slower growth of* **C. botulinum** *cannot occur.*

Source: FDA 1993 *Food Code.*

Examples of potentially hazardous foods include animal products such as fish, meat, and poultry. Also included are some plant products, such as refried beans, cooked rice, seed sprouts (germinated soybeans, mung beans, alfalfa sprouts), processed garlic in oil, and tofu and other moist soy protein products. In some jurisdictions, potentially hazardous foods do not include clean, whole, uncracked, odor-free shell eggs. Other jurisdictions include such eggs as potentially hazardous foods. Check your state and local codes for the specifics in your area.

Time and temperature. Time and temperature requirements are interrelated. Fluctuating temperatures are hazardous to food products because they can favor food spoilage or the proliferation of foodborne illness microbes. Microorganisms can be classified by the temperature conditions in which they thrive. **Psychrophiles** are the cold-loving microorganisms; they can survive at temperatures as low as -19°F (-28°C), yet are able to reproduce at temperatures as high as 68°F (20°C). **Mesophiles** are microbes which prefer intermediate temperatures, generally from 68°F (20°C) to 113°F (45°C). **Thermophiles** prefer temperatures from 113°F (45°C) to 140°F (60°C), and sometimes higher. Most pathogenic bacteria are mesophiles, so they may thrive at normal room temperatures.

The temperature at which raw ingredients are stored influences later bacterial activity; thus storage at intermediate temperatures must be kept to a minimum. In the 1976 Model Ordinance, the temperature range of 45°F (7°C) to 140°F (60°C) is the **temperature danger zone (TDZ)**. The TDZ can vary from state to state and locality to locality around the country. It is critical that you (1) find out the exact TDZ applicable to your food service operation, and (2) minimize the amount of time food spends in the TDZ during storing, preparing, and serving.

More information about time and temperature controls will be presented in Chapters 4, 6, 7, and 8.

The FDA states:

LIMITATION OF GROWTH OF ORGANISMS OF PUBLIC HEALTH CONCERN

3-501.11   Frozen Food.

Stored frozen foods shall be maintained frozen.

"Slacking" means the process of moderating the temperature of a food such as allowing a food to gradually increase from a temperature of -23°C (-10°F) to -4°C (25°F) in preparation for deep-fat frying or to facilitate even heat penetration during the cooking of previously block-frozen food such as spinach.

3-501.12   Potentially Hazardous Food, Slacking.

Frozen potentially hazardous food that is slacked to moderate the temperature shall be held:

(A)   Under refrigeration that maintains the food temperature at 5°C (41°F) or below; or

(B)   At any temperature if the food remains frozen.

3-501.13   Thawing.

Potentially hazardous food shall be thawed:

(A)   Under refrigeration that maintains the food temperature at 5°C (41°F), or below;

(B)   Completely submerged under running water:

(1)   At a water temperature of 21°C (70°F) or below,

(2)   With sufficient water velocity to agitate and float off loose particles in an overflow, and

(3)   For a period of time that does not allow thawed portions of ready-to-eat food to rise above 5°C (41°F), or

(4)   For a period of time that does not allow thawed portions of a raw animal food requiring cooking as specified in Subparagraphs 3-401.11(A)(1)-(4) to be above 5°C (41°F) for more than 4 hours including the time the food is exposed to the running water and the time needed for preparation for cooking or the time it takes under refrigeration to lower the food temperature to 5°C (41°F); or

(C)   As part of a cooking process if the food that is frozen is cooked as specified in Subparagraphs 3-401.11(A)(1)-(4) with no interruption in the process.

3-501.16   Potentially Hazardous Food, Hot and Cold Holding.*

Except during preparation, cooking, or cooling, or when time is used as the public health control as specified under § 3-501.19, potentially hazardous food shall be maintained:

(A)   At 60°C (140°F) or above; or

(B)   At 5°C (41°F) or below.

3-501.17   Ready-to-Eat, Potentially Hazardous Food, Date Marking.*

(A) Refrigerated, ready-to-eat, potentially hazardous food prepared and held for more than 24 hours in a food establishment shall be marked with the date of preparation.

(B) Except as specified in ¶ (C) of this section, a container of refrigerated, ready-to-eat, potentially hazardous food prepared and packaged by another food establishment or a food processing plant shall be marked to indicate the date, as specified under ¶ 3-501.18(C), by which the food shall be sold or served.

(C) *Paragraph (B) of this section does not apply to:*

(1)   *Cured meats and aged cheese; and*

(2)   *Individual meal portions served or repackaged for sale from a bulk container upon a consumer's request.*

3-501.18   Ready-to-Eat, Potentially Hazardous Food, Disposition.*

(A) Refrigerated, ready-to-eat, potentially hazardous food specified in ¶ 3-501.17(A) shall be discarded if not sold or served within 10 calendar days;

(B) Refrigerated, ready-to-eat, potentially hazardous food in vending machines with an automatic shut-off control that is activated at a temperature between 5°C (41°F) and 7°C (45°F) shall be discarded if not sold within 3 days; and

(C) An ingredient or a container of refrigerated, ready-to-eat, potentially hazardous food specified in ¶ 3-501.17(A) or (B) shall be discarded if not sold or served within 10 calendar days after the original package is opened or by the manufacturer's "sell by" or "use by" date, whichever occurs first.

3-501.19   Time as a Public Health Control.*

Time only, rather than time in conjunction with temperature, may be used as the public health control for a working supply of potentially hazardous food before cooking, or for ready-to-eat potentially hazardous food that is displayed or held for service for immediate consumption, if:

(A)   The food is marked or otherwise identified with the time within which it shall be cooked, served, or discarded;

(B)   The food is served or discarded within 4 hours from the point in time when the food is removed from temperature control;

(C)   Food in unmarked containers or packages, or for which the time expires, is discarded; and

(D)   Written procedures that assure compliance with ¶¶ (A)–(C) of this section are maintained in the establishment and made available to the regulatory authority upon request.

Source: FDA 1993 *Food Code.*

Besides the factors already mentioned, bacterial growth is affected by the characteristics of the species, the initial population size, and competition from other organisms in the environment. In any case, sanitization of equipment and utensils is an effective method of controlling bacterial growth. Product thermometers, for example, should be cleaned and sanitized after each changed use.

The FDA states:

"Sanitization" means the application of cumulative heat or chemicals on cleaned food contact surfaces that, when evaluated for efficacy, yield a reduction of 5 logs, which is equal to a 99.999% reduction, of representative disease microorganisms of public health importance.

Source: FDA 1993 *Food Code.*

Other Bacterial Characteristics. Some bacilli have the ability to form a dense, slime-like protective coating around their cell walls. This **encapsulation** protects the organism from chemicals and heat. Encapsulation also increases the bacterial cell's resistance to death from natural causes.

Other types of bacteria form long chains or groups of cells called **cell aggregates.** Examples of bacteria in this category are *Staphylococcus aureus* and *Streptococcus pyogenes.* Cell aggregates are more difficult to kill than individual cells.

Most foodborne pathogens move from place to place by "hitchhiking" on humans, dust, air, food, clothing, or sneezes and coughs. Other cells, however, are capable of moving short distances within their environment, propelled by tiny whip-like appendages called flagella. In general, all of the spirilla, and some of the cocci, bacilli, and vibrio groups have flagella (see Exhibit 3.2).

Parasitic Worms

Foodborne parasitic worms (or nematodes) are found in the intestines of animals; humans become infected when they consume the flesh of infected animals. Most parasitic worms can be destroyed by cooking or freezing.

Trichinosis is a disease caused by a parasite known as *Trichinella spiralis,* found in infected hogs and the flesh of some wild animals (such as bear and walrus). Symptoms, which include muscle soreness, swelling, and weakness, usually appear in about 9 days, but can occur from 4 to 28 days after consumption. This thread-like roundworm can be destroyed by heating meat to an internal temperature of 155°F (68°C) for 15 seconds. It can also be destroyed by quick freezing or storage at 5°F (-15°C) or lower for not less than 20 days. The incidence of trichinosis in the United States is declining. Most hog farmers now feed their animals selected grains to produce lean carcasses; those farmers who still feed garbage to their hogs must first cook the garbage to 212°F (100°C) for 30 minutes. When cooked in a microwave oven, pork and pork products must reach an internal product temperature of at least 180°F (82°C) and be allowed to stand covered for two minutes after cooking to obtain temperature equilibrium.

Other foodborne parasites are found in both freshwater and saltwater fish. Freshwater fish (salmon, for example) are frequently contaminated with the live larvae of *Diphyllobothrium latum,* a fish tapeworm. The disease that results from eating infected fish is known as diphyllobothriasis. Symptoms are hard to detect and usually appear in three to six weeks. Anemia, a condition in which the blood is deficient in red blood cells, hemoglobin, or total volume, occurs in severe infections. The tapeworm can be destroyed by thorough cooking.

Anisakis spp. are nematodes that infect saltwater fish such as salmon, striped bass, and Pacific snapper. Anisakiasis, the illness, takes several days to surface and is characterized by irritation of the throat and digestive tract, along with diarrhea and abdominal pain. The parasite can be destroyed by heavy salting, thorough cooking, and freezing (24 hours at -20°F [-29°C] is sufficient).

Since foodborne parasites are likely to be present in both freshwater and saltwater fish, fresh fish that has never been frozen must be cooked thoroughly to internal temperatures of at least 140°F (60°C). Restaurants serving sushi (raw fish) may only serve fish that has been frozen and thawed. It is a good idea to obtain a guarantee from the fish supplier that the product has been properly frozen (at -31°F [-35°C] or below for 15 hours in a blast freezer, or at -4°F [-20°C] for 168 hours—7 days).

Foodborne Fungi

Molds and yeasts are fungi, and some species are foodborne. Although these foodborne fungi are generally beneficial, some are harmful microorganisms. Molds and yeasts do not usually cause foodborne illness, but they can cause food spoilage. Most yeasts and molds are aerobic mesophiles—that is, they prefer oxygen and medium

Exhibit 3.10 Effects of Molds on Foods

Beneficial	Harmful
Enzyme production	Spoilage
Industrial fermentations	Undesirable pigments
Acid fermentations	Off-flavors
Cheese ripening	Mycotoxins
Soy sauce production	

temperatures. They generally grow best in foods with a pH low enough to stop or slow the growth of bacteria, their natural competitors.

Yeasts are single-celled organisms which are abundant in nature and are often found on fruit. Some species reproduce by a process called budding: a cell produces a bud, which then develops into a cell and separates from the parent cell.

The importance of yeasts to people lies in their ability to ferment carbohydrates. Yeasts are used in the production of wine, beer, alcoholic spirits, cheese, bread and other baked products, and enzymes. Yeasts contain a collection of enzymes called zymase which brings about the breakdown of glucose to form ethanol (ethyl alcohol) and carbon dioxide. Ethanol produces the light-headedness associated with drinking alcoholic beverages, and carbon dioxide gives beer and some sparkling wines their effervescence. In baked products, the ethanol is driven off by the heat of the oven; the carbon dioxide gas provides leavening action during baking. Food spoilage caused by yeasts can be detected by the presence of an alcohol smell, as well as a bubbly appearance.

Molds are multicellular organisms. In general, molds require a lower a_w value than bacteria or yeasts, and most prefer foods with a pH of 4 to 6. Some are extremely salt-tolerant. All molds use spores as a means of reproduction. Molds often cause food spoilage. *Fusarium spp.*, for example, are responsible for fruit and vegetable spoilage. The beneficial and harmful effects of molds are presented in Exhibit 3.10.

Some molds produce poisonous substances called mycotoxins. **Aflatoxin** is a mycotoxin that is produced by a mold called *Aspergillus flavus*. This mold is found worldwide and grows on nuts, corn, wheat, and other grains. As a result, it may be found in finished products like bread and peanut butter. Ingestion of aflatoxin usually only causes low grade fever in humans, but it can produce cancer in trout, rats, and ducks and has been linked to some cases of liver cancer in humans.

Use caution when buying and serving peanuts and freshly ground peanut butter. Discard any moldy-looking, shriveled, or discolored peanuts. Freshly ground peanut butter should be refrigerated. Commercially prepared peanut butter has salt added to help reduce the mold growth. Any moldy peanut butter should be discarded.

Molds can grow on cheese during ripening, curing, or storage. All types of cheeses are susceptible to mold growth, particularly at refrigeration temperatures. Moldy cheese can be restored to a sound and safe condition by carefully cutting off and discarding:

- a layer at least one-half inch (1.3 cm) thick, if the cheese became moldy while being held at or below 41°F (5°C); or

- a layer at least one inch (2.5 cm) thick, if the cheese became moldy while being held above 41°F (5°C).

Careful cutting is important to minimize the likelihood of contaminating the newly exposed surface of the cheese. If the cheese is too small for the required cutting or if it has a high moisture content (for example, ricotta or cottage cheese), or if the mold has penetrated the eyes or holes of the cheese (as in Swiss cheese), it should be discarded.

Some health jurisdictions do not condone cutting the mold from cheese and then serving the restored cheese. They liken it to storing chicken at room temperature, removing the skin, and then serving the chicken. Check with your local health officials.

Penicillium molds are used in the production of antibiotics and cheese. *Penicillium roqueforti* is used to make a blue-veined cheese; if produced in certain caves in France, the cheese is called Roquefort. *Penicillium caseicolum* is used to produce brie and camembert cheeses.

Molds can be destroyed by carefully controlling moisture and by properly applying fungicides.

Viruses

Viruses are microorganisms that are even smaller than bacteria; they average 1/10,000 the size of a pinhead and can only be seen with an electron microscope. Viruses consist of the genetic material RNA (ribonucleic acid) or DNA (deoxyribonucleic acid) surrounded by a protein shell. They are always parasites of other living cells since they cannot grow, feed, or reproduce in isolation.

Viruses do not reproduce in food products, though some viruses can be transmitted through food products. More on foodborne viruses will be presented in a later section of this chapter.

Foodborne Diseases

A foodborne disease results when food containing infectious, toxic, or toxigenic (toxin-producing) agents is eaten. Some groups of people (e.g., the immunocompromised, elderly, and preschool-age children) are highly susceptible to foodborne disease.

The FDA states:

"Highly susceptible population" means a group of persons who are more likely than other populations to experience foodborne disease because they are immunocompromised or elderly and in a facility that provides health care or assisted living services; or preschool age children in a facility that provides custodial care.

Source: FDA 1993 *Food Code.*

As Exhibit 3.11 shows, foodborne diseases are of two general types: infections and poisonings. **Infections** are caused by bacteria and viruses that are transmitted in food and later reproduce inside the body. These agents of food infection invade the gastrointestinal system of humans and can affect other organs. **Poisonings** result: (1) when harmful chemicals are ingested, (2) when poisonous plants or animals are eaten, or (3) when food contaminated with the poisonous waste products (toxins) of toxigenic bacteria or fungi

Exhibit 3.11 A Classification Scheme for Foodborne Diseases

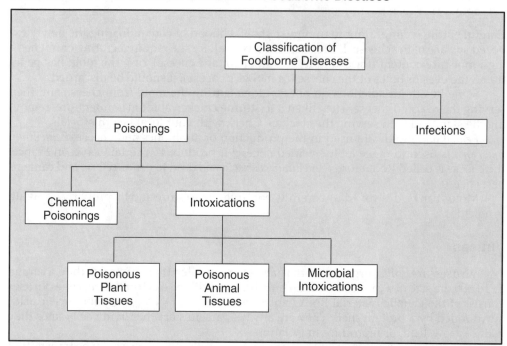

Source: Excerpted from Centers for Disease Control and Prevention, Public Health Service, U.S. Department of Health and Human Services, *Foodborne Diseases and Their Control,* 1980.

is consumed. The illnesses that result from the ingestion of poisonous plants or animals or of toxin-contaminated food are referred to as **intoxications.**

Both infections and microbial intoxications produce similar symptoms: nausea, vomiting, intestinal cramps, and diarrhea. However, microbial intoxications usually have a much shorter **incubation time**—the amount of time between consumption of the contaminated food and the first symptoms of illness—than infections. This is because the agents of infection require time to reproduce in the body.

Bacterial Infections

Bacterial infections result when relatively large numbers of bacteria are consumed, entering the body through contaminated food. Once inside the body, the infectious microorganisms multiply in the intestines. They can also move to other tissues in the body and reproduce.

The pathogens in the genus *Salmonella* are the number one cause of foodborne infection in the United States. There are over 2,000 species of *Salmonella*. These organisms can survive in oxygen-rich or oxygen-poor environments. Some species are mobile rods. In general, *Salmonella* organisms do not form spores and prefer medium temperatures. The most common species associated with the disease known as salmonellosis is *Salmonella typhimurium. Salmonella choleraesuis* and *Salmonella enteritidis* are responsible for two other forms of salmonellosis, while *Salmonella typhi* is the cause of typhoid fever.

Salmonella spp. are most often found in the intestinal tract of animals and humans. These pathogens have been found in turkeys, chickens, hogs, cattle, dogs, cats, frogs, turtles, and birds. The incubation time ranges from 5 to 72 hours, although in most cases symptoms appear in 12 to 48 hours. The symptoms of infection are abdominal pain, diarrhea, fever, chills, vomiting, dehydration, headache, and prostration. Symptoms can be particularly severe for the very young, the elderly, and those already weakened by another disease.

Typical food sources of *Salmonella spp.* are meat, poultry, and egg products. The USDA has estimated that 37% of all chicken, 4% of all beef, and 12% of all pork slaughtered for consumption contain some level of *Salmonella spp.*[3] Other foods which have been implicated in outbreaks are coconut, yeast, chocolate, candy, raw salads, fish, and shellfish. Humans can become carriers of *Salmonella* pathogens after an illness; a carrier does not exhibit the symptoms of the bacterial disease, but can still transfer the microorganisms to humans or food products.

Salmonellosis can be prevented if food products are cooked thoroughly and chilled rapidly. This microorganism is not heat-stable so it can be destroyed by normal cooking procedures. Human carriers are a major source of *Salmonella typhi* contamination. Therefore, food handlers should adhere to rules of good personal hygiene. *Salmonella spp.* can also be transferred by **cross-contamination,** which occurs when a food product comes into contact with a contaminated non-food source (knives, cutting boards, thermometers, and other equipment) or with raw food. The prevention of *Salmonella spp.* contamination is critical to the success of any food service sanitation program.

The FDA states:

3-302.11   Packaged and Unpackaged Food—Separation, Packaging, and Segregation.*

(A) Food shall be protected from cross contamination by:

(1)   Separating raw animal foods during storage, preparation, holding, and display from:

(a)   Raw ready-to-eat food including other raw animal food such as fish for sushi or molluscan shellfish, or other raw ready-to-eat food such as vegetables, and

(b)   Cooked ready-to-eat food;

(2)   *Except when combined as ingredients,* separating types of raw animal foods from each other such as beef, fish, lamb, pork, and poultry during storage, preparation, holding, and display by:

(a)   Using separate equipment for each type, or

(b)   Arranging each type of food in equipment so that cross contamination of one type with another is prevented, and

(c)   Preparing each type of food at different times or in separate areas;

(3)   Cleaning equipment and utensils as specified under ¶ 4-602.11(A) and sanitizing as specified under § 4-703.11;

(4)   Except as specified in ¶ (B) of this section, storing the food in packages, containers, or wrappings;

(5)   Cleaning hermetically sealed food containers of visible soil before opening;

(6)   Protecting food containers that are received packaged together in a case or overwrap from cuts when the case or overwrap is opened;

(7)   Storing damaged, spoiled, or recalled food being held in the establishment as specified under § 6-404.11; and

(8)   Separating fruits and vegetables, before they are washed as specified under § 3-302.15 from ready-to-eat food.

(B)   *Subparagraph (A)(4) of this section does not apply to:*

(1)   *Whole, uncut, raw fruits and vegetables and nuts in the shell, that require peeling or hulling before consumption;*

(2)   *Primal cuts, quarters, or sides of raw meat or slab bacon that are hung on clean, sanitized hooks or placed on clean, sanitized racks;*

(3)   *Whole, uncut, processed meats such as country hams, and smoked or cured sausages that are placed on clean, sanitized racks; or*

(4)   *Food being cooled as specified under Subparagraph 3-501.15(B)(2).*

Source: FDA 1993 *Food Code.*

Shigella spp. constitute a genus of bacteria responsible for shigellosis (bacillary dysentery). These non-mobile rod-like organisms can thrive with or without oxygen. More than ten *Shigella* species have been identified as causes of illness in humans. Most of these pathogens are transmitted to food from the feces of infected humans, by direct contact or through water. *Shigella spp.* have been discovered in moist, mixed foods—for example, tuna, shrimp, turkey, macaroni, and potato salads. Other food sources are milk, beans, apple cider, and contaminated produce. Humans are the most significant reservoir of *Shigella spp.*

The incubation period for *Shigella* pathogens ranges from one to seven days, but it is usually less than four days. Symptoms include abdominal pain, diarrhea, fever, chills, headache, blood in the feces, nausea, dehydration, and prostration. The severity of symptoms varies a great deal, depending on the number and species of *Shigella* microorganisms ingested.

Shigella contamination can be controlled by chilling and heating food products rapidly, practicing good personal hygiene, controlling flies, and preparing food products in a sanitary manner.

Vibrio parahaemolyticus cells are mobile, straight or slightly curved rods. This pathogen generally prefers environments with no oxygen. *Vibrio parahaemolyticus* is often found in marine life and sea water. Most diseases associated with this organism have been seen in Japan, although the number of outbreaks in the United States has risen with the increased popularity of sushi.

Incubation times vary from 2 to 48 hours, but symptoms usually surface 10 to 20 hours after eating the contaminated food. Symptoms are abdominal cramps, diarrhea, nausea, vomiting, mild fever, chills, headache, and prostration. Recovery occurs within two to five days.

Typical food sources of *Vibrio parahaemolyticus* are raw foods of marine origin: saltwater fish, shellfish, and fish products. Salty foods and cucumbers have also been identified as sources. This organism can be controlled by proper cooking and chilling procedures. Raw foods should always be kept separate from cooked foods. Proper icing or refrigeration of seafood can minimize the spread of *Vibrio parahaemolyticus* if it is present. Sea water should never be used for rinsing food that is to be eaten raw.

Escherichia coli is a mobile rod. It survives in environments with or without free oxygen. Many strains of this microorganism are harmless, but some others are responsible for food infections. (Some strains are also toxigenic.) This microbe is found in the feces of infected humans and is transmitted to food by direct contact with carriers; it can also be air- or waterborne. Infants and young people are most susceptible to infection.

The incubation time for this pathogen ranges from 8 to 24 hours, with an average of 11 hours. Symptoms are similar to those of shigellosis. *Escherichia coli* has been isolated from ground beef, cheese, shellfish, and watercress. Any food exposed to sewage-contaminated water can carry *Escherichia coli*. This organism should be controlled in the same way as *Shigella spp.*

Listeria monocytogenes has been recognized for over 50 years, but this pathogen has only recently been positively identified in foodborne disease outbreaks. *Listeria* is a mobile non-spore-forming rod that prefers aerobic conditions. It is a psychrophile, and not only has the ability to survive for long periods of time under refrigeration or freezing, but is also more pathogenic when it reproduces at low temperatures. This pathogen is widely distributed in nature and prefers neutral or slightly alkaline foods.

The disease caused by *Listeria monocytogenes* is called listeriosis. The incubation time is four days to three weeks. Symptoms are typically mild and flu-like, including headache and vomiting. However, pregnant women and people with compromised immune systems (for example, patients undergoing chemotherapy) are particularly susceptible. In these two groups, symptoms can also include meningitis (inflammation of the three membranes that envelop the brain and spinal cord), abortion, and prenatal septicemia. The mortality rate in these two groups is 30 to 40%.

The first confirmed outbreak of listeriosis was linked to commercially prepared coleslaw in Canada. Forty-one people became ill and 18 died. The cabbage used to prepare the coleslaw had been infected with *Listeria* when it was fertilized with contaminated sheep manure. Pasteurized whole and 2% milk have also been implicated in outbreaks; the milk was contaminated after pasteurization. Other food sources include domestic and imported cheeses, chicken broilers, dry sausages (salami), and contaminated meat and meat products.

Fortunately, most healthy people can overcome an attack of listeriosis with their cell-mediated immunity. The organism is heat-sensitive, so it is critical to destroy it during pasteurization or other heat processing and not recontaminate the food products. As an extra precaution, keep all dairy products (milk, ice cream, cheeses) refrigerated or frozen when they are not being used or consumed. Also, proper equipment cleaning and sanitization are essential.

Yersinia enterocolitica is a ubiquitous short rod that prefers anaerobic conditions, but can adapt to the presence of oxygen. Some of these rods are mobile and some are relatively heat-resistant. *Yersinia enterocolitica* is frequently suspected in the diagnosis of many unidentified cases of foodborne illness; however, documented cases are few.

Yersiniosis, the disease, is unique because the symptoms vary with the age of the victim. Children and adolescents experience digestive upset and severe abdominal pain. In fact, the abdominal pain is so much like acute appendicitis that some young people have had their appendix removed unnecessarily. In adults, symptoms include acute abdominal disorders, diarrhea, fever, and arthritis. Skin and eye infections may be present in both groups. Symptoms usually appear in three to seven days.

Yersinia is found in contaminated raw pork and beef, drinking water, ice cream, raw and pasteurized milk, chocolate milk, reconstituted dried milk, and tofu (soybean curd). Milk is usually contaminated after pasteurization.

Sufficient heat treatment, including proper pasteurization, controls this pathogen. It is also important to prevent recontamination after heat processing through proper personal hygiene and equipment and utensil cleaning and sanitization. Always obtain food products from approved sources.

Campylobacter jejuni is a subspecies of *Campylobacter fetus,* which is actually three slightly different bacterial pathogens (or more). Even though this organism has been isolated from animals for over 80 years, it has been implicated in human foodborne disease outbreaks only in the last decade. The name *Campylobacter* means "curved rod," and the organism is generally vibrio- or spiral-shaped. *Campylobacter* is mobile, does not form spores, and survives in environments with little or no oxygen. This microbe prefers medium temperatures.

Some estimate that this pathogen is as common as *Salmonella* and more common than *Shigella. Campylobacter jejuni* is responsible for campylobacteriosis, more commonly known as travelers' diarrhea, and is recognized as among the most frequent causes of bacterial diarrhea in humans. Symptoms surface in one to seven days or longer. The most common symptoms are diarrhea, abdominal pain, fever, and malaise (a vague unhealthy feeling). Symptoms less frequently present are nausea, headache, urinary tract infection, and reactive arthritis.

Campylobacter jejuni is present in the intestinal tract of infected cattle, swine, chicken, turkeys, and other animals. Food sources implicated in outbreaks include raw or inadequately cooked or processed foods of animal origin, such as milk, chicken, turkey, clams, and hamburger, as well as unchlorinated water. It has also been found, in virtually every country, in wild or domesticated dogs, cats, and rodents.

To control *Campylobacter jejuni,* thoroughly cook and properly handle all food products. Since it is sensitive to normal oxygen levels and low temperatures, it is easier to control than some of the other pathogens. It is also sensitive to drying and freezing, as well as the addition of acidic food products such as vinegar, lemon juice, and tomatoes.

Other bacteria are less frequently identified in outbreaks of foodborne illness. *Streptococcus pyogenes* has been found in food containing milk or eggs. *Vibrio cholerae* has been discovered in raw vegetables and mixed, moist foods. These bacteria are generally controlled by the same sanitary practices which control the more common agents of foodborne infection already described. Because of technological advances and better methods of detecting pathogens, other bacterial agents might be identified in the next few years as sources of foodborne illness.

Viral Infections

Although not usually a source of foodborne infections, two infectious viruses have been found in a limited number of foods, particularly those consumed raw.

The virus infectious hepatitis (or hepatitis A) is found in the blood, urine, and feces of human and animal carriers. It is transmitted either by direct, person-to-person contact or through contaminated water. Rodents and insects can also carry this and other viruses. The incubation time ranges from 10 to 50 days, with an average of 30.

The virus infectious hepatitis causes liver infection, fever, nausea, abdominal pain, and a tired feeling. It is often accompanied by jaundice that lasts a few weeks to several months. The virus can be transmitted in uncooked foods likely to be handled, such as bakery items, salads, and sandwiches. It has been detected in shellfish, milk, potato salad, cold cuts, frozen strawberries, orange juice, whipped cream cakes, glazed doughnuts, and sandwiches.

The Norwalk virus is an intestinal pathogen. It is present in fish and shellfish harvested from contaminated waters, probably by inadequately treated domestic sewage. It can also be transmitted person-to-person. The incubation period is usually 24 to 48 hours. Symptoms of the virus include fever, headache, abdominal pain, vomiting, and diarrhea. It has been detected in shellfish, particularly raw clams and oysters. Control this virus by purchasing foods from approved sources, cooking shellfish by steaming for a minimum of four minutes, and adhering to rules of personal hygiene and cleanliness.

Additional foodborne viruses can be positively linked to outbreaks as refined isolation and culture techniques improve detection. Whenever handling potentially hazardous foods, use good personal hygiene and food handling techniques, practice time and temperature control, and vigilantly guard against contamination by any pathogen.

Food Poisoning

Toxic chemicals, poisonous plants and animals, and bacterial and fungal toxins all cause food poisoning when consumed.

Bacterial Intoxications. There are several sources of bacterial intoxication: *Staphylococcus aureus, Clostridium botulinum, Clostridium perfringens,* and *Bacillus cereus.*

Staphylococcus aureus is a spherical, non-mobile, non-spore-forming organism. It has the ability to clump together in clusters like bunches of grapes; this makes the organism more difficult to destroy. *Staphylococcus aureus* can survive with or without oxygen and prefers moderate temperatures. Although the organism itself is not very heat-resistant, the toxin produced by *Staphylococcus aureus* is extremely heat-stable; it is not destroyed by normal cooking procedures. The toxin is a protein which does not alter the texture, color, appearance, odor, or taste of food products.

Staphylococcus aureus is widespread in the environment, which is why it is the number-one agent of bacterial intoxication in the United States. It is found primarily in and on human beings. It has been detected in nose and throat discharges, on hands and skin, in infected wounds and burns, and on pimples and acne. *Staphylococcus aureus* has also been found in feces and hair. It is estimated that this organism is present on 20% of the population who appear healthy. Food products can become contaminated with *Staphylococcus aureus* after cooking as a result of contact with infected food handlers.

This pathogen has an incubation time of one to eight hours, although symptoms usually surface in two to four hours. The incubation period depends on the amount of toxin present in the food. As the toxin level increases, the incubation time decreases. Symptoms include nausea, vomiting, abdominal cramps, diarrhea, dehydration, sweating, weakness, and prostration, and usually last one to two days.

Several foods have been identified as common sources of *Staphylococcus aureus* intoxication. They are cooked ham, poultry and poultry dressings, meat products, gravies and sauces, cream-filled pastries, milk, cheese, hollandaise sauce, bread pudding, and fish, potato, ham, poultry, and egg salads. High-protein leftover foods are frequently involved in outbreaks.

Control of *Staphylococcus aureus* might initially appear to be impossible due to the pathogen's ubiquity; however, a two-sided strategy is effective. First, ill workers are potential carriers and must be excluded from the operation's food production and handling system. Staff members suffering from colds, diarrhea, skin eruptions, or infected cuts should not be allowed to handle food. Second, even staff members who are apparently healthy should concentrate on proper personal hygiene. In addition, food products must be handled with the utmost care. Thorough cooking and reheating, along with rapid chilling and proper refrigeration, will minimize the risks.

Clostridium botulinum is the pathogen responsible for botulism. This bacterium is a spore-forming rod. The spore is extremely heat-stable; it can survive high temperatures and begin to reproduce later as a vegetative cell. This pathogen is characterized by a preference for medium temperatures. It reproduces best in environments with no air (for example, in canned foods). The toxin it produces is very potent and is easily absorbed through the tissues lining the mouth: 1 teaspoon (4 grams) of pure *Clostridium botulinum* toxin is a lethal dose for 400,000 to 500,000 people; 1 gram (20 drops) could kill 100,000 people; and 1 drop is potentially fatal for 5,000 people. Fortunately, botulism is relatively rare in the United States.

Clostridium botulinum is found in the soil, contaminated water, and dust. It has been detected in fruits, vegetables, feed, manure, honey, and sewage. The incubation time is 2 hours to 14 days, although symptoms usually appear in 12 to 36 hours. Since the toxin affects the body's neurological systems, signs of botulism include high fever, dizziness, dry mouth, respiratory difficulties, paralysis, and loss of reflexes. Unless the correct anti-toxin is administered rapidly, death occurs in three to ten days as a result of respiratory failure. If the victim lives, paralysis may last an additional six to eight months. During the past decade the mortality rate of botulism victims has significantly declined.

Inadequately processed or heated canned foods are responsible for outbreaks of botulism more often than any other food product. *Home-canned foods must not be served in a food establishment* for this reason. Low-acid foods (for example, peas, beans, beets, corn, asparagus, mushrooms, chili peppers, figs, tuna, and olives) have been implicated in past outbreaks of botulism. These foods are potentially hazardous; they have a pH in excess of 4.6. Other outbreaks have been linked to commercially-bottled chopped garlic in soybean oil, fish and fish products such as inadequately processed smoked fish, foil-wrapped baked potatoes, sauteed onions, and fermented foods (such as salmon eggs).

Since *Clostridium botulinum* toxins can be destroyed by heating with correct time-temperature combinations, this is the most effective method of control. Other control measures are the addition of acids, refrigeration, and curing food products in sufficient concentrations of salt, nitrites, and nitrates. Since the pathogen sometimes produces a gas under airtight conditions, all bulging cans with off-odors and gas bubbles must be thrown out. *Never taste any product exhibiting these characteristics.*

Clostridium perfringens is a non-mobile spore-forming rod. It proliferates when no oxygen is present. This organism is more likely to form spores in the human body than in food. Because it reproduces within the body, and because the symptoms of ingestion are relatively mild, it is often considered an agent of food infection. But, the toxin produced by *Clostridium perfringens* is responsible for the illness. *Clostridium perfringens* is widely distributed in nature. It has been found in animal manure, human feces, dust, and soil.

The incubation time for this pathogen ranges from 6 to 24 hours, with the majority of symptoms appearing in 8 to 12 hours. Symptoms are acute abdominal cramps, shivering, headache, and diarrhea. Occasionally, dehydration and prostration occur, but nausea, vomiting, chills, and fever are rare. The symptoms clear up in one day or less.

Typical food sources of *Clostridium perfringens* are products that are cooked and then cooled slowly or in large quantities at room temperatures. Examples are cooked meat and poultry, meat pies, gravies, and stews. Insufficient holding or reheating temperatures can also foster growth of this microorganism. Soil-grown vegetables that have not been cleaned properly have also been implicated in *Clostridium perfringens* outbreaks. Thorough cleaning, cooking, and adequate holding temperatures will reduce problems. Good personal hygiene coupled with proper chilling and reheating of leftovers will also minimize the risks.

Bacillus cereus is classified as an agent of food intoxication because some strains produce poisonous waste products in food. The organism is a spore-forming rod capable of reproducing in the presence or absence of free oxygen. It has a tendency to form chains and possesses flagella.

Bacillus cereus is found in the soil, on dust, and on grains and vegetables. The incubation period ranges from 15 minutes to 16 hours, although the symptoms frequently surface 1 to 5 hours after eating the contaminated food. Symptoms are nausea, vomiting, abdominal pain, and diarrhea. Symptoms usually clear up in one day or less and are rarely fatal.

This pathogen has been isolated from a wide variety of food products, including cereal products, puddings and custards, milk and cream, sauces and soups, meat loaf and other meat products, vegetables, and boiled or fried rice. The spores of *Bacillus cereus* can survive ordinary cooking procedures. Susceptible food products should be cooked, served, and eaten immediately. Foods held hot must have internal temperatures of 140°F (60°C) or greater. Hot foods, especially cooked rice, must be chilled rapidly to less than 45°F (7°C) in small quantities. All leftovers must be reheated to a minimum internal temperature of 165°F (74°C) prior to serving.

Poisonous Plants and Animals. A wide variety of plants and animals are toxic if consumed. Most people have read about the fatal hemlock that Socrates was forced to drink. Poisonous plants have long been the cause of accidental (and intentional) deaths.

Toxic plants implicated in food poisoning are usually poisonous mushrooms of the genus *Amanita*. Death Cap, *Amanita philloides*, causes symptoms including nausea, vomiting, and diarrhea. It has resulted in coma and the need for a liver transplant in some infected humans. These poisonous mushrooms are toxic whether they are raw or cooked, and some toxic varieties look like edible varieties. A food service operation should never serve wild or home-canned mushrooms.

Many other plants have been identified as poisonous. Therefore, the practice of foraging for edible plants should be left to experts—it is an extremely risky way to obtain food. *Never serve food obtained this way in a food establishment.*

Several types of fish cause food poisoning when consumed. Scombroid poisoning, which results from eating infected scombroid fish (tuna, bonito, and mackerel), is characterized by intense headache, diarrhea, nausea, dizziness, vomiting, difficulty in swallowing, and itching of the skin. Symptoms usually appear in a few minutes to 1 hour after ingestion; however, they disappear in about 12 hours. These fish should be cooked and either cooled or eaten soon after they are caught.

Puffer fish poisoning causes paralysis of the central nervous system and is followed by death in 50 to 60% of the cases. The poison, found in the liver and ovaries of the fish, is approximately 100 times more deadly than cyanide. Toxic species of puffer fish (such as fugu, blowfish, and balloonfish) should be avoided. In Japan, the sale of puffers is closely regulated by the government; puffer restaurants and cooks are licensed and must operate under a strict set of controls.

Ciguatera poisoning is carried by many marine fish, as well as clams and oysters. The ciguatoxin affects the central nervous system of the victim; however, recovery usually occurs within 24 hours. No reliable method for detecting the presence of this heat-stable neurotoxin is currently known. Therefore, it is best to avoid eating the liver, intestines, and roe (eggs) of tropical fish. Moray eels and contaminated tilefish and mussels are also responsible for ciguatera poisoning.

To minimize the risks posed by poisonous plants and animals, purchase food products only from approved sources.

Chemical Poisonings and Other Toxic Effects. The adulteration of food with undesirable chemicals can occur at any point in the chain of distribution or production. Mislabeling and mishandling must be closely guarded against. In food establishments, it is especially important that all equipment and utensils be made of corrosion-resistant materials.

The FDA states:

"Corrosion-resistant material" means a material that maintains acceptable surface cleanability characteristics under prolonged influence of the food to be contacted, the normal use of cleaning compounds and sanitizing solutions, and other conditions of the use environment.

Source: FDA 1993 *Food Code.*

Zinc poisoning can occur when food products are cooked or stored in galvanized (zinc-coated) containers. Cases of zinc poisoning have been traced to cooked apples, spinach, mashed potatoes, chicken, tomatoes, and fruit punch. In one case, high-acid lemonade was stored in a galvanized container overnight; the acid in the drink leached zinc off the walls of the container and into the liquid. Galvanized containers must not be used for cooking or storing food or beverage products. Cadmium poisoning can occur when food products are cooked or stored in cadmium-coated containers; such containers should also not be used in a food establishment.

Antimony poisoning can occur when antimony-glazed enamel containers are used to store or cook acidic foods. Lemonade, punch, fruit gelatin, sauerkraut, and frozen fruit pops have been implicated in cases of antimony poisoning. Antimony-glazed containers should be avoided.

Copper is a heavy metal that can enter the food supply from copper pipes, containers, and cake decorating tools. When carbonated beverages and acidic foods come into contact with copper, they can carry copper poisoning. Lead poisoning comes from lead pipes, pesticide sprays, and utensils. Lead poisoning has been linked to the storage and service of acidic liquids (tomato juice, orange juice, coffee) in lead-base glazed earthenware. To minimize the risks, wash all fruits and vegetables to be used fresh, protect foods in storage, and do not use lead-based earthenware.

Many food additives are incorporated into the food supply for specific reasons. Approximately 2,800 food additives are used to maintain or increase the nutritional value, preserve freshness, enhance flavor, and aid in the processing and preparation of foods. Food additives are regulated by the FDA through the Food, Drug and Cosmetic Act. Excessive amounts of some additives cause food poisoning. Some examples of additives that are toxic in excessive amounts are nitrites, niacin, and cobalt. Other additives cause an allergic reaction in some people. Excessive use of monosodium glutamate (MSG), a flavor intensifier, is responsible for Oriental (Chinese) Restaurant Syndrome in some sensitive humans.

Chemicals called sulfiting agents were once commonly used as vegetable fresheners and potato whiteners in food service operations. In August of 1986, however, the FDA outlawed the addition of sulfiting agents to fresh fruits and vegetables intended to be sold or served raw. The prohibition was due to the adverse reactions among sensitive individuals, particularly asthmatics. Effective January of 1987, any food containing a detectable (over 10 parts per million) amount of sulfites must carry this information on the label.

Other food products can cause allergic reactions in some guests. Some individuals are sensitive to eggs, fish and shellfish, flavors, food colors, milk, peanuts, or preservatives. Reactions can include hives, diarrhea, swelling, and even death. Food allergies and idiosyncratic reactions are more likely to occur in children than adults and can be caused by protein-containing foods. It is wise to train staff members to be able to answer questions about food preparation techniques and ingredients. In addition, the surfaces of all preparation equipment and utensils should be thoroughly cleaned and sanitized after each changed use.

Toxic chemicals sometimes enter the food supply accidentally. Most of these toxins are insecticides, soil fumigants, roach and rat poisons, and weed killers. Others are present in a food service operation in the form of cleaning and sanitization compounds. These necessary chemicals are potentially poisonous if consumed. They should be used only according to the manufacturer's recommendations.

Cleaners and compounds used for sanitization should be stored separately from other chemicals and may be stored in the area of use, such as under or above sinks or on shelves. Other poisonous chemicals such as oven cleaners and silver polish must be stored in a separate location. Generally, if a product is used in a dilute solution (such as a detergent or compound used for sanitization), it can be stored in the area of use. If, on the other hand, the product is used without dilution (such as oven cleaner), it must be stored separately. Products that are not used in a food establishment (such as motor oil, herbicides, and gasoline) may not be on the premises.

Several potentially toxic chemicals have been discovered in the food supply of the United States. In the early 1970s, polybrominated biphenyl (PBB) was detected in high concentrations in farm animals in the state of Michigan. The PBB entered the food chain when a worker at a farm supply center mistakenly added a poisonous fire-retardant (Firemaster) instead of an animal feed nutrient (Nutrimaster) to a livestock feed formula. Customers of the supplier unknowingly fed this mixture to their animals. Over the next few years, the fire-retardant entered tons of meat, milk, and other foods consumed by millions of the state's residents. At least 23,000 cattle, 1.5 million chickens, and thousands of pigs, sheep, and other animals died or were intentionally slaughtered due to contamination. To date, the Michigan Department of Agriculture has spent more than $21 million on the PBB incident.

Polychlorinated biphenyl (PCB) is a fire-retardant used as an insulator in electrical transformers. This toxic chemical is present in some of the Great Lakes. It enters the human system if fatty fish (for example, lake trout and salmon) from the affected lakes are consumed. Both PBB and PCB are stored in fat cells in the human body. Toxic concentrations of mercury and the pesticide Mirex have also contaminated parts of Lake Ontario.

In recent years it has been discovered that Americans eat about eight times more toxic chemicals in food than they breathe in the air or drink in the water. Dioxins and dibenzofurans have been detected in fresh meat, fruits, vegetables, and milk. Imported fruits and vegetables have also been discovered with toxic levels of pesticide residues.

You must obtain all food and beverage products from approved sources. In addition, proper food handling techniques, personal hygiene and cleanliness, acceptable cleaning and sanitization procedures, and caution and common sense can prevent a tragedy.

Foodborne Physical Hazards

Physical hazards present in food service businesses should never be allowed to endanger the safety of guests. The possible hazards are numerous.

Metal fragments can end up in foods if can openers are not cleaned frequently and if knives, forks, spoons, pots, and pans are used and cleaned carelessly. When a cook opens a container with a knife blade, the risk of contaminating food with metal slivers increases. This practice should be forbidden.

Glass is frequently used for food and beverage containers. When handled or stacked carelessly, glass fragments can find their way into food products. Broken glass chips have been discovered on salad bars and in glasses containing beverages. Ice should be transferred with a metal or plastic scoop designed for that purpose. Never scoop ice with a glass container. If a glass breaks in or near ice, the ice in the ice bin should be discarded and the bin flushed with hot water, washed, and rinsed before refilling.

Cigarette butts and matches, when discovered in food, are a nauseating turn-off. It is best to have a clearly written and understood set of smoking guidelines in your operation. In addition to applying to public areas, the guidelines should cover all areas of the facility. Never permit food staff members to smoke in storage, production, or service areas.

Hair in food is unsanitary, distasteful, and the greatest dissatisfier for many restaurant guests. All staff members must wear approved hair restraints. This is required by all state and federal sanitation codes.

Other foodborne physical hazards that have been discovered in food products served to guests include bandages, twist ties, staples, and rocks. In more than one case, a disgruntled staff member added the foreign object to the food.

Physical hazards can be minimized if staff members are made aware of the hazards and take steps to reduce the risks. As with the other forms of food contamination, specific controls must be built into the operation's sanitation risk management (SRM) program.

The Importance of Health and Hygiene

Good health and personal cleanliness are important for every staff member in the food service business. Strict sanitation standards are necessary throughout the operation to prevent the contamination of food and food-contact surfaces with diseases or pathogenic organisms. These standards should be adapted to the individual operation and presented to all staff members during orientation and training. Management should follow up to ensure that each staff member upholds the standards.

All staff members must practice good personal hygiene. Food service staff members must also be in good health; some operations require job applicants to pass a physical examination before considering them for employment. Staff member uniforms must be clean and well-maintained; if possible, staff members should change into their uniforms after arriving at the workplace, thus minimizing possible contamination from street clothes. Frequent handwashing while working is especially important.

Food staff members must keep their hands and exposed portions of their arms clean. The hands and exposed portions of the arms must be cleaned by vigorously rubbing together the surfaces of the lathered hands and arms for at least 20 seconds and thoroughly rinsing with clean water. Special attention should be paid to areas beneath the fingernails and between the fingers.

Using the same cleaning procedure after defecating, contacting body fluids and discharges, or handling waste containing fecal matter, body fluids, or body discharges, and before beginning or returning to work, staff members should wash their hands *twice*, using a nailbrush during the first washing to clean their fingertips, under their fingernails, and between their fingers. Food employees are required to clean their hands and exposed portions of their arms at the following times:

- After touching bare human body parts other than clean hands and clean, exposed portions of arms;

- After using the toilet room;

- After caring for or handling support animals;

- After coughing, sneezing, using a handkerchief or disposable tissue, using tobacco, eating, or drinking;

- After handling soiled equipment or utensils;

- Immediately before engaging in food preparation, including working with exposed food, clean equipment and utensils, and unwrapped single-service and single-use articles;

- During food preparation, as often as necessary to remove soil and contamination and prevent cross-contamination when changing tasks;

- When switching between working with raw foods and working with ready-to-eat foods; or

- After engaging in other activities that contaminate the hands.

An alcohol-based instant hand sanitizer lotion or a chemical hand sanitizing solution should be applied to the clean hands.

The FDA states:

SUPERVISION

2-101.11   Assignment.*

The permit holder shall be the person in charge or shall designate a person in charge and shall assure that a person in charge is present at the food establishment during all hours of operation.

2-102.11   Demonstration.*

Based on the risks of foodborne illness inherent to the food operation, during inspections and upon request the person in charge shall demonstrate to the regulatory authority knowledge of foodborne disease prevention, application of the Hazard Analysis Critical Control Point principles, and the requirements of this Code, as it relates to the food operation, by:

(A)   Describing the relationship between the prevention of foodborne disease and the personal hygiene of a food employee;

(B) Explaining the responsibility of the person in charge for preventing the transmission of foodborne disease by a food employee who has a disease or medical condition that may cause foodborne disease;

(C) Describing diseases that are transmissible through food and the symptoms associated with the diseases;

(D) Explaining the significance of the relationship between maintaining the time and temperature of potentially hazardous food and the prevention of foodborne illness;

(E) Explaining the hazards involved in the consumption of raw or under-cooked meat, poultry, eggs, and fish;

(F) Stating the required food temperatures and times for safe cooking of potentially hazardous food including meat, poultry, eggs, and fish;

(G) Stating the required temperatures and times for the safe refrigerated storage, hot holding, cooling, and reheating of potentially hazardous food;

(H) Describing the relationship between the prevention of foodborne illness and the management and control of the following:

    (1) Cross contamination,

    (2) Hand contact with ready-to-eat foods,

    (3) Handwashing, and

    (4) Maintaining the food establishment in a clean condition and in good repair;

(I) Explaining the relationship between food safety and providing equipment that is:

    (1) Sufficient in number and capacity, and

    (2) Properly designed, constructed, located, installed, operated, maintained, and cleaned;

(J) Explaining correct procedures for cleaning and sanitizing utensils and food-contact surfaces of equipment;

(K) Identifying the source of water used and measures taken to assure that it remains protected from contamination such as providing protection from backflow and precluding the creation of cross connections;

(L) Identifying poisonous and toxic materials in the food establishment and the procedures necessary to assure that they are safely stored, dispensed, used, and disposed of according to law;

(M) Identifying critical control points in the operation from purchasing through sale or service that may contribute to foodborne illness and explaining steps taken to assure that the points are controlled in accordance with the requirements of this Code;

(N)   Explaining the details of how the person in charge and food employees comply with the HACCP plan if a plan is required by the law, this Code, or an agreement between the regulatory authority and the establishment; and

(O)   Explaining the responsibilities, rights, and authorities assigned by this Code to the:

> (1)   Food employee,
>
> (2)   Person in charge, and
>
> (3)   Regulatory authority.

2-103.11   Person in Charge.

The person in charge shall assure that:

(A)   Food establishment operations are not conducted in a private home or in a room used as living or sleeping quarters as specified under § 6-202.111;

(B)   Persons unnecessary to the food establishment operation are not allowed in the food preparation, food storage, or warewashing areas, *except that brief visits and tours may be authorized by the person in charge if steps are taken to assure that exposed food; clean equipment, utensils, and linens; and unwrapped single-service and single-use articles are protected from contamination;*

(C)   Employees and other persons such as delivery and maintenance persons and pesticide applicators entering the food preparation, food storage, and warewashing areas comply with this Code;

(D)   Employees are effectively cleaning their hands, by routinely monitoring the employees' handwashing;

(E)   Employees are visibly observing foods as they are received to determine that they are from approved sources, delivered at the required temperatures, protected from contamination, unadulterated, and accurately presented, by routinely monitoring the employees' observations and periodically evaluating foods upon their receipt;

(F)   Employees are properly cooking potentially hazardous food, being particularly careful in cooking those foods known to cause severe foodborne illness and death, such as eggs and comminuted meats, through daily oversight of the employees' routine monitoring of the cooking temperatures;

(G)   Employees are using proper methods to rapidly cool potentially hazardous foods that are not held hot and are not for consumption within 4 hours, through daily oversight of the employees' routine monitoring of food temperatures during cooling;

(H)   Consumers who order raw or partially cooked foods of animal origin are informed as specified under § 3-603.11 that the food is not cooked sufficiently to assure its safety;

(I)   Employees are properly sanitizing cleaned multiuse equipment and utensils before they are reused, through routine monitoring of solution temperature and exposure time for hot water sanitizing, and chemical concentration, pH, temperature, and exposure time for chemical sanitizing; and

(J)   Consumers are notified that clean tableware is to be used when they return to self-service areas such as salad bars and buffets.

2-201.11   Responsibility of the Person in Charge to Require Reporting by Food Employees and Applicants.*

The permit holder shall require food employees and food employee applicants to report to the person in charge, information about their health and activities as they relate to diseases that are transmissible through food. A food employee or applicant shall report the information in a manner that allows the person in charge to prevent the likelihood of foodborne disease transmission, including the date of onset of jaundice or of an illness specified in ¶ (C) of this section, if the food employee or applicant:

(A)   Is diagnosed with an illness due to:

    (1)   *Salmonella typhi,*

    (2)   *Shigella* spp.,

    (3)   *Escherichia coli* O157:H7, or

    (4)   Hepatitis A virus infection;

(B)   Has a symptom caused by illness, infection, or other source that is:

    (1)   Associated with an acute gastrointestinal illness such as:

        (a)   Abdominal cramps or discomfort,

        (b)   Diarrhea,

        (c)   Fever,

        (d)   Loss of appetite for 3 or more consecutive days,

        (e)   Vomiting, or

        (f)   Jaundice, or

    (2)   A pustular lesion such as a boil or infected wound that is open or draining and is:

        (a)   On the hands, wrists, or exposed portions of the arms, or

        (b)   On other parts of the body, unless the lesion is covered by a dry, durable, tight-fitting bandage;

(C)   Had a past illness from an infectious agent specified in ¶ (A) of this section; or

(D)   Meets one or more of the following high-risk conditions:

(1)   Is suspected of causing, or being exposed to, a confirmed disease outbreak caused by *S. typhi*, *Shigella* spp., *E. coli* O157:H7, or hepatitis A virus illness including an outbreak at an event such as a family meal, church supper, or ethnic festival because the food employee or applicant:

(a)   Prepared food implicated in the outbreak,

(b)   Consumed food implicated in the outbreak, or

(c)   Consumed food at the event prepared by a person who is infected or ill with the infectious agent that caused the outbreak or who is suspected of being a carrier of the infectious agent, or

(2)   Lives in the same household as a person who is diagnosed with a disease caused by *S. typhi*, *Shigella* spp., *E. coli* O157:H7, or hepatitis A virus infection,

(3)   Lives in the same household as a person who attends or works in a setting where there is a confirmed disease outbreak caused by *S. typhi*, *Shigella* spp., *E. coli* O157:H7, or hepatitis A virus infection,

(4)   Traveled out of the country within the last 50 calendar days.

2-201.12   Exclusions and Restrictions.*

The person in charge shall:

(A)   Exclude a food employee from a food establishment if the food employee is diagnosed with an infectious agent specified in ¶ 2-201.11(A);

(B)   Except as specified under ¶ (C) of this section, restrict a food employee from working with exposed food; clean equipment, utensils, and linens; and unwrapped single-service and single-use articles, in a food establishment if the food employee is:

(1)   Suffering from a symptom specified in ¶ 2-201.11(B), or

(2)   Is not experiencing a symptom of acute gastroenteritis specified in Subparagraph 2-201.11(B)(1) but has a stool that yields a specimen culture that is positive for *Salmonella typhi*;

(C)   If the population served is a highly susceptible population, exclude a food employee or an applicant who:

(1)   Is experiencing a symptom of acute gastrointestinal illness specified in Subparagraph 2-201.11(B)(1) and meets a high-risk condition specified in Subparagraphs 2-201.11(D) (1)–(4),

(2)   Is not experiencing a symptom of acute gastroenteritis specified in Subparagraph 2-201.11(B)(1) but has a stool that yields a specimen culture that is positive for *S. typhi*, *Shigella* spp., or *Escherichia coli* O157:H7,

(3)   Had a past illness from *S. typhi* within the last 3 months, or

(4)   Had a past illness from *Shigella* spp. or *E. coli* O157:H7 within the last month; and

(D)   For a food employee or an applicant who is jaundiced:

(1)   If the onset of jaundice occurred within the last 7 calendar days, exclude the food employee or applicant from the food establishment, or

(2)   If the onset of jaundice occurred more than 7 calendar days before:

(a)   Exclude the food employee or applicant from a food establishment that serves a highly susceptible population, or

(b)   Restrict the food employee or applicant from activities specified in ¶ 2-201.12(B), if the food establishment does not serve a highly susceptible population.

2-201.13   Removal of Exclusions and Restrictions.

(A) The person in charge may remove an exclusion specified in ¶ 2-201.12(A) if the person in charge obtains approval from the regulatory authority and if the person excluded as specified in ¶ 2-201.12(A) provides to the person in charge written medical documentation from a physician licensed to practice medicine that specifies that the excluded person:

(1)   May work in an unrestricted capacity in a food establishment, including an establishment that serves a highly susceptible population, because the person is free of:

(a)   The infectious agent of concern as specified in § 8-501.40, or

(b)   Symptoms, if hepatitis A virus is the infectious agent of concern; or

(2)   May only work in an unrestricted capacity in a food establishment that does not serve a highly susceptible population because the person:

(a)   Is free of the symptoms specified in Subparagraphs 2-201.11(B)(1)(a)–(f), and

(b)   Has a stool that yields a specimen culture that is positive for *Shigella* spp., or *Escherichia coli* O157:H7.

(B) The person in charge may remove a restriction specified in:

(1)   Subparagraph 2-201.12(B)(1) if the restricted person:

(a)   Is free of the symptoms specified in ¶ 2-201.11(B) and no foodborne illness occurs that may have been caused by the restricted person,

(b)   Is suspected of causing foodborne illness but:

(i)   Is free of the symptoms specified in ¶ 2-201.11(B), and

(ii)   Provides written medical documentation from a physician licensed to practice medicine stating that the restricted person is free of the infectious agent that is suspected of causing the person's symptoms or causing foodborne illness, as specified in § 8-501.40, or

(c)   Provides written medical documentation from a physician licensed to practice medicine stating that the symptoms experienced result from a chronic noninfectious condition such as ulcerative colitis or irritable bowel syndrome; or

(2)   Subparagraph 2-201.12(B)(2) if the restricted person provides written medical documentation according to the criteria specified in § 8-501.40 that indicates the stools are free of *Salmonella typhi*.

(C) The person in charge may remove an exclusion specified under ¶ 2-201.12(C) if the excluded person provides written medical documentation from a physician licensed to practice medicine that the person is free of *S. typhi*, *Shigella* spp., *E. coli* O157:H7, or hepatitis A virus infection, whichever is the infectious agent of concern, as specified in § 8-501.40.

(D) The person in charge may remove an exclusion specified in Subparagraph 2-201.12(D)(1) and Subparagraph 2-201.12(D)(2)(a) and a restriction specified in Subparagraph 2-201.12(D)(2)(b) if:

(1)   No foodborne illness occurs that may have been caused by the excluded or restricted person and the person:

(a)   Provides written medical documentation from a physician licensed to practice medicine stating that the person is free of hepatitis A virus as specified in ¶ 8-501.40 (D), or

(b)   Is no longer jaundiced; or

(2)   The excluded or restricted person is suspected of causing foodborne illness and complies with Subparagraphs (D)(1)(a) and (b) of this section.

2-201.14   Responsibility of a Food Employee or an Applicant to Report to the Person in Charge.*

A food employee or a person who applies for a job as a food employee shall:

(A)   In a manner specified in § 2-201.11, report to the person in charge the information specified in ¶¶ 2-201.11(A)–(D); and

(B)   Comply with exclusions and restrictions that are specified in ¶¶ 2-201.12(A)–(D).

2-201.15   Reporting by the Person In Charge.*

The person in charge shall notify the regulatory authority of a food employee or a person who applies for a job as a food employee who is diagnosed with, or is suspected of having an illness due to, *Salmonella typhi*, *Shigella* spp., *Escherichia coli* O157:H7, or hepatitis A virus infection.

2-301.11   Clean Condition (Hands and Arms).*

Food employees shall keep their hands and exposed portions of their arms clean.

2-301.12   Cleaning Procedure.*

Except as specified under § 2-301.13, food employees shall clean their hands and exposed portions of their arms with a cleaning compound in a lavatory that is equipped as specified under ¶ 5-202.12(A) by vigorously rubbing together the surfaces of their lathered hands and arms for at least 20 seconds and thoroughly rinsing with clean water. Employees shall pay particular attention to the areas underneath the fingernails and between the fingers.

2-301.13   Special Handwash Procedures.*

After defecating, contacting body fluids and discharges, or handling waste containing fecal matter, body fluids, or body discharges, and before beginning or returning to work, food employees shall wash their hands:

(A)   Twice, using the cleaning procedure specified in § 2-301.12; and

(B)   By using a nailbrush during the first washing to clean their fingertips, under their fingernails, and between their fingers.

2-301.14   When to Wash.*

Food employees shall clean their hands and exposed portions of their arms as specified under §§ 2-301.12 or 2-301.13 at the following times:

(A)   **After touching bare human body parts** other than clean hands and clean, exposed portions of arms;

(B)   **After using the toilet room;**

(C)   **After caring for or handling support animals as allowed under** § 2-403.11;

(D)   **After coughing, sneezing, using a handkerchief or disposable tissue, using tobacco, eating, or drinking;**

(E)   **After handling soiled equipment or utensils;**

(F)   **Immediately before** engaging in **food preparation** including working with exposed food, clean equipment and utensils, and unwrapped single-service and single-use articles;

(G)   **During food preparation, as often as necessary to remove soil and contamination and to prevent cross contamination when changing tasks;**

(H)   **When switching between** working with **raw foods and** working with **ready-to-eat foods;** or

(I)   **After** engaging in other **activities that contaminate** the hands.

2-301.15   Hand Sanitizers.

(A) An alcohol-based, instant hand sanitizer lotion and a chemical hand sanitizing solution used as a hand dip shall:

(1)   Consist of, or be made up of, a chemical formulation **specifically listed for use as a hand sanitizer** in 21 CFR 178.1010. Sanitizing solutions or their components shall be generally recognized as safe as specified in 21 CFR 182—Substances Generally Recognized As Safe and 21 CFR 184—Direct Food Substances Affirmed As Generally Recognized As Safe.

(2)   Consist of, or be made up of, a chemical formulation that is not generally recognized as safe or listed for use as a hand sanitizer, and:

(a)   Is followed by thorough hand rinsing in clean water or the use of gloves, or

(b)   Is used only where there is no direct contact with food by the hands; and

(3)   Be applied only to hands that are cleaned as specified under §§ 2-301.12 or 2-301.13.

(B) A chemical hand sanitizing solution used as a hand dip shall be maintained clean and at a strength equivalent to 100 mg/L chlorine or above.

2-302.11   Maintenance (Fingernails).

Food employees shall keep their fingernails trimmed, filed, and maintained so the edges and surfaces are smooth and cleanable.

2-303.11   Prohibition (Jewelry).

While preparing food, food employees may not wear jewelry on their arms and hands. *This section does not apply to a plain ring such as a wedding band.*

2-304.11   Clean Condition (Outer Clothing).

Food employees shall wear clean outer clothing. When moving from a raw food operation to a ready-to-eat food operation, food employees shall wear a clean outer covering over clothing or change to clean clothing if their clothing is soiled.

2-401.11   Eating, Drinking, or Using Tobacco.*

(A) Except as specified in ¶ (B) of this section, an employee shall eat, drink, or use any form of tobacco only in designated areas where the contamination of exposed food; clean equipment, utensils, and linens; unwrapped single-service and single-use articles; or other items needing protection can not result.

(B) *A food employee may drink from a closed beverage container if the container is handled to prevent contamination of:*

(1)   *The employee's hands;*

(2)   *The container; and*

(3) *Exposed food; clean equipment, utensils, and linens; and unwrapped single-service and single-use articles.*

2-401.12   Discharges from the Eyes, Nose, and Mouth.*

Food employees experiencing persistent sneezing, coughing, or a runny nose that causes discharges from the eyes, nose, or mouth may not work with exposed food; clean equipment, utensils, and linens; or unwrapped single-service or single-use articles.

2-402.11   Effectiveness (Hair Restraints).

(A) Except as provided under ¶ (B) of this section, food employees shall wear hair restraints such as hats, hair coverings or nets, beard restraints, and clothing that covers body hair, that are designed and worn to effectively keep their hair from contacting exposed food; clean equipment, utensils, and linens; and unwrapped single-service and single-use articles.

(B) *This section does not apply to food employees such as counter staff who only serve beverages and wrapped or packaged foods, hostesses, and wait staff if they present a minimal risk of contaminating exposed food; clean equipment, utensils, and linens; and unwrapped single-service and single-use articles.*

2-403.11   Handling Prohibition (Animals).*

(A) Except as specified in ¶ (B) of this section, food employees may not care for or handle animals that may be present such as patrol dogs, support animals, or pets that are allowed under Subparagraphs 6-501.115(B)(2)–(4).

(B) *Food employees with support animals may care for their support animals if they wash their hands as specified under § 2-301.13 before working with exposed food; clean equipment, utensils, and linens; or unwrapped single-service and single-use articles.*

Source: FDA 1993 *Food Code.*

A food service operation must have adequate facilities to ensure compliance with these sanitation standards. Proper handwashing and restroom facilities must be available to all staff members. Usually, staff members should not share restroom facilities with guests, although the number of restrooms required depends on the seating capacity of the food establishment's serving area. (More about restrooms is presented in Chapter 10.) If staff members change into uniforms at the workplace, they should have adequate dressing areas and lockers. These areas should be used for no other purpose.

The FDA states:

5-202.12   Handwashing Lavatory, Water Temperature, and Flow.

(A) A handwashing lavatory shall be equipped to provide water at a temperature of at least 43°C (110°F) through a mixing valve or combination faucet.

(B)   A steam mixing valve may not be used at a handwashing lavatory.

(C)   A self-closing, slow-closing, or metering faucet shall provide a flow of water for at least 15 seconds without the need to reactivate the faucet.

5-203.11   Handwashing Lavatory.*

(A) Except as specified in ¶ (B) of this section, at least 1 handwashing lavatory, a number of handwashing lavatories necessary for their convenient use by employees in areas specified under § 5-204.11, and not fewer than the number of handwashing lavatories required by law shall be provided.

(B)   *If approved by the regulatory authority, when food exposure is limited and handwashing lavatories are not conveniently available, such as in some mobile or temporary food establishments or at some vending machine locations, employees may use chemically treated towelettes for handwashing.*

5-204.11   Handwashing Lavatory (Location and Placement).*

A handwashing lavatory shall be located:

(A)   To allow convenient use by employees in food preparation, food dispensing, and warewashing areas; and

(B)   In, or immediately adjacent to, toilet rooms.

5-205.11   Using a Handwashing Lavatory.

(A) A handwashing lavatory shall be maintained so that it is accessible at all times for employee use.

(B) A handwashing lavatory may not be used for purposes other than handwashing.

6-301.10   Minimum Number.

Handwashing lavatories shall be provided as specified under § 5-203.11.

6-301.11   Handwashing Cleanser and Nailbrush, Availability.

Each handwashing lavatory or group of 2 adjacent lavatories shall have available:

(A)   A supply of hand cleaning liquid, powder, or bar soap; and

(B)   A nailbrush, if the lavatories are used by food employees.

6-301.12   Hand Drying Provision.

Each handwashing lavatory or group of adjacent lavatories shall be provided with:

(A)   Individual, disposable towels;

(B)   A continuous towel system that supplies the user with a clean towel; or

(C)   A heated-air hand drying device.

6-301.13   Disposable Towels, Waste Receptacle.

A waste receptacle shall be provided for each handwashing lavatory or group of adjacent lavatories that is provided with individual, disposable towels as specified in § 6-301.12(A), as specified under ¶ 5-501.17(B).

Source: FDA 1993 *Food Code.*

Staff members who regulatory authorities have reasonable cause to believe have transmitted a foodborne disease may be interviewed and/or required to have appropriate medical examinations. As a result, an infected staff member may be restricted or excluded from the food establishment. Additionally, the establishment's permit may be summarily suspended. Release of a staff member from restriction or exclusion may require additional medical tests as well as minimum time periods.

It is a wise idea to reduce risks by requiring staff members to provide information by completing the Applicant and Food Employee Interview (see Exhibit 3.12), Food Employee Reporting Agreement (see Exhibit 3.13), and the Applicant and Food Employee Medical Referral form (see Exhibit 3.14). Such a concentrated effort will help lower food safety risks.

The FDA states:

PREVENTION OF FOODBORNE DISEASE TRANSMISSION BY EMPLOYEES

8-501.10   Obtaining Information: Personal History of Illness, Medical Examination, and Specimen Analysis.

The regulatory authority shall act when it has reasonable cause to believe that a food employee has possibly transmitted disease; may be infected with a disease in a communicable form that is transmissible through food; may be a carrier of infectious agents that cause a disease that is transmissible through food; or is affected with a boil, an infected wound, or acute respiratory infection, by:

(A)   Securing a confidential medical history of the employee suspected of transmitting disease or making other investigations as deemed appropriate; and

(B)   Requiring appropriate medical examinations, including collection of specimens for laboratory analysis, of a suspected employee and other employees.

8-501.20   Restriction or Exclusion of Food Employee, or Summary Suspension of Permit.

Based on the findings of an investigation related to an employee who is suspected of being infected or diseased, the regulatory authority may issue an order to the

Exhibit 3.12 Applicant and Food Employee Interview

FORM
1

Applicant and Food Employee Interview

Preventing Transmission of Diseases through Food by Infected Food Employees with Emphasis on ***Salmonella typhi, Shigella spp., Escherichia coli*** O157:H7, and Hepatitis A Virus.

The purpose of this form is to assure that Applicants and Food Employees advise the Person in Charge of past and current conditions described so that the Person in Charge can take appropriate steps to preclude the transmission of foodborne illness.

Applicant or Employee name (print) _____
Address _____
_____

Telephone *Daytime:*_____   *Evening:*_____

TODAY:

Are you suffering from any of the following:
    1. Symptoms
        Abdominal cramps ?   YES/NO
        Diarrhea ?   YES/NO
        Fever ?   YES/NO
        Prolonged loss of appetite (more than 3 days) ?   YES/NO
        Jaundice ?   YES/NO
        Vomiting ?   YES/NO
    2. Pustular lesions
        Pustular lesion on the hand, wrist or an exposed body part ?
        (*such as boils and infected wounds, however small*)   YES/NO

PAST:

Have you ever been diagnosed as being ill with typhoid or paratyphoid fever *(Salmonella typhi)*, shigellosis *(Shigella* spp.), *Escherichia coli* O157:H7 infection, or hepatitis (hepatitis A virus)?   YES/NO
If you have, what was the date of the diagnosis _____

HIGH-RISK CONDITIONS

1. Do you have a household member attending or working in a setting where there is a confirmed outbreak of typhoid fever, shigellosis, *Escherichia coli* O157:H7 infections, or hepatitis A?   YES/NO
2. Do you live in the same household as a person diagnosed with typhoid fever, shigellosis, hepatitis A, or illness due to *E. coli* O157:H7?   YES/NO
3. Have you been exposed to or suspected of causing a confirmed outbreak of typhoid fever, shigellosis, *E. coli* O157:H7 infections, or hepatitis A?   YES/NO
4. Have you traveled outside the United States within the last 50 days ?   YES/NO

Name, Address, and Telephone Number of your Doctor:
Name   _____
Address   _____
        _____

Telephone - *Daytime* _____   *Evening* _____

Signature of Applicant or Food Employee _____ **Date** _____

Signature of Permit Holder's Representative _____ **Date** _____

Source: FDA 1993 *Food Code.*

Exhibit 3.13 Food Employee Reporting Agreement

FORM 2	**Food Employee Reporting Agreement**

Preventing Transmission of Diseases through Food by Infected Food Employees with Emphasis on *Salmonella typhi, Shigella spp., Escherichia coli* O157:H7, and Hepatitis A Virus.

The purpose of this agreement is to assure that Food Employees notify the Person in Charge when they experience any of the conditions listed so that the Person in Charge can take appropriate steps to preclude the transmission of foodborne illness.

I AGREE TO REPORT TO THE PERSON IN CHARGE:

FUTURE SYMPTOMS and PUSTULAR LESIONS:

    1. Abdominal cramps
    2. Diarrhea
    3. Fever
    4. Prolonged loss of appetite (more than 3 days)
    6. Jaundice
    5. Vomiting
    7. Pustular lesions:
          ·Pustular lesion on the hand, wrist, or an exposed body part
          (*such as boils and infected wounds, however small*)

FUTURE MEDICAL DIAGNOSIS:

Whenever diagnosed as being ill with typhoid or paratyphoid fever (*Salmonella typhi*), shigellosis (*Shigella* spp.), *Escherichia coli* O157:H7 infection, or hepatitis (hepatitis A virus).

FUTURE HIGH-RISK CONDITIONS:

1. A household member attending or working in a setting experiencing a confirmed outbreak of typhoid fever, shigellosis, *Escherichia coli* O157:H7 infection, or hepatitis A
2. A household member diagnosed with typhoid fever, shigellosis, illness due to *E. coli* O157:H7, or hepatitis A
3. Exposure to or suspicion of causing any confirmed outbreak of typhoid fever, shigellosis, *E. coli* O157:H7, or hepatitis
4. Travel outside the United States within the last 50 days

I have read (or had explained to me) and understand the requirements concerning my responsibilities under the **Food Code** and this agreement to comply with:

    (1) Reporting requirements specified above involving symptoms, diagnoses, and high-risk conditions specified;
    (2) Work restrictions or exclusions that are imposed upon me; *and*
    (3) Good hygienic practices.

I understand that failure to comply with the terms of this agreement could lead to action by the food establishment or the food regulatory authority that may jeopardize my employment and may involve legal action against me.

Applicant or Food Employee Name (please print) _____

Signature of Applicant or Food Employee _____Date _____

Signature of Permit Holder's Representative _____Date _____

Source: FDA 1993 *Food Code.*

Exhibit 3.14 Applicant and Food Employee Medical Referral

FORM
3

Applicant and Food Employee Medical Referral

Preventing Transmission of Diseases through Food by Infected Food Employees with Emphasis on *Salmonella typhi, Shigella spp., Escherichia coli* O157:H7, and Hepatitis A Virus.

The Food Code specifies, under *Part 2-2 Employee Health Subpart 2-201 Disease or Medical Condition*, that Applicants and Food Employees obtain medical clearance from a physician licensed to practice medicine whenever the individual:

1. Is chronically suffering from a symptom such as **diarrhea;** *or*
2. Meets one of the high-risk conditions specified in Paragraph 2-201.11(D) and is suffering from any symptom specified in Subparagraph 2-201.11(B)(1).
3. Has a **current illness** involving *Salmonella typhi* (typhoid or paratyphoid fever), *Shigella* spp. (shigellosis), *Escherichia coli* O157:H7 infection, or hepatitis A virus (hepatitis), *or*
4. Reports *past illness* involving *Salmonella typhi* (typhoid or paratyphoid fever), *Shigella* spp. (shigellosis), *Escherichia coli* O157:H7 infection, or hepatitis A virus (hepatitis), if the establishment is serving a highly susceptible population such as preschool age children or immunocompromised, physically debilitated, or infirm elderly.

Name of Applicant or Food Employee being referred and population served:
(_____ (Name, please print) _____). **Highly susceptible population YES ☐ NO ☐**

REASON FOR MEDICAL REFERRAL:

The reason for this referral is checked below:
☐ Chronic diarrhea or other chronic symptom _____(specify)_____ .
☐ Meets a high-risk condition specified in Paragraph 2-201.11(D) ____(specify)____ and suffers from a symptom specified in Subparagraph 2-201.11(B)(1). ____(specify)____ .
☐ Diagnosed or suspected typhoid or paratyphoid fever, shigellosis, *E. coli* O157:H7 infection, or hepatitis.
☐ Reported past illness from typhoid or paratyphoid fever, shigellosis, *E. coli* O157:H7 infection, or hepatitis.
☐ Other medical condition of concern per the following description:
_____

PHYSICIAN'S CONCLUSION:

☐ Applicant or food employee is free of *Salmonella typhi, Shigella* spp., *Escherichia coli* O157:H7, or hepatitis A and may work as a food employee without restrictions.
☐ Applicant is an asymptomatic carrier of *Salmonella typhi* and is restricted from direct food handling duties in establishments not serving highly susceptible populations.
☐ Applicant or food employee is not ill but continues as an asymptomatic carrier of ____(pathogen)____ and should be excluded from working as a food employee in food establishments serving highly susceptible populations such as those who are preschool age, physically debilitated, immunocompromised, or infirm elderly.
☐ Applicant or food employee is suffering from *Salmonella typhi, Shigella* spp., *Escherichia coli* O157:H7, or hepatitis A virus and should be excluded from working as a food employee.

COMMENTS:

Signature of Physician _____ **Date** _____ .

Source: FDA 1993 *Food Code.*

suspected employee or permit holder instituting one or more of the following control measures:

(A)   Restricting the employee's services to specific areas and tasks in a food establishment that present no risk of transmitting the disease;

(B)   Excluding the employee from a food establishment; or

(C)   Closing the food establishment by summarily suspending a permit to operate in accordance with law.

8-501.30   Restriction or Exclusion Order: Warning or Hearing Not Required, Information Required in Order.

Based on the findings of the investigation as specified in § 8-501.10 and to control disease transmission, the regulatory authority may issue an order of restriction or exclusion to a suspected employee or the permit holder without prior warning, notice of a hearing, or a hearing if the order:

(A)   States the reasons for the restriction or exclusion that is ordered;

(B)   States the evidence that the employee or permit holder shall provide in order to demonstrate that the reasons for the restriction or exclusion are eliminated;

(C)   States that the suspected employee or the permit holder may request an appeal hearing by submitting a timely request as provided under law; and

(D)   Provides the name and address of the regulatory authority representative to whom a request for an appeal hearing may be made.

8-501.40   Release of Employee from Restriction or Exclusion.

The regulatory authority shall release an employee from restriction or exclusion according to law and the following conditions:

(A)   An employee who was infected with *Salmonella typhi* if the employee's stools are negative for *S. typhi* based on testing of at least 3 consecutive stool specimen cultures that are taken:

(1)   Not earlier than 1 month after onset,

(2)   At least 48 hours after discontinuance of antibiotics, and

(3)   At least 24 hours apart; and

(B)   If one of the cultures taken as specified in ¶ (A) of this section is positive, repeat cultures are taken at intervals of 1 month until at least 3 consecutive negative stool specimen cultures are obtained.

(C)   An employee who was infected with *Shigella* spp. or *Escherichia coli* O157:H7 if the employee's stools are negative for *Shigella* spp. or *E. coli* O157:H7 based on testing of 2 consecutive stool specimen cultures that are taken:

(1)   Not earlier than 48 hours after discontinuance of antibiotics; and

(2)   At least 24 hours apart.

(D)   An employee who was infected with hepatitis A virus if:

(1)   Symptoms cease; or

(2)   At least 2 blood tests show falling liver enzymes.

Source: FDA 1993 *Food Code.*

Incidence of Foodborne Disease in the United States

Reports of foodborne and waterborne diseases are published periodically in the United States. The number of outbreaks reported are thought to be fewer than the number of outbreaks which have actually occurred. Every year, about 9,000 Americans die of food poisoning. The most frequent victims are the very young and the elderly with weakened immune systems.[4] Since many symptoms of foodborne disease resemble symptoms of the 24-hour flu, the actual number of outbreaks occurring in the United States is probably far greater than the number being reported. Some experts estimate that only about 10% of all salmonellosis outbreaks are reported. In any case, foodborne disease outbreaks in the United States are preventable.

An outbreak of foodborne disease only occurs under certain conditions. These conditions are illustrated in the form of a flow diagram in Exhibit 3.15. Initially, disease agents must be present in humans, animals, food, or the environment. These pathogenic agents can enter the food before they get to the food establishment. The agents can also enter food products once they are in the establishment. The critical factor is the contamination of food with the disease agents or their toxins. Once in the food service operation, the pathogens can reproduce in food. Some simply increase in numbers while others produce toxic waste products in the food. When contaminated food is then eaten, foodborne illness results. Any SRM program must be designed to eliminate the risks throughout this chain of distribution and processing.

Periodically, the Centers for Disease Control and Prevention report surveillance summaries in the *Morbidity and Mortality Weekly Report.* Exhibit 3.16 presents a summary of foodborne disease outbreaks, by etiologic agent and contributing factors, in the United States from 1983 to 1987. In this summary, a foodborne disease outbreak is defined as an incident in which (a) two or more persons experience a similar illness after ingestion of a common food, and (b) epidemiologic analysis implicates the food as the source of the illness. A few exceptions exist; for example, one case of botulism or chemical poisoning constitutes an outbreak.

Outbreaks of known etiology are those for which laboratory evidence of a specific agent is obtained and specified criteria are met. Outbreaks of unknown etiology are those for which epidemiologic analysis implicates a food source, but adequate laboratory confirmation is not obtained. Outbreaks of unknown etiology are subdivided into four subgroups by incubation period of the illnesses: less than 1 hour (probable chemical poisoning), 1–7 hours (probable *Staphylococcus* food poisoning), 8–14 hours (probable *Clostridium perfringens* food poisoning), and more than 14 hours (other infections or toxic agents).

Exhibit 3.15 Conditions Leading to a Foodborne Illness Outbreak

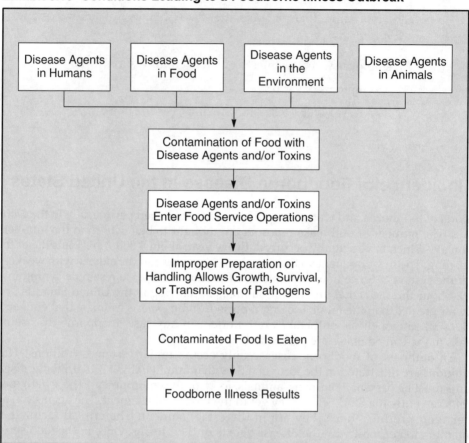

The CDC have repeatedly stated that the number of outbreaks of foodborne disease reported by the surveillance system clearly represents only a small fraction of the outbreaks that occur. Nevertheless, these data show that the vast majority (over 80%) of known factors occur due to human error or carelessness. The most significant contributing factor is improper holding temperatures. While bacteria are responsible for the largest number of outbreaks, *Salmonella spp.* are most often identified as the etiologic agent.

The sanitation risk management program in a food service operation should guard against improper holding temperatures, inadequate cooking, contaminated equipment, poor personal hygiene, and food from unsafe sources. Each of the factors contributing to outbreaks of foodborne disease must be addressed by the SRM program, and the program must follow the requirements of state and local sanitation codes. The SRM program design, using the control points described earlier, should focus on controlling these five contributing risk factors. Whenever possible, the utmost care and caution must be practiced to minimize or eliminate the risks. If food does become contaminated, it should be discarded.

Exhibit 3.16 Foodborne Disease Outbreaks by Etiologic Agent and Contributing Factors

Etiologic Agent	Number of Reported Outbreaks	Number of Outbreaks in which Factors Reported	Improper Holding Temperatures	Inadequate Cooking	Contaminated Equipment	Food from Unsafe Source	Poor Personal Hygiene	Other
BACTERIAL								
Bacillus cereus	16	12	11	1	3	—	2	—
Brucella	2	1	—	1	—	1	—	—
Campylobacter	28	17	3	3	3	9	3	1
Clostridium botulinum	74	7	2	2	—	—	—	5
Clostridium perfringens	24	22	21	13	4	1	4	3
Escherichia coli	7	3	—	1	—	—	—	2
Salmonella	342	220	157	92	79	18	80	25
Shigella	44	24	8	1	6	3	18	6
Staphylococcus aureus	47	35	33	1	11	—	15	3
Streptococcus	9	6	5	—	—	1	4	1
Vibrio parahaemolyticus	3	2	—	2	—	2	—	—
Other bacterial	4	3	1	—	—	1	—	2
Total	600	352	241	117	106	36	126	48
CHEMICAL								
Ciguatoxin	87	27	2	—	—	10	—	15
Heavy metals	13	11	1	—	2	—	—	8
Mushrooms	14	7	—	—	—	7	—	—
Scombrotoxin	83	37	30	—	—	12	1	4
Shellfish	2	1	—	—	—	1	—	—
Other chemical	33	15	1	—	2	1	—	15
Total	232	98	34	—	4	31	1	42
PARASITIC								
Trichinella spiralis	33	5	1	3	1	1	—	—
Other parasitic	3	1	—	—	—	—	1	—
Total	36	6	1	3	1	1	1	—
VIRAL								
Hepatitis A	29	14	1	—	—	—	8	1
Norwalk virus	10	8	2	1	1	2	3	2
Other viral	2	2	—	—	—	—	1	—
Total	41	24	3	1	2	2	12	4
Confirmed Total	909	480	279	121	113	70	140	94
Unknown	1,488	775	513	144	173	79	204	152
TOTAL	2,397	1,255	792	265	286	149	344	246

Source: Centers for Disease Control and Prevention, "Foodborne Disease Outbreaks, 5-Year Summary, 1983–1987," *Morbidity and Mortality Weekly Report*, March 1990, 39 (No. SS-1): 15–57.

The FDA states:

3-701.11   Discarding Food Contaminated by Persons.*

(A) Food that may have been contaminated by an employee who has been re-stricted or excluded as specified in § 2-201.12 shall be discarded.

(B) Food that is contaminated by food employees, consumers, or other persons through contact with their hands, bodily discharges, such as nasal or oral dis-charges, or other means shall be discarded.

Source: FDA 1993 *Food Code.*

What If a Foodborne Illness Outbreak Is Suspected?

Assume you are a food service manager and a guest calls to inform you that she and her husband became ill after eating in your establishment. What will you say, and what action will you take? How will you handle the guest's accusation that your facility might be a source of foodborne illness? What steps will you take to close this complaint with the guest? The answers to these questions might depend on whether or not your operation has an established procedure for dealing with suspected outbreaks of foodborne illness.

If you have a written procedure detailing what to do and when, you will probably respond to this potential crisis in a logical and systematic way. If no set of procedures exists, your response is likely to be rash and disorganized. Having a detailed procedure can save you time when you need it most. In such an emergency situation, prompt ac-tion will prevent further problems and will minimize the likelihood of other outbreaks. With your reputation, your guest's health, and the image of your operation at stake, you cannot afford to be unprepared.

The regulations and recommendations discussed throughout this book are aimed at preventing the situation just described from occurring. But with so many potential sources of food contamination, it is only sensible to be ready to deal with a foodborne disease outbreak. Such readiness is not a sign that the operation is negligent; rather, it shows that management is realistic and follows the principles of risk management.

Before we consider the procedures for handling guest foodborne illness complaints, think about the following findings from a White House Study of Consumer Affairs:

- Customers who take the time to complain are more likely to return to a business, even if the problem wasn't resolved satisfactorily.

- Of those who take the time to complain, 54 to 70% will return if their complaints are resolved. If the complaint is resolved quickly, 95% will return.

- The average customer who has a complaint tells 9–10 other people. Thirteen percent will tell 20 or more other people.

- Customers who have had complaints satisfactorily resolved tell an average of 5 other people.[5]

Many of these "other people" are potential guests. Thus it makes sense to resolve complaints quickly: such action can be a source of positive word-of-mouth advertising.

The following 11-step procedure for handling guest foodborne illness complaints should prove valuable to food service and lodging managers in their risk management programs.

Step 1—Just one person in the operation, usually the manager, should be responsible for the investigation. It is important that this person keep accurate, detailed records, since these records may be beneficial during a health department investigation.

If public statements are necessary, the responsible person should also act as the only authoritative spokesperson for the establishment. This individual should handle all communications with the media and others who need information. All inquiries should be referred to this spokesperson. If more than one spokesperson is used to explain the same circumstances, there might be a loss of credibility. All relevant information should be made public unless it involves security or a confidential issue. When in doubt, the person in charge should check with legal counsel. If the outbreak is prolonged, the responsible person must provide regular updates to the media, staff members, and others. The less people know about the situation, the more they fear possible consequences. Above all, the spokesperson should be truthful and credible.

Step 2—Listen to the complaint. The interviewer should be courteous and should avoid arguing with the complainant. The responsible person should not talk about similar problems which have occurred in the past. No mention of insurance or claim settlements should be made at this point.

When listening, focus all of your attention on the guest who is complaining. Never argue, defend, or try to explain away the guest's concerns. These reactions only cause the complainant to grow angrier. Above all, do not admit liability. Show your sympathy and concerns, but do not say "I'm so sorry that our food made you sick."

If an insurance claim or lawsuit has been filed against the establishment, other strategies might be necessary. The person being served should say nothing to the process server and should get a lawyer as soon as possible. If the situation that caused the outbreak can be shown to be an isolated incident, the liability may not be as severe as when the facility has persisted in unsanitary practices against health department recommendations. The insurance company and lawyers might wish to subpoena past inspection reports. Managers subject themselves to the possibility of punitive damages if an illness or injury results from a practice or condition about which the health department has issued prior warnings.

Step 3—Get the facts. The person designated as the complaint investigator should keep a supply of complaint recording forms on hand. By using a standard form such as the one shown in Exhibit 3.17, the investigator is sure to get all of the essential information. The complaint record form should include the menu items eaten, meal period, symptoms, time, date, and the names, addresses, and telephone numbers of others who ate with the complainant.

Before completing the form, ask the complainant if he or she minds if you take notes. This shows the complainant that you are focusing on the facts. When recording the facts, do not admit liability. Before leaving the complainant, summarize the facts to be certain that you understand what was said.

Step 4—Promptly and properly evaluate the guest complaint. The investigator should then contact the people who dined with the complainant to determine whether these guests have experienced similar symptoms. If so, the investigator should sort through the other guest checks to identify those who also consumed the same food. By matching credit card receipts to guest checks, the person in charge can gather the information necessary to contact these other guests. Detailed records should be kept on every conversation related to the suspected outbreak.

Exhibit 3.17 Sample Food-Related Complaint Record

Name of Complainant		
Address		
Telephone Number		
Summary of the Complaint		
Number Affected	**Date of Meal**	**Time Eaten**
Food and Beverages Consumed		

Symptoms

_____	Nausea	_____	Abdominal Cramps
_____	Diarrhea	_____	Prolonged loss of appetite
_____	Fever		(more than 3 days)
_____	Jaundice	_____	Other (specify) _____
_____	Vomiting		_____

Did others consume the same food and beverage?

Names, Telephone Numbers, and Addresses of Other Consumers

Management Action to Resolve the Complaint

Date _____ Signature _____

In the event that the complaint is totally unfounded, the manager might choose to handle it in-house. In most cases, however, it is advisable to call in the health department to assist in the investigation of the complaint. In any case, be certain that the complaint is handled professionally and quickly.

Step 5—The health department should be promptly notified if the complaint appears to be valid. It is the obligation of the health department to investigate foodborne illness outbreaks. An outbreak is a situation in which more than one person becomes ill from eating the same food.

Step 6—Isolate the suspected food products, if samples are still available. By this time the responsible person should have an idea of what food caused the suspected outbreak. The person in charge should promptly take possibly contaminated ingredients or batches of finished menu items out of circulation. These samples should be placed in clean, sanitized containers and then covered, dated, and labeled "DO NOT USE—SUSPECTED SOURCE OF FOODBORNE ILLNESS." All suspected food should be refrigerated and all staff members informed that the containers are not to be tampered with until further notice.

Step 7—Cooperate with the health department. Cooperation with health department officials is essential. Tell them everything, accurately and quickly. They will be able to determine whether guests who could not be identified or located have filed similar complaints with the health department office.

In cases of foodborne illness outbreaks, the health department conducts detailed interviews with complainants to determine symptoms and the food history. The health department might be able to draw a preliminary conclusion regarding the organisms responsible for the symptoms based on these interviews; officials can also identify which one of the complainants' meals is most likely to have caused the problem. This input from the health department helps determine whether the complaint against the operation is valid or not. The health department might uncover other causes for the complainants' symptoms. This is especially helpful in cases involving infections, which are slow to surface. People naturally associate illness with the last meal consumed away from home, but if the illness can be traced to a much earlier meal eaten elsewhere, the operation can be cleared of the accusation.

The health department might also interview staff members and managers. Swabs of equipment, surfaces, and staff members might be required. Food samples might be sent to a lab for analysis. Fecal samples might be requested from staff members. Naturally, the health department checks the sanitary condition of the operation in question. The authorities might immediately exclude one or more staff members from employment in the facility. If a staff member presents a potential risk, his or her services can be restricted to an area of the operation where no possibility of foodborne disease transmission exists.

Step 8—Take corrective action to reduce future risks. The manager of a business implicated in an outbreak of foodborne disease has a powerful incentive to evaluate the operation's staff member training, its system of food handling, and its overall sanitation risk management program. The results of this evaluation should be improvements which will minimize the risk of another outbreak. Corrective action should address the four resources under the manager's control and the problems associated with them— that is, human hazards, product hazards, equipment hazards, and facilities hazards.

The health department is usually willing to suggest procedures for corrective action. Following these recommendations helps the operation avoid future incidents similar to the one under investigation. It is important to keep all staff members updated and provide instructions regarding corrective actions.

Step 9—Close the complaint with the guest. When the investigation is completed, it is time to contact the complainant and apologize. Some operations have a policy of offering a gift, a free meal, a coupon, or a small check.

When closing the complaint with the guest, ask "What would you like me to do to resolve your complaint?" Most complainants will ask for less than you anticipate. Most guests want you to listen to their complaints with understanding and reassure them that the problems will not recur. It is a good strategy to do what the guest suggests, regardless

Exhibit 3.18 Suggested Procedures for Handling Foodborne Illness Complaints from Guests

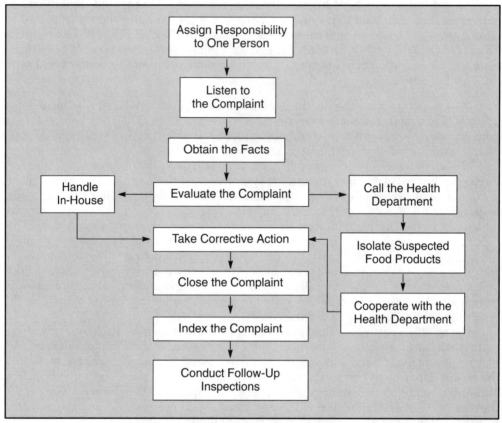

of the short-term cost. If the end result is a satisfied guest, then closing the complaint is one of the best investments that you can make.

Step 10—Index all complaints. The person responsible for the investigation should maintain a file of complaint record forms. This file should contain all relevant information obtained as a result of the investigation. Validated complaints should be flagged for future reference. This file is helpful in planning the corrective action phase (Step 8) and the follow-up phase (Step 11).

Step 11—Follow up to ensure that corrective action has been taken. Regardless of who handles the in-house investigation of a suspected foodborne illness outbreak, management is ultimately responsible for preventing a recurrence. Thus, the operation's manager should conduct an in-house follow-up inspection. This inspection should be documented in the complaint file. The manager should also periodically spot-check the critical areas associated with past problems to make sure they are under control.

The 11-step procedure for handling guest complaints of foodborne illness is summarized in Exhibit 3.18. The basic procedure suggested here applies to both independent and chain food service and lodging operations. The chain's single-unit manager is advised to contact the corporate office as soon as it is determined that the unit might be involved in an outbreak. The corporate office might have its own written procedures to follow.

Without a doubt, the best time to counteract foodborne illness is before it starts. An outbreak could cost your business thousands of dollars. Weighed against the costs of proper training, correct sanitation and maintenance of equipment and facilities, and proper inventory control, the outbreak is certainly costlier. Furthermore, a foodborne disease outbreak can disrupt or close your business. Finally, the damage done to your establishment's image lasts long after the outbreak has been handled. Many of the remaining chapters of this book outline specific preventive measures you can take to protect your guests' health and your operation's future.

Other Concerns in the Food Service Industry

Two other viruses—herpes simplex and AIDS—are *not* foodborne according to current scientific information. However, a discussion of these two viruses is included because of the growing concern on the part of food service owners, managers, staff members, and guests.

AIDS is an abbreviation for Acquired Immune Deficiency Syndrome. AIDS is caused by a virus that attacks a person's immune system. The technical term for the virus that causes AIDS is the Human Immunodeficiency Virus (HIV). As the AIDS virus reproduces in the body, it reduces the body's natural ability to resist infections. The AIDS virus can survive in the human body for years before actual symptoms appear. AIDS is transmitted in the following four ways:

- Sexual contact with a person infected with the AIDS virus

- Sharing drug needles and syringes with a person infected with the AIDS virus

- Transfusions of AIDS-infected blood

- Perinatal transmission from mother to child during pregnancy or through breast-feeding after birth

There is no medical evidence that proves the AIDS virus can be transmitted through saliva, tears, perspiration, mosquito bites, or by using telephones, drinking fountains, toilet seats, toothbrushes, or typewriters used by someone infected with the AIDS virus. The Centers for Disease Control and Prevention have stated: "All epidemiologic and laboratory evidence indicates that blood-borne and sexually transmitted infections are not transmitted during the preparation or serving of food or beverages . . . ." The CDC guidelines on AIDS in the workplace state, "Food service workers known to be infected [with the AIDS virus] need not be restricted from work unless they have evidence of other infection or illness for which any food service worker should be restricted."

The U.S. Supreme Court ruled in 1985 that someone infected with the AIDS virus must be classified as handicapped. The court held that persons impaired by contagious diseases are entitled to protection from discrimination. As with any legal matter, your specific questions can only be answered by legal counsel. Perhaps the best way to handle AIDS is to initiate an educational campaign that clearly presents the facts to staff members. Exhibit 3.19 presents a list of resources for AIDS information.

Because of its increasing incidence, herpes simplex virus (HSV) has received a great deal of attention, although it has been overshadowed by the AIDS virus. HSV consists of two different but closely related viruses. HSV-type 1 causes approximately 90% of oral (fever blisters and cold sores) and ocular herpes infections. HSV-type 2 causes about 85% of genital herpes infections.

Exhibit 3.19 Sources of Information About AIDS

American Hotel & Motel Assocication
1201 New York Avenue, NW
Washington, DC 20005-3917
Phone: 202/289-3100
"AIDS: Questions and Answers for Lodging Industry Employees"
Available in English and Spanish

U. S. Public Health Service Public Affairs Office
Hubert H. Humphrey Building, Room 725-H
200 Independence Avenue, SW
Washington, DC 20201
Phone: 202/245-6867

Local Red Cross or American Red Cross AIDS Education Office
1730 D Street, NW
Washington, DC 20006
Phone: 202/737-8300

AIDS Action Council
728 Eighth Street, SE, Suite 200
Washington, DC 20003
Phone: 202/547-3101

Hispanic AIDS Forum c/o APRED
853 Broadway, Suite 2007
New York, NY 10003
Phone: 212/463-8264

Service Employees International Union
AFL-CIO, CLC
1313 L Street, NW
Washington, DC 20003
Phone: 202/898-3200

National AIDS Hotline: 800/342-AIDS

Free Brochures about AIDS: 800/342-7514

National Sexually Transmitted Diseases Hotline/
  American Social Health Association: 800/227-8922

HSV can be transmitted when any part of a person's body directly touches active HSV or sores containing active HSV. Mucous membranes and broken or damaged skin are easy points of entry into the body. Even though HSV cannot survive very long outside of the human body, recent data suggest that HSV might be able to survive in warm, damp towels.

HSV is not known to be transmitted by food or drinking water, through the air, by water in hot tubs and swimming pools, or by toilet seats. HSV is not transmitted by food-contact surfaces or equipment. Nevertheless, it is critical for all staff members to practice good personal hygiene and personal cleanliness procedures, including proper handwashing.

Summary

There are many potential sources of food contamination. Agents of food poisoning and agents of food infection produce foodborne diseases. Food-contaminating organisms can be broadly categorized as bacteria, parasites, fungi, or viruses. Food service managers and staff members should understand the characteristics, factors affecting reproduction, common food sources, incubation times, symptoms produced, and techniques for prevention and control of microbial contaminants. Pathogenic organisms can be broadly categorized as bacteria, parasites, fungi, and viruses. Other sources of food contamination include poisonous plants and animals, heavy metals, food additives, harmful chemicals, and foodborne physical hazards.

The events which cause outbreaks of foodborne illness are controllable. Of all factors affecting the introduction, survival, and reproduction of pathogens in food, the factor most often responsible for contamination is the failure to properly refrigerate food. Negligence here is probably responsible for more foodborne disease outbreaks than any other single factor. Natural contamination and additional contamination through improper handling also contribute to outbreaks.

Endnotes

1. Some states specify that a foodborne illness outbreak occurs when two or more persons not of the same household become ill from eating the same food.
2. FDA 1993 *Food Code*, p. vii.
3. Kathleen McAuliffe and Nancy Linnon, "Will Your Dinner Make You Sick?" *U.S. News and World Report*, November 16, 1987, p. 73.
4. McAuliffe and Linnon.
5. William D. Stevens, "Turn Complaints Into Gold," *Restaurants USA*, May 1989, p. 17.

Key Terms

aerobic • aflatoxin • anaerobic • cell aggregates • colony • cross-contamination • death phase • encapsulation • facultatively anaerobic • generation time • incubation time • infection • intoxication • lag phase • log phase • mesophile • pathogen • pH • poisoning • potentially hazardous foods • psychrophile • spore • stationary phase • temperature danger zone (TDZ) • thermophile • vegetative bacterial cell • water activity (a_w)

Discussion Questions

1. How do pathogens differ from spoilage organisms?

2. What are the four types of microorganisms responsible for most food contamination?

3. What are the four phases of bacterial growth, and what factors influence the rate of bacterial reproduction?

4. Most foodborne parasitic worms can be controlled by which methods?

5. How do molds differ from yeasts, including their harmful and beneficial effects? What control methods should be used?

6. What are the two general types of foodborne diseases and their causes?

7. What are the seven most important agents of food infection?

8. What two viruses cause foodborne diseases?

9. What are the five most important bacterial intoxicants?

10. What are the most effective control measures for foodborne poisonings caused by (1) toxic plants and animals and (2) chemical poisons and foodborne physical hazards?

11. What personal health and hygiene practices must be observed in a food establishment?

12. What conditions lead to an outbreak of foodborne illness, and what are the three most frequent causal factors?

13. What are the 11 steps that should be followed in handling a foodborne illness complaint?

14. What should food service managers know about AIDS and HSV?

Case Study

You are the manager-on-duty at a 400-room suburban hotel. Your responsibilities include overseeing the operations of the entire hotel when the general manager is not present. The hotel has a 150-seat dining room, catering and banquet function space to accommodate 800 guests, and room service throughout the hotel.

The hotel has been completely filled this past week with a group of association executives and members. It is Saturday afternoon and the general manager is not on duty. The food and beverage director is also not available.

You are in your office and receive a call from a guest, the chief executive officer of the association. He tells you that his entire group of 750 people attended a reception and dinner last night in the hotel as part of the closing ceremonies for their convention, and that nearly 100 of his executives and guests have been complaining to him about nausea, vomiting, cramps, and diarrhea.

"Listen, buddy," the guest says, "I've been on the phone all night, listening to people tell me how sick they are from *your* food. What kind of place is this? What did you serve us, rotten leftovers?"

You listen carefully to the complaint. Although the guest is becoming more and more upset, you manage to learn that the entrée last night was stuffed Cornish hen with a poulet sauce and that the oysters on the buffet table tasted strange.

The guest tells you that his association is planning to take action. He has met with the executive committee of the association's officers and he plans to speak with his legal counsel about a lawsuit. He wants you to investigate the situation and get back to him. In the meantime, he wants you to give him the names and phone numbers of several local doctors and hospitals.

You decide to go to the kitchen and talk to the executive chef. The chef tells you that he supervised the banquet last night and that there was nothing wrong with the oysters, the Cornish hen, or any of the other food. You ask the chef if there are any leftovers from the banquet. He says that he will check and call you, but that most of the leftover entrées were served to the staff members who worked the banquet.

On your way back to the office, you meet the banquet manager. He seems worried and tells you that he doesn't have time to talk to you right now since four of his servers have called in sick and he needs to find replacements for tonight's banquets. As you arrive at your office, the secretary tells you that the chef called and has found three Cornish hens, along with some of the fresh oysters, in the walk-in cooler.

You enter your office and sit down, thinking about your next move.

1. Clearly define the problems in this case from the standpoint of the owners/managers, guests, and staff members.

2. Develop strategies to handle this situation and solve the problems in item #1.

3. Complete the form in Exhibit 3.14 according to the facts in this case.

4. Using the facts presented in the case and the 11-step procedure in the chapter, develop ways to resolve this situation.

References

"AIDS Cases Can Create 'Catch 22'." *Restaurants & Institutions*, February 6, 1989, p. 36.

"Bacteria Clean Up Toxic Wastes." *Management Review*, June 1987, p. 11.

Bain, Laurie. "Salmonella Scare." *Restaurant Business*, May 20, 1987, p. 102.

Banwart, George J. *Basic Food Microbiology*, abridged ed., New York: Van Nostrand Reinhold, 1981.

Berlinski, P. "Special Report on Sanitation and Safety." *Restaurant Business*, December 1975, p. 34.

Beuchat, L. R. "*Yersinia Enterocolitica*: Recovery from Foods and Virulence Characterization." *Food Technology*, March 1982, pp. 84–88.

Bohl, Don L., ed. *AIDS - The New Workplace Issues.* New York: Human Resources Division of the American Management Association, 1988.

"Botulism Feared in Illness." *Winnipeg Free Press*, Friday, February 20, 1987, p. 1.

Bryan, F. L. "Current Trends in Foodborne Salmonellosis in the United States and Canada." *Journal of Food Protection*, May 1981, pp. 341–350.

————. "Epidemiology of Foodborne Diseases Transmitted by Fish, Shellfish, and Marine Crustaceans in the United States, 1970-1978." *Journal of Food Protection*, November 1980, pp. 859–876.

Burris, Jerry. "3rd Salmonella Outbreak Here After Fund-Raiser Chicken Sale." *The Honolulu Advertiser*, Thursday, December 3, 1987, p. A-1.

Centers for Disease Control. *Diseases Transmitted by Food.* Atlanta, Ga.: Public Health Service, U.S. Department of Health, Education, and Welfare, 1979.

————. *Foodborne Diseases and Their Control.* Atlanta, Ga.: Public Health Service, U.S. Department of Health and Human Services, 1980.

————. *Foodborne Disease Outbreaks—Annual Summary 1982.* Washington, D.C.: U.S. Government Printing Office, 1985.

————. *Water-Related Disease Outbreaks—Annual Summary 1984.* Washington, D.C.: U.S. Government Printing Office, 1985.

Chapman, Fien Schumer. "AIDS & Business—Problems of Costs and Compassion." *Fortune*, September 15, 1986, pp. 122-124, 126-127.

Childers, A. B., and C. Vanderzant. "*Yersinia Enterocolitica:* A New Problem in Foodborne Illness." *Dairy and Food Sanitation,* September 1981, pp. 364–366.

"'Concentrated Plan' for Food Safety Is Urged." *Restaurant Business,* November 20, 1987, p. 22.

Corwin, E. "A Food Poisoning Whodunit." *Dairy and Food Sanitation,* April 1981, pp. 144–147.

Cummings, G. "Foodborne Illnesses Are Rare, Precautions Are Mandatory." *Restaurant Business,* December 1981, p. 130.

Fabricant, Florence. "Experts Warn of Certain Risks Involved with Eating Raw Fish." *Nation's Restaurant News,* November 10, 1986, p. 11.

"FDA May Target Vegetables in Bacteria Investigation." *Nation's Restaurant News,* October 20, 1986, p. 67.

Food and Drug Administration, Center for Food Safety and Applied Nutrition, Retail Food Protection Branch. *Interpretation: Employee Health—Transmission of Herpes by Food or Food Contact Surfaces,* June 25, 1984.

————. *Interpretation: Food Supplies—Moldy Cheese,* February 20, 1985.

————. *Interpretation: Food Supplies—Sulfiting Agents on Food in Retail Food Establishments,* August 13, 1986.

————. *Interpretation: Definitions—Potentially Hazardous Food,* May 9, 1986.

————. *Interpretation: Definitions—Soy Protein Products Considered to be Potentially Hazardous Foods,* May 23, 1984.

————. *Interpretation: Definitions—Potentially Hazardous Food—Hard Boiled Eggs with Shells Intact,* July 8, 1985.

————. *Interpretation: Food Protection—Baked or Boiled Potatoes Considered to be Potentially Hazardous Foods,* March 30, 1984.

————. *Interpretation: Definitions—Potentially Hazardous Food—Cooked Bacon,* April 23, 1984.

Food and Drug Administration, Public Health Service, U.S. Department of Health, Education, and Welfare. *Food Code.* 1993.

"Food Poisoning: Everybody's Problem." *Cooking for Profit,* July 1978, pp. 17–18.

Franco, Don A. "Campylobacter Species: Considerations for Controlling a Foodborne Pathogen." *Journal of Food Protection,* February 1988, pp. 145–153.

Frazier, W. C., and D. C. Westhoff. *Food Microbiology,* 3d ed. New York: McGraw-Hill, 1978.

Frydman, Ken. "Deadly Delicacy." *Nation's Restaurant News,* January 30, 1989, pp. 1, 66.

Girdin, Rons. "A Costly Reminder." *Restaurant Business,* January 20, 1985, p. 90.

Hauschild, A. H. W., and F. L. Bryan. "Estimate of Food- and Waterborne Illness in Canada and the United States." *Journal of Food Protection,* June 1980, pp. 435–440.

Hopkins, H. "Danger Lurks Among the Molds." *Dairy and Food Sanitation,* June 1981.

"Illness Hits 13, Causes Closing." *Nation's Restaurant News,* March 9, 1987, p. 58.

Jay, M. M. *Modern Food Microbiology,* 2d ed. New York: Van Nostrand, 1978.

Kahn, Sharon. "Fighting Back Against Foodborne Illness." *Restaurant Business,* December 10, 1986, pp. 239–241, 244–246.

Kaufmann, O. W. "Public Enemy Number One." *Dairy and Food Sanitation,* July 1981, pp. 280–284.

"Keeping an Eye on Peanuts." *University of California, Berkeley Wellness Letter,* November 1986, p. 1.

Klein, James A. *AIDS: An Employer's Guide.* Washington, D.C.: U.S. Chamber of Commerce, 1988.

Kochak, Jacque White. "When the Unthinkable Happens." *Restaurant Business,* March 1, 1988, p. 102.

Larkin, E. P. "Food Contaminants—Viruses." *Journal of Food Protection,* April 1981, pp. 320–325.

Levine, Donna. "The Food Safety Challenge." *Restaurant Business,* December 10, 1987, pp. 92–94, 96.

"Life in the Kitchen." *Food Management,* July 1982, p. 34.

Longree, Karla. *Quantity Food Sanitation,* 2d ed. New York: Wiley-Interscience, 1972.

McAuliffe, Kathleen, and Linnon, Nancy. "Will Your Dinner Make You Sick?" *U.S. News & World Report,* November 16, 1987, p. 73.

McBean, Lois D. "A Perspective on Food Safety Concerns." *Dairy Council Digest,* January-February 1987, pp. 1–6.

McGrath, Anne. "Fatal Salmonella Outbreak Probed." *Lansing State Journal,* November 30, 1986, p. 3A.

Nichols, Sue. "Officials Call Commitment Key to Avoiding Violations." *Lansing State Journal,* January 18, 1988, p. 5A.

———. "Unsanitary Habits Can Be Deadly." *Lansing State Journal,* April 18, 1985, p. 3C.

Ockerman, H. W. *Source Book for Food Scientists.* Westport, Conn.: AVI, 1978.

"Pesticide-Contaminated Foods Reach American Tables." *Nation's Restaurant News,* November 3, 1986, p. 82.

Pierson, Dudley K. "Toxic Level Found High in Foods." *The Detroit News,* Tuesday, May 20, 1986, p. 1A.

Rankin, Ken. "FDA Outlaws Sulfites." *Nation's Restaurant News,* July 21, 1986, pp. 1, 105.

"Sanitation: The Dirty Word in Foodservice." *Food Management,* April 1976, p. 32.

Schaffner, R. M. "Government's Role in Preventing Foodborne Botulism." *Food Technology,* December 1982, pp. 87–89.

"Shellfish Alert." *U.S. News & World Report,* March 24, 1986, p. 73.

Silliker, J. H. "Status of Salmonella—Ten Years Later." *Journal of Food Protection,* April 1980, pp. 307–313.

Smith, J. L., and S. A. Palumbo. "Microorganisms as Food Additives." *Journal of Food Protection,* December 1981, pp. 936–955.

Stiles, Edward. "Feeling Low? Probably Something You Ate." *The Detroit News,* Thursday, October 20, 1988, p. 1F.

Surgeon General and The Centers for Disease Control and Prevention. *Understanding AIDS.* Washington, D.C.: U.S. Government Printing Office, 1988.

"Tampering Leads to One Indictment." *Nation's Restaurant News,* July 21, 1986, p. 86.

"Typhoid Outbreak Hits 7." *Restaurant Business,* November 1, 1986, p. 36.

Wallis, Claudia. "Viruses." *Time,* November 3, 1986, pp. 66–70, 73–74.

Zottola, E. A. *Botulism.* St. Paul, Minn.: University of Minnesota Agricultural Extension Service, 1976.

———. *Clostridium Perfringens Food Poisoning.* St. Paul, Minn.: University of Minnesota Agricultural Extension Service, 1979.

———. *Staphylococcus Food Poisoning.* St. Paul, Minn.: University of Minnesota Agricultural Extension Service, 1968.

REVIEW QUIZ

When you feel you have covered all of the material in this chapter, answer these questions. Choose the *best* answer. Check your answers with the correct ones found on the Review Quiz Answer Key at the end of this book.

1. Mesophiles reproduce most quickly in which of the following temperature ranges?

    a. –19°F (–28°C) to 12°F (–11°C)
    b. 0°F (–18°C) to 42°F (5°C)
    c. 45°F (7°C) to 77°F (25°C)
    d. 68°F (20°C) to 113°F (45°C)

2. Illness resulting from the ingestion of harmful chemicals is called:

    a. bacterial intoxication.
    b. infection.
    c. poisoning.
    d. cross-contamination.

3. Which of the following are symptoms of yersiniosis?

    a. digestive upset and severe abdominal pain
    b. diarrhea and fever
    c. arthritis and eye infections
    d. all of the above

4. In which of the following have *Shigella spp.* been found?

    a. moist mixed foods
    b. chicken and eggs
    c. canned vegetables
    d. unpasteurized dairy products

5. What is the incubation time for listeriosis?

    a. 24 to 72 hours
    b. 2 to 7 days
    c. 1 day to 2 weeks
    d. 4 days to 3 weeks

6. The FDA has outlawed the use of _____ on fresh vegetables intended to be served raw.

    a. sulfiting agents
    b. monosodium glutamate
    c. nitrites
    d. all of the above

7. In which of the following instances is it *unnecessary* for food service employees to wash their hands?

    a. after drinking a glass of water
    b. after touching their face
    c. after setting a table
    d. after clearing a table

8. The most significant contributing factor with respect to foodborne illness outbreaks is:

    a. improper holding temperatures.
    b. inadequate cooking.
    c. poor personal hygiene.
    d. contaminated equipment.

9. If an outbreak of foodborne illness is suspected at a food establishment, the suspected food products should be:

    a. put in clearly labeled sanitized containers and placed in a secure storeroom.
    b. put in clearly labeled sanitized containers and placed in a freezer.
    c. put in clearly labeled sanitized containers and refrigerated.
    d. destroyed except for a sample, which should be put in a clearly labeled sanitized container and placed in chilled storage.

10. Herpes simplex viruses may be transmitted through:

    a. drinking water.
    b. direct contact with sores.
    c. food-contact surfaces.
    d. none of the above.

Chapter Outline

Learning Objectives

4

Food Spoilage and Preservation

A discussion of food service sanitation would be incomplete if it failed to include food spoilage and food preservation. Microorganisms are responsible for much of the food spoilage that occurs in the channels of distribution and in food service operations. This chapter focuses on how food products spoil and the short- and long-term methods used to minimize this spoilage.

Food Spoilage

Almost all food products are composed largely of organic material (material containing carbon compounds). Once the food is harvested or slaughtered, the organic material in it begins to break down chemically. Two distinct processes occur during food breakdown: autolysis and spoilage.

Autolysis is the chemical breakdown of food products caused by substances (primarily enzymes) within the food. **Enzymes** are proteins that catalyze this chemical reaction; that is, they speed up the rate of autolysis. In living cells, enzyme activity is held in check by various processes. The enzymatic autolysis of some foods is desirable; for example, meat tenderization and the ripening of fruits and vegetables are the results of autolysis. Autolysis destroys the cell walls of food products. This physical change in turn facilitates food spoilage.

Food spoilage occurs primarily through the action of bacteria, molds, and yeasts. Spoilage organisms break down the complex organic substances in foods into their simple, inorganic components. This process is responsible for the changes in the odor, color, texture, appearance, and taste of food products which indicate spoilage. Spoiled food is unfit for human consumption.

Many factors contribute to food spoilage. A variety of microorganisms are often involved in the breakdown of organic substances. Enzymatic autolysis accelerates the rate of spoilage. Insects and rodents also damage food products and make them unfit for human consumption. Physical changes (exposure to extreme temperatures or excessive pressure) and careless handling cause bruising. Chemical reactions other than autolysis can also be responsible for food spoilage. This chapter deals primarily with food spoilage caused by microorganisms. (Food spoilage caused by insects and rodents is discussed in Chapter 9.)

The spoilage of food products in a food establishment is often linked to one or more of the following causes:

- Improper storage temperatures
- Incorrect or excessive storage times

- Unacceptable levels of ventilation in storage areas
- Failure to segregate foods in storage
- Excessive delays between receiving and storing of food products
- Inadequate or unacceptable sanitation standards resulting in exposure of food products to contaminants

As this list suggests, most food spoilage occurs when foods are at the storing control point. Storage area standards must be designed to prevent or minimize food spoilage and exposure of food products to pathogenic organisms. A detailed discussion of the storing control point is presented in Chapter 6.

In general, raw food products can be placed in one of three broad categories—perishable, semi-perishable, non-perishable—based on their susceptibility to microbial spoilage. **Perishable** food products spoil readily without special processing or preservation techniques. This category includes most products used daily in a food service facility: meats, poultry, fish, shellfish, eggs, dairy products, and most fruits and vegetables. **Semi-perishable** food products have a longer shelf life than perishable foods. These products spoil more slowly when stored under recommended time-temperature combinations. Included in this category are nuts, apples, potatoes, and waxed vegetables such as cucumbers. **Non-perishable** food products are the most resistant to spoilage unless they are improperly handled and stored. This category includes most dry grocery items, such as sugar, flour, spices, and dry beans. Food preservation methods are designed to increase the shelf life and maintain the desirable physical and chemical properties of food.

Food Preservation

The United States was once an agricultural society. Most people lived and worked on or close to farms, so a wide variety of fresh food products were readily available. This pattern of rural living changed with the Industrial Revolution. Americans began moving from farms to industrialized cities, and this migration radically altered the food supply needs of the population. Americans no longer had easy access to a supply of fresh food products; as cities absorbed more of what was once farmland, the sources of fresh food grew increasingly distant.

The food processing industry responded to this challenge by improving methods of food preservation. Food processors discovered that one of the best ways to preserve food was to practice strict microbiological control. Along with controlling pathogenic organisms, food processors and manufacturers learned to control organisms responsible for food spoilage. They succeeded in increasing the shelf life and availability of food products for the growing number of city dwellers. In time, processed food products even became popular with farm families. Today, food processing plants use a variety of methods to provide wholesome food products to industrialized America.

The FDA states:

Food Processing Plant.

(a) **"Food processing plant"** means a commercial operation that manufactures, packages, labels, or stores food for human consumption and does not provide food directly to a consumer.

(b) *"Food processing plant"* does not include a food establishment as defined in Subparagraph 1–201.10(B)(31).

Source: FDA 1993 *Food Code.*

In recent years, several self-proclaimed "food experts" have tried to persuade the American public that the food supply is loaded with unnecessary levels of food additives. But these food additives control undesirable microbes and increase the availability of food. To condemn food additives without acknowledging their benefits does a disservice to the uninformed consumer. Without such additives, we would be buying food products like those in turn-of-the-century general stores. Few of us would be willing to give up the convenience of modern supermarkets just to avoid additives.

Nevertheless, recent studies indicate that many consumers are increasingly concerned with the safety of the food supply.[1] Many are worried about residues from agricultural chemicals, herbicides, and pesticides. A few red grapes tainted with minute traces of cyanide caused a national scare. A substance called alar, a growth regulator that helps maintain the red color of apples during storage, also raised concern: several cities temporarily banned apples and apple products in their school districts. In a public opinion survey released by the Food Marketing Institute (FMI), nine out of ten respondents described food additives and preservatives as hazardous.[2]

Food additives are already closely regulated in the United States. Unsafe or unapproved food or color additives may not be incorporated into food products. However, consumer interest in this area is unlikely to diminish. The best protection that a food service operation has is to be informed and to obtain food products only from approved sources.

The FDA states:

"Safe material" means:

(a) An article manufactured from or composed of materials that may not reasonably be expected to result, directly or indirectly, in their becoming a component or otherwise affecting the characteristics of any food;

(b) A food additive or color additive as defined in § 201(s) or (t) of the Federal Food, Drug, and Cosmetic Act that is used as specified in § 409 or 706 of the Act; or

(c) Other materials that are not a food additive or color additive as defined in § 201(s) or (t) of the Federal Food, Drug, and Cosmetic Act and that are used in conformity with applicable regulations of the Food and Drug Administration.

Source: FDA 1993 *Food Code.*

There are four main objectives of food preservation. As noted in Chapter 3, some preservation methods are designed to lengthen the lag phase of bacterial growth. Another objective of food preservation is to delay undesirable autolysis. This is achieved by destroying enzymes or preventing enzymatic action. The third objective is to minimize the damage caused by insects, rodents, and physical trauma. The fourth objective, the prevention of microbiological breakdown of food, is probably the most important. All methods of food preservation are designed to achieve one or more of these objectives.

Low-Temperature Food Preservation

Low temperatures preserve food products during their flow through the control points of a food service operation. They slow the growth of spoilage organisms and decrease the rate of chemical reactions and enzyme activity. The rate of microbial reproduction decreases as the temperature drops, and eventually stops altogether. Some organisms may survive the low temperatures and form spores which, when temperatures again become favorable, can germinate to form vegetative cells capable of reproduction. Some psychrophiles remain active at refrigerator temperatures, and some spores can even survive freezer temperatures.

Thus, low-temperature preservation cannot be expected to thoroughly destroy spoilage or pathogenic microorganisms in food. However, a reduction in the rate of microbial reproduction (along with a decrease in the number of cells) can be expected if correct time-temperature combinations are followed. The number of microorganisms killed, deactivated, or unaffected by low-temperature food preservation methods depends on the type and number of microbes present, the rate of cooling, the time-temperature combinations, the characteristics of the food, and other variables. Low-temperature food preservation is effective in many applications, particularly in controlling thermophiles and mesophiles.

There are three kinds of low-temperature food preservation: chilled storage, refrigerated storage, and freezer storage.

Chilled Storage. Temperatures for chilled storage are lower than room temperature but higher than those for refrigerated temperatures. A typical range for chilled storage is between 50°F (10°C) and 59°F (15°C). Some fruits and vegetables (potatoes and cucumbers, for example) should be stored in this range. Chilled storage may not be used for potentially hazardous foods.

Refrigerated Storage. Temperatures for refrigerated storage range from 32°F (0°C) to 45°F (7°C). Some jurisdictions specify 41°F (5°C) as the highest refrigerated temperature; check your local regulations. Most food products that are classified as perishable are best stored at refrigerator temperatures. Storage at these temperatures slows the growth rate of spoilage organisms and most pathogenic bacteria (with the exception of some strains of *Clostridium botulinum* and certain psychrophiles). Enzymatic and chemical reactions are also significantly reduced at refrigerator temperatures.

Several factors affect the ability of refrigerator temperatures to control spoilage organisms. One factor is the relative humidity—the ratio of water vapor present in the air to the quantity of water vapor that would be present if the air were saturated at the same temperature. In other words, the relative humidity reports the amount of moisture in the air as a percentage. The relative humidity of a storage area affects microbial growth and, therefore, storage times. Excessive moisture encourages the growth of microorganisms. If the relative humidity is too low, food in storage loses moisture to the environment. Moisture loss in fresh fruits and vegetables is characterized by wilting, softening, shrinkage, and reduced weight.

Ventilation or air flow maintains a uniform level of relative humidity. Ventilation in storage areas also helps maintain an optimum storage environment by removing undesirable odors. In some cases, ventilation systems are used to alter the storage area atmosphere. The use of carbon dioxide gas or nitrogen gas makes it possible to maintain higher storage temperatures and relative humidities. It also prolongs the shelf life of food products. Such controlled-atmosphere storage methods are useful in maintaining the quality of fresh fruits and vegetables.

Freezer Storage. Freezer storage temperatures are generally 0°F (–18°C) and below. As one would expect, these very low temperatures reduce the growth rate of microorganisms even further. But some spores can survive freezer storage temperatures. One advantage of freezing over refrigeration is that freezing also reduces the a_w (water activity) of food products: when water is converted from liquid to solid form, microbes can no longer use it. Only high-quality food products should be selected for freezer storage because most food products lose quality after being frozen.

Any physical evidence of food spoilage or damage should be removed before freezing food products. All inedible parts of the food should also be removed. Fruit and vegetable products must be sorted, washed, and blanched before freezing. **Blanching,** the process of exposing the product to either steam or hot water for a short time, sets the color of green vegetables and renders enzymes inactive. The blanching process also destroys some microorganisms, forces trapped air out of the plant cells, and causes leafy vegetables to wilt, making them easier to pack.

Chemicals may be added to food products prior to freezing. Antioxidants are incorporated into some bakery products to prevent rancidity, a chemical change or decomposition in fats and oils which produces a disagreeable taste or odor in foods. Ascorbic acid (vitamin C) is added to some fruits and vegetables to minimize browning during frozen storage.

Many people are surprised to learn that frozen fruits and vegetables may have a *higher* nutritive value than their "fresh" counterparts. Consider fresh grapefruit harvested in Florida and shipped to Michigan. The citrus fruit might take one or two days to reach the northern state. Once it is received by the food distributor in Michigan, it could be stored under refrigeration for a couple of weeks until a food service operation places an order. Upon delivery, it could be stored for as long as a week before it is actually used. Throughout this period, the fruit loses vitamin C. On the other hand, grapefruit to be commercially frozen is processed much more quickly, sometimes immediately after harvest. Therefore, the vitamin C content of frozen grapefruit is often higher than that of "fresh" grapefruit.

Quick freezing reduces the temperature of a product to –4°F (–20°C) in 30 minutes or less, while slow freezing takes 3 to 72 hours. Quick freezing is more desirable than slow freezing for a number of reasons. First, quick freezing better preserves product quality. Quick freezing causes small ice crystals to form within food, which minimizes damage to the food's cell structure, thus preserving its flavor and texture. Second, when thawed, products that have been quick-frozen exhibit less drip loss than similar products that have been slow-frozen. (Drip loss is the moisture eliminated from frozen foods when they are thawed.) Third, quick freezing slows enzymatic and microbial activity more promptly. However, the specialized equipment needed for quick freezing is seldom present in a food establishment, so slow-freezing methods are often used. In fact, most food service freezers are storage freezers designed to hold already-frozen products—not to freeze them.

A variety of quick-freezing methods are used for food products, depending on the individual characteristics of the product type. Immersion freezing entails dipping food products (such as fish fillets) directly into a low-temperature coolant. Liquid nitrogen, brine, or sugar solutions are used in this technique. Plate freezing is used for boxes and packages of food, such as 2 or 2 1/2 pound (0.91 or 1.14 kg) boxes of frozen vegetables: each package is placed between two plates that have a low-temperature coolant passing through them. Blast freezing requires exposure of food to temperatures as low as 0°F (–18°C) to –30°F (–34°C). This technique is used for freezing meats, fish, poultry, fruits, and vegetables.

Even when a food product is frozen and stored at freezer temperatures, several changes that adversely affect quality can still take place. Freezer burn is a dehydration that occurs when frozen products are not wrapped or packaged properly. This loss of moisture takes place on the surface of fruits, vegetables, meats, fish, and poultry. Unfortunately, freezer burn is irreversible. It is a form of food spoilage because it renders food products unusable. Furthermore, the texture, color, odor, appearance, and taste of foods are slowly altered under freezer storage conditions. Maximum storage times for various types of food are discussed later in this chapter.

Low-temperature preservation needs in food service operations have changed dramatically over the past several years. Operations that once relied heavily on dry storage areas for canned goods and frozen storage areas for frozen products have experienced a number of changes. The demand for fresh produce and fresh fish has created the need for more refrigerated storage space. Also, the move by some food distributors to minimize daily deliveries has led to bulk sale incentives and larger inventories of refrigerated items in food service operations.

Unfortunately, many older food service facilities were not designed with adequate refrigerated storage space for today's menu items. However, when replacement refrigeration equipment is purchased or when new facilities are constructed, many operators now install a single unit called a refrigerator-freezer or dual temperature unit. More information about these flexible refrigeration units is presented in Chapter 6.

Thawing. Frozen food products may be cooked directly from the frozen state or thawed prior to cooking. But frozen food thawing is potentially hazardous if food products are exposed to the temperature danger zone—the range of temperatures from 41°F (5°C) to 140°F (60°C). Remember, the TDZ may be different in your locality. The defrosting method selected should minimize contact with the TDZ. *Never thaw frozen foods at room temperature.* The risks are too great.

Recall that some frozen foods undergo a process known as *slacking* that allows the temperature of the food to gradually increase from –10°F (–23°C) to 25°F (–4°C). Slacking is done in preparation for deep-fat frying or to facilitate even heat penetration during the cooking of previously block-frozen food such as spinach.

Thawing under refrigeration at temperatures of 41°F (5°C) or less is recommended since it minimizes contact with the TDZ. This method also minimizes product quality loss and exposure to contamination. It works well for frozen fruit, poultry, fish, shellfish, and large cuts of meat. There is an added advantage to thawing under refrigeration: frozen food placed in a refrigerator to thaw will draw heat from the other refrigerated products. This heat exchange saves energy by reducing the amount of time the refrigerator's cooling equipment has to run. Today's food establishments are often designed with back-to-back walk-in freezer and refrigerator combinations. This design allows the (outer) refrigerator to serve as a buffer zone between the heat of the kitchen and the freezer, thus reducing the amount of cold air lost from the freezer.

Thawing under cold running water (70°F [21°C] or less) is also acceptable. Items thawed in this manner must be protected from water damage by being tightly wrapped or placed in watertight containers. This method works well with frozen fruit. Some jurisdictions do not recommend thawing potentially hazardous foods under cold running water.

With some food products, defrosting as part of the cooking process can save time and still be safe. Small cuts of meat, poultry, fish, and frozen vegetables are usually defrosted and cooked simultaneously. Breaded vegetables, fish, and shellfish are actually better when they are cooked directly from the frozen state.

Microwave oven thawing may be used for some food products, although there are limitations. Microwave thawing is acceptable only when it is part of the cooking process or when it is followed immediately by cooking. Bread and rolls are toughened when heated in a microwave oven, and large pieces of meat may not fit into the chamber.

It is important to remember that since foods are not pure water, they are not frozen at 32°F (0°C) as water is. Foods freeze and thaw at temperatures between 25°F (-4°C) and 32°F (0°C). Frozen foods have several opportunities to defrost during handling, transportation, and storing. If the food is thawed and then refrozen, large ice crystals will form and will reduce the product's quality.

Another low-temperature food preservation technique uses reduced oxygen packaging and is rapidly emerging due to technological advances. *Sous vide* (literally "under vacuum") was invented by French chef George Pralus. The method consists of packaging food items into plastic bags or pouches, vacuum-sealing the pouches, and cooking the pouches of food while carefully controlling both moisture and temperature. The food is then immediately chilled to stop the cooking and stored refrigerated. The pouches may be reheated in hot water for service, or the fully cooked food may be served chilled.

Initially, the FDA banned on-premises *sous vide* preparation in restaurants, citing the section of the 1976 Model Ordinance that refers to home-canned foods. The concern was due to the possibility of inadequate heat treatment, followed by the growth of *Clostridium botulinum* and the psychrophilic pathogens such as *Listeria monocytogenes* and *Yersinia enterocolitica*. Because of strict processing controls, *sous vide* preparation was only permitted in food processing plants and sold to food service operations.

The FDA states:

Reduced Oxygen Packaging.

(a) **"Reduced oxygen packaging"** means the reduction of the amount of oxygen in a package by mechanically evacuating the oxygen; displacing the oxygen with another gas or combination of gases; or otherwise controlling the oxygen content in a package to a level below that normally found in the surrounding atmosphere, which is 21% oxygen.

(b) **"Reduced oxygen packaging"** includes methods that may be referred to as altered atmosphere, modified atmosphere, controlled atmosphere, low oxygen, and vacuum packaging including sous vide.

3-502.11   Variance Requirement.*

A food establishment shall obtain a variance from the regulatory authority as specified in § 8-103.10 and under § 8-103.11 before smoking or curing food; brewing alcoholic beverages; using food additives as a method of food preservation rather than as a method of flavor enhancement; using a reduced oxygen method of packaging food except as specified in § 3-502.12 where a barrier to *Clostridium botulinum* exists; custom processing animals that are for personal use as food and not for sale or service in a food establishment; or preparing food by another method that is determined by the regulatory authority to require a variance.

3-502.12   Reduced Oxygen Packaging, Criteria.*

(A) A food establishment that packages food using a reduced oxygen packaging method shall have a HACCP plan that contains the information specified under § 8-201.14(D) and that:

(1)   Identifies the food to be packaged;

(2)   Limits the food packaged to a food that does not support the growth of *Clostridium botulinum* because it:

(a)   Has an a_w of 0.91 or less,

(b)   Has a pH of 4.6 or less,

(c)   Is a meat product cured at a processing plant regulated by the U.S. Department of Agriculture using a combination of nitrites, nitrates, and salt that at the time of processing consists of 120 mg/L or higher concentration of sodium nitrite and a brine concentration of at least 3.50% and is received in an intact package, or

(d)   Is a food with a high level of competing organisms such as raw meat or raw poultry;

(3)   Specifies methods for maintaining food at 5°C (41°F) or below;

(4)   Describes how the packages shall be prominently and conspicuously labeled on the principal display panel in bold type on a contrasting background, with instructions to:

(a)   Maintain the food at 5°C (41°F) or below, and

(b)   Discard the food if within 14 calendar days of its packaging it is not served for on-premises consumption, or consumed if served or sold for off-premises consumption;

(5)   Limits the shelf life to no more than 14 calendar days from packaging to consumption or the original manufacturer's "sell by" or "use by" date, whichever occurs first;

(6)   Includes operational procedures that:

(a)   Prohibit contacting food with bare hands,

(b)   Identify a designated area and the method by which:

(i)   Physical barriers or methods of separation of raw foods and ready-to-eat foods minimize cross contamination, and

(ii)   Access to the processing equipment is restricted to responsible trained personnel familiar with the potential hazards of the operation, and

(c)   Delineate cleaning and sanitization procedures for food-contact surfaces; and

(7)   Describes the training program that assures that the individual responsible for the reduced oxygen packaging operation understands the:

(a)   Concepts required for a safe operation,

(b)   Equipment and facilities, and

(c)   Procedures specified in Subparagraph (A)(6) of this section and ¶ 8-201.14(D).

(B)   *Except for fish that is frozen before, during, and after packaging,* a food establishment may not package fish using a reduced oxygen packaging method.

Source: FDA 1993 *Food Code.*

In January 1989, the FDA outlined control steps that, if strictly followed, would permit on-premises *sous vide* preparation. However, many states do not permit vacuum packaging in any facility except a food processing plant. The control steps are:

1. A food establishment that packages food using a reduced oxygen packaging method shall have a HACCP plan that:

    a. identifies the food to be packaged;

    b. limits the food packaged to a food that does not support the growth of *Clostridium botulinum* because it:

       (1)   has an a_w of 0.91 or less,

       (2)   has a pH of 4.6 or less,

       (3)   is a meat product cured at a processing plant regulated by the USDA using a combination of nitrites, nitrates, and salt that at the time of processing consists of 120 mg/L or higher concentration of at least 3.50% and is received in an intact package, or

       (4)   is a food with a high level of competing organisms such as raw meat or raw poultry;

    c. specifies methods for maintaining food at 41°F (5°C) or below;

    d. describes how the packages shall be prominently and conspicuously labeled on the principal display panel in bold type on a contrasting background, with instructions to:

       (1)   maintain the food at 41°F (5°C) or below, and

       (2)   discard the food if, within 14 calendar days of its packaging, it is not served for on-premises consumption, or consumed if served or sold for off-premises consumption,

    e. limits the shelf life to no more than 14 calendar days from packaging to consumption or the original manufacturer's "sell by" or "use by" date, whichever occurs first;

    f. includes operational procedures that:

       (1)   prohibit contacting food with bare hands,

(2)   identify a designated area and the method by which:

(a)   physical barriers or methods of preparing raw foods and ready-to-eat foods minimize cross-contamination, and

(b)   access to the processing equipment is restricted to responsible trained personnel familiar with the potential hazards of the operation, and

(3)   delineate cleaning and sanitization procedures for food-contact surfaces; and

g.   describes the training program that ensures that the individual responsible for the reduced oxygen packaging operation understands the:

(1)   concepts required for safe operation,

(2)   equipment and facilities, and

(3)   procedures specified.

2.   Except for fish that is frozen before, during, and after packaging, a food establishment may not package fish using a reduced oxygen packaging method.

Many food service operators have explored the benefits of *sous vide* preparation techniques. Some of the benefits frequently mentioned are:

- Retention and enhancement of taste and odor

- Reduced amounts of seasonings, including salt, needed since the essences do not evaporate during cooking

- Extended shelf life (up to 10 days in some products)

- Reduced labor needs

- Batch production and increased consistency

- Reduced food costs due to extended shelf life

- Increased menu variety

Expect to see greater applications of *sous vide* techniques in the future as labor becomes more scarce and food service operators continue to focus on quality.

High-Temperature Food Preservation

High temperatures are effective in food preservation because they control the growth of microorganisms. When most microbial cells are heated, they are either injured and deactivated or destroyed. The exceptions are thermophiles, which prefer higher temperatures, and other microorganisms which have the ability to form heat-resistant spores. The heat stability of vegetative cells and spores varies considerably among species.

Several variables affect the survival rate of cells and spores exposed to high temperatures. First, the time-temperature relationship is critical to controlling the growth of microorganisms. With sufficiently high temperatures, the time required for microbial deactivation or destruction is reduced as the temperature is increased. Second, the initial colony size influences the rate of deactivation or destruction. Everything being equal, as the number of cells or spores initially present increases, the amount of heat needed to accomplish deactivation or destruction also rises.

Finally, the composition of a food product also determines the effectiveness of high-temperature food preservation. In general, carbohydrates, proteins, and fats in food protect some organisms from destruction by heat. When the a_w is reduced, some microbes become more heat-resistant. A pH near 7.0 (neutral) also makes microorganisms more heat-resistant. Some food products may require added chemicals such as nitrites or preservatives to overcome microbial resistance to heat.

There are two methods of high-temperature food preservation: **pasteurization** and **sterilization.**

Pasteurization. Pasteurization temperatures are used either to extend the shelf life of food by reducing spoilage organisms or to destroy all pathogenic microorganisms present in the food. Pasteurization may be done in one of two ways. The holder process of pasteurization involves heating the food product to 145°F (63°C) for 30 minutes. In the **high temperature-short time (HTST)** method of pasteurization, the product is heated to 161°F (72°C) for 15 seconds. Both techniques require the heated food to be immediately cooled to 50°F (10°C) or less.

The most common example of pasteurized food is fluid milk. Either pasteurization method can be used for milk and milk products, although the HTST process is preferred since it is so rapid. In either case, the time-temperature combination is sufficient to eliminate the possible presence of two pathogens: *Mycobacterium tuberculosis* and *Coxiella burnetti.* These non-spore-forming pathogens cannot survive either pasteurization method. The importance of the pasteurization process is readily apparent when one considers that more than 17 billion gallons of milk are produced annually in the United States.

In addition to milk, the government requires that ice cream mixes and liquid egg products (such as shelled whole eggs) be pasteurized. This process minimizes the risk of *Salmonella spp.* microorganisms. Canned hams are also pasteurized. Pasteurization eliminates pathogens, but since it does not destroy *all* microorganisms present in the food products, pasteurized foods must still be stored under refrigeration.

Sterilization. Sterilization destroys virtually all microorganisms and their spores. Once the food is batch-sterilized, or before it is individually sterilized, it must be stored in a hermetically sealed container, such as a can, glass bottle, or jar. With advances in food technology, flexible plastic containers can now be used for sterilized food products as well. Because the food is sterilized and hermetically sealed, it need not be refrigerated until the containers are opened.

The canning process is designed to achieve commercial sterilization of food products. The process has improved greatly since Nicolas Appert did his pioneer work in canning in the late 1700s and early 1800s. The modern canning process begins with the arrival of the freshly harvested or slaughtered food. The food is cleaned and all inedible parts are removed. Some vegetables are blanched prior to being placed in cans. The food is placed in washed cans, and brine (salt water) is added to vegetables. (The exception is pickled vegetables, which are preserved by the acetic acid formed during fermentation.) Fish products such as tuna may be packed in either brine or oil. A sugar-water solution is usually added to fruits during filling, although fruits packed in their own juices have gained popularity among consumers in recent years.

Once they are filled, the containers are evacuated; that is, a partial vacuum is created in the container. During the sealing stage, the lids are added and sealed to the body of the containers to form an airtight or hermetic seal. After the containers are sealed, they are heated to sterilization temperatures for carefully controlled time periods.

The FDA states:

"Hermetically sealed container" means a container that is designed and intended to be secure against the entry of microorganisms and, in the case of low acid canned foods, to maintain the commercial sterility of its contents after processing.

3-201.12   Hermetically Sealed Food.*

Food in a hermetically sealed container shall be obtained from a food processing plant that is regulated by the food regulatory agency that has jurisdiction over the plant.

Source: FDA 1993 *Food Code.*

A number of variables affect the amount of heat required for sterilization. First, the size, shape, and material of the container affect the heat transfer rate. Smaller cans permit a faster heat transfer than larger cans or glass bottles. Second, the contents of the container have a tremendous effect on the heat transfer rate. Extremely viscous food products (for example, tomato paste) have a slower heat transfer rate than food products that are largely liquid (tomato purée). The pH of the food also influences the amount of heat necessary for sterilization. In general, food products can be placed in one of three categories based on their pH:

1. Low-acid foods (pH above 4.5) include meats, fish, poultry, milk, spinach, asparagus, pumpkin, corn, and lima beans. Because of their low acid content, these products require a relatively severe heat treatment to guard against the growth of *Clostridium botulinum.* The sterilization process is frequently used to achieve a desirable level of microbial destruction, while minimizing the negative effects on the product's texture, taste, odor, color, and appearance.

2. Medium-acid foods (pH of 3.7 to 4.5) include some tomatoes, pineapples, and pears. The acidity in this group of food products inhibits the growth of *Clostridium botulinum.* However, spoilage organisms can grow at this level of acidity, so the heat treatment must be severe enough to destroy these undesirable microbes.

3. High-acid foods (pH below 3.7) include sauerkraut and berries. Few pathogenic or spoilage organisms can survive in such high acidity. A relatively mild heat treatment is required for this group.

Heating for sterilization usually takes place in a large container which is pressurized according to the food product and its ability to withstand heat. Food products that are particularly sensitive to heat are processed using a variation of the normal canning process known as **aseptic canning.** This process involves the separate sterilization of containers (using hydrogen peroxide) and contents, and uses more heat for substantially shorter periods of time than conventional canning. Once sterilized, the contents are placed into the containers and packed in a sterile environment. This process conserves nutrients, color, taste, odor, and texture but is relatively expensive.

After the heating process is completed, the containers are cooled. The cooling process must be gradual to prevent cans from bending and bottles from cracking. Once they have cooled, the containers are labeled and placed in boxes or cases for later shipment. Modern technology has made commercial canning a highly automated, continuous process.

Food Preservation by Dehydration

Food **dehydration** may be the oldest method of food preservation. Primitive people probably discovered this method when they accidentally left food out in the sun. Dehydration is an effective method of preservation because it reduces the a_w of food and thus inhibits microbial activity. There are four methods of drying food: sun drying, mechanical drying, freeze-drying, and drying during smoking.

Sun Drying. This is effective in areas with low humidity and high temperatures. Fruits and vegetables have been dehydrated this way for centuries. Today, grapes, plums, currants, and apricots are dehydrated by this method.

Mechanical Drying. This is the drying method of primary commercial importance. Food products are prepared for mechanical drying by trimming, washing, and removing the inedible parts. Then heat is applied, usually in combination with moving air. The three mechanical drying methods are spray drying, tunnel drying, and drum drying.

Spray drying is used for liquid foods. The liquid is sprayed continuously into the top of a drying chamber that may be several stories high. Hot air mixes with the falling food and evaporates the moisture. The result is a fine powder of dried food which exits at the bottom of the chamber. Milk, tea, eggs, coffee, and fruit purées are spray dried.

Tunnel drying uses a conveyor belt to move the food products into and out of a drying chamber. Like spray drying, tunnel drying is a continuous process. Once in the chamber, the food is exposed to blasts of hot air that evaporate moisture. Tunnel drying is used for vegetables, fruits, nuts, confectionery products, and breakfast cereals.

Drum drying uses a large rotating drum heated from within by steam. Liquid food is applied to the drum in a thin film as it rotates. A scraper is used to remove the dried food from the drum in this continuous process. Potatoes, breakfast cereals, infant foods, soups, and sauces are dried using this mechanical process.

Freeze-Drying. This technique uses a process known as sublimation—the direct conversion of solid water (ice) to water vapor without the usual intermediate step of melting into a liquid. To freeze-dry a product, the product must first be frozen. Sublimation takes place in a drying chamber where a vacuum and a small amount of heat are applied. This process results in a dried product that is porous and easy to rehydrate. The food product suffers minimal damage because only a small amount of heat is required for this process. However, freeze-drying is relatively expensive. Freeze-drying has been used for meat, fish, shellfish, poultry, vegetables, fruits, and coffee.

Drying During Smoking. This method is quite slow compared to other means of drying, but its results are unique. Smoking alters the odor, color, appearance, texture, and taste of food products. It also has a tenderizing effect on proteins. Since colonial times, Americans have enjoyed the taste of foods hung up to dry in closed sheds filled with the smoke of hardwoods, especially hickory. This method of drying is used for meats, fish, and cheese.

Drying is an effective preservation method because it reduces the a_w of foods and destroys some, but not all, of the organisms present. To achieve the desired results, strict time-temperature combinations must be adhered to during drying. In addition, the relative humidity and the air speed must be carefully controlled.

Once a food product is dried, its storage stability varies according to the natural components of the food. Dried foods that contain a relatively high percentage of fats or oils (meats, for example) are more susceptible to rancidity reactions. Some food products such as apricots brown when dried. However, chemical additives can be incorporated before drying to prevent this undesirable oxidation. Regardless of their ingredients, dried food products must be stored in airtight containers to prevent them from absorbing moisture from the environment. Many dried foods must be reconstituted before they can be served. Once they are reconstituted (recombined with water or other liquids), these foods should be handled carefully.

Chemical Food Preservation

In the United States, several chemical food additives have been approved by the Food and Drug Administration for food preservation applications. These chemical preservatives inhibit the activity of selected pathogens and spoilage organisms. The FDA strictly monitors the use of chemical preservatives. The categories of chemical preservatives are nitrites and nitrates, sugar and salt, sulfur dioxides and sulfites, ethylene and propylene oxides, alcohol, organic acids and their salts, and spices and other condiments.

Nitrites, nitrates, and their salts are used in the preservation of meat products. They inhibit the activity of *Clostridium botulinum*, give cured meats their typical color, and contribute to flavor. Nitrites and nitrates are added to bacon, lunch meats, ham, and other cured meats. Recently, the USDA approved a reduction in the amount of nitrite preservatives added to bacon, from 120 parts per million (ppm) to 100 ppm. Note that milligrams/liter (mg/L) is the metric equivalent. An alternative approved method is to use lactic acid starter cultures and sugar in a curing solution, with 40 mg/L to 80 mg/L of sodium nitrite. This will result in savings for food service operations while maintaining safety.

The FDA states:

"**mg/L**" means milligrams per liter, which is the metric equivalent of parts per million (ppm).

Source: FDA 1993 *Food Code.*

Sugar and salt bind water and lower a food product's a_w. Salt is used in brines in which canned fish, meats, and vegetables are packed, and enhances their flavor. Sugar is found in the syrups in which canned fruits are packed; it also contributes to their flavor. Salt and sugar are added to a wide variety of processed foods as preservatives.

Sulfiting agents (sulfur dioxide, sodium sulfite, sodium and potassium bisulfite, and sodium and potassium metabisulfite) have been used to retard oxidative or enzymatic browning of fruits and vegetables, to inhibit "black spot" on shrimp, and to control gray mold on table grapes. Since sulfites bind to food constituents, they remain in or on food in spite of washing. Cooking, particularly the high heat of frying, reduces sulfite residues but does not eliminate them.

The FDA has banned the use of sulfites in raw fruits and vegetables intended to be served or sold raw. The FDA has also proposed to ban sulfites in fresh potato products and limit sulfite levels in beer, wine, baked goods, tea, and fruit juices. Sulfites have been known to cause severe reactions and even death in asthmatics. The FDA has reminded food service operators that the federal rules do not replace state and local rules. Some states (for example, Michigan) have banned the application of sulfites in food establishments. It is a good idea to be certain that your food and beverage operation complies with regulations issued by local health authorities.

Ethylene and propylene oxides are used to sterilize containers in which food is packaged. For example, wine bottles and juice packages are sterilized with these oxides before the beverages are added.

Ethanol (ethyl alcohol), which functions as a preservative, is produced by fermentation in wine, beer, and spirits. The natural flavorings in these beverages are dissolved in the ethanol. Ethanol is also the main flavor carrier in extracts used for cooking (for example, almond and vanilla extracts).

Organic acids and their salts are sometimes added to food products as preservatives. Salts are formed when organic acids and metals (for example, sodium, calcium, and potassium) are combined. However, in some foods, these acids and salts form naturally during normal fermentation. Benzoates are salts derived from benzoic acid and are added to carbonated beverages, pickled vegetables, fruit jams and jellies, and margarine. Propionates are salts made from propionic acid. They control mold growth in baked products and cheeses. Sorbates, derived from sorbic acid, inhibit mold and yeast activity. Sorbates are added to cheeses, beverages, fruits, margarine, pickled vegetables, and jams and jellies. Acetates are derivatives of acetic acid, better known as vinegar. Acetates are used in pickled vegetables, condiments, pickled sausages, and mayonnaise. Ascorbic acid, erythorbic acid, citric acid, sodium ascorbate, and sodium citrate are used to maintain the color and overall appearance of fresh pork.

One major advance in chemical food preservation is the use of organic acids to lower the pH of food products. Certain operations (commissaries and chain operations, for example) can afford the equipment, technology, and monitoring systems to use pH adjustments as a complement to correct time-temperature combinations. Standard recipes can be adjusted by the addition of organic acids and high-acid food ingredients to produce a product with a lower pH. While pH adjustments are currently not suitable for every food item or operation, this method of preservation has the potential for widespread application in the future.

Spices and other condiments constitute the last class of chemical preservatives. Not all spices and condiments have the effect of inhibiting bacterial activity in food products, but some have been valued for centuries as flavor enhancers and preservatives. Cinnamon and cloves have anti-microbial properties. Condiments that contain vinegar also discourage the growth of pathogens and spoilage organisms. Mayonnaise, which is often wrongly blamed for foodborne illness outbreaks traced to salads, kills *Staphylococcus aureus*, *Escherichia coli*, and *Salmonella spp.* However, high protein foods (such as meat, poultry, fish, and eggs), when added to mayonnaise, raise the product's pH and increase the likelihood of microbial growth. Holding salads in the temperature danger zone (41° to 140°F [5° to 60°C]) compounds the risks.

Food Preservation by Radiation

The use of radiation in food preservation is presently limited, although further research may reveal new applications. This method of preservation, called irradiation, involves exposing food to ultraviolet light, gamma rays, or X rays to destroy harmful organisms. Ultraviolet light acts only on the surface of food products. In the past, it was used in the aging (tenderization) of meats at relatively high temperatures. Ultraviolet light is now used to reduce bacterial activity on the surface of fruitcakes before they are wrapped.

Gamma rays are produced by radioactive elements such as cobalt. These short-length waves disrupt cell components and kill harmful microorganisms and insects.

They can be used to sterilize or pasteurize food products such as meat and poultry. In some instances, they are used to reduce insect infestation in newly harvested grains.

Low doses of gamma rays add little heat to food while allowing flavors to remain intact and extending shelf life significantly. High doses of gamma rays negatively alter the color, odor, taste, and appearance of foods. Current research and development of low dosage gamma radiation may result in a preservation technique that will not significantly alter either the appearance or taste of food. Fruits, vegetables, fish, and poultry are some of the products that could be preserved by low dosage gamma radiation in the future. X rays are essentially the same as gamma rays.

Food irradiation can help extend shelf life by keeping grains from sprouting, deactivating molds, and killing spoilage bacteria. It can also make food safer. At low to medium doses, radiation kills *Salmonella spp.* and other pathogens, including the parasite *Trichinella spiralis.*

Consumer concerns have been raised that irradiation will produce new chemical compounds in foods. However, researchers have concluded that the changes in food resulting from irradiation are too small to affect the safety of the food product. Irradiated foods contain chemicals identical to those found in baked or broiled foods, and contain fewer altered chemicals than barbecued steak. Consumers are not exposed to radiation by eating irradiated food, since the process of irradiation is low in intensity and the energy passes through the food leaving no radioactivity. One scientist has said that consumers run no more risk of being exposed to radiation from irradiated food than they do from a briefcase that has been X-rayed by a machine at an airport.[3]

Nevertheless, consumers and health groups concerned with the effects of food irradiation petitioned the FDA to require warnings on menus and on the doors of restaurants offering irradiated foods for sale. The groups asked the FDA to require the word "picowaved" and the international symbol for food irradiation. In a survey conducted by the Food Marketing Institute (FMI), over 70% of the respondents characterized irradiated foods as a hazard. Fewer than 30% of the respondents indicated that they had even heard of food irradiation two years earlier.[4] The FDA has ruled that even though foods preserved through irradiation must be labeled to show this fact at both the wholesale and retail levels, "multiple-ingredient foods" such as restaurant meals are exempt from this requirement. The FDA's ruling stated that the effects of radiation on individual ingredients would likely have no significant effect on the final product. Further changes can be expected as technology improves and consumer groups become more active and vocal.

One additional method of preserving foods is known as pulsed-power. This method uses tens of thousands of volts of electricity in bursts as brief as millionths of a second to kill bacteria and extend shelf life. Other technological advances may permit the use of pulsed electromagnetic fields to do the same thing.

Having explored the causes of food spoilage and the methods of commercial preservation, we can now consider specific recommendations for preserving various types of food. The recommendations which follow should be valuable to food service and lodging businesses, considering the large sums of money they spend on food products. These recommendations can help eliminate the risk of serving spoiled food products to guests.

Preservation Methods for Various Types of Foods

The characteristics of each category of food provide insight into the spoilage problems food service companies might encounter. This section covers the characteristics, spoilage potential, and preservation methods for each group of food products. Since most of the food preservation methods have already been described in the previous section, the details are not repeated here. The two main categories are foods from animal sources and foods from plant sources, although fats and oils overlap these categories somewhat. Within each main category, some foods have their own unique preservation methods.

Preservation of Foods from Animal Sources

Foods from animal sources include meat, poultry, fish and shellfish, eggs, dairy products, and fats. These foods represent a large portion of the food dollars spent by the average food service operation, so their preservation is important.

The FDA states:

"Meat" means the flesh of animals used as food including the dressed flesh of cattle, swine, sheep, or goats and other edible animals, *except fish and poultry,* that is offered for human consumption.

Game Animal.

(a) **"Game animal"** means an animal, the products of which are food, that is not classified as cattle, sheep, swine, or goat in 9 CFR Subchapter A - Mandatory Meat Inspection, Part 301, as poultry in 9 CFR Subchapter C - Mandatory Poultry Products Inspection, Part 381, or as fish as defined in Subparagraph 1-201.10(B)(25).

(b) **"Game animal"** includes:

(i) Animals such as reindeer, elk, deer, antelope, water buffalo, bison, rabbit, squirrel, bear, and muskrat; aquatic and nonaquatic birds such as wild ducks and geese, quail, and pheasant; nonaquatic reptiles such as rattlesnakes; and aquatic mammals; and

(ii) Exotic animals as defined in 9 CFR Subchapter A - Animal Welfare, Part 1, such as lion, tiger, leopard, elephant, camel, antelope, anteater, kangaroo, and water buffalo, and species of foreign domestic cattle, such as Ankole, Gayal, and Yak.

3-201.17   Game Animals, Prohibition.*

(A) Except as specified in ¶ (B) of this section, game animals may not be received for sale or service.

(B) *This section does not apply to the sale or service of:*

(1) *Game animals commercially raised for food that:*

(a) *Are raised, slaughtered, and processed under a voluntary inspection program that is conducted by the agency that has animal health jurisdiction, or*

(b) *Are under a routine inspection program conducted by a regulatory agency other than the agency that has animal health jurisdiction and are raised, slaughtered, and processed according to laws governing meat and poultry as determined by the agency that has animal health jurisdiction and the agency that conducts the inspection program. The agencies shall consider factors such as the need for antemortem and postmortem examination by a veterinarian or a veterinarian's designee, approved by the regulatory authority.*

(2) *As allowed by law, field-dressed wild game animals that are under a routine inspection program under which the animals:*

(a) *Receive a postmortem examination by a veterinarian or a veterinarian's designee, approved by the regulatory authority,*

(b) *Are field-dressed and transported according to requirements specified by the agency that has animal health jurisdiction and the agency that conducts the inspection program, and*

(c) *Are processed according to laws governing meat and poultry as determined by the agency that has animal health jurisdiction and the agency that conducts the inspection program; or*

(3) *Exotic species of animals including animals raised for exhibition purposes in a zoo or circus that:*

(a) *Meet Subparagraph (B)(1)(a) of this section, or*

(b) *Receive antemortem and postmortem examination by a veterinarian or a veterinarian's designee, approved by the regulatory authority, and*

(c) *Are slaughtered and processed according to laws governing meat and poultry as determined by the agency that has animal health jurisdiction and the agency that conducts the inspection program.*

Source: FDA 1993 *Food Code.*

Meat. Meat is generally defined as the flesh of any animal used for food. For purposes of this discussion, meat includes beef, lamb, veal, and pork. The USDA includes all edible parts of skeletal muscles, variety meats (tongue, diaphragm, esophagus, heart) and glandular meats (liver, kidney, brain, spleen, pancreas, thymus, and stomach linings) in this category. However, lean muscle is what most Americans think of as meat. The components of lean muscle tissue are listed in Exhibit 4.1. In light of the fact that lean muscle is mostly moisture, it is not surprising that meat is capable of supporting rapid bacterial growth. Because meat and meat products have a relatively high a_w and are not highly acidic, they are considered potentially hazardous foods.

Several pathogenic bacteria have been detected in fresh meat products. Among the most prominent are *Staphylococcus aureus, Salmonella spp., Clostridium perfringens, Listeria monocytogenes, Yersinia enterocolitica, Campylobacter jejuni,* and the parasite *Trichinella spiralis.* Spoilage organisms have also been detected in fresh meat products. (These organisms are discussed in detail later in this section.)

Generally, the normal muscle tissue of healthy living animals does not harbor pathogenic microorganisms. However, spoilage organisms and pathogens can invade the muscle tissue from the animal's intestinal tract when the animal is slaughtered. The extent of the invasion depends on the following factors:

Exhibit 4.1 The Composition of Meat

Component	Percentage Range
Moisture	65.0 – 80
Proteins	16.0 – 22
Fats and Lipids*	1.5 – 42
Cartilage and Bone	0.0 – 26
Carbohydrates	1.0 – 2
Minerals	0.5 – 1
Vitamins	trace

*"Lipids" is a term for fats and oils and other substances that do not dissolve in water.

- The microbial content of the animal's intestines

- The physiological condition of the animal before slaughter

- The method of slaughter

- The method of carcass cooling

The microbial content of the animal's intestines probably exerts the greatest influence over potential contamination. For this reason, meat animals are usually starved for 24 hours before they are slaughtered.

The animal's physiological condition determines its internal body chemistry to some extent. Normally, after an animal is slaughtered, its muscles become stiff—a condition known as rigor mortis. Rigor mortis takes place in meat animals about 6 to 12 hours after slaughter, depending on the carcass size. As rigor mortis sets in, a chemical reaction called **anaerobic glycolysis** takes place, during which glycogen (a chemical form of energy stored in muscle tissue) is converted to lactic acid. Calm, rested animals have more glycogen in their muscle tissues; thus, the production of lactic acid after slaughter causes a dramatic pH drop (from 7.0 to 5.6). An animal that is excited or fatigued before slaughtering will have used up its stored glycogen, and thus less lactic acid will be produced and the pH drop will not be as dramatic. The result is dark cutting meat, which is less tender and more susceptible to microbial attack.

The method of slaughter should be quick and efficient. Besides being more humane, quick slaughtering can accomplish the objective of rapid bleeding in a relatively sanitary environment. The method of carcass cooling is also important to meat preservation. Carcasses must be cooled quickly to reduce contact with the temperature danger zone.

Additional microorganisms might be introduced after an animal is slaughtered. Contaminants might enter the meat tissue from the animal's hide when it is skinned. When meat products are cut up or boned, further contamination might be introduced through knives and cutting surfaces. Ground (comminuted) meats and finely chopped meats are most susceptible to contamination because of their large surface areas, due to a reduction in size by chopping, flaking, grinding, or mincing, and the additional handling they receive.

The FDA states:

Comminuted.

(a) **"Comminuted"** means reduced in size by methods including chopping, flaking, grinding, or mincing.

(b) **"Comminuted"** includes fish or meat products that are reduced in size and restructured or reformulated such as gefilte fish, formed roast beef, gyros, ground beef, and sausage; and a mixture of 2 or more types of meat that have been reduced in size and combined, such as sausages made from 2 or more meats.

Source: FDA 1993 *Food Code.*

Nevertheless, most meat contamination comes from the penetration of pathogens from the intestinal tract of the animal.

The survival and growth of microorganisms in meat are influenced by the kinds of organisms present, the physical and chemical characteristics of the meat, the storage temperature, and the amount of available oxygen. Besides being subject to contamination with pathogens, which has already been discussed, meats are susceptible to two broad types of spoilage: anaerobic and aerobic.

Anaerobic spoilage of meat tissue takes place under conditions with a limited amount of oxygen. **Putrefaction** is a bacterial splitting of meat proteins, resulting in the formation of foul odors. *Pseudomonas spp.* are the bacteria responsible for this type of spoilage. Souring is a form of anaerobic spoilage caused by the production of acids. This process results in a sour odor and taste in meats.

Aerobic spoilage of meat tissue is likelier to occur since fresh meat is rarely stored in an oxygen-free environment. Bacteria are responsible for the greatest amount of aerobic meat spoilage. Some bacteria form slimy capsules and surface slime on meat. Other bacteria change the color of meat to gray, green, and shades of brown. Still others cause fat rancidity in meats. Finally, surface colors on meat can be changed to red, green, blue, or yellow by bacteria that produce pigments.

Molds are aerobic organisms that cause fuzziness or stickiness on meats. Color changes (green, black, and white) are caused by molds. Other molds can decompose fats and proteins in meats because they have enzymes that accelerate the breakdown. This results in an unacceptable odor, color, taste, texture, and appearance. The genus of molds called *Penicillium* is often responsible for meat spoilage.

Food preservation methods for meat products are designed to prevent the activity of pathogenic and spoilage microorganisms. Meat products may be rendered commercially sterile by the canning process. Meat products may also be pasteurized and then stored under refrigeration. Low-temperature preservation is the commonest method of preserving fresh meats. Freezing and refrigerating are preferable to canning in that they do not significantly alter the taste and texture of meat. However, some psychrophilic spoilage organisms (*Pseudomonas spp.*) can grow on meats stored at refrigerator temperatures. Whenever meat products are chilled or frozen, they should be carefully wrapped to minimize contamination and dehydration. Recommended temperatures, times, and relative humidities for storage of fresh and frozen meats are presented in Exhibit 4.2.

Some meat products are preserved by drying. This was a common practice among the pioneers who settled the western part of the United States: they made jerky by cutting meat into strips and drying it in the sun. Modern-day adventurers who backpack in

Exhibit 4.2 Recommended Storage Conditions for Fresh and Frozen Meats

PRODUCT	STORAGE TEMPERATURES	RELATIVE HUMIDITY (Percent)	STORAGE TIMES
Refrigerated Storage			
Beef			
Wholesale Cuts	34 to 36°F (1 to 2°C)	85	1–2 weeks
Portion Cuts	34 to 36°F (1 to 2°C)	85	4–6 days
Ground Beef	34 to 36°F (1 to 2°C)	85	1–2 days
Pork			
Wholesale Cuts	34 to 36°F (1 to 2°C)	85	5 days
Portion Cuts	34 to 36°F (1 to 2°C)	85	3 days
Ground Pork	34 to 36°F (1 to 2°C)	85	1–2 days
Lamb			
Wholesale Cuts	34 to 36°F (1 to 2°C)	85	1 week
Portion Cuts	34 to 36°F (1 to 2°C)	85	3–4 days
Veal			
Wholesale Cuts	34 to 36°F (1 to 2°C)	90	5 days
Portion Cuts	34 to 36°F (1 to 2°C)	90	3 days
Cured Meats	34 to 36°F (1 to 2°C)	75	2 weeks
Variety Meats	34 to 36°F (1 to 2°C)	85	3–5 days
Freezer Storage			
Beef			
Wholesale Cuts	−10 to 0°F (−23 to −18°C)	—	6–10 months
Portion Cuts	−10 to 0°F (−23 to −18°C)	—	4–8 months
Ground Beef	−10 to 0°F (−23 to −18°C)	—	4–6 months
Pork			
Wholesale Cuts	−10 to 0°F (−23 to −18°C)	—	4–8 months
Portion Cuts	−10 to 0°F (−23 to −18°C)	—	2–6 months
Cured/Smoked	−10 to 0°F (−23 to −18°C)	—	1–2 months
Lamb			
Wholesale Cuts	−10 to 0°F (−23 to −18°C)	—	6–10 months
Portion Cuts	−10 to 0°F (−23 to −18°C)	—	4–8 months
Veal			
Wholesale Cuts	−10 to 0°F (−23 to −18°C)	—	4–8 months
Portion Cuts	−10 to 0°F (−23 to −18°C)	—	2–6 months

the wilderness often take foil-packaged, freeze-dried meat products which are easy to carry and prepare. Freeze-dried meat products are shelf stable as long as they are stored properly and their packages are not opened. Other dried meat products are often cured and/or smoked. Curing is the addition of common table salt, sugar, nitrites, or nitrates to meats. Smoking provides additional flavor to cured meats and helps to tenderize beef and pork products. Meats can also be dried by smoking alone.

The USDA has developed a simple, fast, and inexpensive test to measure potential spoilage in ground beef. The test measures lactic acid; high levels of this organic acid indicate that the beef will spoil quickly and develop a sour odor. The test is being used by food service distributors and may find its way into food service operations.

An increasing number of food service operations are offering "exotic meats" on their menus. Wild game, for example, may be served in a food service operation provided the food products have been obtained from an approved and safe source. Since these food products are not usually raised commercially, extra caution is necessary.

Poultry. This category includes chicken, turkey, duck, goose, and game birds. Like meats, poultry products are classified as potentially hazardous foods. Pathogenic and spoilage organisms prefer poultry products because they have a favorable pH, high moisture content, and high nitrogen content. The intestinal tract and skin of poultry may contain a variety of pathogenic bacteria, including *Staphylococcus aureus, Salmonella spp.,* and *Escherichia coli.* Recall the USDA's estimate that over a third of all chicken carcasses carry *Salmonella spp.* (see Chapter 3). Other pathogens that have been associated with poultry products include *Clostridium perfringens, Listeria monocytogenes,* and *Campylobacter jejuni.* The frequent identification of poultry products with cases of human salmonellosis makes it especially important to properly handle and preserve poultry products.

Spoilage is apparent when poultry is sticky, slimy, and has an objectionable odor. Generally, two types of spoilage affect poultry products. Enzymes, present within the poultry cells, can cause chemical changes and deterioration. Fortunately, enzymatic changes are significantly slowed by refrigeration or freezing. Bacteria are responsible for even more poultry spoilage. Bacterial spoilage is usually traceable to the *Pseudomonas* and *Flavobacterium* genera. As with meat, most spoilage bacteria come from the live animal's skin and intestinal tract. Bacteria reproduce on the skin of slaughtered birds, in the cavity of whole carcasses, and on any cut tissue. Slowly, these spoilage organisms penetrate into the poultry tissue. Molds also accelerate the spoilage of poultry products.

Many precautionary measures are taken to properly process poultry products. After the birds are slaughtered, the carcasses are washed with chlorinated water to kill germs. Then the carcasses are immediately chilled by cold air, ice, or iced water. The cold air method is preferred because it rapidly brings the temperature down to 32°F (0°C) and does not add extra moisture to the carcass. If the poultry is cut up, additional steps must be taken to ensure that contamination is not added.

Low-temperature preservation is frequently used for poultry products. Poultry products can be refrigerated or frozen successfully if they are carefully wrapped to minimize dehydration, contamination, and quality deterioration. Rapid freezing is desirable for the reasons previously discussed. Recommended temperatures, times, and relative humidities for storage of fresh and frozen poultry are presented in Exhibit 4.3.

Poultry products may also be preserved with the addition of heat. Poultry may be canned whole, in pieces, or completely boned. Some canned poultry products have a chemical preservative added. Organic acids, such as acetic acid, lengthen the shelf life of poultry products by lowering the pH. Some turkey products are cured; others are cured and then smoked.

Fish. Consumption of fish is on the rise in the United States. Fish products may be subdivided into a number of categories, the most common being finfish and shellfish.

Exhibit 4.3 Recommended Storage Conditions for Fresh and Frozen Poultry

PRODUCT	STORAGE TEMPERATURES	RELATIVE HUMIDITY (Percent)	STORAGE TIMES
Refrigerated Storage			
Chickens			
Whole	28 to 32°F (–2 to 0°C)	85	2–4 days
Pieces	28 to 32°F (–2 to 0°C)	85	1–2 days
Turkeys			
Whole	28 to 32°F (–2 to 0°C)	85	2–4 days
Pieces	28 to 32°F (–2 to 0°C)	85	1–2 days
Ducks	28 to 32°F (–2 to 0°C)	85	2–4 days
Geese	28 to 32°F (–2 to 0°C)	85	2–4 days
Freezer Storage			
Chickens			
Whole	–10 to 0°F (–23 to –18°C)	—	4–10 months
Pieces	–10 to 0°F (–23 to –18°C)	—	3–6 months
Turkeys	–10 to 0°F (–23 to –18°C)	—	4–10 months
Ducks	–10 to 0°F (–23 to –18°C)	—	4–10 months
Geese	–10 to 0°F (–23 to –18°C)	—	4–10 months

The FDA states:

"Fish" means fresh or saltwater finfish, molluscan shellfish, crustaceans, and other forms of aquatic animal life other than birds or mammals and includes any edible human food product derived in whole or in part from fish, including fish that has been processed in any manner.

"Molluscan shellfish" means any edible species of fresh or frozen oysters, clams, mussels, and scallops or edible portions thereof, except when the scallop product consists only of the shucked adductor muscle.

"Shellfish control authority" means a state, federal, foreign, or other government entity legally responsible for administering a program that includes certification of molluscan shellfish harvesters and dealers for interstate commerce.

"Shellstock" means raw, in-shell molluscan shellfish.

"Shucked shellfish" means molluscan shellfish that have one or both shells removed.

3-201.14   Fish.*

(A) Fish may not be received for sale or service unless they are:

    (1)   Commercially and legally caught or harvested; or

(2)   Except as specified under ¶ (B) of this section, caught recreationally and:

(a)   Approved for sale or service by the regulatory authority, and

(b)   If the fish are scombrotoxin-prone or are reef fish subject to ciguatera toxin, their source, preparation, and distribution are controlled under conditions of a variance granted by the regulatory authority as specified in § 8-103.10.

(B)   Molluscan shellfish that are recreationally caught may not be received for sale or service.

3-201.15   Molluscan Shellfish.*

(A)   Molluscan shellfish shall be obtained from sources according to law and the requirements specified in the Department of Health and Human Services, Public Health Service, Food and Drug Administration, National Shellfish Sanitation Program Manual of Operations.

(B)   Molluscan shellfish received in interstate commerce shall be from sources that are listed in the Interstate Certified Shellfish Shippers List.

3-402.11   Parasite Destruction.*

Before service or sale in ready-to-eat form, raw, marinated, or partially cooked fish other than molluscan shellfish shall be frozen throughout to a temperature of:

(A)   –20°C (–4°F) or below for 168 hours (7 days) in a freezer; or

(B)   –35°C (–31°F) or below for 15 hours in a blast freezer.

3-402.12   Records, Creation and Retention.

(A)   Except as specified in ¶ (B) of this section, if raw, marinated, or partially cooked fish are served or sold in ready-to-eat form, the person in charge shall record the freezing temperature and time to which the fish are subjected and shall retain the records at the food establishment for 90 calendar days beyond the time of service or sale of the fish.

(B)   *If the fish are frozen by a supplier, a written agreement or statement from the supplier stipulating that the fish supplied are frozen to a temperature and for a time specified under § 3-402.11 may substitute for the records specified under ¶ (A) of this section.*

Source: FDA 1993 *Food Code.*

Finfish come from freshwater lakes and rivers and from the ocean. Finfish can be classified as either fatty or lean. Fatty finfish include bluefish, bonito, mackerel, pompano, salmon, shark, smelt, swordfish, trout, tuna, and whitefish. Other species of finfish are generally classified as lean. Bass, cod, flounder, grouper, haddock, halibut, monkfish, ocean perch, snapper, sole, tilefish, turbot, and whiting fall into this category.

Shellfish are also considered lean. Shellfish are classified as crustaceans, which include crab, lobster, and shrimp, or mollusks, which include abalone, clams, octopus, oysters, scallops, snails, and squid.

Finfish and shellfish have less connective tissue and a relatively high moisture content compared with meat and poultry. Therefore, finfish and shellfish are more susceptible than meats and poultry to enzymatic autolysis and microbial spoilage.

Unlike meat and poultry processors, fish processors have no mandatory government inspections for quality or wholesomeness. However, there is increasing pressure to move toward mandatory government inspections because of the number of foodborne illness outbreaks associated with fish. The industry is fragmented; East Coast fish are primarily harvested wild, while West Coast fish are usually farmed. Inspections are currently made at the supplier's discretion and cost. Fish inspection is further complicated by the absence of any safe sensory method for differentiating between toxic and nontoxic seafood. It is therefore very important for food service operators to get to know their fish suppliers and be assured that they are safe sources.

One of the trends in the production of fish and shellfish is cultivation, or aquaculture. After starting with trout farming, processors are now commercially raising catfish, clams, shrimp, oysters, mussels, crayfish, striped bass, and salmon. Research is ongoing in the aquaculture of lobsters, scallops, redfish, and sturgeon. Fish cultivation provides readily renewable supplies, and the size, flavor, and nutrients can be tailored to market needs. In addition, the freedom from contact with pollutants and pathogenic organisms in the natural habitat is a major advantage. Aquaculture, along with more rigorous inspection procedures, will go a long way toward reducing the potential hazards of serving these products.

Contamination of fish can come from the natural slime present on the skin of fish. Most of this natural coating is harmless, but if the fish are taken from contaminated waters, their slime covering may be expected to contain contaminants. Typical pathogens on the skin of fish are *Vibrio parahaemolyticus, Clostridium botulinum, Salmonella spp.,* and the virus of infectious hepatitis. Further contamination can be introduced during processing and handling. The intestinal tract of fish could contain pathogens of the genera *Escherichia, Clostridium,* and *Bacillus.* Other pathogens that could be associated with fish are *Staphylococcus aureus,* the Norwalk virus, and the parasites *Diphyllobothrium latum* (freshwater fish) and *Anisakis spp.* (cod and herring). Spoilage organisms responsible for an ammonia-like odor are *Pseudomonas spp.* and *Proteus spp.,* while *Acinetobacter spp.* and *Aeromonas spp.* produce unpleasant fruity or sweet odors in spoiled fish.

During receiving of fish or shellfish, a trained representative of the food service operation should check product temperature, condition of the cases the products are received in, freshness, wholesomeness, and integrity. These inspections should be completed before storing the products.

The products should be well iced or solidly frozen when received. Use a probe thermometer to determine product temperature, which should then be checked against the following temperature guidelines:

- 32° to 38°F (0° to 3°C) for fresh fish

- 0° to 10°F (–18° to –12°C) for frozen fish

- 41°F (5°C) or less for live mollusks

- 40°F (4°C) for live crabs and lobsters

- 38°F (3°C) or less for vacuum-packed, modified atmosphere-packed, and pasteurized products

Any damaged cases should be opened, and any moisture or signs of dried moisture should be investigated.

The quality of fish and shellfish is measured by smell and appearance. Fresh finfish has a mild, agreeable odor. The skin should be bright and shiny with scales (if present) tightly attached. If the head is left on the fish, the eyes should be bright, clear, and full. The flesh of fresh fish is firm and elastic to the touch. Frozen fish should be solid with no discoloration on the firm flesh. Prior to freezing, the fish should be tightly wrapped or carefully packaged to withstand the low temperatures. Smoked fish appears bright and glossy and has a clean, smoky odor.

Many food service businesses in coastal areas have access to live shellfish; others must settle for frozen shellfish or fresh shellfish meat. (Some outstanding inland restaurants overcome this limitation by having a fresh catch flown in daily from coastal cities.) Fresh clams and oysters in the shell should be alive; this is indicated by a closed shell or one that closes tightly when tapped. If taken out of the shell, the meat of shellfish should be plump and free from off-odors. Live lobsters should show movement in their claws and tails and have bluish-green shells. Live crabs possess a sweet odor and show movement in their legs. Any frozen shellfish is undesirable if it has slimy or sticky flesh and a sour ammonia odor.

Shucked clams, oysters, and mussels should have a creamy color and be plump. Excessive liquid should not be present in the containers. Scallops should be firm and have a sweet, fresh odor. Shrimp should have firm flesh, a mild odor, and firmly-attached shells. Cooked lobsters and crabs should have creamy or snowy white meat and bright red shells.

Regarding wholesomeness, check packing ice to be certain that it is clean. Raw, cooked, and live products should be delivered in separate containers to prevent cross-contamination. Carefully check fresh fish for visible signs of parasites. If a product is discovered in contact with foreign objects or filth, reject it.

Finally, check the standard purchase specifications, including the size, weight, and other factors ordered during receiving. Store fish and shellfish as quickly as possible to maintain product temperature, quality, and safety.

Finfish and shellfish may be preserved by canning. In most cases, a brine solution or oil is added to finfish and shellfish during the canning process. However, low-temperature preservation is most frequently used for fish and shellfish. At all temperatures above freezing, the enzymatic autolysis of finfish and shellfish continues. However, at refrigerator temperatures, this process is slower than it would be at room temperatures.

Today's freezing techniques permit the quick freezing of finfish and shellfish immediately after they are caught. Many modern fishing ships are actually floating processing plants, where fresh fish can be efficiently cleaned, packaged, and refrigerated or frozen. Freezing prevents autolysis and destroys parasites if the fish is frozen throughout at -4°F (-20°C) or below for 168 hours (7 days) or -31°F (-35°C) or below for 15 hours in a blast freezer, but it does not prevent fat oxidation from occurring, especially in fatty finfish. Recommended temperatures, times, and relative humidities for storage of fresh and frozen finfish and shellfish are shown in Exhibit 4.4.

Some fish products are preserved by drying, often with the addition of salt and/or smoke. Besides contributing flavor, salt added during drying can also act as a chemical preservative. Other chemical preservatives used with fish are nitrites, nitrates, and sorbic acid. The acetic acid in sauces made of wine, vinegar, or sour cream is used to pickle fish such as herring. Antioxidants are frequently added to fatty fish to prevent their natural fats and oils from becoming rancid.

Eggs. Eggs, the fourth category of foods from animal sources, are an excellent source of high quality protein, both for humans and microorganisms. The inside of an egg is protected by its shell, a porous and often contaminated covering. If the laying flock is

Exhibit 4.4 Recommended Storage Conditions for Fresh and Frozen Fish and Shellfish

PRODUCT	STORAGE TEMPERATURES	RELATIVE HUMIDITY (Percent)	STORAGE TIMES
Refrigerated Storage			
Finfish			
Fatty	28 to 32°F (–2 to 0°C)	95	1–2 days
Lean	28 to 32°F (–2 to 0°C)	95	1–3 days
Shellfish			
Mollusks	34 to 36°F (1 to 2°C)	85	1–7 days
Crustaceans	30 to 34°F (–1 to 1°C)	90	1–3 days
Freezer Storage			
Finfish			
Fatty	–10 to 0°F (–23 to –18°C)	—	2–6 months
Lean	–10 to 0°F (–23 to –18°C)	—	2–6 months
Shellfish			
Mollusks	–10 to 0°F (–23 to –18°C)	—	2–6 months
Crustaceans	–10 to 0°F (–23 to –18°C)	—	2–6 months

contaminated, pathogens may be present on the shell and can penetrate to the inside. Pathogens which have been known to contaminate eggs are *Salmonella spp., Bacillus spp., Escherichia coli,* and *Staphylococcus aureus. Salmonella spp.* are the pathogens most frequently found on fresh eggs. These microbes can come from the hen's intestinal tract or feathers, from the hands of humans, and from pests such as mice and rats.

Two types of spoilage take place during the storage of shell eggs. The first type is non-microbial. Since the shell of an egg is porous, moisture gradually passes out of the egg. This moisture is displaced by oxygen entering the egg through the shell. Thus, as an egg ages, the size of the inner airspace increases. The albumen (the white of the egg) also thins and the egg yolk membrane weakens, producing a "watery" egg. In addition, the pH increases from 7.6 to 9.5 as the egg gets older. This type of deterioration is not caused by microorganisms, but it is clearly undesirable.

The second type of spoilage affecting shell eggs is caused by microorganisms. A high level of moisture in the air enhances the rate of microbial penetration from the shell to the interior of the egg; thus, the spoilage rate of fresh eggs increases as the relative humidity rises. Several forms of microbial spoilage have been identified in eggs. Green rot in egg whites, colorless rot, black rot, and some mold spoilage may occur in eggs and egg products.

Egg products may be preserved in a number of ways. Heat preservation is somewhat limited because egg whites have a tendency to coagulate when heated. Nevertheless, the USDA requires that liquid whole eggs and egg whites be pasteurized to control the proliferation of *Salmonella spp.* Eggs can also be successfully dried, usually by means of the spray-drying technique. Before drying, egg whites are treated with an enzyme to prevent the appearance of brown colors. Dried eggs must be stored carefully due to their tendency to absorb excess moisture and contaminants.

Exhibit 4.5 Recommended Storage Conditions for Fresh and Frozen Eggs

PRODUCT	STORAGE TEMPERATURES	RELATIVE HUMIDITY (Percent)	STORAGE TIMES
Refrigerated Storage			
Shell Eggs*	29 to 35°F (−2 to 2°C)	80–85	2–4 weeks
Dried Eggs	35°F (2°C)	minimum	6–12 months
Reconstituted Eggs	29 to 35°F (−2 to 2°C)	80–85	2–4 weeks
Freezer Storage			
Whole Eggs	−10 to 0°F (−23 to −18°C)	—	6–8 months

*Some states do not consider clean, whole, uncracked, odor-free shell eggs potentially hazardous.

Low-temperature preservation techniques are effective for eggs. To lengthen the shelf life of refrigerated shell eggs, some egg-producing companies coat the shells with a colorless, odorless, tasteless mineral oil. Whole (shelled) eggs and egg whites can be successfully frozen, although sugar or salt must first be added; without the addition of sugar or salt, frozen yolks form a gel which persists even after thawing. Because their ease of handling and long shelf life make them practical, frozen eggs are frequently purchased in 30- to 50-pound (13.62 to 22.70 kg) containers. A summary of temperatures, times, and relative humidities for storage of various forms of eggs is presented in Exhibit 4.5.

Both the FDA and the USDA have issued guidelines for the safe handling of eggs in food service operations. First, avoid serving raw eggs and foods containing raw eggs. Second, cook eggs thoroughly in order to serve the yolk and white firm. Third, lightly cooked foods containing eggs (for example, meringues, french toast, and soft custards) may be risky for people with weakened immune systems. And finally, review food-handling practices and recipes to consider substituting pasteurized egg products for shell eggs whenever possible.

Dairy Products. These products constitute the fifth category of foods from animal sources. This large category encompasses milk, cream, butter, cheese, frozen desserts, and fermented milk products. Most of these products begin with cows' milk.

The milk of healthy cows contains few pathogens or spoilage organisms. However, contamination has been traced to equipment and handlers. Equipment may harbor *Staphylococcus aureus* and *Salmonella spp.* organisms. Other pathogens responsible for foodborne outbreaks with dairy products include *Listeria monocytogenes, Campylobacter jejuni,* and *Yersinia enterocolitica.* Because milk and milk products are highly perishable, they are classified as potentially hazardous foods.

Dairy products may spoil in a variety of ways. Fresh milk may sour by the action of *Streptococcus lactis, Lactobacillus bulgaricus,* or *Lactobacillus thermophilus,* depending on its temperature. While this souring is undesirable in milk and most other dairy products, it adds to the characteristic flavor of yogurt. When *Bacillus, Clostridium,* and *Pseudomonas* organisms are present in milk, a protein breakdown results. Other organisms are responsible for the rancidity of milk fat, flavor changes, and color changes in milk.

Exhibit 4.6 Approximate Compositions of Fresh Whole, Evaporated, Condensed, and Dried Milk

Component	Type of Milk			
	Fresh Whole	**Evaporated**	**Condensed**	**Dried**
Water	88.0%	74%	30%	3%
Fat	3.5	8	8	27
Nonfat Solids	8.5	18	20	70
Sugar	—	—	42	—

Dairy products are primarily preserved by pasteurization, because the fresh milk used to make them is pasteurized. The USDA also requires that ice cream mixes be pasteurized.

A comparison of the components of the four basic types of milk—fresh whole, evaporated, condensed, and dried—is given in Exhibit 4.6.

Fresh milk is potentially hazardous and must be stored under exact time-temperature combinations. In the United States, fresh whole milk is usually homogenized, although this does not contribute to its preservation. **Homogenization** is a process that uses pressure to force milk through tiny openings. This breaks up the fat globules present in whole milk so that they are permanently suspended in the whey (liquid portion of the milk). There the fat globules cannot recombine and rise to the top as cream. Before the process of homogenization was widely used, consumers had to vigorously shake bottles of unhomogenized milk to distribute the milk fat—which recombined quickly. Many people prefer to drink low fat or skim milk; these products have some of the fat skimmed off before homogenization.

In addition to being pasteurized, condensed milk and evaporated milk are canned, so they last much longer than fresh milk. Few spoilage problems arise as long as their containers have been properly sealed and heat processed. The high sugar content of condensed milk also helps to preserve it.

Dried milk is made by heating milk and then spray-drying it. The combination of heat and drying usually results in low bacterial counts. Dried milk is relatively safe as long as it is properly stored to prevent the addition of moisture.

Ice cream is generally free of bacteria. It benefits from the combination of pasteurization and freezer temperatures which kill most organisms and prevent the reproduction of survivors.

Butter is made from pasteurized cream. Once butter is produced, it is held at freezer temperatures. Butter containing salt is more inhibiting to bacteria than salt-free butter. The low moisture content of butter provides favorable conditions for mold growth.

Cheese is manufactured from pasteurized milk. Some cheeses, such as Romano and Parmesan, are so low in moisture that they may not support the normal growth of bacteria. However, molds frequently attack cheeses. Cheese may be salted or smoked during processing.

Selected temperatures, times, and relative humidities for storing various dairy products are presented in Exhibit 4.7.

Fats and Oils. Fats and oils constitute an important food category because they are part of a wide variety of food products, including cookies, crackers, butter, cheese, breakfast cereals, salad dressings, milk, nuts, snack foods, meats, poultry, some fish, and some fruits and vegetables. Fats and oils in their pure form may be differentiated in three

Exhibit 4.7 Recommended Storage Conditions for Dairy Products

PRODUCT	STORAGE TEMPERATURES	RELATIVE HUMIDITY (Percent)	STORAGE TIMES
Refrigerated Storage			
Butter	32 to 36°F (0 to 2°C)	85	2–4 weeks
Cheese, Hard	38 to 40°F (3 to 4°C)	75	4–6 months
Cheese, Soft	38 to 40°F (3 to 4°C)	75	13–14 days
Fluid Milk	36 to 38°F (2 to 3°C)	85	6–14 days
Reconstituted Dried Milk	36 to 38°F (2 to 3°C)	85	5–8 days
Freezer Storage			
Ice Cream and Frozen Desserts	0 to 10°F (−18 to −12°C)	—	2–4 months
Dry Storage			
Condensed Milk	50 to 70°F (10 to 21°C)	50–60	2–4 months
Evaporated Milk	50 to 70°F (10 to 21°C)	50–60	8–10 months
Dried Milk	50 to 70°F (10 to 21°C)	50–60	8–10 months

ways. Fats come from animal sources, are solid at room temperature, and are usually saturated. Oils are generally from plant sources, are liquid at room temperature, and are unsaturated. Saturated fats contain the maximum amount of hydrogen in the molecule and are therefore less susceptible to breakdown than unsaturated oils.

Foods containing fats and oils can undergo three types of breakdown reactions: autoxidation, hydrolytic rancidity, and flavor reversion. Autoxidation is a form of oxidative rancidity caused by the exposure of the fat or oil to oxygen. The reaction is accelerated by the presence of heat, metals, salt, and light. Unsaturated oils are more susceptible to autoxidation than saturated fats. Oxidative rancidity gives off-odors and flavors to food products. It is controlled by the addition of antioxidants such as BHA (butylated hydroxyanisole) and BHT (butylated hydroxytoluene). BHA and BHT are added to many bakery products to control autoxidation.

Hydrolytic rancidity is responsible for flavor, odor, and taste changes in butter and products containing milk fat. It is caused by an enzyme called lipase. Lipase breaks down milk fat into its components. Since the fatty acids in milk fat are saturated, they possess a noticeable odor at room temperature. This reaction is controlled by heating the milk fat to destroy the lipase enzyme.

Flavor reversion is another form of oxidative rancidity. It occurs in vegetable oils that are highly unsaturated and contain linolenic acid, a polyunsaturated fatty acid. The result of flavor reversion is an unacceptable beany, fishy, or paint-like odor. Flavor reversion is controlled by a process known as **partial hydrogenation.** Hydrogen gas is added so that the polyunsaturated linolenic fatty acid becomes saturated and the problem is eliminated. Soybean oils used in the manufacture of salad dressings are partially hydrogenated to control flavor reversion, as are other oils found in many processed foods.

Fats and oils generally contain few, if any, pathogenic organisms. Recall that Chapter 3 referred to commercially processed garlic in soybean oil as a source of botulism. The

Clostridium botulinum organisms survived due to inadequate heat treatment and then were able to produce their toxin under the anaerobic conditions inside the container. The outbreak had little to do with the soybean oil.

The reasons for the proper preservation of foods obtained from animal sources are obvious. First, proper preservation controls pathogenic microorganisms which could cause a foodborne disease outbreak. Thus, it contributes to the operation's sanitation risk management program. Second, effective control of spoilage reduces food waste. Because foods from animal sources constitute the majority of purchases made by most food establishments, proper preservation of these products is essential to any operation's cost control program. Finally, proper storage of foods preserves their desirable qualities and thus contributes to overall guest satisfaction.

Preservation of Foods from Plant Sources

Foods from plant sources have increased in popularity over the last several years; per capita consumption is up by nearly 30% since 1970.[5] Fresh vegetables are preferred to frozen and canned by almost 2 to 1.[6] In keeping with the trends toward physical fitness, weight consciousness, and nutritious, high-fiber diets, food service guests are demanding more fruits, vegetables, grains, cereals, and nuts.

Fresh Fruits and Vegetables. These products generally continue respiring (living) after they are harvested. As they pass through the distribution channels, their respiration is counteracted by autolysis and microbial spoilage. The rate of enzymatic autolysis in fruits and vegetables varies directly with the temperature. Autolysis is substantially reduced when temperatures are decreased.

A number of microorganisms may be present on the exteriors of fresh fruits and vegetables. The microbes include *Pseudomonas spp., Shigella spp., Bacillus spp., Streptococcus faecalis, Staphylococcus aureus, Clostridium botulinum,* and a variety of molds. Most of these are spoilage organisms, although a few are pathogenic to humans.

Bacteria are responsible for several types of vegetable spoilage. *Psuedomonas spp.* cause a mushy, soft, malodorous spoilage called soft rot. Other bacteria cause vegetables to rot and develop sour odors. *Botrytis cinerea* is a mold which causes gray rot on vegetables. Other molds can cause soft rot, black rot, and sour rot.

Most fruit spoilage is the result of mold growth. Molds may produce gray, green, blue, and white pigments on fruit. For example, *Botrytis cinerea* causes a gray rot, while *Penicillium spp.* are responsible for a blue-colored rot. The activity of molds can also cause softening, souring, and the development of bitter flavors in fresh fruits.

Fresh fruits and vegetables acquire their microbial populations from the water and the soil as they grow. Since plants consist largely of moisture and carbohydrates, organisms which prefer these nutrient sources are most frequently found on fruits and vegetables. Surface washing reduces the exterior microbial population.

Fresh fruits and vegetables are preserved by the use of low temperatures. When they are harvested, their temperature is immediately dropped for preservation purposes. Many fruits and vegetables can be frozen, as described earlier in this chapter. Others are refrigerated as they move to fresh produce markets. However, some fruits (such as bananas) are susceptible to chill shock and must be stored at higher temperatures. Some recommended temperatures, times, and relative humidities for storage of fresh, canned, and frozen fruits and vegetables are presented in Exhibits 4.8 and 4.9.

The year-round availability of fruits and vegetables throughout the United States is largely due to freezing and canning. Of course, some canned foods still spoil due to can

Exhibit 4.8 Recommended Storage Conditions for Fruits

PRODUCT	STORAGE TEMPERATURES	RELATIVE HUMIDITY (Percent)	STORAGE TIMES
Fresh Fruits			
Apples	30 to 32°F (–1 to 0°C)	85	2–6 months
Grapefruits	32 to 45°F (0 to 7°C)	85	1–2 months
Lemons	46 to 50°F (8 to 10°C)	85	1–4 months
Limes	46 to 50°F (8 to 10°C)	85	1–2 months
Melons	40 to 45°F (4 to 7°C)	85	2–4 weeks
Oranges	32 to 36°F (0 to 2°C)	85	2–3 months
Peaches	30 to 32°F (–1 to 0°C)	85	2–4 weeks
Berries	30 to 32°F (–1 to 0°C)	85	1–2 weeks
Grapes	30 to 32°F (–1 to 0°C)	85	1–2 months
Strawberries	30 to 32°F (–1 to 0°C)	85	4–8 days
Canned Fruits	50 to 72°F (10 to 22°C)	50–60	8–12 months
Frozen Fruits	–10 to 0°F (–23 to –18°C)	—	6–12 months

Exhibit 4.9 Recommended Storage Conditions for Vegetables

PRODUCT	STORAGE TEMPERATURES	RELATIVE HUMIDITY (Percent)	STORAGE TIMES
Fresh Vegetables			
Asparagus	32 to 34°F (0 to 1°C)	90	2–4 weeks
Beans	40 to 45°F (4 to 7°C)	85	7–10 days
Cabbage	32 to 34°F (0 to 1°C)	90	2–3 months
Carrots	32 to 34°F (0 to 1°C)	90	1–3 weeks
Cauliflower	32 to 34°F (0 to 1°C)	85	2–3 weeks
Corn	31 to 32°F (–1 to 0°C)	85	4–7 days
Cucumbers	45 to 48°F (7 to 9°C)	90	1–2 weeks
Lettuce	32 to 34°F (0 to 1°C)	90	2–4 weeks
Onions	32 to 34°F (0 to 1°C)	75	5–8 months
Potatoes	50 to 55°F (10 to 13°C)	85	2–4 months
Spinach	32 to 34°F (0 to 1°C)	90	1–2 weeks
Squash, Zucchini	32 to 36°F (0 to 2°C)	85	1–2 weeks
Tomatoes, Ripe	32 to 34°F (0 to 1°C)	85	7–10 days
Canned Vegetables	50 to 70°F (10 to 21°C)	50–60	8–12 months
Frozen Vegetables	–10 to 0°F (–23 to –18°C)	—	6–10 months

corrosion, leakage, or insufficient heating during the canning process. Three types of canned food spoilage are flat sour spoilage, thermophilic gas spoilage, and carbon dioxide gas spoilage.

Flat sour spoilage of canned foods is caused by the anaerobic growth of heat-resistant, spore-forming bacteria. *Bacillus coagulans* is responsible for this kind of spoilage in tomatoes and tomato juice. These organisms change the flavor (but not the appearance) of canned foods.

Thermophilic gas spoilage is also caused by heat-resistant microbes that form spores. However, when these microorganisms survive the heating process (due to insufficient time-temperature combinations), they produce gas. Examples are *Clostridium sporogenes, Clostridium putrefaciens,* and *Clostridium thermosaccharolyticum.* These organisms cause food cans to swell and become distorted. A "flipper" is a can with flat ends that bulge when the can is warm. A "springer" is a can with moderate bulges on both top and bottom. A "soft swell" is similar to a springer; however, the bulges can be pushed back with finger pressure. A "hard swell" has bulges at both ends which cannot be pushed back with finger pressure. In general, if the top and the bottom of a can are flat, it is a safe product.

Carbon dioxide gas spoilage occurs when non-spore-forming bacteria enter the product after processing. These spoilage organisms get into the can through faulty seals or leaks. For example, *Micrococcus spp.* and *Streptococcus thermophilus* can make the contents of a can frothy and slimy. Carbon dioxide gas spoilage produces flippers, springers, soft swells, and hard swells.

Of course, there is always the possibility that the deadly toxin of the pathogen *Clostridium botulinum* may be present in a swollen can. If you ever observe *any* abnormal conditions in canned products, *throw them out.* Do not take a chance with your own life or the lives of your guests and staff members.

Canned foods, with the exception of ethnic products and boxed fruit juices, are losing popularity in the United States. This is due largely to the increasing popularity of fresh fruits and vegetables.

In addition to freezing and canning, drying is used to preserve some fruits and vegetables. This process destroys molds and yeasts, as well as non-spore-forming bacteria. Freeze-drying is very effective with fruits and vegetables. Regardless of how fruits and vegetables are preserved, care must be taken to avoid introducing pathogenic and spoilage organisms during processing and handling.

With advances in technology, hydroponics might one day help meet the food service industry's demand for fresh vegetables, fruits, and herbs. Hydroponics is the growing of fresh produce in a nutrient-enriched water solution. No soil is used, and nutrient levels are controlled by computer. A major advantage of this method is that it produces cleaner, less contaminated products. Even though it is relatively expensive at this time, hydroponics might be the wave of the future.

Cereals, Grains, and Flours. These products are various forms of wheat, oats, rice, barley, corn, rye, and chicory plants. They can be grouped together because they have similar contamination problems. The exterior of these products can be contaminated by soil, insects, and equipment. *Bacillus cereus* is an organism frequently found on cereal grains. Most microbial contamination is removed from grains during milling; thus flours are relatively free of pathogens and spoilage organisms. However, if the moisture content of flour is raised, certain bacteria can cause a fermentation which results in spoilage. Molds frequently attack baked products made from flours.

Among the most familiar spoiled foods in this category are bakery products which exhibit *Rhizopus nigricans* (a black mold) or *Penicillium expansum* (a green mold). Mold growth can be controlled in baked products by fast cooling, followed by prompt wrapping. The addition of chemicals (for example, calcium propionate or sodium propionate) to doughs and batters prior to baking also inhibits mold activity.

The formation of rope in bakery products is characterized by an odor of ripe melons, yellow crumb color, sticky crumbs, and a slimy, thread-like material evident when the product is sliced. Rope is caused by a spore-forming group of *Bacillus* organisms. It is controlled by the addition of acid prior to baking, fast cooling, and freezing.

Spices. Spices are normally not prone to spoilage, although they may have molds present. Some spices exhibit bacterial spoilage if their water content is excessively increased.

Nuts. Nuts do not normally spoil by the action of bacteria because their moisture content is too low and their fat content too high. They are susceptible to rancidity reactions, however. Molds can also cause some problems if the water content of the nuts is raised. As discussed in Chapter 3, *Aspergillus flavus* molds produce aflatoxins in peanuts.

Carbonated beverages. These products generally do not spoil if stored properly. The trapped carbon dioxide gas lowers the pH, and added acids (for example, citric and benzoic acids) inhibit microbial activity. Because yeasts can spoil carbonated beverages containing sugar, beverage canners and bottlers carefully control the yeast content of their products.

Beer should be stored where it is not exposed to heat or light. Most bottled and canned beer is pasteurized and, if stored below 70°F (21°C), will not spoil if used within 90 to 120 days of packaging.[7] Keg beer is more delicate since it is usually not pasteurized. Table wine may be attacked by yeasts and bacteria; the result is the formation of acetic acid. Alcoholic spirits and liqueurs contain so much alcohol they are virtually free from all forms of spoilage.

New packaging called bag-in-box is expanding the offerings of carbonated soft drinks in food service operations. This packaging system consists of a strong, flexible bag with a dispensing spout inside a rigid container. This system would replace the need to store the heavy, reusable metal tanks currently used by most operations.

Summary

Food spoilage and food contamination are intimately related in that they are caused largely by the action of bacteria and molds. One major difference separates the pathogens from the spoilage organisms. Pathogens, which cause foodborne disease, are often undetectable until after the food products are consumed; whereas spoilage organisms, which are not responsible for foodborne disease outbreaks, are usually readily detectable by sight and smell.

Many food preservation techniques can lengthen the lag phase of bacterial growth. Food products are preserved by techniques that fall into five categories: high temperatures, low temperatures, dehydration, chemical preservatives, and irradiation. Each preservation process has its own advantages in food processing.

Foods from animal sources spoil readily through the action of spoilage bacteria and molds. These potentially hazardous foods also harbor a variety of pathogenic microorganisms. Foods from plant sources can be attacked by spoilage bacteria, though mold spoilage is more frequent.

Recommended storage temperatures, times, and relative humidities for various food types presented in the chapter show how food service operations can minimize food contamination and spoilage. A reduction in food waste alone can have a positive impact on a hospitality operation's bottom line.

Endnotes

1. Ken Rankin, "Consumers Concerned Over Hazards in Nation's Food Supply," *Nation's Restaurant News,* August 31, 1987, p. 43.

2. Rankin.

3. Kathleen A. Meister, *Irradiated Foods,* Summit, N.J.: American Council of Science and Health, July 1985.

4. Rankin.

5. "Vegetable Consumption Up Since '70s," *Nation's Restaurant News,* March 9, 1987, p. 48.

6. "USDA Study Indicates Vegetable Consumption Is Up," *Nation's Restaurant News,* January 27, 1986, p. 40.

7. Lendal H. Kotschevar and Mary L. Tanke, *Managing Bar and Beverage Operations* (East Lansing, Mich.: Educational Institute of the American Hotel & Motel Association, 1991), pp. 238–239.

Key Terms

aerobic spoilage • anaerobic glycolysis • anaerobic spoilage • aseptic canning • autolysis • blanching • dehydration • enzyme • high temperature-short time (HTST) pasteurization • homogenization • non-perishable • partial hydrogenation • pasteurization • perishable • putrefaction • reconstitute • semi-perishable • *sous vide* • sterilization

Discussion Questions

1. What are the common causes of food spoilage in a food establishment?

2. How do perishable, semi-perishable, and non-perishable food products differ? Suggest examples of each type.

3. What are the four objectives of food preservation?

4. Low-temperature food preservation comprises what three types of storage?

5. What thawing procedures are acceptable for a food establishment?

6. What are the two methods of high-temperature food preservation?

7. Why is dehydration an effective method of food preservation? What are the four methods of dehydration?

8. What are some common chemical food preservatives and how are they used?

9. How would you describe the advantages of food preservation by irradiation in relation to consumer concerns about the effects of irradiation on food products?

10. In the categories of foods from animal sources and foods from plant sources, what preservation methods are unique to each category?

Case Study

You are the executive chef and food production manager of an independent restaurant in the Midwest. This restaurant now features fresh fish and shellfish, since guest demand has risen for these menu items in recent years. In fact, you have seen a dramatic increase in guest preferences for fresh food in your restaurant—not only for fish and shellfish but also for fruits and vegetables.

It is Monday morning and you are preparing your preliminary orders for your suppliers for the week. As you enter the walk-in cooler, you meet one of your cooks, who says, "Chef, there is a pan of fresh whitefish that looks and smells spoiled in here." You check it out and verify that the cook is right. The cook tells you that this has happened about three other times in the past two months. He says that you should consider not ordering whitefish from this supplier, since the quality is not up to your operation's standards. You note the supplier and leave the walk-in.

You decide to check the reasons for food spoilage, take steps to eliminate them, and develop an action plan. You begin by checking your purchase specifications for fresh whitefish. After reviewing the specifications in detail, you monitor the receiving of products on the loading dock. Since it is Monday morning, several deliveries have arrived. You notice that there are a number of products sitting on the dock, including fresh fish and shellfish, frozen products, and canned goods.

You ask the receiver if this is normal practice and she tells you, "When we are busy here like we are this morning, I have no choice. I try to store these items as soon as possible, but I can't do it all at the same time." As you leave the receiving area, you notice that some of the containers and cases of products appear to be damaged even though they were just received.

Next, you return to the walk-in where the fish and shellfish are stored. You see fresh fish stored in cold water in large hotel pans. Some of the cases of fish are stored on the floor. Most of the products are covered with damp cloths, but some are uncovered. As you check a pan of fish, you note that the product temperature is 38°F (3°C). You notice that the temperature reading on the built-in thermometer for the walk-in is 45°F (7°C).

As you are walking back to your office, you notice several sheet pans of shrimp-in-the-shell on a counter top in the kitchen. You ask one of the cooks nearby and she says, "We have a party tonight and we're thawing the shrimp so we can prepare it this afternoon." You return to your office, sit down, and try to formulate a solution to your food spoilage problem.

Test Your Understanding

1. What are the six causes of food spoilage in a food service operation?
2. Describe the characteristics of fish and shellfish, including the pathogenic and spoilage microorganisms.
3. Outline a plan to minimize food spoilage of fresh fish and shellfish during receiving.
4. What recommendations do you have to maintain the quality levels and safety of the fish and shellfish during storing?
5. Describe some safe methods for thawing frozen fish and shellfish.

References

Alva, Marilyn. "Operators: Sulfite Ban Should Ease Consumer Worries." *Nation's Restaurant News,* August 11, 1986, p. 3.

Backas, Nancy. "Consumers Question Use of Pesticides." *Restaurants & Institutions,* June 12, 1989, pp. 22-23.

Baird, Patricia. "Using Eggs Safely." *Restaurant Business,* April 10, 1989, pp. 82, 84-85.

Banwart, George J. *Basic Food Microbiology,* abridged ed. New York: Van Nostrand, 1981.

Boyle, Kathy. "Hydroponics—The Wave of the Future?" *Restaurants USA,* September 1986, pp. 16-19.

"Canned Foods Lose to Frozen Goods in 1987." *Nation's Restaurant News,* March 21, 1988, p. 30.

Cichy, R. F., and J. Kosec. "Variety, Versatility, Economy—Eggscetera . . ." *Cooking for Profit,* November 15, 1983, pp. 10-13.

"Cultivated Fish: More Chefs Using Alternative to Fisherman's Catch." *Nation's Restaurant News,* May 12, 1986, p. 10.

D'Ambrosio, Elizabeth. "Seafood Inspection a Must." *Restaurant Business,* April 10, 1988, p. 104.

Dawson, L. E., J. R. Chipley, F. E. Cunningham, and A. A. Kraft. "Incidence and Control of Microorganisms on Poultry Products." *North Central Regional Research Publication No. 260,* November 1979, pp. 3-36.

Denny, C. B. "Thermophilic Organisms Involved in Food Spoilage: Introduction." *Journal of Food Protection,* February 1981, pp. 144-145.

Durocher, Joseph F. "The Cold Truth." *Restaurant Business,* November 20, 1987, pp. 188, 190.

Evans, Deane. "Petition Urges Labeling of Radiation-Treated Food." *Nation's Restaurant News,* March 10, 1986, p. 33.

———. "*Sous Vide* Safe? Yes, Concedes FDA, If It's Done Carefully." *Nation's Restaurant News,* July 11, 1988, pp. 1, 114.

———. "USDA Develops New Shelf-Life Test." *Nation's Restaurant News,* February 24, 1986, p. 50.

———. "USDA: Food Irradiation Benefits Out-Weigh Problems." *Nation's Restaurant News,* August 11, 1986, p. 154.

"FDA Bans Sulfites in Fruits, Vegetables." *Restaurants USA,* August 1986, p. 7.

"FDA Spares Food Service from Irradiation Ruling." *Nation's Restaurant News,* February 6, 1989, p. 2.

Fennema, O.R., ed. *Principles of Food Science Part II—Physical Principles of Food Preservation.* New York: Dekker, 1975.

Food and Drug Administration, Center for Food Safety and Applied Nutrition, Retail Food Protection Branch. *Interpretation: Food Preparation—Raw, Marinated, or Partially Cooked Fishery Products,* August 21, 1987.

———. *Interpretation: Food Suppliers—Sulfiting Agents on Food in Retail Food Establishments,* August 13, 1986.

Food and Drug Administration, Public Health Service, U.S. Department of Health, Education, and Welfare. 1993 *Food Code.*

Food and Drug Administration and United States Department of Agriculture. "Safe Handling of Eggs in Quantity." *Food Service Institutions Bulletin,* September 1988.

Frazier, W. C., and D. C. Westhoff. *Food Microbiology,* 3d ed. New York: McGraw-Hill, 1978.

Frumkin, Paul. "FDA Bans On-Premises *Sous Vide.*" *Nation's Restaurant News,* February 15, 1988, pp. 1, 98.

"The Gamma Ray Gourmet." *INC.,* August 1983, p. 23.

Gordon, Stephanie, and Denise Roach. "New Limits for Sulfite Use Proposed." *Restaurants USA,* February 1989, p. 7.

Gotschall, Beth. "FDA Modifies Ruling on Retail Vacuum Packing." *Restaurants & Institutions,* April 17, 1989, pp. 22–23.

"Health Group: Irradiation Is Food Roulette." *Nation's Restaurant News,* September 8, 1986, p. 55.

Jay, J. M. *Modern Food Microbiology,* 2d ed. New York: Van Nostrand, 1978.

Kaufman, O. W. "Microbiology in Food Processing." *Dairy and Food Sanitation,* January 1982, pp. 18–19.

Levine, Donna. "The Food Safety Challenge." *Restaurant Business,* December 10, 1987, pp. 92–94, 96.

Longree, Karla. *Quantity Food Sanitation,* 2d ed. New York: Wiley-Interscience, 1978.

McAuliffe, Kathleen, and Nancy Linnon. "Will Your Dinner Make You Sick?" *U.S. News & World Report,* November 16, 1987, p. 73.

Meister, Kathleen A. *Irradiated Foods.* Summit, N.J.: American Council of Science and Health, July 1985.

Mutkoski, S. A., and M. L. Schurer. *Meat and Fish Management.* North Scituate, Mass.: Breton, 1981.

"New Packaging Could Expand Soft-Drink Offerings." *Nation's Restaurant News,* March 24, 1986, p. 15.

Ockerman, H. W. *Source Book for Food Scientists.* Westport, Conn.: AVI, 1978.

"Proposed Sulfite Ban Irks Operators." *Nation's Restaurant News,* January 25, 1988, p. 25.

Ramirez, Anthony. "In Hot Pursuit of High-Tech Food." *Fortune,* December 23, 1985, pp. 85, 86, 90, 94.

Rankin, Ken. "Consumers Concerned Over Hazards in Nation's Food Supply." *Nation's Restaurant News,* August 31, 1987, p. 43.

Richter, R. "Microbiological Problems in Dairy Foods in the 1980's." *Journal of Food Protection,* June 1981, pp. 471–475.

"Rule: Suppliers Allowed to Restore Color to Fresh Pork." *Nation's Restaurant News,* January 30, 1989, p. 14.

Schwarz, Thomas. "*Sous Vide* Guidelines." *Restaurant Business,* April 10, 1988, pp. 94, 96, 97.

Shapiro, Laura. "Warning! Your Food, Nutritious and Delicious, May Be Hazardous to Your Health." *Newsweek,* March 27, 1989, pp. 16–20, 22–25.

Smith, J. L., and S. A. Palumbo. "Microorganisms as Food Additives." *Journal of Food Protection,* December 1981, pp. 936–955.

Sofos, J. N., F. F. Busta, and C. E. Allen. "Botulism Control by Nitrite and Sorbate in Cured Meats: A Review." *Journal of Food Protection,* September 1979, pp. 739–770.

"Sulfite Labeling to Appear On Alcoholic Beverages." *Nation's Restaurant News,* October 27, 1986, p. 90.

Tiwari, N. P., and V. W. Kadis. "Microbiological Quality of Some Delicatessen Meat Products." *Journal of Food Protection,* November 1981.

"USDA Approves Additives to Maintain Pork's Color." *Nation's Restaurant News,* January 16, 1989, p. 2.

"USDA Recalls Tainted Canned Ham." *Nation's Restaurant News,* February 24, 1986, p. 59.

"USDA Study Indicates Vegetable Consumption Is Up." *Nation's Restaurant News,* January 27, 1986, p. 40.

"USDA To Permit Two Alternative Procedures for Processing Bacon." *Nation's Restaurant News,* July 28, 1986, p. 30.

"Vegetable Consumption Up Since '70s." *Nation's Restaurant News,* March 9, 1987, p. 48.

REVIEW QUIZ

When you feel you have covered all of the material in this chapter, answer these questions. Choose the *best* answer. Check your answers with the correct ones found on the Review Quiz Answer Key at the end of this book.

1. Most food spoilage occurs when foods are at the _____ control point.

    a. receiving
    b. storing
    c. preparing
    d. holding

2. Non-perishable food items are likely to spoil if:

    a. they are not refrigerated.
    b. they have not been subject to processing or preservation techniques.
    c. they are stored improperly.
    d. all of the above

3. Which of the following is an example of a semi-perishable food item?

    a. shellfish
    b. cucumbers
    c. lettuce
    d. none of the above

4. Which of the following represents an advantage of freezer storage?

    a. It destroys almost all spores.
    b. It reduces the a_w of food products.
    c. Reduction in food quality is minimal.
    d. all of the above

5. *Sous vide* is the process of:

    a. packaging cooked food items with a specific level of moisture content in vacuum-sealed pouches, then quick-freezing them.
    b. cooking food items under controlled conditions, vacuum-sealing the warm food in plastic pouches, then chilling them quickly.
    c. cooking vacuum-sealed pouches of food under controlled conditions then chilling them immediately.
    d. vacuum-sealing pouches of blanched fruits or vegetables, then slow-freezing them under controlled conditions.

6. Microwave thawing is acceptable when:

    a. it is part of the cooking process.
    b. the thawed food will be cooked immediately.
    c. either a or b
    d. neither a nor b

7. Stiffening of an animal's muscles after slaughter is called:

    a. reversion.
    b. rigor mortis.
    c. anaerobic glycolysis.
    d. putrefaction.

8. An ammonia-like odor in fish generally means the fish have been:

    a. preserved with organic acids.
    b. quick-frozen in liquid nitrogen.
    c. contaminated with *Pseudomonas spp.* or *Proteus spp.*
    d. harvested in contaminated waters.

9. Mold growth can be controlled in baked products by:

    a. fast cooling and prompt wrapping.
    b. microwave dehydration.
    c. the addition of acid prior to baking.
    d. decreasing water content and freezing.

10. In general, a can of food is safe if the top and bottom:

    a. are slightly bulged but cannot be pushed back with finger pressure.
    b. are flat when the can is cold and only slightly bulged when the can is warm.
    c. are flat when the can is warm.
    d. none of the above

Chapter Outline

Learning Objectives

1. Describe the relationship between menu planning and inventory, and note the effects of rationalization, diversification, and convenience foods. (pp. 169–170)

2. Identify important staff member considerations at the menu planning control point. (pp. 170–171)

3. Identify important equipment and facilities considerations at the menu planning control point. (pp. 171–174)

4. Identify factors that influence menu changes. (p. 174)

5. Identify factors that influence purchasing needs, and list the functions of the purchasing control point. (pp. 177–178)

6. Explain the relationship between purchasing and inventory. (pp. 178–183)

7. Outline the skills of a successful buyer, including what one should know about dealing with suppliers. (pp. 184–187)

8. Explain how a buyer can reduce risks at the purchasing control point. (p. 197)

5

The Menu Planning and Purchasing Control Points

The Menu Planning Control Point

Menu planning is the first control point in the food service system. In many respects, the menu is the mission statement for a food establishment. It defines the operation's concept and communicates that concept to guests. The menu attempts to provide what guests expect from their overall hospitality experience. It also serves as a plan for the entire food service system. The success of menu planning determines the success of the other basic operating activities.

When a menu is presented to a guest, a sales transaction begins. If properly designed, the menu can stimulate sales and increase the guest check average. The menu also presents an image of the establishment. Therefore, the appearance of the menu should be in harmony with the image the food establishment wants to project. The image may be elegant, businesslike, fun, ethnic, or trendy, depending on the target markets. The physical condition of the menu is also important. Dirty, worn, out-of-date, or unattractive menus indicate management's lack of concern for the establishment's image. Because they create a negative first impression, such menus should be discarded. Someone should be responsible for checking the condition of each menu before each meal period begins.

Guests are influenced by visual cues provided by the menu, such as design and layout, artwork, and type styles. As with other communication tools, the way the information is conveyed is as important as the information itself. For example, fast-food restaurants offer a limited number of menu items but sell these items in large quantities. Since guests are served at a common sales counter, separate menus are not needed. Most guests are familiar with the standardized menu offerings, so long, elaborate descriptions are unnecessary; they would only slow down the guests' decision-making process. Fast-food restaurants simply post the names and prices of their products near the sales counter. Enlarged color photographs of menu items show their color and texture and thus may contribute to increased sales. (However, it is important that the items served look like the pictured items.) The overall effect is to convey simplicity, speed, and a limited selection of products prepared the same way at every unit.

On the other hand, a specialty restaurant catering to wealthy, sophisticated guests would have an altogether different menu. To project an image of elegance, such a restaurant might have a menu as large as a book, with detailed descriptions of a wide range of food products. This type of menu offers guests a feeling of endless possibilities. Since the establishment's guests probably seek a leisurely and pleasurable dining experience, the time it takes them to peruse a large menu is no problem.

Another element distinguishes the menu of an elegant restaurant from that of a fast-food restaurant: prices. Prices are sometimes omitted from extensive menus due to seasonal fluctuations in the cost of some items. In such cases, the management assumes either that money is no object or that, if it is, guests will inquire about current prices. When setting menu prices, it is important to remember that today's sophisticated guest is searching for the best price-value relationship. If an operation's prices far exceed the perceived value of its menu items, guests are unlikely to return.

To draw attention to daily specials and highlight signature items, some restaurants box these items on the menu. Another way to increase sales of featured items is to write them on an illuminated board near the entrance. Some restaurants specializing in fresh seafood use a chalkboard to list the flight arrival times of the jet-fresh catch of the day. While this approach sacrifices a degree of elegance, it provides convincing evidence of the freshness and variety of the operation's offerings.

Generally, dynamic menus are preferable to static menus. However, menu variability depends on the seasonal availability of raw ingredients, the number and kinds of courses offered, the potential for using leftovers and local ingredients, the operation's image, and the demands of its target markets. In many respects, the menu is never complete; menu planning is an ongoing process.

Menu Trends

In recent years, several menu trends have had a dramatic impact on the menu planning control points of all food service operations. These trends are the result of changing consumer preferences throughout the country. Today's consumers are increasingly demanding smaller portions, regional cuisine, lighter, healthier foods, and ethnic and exotic foods.

Smaller Portions. Guests are interested in sampling a variety of foods in smaller portions, as part of the more casual approach to dining that emerged in the 1980s. (Spanish *tapas* and Oriental *dim sum* are examples of this concept.) This approach calls for mini-meals that can be shared and offers guests a great deal of flexibility. Some restaurants feature expanded appetizer and finger food selections, half portions, and a variety of smaller desserts in response to this trend. Known variously as "grazing" or "modular cuisine," interchangeable courses appeal to today's guest.

However, this menu strategy has its disadvantages. It can overwork a kitchen at peak times, slow table turnover since it takes longer to serve guests, and raise labor costs because of the small, hand-prepared food items and elaborate plate presentations. Food handling may increase and present more potential for contamination and loss of temperature control.

Regional Cuisine. Regional foods include Cajun cuisine with its blackened entrées, Southwestern cuisine with its liberal use of chiles, and California cuisine with its fresh vegetables and goat cheese. Nostalgic cuisine, also known as "comfort food," features foods such as pot roast, meat loaf, and mashed potatoes with real lumps, as well as grilled burgers and blue plate specials. Regional cuisine enables food service operations to feature fresh, high-quality local produce that often costs less than imported items. As the number of fresh items on the menu increases, procedures at the various control points change.

Lighter, Healthier Foods. Perhaps no other trend has so dramatically affected menu planning as the consumer demand for lighter, fresher, more healthful food choices. Americans are ordering smaller portions of fresh and light food, such as meatless entrées and grilled rather than fried items. Salads, pasta, chicken, and some seafood are gaining popularity, as are new ways to offer them: for example, Northern Italian cuisine is a lighter version of

America's favorite ethnic food. Appetizing foods with reduced sodium, cholesterol, fat, and calories are much in demand. Some operators present nutritional information on their menus, and some use the American Heart Association symbol to highlight items with controlled fat and cholesterol. Others emphasize fresh, seasonal, wholesome food choices. Fresh menu items call for adjustments in purchasing frequencies, receiving schedules, storage procedures, and production techniques. As preparation and cooking methods change, the skill levels of staff members and managers must also change.

Ethnic and Exotic Foods. Conventional ethnic cuisines such as Italian, Mexican, and Asian come under this heading. Food products with exotic flavors or combinations, such as Cajun, sweet and sour, and cold and spicy, are also included. Such items, though popular, should be added to a menu with care. Caution must be exercised whenever ingredients or preparation and cooking processes are altered and staff members are not familiar with them. Adding new menu items can result in sanitation and quality problems if staff members are not properly trained.

Other menu trends will likely surface. While many of the trends discussed here affect menu planning only in certain segments of the food service industry, some influence the entire industry. For example, lighter, healthier foods are being added to institutional, table service, and fast-food restaurant menus. In all segments, food service operators are incorporating some menu trends in order to put more value on the guest's plate.

Along with these menu trends, there are other factors to consider when planning a menu. These factors include the resources available to a manager at this and all of the control points. These resources are inventory, people, equipment, and facilities.

Menu Planning and Inventory

Inventory is the total supply of items an operation has in stock. The menu helps create demand for the finished food products prepared from the items in inventory. The guest's order depletes the inventory on hand. The operation must periodically replenish the inventory if it is to continue offering the items guests are buying. It is important to keep detailed records on the relative popularity of every menu item. This information is useful at the purchasing control point, the next step of the food service system (discussed in the second half of this chapter).

The menu directly affects the establishment's purchasing, receiving, and storage requirements. The size of storage areas needed for raw ingredients and finished menu items depends on the menu. One of the primary advantages of a limited menu is that it reduces storage area requirements.

In the past, food service managers attempted to diversify their menus, offering a wide variety of items. Since most items were made on-site, the number and variety of raw ingredients needed increased significantly with each new item. Now, however, there is a trend toward **rationalization** of menu items: the creation of a simplified, balanced menu for the sake of operational efficiency and guest satisfaction. Although this strategy frequently results in a limited menu, the operation can offer several menu items which use the same raw ingredients. The objective of this **cross-utilization** is to prepare and serve as many menu items as possible with a limited number of raw ingredients. Planning the menu to ensure a balance of menu selections in each category helps streamline the purchasing, receiving, and storing functions.

The decision of whether or not to diversify the menu is driven to a great extent by guest demands. Guests who dine out frequently are looking for diversity in menu choices. Some food service operators reason that, due to increased competition, they must diversify in order to build guest loyalty and repeat business, expand business into new meal periods, and draw on a wider guest base. However, while a constantly changing menu offers variety, it can cause confusion in the operation and result in lowered sanitation and quality standards. Alternatives to extensive diversification include highlighting items on the existing menu and adding a few daily specials.

Proponents of menu rationalization say that a food establishment should discover what it does best and continually refine it. Menu diversification requires additional staff training and additional time for taking orders and answering guest questions. Perhaps the best strategy is to create a balanced menu by choosing items from a limited inventory—in other words, create a rational, consolidated menu that maximizes cross-utilization.

The proliferation of high-quality **convenience foods** has made it easier for food service operations to offer new items without buying additional raw ingredients or elaborate equipment. High-quality convenience products can be purchased in semi- or fully-prepared forms. These products reduce in-house labor requirements. Of course, convenience food products usually have a higher AP (as purchased) price than the raw ingredients from which they are made.

It is always best to base initial menu plans on the needs and expectations of the target markets. Several other factors may influence the selection of menu items as well. Among these factors are recommended storage conditions; staff member skill levels; product availability and seasonality; the stability of quality and price levels; and the operation's ability to purchase, prepare, and serve the menu item in a safe and sanitary way.

Menu Planning and People

An operation's staff members are important to the success of its menu. Before management begins menu planning, the skill levels of production and service staff must be assessed. It may be helpful to consider the production staff and service staff separately, although their functions are closely related in practice.

The production staff produces menu items within the confines of the kitchen. In planning the operation's menu, the objective is to avoid overloading any one person or work station. A well-planned menu features items that the operation's kitchen staff can consistently produce while maintaining the operation's quality, cost, and sanitation standards.

Management should be realistic in determining what can be accomplished with the existing staff. For example, consider a kitchen in a metropolitan hotel where every menu item is prepared from scratch. If all meats are received in the wholesale-cut form (which is less expensive than the retail- or portion-cut form), the staff has to do the retail butchering. If the production staff is not properly trained in butchering wholesale cuts into retail cuts of meat, a lot of time and money will be wasted, and unnecessary sanitation hazards will abound. Rather than saving the business money, this poorly conceived arrangement increases the food cost, adds to the labor cost, and destroys the quality control system. Such problems can be avoided by organizing the menu planning function with personnel limitations in mind.

The service staff transfers the menu items from the production staff to the guests. In order to properly serve guests, servers should be ready to answer their questions. For example, servers should know what items are on the menu, the portion sizes offered, how the items are prepared, and the prices. Even if the menu contains all of this information, a server can provide a personal touch by answering guests' questions directly. Servers should also know the meanings of all terms used on the menu so they can explain them to any guests who are puzzled. This is particularly true if the menu includes ethnic foods, since these items may be unfamiliar to the average guest.

Again, staff training is critical. In addition to thoroughly training new servers, some managers call a five- to ten-minute **line-up meeting** with service staff members before each meal period. These brief meetings are informal training sessions. They give the chef and the manager an opportunity to explain daily specials, and they give the servers an opportunity to sample portions of new menu items and to ask questions.

Like the skill levels of production staff, the skills of service staff must be considered in menu planning. This is particularly true if management is considering menu items to be prepared in the dining room, such as tossed salads and flambéed desserts. Whether an operation uses tableside preparation methods depends, in part, on the image it seeks. Whatever style of service an operation offers, the service staff must be trained in the skills dictated by the menu.

Suppliers must also be considered when planning a menu. Although suppliers are not, strictly speaking, under the manager's control, they can contribute to the success of the business. Particularly at the menu planning control point, their input and suggestions can help make the business more profitable while enhancing the guest's satisfaction. For example, suppliers can offer preparation and merchandising suggestions for various menu items. Excellent food service operations use their suppliers as sources of market trend information, new promotion ideas, and informal competitive analyses.

Menu Planning and Equipment

Any food service operation must make a large investment in equipment before it can open for business. Naturally, the amount and type of production and service equipment owned by the business determines what items it can produce and place on the menu. It is imperative to select equipment based on capacity, skill levels of staff members, energy and maintenance costs, and initial purchase price. Equipment should be constructed according to nationally recognized sanitation standards and/or be listed by accredited testing and listing organizations such as the National Sanitation Foundation and Underwriters Laboratories. But above all, it is critical that equipment be easy to clean and sanitize.

The FDA states:

Equipment.

(a) **"Equipment"** means an article that is used in the operation of a food establishment such as a freezer, grinder, hood, ice maker, meat block, mixer, oven, reach-in refrigerator, scale, sink, slicer, stove, table, temperature measuring device for ambient air, vending machine, or warewashing machine.

(b) *"Equipment" does not include items used for handling or storing large quantities of packaged foods that are received from a supplier in a cased or overwrapped lot, such as hand trucks, forklifts, dollies, pallets, racks, and skids.*

Easily Cleanable.

(a) **"Easily cleanable"** means a characteristic of a surface that:

(i)   Allows effective removal of soil by normal cleaning methods;

(ii)   Is dependent on the material, design, construction, and installation of the surface; and

(iii)   Varies with the likelihood of the surface's role in introducing pathogenic or toxigenic agents or other contaminants into food based on the surface's approved placement, purpose, and use.

(b)   **"Easily cleanable"** includes a tiered application of the criteria that qualify the surface as easily cleanable as specified in Subparagraph (a) of this definition to different situations in which varying degrees of cleanability are required such as:

(i)   The appropriateness of stainless steel for a food preparation surface as opposed to the lack of need for stainless steel to be used for floors or for tables used for consumer dining; or

(ii)   The need for a different degree of cleanability for a utilitarian attachment or accessory in the kitchen as opposed to a decorative attachment or accessory in the consumer dining area.

Source: FDA 1993 *Food Code.*

Adding a new menu item may require purchasing new production equipment. Such purchases should not be made without an analysis of the flow of products and people through the work area. This analysis helps management anticipate where cross-traffic may create safety and sanitation hazards. Many operations use equipment on wheels or casters which can be moved easily when necessary. In addition to allowing for adjustments to the product and staff traffic patterns, this mobility facilitates cleaning. Before a new menu item is added, the proper equipment should be available to reduce sanitation hazards. For example, if the proposed menu change involves adding a soup bar to the dining room, the kitchen must have adequate steam-table, steam-jacketed kettle, or range equipment to reach and maintain safe product temperatures during preparing and cooking.

A change in menu may also have implications for the operation's service equipment. Again, the sanitation hazards must be considered beforehand. In the case of the soup bar, for example, the dining room should be equipped with suitable hot-holding equipment before these new items are added to the menu.

A dramatically modified menu can have a devastating effect on the system if proper equipment is not available. Consider what might happen if the owner of a bar that serves a wide selection of drinks and cold snack foods decides to add hot barbecued meatballs to the snack food menu. She realizes that equipment to produce and hold the product is necessary; however, she fails to realize the significance of the serving containers. She chooses reusable dishes, thinking that these will be less expensive in the long run than disposable containers. Making a hasty decision on cost alone, the owner neglects to consider the fact that if the meatballs are served in reusable containers, proper provisions must be made for washing, sanitizing, and storing the dishes. It is not acceptable to wash the sauce-laden meatball dishes in the bar's glass-washing equipment. In the end, she realizes that the addition of this new food item is an expensive endeavor.

The addition of banquet service to a traditional food service operation must also be carefully considered in light of the additional constraints banquets place on menu planning and equipment. For example, if a hotel is planning to serve a banquet for 800, all of the food items cannot be dished for all 800 guests immediately prior to service. Therefore, extra hot-holding and cold storage equipment is essential. The hotel must also limit its banquet menu to items which can safely withstand the extra handling and holding times involved.

Menu Planning and Facilities

The facilities, both indoor and outdoor, affect the image of a food establishment.

> The FDA states:
>
> **"Physical facilities"** means the structure and interior surfaces of a food establishment including accessories such as soap and towel dispensers and attachments such as light fixtures and heating or air conditioning system vents.

Source: FDA 1993 *Food Code.*

The layout and design of the facilities are also important considerations in menu planning, because they establish the physical limits within which food preparation and service take place. The facilities must be adequate for the purchasing, receiving, storing, issuing, preparing, cooking, holding, and serving of every item on the menu. Thus, a major change in the menu may necessitate remodeling the physical facilities. By the same token, a change in facilities may force an operation to revise its menu. This mutual influence can be illustrated by the following examples.

Consider a country club food service operation in which 80% of the space is allocated to the dining room and 20% to the kitchen. Since the kitchen generally prepares menu items from scratch, the production facilities are often pushed to the limit. The kitchen facilities are almost always overtaxed during the summer, when there are more parties and special functions.

Suppose the country club manager decides to expand the dining and banquet facilities by adding a 90-seat patio service area with a clear glass roof. He is convinced that this area will appeal to guests planning parties and banquets because it offers a breathtaking view of the golf course. However, the manager has not considered the production capabilities of the kitchen; to increase the dining facilities without adding to the production area would be a critical error. Such a decision would likely result in lower productivity and morale among production staff. A corresponding reduction in guest satisfaction could be expected to follow.

Another hotel decides to add room service in an attempt to generate more revenue. Again, the size and layout of the facility have an impact on the success of the effort. For example, the kitchen might produce a beautiful and tasty eggs Benedict entrée for breakfast, but by the time room service delivers the order to the farthest wing of the hotel, the product is cold and unappealing. Room service menus must be limited to those items that can be successfully and safely delivered to the guest.

Yet another problem occurs when an overly ambitious hotel sales force convinces meeting planners that special entrées or desserts will add a touch a elegance to their banquets. These salespeople sometimes fail to consider the limitations of the hotel's production and service facilities. Likewise, an outdoor barbecue for 500 people in the hotel's gardens may sound like an exciting affair; but if the kitchen or service staff cannot deliver the products, the guests will not be satisfied.

In all of these examples, the unfortunate results could be prevented. An operation must design its menu around what the physical facilities can realistically handle. Menu planning is a complex process, but it can be successful when the establishment's resources are taken into consideration.

Changing the Menu

Because conditions change, a food service operation's menu must also change. Menu changes are influenced by both external and internal factors.

External factors include guest demands, economic factors, the competition, supply levels, and industry trends. Guest demands are perhaps the most important factor to consider in changing a menu. Management should first decide which potential markets it wants to attract with a modified menu. The proposed menu change should then be evaluated in light of its potential impact on the current markets.

Economic factors include the cost of ingredients and the potential profitability of new menu items. The competition's menu offerings can also influence menu decisions. For example, a hotel food service operation located next door to a restaurant offering the "best Chinese food in town" might elect not to serve Chinese cuisine. Supply levels affect the price and the quality and quantity of the proposed menu items. Supply levels are highly variable for some seasonal raw ingredients such as fresh fruits and vegetables. Industry trends are general observations about how the industry is responding to new demands. At present, the overall trend is to attempt to satisfy a more sophisticated, value-conscious guest.

Internal factors that may result in a proposed menu change are the facility's meal pattern, concept and theme, operational system, and menu mix. The typical meal pattern is breakfast, lunch, and dinner. Management must decide if existing meal periods should be continued or altered. The target markets' expectations directly influence this decision. Any menu change must also be compatible with the establishment's concept and theme; a restaurant that is known as the best steakhouse in the city may do itself a disservice by offering fewer steak selections in order to add fresh fish and shellfish to the menu. An establishment's image may also rule out certain foods which do not blend with its theme and decor.

Menu changes are also modified by the establishment's operational system. For example, a menu change may raise both food and labor costs to unacceptable levels. The production and service staff members may lack the necessary skills to produce and present the new menu item. If extensive new equipment is crucial to the successful production and service of a new item, the change may be too costly. Many operations deal with this factor by designing flexible kitchens with multi-purpose equipment. For example, a combination convection oven/steamer can bake, roast, and steam. Tilt skillets can be used for baking, braising, frying, griddling, or steaming.

An operation's existing menu has a certain overall combination or mix of items. This menu mix will be affected by any change in individual items. All of these factors should be evaluated before menu changes are finalized.

Truth-in-Menu Regulations

Due to rising consumerism in the United States, **truth-in-menu regulations** are an increasingly important menu planning consideration. Although such regulations exist primarily at the state and local levels, federal regulations are likely to be strengthened in the future. The FDA Food Code specifies that food shall be safe, unadulterated, and honestly presented.

The FDA states:

3-101.11   Safe, Unadulterated, and Honestly Presented.*

Food shall be safe, unadulterated, and, as specified under § 3-601.12, honestly presented.

3-601.12   Honestly Presented.

(A) Food shall be offered for human consumption in a way that does not mislead or misinform the consumer.

(B) Food or color additives, colored overwraps, or lights may not be used to misrepresent the true appearance, color, or quality of food.

Source: FDA 1993 *Food Code.*

According to truth-in-menu regulations, accurate descriptions of raw ingredients and finished menu items are essential. For example, the correct quality or grade of food products must be stated; care must be exercised when (USDA) grades are printed on the menu. A "choice top butt steak" implies that the meat is USDA Choice grade. It is also important that items billed as "fresh" have not been frozen, canned, or preserved in any way. A product's point of origin must also be represented accurately; for example, "fresh Lake Superior whitefish" should indeed be fresh whitefish from Lake Superior. A sample list of common points of origin is presented in Exhibit 5.1.

The size, weight, and portion advertised on the menu must also be accurate. A bowl of soup should contain more than a cup of soup. Descriptions like "extra tall" drinks or "extra large" salads can open the door to possible guest complaints. "All you can eat" implies that the guest is entitled to exactly that: as much as he or she can eat. For meat items, it is a generally accepted practice to list the precooked weight.

The preparation technique must be accurately described. If there are additional charges for extras (such as substitutions or coffee refills), such charges must be clearly stated on the menu. Any pictures of food products should be accurate. Dietary or nutritional claims, if used, must be precise. "Low calorie," for example, is vague because it implies that the product is lower in calories but does not specify what the product is being compared to. Servers' descriptions should also accurately portray the menu selections.

Truth-in-menu violations can be costly for a food service business. For example, one fast-food operation that advertised maple syrup and fresh orange juice on its breakfast menu had to pay $10,500 in fines and court costs because the syrup was not pure maple syrup and the orange juice was frozen.[1]

Another issue has been stirring controversy for over five years. Federal legislation is pending which calls for the disclosure of the ingredients and nutritional value of fast food. While the legislation is being promoted by the Center for Science in the Public Interest (CSPI), it has been denounced by the National Restaurant Association. Other groups have recommended that all types of food, wrapped and unwrapped, from all types of food establishments, carry such labels.

Some chains (for example, KFC and McDonald's) have developed descriptive brochures and pamphlets that provide nutritional information on their products. This information is available upon request; however, most participating chains report little guest interest. While such brochures may be useful and interesting to only a relatively small

Exhibit 5.1 Typical Representations of Point of Origin

Dairy Products
Danish Bleu Cheese
Domestic Cheese
Imported Swiss Cheese
Roquefort Cheese
Wisconsin Cheese

Fish and Shellfish
Cod, Icelandic (North Atlantic)
Crab
    Alaskan King Crab
    Florida Stone Crab
    North Atlantic Crab
    Snow Crab
Frog Legs
    Domestic Frog Legs
    Imported Frog Legs
    Louisiana Frog Legs
Lobster
    Australian Lobster
    Brazilian Lobster
    Maine Lobster
    South African Lobster
Oysters
    Blue Point Oysters
    Chesapeake Bay Oysters
    Olympia Oysters
Salmon
    Nova Scotia Salmon
    Puget Sound Sockeye Salmon
    Salmon Lox
Scallops
    Bay Scallops
    Sea Scallops

Scrod, Boston
Shrimp
    Bay Shrimp
    Gulf Shrimp
Trout
    Colorado Brook Trout
    Idaho Brook Trout
Whitefish, Lake Superior

Meats
Beef, Colorado
Ham
    Country Ham
    Danish Ham
    Imported Ham
    Smithfield Ham
    Virginia Style Ham
Pork, Iowa

Poultry
Long Island Duckling
Maryland Milk-Fed Chicken

Vegetables and Fruits
Orange Juice, Florida
Pineapples
    Hawaiian Pineapples
    Mexican Pineapples
Potatoes
    Idaho Potatoes
    Maine Potatoes

number, the information should be available to those who request it. Some people use this information to avoid allergenic foods; others simply like to know exactly what they are eating.

Some state and local governments are also promoting the disclosure of ingredients and nutritional information in food establishments, particularly fast-food operations. California and Texas have led the way in enacting such legislation. San Francisco adopted the first and most stringent ordinance, requiring ingredient disclosure as well as the caloric, fat (total, polyunsaturated, and saturated), carbohydrate, protein, cholesterol, sodium, vitamin, and mineral content of fast food. Even though the city ordinance expresses a preference for package labeling, it allows pamphlets, tray liners, fact sheets, and brochures. Failure to comply carries a maximum penalty of $500 per day.[2]

The food service industry argues that package labeling is too time-consuming and expensive because of the space it requires. For example, a pizza restaurant offering four sizes and twelve different toppings would need over 4,000 different package labels. The industry also questions the ability of a "typical customer" to analyze scientific data (for example, milligrams of sodium). The government and private interest groups (CSPI and others) argue that it is time to provide consumers with information that could help them improve their health. In addition, labeling would enable individuals who are allergic to certain foods to avoid them.

The San Francisco ordinance may blaze the trail for others to follow at the state and local levels. Whether you are for or against mandatory labeling of fast food or food in all restaurants, your guests will ultimately decide how important this information is to them. Be aware of their needs and expectations, and consider what might happen if you ignore them: they may choose to spend their money elsewhere.

Menu Planning and the SRM Program

Menu planning sets the direction for each of the other control points. Thus, the sanitation risk management (SRM) program begins with menu planning. Management must consider each menu item in light of possible sanitation hazards at every control point. Once potential hazards are identified, risks can be reduced. Several questions must be considered before the menu planning process is complete. Can the operation procure the necessary raw ingredients from safe, approved sources? Can the raw ingredients be received and stored easily? Is the production staff able to prepare the menu items efficiently and in a sanitary manner? Can the finished products be served in a safe and sanitary way? All of these factors are important in menu planning decisions.

The Purchasing Control Point

Once menu planning is completed, purchasing is the next step in the flow of basic operating activities. The menu determines what ingredients must be purchased and in what amounts. One of the major objectives of purchasing is to obtain the right quality and quantity of items at the right price from the right supplier. The goals are to maintain quality and value, strengthen the establishment's competitive position, and minimize the investment in inventory.

Purchasing is one of the most important control points for cost and quality controls. Most food service businesses spend 30 to 50% of their total sales revenues on product purchasing. Reducing purchasing costs can translate directly to the operation's bottom line. Failing to properly control food costs can have a more devastating effect than overspending in most other cost categories. It is not surprising that the primary concern of many operators is their food costs. Rising food costs often force management to reexamine the operation's purchasing needs.

In addition to the menu, several other factors dictate purchasing needs. The forecasted sales volume is an estimate of how much business a facility will have on a given day. This information, along with the operation's standard recipes, can be used to calculate the amounts of ingredients needed. Certain external factors also affect purchasing needs. The size and frequency of orders, for example, is affected by how much lead time the supplier requires before a delivery can be made. The facility's distance from the supplier may also affect quantities purchased. For example, a steakhouse located high in the mountains or in a rural area would probably receive less frequent deliveries than a steakhouse in a downtown metropolitan area. More frequent deliveries usually mean smaller orders, which results in less money tied up in inventory.

Of course, the quantities of food ordered and the money invested in inventory are not the only purchasing concerns. Quality and sanitation standards must also be considered

Exhibit 5.2 Overview of Purchasing Activities

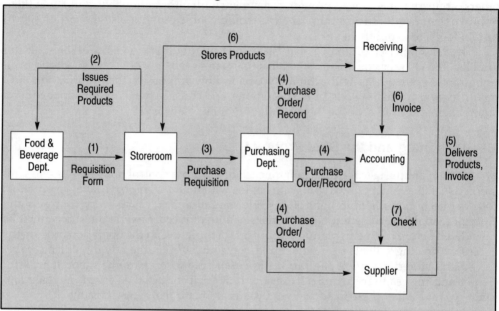

Source: Jack D. Ninemeier, *Planning and Control for Food and Beverage Operations*, 3d ed. (East Lansing, Mich.: Educational Institute of the American Hotel & Motel Association, 1991), p. 132.

at this control point. A low-quality or unsanitary product is never a bargain, no matter how inexpensive it is. It can unnecessarily increase the operation's risks.

The factors affecting purchasing needs are directly related to the functions of the purchasing control point. These purchasing functions are:

- Establishing and maintaining an adequate supply of food and non-food products

- Minimizing the operation's investment in inventory

- Maintaining the operation's quality, sanitation, and cost standards while reducing risks

- Maintaining the operation's competitive position

- Buying the product, not the deal

Each of these purchasing objectives will be discussed as it relates to the four resources under a manager's control.

Purchasing and Inventory

Many functions of the food service operation can be delayed or stopped entirely if the necessary quantity and quality of inventory is not available. As Exhibit 5.2 illustrates, the purchasing department plays a major role in the flow of products through the food service facility. The overall goal of purchasing is to obtain quality food and non-food items in the proper quantities at a reasonable price. To reach this goal, buyers have many tools at their disposal. The first tool is a set of standard purchase specifications.

Standard purchase specifications precisely define the quality, quantity, and other characteristics of the products an establishment buys. Standard purchase specifications are communication tools. They require management to define exactly what is needed; thus they eliminate supplier confusion and facilitate the bidding process. A sample standard purchase specification format is presented in Exhibit 5.3. Note that the form calls for precise details in describing the product. These specifications can be developed by a management team consisting of the food and beverage director, the executive chef, the buyer, and other users. Although it might take this team some time to develop standard purchase specifications for all products normally purchased by the operation, the results are well worth the investment of time. Once they are developed, the specifications can be used over and over again and are especially useful for new suppliers, menu changes, and quality control.

The standard purchase specification defines quality with government grades or brand names. For example, the "fancy" or "A" government grade indicates a certain quality level in fruits and vegetables. Likewise, the quality of Heinz tomato ketchup, Swift's Premium ham, and Minor's beef base are implied by their brand names. Quantity may be indicated as the number of units per container, box, or case, and by the size of standardized containers (for example, #10 cans). Other descriptions complete the standard purchase specification, telling the supplier exactly what kind of product is desired.

Standard purchase specifications are only useful if they accurately reflect the particular needs of the operation. Although several specification manuals such as *The Meat Buyer's Guide* and *NIFDA Canned Foods Manual* are available, the general specifications in these references should be modified as necessary. In-house kitchen or performance tests can be used to alter general specifications to fit the establishment's needs. Market conditions which affect availability may also modify an operation's specifications. Ultimately, standard purchase specifications for each product must be based on the intended use of the product.

A second tool available to buyers is the **food sample data sheet** (see Exhibit 5.4). This form helps standardize the evaluations of products that an operation is considering for purchase. It can be used to record purchasing, storing, preparing, and serving information about such products. Note that this sheet can also be used to request nutritional and ingredient analysis information. The food sample data sheet makes product selection more objective and less likely to be the result of a buyer's personal preferences.

Once standard purchase specifications are developed and suppliers are selected, a third tool—the **purchase order**—assists in maintaining purchasing control. The purchase order contains the details of an order placed with a supplier. This standard form is filled in by the operation's buyer and sent to the supplier. A copy of the purchase order is retained to facilitate in-house recordkeeping. A sample purchase order is displayed in Exhibit 5.5.

Federal and state agencies provide guidelines for obtaining food supplies. These guidelines serve to prevent both food spoilage and contamination. Note that the federal code focuses on potentially hazardous foods, although all food intended for human consumption is covered.

The FDA states:

3-201.11   Compliance with Food Law.*

(A) Food shall be obtained from sources that comply with law.

Exhibit 5.3 Purchase Specification Format

(name of food and beverage operation)

1. Product name: _____

2. Product used for:

> Clearly indicate product use (such as olive garnish for beverage, hamburger patty for grill frying for sandwich, etc.)

3. Product general description:

> Provide general quality information about desired product. For example, "iceberg lettuce; heads to be green, firm without spoilage, excessive dirt or damage. No more than 10 outer leaves; packed 24 heads per case."

4. Detailed description:

> Purchaser should state other factors which help to clearly identify desired product. Examples of specific factors, which vary by product being described, may include:
>
> | | | |
> |---|---|---|
> | • Geographic origin | • Product size | • Medium of pack |
> | • Variety | • Portion size | • Specific gravity |
> | • Type | • Brand name | • Container size |
> | • Style | • Density | • Edible yield, trim |
> | • Grade | | |

5. Product test procedures:

> Test procedures occur at time product is received and as/after product is prepared/used. Thus, for example, products to be at a refrigerated temperature upon delivery can be tested with a thermometer. Portion-cut meat patties can be randomly weighed. Lettuce packed 24 heads per case can be counted.

6. Special instructions and requirements:

> Any additional information needed to clearly indicate quality expectations can be included here. Examples include bidding procedures, if applicable, labeling and/or packaging requirements and special delivery and service requirements.

Source: Jack D. Ninemeier, *Planning and Control for Food and Beverage Operations*, 3d ed. (East Lansing, Mich.: Educational Institute of the American Hotel & Motel Association, 1991), p. 136.

Exhibit 5.4 Food Sample Data Sheet

1. Product: _____

2. Brand Name: _____

3. Presented By: _____ Date: _____

4. Varieties Available: _____

5. Shelf Life: (Frozen) _____ (Thawed, Refrigerated, Dry) _____

6. Preparation and Sanitation Considerations: _____

_____

_____

_____

7. Menu Suggestions: _____

8. Merchandising Aids Available (Poster, Table Tents, etc.): _____

9. Case Size (Number of Portions): _____

10. Portion Size: _____

11. Distributed By: _____

12. Minimum Order: _____

13. Any Additional Ordering Information: _____

_____

14. Lead Time: _____

15. Approximate Price Per Serving: _____

NOTE: Were the following information sheets received with products?

   a. Nutritional and Ingredient Analysis: Yes _____ No _____

   b. Specification Sheet: Yes _____ No _____

(B) Food prepared in a private home may not be used or offered for human consumption in a food establishment.

(C) Packaged food shall be labeled as specified in law.

(D) Fish, other than molluscan shellfish, that are intended for consumption in their raw form and allowed as specified under Subparagraph 3-401.11(B)(1) shall be obtained from a supplier that freezes the fish as specified under § 3-402.11; or shall be frozen on the premises as specified under § 3-402.11 and records shall be retained as specified under § 3-402.12.

Exhibit 5.5 Purchase Order

Purchase Order
Number: _____

Order Date: _____

Payment Terms: _____

From/

To: _____
(supplier)

Ship to: _____
(name of food service operation)

_____
(address)

_____

_____
(address)

Delivery Date: _____

Please Ship:

Quantity Ordered	Description	✓	Units Shipped	Unit Cost	Total Cost

Total Cost _____

Important: This Purchase Order expressly limits acceptance to the terms and conditions stated above, noted on the reverse side hereof, and any additional terms and conditions affixed hereto or otherwise referenced. Any additional terms and conditions proposed by seller are objected to and rejected.

_____
(Authorized Signature)

Source: Jack D. Ninemeier, *Planning and Control for Food and Beverage Operations*, 3d ed. (East Lansing, Mich.: Educational Institute of the American Hotel & Motel Association, 1991), p. 142.

3-201.16   Wild Mushrooms.*

(A) Except as specified in ¶ (B) of this section, mushroom species picked in the wild shall be obtained from sources where each mushroom is individually inspected and found to be safe by a mushroom identification expert approved by the regulatory authority.

(B) *This section does not apply to:*

(1) *Cultivated wild mushroom species that are grown, harvested, and processed in an operation that is regulated by the food regulatory agency that has jurisdiction over the operation; or*

(2) *Wild mushroom species if they are in packaged form and are the product of a food processing plant that is regulated by the food regulatory agency that has jurisdiction over the plant.*

3-603.11   Consumption of Raw or Undercooked Animal Foods.*

If a raw or undercooked animal food such as beef, eggs, fish, lamb, milk, pork, poultry, or shellfish is offered in a ready-to-eat form as a deli, menu, vended, or other item; or as a raw ingredient in another ready-to-eat food, the permit holder shall inform consumers by brochures, deli case or menu advisories, label statements, table tents, placards, or other effective written means of the significantly increased risk associated with certain especially vulnerable consumers eating such foods in raw or undercooked form.

Source: FDA 1993 *Food Code.*

A list of typical violations may serve to reinforce this section of the ordinance. Home-canned products such as fruits, vegetables, and meats may not be stored in or served by a food service business because home-canned products are not prepared by processors licensed and inspected by governmental agencies. Unpasteurized (raw) milk cannot be served in a food service facility. Fish and shellfish may be purchased only from sources approved by the United States government. Egg products are expected to undergo preservation processing and handling under carefully controlled conditions. Rigorous requirements are imposed on all of these products because they are common food sources of pathogenic bacteria.

An operation should never purchase a product after the expiration date printed on the package has passed. Suppliers should employ the **first-in-first-out (FIFO) inventory system;** however, once a food service operation buys, uses, and sells a bad product, it is liable for any resulting damages.

Another important inventory item is water. While it is used in more food recipes than any other item purchased by a food service business, the quality of water is often taken for granted in developed countries like the United States. Check with your state and local regulatory authorities for additional regulations affecting your food service operation.

Purchasing and People

A number of people have responsibilities related to the purchasing control point; however, purchasing itself is a management function. Hotels often have a full-time purchasing agent, or, if the hotel is large, a purchasing department responsible for all food and non-food buying. Of course, not all operations need a full-time buyer. In smaller operations, the manager or a key assistant (such as the assistant manager, executive chef, steward, or food and beverage director) might serve as a part-time buyer. The buyer is responsible for the operation's purchasing control point.

The Successful Buyer. To be successful, the buyer must possess many skills, including managerial and technical skills and knowledge. Managerial skills are necessary because the buyer is a part of the operation's management team. He or she must understand the establishment's present position and its short- and long-term goals. This knowledge assists the buyer in carrying out purchasing activities according to management's overall plan.

Technical knowledge enables the buyer to do a more efficient job. Textbooks, trade journals, industry associations, and the operation's suppliers are good sources of new information on food marketing, packaging, distribution, and product yields. The buyer's level of technical expertise also depends upon his or her knowledge of the operation's quality, sanitation, and cost standards, and of which products meet these standards. A certain amount of purchasing experience might be necessary to develop these skills.

The buyer should also have good interpersonal skills and high ethical standards. Interpersonal skills are critical because the buyer must be a communicator; he or she regularly interacts with department heads, staff members in the purchasing department, and other management staff. The buyer's communication skills are also important when working with suppliers. Ethical standards may be difficult to specify, but certainly honesty and trustworthiness are two important considerations. A buyer frequently faces temptation in the form of opportunities for personal rebates and under-the-table kickbacks. It is management's responsibility to spot-check the purchasing function to keep its buyer honest. Unannounced checks also provide a stimulus for the buyer to avoid compromising the establishment's sanitation, quality, and cost control standards.

To perform well, a buyer must accomplish the five functions of purchasing. Although the amount of time devoted to purchasing can vary with the facility's size, all five functions are addressed by a well-planned purchasing control point. First, the buyer is responsible for maintaining adequate inventory levels, in order to reduce or eliminate stockouts which inconvenience production staff and disappoint guests. Second, the buyer should minimize the operation's dollar investment in inventory. There are two reasons for this: excessive inventories promote spoilage and potential contamination, and they tie up dollars without earning interest. Third, the buyer must maintain the operation's quality, sanitation, and cost standards. Fourth, the buyer must work to maintain the operation's competitive position. And fifth, the buyer must purchase the product, not the deal. He or she should never compromise the establishment's standards for a better price.

The buyer is responsible for conducting negotiations with the operation's suppliers. The negotiations typically cover the as purchased (AP) price, quantities to be purchased, delivery schedules, and other supplier services. An intimate knowledge of the establishment's standards and product needs is necessary if the buyer is to obtain acceptable products. The buyer must communicate quality, sanitation, and cost standards to suppliers. He or she should also keep suppliers informed of ways in which they can improve their services to the operation. Good relationships with suppliers help guarantee that the buyer will get the best value each supplier can offer.

Of course, suppliers cannot always fill orders promptly. Some buyers have circumvented this problem by establishing a reciprocal relationship with competitors. Under such an agreement, when a competitor is temporarily out of a product, the operation supplies it from its own stock until the competitor's order is shipped in. When the operation runs out of a product, the buyer can then call on the competitor and request a temporary loan.

Suppliers. Suppliers are another human component of the purchasing function. The role of suppliers has changed significantly in recent years. In the past, most suppliers distributed certain categories of food products or supplies, such as produce, meats, dairy products, or coffee. By the early 1970s, however, the supplier's role had evolved into the full-line or one-stop shopping distributor. This trend in food service distribution is known as the **master distributor** concept. Many of the full-line distributors carry from 5,000 to 10,000 different products. One master distributor may be able to satisfy 90 to 100% of an operation's purchasing needs. Many businesses currently purchase most of their supplies from a small number of full-line distributors who sell meat, produce, fresh fish, canned foods, frozen foods, cleaning supplies, paper products, flowers, utensils, and kitchen equipment. Larger operations may still buy a few specialty items (for example, exotic fruits and vegetables or dairy products) from specialty suppliers. However, a full-line distributor can usually satisfy all the purchasing needs of a small business.

This one-stop purchasing arrangement increases product consistency and provides purchasing leverage for the facility. It also builds the supplier's trust in the operation and gives management more time for other duties. Furthermore, master distributors often provide services that a specialist cannot offer. These additional services include menu consulting, employee training programs and seminars, and new product presentations. These advantages make it likely that the master distributor concept will increase in popularity.

One of the disadvantages of the master distributor is that deliveries tend to be weekly rather than daily. This means that planning is more important, both in terms of inventory levels and storage space. For extremely perishable products, a specialty supplier may be the distributor of choice if more frequent deliveries can be obtained.

Regardless of whether a specialty or full-line distributor is used, the establishment should periodically evaluate its suppliers based on the following criteria:

- Sanitation policies

- Size and services

- Staff and labor relations

- Purchasing power and financial position

- Products and prices

- Reputation

- Value

A supplier's sanitation policies can easily be spot-checked through periodic informal, unannounced visits to the distributor's warehouse or processing plant. The food service operation's representative should check to see if the operation is clean and adequately maintained by taking a walking tour of the facility. The person who receives deliveries can periodically inspect the supplier's delivery vehicles as food is unloaded. Refrigerated and frozen products must be delivered in vehicles equipped with refrigerated storage. The health department may be able to provide the food establishment with a general impression of the distributor's facilities based on past inspections. Above all, the supplier must be approved—that is, acceptable to the regulatory authority. Always check with your state or local health department for guidelines pertaining to approved sources.

The FDA states:

"**Approved**" means acceptable to the regulatory authority based on a determination of conformity with principles, practices, and generally recognized standards that protect public health.

Source: FDA 1993 *Food Code.*

The size of the distributing company must be adequate to meet the operation's needs. Supplier services include arranging delivery schedules at the food service operation's convenience, which can help the operation avoid both the overcrowding of storage areas and stockouts. Most suppliers are also willing to carry unusual items as a special service to the operation if these items are needed on a regular basis. Other supplier services include a computer printout of all the products ordered during a given period (such as a week, a month, or a year). This report, called a **velocity report,** gives management a tool to analyze loss, waste, and theft.

A distributing company's sales and delivery personnel must also be evaluated. A supplier should have salespeople who know their products and can help the buyer become familiar with product alternatives that will meet the operation's needs. The supplier's sales representatives can also provide valuable market information. For example, if the distributor learns that California is experiencing heavy rains, its sales representatives should inform the operation's buyer that the price of California lettuce will be higher in approximately six weeks. Similarly, the supplier should keep the establishment abreast of market conditions which change with growing seasons. Sales personnel should also keep the establishment informed of promotional discounts offered by processors and manufacturers.

Delivery personnel also represent the supplier. Their appearance and attitude, as well as other labor relations factors such as the supplier's ability to create a team spirit among its staff members, should be considered.

The purchasing power and financial position of the supplier are important. High-volume distributors buy in large quantities at a low cost per unit; thus, a portion of the savings can be passed on to the food service business. A supplier that is on sure financial ground is likely to give the operation good value for its food and non-food product dollars.

Naturally, products and prices are a critical evaluation point. Products should meet the establishment's stated specifications. Distributors offering greater product variety are able to serve more types of food service businesses. Suppliers are obligated to charge a fair price. When evaluating prices, however, it is essential to compare like items. In many cases, the edible portion (EP) price is more important than the AP price because the EP price takes into account the product's yield.

The supplier's reputation is built on the company's reliability, consistency, and predictability. The food service operation should select suppliers who stand behind their products and services. It is a good idea to ask for references from the local health department and restaurant and hotel associations before choosing suppliers. In one sense, suppliers are partners in the food service business because they have a stake in its success.

Exhibit 5.6 Examples of Value-Added Services

Automated Order Entry

Full Test Kitchens

Group Insurance Plans for Independent Small Operators

Market Specialists (chain/national accounts)

Monitoring of Rebates from Manufacturers

On-line Computer Access to Current Product and Pricing Information

On-staff Chefs for Menu Ideas and Recipe Development

On-staff Dietitians for Nutritional Analysis and Special Diets

Operator Newsletters

Placement Services for Personnel

Produce Processing

Product Specialists and Merchandising Ideas

Professionally-Accredited Seminars

Quality Control Testing

"Segmented Idea" Shows

Training for Staff Members

Buyers and suppliers can work together to satisfy the needs of the operation's target markets.

Value, the final criterion, is an overall assessment of the other six factors. Today, **value-added distributors** are revolutionizing the operator-distributor relationship. Value-added distributors offer services beyond those normally expected, including nutritional analysis, quality control testing, idea shows geared toward certain market segments, product education, computer services, and others (see Exhibit 5.6). Some distributors may require a certain volume of business before offering some of these value-added services. Check with your suppliers to determine their value-added offerings and any restrictions that may apply.

Purchasing and Equipment

Food service businesses purchase a variety of utensils and equipment from suppliers. Utensils are food contact implements or containers.

The FDA states:

"Utensil" means a food-contact implement or container used in the storage, preparation, transportation, dispensing, sale, or service of food, such as kitchenware or tableware that is multiuse, single-service, or single-use; gloves used in contact with food; and food temperature measuring devices.

4-302.11   Utensils, Consumer Self-Service.

A food dispensing utensil shall be available for each container displayed at a consumer self-service unit such as a buffet or salad bar.

4-502.11   Good Repair and Proper Calibration.

(A) Utensils shall be maintained in a state of repair or condition that complies with the requirements specified in Parts 4-1 and 4-2 or shall be discarded.

(B) Temperature measuring devices shall be calibrated in accordance with manufacturer's specifications as necessary to assure their accuracy.

Source: FDA 1993 *Food Code.*

The material content, design, and fabrication of these items should be in accordance with nationally recognized standards and/or tested and listed by nationally recognized organizations, such as the National Sanitation Foundation, Environmental Testing Laboratories, or Underwriters Laboratories. Generally, the materials from which equipment and utensils are constructed must be safe (non-toxic), durable, able to withstand repeated warewashing, smooth, and easily cleanable.

Chapter 3 described the dangers of using equipment and utensils made of certain toxic materials: when they come into contact with acidic foods (such as fruit juices and tomato products), their surfaces can corrode and cause metal poisoning from zinc, cadmium, or lead. To prevent this, most regulatory agencies only allow equipment and utensils which neither contaminate nor impart odors, colors, or tastes to food. For example, only food-grade plastic bags may be purchased for food storage; using utility (non-food-grade) plastic bags can result in the addition of undesirable colors and odors to stored food products. Any equipment or utensils which do not meet these requirements should be eliminated from food service facilities.

The FDA states:

4-101.11   (Multiuse) Characteristics.*

Materials that are used in the construction of utensils and food-contact surfaces of equipment may not allow the migration of deleterious substances or impart colors, odors, or tastes to food and under normal use conditions shall be:

  (A)   Safe;

  (B)   Durable, corrosion-resistant, and nonabsorbent; [N]

  (C)   Sufficient in weight and thickness to withstand repeated warewashing; [N]

  (D)   Finished to have a smooth, easily cleanable surface; [N] and

  (E)   Resistant to pitting, chipping, crazing, scratching, scoring, distortion, and decomposition. [N]

4-101.12   Cast Iron, Use Limitation.

(A) Except as specified in ¶¶ (B) and (C) of this section, cast iron may not be used for utensils or food-contact surfaces of equipment.

(B) *Cast iron may be used as a surface for cooking.*

(C) *Cast iron may be used in utensils for serving food if the utensils are used only as part of an uninterrupted process from cooking through service.*

4-101.13   Ceramic, China, and Crystal Utensils, Use Limitation.

Ceramic, china, crystal utensils, and decorative utensils such as hand painted ceramic or china that are used in contact with food shall be lead-free or contain levels of lead not exceeding the limits of the following utensil categories:

Utensil Category	Description	Maximum (mg/L)
Hot Beverage Mugs	Coffee Mugs	0.5
Large Hollowware	Bowls > 1.1 L (1.16 QT)	1
Small Hollowware	Bowls < 1.1 L (1.16 QT)	2.0
Flat Utensils	Plates, Saucers	3.0

4-101.14   Copper, Use Limitation.*

Copper and copper alloys such as brass may not be used in contact with a food that has a pH below 7 such as vinegar, fruit juice, or wine or for a fitting or tubing installed between a backflow prevention device and a carbonator.

4-101.15   Galvanized Metal, Use Limitation.*

Galvanized metal may not be used for utensils or food-contact surfaces of equipment that are used for beverages, moist food, or hygroscopic food. ᔆ

4-101.16   Linens, Napkins, and Sponges, Use Limitation.

(A) Except as specified in ¶¶ (B) and (C) of this section, linens, napkins, and sponges may not be used in contact with food.

(B) *Linens and napkins may be used to line containers used for the service of foods if the linens and napkins are replaced each time the container is refilled for a new consumer.*

(C) *Cloth gloves may be used in direct contact with food that is subsequently cooked as required under Part 3-4 such as frozen food or a primal cut of meat.*

(D) Sponges may not be used in contact with cleaned and sanitized or in-use food-contact surfaces.

4-101.17   Pewter, Use Limitation.

Pewter may not be used as a food-contact surface. Imitation pewter meeting the characteristics of multiuse utensils specified under § 4-101.11 may be used as a food-contact surface.

4-101.18   Solder and Flux, Use Limitation.

Solder and flux containing lead in excess of 0.2% may not be used on surfaces that contact food.

4-101.19   Wood, Use Limitation.

(A) Except as specified in ¶¶ (B), (C), and (D) of this section, wood and wood wicker may not be used as a food-contact surface.

(B) *Hard maple or an equivalently hard, close-grained, nonabsorbent wood may be used for:*

(1) *Cutting boards; cutting blocks; bakers' tables; and utensils such as rolling pins, doughnut dowels, salad bowls, and chopsticks; and*

(2) *Wooden paddles used in confectionery operations for pressure scraping kettles when manually preparing confections at a temperature of 110°C (230°F) or above.*

(C) *Whole, uncut, raw fruits and vegetables, and nuts in the shell may be kept in the wood shipping containers in which they were received, until the fruits, vegetables, or nuts are used.*

(D) *If the nature of the food requires removal of rinds, peels, husks, or shells before consumption, the whole, uncut, raw food may be kept in:*

(1) *Untreated wood containers; or*

(2) *Treated wood containers if the containers are treated with a preservative that meets the requirements specified in 21 CFR 178.3800 Preservatives for wood.*

4-101.110   Nonfood-Contact Surfaces.

Nonfood-contact surfaces of equipment that are exposed to splash, spillage, or other food soiling or that require frequent cleaning shall be constructed of a corrosion-resistant, nonabsorbent, and smooth material.

4-202.11   Food-Contact Surfaces.*

Multiuse food-contact surfaces shall be:

(A) Smooth;

(B) Free of breaks, open seams, cracks, chips, pits, and similar imperfections;

(C) Free of sharp internal angles, corners, and crevices;

(D) Finished to have smooth welds and joints; and

(E) Accessible for cleaning and inspection by one of the following methods:

(1) Without being disassembled,

(2) By disassembling without the use of tools, or

(3) By easy disassembling with the use of only simple tools such as mallets, screw drivers, or wrenches that are kept near the equipment and are accessible for use.

4-502.14   Shells, Use Limitation.

Mollusc and crustacea shells may not be used more than once as serving containers.

Source: FDA 1993 *Food Code.*

Single-service and single-use articles must meet similar standards to prevent undesirable additives from entering food. These items may not be reused. For example, plastic flatware used by guests at an outdoor buffet must be discarded after the buffet.

The FDA states:

"Single-service articles" means tableware, carry-out utensils, and other items such as bags, containers, placemats, stirrers, straws, toothpicks, and wrappers that are designed and constructed for one time, one person use.

Single-Use Articles.

(a) **"Single-use articles"** means utensils and bulk food containers designed and constructed to be used once and discarded.

(b) **"Single-use articles"** includes items such as wax paper, butcher paper, plastic wrap, formed aluminum food containers, jars, plastic tubs or buckets, bread wrappers, pickle barrels, ketchup bottles, and number 10 cans.

4-102.11   Characteristics.*

Materials that are used to make single-service and single-use articles:

(A) May not:

(1) Allow the migration of deleterious substances; or

(2) Impart colors, odors, or tastes to food; [N] and

(B) Shall be:

(1) Safe; and

(2) Clean. [N]

4-201.11   Equipment and Utensils.

Equipment and utensils shall be designed and constructed to be durable and to retain their characteristic qualities under normal use conditions.

4-502.12   Single-Service and Single-Use Articles, Required Use.*

A food establishment without facilities specified in Parts 4-6 and 4-7 for cleaning and sanitizing kitchenware and tableware shall provide only single-use kitchenware, single-service articles, and single-use articles for use by food employees and single-service articles for use by the consumer.

4-502.13   Single-Service and Single-Use Articles, Reuse Limitation.

Single-service and single-use articles may not be reused.

Source: FDA 1993 *Food Code.*

Equipment and utensils purchased by the operation must also be easy to clean. They must be constructed and repaired with materials that are safe, corrosion-resistant, and non-absorbent. Multi-use equipment and utensils must also be smooth, durable, and easily cleanable. (Since single-service articles may not be reused, they need not be easy to clean.) Non-absorbent hardwood (such as hard maple) may be used for baker's tables, salad bowls, and cutting blocks or boards. Wood is not permitted for any other food-contact surfaces. Rubber or plastic materials are permitted if they are easily cleanable and resistant to scoring, decomposition, scratching, and chipping under normal conditions. Rubber or plastic cutting boards are often preferable to wooden boards because they are easier to clean and maintain.

When purchasing cookware, including pots and pans, it is important to consider not only the useful life, but also cleaning and sanitization. Heavy cookware with riveted construction may cost more initially but can last at least ten years if properly maintained. Heavy-gauge stainless steel and aluminum cookware, for example, is designed to withstand the abuses of a commercial kitchen. Avoid purchasing thin-walled aluminum cookware; such items can cause discoloration of sauces or aluminum poisoning when they come into contact with acidic foods. In addition, the bleach in some solutions can wear down the aluminum. All cookware should be hand-washed with pot and pan soap and treated with a sanitizer designed for the purpose.

The important factors in design and fabrication of equipment and utensils are durability and cleanability. In particular, all food-contact surfaces must be designed and fabricated to be smooth and free from cracks, chips, breaks, and difficult-to-clean crevices and corners. Cast iron is permitted only on grills, griddles, skillets, and other heated surfaces. Materials used as lubricants should not come in contact with food or food-contact surfaces.

The FDA states:

4-601.11   Equipment, Food-Contact Surfaces, Nonfood-Contact Surfaces, and Utensils.*

(A) Equipment food-contact surfaces and utensils shall be clean to sight and touch.

(B) The food-contact surfaces of cooking equipment and pans shall be kept free of encrusted grease deposits and other soil accumulations.[N]

(C) Nonfood-contact surfaces of equipment shall be kept free of an accumulation of dust, dirt, food residue, and other debris.[N]

4-602.11   Equipment Food-Contact Surfaces and Utensils.*

(A) Equipment food-contact surfaces and utensils shall be cleaned:

(1)   Except as specified in ¶ (B) of this section, before each use with a different type of raw animal food such as beef, fish, lamb, pork, or poultry;

(2)   Each time there is a change from working with raw foods to working with ready-to-eat foods;

(3)   Between uses with raw fruits or vegetables and with potentially hazardous food;

(4)   Before using or storing a food temperature measuring device; and

(5)   At any time during the operation when contamination may have occurred.

(B) *Subparagraph (A)(1) of this section does not apply if raw animal foods that require cooking temperatures specified under Subparagraph 3-401.11(A)(4) are prepared after foods that require cooking temperatures specified under Subparagraphs 3-401.11(A)(2)-(3).*

(C) Except as specified in ¶ (D) of this section, if used with potentially hazardous food, equipment food-contact surfaces and utensils shall be cleaned throughout the day at least every 4 hours.

(D) *Equipment food-contact surfaces and utensils may be cleaned less frequently than every 4 hours if:*

(1)   *In storage, containers of potentially hazardous food and their contents are maintained at temperatures specified under Chapter 3 and the containers are cleaned when they are empty;*

(2)   *Utensils and equipment are used to prepare food in a refrigerated room that maintains the utensils, equipment, and food under preparation at temperatures specified under Chapter 3 and the utensils and equipment are cleaned at least every 24 hours;*

(3)   *Containers in serving situations such as salad bars, delis, and cafeteria lines hold ready-to-eat potentially hazardous food that is maintained at the temperatures specified under Chapter 3, are intermittently combined with additional supplies of the same food that is at the required temperature, and the containers are cleaned at least every 24 hours;*

(4)   *Temperature measuring devices are maintained in contact with foods, such as when left in a container of deli food or in a roast, held at temperatures specified under Chapter 3; or*

(5)   *The regulatory authority approves the cleaning schedule based on consideration of:*

(a) *Characteristics of the equipment and its use,*

(b) *The type of food involved,*

(c) *The amount of food residue accumulation, and*

(d) *The temperature at which the food is maintained during the operation and the potential for the rapid and progressive multiplication of pathogenic or toxigenic microorganisms that are capable of causing foodborne disease.*

CIP.

(a) "**CIP**" means cleaned in place by the circulation or flowing by mechanical means through a piping system of a detergent solution, water rinse, and sanitizing solution onto or over equipment surfaces that require cleaning, such as the method used, in part, to clean and sanitize a frozen dessert machine.

(b) "**CIP**" does not include the cleaning of equipment such as band saws, slicers or mixers that are subjected to in-place manual cleaning without the use of a CIP system.

4-202.12 CIP Equipment.

(A) CIP equipment shall meet the characteristics specified under § 4-202.11 and shall be designed and constructed so that:

(1) Cleaning and sanitizing solutions circulate throughout a fixed system and contact all interior food-contact surfaces, and

(2) The system is self-draining or capable of being completely drained of cleaning and sanitizing solutions; and

(B) CIP equipment that is not designed to be disassembled for cleaning shall be designed with inspection access points to assure that all interior food-contact surfaces throughout the fixed system are being effectively cleaned.

Source: FDA 1993 *Food Code.*

Equipment or utensils that do not meet design and fabrication requirements are virtually impossible to keep clean. Violations (such as using dented or chipped equipment and utensils) invite sanitation problems. For example, the common practice of lubricating a food mixer with a petroleum-based lubricant may result in the lubricant dripping into and contaminating food.

Glass-stemmed thermometers may not be used to check food temperatures or the temperature of oil in a deep fryer. Soft wood is not permitted for non-food-contact surfaces which are exposed to splash or food debris and thus require frequent cleaning. Improperly designed and fabricated ventilation hoods may allow possibly contaminated grease to drip into food. Sinks and drain boards should be self-draining. If a piece of equipment must be taken apart for cleaning, the equipment should be designed to be easily disassembled.

Buyers should be aware that equipment from foreign suppliers (for example, East Indian ovens or Italian pasta machines) may not meet nationally recognized construction codes and specifications. However, there is no law preventing foreign manufacturers from selling their equipment in the United States. Ask state or local health officials to evaluate the equipment based on existing codes.

When purchasing new or used equipment, evaluate it with sanitation in mind. Consider asking suppliers for a written guarantee that their equipment is in compliance with relevant codes and standards. Also consider asking suppliers to furnish you with state or local inspection reports on their facilities, or for permission to conduct your own unannounced inspections.

The National Sanitation Foundation (NSF) is a non-profit organization that develops standards and criteria for equipment, products, and services in the interest of public health. The NSF seal on equipment and utensils indicates that these items meet most public health standards: the seal only appears on items that have passed a rigorous inspection. NSF's *Standard No. 2 for Food Service Equipment* and the FDA's Food Code are the basis for the recommendations NSF makes to manufacturers and others. NSF is the only organization that develops industry standards. Other organizations use these standards to test equipment. Three independent organizations test and evaluate food service equipment. Underwriters Laboratories (UL) evaluates electrically powered equipment, while the American Gas Association (AGA) performs similar testing on gas equipment. Environmental Testing Laboratories (ETL) also tests equipment against NSF standards. When applicable, it is a good idea to specify evaluated and tested equipment.

It is important to realize that NSF and FDA set *minimum* standards. Just because an item meets these minimum standards does not guarantee that it is suitable for the intended purpose. For example, equipment designed for home use (non-commercial equipment) may seem a bargain at first glance. However, this equipment is not designed for frequent, large-quantity use. In fact, commercial use of such equipment usually voids the warranty.

One piece of equipment is absolutely essential in virtually all of the control points: a temperature measuring device. This category includes a thermometer, thermocouple, thermistor, or other device. For example, a food thermometer provides an accurate determination of internal product temperature as a product moves through the control points. The recommended accuracy for a product thermometer is $\pm 2°F$ ($\pm 1°C$).

The FDA states:

"Temperature measuring device" means a thermometer, thermocouple, thermistor, or other device that indicates the temperature of food, air, or water.

4-302.12   Food Temperature Measuring Devices.

Food temperature measuring devices shall be provided and readily accessible for use in assuring attainment and maintenance of food temperatures as specified under Chapter 3.

4-201.12   Food Temperature Measuring Devices.*

Food temperature measuring devices may not have sensors or stems constructed of glass, *except that thermometers with glass sensors or stems that are encased in a shatterproof coating such as candy thermometers may be used.*

4-203.11   Food Temperature Measuring Devices.

(A) Food temperature measuring devices that are scaled only in Celsius or dually scaled in Celsius and Fahrenheit shall be accurate to $\pm 1°C$ ($1.8°F$).

(B) Food temperature measuring devices that are scaled only in Fahrenheit shall be accurate to $\pm 2°$F.

4-204.112   Temperature Measuring Devices.

(A) In a mechanically refrigerated or hot food storage unit, the sensor of a temperature measuring device shall be located to measure the air temperature in the warmest part of a mechanically refrigerated unit and in the coolest part of a hot food storage unit.

(B) Except as specified in ¶ (C) of this section, cold or hot holding equipment used for potentially hazardous food shall be designed to include and shall be equipped with at least one integral or permanently affixed temperature measuring device that is located to allow easy viewing of the device's temperature display.

(C) *Paragraph (B) of this section does not apply to equipment for which the placement of a temperature measuring device is not a practical means for measuring the ambient air surrounding the food because of the design, type, and use of the equipment, such as calrod units, heat lamps, cold plates, bainmaries, steam tables, insulated food transport containers, and salad bars.*

(D) Temperature measuring devices shall be designed to be easily readable.

(E) Food temperature measuring devices shall have a numerical scale, printed record, or digital readout in increments no greater than $1°$C or $2°$F.

Source: FDA 1993 *Food Code.*

Purchasing and Facilities

A food service operation's facilities help determine the operation's purchasing method. If the facilities are spacious and accommodate many guests, the operation will likely use a formal purchasing method. This method involves relatively large orders. Therefore, competitive buying is used to help control costs. The operation prepares written specifications to communicate product needs to suppliers, and suppliers submit written bids to the operation's buyer. These bids indicate the price they will charge for the desired products if their bid is accepted. Depending on the operation's needs, the buyer may use written negotiations during the formal purchasing process.

In smaller businesses, orders are usually smaller and purchasing procedures tend to be informal. Written specifications, bids, and negotiations are usually not used; the operation provides specifications, suppliers quote prices, and negotiations are conducted either in person or by telephone. While this method is less exact, it is simple and saves time for the small operation. It does, however, result in less operator control.

Purchasing and Change

Perhaps more than any other control point, the purchasing activity is in a constant state of flux. Conditions change from season to season, from week to week, and in some cases, overnight. For example, the availability, prices, and supply levels of products purchased by a food service business often change. Purchasing patterns must be altered when conditions change. However, before a change is implemented, it is important to systematically predict and evaluate its impact on the operation's sanitation, quality, and cost standards. As part of this systematic evaluation, the risks must be clarified, analyzed, and reduced, when possible.

In an attempt to minimize uncertainty at the purchasing control point, standards (such as purchase specifications), as well as sensory and temperature checks, should be used to determine product quality and assess the sanitation risks. If a system of SRM is in place, it is relatively easy to change a product or update standards. When such a system is not in place, it becomes all the more difficult to control purchasing activities.

Purchasing and the SRM Program

Purchasing can be risky if menu planning is haphazard and the objectives of purchasing are not clearly understood. The risks can be reduced if the buyer is armed with knowledge about the operation's:

- Quality, sanitation, and cost standards

- Food production methods

- Purchasing procedures

- Suppliers and competitors

Knowledge of quality, sanitation, and cost control standards is most important. Jeopardizing the operation's SRM program in order to save a few dollars on the purchase price can be a costly mistake. Similarly, to compromise the establishment's quality standards is to risk losing guests. The buyer must strike a balance between these three types of control, all of which determine the guest experience and the success of the business.

Knowledge of food production methods is also important at the purchasing control point. A buyer must know the yield of a raw ingredient, based on preparation and serving techniques, in order to calculate its EP cost.

The buyer must know purchasing procedures to operate efficiently. A planned, organized system—complete with written product specifications, purchase orders, and product evaluation forms—increases the buyer's control. By carefully reviewing issuing records, the buyer can establish par stocks (minimum quantities) for each item the facility should have on hand. This helps eliminate costly stockouts. An operation cannot negotiate either price or quality when it always buys at the last minute.

Knowledge of suppliers and competitors completes the purchasing success formula. Suppliers can be a valuable source of market information. They can assist the operation in solving yield, sanitation, quality, and cost problems. Successful operations are also not afraid to develop reciprocal supply loan relationships with competitors; such relationships are usually beneficial.

Summary

The menu, which details an operation's product offerings, is the blueprint for the success of a food establishment. The menu greatly influences the other control points in the food service system. Menu planning must take into account the resources under a manager's control: inventory, people, equipment, and facilities. The trend today is toward limited menus and cross-utilization of raw ingredients.

Purchasing needs are dictated by a careful analysis of the menu and its standard recipes. Purchasing patterns evolve as market trends, supply sources, and guest needs change. Successful purchasing is the rule rather than the exception when the establishment's representatives arm themselves with knowledge. Control of the quality, sanitation, and cost of purchases is possible when a set of controls is systematically used. These controls help reduce the risks of operating a food establishment.

Endnotes

1. *Accuracy in Menu Guidelines* (Denver, Colo.: Colorado-Wyoming Restaurant Association, 1981).
2. Robert Keane, "Ingredient-Labeling Battle Continues," *Restaurants & Institutions*, April 15, 1987, p. 24.

Key Terms

convenience foods • cross-utilization • first-in-first-out (FIFO) inventory system • food sample data sheet • inventory • line-up meeting • master distributor • purchase order • rationalization • standard purchase specification • truth-in-menu regulations • value-added distributor • velocity report

Discussion Questions

1. What are four important trends affecting menu development?
2. What is the relationship between menu planning and inventory? How do rationalization, diversification, and convenience foods fit into this relationship?
3. The menu planning control point requires considerations for three other major resources besides inventory. What are these resources and their considerations?
4. Why are menu changes implemented? What factors are influential?
5. What are the major truth-in-menu regulations?
6. The purchasing control point is influenced by which factors? What are the functions of this control point?
7. Why are inventory standards important at the purchasing control point?
8. What types of skills are required of a successful buyer?
9. What are the basic guidelines for purchasing equipment? How do facilities influence purchasing procedures?
10. How can a buyer reduce risks at the purchasing control point?

Checklist for Menu Planning

Inventory

____   The menu achieves the financial objectives, helps create the image, and functions as the plan for the entire operation.

_____ Records are maintained on the menu's sales mix and the popularity of every menu item.

_____ The menu incorporates relevant menu trends.

_____ The menu's effect on the other control points is considered when planning the menu.

_____ Menu items are rationalized and ingredients cross-utilized as much as possible.

_____ High-quality convenience foods are evaluated and used when appropriate.

_____ Menu offerings are based on the expectations of the target markets.

People

_____ The menu communicates the strategy for meeting or exceeding guest expectations.

_____ The appearance, readability, clarity, and pricing strategies of the menu are evaluated regularly.

_____ The skill levels of production staff are evaluated.

_____ The skill levels of service staff are evaluated.

_____ Suppliers are asked for preparation and merchandising suggestions.

_____ Sanitation, quality, and cost control standards are maintained.

_____ Servers know the meaning of terms used to describe menu items and their preparation.

Equipment

_____ Equipment is selected based on initial costs, capacity, availability of energy sources, operating costs, maintenance costs, and skill levels of staff members.

_____ Equipment is easy to clean and sanitize.

_____ Equipment design, layout, and installation facilitate both product and people movement in the kitchen and service areas.

_____ Special functions, banquets, and room service menus are planned realistically, based on the operation's equipment resources.

Facilities

_____ Traffic flow in the kitchen and dining room is evaluated, and the design and layout of the facilities are changed when necessary.

_____ The ambience of the facilities is appropriate for the menu and the expectations of the target markets.

_____ Special functions and banquets are booked with the limitations of the establishment's facilities in mind.

_____ The facilities are maintained in a clean and sanitary manner.

Truth-in-Menu

_____ Accurate descriptions are used for raw ingredients and finished menu items.

_____ Quality or grade statements are factual.

_____ Sizes, weights, or counts are depicted accurately on the menu.

_____ Frozen or canned items are never billed as fresh.

_____ Preparation techniques are described accurately.

_____ Additional charges for extras are clearly stated on the menu.

_____ Pictures on the menu accurately represent the product served.

_____ Server descriptions are accurate.

_____ Dietary or nutritional claims are precise.

_____ Points of origin are described accurately.

_____ Ingredient and nutritional information is available to those who request it.

SRM Program

_____ Menu items are considered in light of possible sanitation hazards at every control point.

_____ Once the potential hazards are identified, steps are taken to reduce the risks.

Checklist for Purchasing

Inventory

_____ Inventory and stock levels are established based on the intended use of the product and the volume of business.

_____ The functions of purchasing are used to guide activities.

_____ Written standard purchase specifications are used and updated periodically as conditions change.

_____ Market conditions are evaluated regularly.

_____ Food sample data sheets are used to select and evaluate products.

_____ Written purchase orders are used to define the details of each order.

_____ All inventory items are obtained from approved and safe sources.

_____ The FIFO inventory system is used by the operations and its suppliers.

People

_____ Purchasing is done by a manager or a key assistant.

_____ The buyer establishes and maintains an adequate supply of food and non-food products.

_____ The buyer minimizes the investment in inventory.

_____ The sanitation, quality, and cost standards are defined and maintained while risks are reduced.

_____ The operation's competitive position is maintained.

_____ The buyer purchases the product, not the deal.

_____ The buyer understands the operation's short- and long-term goals.

_____ The buyer possesses managerial, technical, and interpersonal skills.

_____ The buyer is ethical and loyal to the business.

_____ The buyer has an intimate knowledge of the operation and its product needs.

_____ The buyer establishes reciprocal supply loan relationships with the operation's competitors.

_____ The buyer evaluates the master distributor versus the specialty supplier.

_____ The buyer periodically checks the supplier's sanitation policies, size, services, staff and labor relations, purchasing power and financial position, products, quality, prices, reputation, and value.

_____ The buyer builds relationships with value-added suppliers.

_____ The buyer uses the supplier as a source of market information.

_____ Staff members in the purchasing department have a formal training program.

Equipment

_____ The materials, design, and fabrication of equipment purchased by the facility meet local, state, and federal health codes.

_____ The operation purchases equipment made of non-toxic materials.

_____ The operation purchases equipment that is easy to clean and maintain.

_____ Single-service items are not washed and re-used.

_____ Food-contact surface are free from cracks, chips, breaks, and difficult-to-clean crevices and corners.

_____ Materials used as lubricants do not contaminate food or food-contact surfaces.

_____ When considering equipment manufactured by foreign suppliers, local or state regulatory officials evaluate it based on existing codes.

_____ Equipment has been tested and evaluated by NSF and AGA, ETL, or UL where appropriate.

_____ Equipment designed for home use is not purchased.

_____ Product thermometers are purchased and used to measure internal product temperature as a product moves through the control points.

_____ Cookware is purchased based on durability and considerations of cleaning and sanitization.

Facilities

_____ The formality or informality of the purchasing arrangement is based on the establishment's facilities.

_____ Facilities are maintained in a clean and sanitary manner.

SRM Program

_____ Risks are reduced by knowledge of quality, sanitation, and cost standards; food production methods and purchasing procedures; and suppliers and competitors.

_____ Inventory is purchased carefully.

_____ Staff members are trained to maintain standards and reduce risks during purchasing.

_____ Adequate equipment and facilities are present, used, and frequently cleaned, sanitized, and maintained to reduce the risks during purchasing.

Case Study

This case study challenges you to use concepts presented in this chapter to apply the principles of the sanitation risk management program to the menu planning and purchasing control points.

In this case study, you are to select a menu item from the second edition of *Professional Cooking* by Wayne Gisslen (New York: Wiley, 1989), the fifth edition of *The Professional Chef* by the Culinary Institute of America (New York: CBI, 1991), or another source of quantity food production recipes. Select an item which uses a potentially hazardous food product.

Transcribe the standard recipe into the format used for the baked whitefish Florentine. Then develop the standard purchase specifications for the main ingredient and any other potentially hazardous ingredients (use Exhibit 5.3). You may also choose to complete the food sample data sheet (Exhibit 5.4) after interviewing a broker or supplier's sales representative.

Develop a set of criteria to evaluate potential suppliers for the main ingredient. Assuming you will sell 300 orders per week, complete the purchase order in Exhibit 5.5. Determine any value-added services you might expect with the order. Use the checklists in this chapter to review the resources under each control point and define standards. Outline your approach using these checklists.

Next, think of at least three other menu items that you can feature (either at lunch or dinner) to cross-utilize the main ingredient. For example, if the main ingredient is beef sirloin, consider using it in a stir-fry and as a marinated steak menu item.

Your development of this case study depends in part on the menu item you select. Nevertheless, the basic principles of the menu planning and purchasing control points can be analyzed even without applying them to an actual food establishment. If you are currently employed in a food establishment, you may wish to choose a menu item that is either currently offered there or one that is under consideration for future addition to the menu.

An SRM Program Example: Whitefish and the Menu Planning and Purchasing Control Points

In Chapter 1, we introduced a sanitation risk management (SRM) program that uses principles of the Hazard Analysis Critical Control Point (HACCP) approach to identify potentially hazardous foods, create a product flow diagram, establish critical control points, and develop and monitor a system of controls. In this and the next four chapters, we will follow a sample menu item through the relevant control points of the SRM program, discussing control measures for inventory, people, equipment, and facilities. This feature, which appears near the end of each chapter, helps illustrate methods for reducing risks at each control point.

The menu item selected is fresh Lake Superior whitefish. This entrée was selected because it is potentially hazardous and is a popular addition to many menus.

Whitefish is a freshwater finfish found in the Great Lakes and other freshwater lakes. It is a fatty fish and therefore less likely to dry out when cooked with dry heat (for example, broiling, baking, or grilling). It has flaky white flesh with a distinctively sweet flavor. Whitefish has an a_w of .99 to .99+ and a pH of approximately 6.0 to 6.9. It can be classified as a potentially hazardous food because it is of animal origin and is raw.

Recall that fish have less connective tissue than meat and poultry; therefore, they are more susceptible to enzymatic autolysis and microbial spoilage than other foods. Contamination can come from the skin of the fish and can be introduced or spread during processing and handling. Also recall that quality or wholesomeness inspections for fish are not mandatory in the United States, although they may be in the near future. The product flow diagram for this potentially hazardous food is presented in Exhibit 5.7.

The whitefish can be featured as baked whitefish Florentine on the menu. Exhibit 5.8 shows the standard recipe for this entrée. The same inventory item can be cross-utilized as broiled whitefish with lemon and herbs and baked whitefish with a sauce. It can be served at both lunch and dinner.

The staff members in the kitchen should be able to prepare and cook the whitefish while maintaining quality and sanitation standards. In addition, the staff members responsible for purchasing, receiving, storing, and issuing must understand that fresh fish is one of the most perishable foods they will handle. They must be trained to handle the fish carefully during receiving, store the fish properly, and use the fish quickly. Service staff members must understand how to serve the fish quickly and safely. If, after an assessment of staff member skills and guest expectations, it appears that whitefish is a wise choice for the operation, it will be added to the menu. All available suppliers of fresh whitefish will be checked and their input and suggestions will be solicited.

Equipment to properly receive, store, prepare, cook, hold, and serve fresh whitefish must be present before the item is added to the menu. This includes scales, thermometers, refrigeration systems, pans for storing, preparation and portioning equipment, ovens for baking, and the proper tableware for serving the entrée. Facilities for receiving and inspecting the fresh fish must be available. Adequate facilities must also be present for storing, preparing, cooking, and serving the whitefish.

The standard purchase specification is presented in Exhibit 5.9. Quality is defined through sensory test procedures to be conducted during receiving. A purchase order must be developed. Since this is a new item from a new supplier, the food sample data sheet (see Exhibit 5.4) is used to evaluate the product. The quantity ordered depends on the delivery frequency and forecasted sales. The fish will be purchased in 10-lb units as specified. If the fish is rinsed in water before preparing, the water used must be potable and meet the state drinking water quality standards.

The buyer has selected a specialty supplier who supplies only fish and shellfish. One of the main reasons for this choice was the frequency of deliveries: daily on Monday through Saturday with a minimum order of $100. Purchasing department representatives have inspected the distributor's facilities, checked with the local health department for past inspection scores, compared quality and price, and have found all criteria to be acceptable. Written specifications are used to establish a fixed price in effect for one week.

References

Accuracy in Menu Guidelines. Denver, Colo.: Colorado-Wyoming Restaurant Association, 1981.

Andrews, Edmund. "Is the Menu Labeling Controversy Overblown?" *Restaurant Business*, February 10, 1987, pp. 78, 80–82, 87.

Backas, Nancy. "Quick Bites: Menus to Graze By." *Restaurants & Institutions*, October 1, 1986, p. 153.

Exhibit 5.7 Product Flow Diagram for Fresh Whitefish

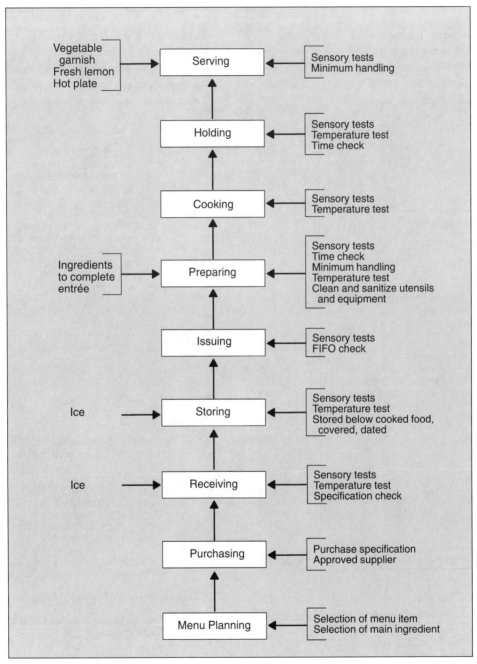

Balestreri, Ted. "Labeling: Farfetched Response." *Nation's Restaurant News,* February 3, 1986, p. F1.

Berlinski, Peter. "Is Your Menu Tasty?" *Restaurant Business,* November 20, 1987, p. 16.

Exhibit 5.8 Standard Recipe for Baked Whitefish Florentine

Standard Recipe No.: 413
Product Name: Baked Whitefish Florentine
Pan Size: Large sheet pan
Temperature: 350°F (176°C)
Cooking Time: 20 minutes

Yield (No. of Servings): 25
Portion Size: 2 fillets, stuffed
Portion Utensil: Spatula; stainless spoon
Special Directions: May be served with a fish velouté sauce on the side.

Ingredients	Quantity	Method
Whitefish, fresh	50 6-oz (170 g) fillets	1. Select the tail sections of the fillets, no thicker than $1/2$" (1.3 cm).
Spinach	3 lb (1,361 g)	2. Clean the spinach and remove the stems. Blanch the spinach, drain, squeeze dry, and finely chop. Alternately, use a $2^1/2$ lb (1,134 g) box of frozen chopped spinach.
Bread crumbs Butter, melted	20 oz (567 g) 6 oz (170 g)	3. Mix the spinach, crumbs, and butter with a fork.
Parsley, chopped Eggs, beaten Sorrel leaves, fresh, chopped Thyme, fresh, chopped Tarragon, fresh, chopped Lemon zest, grated Pepper, white, ground	8 oz (227 g) 3 8 oz (227 g) 2 T (28 g) 2 T (28 g) 1 T (14 g) 1 T (14 g)	4. Add the remaining ingredients and mix well.
Oil	4 oz (113 g)	5. Oil the sheet pans. Place 25 fillets on the pans, skin side down. 6. Top each fillet with $1^1/2$ oz (42 g) of stuffing. Shape the stuffing to fit the shape of the fish. Place the second fillet on top and press down lightly.
Butter, melted	8 oz (227 g)	7. Drizzle the melted butter over the fish. 8. Bake at 350°F (176°C) until the internal product temperature is at least 145°F (63°C); about 20 minutes.
Lemon crowns Vegetable du jour	25 25 portions	9. Serve with lemon crown and vegetable garnish.

Special Equipment Needed: Metal-stemmed product probe thermometer

Exhibit 5.9 Standard Purchase Specification for Fresh Whitefish

1. **Product name:** Fresh Lake Superior Whitefish
2. **Product used for:**
   Entrée in a variety of forms at both lunch and dinner. It will be served as baked whitefish Florentine, broiled whitefish, and grilled whitefish.
3. **Product general description:**
   Fresh Lake Superior whitefish delivered at 32° to 38°F (0° to 3°C) on clean crushed ice. Pack 10 fillets per box with ice to make 10-lb boxes.
4. **Detailed description:**
   Whitefish must be fresh and come from Lake Superior. Portion size is 10- to 12-oz (280- to 340-g) boneless fillets. The skin should be shiny and bright with no scales.
   Fillets should be packed in a separate box with no other products besides crushed ice. Flesh should be firm. Product should be in sound condition, free from spoilage, filth, or other contamination, and shall be safe for human consumption.
5. **Product test procedures:**
   Sensory tests will include checking for a mild, sweet, fresh, agreeable odor. Firm flesh and condition of the skin will also be checked during receiving. A visual check of the cleanliness of the ice and the condition of the delivery container will be made. No damaged cases or cases in which other products are stored will be accepted. Internal temperature will be checked with a metal-stemmed probe thermometer and should be between 32° and 38°F (0° and 3°C). Fillets will be randomly weighed.
6. **Special Instructions and requirements:**
   Whitefish will be randomly inspected for the presence of parasites. If parasites are detected, the entire box will be rejected.

Bertagnoli, Lisa. "Time Shows the Value of Pots, Pans." *Restaurants & Institutions,* February 4, 1987, pp. 164–166.

Cichy, Ronald F. "Inflation Fighting Through Profitable Purchasing, Rational Receiving, and Secure Storage." *Michigan Hospitality,* July/August 1980, p. 40.

———. "The Magic of Menus." *Food Management,* June 1983, p. 52.

———. "The Menu Is a Marketing Tool." *Rocky Mountain Chefs Magazine,* January 1983, p. 10.

———. "Sanitation Tips—Personnel Standards." *Restaurant Business,* October, 1985, p. 36.

Cichy, R. F. and R. P. Krump. "Cost Control Part I: Control vs. Controls." *Rocky Mountain Chefs Magazine,* November, 1984, p. 8.

———. "Cost Control Part II: Efficient and Effective." *Rocky Mountain Chefs Magazine,* January 1985, pp. 20, 21.

The Editors of Time-Life Books. *The Good Cook—Fish.* Alexandria, Va.: Time-Life Books, 1979.

Frumkin, Paul. "Menu Strategy Offers New Freedom of Choice." *Nation's Restaurant News,* October 27, 1986, pp. F3–F4.

———. "Tapas Step into High Fashion." *Nation's Restaurant News,* April 28, 1986, pp. 1, 59.

"FTC Supports New FDA Proposal on Food Labeling." *Nation's Restaurant News,* February 15, 1988, p. 14.

Gindin, Rona. "The Healthy Foods Phenomenon." *Restaurant Business,* February 10, 1986, pp. 125, 128, 132, 136, 138, 142.

Gindin, Rona, and Dolores Long. "New Trends to Watch." *Restaurant Business*, August 10, 1986, pp. 179–189.

Gisslen, Wayne. *Professional Cooking*. 2d ed. New York: Wiley, 1989.

Goebeler, George. "Maintaining Relationships." *Restaurant Business*, July 1, 1989, p. 56.

Keane, Robert. "Ingredient-Labeling Battle Continues." *Restaurants & Institutions*, April 15, 1987, p. 24.

Liddle, Alan. "S.F. Labeling Czar to Deal 'Reasonably' With Chains." *Nation's Restaurant News*, September 15, 1986, p. 21.

Long, Dolores. "Food Trends: Menus for the '80s." *Restaurant Business*, November 1, 1986, pp. 161–171.

McClane, A. J. *The Encyclopedia of Fish Cookery*. New York: Holt, Rinehart and Winston, 1977.

McKennon, J. E. "How to Control Rising Food Costs, Part V: Purchasing, Receiving, Storing, Issuing." *Lodging*, October 1980, p. 77.

Ninemeier, Jack D. *Planning and Control for Food and Beverage Operations*. 3d ed. East Lansing, Mich.: Educational Institute of the American Hotel & Motel Association, 1986.

Riell, Howard. "Fashionable Foods." *Restaurant Business*, January 20, 1988, pp. 114–117, 122, 123, 126–128.

Salkin, Stephanie. "New Age of Distribution." *Restaurant Business*, July 1, 1989, pp. 64, 66, 72–73.

Scarpa, James. "Developing an Approach." *Restaurant Business*, November 20, 1987, pp. 132–135, 144–146.

REVIEW QUIZ

When you feel you have covered all of the material in this chapter, answer these questions. Choose the *best* answer. Check your answers with the correct ones found on the Review Quiz Answer Key at the end of this book.

1. The objective of cross-utilization is to:

    a. prepare and serve as many menu items as possible with a limited number of raw ingredients.
    b. keep to a minimum the equipment required to prepare menu items.
    c. train food preparation workers to do as many tasks as possible.
    d. streamline the preparation process for each menu item.

2. When planning a menu, it is important to consider the skill level of:

    a. the production staff.
    b. the service staff.
    c. both a and b.
    d. neither a nor b.

3. Adding banquet service to a traditional food service operation usually requires:

    a. more holding and storage equipment.
    b. designing a banquet menu that is more limited than the regular menu.
    c. an expansion of production facilities.
    d. all of the above.

4. Which of the following is an external factor influencing the menu?

    a. concept and theme
    b. the competition
    c. meal pattern
    d. the operational system

5. Which of the following is *not* one of the functions of purchasing?

    a. minimizing the operation's investment in inventory
    b. buying the product, not the deal
    c. adjusting sanitation standards to compensate for supply levels
    d. establishing and maintaining an adequate supply of inventory items

6. What is the primary factor in determining the quantity and quality of food items to be purchased?

    a. standard purchase specifications
    b. food costs
    c. suppliers' inventory
    d. the menu

7. Standard purchase specifications define the _____ of products a food establishment buys.

    a. quality
    b. quantity
    c. both a and b
    d. neither a nor b

8. Which of the following should be included on a purchase order?

    a. expected shelf life
    b. the quantity ordered
    c. product uses
    d. all of the above

9. A computer printout provided by a supplier of all the products ordered by a company during a given period is called a:

    a. velocity report.
    b. food sample data sheet.
    c. requisition.
    d. purchase specification.

10. Suppliers can be a valuable source of information regarding:

    a. sanitation problems.
    b. quality control.
    c. both a and b.
    d. neither a nor b.

Chapter Outline

The Receiving Control Point
  Receiving and Inventory
  Receiving and People
  Receiving and Equipment
  Receiving and Facilities
  Receiving and Change
  Receiving and the SRM Program
The Storing Control Point
  Storing and Inventory
  Storing and People
  Storing and Equipment
  Storing and Facilities
  Storing and Change
  Storing and the SRM Program
The Issuing Control Point
  Issuing and Inventory
  Issuing and People
  Issuing and Equipment
  Issuing and Facilities
  Issuing and Change
  Issuing and the SRM Program
Summary

Learning Objectives

1. Describe inventory controls, standards, and procedures at the receiving control point. (pp. 211–218)

2. Explain the qualifications necessary to perform the receiving function. (pp. 218–219)

3. Describe the elements of proper receiving facilities. (pp. 221–222)

4. Explain the importance of maintaining an optimum inventory. (p. 223)

5. Describe the A-B-C-D scheme of inventory classification, perpetual and physical inventories, and other inventory control measures. (pp. 223–227)

6. Describe the major responsibilities of the storeroom person. (pp. 227–228)

7. Describe the use of thermometers at the storing control point. (pp. 228–229)

8. Describe the three types of storage facilities in a food establishment. (pp. 230–235)

9. Explain what food service managers should know about the issuing control point. (pp. 235–238)

6

The Receiving, Storing, and Issuing Control Points

The receiving, storing, and issuing control points are presented together in this chapter because these three activities are interrelated. They are essential to the success of the operation's sanitation, quality, and cost control systems. By following the principles of the sanitation risk management (SRM) program at these control points, you will be able to implement and monitor a system to reduce risks.

The Receiving Control Point

The receiving control point follows menu planning and purchasing. The objectives of the receiving function include inspecting deliveries for quality and quantity, checking prices, and deciding whether to accept or reject deliveries. In reality, receiving practices vary: one operation may carefully check each item delivered; another might allow the supplier's truck driver to put the order away. From a control standpoint, the former method is certainly preferable.

The receiving function is critical because at this control point an operation assumes ownership of the products. Careful menu planning and skillful purchasing are wasted if an operation accepts inferior products. Good receiving techniques can maximize the results of the other control points. Risk reduction during receiving requires competent personnel, proper equipment, adequate receiving facilities, established receiving hours, and several types of receiving control forms.

Receiving and Inventory

When inventory items are received at a food establishment, a critical control point must be monitored. The receiver must check inventory quality, cleanliness, and labels very carefully. A temperature check is a good idea for all potentially hazardous foods; improper temperatures should prompt further quality inspection. Refrigerated potentially hazardous foods should generally be received at 41°F (5°C) or less.

Egg products, if liquid, frozen, or dried, should be obtained pasteurized. Shell eggs should be clean and whole and without cracks or checks. Fluid and dry milk and milk products should also be obtained pasteurized.

Food packages should be in good condition upon receipt, and they must be labeled. Raw and frozen molluscan shucked shellfish must be delivered in non-returnable packages labeled with the processor's name, address, and authorized certification number. Shellstock packages must also show the "sell by" or shucked date and location. An operation should retain this source identification for 90 days after the container is empty.

Molluscan shellstock should be received reasonably free of mud, dead shellfish, and shellfish with broken shells. Fish, however, may not be received unless they are commercially and legally caught or harvested or caught recreationally and approved for sale or service by the regulatory authority. Molluscan shellfish that are recreationally caught may not be approved for sale or service.

The FDA states:

3-201.14   Fish.*

(A) Fish may not be received for sale or service unless they are:

    (1)   Commercially and legally caught or harvested; or

    (2)   Except as specified under ¶ (B) of this section, caught recreationally and:

        (a)   Approved for sale or service by the regulatory authority, and

        (b)   If the fish are scombrotoxin-prone or are reef fish subject to ciguatera toxin, their source, preparation, and distribution are controlled under conditions of a variance granted by the regulatory authority as specified in § 8-103.10.

(B) Molluscan shellfish that are recreationally caught may not be received for sale or service.

3-202.11   Temperature.*

(A) Except as specified in ¶ (B) of this section, refrigerated, potentially hazardous food shall be at a temperature of 5°C (41°F) or below when received.

(B) *Fluid milk and milk products, molluscan shellstock, and shell eggs may be received at their respective temperatures according to laws governing their distribution.*

(C) Except as specified under ¶ (D) of this section, potentially hazardous food that is cooked to a temperature and for a time specified under §§ 3-401.11–3-401.15 and received hot shall be at a temperature of 60°C (140°F) or above.

(D) Upon receipt, potentially hazardous food shall be free of evidence of previous temperature abuse.

3-501.14   Cooling.*

Fluid milk and milk products, shell eggs, and molluscan shellstock received in compliance with laws regulating the respective food during shipment from the supplier shall be cooled to 5°C (41°F) or below within 4 hours.

3-202.13   Shell Eggs.*

Shell eggs shall be clean and received whole and without cracks or checks.

3-202.14   Liquid, Frozen, and Dry Eggs.*

Liquid, frozen, and dry eggs and egg products shall be obtained pasteurized.

3-202.15   Fluid, Frozen, and Dry Milk and Milk Products.*

Fluid, frozen, and dry milk and milk products shall be obtained pasteurized *unless alternative procedures to pasteurization are provided for in the CFR, such as in 21 CFR 133 – Cheeses and Related Cheese Products, for curing certain cheese varieties.*

3-202.16   Package Integrity.*

Food packages shall be in good condition and protect the integrity of the contents so that the food is not exposed to adulteration or potential contaminants.

3-202.18   Shucked Molluscan Shellfish, Packaging and Identification.

Raw and frozen shucked molluscan shellfish shall be obtained in nonreturnable packages legibly bearing the name of the person who shucks and packs the shellfish, the person's authorized certification number, and the "sell by" date for packages with a capacity of less than 1.87 L (one-half gallon) or the date shucked for packages with a capacity of 1.87 L (one-half gallon) or more.

3-202.19   Molluscan Shellstock Identification.*

Molluscan shellstock shall be obtained in containers bearing legible source identification tags or labels that are affixed by the harvester and each dealer that depurates, ships, or reships the shellstock, as specified in the National Shellfish Sanitation Program Manual of Operations, Part II Sanitation of the Harvesting, Processing and Distribution of Shellfish, and that list:

(A)   Except as specified under ¶ (C) of this section, on the harvester's tag or label, the following information in the following order:

(1)   The harvester's identification number that is assigned by the shellfish control authority,

(2)   The date of harvesting,

(3)   The most precise identification of the harvest location or aquaculture site that is practicable based on the system of harvest area designations that is in use by the shellfish control authority and including the abbreviation of the name of the state or country in which the shellfish are harvested,

(4)   The type and quantity of shellfish, and

(5)   The following statement in bold, capitalized type: "This tag is required to be attached until container is empty or retagged and thereafter kept on file for 90 days"; and

(B)   Except as specified under ¶ (D) of this section, on each dealer's tag or label, the following information in the following order:

(1)   The dealer's name and address, and the certification number assigned by the shellfish control authority,

(2)   The original shipper's certification number including the abbreviation of the name of the state or country in which the shellfish are harvested,

(3)   The information specified in Subparagraphs (A)(2)–(4) of this section, and

(4)   The following statement in bold, capitalized type: "This tag is required to be attached until container is empty and thereafter kept on file for 90 days."

(C)   If a place is provided on the harvester's tag or label for a dealer's name, address, and certification number, the dealer's information shall be listed first.

(D)   *If the harvester's tag or label is designed to accommodate each dealer's identification as specified under Subparagraphs (B)(1) and (2) of this section, individual dealer tags or labels need not be provided.*

3-202.110   Molluscan Shellstock, Condition.

When received by a food establishment, molluscan shellstock shall be reasonably free of mud, dead shellfish, and shellfish with broken shells. Dead shellfish or shellstock with badly broken shells shall be discarded.

3-203.11   Molluscan Shellfish, Original Container.

(A) Except as specified in ¶¶ (B) and (C) of this section, molluscan shellfish may not be removed from the container in which they were received other than immediately before sale or preparation for service.

(B) *Molluscan shellstock may be removed from the container in which they were received, displayed on drained ice, or held in a display container, and a quantity specified by a consumer may be removed from the display or display container and provided to the consumer if:*

(1)   *The source of the shellstock on display is identified as specified under § 3-202.19 and recorded as specified under § 3-203.12; and*

(2)   *The shellstock are protected from contamination.*

(C) *Shucked molluscan shellfish may be removed from the container in which they were received and held in a display container from which individual servings are dispensed upon a consumer's request if:*

(1)   *The labeling information for the shellfish on display as specified under § 3-202.18 is retained and correlated to the date when, or dates during which, the shellfish are sold or served; and*

(2)   *The shellfish are protected from contamination.*

3-203.12   Shellstock, Maintaining Identification.*

The identity of the source of shellstock that are sold or served shall be maintained by retaining shellstock tags or labels for 90 calendar days from the date the container is emptied by:

(A)   Using a record keeping system approved by the regulatory authority that keeps the tags or labels in chronological order correlated to the date when, or dates during which, the shellstock are sold or served; and

(B)   If shellstock are removed from their tagged or labeled container:

(1)   Using only 1 tagged or labeled container at a time, or

(2)   Using more than 1 tagged or labeled container at a time and obtaining a variance from the regulatory authority as specified in § 8-103.10 based on a HACCP plan that:

(a)   Is submitted by the permit holder and approved by the regulatory authority as specified under § 8-103.11,

(b)   Preserves source identification by using a record keeping system as specified under ¶ (A) of this section, and

(c)   Assures that shellstock from one tagged or labeled container are not commingled with shellstock from another container before being ordered by the consumer.

Source: FDA 1993 *Food Code.*

Before they become inventory items, all product deliveries should be verified. This verification is a two-step process. First, the supplier's invoice is checked against the establishment's purchase order and standard purchase specifications. The **invoice** details all the products being delivered to the facility and their corresponding prices. In some cases, it also shows products that are back-ordered or not yet available for delivery. Since the supplier uses the invoices to calculate the amount due, each invoice must be verified for accuracy. The second step entails checking the products against the supplier's invoice. Any products that are priced by weight should be weighed on an accurate scale. Packaged products should be removed from their packing containers, or the weight of the containers should be subtracted from the gross weight. Different cuts of meat which are delivered together must be weighed separately because of varying per-pound prices. Any products purchased on a per-unit basis should be counted before they are accepted. If more than one container of the same product is delivered, a random spot-check may be sufficient to verify the count.

The invoice may need to be modified if some products are spoiled, do not meet the establishment's specifications, or are delivered in the wrong quantities. In such cases, the receiver may fill out a request-for-credit memo stating why the products are unacceptable and asking the supplier to credit the invoice. The supplier should then issue a **credit memo** to adjust the account. A sample request-for-credit memo is shown in Exhibit 6.1. This form helps to ensure that the food establishment is charged only for the products that conform to its standards. Products that are held for credit for return to the

Exhibit 6.1 Request-for-Credit Memo

Request-for-Credit Memo

(prepare in duplicate)   Number: _____

From: _____   To: _____

        _____   _____

        _____   _____

        _____   _____

Credit should be given on the following:

Invoice Number: _____   Invoice Date: _____

Product	Unit	Number	Price/Unit	Total Price

Reason: Total: _____

_____   _____
        (delivery person)   (authorizing signature)

Source: Jack D. Ninemeier, *Planning and Control for Food and Beverage Operations,* 3d ed. (East Lansing, Mich.: Educational Institute of the American Hotel & Motel Association, 1991), p. 151.

distributor shall be segregated and held in areas away from food, equipment, utensils, linens, and single-service and single-use articles.

The FDA states:

6-404.11   Segregation and Location.

Products that are held by the permit holder for credit, redemption, or return to the distributor, such as damaged, spoiled, or recalled products, shall be segregated and held in designated areas that are separated from food, equipment, utensils, linens, and single-service and single-use articles.

Source: FDA 1993 *Food Code.*

Product inspection is essential during receiving. Sensory tests (evaluating a product by its appearance, odor, and feel) are useful in quality inspections. In addition, a temperature check verifies that potentially hazardous foods are not in the temperature danger

Exhibit 6.2 Storage Tag

Tag Number	1005		Tag Number	1005
Date of Receipt	8/1/00		Date Received	8/1/00
Weight/Cost			Weight	35#
35 × $2.85 = $99.75			Price	$2.85
(No. of #s) (Price) (Cost)			Cost	$99.75
Name of Supplier:			Supplier	Jacob Meats
Jacob Meats			Date Issued	
Date of Issue				

Source: Jack D. Ninemeier, *Planning and Control for Food and Beverage Operations*, 3d ed. (East Lansing, Mich.: Educational Institute of the American Hotel & Motel Association, 1991), p. 152.

zone (TDZ). Once products pass the inspection, they should be dated immediately with a marking pen, either on the outer container or the individually wrapped packages. Some operators also mark the price on each product unit, since this helps facilitate physical inventory and helps remind staff members how much food products cost.

A thorough inspection of every product delivery may be a time-consuming task. However, a food service business can only gain from a policy of consistent inspection. It keeps honest suppliers honest and discourages dishonest suppliers from dealing with the operation. Regular inspections also help reduce risks by preventing the acquisition of unacceptable inventory.

Once the products have been legally accepted, it is time to record the new inventory items and prepare them for storage. Tagging products when they are delivered aids in inventory control later. A sample product storage tag is presented in Exhibit 6.2. The date on the tag facilitates stock rotation, which is the goal of the FIFO (first-in-first-out) inventory system. Inventory tags with prices also speed up the physical inventory process. In addition, the tagging system provides an audit trail for food products. Initially, one part of the tag is attached to the product, while the other portion is affixed to the invoice. Later, when the product is issued for use, the portion of the tag attached to the product is removed and sent to the operation's accounting office. By matching the product portion of the tag to the invoice portion, the accounting department helps maintain inventory control.

If products are to be used immediately, they are sent directly to kitchen production areas without going through the usual storing and issuing control points. Nevertheless, everything that the facility receives must be recorded on the **daily receiving report**. A sample daily receiving report is shown in Exhibit 6.3. It lists what was received, the date of the delivery, the name of the supplier, the quantity, the price, and any other relevant comments. The report also provides a record of delivery distribution. The "Food Directs" column indicates the dollar value of products to be sent directly to kitchen production areas. The "Food Stores" column records the dollar value of products to be placed into storage. Generally, the food items placed in storage vastly outnumber the food items sent directly to production.

Exhibit 6.3 Daily Receiving Report

Date: 8/1/00													Page 1 of 2
				No. of	Purchase		Distribution						Transfer
	Invoice		Purchase	Purchase	Unit	Total	Food		Beverages				to
Supplier	No.	Item	Unit	Units	Price	Cost	Directs	Stores	Liquor	Beer	Wine	Soda	Storage
1	2	3	4	5	6	7	8	9	10	11	12	13	14
AJAX	10111	Gr. Beef	10#	6	$ 28.50	$171.00		$171.00					Bill
ABC Liquor	6281	B. Scotch	cs(750)	2	$ 71.80	$143.00			$143.60				Bill
		H. Chablis	gal	3	$ 8.50	$ 25.50					$ 25.50		Bill
B/E Produce	70666	Lettuce	cs	2	$ 21.00	$ 42.00	$ 42.00						
					Totals		$351.00	$475.00	$683.50	—	$102.00		

Source: Jack D. Ninemeier, *Planning and Control for Food and Beverage Operations*, 3d ed. (East Lansing, Mich.: Educational Institute of the American Hotel & Motel Association, 1991), p. 150.

Storing new inventory items in the proper order can preserve product quality and food safety. The most perishable items—frozen products—should be stored first. Refrigerated meats, fish, poultry, dairy products, and produce should be stored next. The least perishable items—staple foods and non-food supplies—should be stored last. Adhering to this order minimizes product deterioration. At the moment the delivery is accepted, the safety of the food becomes the responsibility of the food establishment. The receiver should strive to keep the time between delivery and storage as short as possible, particularly for frozen and refrigerated food products.

Receiving and People

The number of people working at the receiving control point varies among food service operations. The major determining factors are the size of the operation and its annual sales volume. In a relatively small operation, the manager or the assistant manager is usually in charge of receiving. In larger operations, one full-time or two part-time people typically handle the receiving function. The person in charge of receiving may be called a receiving clerk, steward, or storeroom person. This individual usually reports either to the food controller, the assistant manager, or the food and beverage manager.

Regardless of how many individuals are assigned to the receiving function, the general requirements are the same:

- Good health and personal cleanliness

- Familiarity with the necessary forms, tools, and equipment

- Literacy

- Product knowledge

- Quality and sanitation judgment

- Personal integrity, accuracy, and commitment to the interests of the organization

- Ability to coordinate the needs of the operation's departments with the supplies being delivered

Good health and personal cleanliness are important for the receiver, as for all other staff members. (See Chapter 3 for a complete discussion of staff member health and hygiene.) The person in charge of receiving should also be able to effectively use all equipment, facilities, and forms required at this control point. More will be said about these tools in later sections of the chapter.

Because of the volume of written information used at this control point, the operation's receiver must be able to read and write. Among other things, the receiver must be able to check the actual products delivered against the written purchase specifications and purchase orders. A receiver who is illiterate would not see, for example, that the purchase order says "50 ten-ounce USDA Prime tenderloin steaks" and could mistakenly accept 40 twelve-ounce USDA Choice tenderloin steaks instead.

The receiver should know the quality characteristics outlined in the operation's standard purchase specifications. A knowledge of product grades, weight ranges, and fat trim factors is also necessary. In addition, the receiver must be able to judge the sanitary condition of the products and the delivery vehicle.

The receiver should demonstrate both honesty and attention to detail. The receiver's integrity ensures that the establishment's standards, policies, and procedures will not be compromised. He or she must take this important job seriously. Negligence or inaccuracy may cause the business to suffer financial damage. Its reputation may also suffer if hazardous foods are carelessly accepted into the food service system. The receiver must be committed to protecting the interests of the operation.

The receiver must coordinate supply requisitions from all departments with the delivery schedules of suppliers. Ideally, receiving should take place during slow periods in the operation's daily business cycle. This is particularly important when the receiver is also the chef, assistant manager, or manager. The establishment's delivery hours should be posted on the back door as a guide for suppliers. The receiver should be available when deliveries are expected. Staggering food deliveries avoids overloading the storage area facilities. A smoothly run receiving control point is an indication of the receiver's competence and reliability.

Food production experience is essential for the receiver; however, this does not imply that any kitchen staff member in the operation is qualified to perform the receiving function. Only selected and trained staff members should be permitted to receive food and non-food products. A facility that allows the janitor, dishwasher, or busperson to do its receiving is opening the door for trouble; these individuals lack the training to recognize and resolve product problems. A properly trained receiver, on the other hand, knows what to do when there is a problem with product deliveries. The receiver can use his or her clout with the supplier to point out problems to the delivery person and see that they are corrected.

Receiving and Equipment

The receiver must be able to use a variety of equipment. Some equipment is used to gain access to the food for the usual quality and quantity checks. The operation should keep such tools as hammers, pliers, and screwdrivers on hand for the receiver to use in opening crates and boxes. Other equipment serves to verify product quality, quantity, and price. These tools include scales, thermometers, rulers, and calculators.

An accurate scale is crucial to the success of the receiving control point because many products purchased by a food service facility are priced by weight. The receiver should weigh all such products, checking the actual weight against that shown on the invoice. Several types of scales are available for use during receiving. Electronic readout scales are both easy to use and precise. Some of these scales are equipped with a device to stamp the recorded weight directly on the package. Tabletop or counter scales are suitable for checking the weight of lighter products. A large-capacity floor or platform scale is used for bulky or heavy products, which can often be rolled onto the scale with the aid of a handcart. To record the product's net weight, subtract the weight of the cart and packaging material.

Some operations attempt to save money by buying inexpensive scales. However, these scales are often inaccurate and, as a result, not useful. An accurate scale is an investment that pays for itself in the long run by allowing the receiver to verify invoices precisely. Scales should be checked for accuracy at least every three months by a qualified expert such as a representative of the state or local bureau of weights and measures.

Thermometers are also indispensable for proper receiving. In the hands of a knowledgeable receiver, an accurate metal-stemmed pocket probe thermometer is a valuable tool. The temperatures of all perishable products (meats, fish, poultry, produce, and all frozen foods) should be monitored. The internal temperature of refrigerated products must be less than or equal to 41°F (5°C), while frozen foods must be at 0°F (–18°C) or below. If products are delivered at higher temperatures, they must be further evaluated on the basis of appearance, odor, feel, and perhaps taste. Exhibit 6.4 shows one method of testing the internal product temperatures of frozen foods without opening the packages.

In the last few years, perishable product inspection at receiving has been made easier by the **time-temperature monitor**. This is a relatively inexpensive device that is attached to boxes or cartons of refrigerated and frozen products just before they leave the processing plant. It measures the combined effects of heat and age by changing color in response to the chemical and physical reactions that take place when a product's temperature exceeds a certain level for an excessive length of time.

Time-temperature monitors benefit a food service business by identifying weaknesses in the distribution system. This new technology allows the operation's receiver to quickly see whether a product has been thawed and then refrozen, making the accept/ reject decision faster and more objective. The widespread use of these monitors may also provide a stimulus for suppliers and distributors to maintain correct product temperatures and storage times.

A ruler is useful for checking the size of steaks and roasts and the amount of fat covering them. A calculator allows the receiver to quickly verify the accuracy of the supplier's invoice.

After a delivery is accepted, other equipment is used to prepare and transport items to storage. Marking pens are used to record the product's AP (as purchased) price directly on the package. This practice prompts other food handlers in the operation to think about the products as being equivalent to money; it also encourages proper food care to reduce contamination and spoilage losses. Marking pens are also used to record the delivery date in order to ensure proper product rotation (FIFO). Dollies and other

Exhibit 6.4 Measuring Frozen Food Temperatures Without Opening Packages

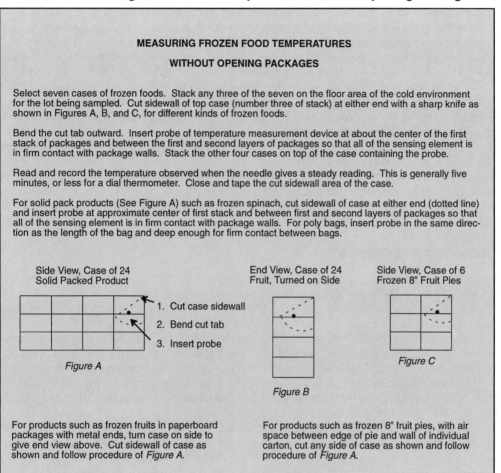

MEASURING FROZEN FOOD TEMPERATURES

WITHOUT OPENING PACKAGES

Select seven cases of frozen foods. Stack any three of the seven on the floor area of the cold environment for the lot being sampled. Cut sidewall of top case (number three of stack) at either end with a sharp knife as shown in Figures A, B, and C, for different kinds of frozen foods.

Bend the cut tab outward. Insert probe of temperature measurement device at about the center of the first stack of packages and between the first and second layers of packages so that all of the sensing element is in firm contact with package walls. Stack the other four cases on top of the case containing the probe.

Read and record the temperature observed when the needle gives a steady reading. This is generally five minutes, or less for a dial thermometer. Close and tape the cut sidewall area of the case.

For solid pack products (See Figure A) such as frozen spinach, cut sidewall of case at either end (dotted line) and insert probe at approximate center of first stack and between first and second layers of packages so that all of the sensing element is in firm contact with package walls. For poly bags, insert probe in the same direction as the length of the bag and deep enough for firm contact between bags.

Side View, Case of 24
Solid Packed Product

1. Cut case sidewall
2. Bend cut tab
3. Insert probe

Figure A

End View, Case of 24
Fruit, Turned on Side

Figure B

Side View, Case of 6
Frozen 8" Fruit Pies

Figure C

For products such as frozen fruits in paperboard packages with metal ends, turn case on side to give end view above. Cut sidewall of case as shown and follow procedure of *Figure A*.

For products such as frozen 8" fruit pies, with air space between edge of pie and wall of individual carton, cut any side of case as shown and follow procedure of *Figure A*.

Source: National Sanitation Foundation, *Product Temperature Management.*

transportation equipment help the receiver move marked products rapidly into storage, thereby retaining product safety and quality.

Receiving and Facilities

Proper receiving facilities are essential to the maintenance of the establishment's sanitation, quality, and cost standards at the receiving control point. Receiving facilities include the inside and outside areas surrounding the loading dock, the back door, and the receiving office.

The sanitary condition of the receiving area is critical. Inside floors and walls as well as the receiving dock must be free of debris and food particles; these unclean conditions could contaminate food or food containers before storage. Empty shipping containers and packaging materials should be taken to disposal areas promptly. Some operations put their trash areas near the receiving dock. This practice may create sanitation risks and the potential for inventory thefts. Whenever possible, trash containers should be placed in an area that is physically separated from the receiving area.

An operation's outdoor receiving facilities present an image of the establishment to suppliers and competitors. Ideally, receiving docks should be constructed so that deliveries are easy to manage. Adequate ramps, platforms, and truck maneuvering space should be provided. For safety as well as security, the outdoor and indoor receiving areas should be well-lit. The receiving door should also be locked when not in use. Whenever possible, the receiving office should be located between the receiving dock and storage areas. This will minimize the effort and, more important, the time it takes to transport products to storage.

Costs are easier to control when the receiving facilities are equipped with the necessary tools and work surfaces. A work table or desk is essential for recordkeeping and administrative responsibilities. Additional table space should be available for opening product containers during inspection of deliveries. Adequate floor space is necessary so that orders do not pile up in the receiving area. Overcrowding in the delivery area results in safety and sanitation hazards.

Receiving and Change

There is no room for negligence, waste, or error at the receiving control point. Evidence of any of these problems should prompt a thorough evaluation of the receiving function. Management should periodically review receiving practices to identify areas for possible improvement.

Because the control points are all interrelated, receiving should also be re-evaluated when menu planning or purchasing activities change. For example, if a small operation changes its menu and business improves dramatically, the operation's increased sales volume might justify hiring a full-time receiving person and expanding receiving facilities. The operation's orders can only be checked in properly if the receiver has enough time and the proper tools.

Regardless of the size of the business, the more consistent and routine the receiving function becomes, the fewer problems there will be. As with all the other control points, an evaluation of the costs versus the benefits indicates the degree to which more sophisticated controls are required.

Receiving and the SRM Program

When food products are delivered to the back door of a food establishment, the risks are transferred from the supplier to the owners and managers of the establishment. A food service operation needs strategies to reduce the risks at this critical control point.

All products must go through a detailed inspection during receiving. Important inspection points include temperature, freshness, wholesomeness, integrity, and case condition. Each product has its own temperature requirements and quality (freshness and wholesomeness) indicators. Freedom from filth, spoilage, or other contamination indicates product integrity. The condition of the cases or containers in which products are delivered indicates how products have been handled before arriving at the food establishment. All food products must also be checked against the establishment's standard purchase specifications.

The receiver must maintain high standards of personal hygiene and cleanliness. Equipment and forms used during receiving enhance cost, sanitation, and quality control. The receiver should use these tools at all times. Careful adherence to the receiving standards of the SRM program will help reduce the risks inherent in this control point.

The Storing Control Point

The storing control point serves to protect the operation's food and non-food purchases until they are put to work as income producers. To maximize income, profits, and guest satisfaction, spoilage and contamination must be minimized. The inventory must also be protected from theft and pilferage. Several storage area controls are useful in maintaining a high level of sanitation and quality while keeping down costs and risks.

The keys to proper food storage are knowing how items should be stored and having the facilities and equipment to keep the products in optimal condition. Recommended storage times, temperatures, and relative humidities for selected food products may be found in Chapter 4.

Storing and Inventory

Generally, the larger the inventory dollar value, the more difficult it is to achieve control of the storing function. While too small an inventory can lead to frequent stockouts, an excessively large inventory can cause a number of problems. Most food products, including frozen items, lose volume and quality if stored too long. Pilferage and spoilage losses also tend to increase in direct proportion to the amount of inventory on hand. When staff members see a large quantity of products in stock, they might be tempted to steal, reasoning that no one will notice one less item. Large inventories also encourage waste; staff members are not as likely to conserve food products that are obviously overstocked.

If storage areas are inadequate, excessive inventory might require more labor to handle and rehandle the products. It is more difficult to take inventory in overstocked storage areas, and excessive inventories can tie up the operation's money for long periods of time. They can also enhance the potential for contamination and raise the risks of a foodborne illness outbreak.

In light of these problems, managers may wonder how to achieve an optimum inventory level, avoiding both shortages and overstocking. If sales are properly forecast, purchasing is more accurate and inventory is easier to control. But suppose an establishment finds it necessary to maintain a large inventory, perhaps due to high sales volume and infrequent supplier deliveries. Is a detailed security system necessary for every product in stock? Such a system might require a large storeroom staff and end up costing more than the losses from theft, spoilage, and contamination it is designed to prevent. The dollar value of food products must determine the amount of inventory control necessary to guarantee security.

The value of food products can be compared by price per unit of weight or volume. Relatively few food products have a high dollar value per unit of measure. On the average, less than 20% of the total items in a food service operation's inventory account for over 80% of the total dollar value of the food inventory. The operation's inventory control measures should therefore focus on these high-cost items.

A-B-C-D Inventory Classification. Several techniques for categorizing inventories have been developed. Perhaps the most useful is the **A-B-C-D scheme**. This technique classifies inventory items according to perishability and cost per serving. The categories of the A-B-C-D scheme are presented in Exhibit 6.5.

Class A inventory items are high in both perishability and cost per serving. Class A items may account for up to 40% of a food service operation's total annual purchases. Class B inventory items are relatively high in cost but low in perishability. These may account for another 20% of a facility's total annual purchases. Class C inventory items

Exhibit 6.5 The A-B-C-D Classification Scheme for Food Items in Inventory

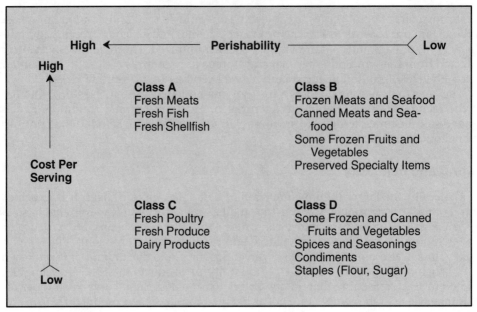

are relatively low in cost per serving, but relatively high in perishability. Class D inventory items have both the lowest perishability and the lowest cost per serving.

There are many advantages of using the A-B-C-D classification scheme, particularly when the storeroom staff is limited. Analyzing the operation's inventory according to this scheme forces the inventory person to consider both relative perishability and cost per serving. The scheme is also straightforward and easy to use. Inventory control should focus primarily on Class A and Class B items, since these account for the greatest dollar volume of inventory and comprise the products likeliest to be stolen by staff members. Of secondary importance are the Class C items, which should be monitored frequently for contamination and spoilage.

Like most classification schemes, the A-B-C-D system is a simplification of reality. Because relative costs vary from operation to operation, some food items may not be categorized exactly as shown in Exhibit 6.5. However, regardless of individual variations, a facility's control system should focus primarily on foods high in cost and perishability. Strict accounting for these items should protect more than half of the total dollar value of all food products purchased by the business.

Physical and Perpetual Inventories. Of course, to adapt the A-B-C-D classification scheme to an operation's own needs, management must know exactly what the operation's inventory consists of. There are two widely accepted methods of inventory control: physical inventory and perpetual inventory.

A **physical inventory** is an actual count of what is on the shelves. It must be taken each time an income statement is prepared. A sample physical inventory form is shown in Exhibit 6.6. The physical inventory must be accurate because it is used to calculate the operation's food costs and **food cost percentage**. The relevant calculations are as follows:

Exhibit 6.6 Physical Inventory Form

		Physical Inventory						
Type of Product:				Month		Month		
Product	Unit	Amount in Storage	Purchase Price	Total Price	Amount in Storage	Purchase Price	Total Price	
Col. 1	Col. 2	Col. 3	Col. 4	Col. 5	Col. 6	Col. 7	Col. 8	
Applesauce	6 #10	4 1/3	$15.85	$68.63				
Green Beans	6 #10	3 5/6	18.95	72.58				
Flour	25# bag	3	4.85	14.55				
Rice	50# bag	1	12.50	12.50				
			Total	$486.55				

Source: Jack D. Ninemeier, *Planning and Control for Food and Beverage Operations*, 3d ed. (East Lansing, Mich.: Educational Institute of the American Hotel & Motel Association, 1991), p. 165.

Gross Food Cost	=	Beginning Inventory Dollar Value + Purchases − Ending Inventory Value
Net Food Cost	=	Gross Food Cost + Bar Transfers to the Kitchen − Food Transfers to the Bar − Staff Member Meals − Complimentary Meals
Food Cost Percentage	=	$\dfrac{\text{Net Food Cost}}{\text{Total Food Sales During the Period}}$

A physical inventory is also necessary in order to calculate **inventory turnover**—the rate at which inventory is converted to revenue during a given period. An excessively low inventory turnover rate can lead to increased spoilage and contamination as well as tie up cash in inventory. However, if turnover rates are too high, production may be hampered by insufficient inventory. High inventory turnover might also indicate that the business is not taking advantage of quantity discounts. Ideal inventory turnover rates can only be established by tracking past rates and calculating averages. Inventory turnover is calculated as follows:

$$\text{Average Inventory} = \frac{\text{Beginning Inventory Dollar Value} + \text{Ending Inventory Dollar Value}}{2}$$

Exhibit 6.7 Perpetual Inventory Form

	**Perpetual Inventory**
colspan="4"	**Product Name:** _P.D.Q. Shrimp_	colspan="5"	**Purchase Unit Size:** _5 lb bag_

Date	In Carried Forward	Out	Balance 15	Date	In Carried Forward	Out	Balance
Col. 1	Col. 2	Col. 3	Col. 4	Col. 1	Col. 2	Col. 3	Col. 4
5/16		3	12				
5/17		3	9				
5/18	6		15				
5/19		2	13				

Source: Jack D. Ninemeier, *Planning and Control for Food and Beverage Operations*, 3d ed. (East Lansing, Mich.: Educational Institute of the American Hotel & Motel Association, 1991), p. 167.

$$\text{Inventory Turnover} \quad = \quad \frac{\text{Net Food Cost}}{\text{Average Inventory}}$$

The person in charge of inventory control may track turnover in each of the four classes of inventory items. Class A and Class C items should have higher turnover rates than Class B and Class D items. It might also be useful to calculate turnover rates for all categories of potentially hazardous foods, as part of the SRM program. The frequency of deliveries must be considered when establishing inventory control standards.

A **perpetual inventory** is an ongoing record of what is in storage at any given time. As products are added to or removed from storage, the balance figure for each item is adjusted. The actual amount of any item on the shelves should agree exactly with the corresponding balance figure at all times. A perpetual inventory form is presented in Exhibit 6.7.

Although the perpetual inventory system requires more recordkeeping, it offers several advantages over periodic physical inventories. The perpetual inventory is always up to date, and the close monitoring involved in this system prevents food spoilage from progressing uncontrolled in storage areas. In addition, the perpetual inventory form, if accurate, allows tight control over food products. The perpetual inventory system is used mainly for expensive (Class A and B) menu items such as meat, fish, shellfish, specialty foods, and expensive spices. The perpetual inventory of such costly items lets staff members know that these items are being watched.

Other Inventory Controls. Another important inventory management technique is the rotation of food supplies on a first-in-first-out (FIFO) basis. According to the FIFO system, new stock is stored *behind* old stock so that the older products will always be used first. If products are dated upon receipt, managers can check each storage area during physical inventory to be sure that the FIFO system is being followed. The food production supervisor (usually the chef or assistant manager) should also make a daily FIFO check.

All stored food products, especially those that are potentially hazardous, should be regularly checked for acceptable sensory qualities. Any damaged products or items with abnormal colors, textures, or odors should be discarded. Keeping records on all spoiled food products helps management identify areas for improvement and helps the accounting department maintain accurate inventory values.

Potentially hazardous foods should not be stored in contact with other foods. Cooked foods should be stored above raw foods, and all foods in storage should be dated and wrapped or covered. Remember that foods should never be frozen or refrozen in a food establishment because these freezers are designed to *store* already-frozen foods.

Toxic and poisonous materials—such as cleaners, sanitizers, and pesticides—must be clearly labeled and stored in areas that are physically away from food products. It is a good idea to keep these storage areas locked. These substances should be stored in their original containers, which should not be re-used.

The FDA states:

"Poisonous or toxic materials" means substances that are not intended for ingestion and are included in 4 categories:

(a) Cleaners and sanitizers, which include cleaning and sanitizing agents and agents such as caustics, acids, drying agents, polishes, and other chemicals;

(b) Pesticides, which include substances such as insecticides and rodenticides;

(c) Substances necessary for the operation and maintenance of the establishment such as nonfood grade lubricants and personal care items that may be deleterious to health; and

(d) Substances that are not necessary for the operation and maintenance of the establishment and are on the premises for retail sale, such as petroleum products and paints.

Source: FDA 1993 *Food Code.*

Storing and People

The storing function is a weak link in the control systems of some food service operations. These operations experience large losses due to contamination, spoilage, and deterioration of their food products, usually because no one is in charge of monitoring storage areas. Although a small business may not be able to justify hiring a storeroom person on a full-time basis, responsibility for storage areas must be given to one dependable person (for example, the chef or assistant manager). The establishment's investment in food and non-food products is too great to be treated haphazardly.

The responsibilities of the storeroom person vary with the operation and the dollar value of its inventory. In smaller operations, the storeroom person often has other responsibilities such as receiving, issuing, and/or production. However, these multiple responsibilities need not be a problem if the person follows the proper routines at each control point.

The major responsibilities of the storeroom person are:

- To conduct frequent, careful inspections of product storage areas in the facility
- To prevent waste in the form of spoilage and decreased product quality
- To discard food that is contaminated or spoiled and thus reduce risks
- To reduce financial losses due to theft and pilferage
- To monitor usage rates of each product
- To record inventory dollar amounts using the perpetual inventory and/or physical inventory system

The purpose of a storeroom person's inspections is to ensure that the operation's quality and safety standards are being maintained. Proper care of inventory items also contributes to the cost control program. Waste in the form of spoilage and decreased product quality increases the cost of goods sold and therefore lowers profits. By preserving food properly (see Chapter 4), the storeroom person makes a major contribution to the operation's bottom-line performance.

Contaminated food must be removed from inventory in order to protect the health of guests and the reputation of the establishment. When in doubt about the safety of an inventory item, it is better to throw it out than to risk an outbreak of foodborne disease. When checking for contamination or spoilage, check the product pull dates on milk and other dairy products.

Unfortunately, theft and pilferage are common in the food service industry. Security is therefore as important in storage areas as it is in the rest of the operation. The establishment of inventory controls can make losses easier to detect.

There are several good reasons for monitoring product usage rates. The information gained in this process can help the purchasing agent to establish par stocks and automatic reorder points, thus minimizing stockouts. The production department can be alerted to surplus products which are not being used up fast enough; these inventory items can then be worked into production before they spoil.

Storing and Equipment

Equipment is an important consideration in each of the three storage areas—dry, refrigerated, and frozen. Ambient storage temperatures in all three of these areas must be monitored with thermometers that are accurate to $\pm 3\,°F$ ($\pm 2\,°C$). A thermometer should be placed in the warmest part of each storage area; the warmest part of a refrigerator or freezer is usually near the door.

The FDA states:

4-203.12   Ambient Temperature Measuring Devices.

(A) Ambient temperature measuring devices that are scaled in Celsius or dually scaled in Celsius and Fahrenheit shall be designed to be easily readable and accurate to $1.5\,°C$ ($2.7\,°F$) at the use range.

(B) Ambient temperature measuring devices that are scaled only in Fahrenheit shall be accurate to ±3°F at the use range.

Source: FDA 1993 *Food Code.*

Thermometers should be positioned to be easily readable. A product thermometer with an accuracy of ±2°F (±1°C) should also be used regularly to monitor the internal product temperatures of potentially hazardous foods in storage.

Many types of storage containers are used to hold food inventory, from pans and pots to plastic containers. When purchasing plastic containers and bags for food storage, buy them from a restaurant supplier and specify food-grade materials. Food products should not be stored in galvanized cans, non-food-grade bags or containers, or cardboard boxes. All containers must be properly labeled with the common name.

The FDA states:

3-302.12   Food Storage Containers, Identified with Common Name of Food.

Working containers holding food or food ingredients that are removed from their original packages for use in the establishment, such as cooking oils, flour, herbs, potato flakes, salt, spices, and sugar shall be identified with the common name of the food *except that containers holding food that can be readily and unmistakably recognized such as dry pasta need not be identified.*

Source: FDA 1993 *Food Code.*

The proper storage of equipment and utensils provides protection from food, splash, and dust in storage areas. Cleaned and sanitized equipment and utensils must be stored in a clean, dry location, in a self-draining position, and covered or inverted at least 6 inches (15.2 cm) above the floor. Utensils should be hung overhead or stored on utensil racks, not in cluttered drawers. Knives and special tools should be stored on trays. The best way to store cutting boards is vertically under counters or in a cutting board rack.

The FDA states:

3-305.11   Food Storage.

(A) Except as specified in ¶¶ (B) and (C) of this section, food shall be protected from contamination by storing the food:

   (1)   In a clean, dry location;

   (2)   Where it is not exposed to splash, dust, or other contamination; and

   (3)   At least 15 cm (6 inches) above the floor.

(B) *Food in packages and working containers may be stored less than 15 cm (6 inches) above the floor on case lot handling equipment as specified under § 4-204.121.*

(C) *Pressurized beverage containers, cased food in waterproof containers such as bottles or cans, and milk containers in plastic crates may be stored on a floor that is clean and not exposed to floor moisture.*

3-305.12   Food Storage, Prohibited Areas.

Food may not be stored:

    (A)   In locker rooms;

    (B)   In toilet rooms;

    (C)   In dressing rooms;

    (D)   In garbage rooms;

    (E)   In mechanical rooms;

    (F)   Under sewer lines that are not shielded to intercept potential drips;

    (G)   Under leaking water lines, including leaking automatic fire sprinkler heads, or under lines on which water has condensed;

    (H)   Under open stairwells; or

    (I)   Under other sources of contamination.

6-501.113   Storing Maintenance Equipment.

Maintenance tools such as brooms, mops, vacuum cleaners, and similar equipment shall be:

    (A)   Stored so they do not contaminate food, equipment, utensils, linens, and single-service and single-use articles; and

    (B)   Stored in an orderly manner that facilitates cleaning of the maintenance equipment storage location.

Source: FDA 1993 *Food Code.*

Tableware, including dishes, bowls, platters, and plates of all sizes, can present a unique storage problem. A self-leveling plate dispenser can help prevent breakage and contamination. The spring-loaded dispenser can be loaded with clean, sanitized tableware at the dishwashing machine and wheeled to kitchen areas for service. Some plate dispensers also heat or chill tableware.

Storing and Facilities

Each of the three types of food storage areas—dry, refrigerated, and frozen—has its own standards and requirements.

Dry Storage. Dry storage areas are designed to secure shelf-stable foods that do not require refrigeration. A properly designed dry storage area is clean, orderly, and well-ventilated. Good housekeeping in dry storage reduces contamination risks as well as fire hazards.

Dry storage areas should not house motors, compressors, machinery, water and heating pipes, or other utility structures. The walls and floors should be constructed of easy-to-clean materials. Protection from insects and rodents is essential. There should be adequate light for reading product labels. Security measures should include locked doors and proper key control.

All food in the dry storage area must be on shelves at least two inches (5.1 cm) from walls and six inches (15.2 cm) from the floor. This clearance not only facilitates inspection and cleaning, but also aids ventilation, prevents contamination, and eliminates pest harborage areas. All products should be stored at least 18 inches (45.7 cm) away from light bulbs and tubes. Bulbs and tubes should be shielded to protect food supplies from glass fragments in case of breakage.

Many operations use shelving on wheels to facilitate storage area cleaning. Open wire shelving is generally best for all three storage areas because it gives an unobstructed view of the products, permits free air circulation, and is usually more adaptable to changing storage needs. Shelves that are open on both sides and located in the center of the room provide the most efficient use of floor space. This center-aisle arrangement (often called library) also makes stock rotation easier.

Each type of product in inventory should have its own assigned location in the storeroom. Bulky and heavy items should be placed on lower shelves, and frequently-used items should be placed near the entrance. Whenever a product is opened in storage, it must be kept away from containers that may be contaminated with dirt, wire, splinters, or other debris. The storeroom person must guard the food against physical hazards such as glass fragments and metal chips.

Storage time-temperature combinations are important because they keep food products high in nutrients, at peak flavor and texture, and safe to eat. All food in dry storage areas should be covered, labeled, and dated. Ideal storage temperatures are 50° to 70°F (10° to 21°C). Relative humidity should be about 50 to 60%. A thermometer should be mounted in the dry storage area, and the storeroom person should record the temperature at least twice each day. This and other information may be recorded on a **storage area condition report.** A sample of this form, which is useful for all three types of storage, is presented in Exhibit 6.8.

Federal and state codes specify dry food storage requirements. The objective in dry storage is to minimize contamination and the proliferation of pathogens. By monitoring storage times and temperatures, an operation protects the quality and safety of its food products and reduces risks.

The FDA states:

"Premises" means:

(a) The physical facility, its contents, and the contiguous land or property under the control of the permit holder; or

(b) The physical facility, its contents, and the contiguous land or property and its facilities and contents that are under the control of the permit holder that may

Exhibit 6.8 Storage Area Condition Report

AREA

☐ Dry

☐ Refrigerated

☐ Freezer   Date _____

Storage Area	Location	Temperature	Relative Humidity	Time Recorded	Signature of Recorder	Comments

impact food establishment personnel, facilities, or operations, if a food establishment is only one component of a larger organization such as a health care facility, hotel, motel, school, recreational camp, or prison.

6-403.11   Designated Areas.

(A) Areas designated for employees to eat, drink, and use tobacco shall be located so that food, equipment, linens, and single-service and single-use articles are protected from contamination.

6-202.11   Light Bulbs, Protective Shielding.

(A) Except as specified in ¶ (B) of this section, light bulbs shall be shielded, coated, or otherwise shatter-resistant in areas where there is exposed food; clean equipment, utensils, and linens; or unwrapped single-service and single-use articles.

(B) *Shielded, coated, or otherwise shatter-resistant bulbs need not be used in areas used only for storing food in unopened packages, if:*

(1)   The integrity of the packages can not be affected by broken glass falling onto them; and

(2) *The packages are capable of being cleaned of debris from broken bulbs before the packages are opened.*

(C) An infrared or other heat lamp shall be protected against breakage by a shield surrounding and extending beyond the bulb so that only the face of the bulb is exposed.

Source: FDA 1993 *Food Code.*

Refrigerated Storage. Refrigerated storage areas are designed to maintain food products at temperatures of 41°F (5°C) or less. Remember to check the health department specifications in your area. Refrigerators must have visible thermometers, and temperatures should be checked at least four times per day.

Most operators complain that they lack adequate refrigerated and frozen storage space. While in some cases modification of the facilities may be in order, limited refrigerated and frozen storage space has its advantages. It can force the production supervisor to control food inventories more carefully, to organize the areas more efficiently, and to work to avoid spoilage.

Because refrigerated storage serves to prolong the shelf life of perishable foods, the FIFO system is indispensable. Foods in refrigerated storage must be at least six inches (15.2 cm) off the floor and two inches (5.1 cm) away from walls to allow for air movement and to reduce insect and rodent harborage areas. Doors on refrigeration units should only be opened for a short time and only when necessary. To avoid having to search for an item, it is a good idea to post the contents of each cooling unit on its door. Placing frequently-used foods near the door of the unit also reduces the amount of time the door is open. Food products on shelves must not be jammed against the cooling unit doors when closed. This may damage the door gaskets and thus cause leaks.

Once canned products are opened, they must be removed from their original containers and placed in clean, labeled, dated, covered containers. Perishable or potentially hazardous foods should be refrigerated in pans not more than four inches (10.2 cm) deep.

Leftover food products should be covered to prevent contamination during refrigeration. However, they should not be covered airtight until chilled to 41°F (5°C); placing an airtight cover on food before it is chilled encourages the growth of anaerobic microorganisms during product cooling. (Chilling is discussed more fully in Chapter 7.) Leftover prepared food must be stored above raw ingredients to prevent cross-contamination. Storing warm foods above already-refrigerated foods will allow the heat to dissipate more quickly. Refrigerated leftovers should be labeled with the date they were first stored; potentially hazardous leftovers should be used within 24 hours of storage or thrown out. Any spoiled foods discovered in storage areas should be discarded immediately.

Refrigeration needs have changed with the addition of fresh items to food service menus; these items require more refrigerated storage space. Recently-designed food establishments use a number of refrigeration units to build a refrigeration system. Walk-in refrigerators are used to store large quantities of food in bulk. Some walk-in refrigerators have a thermal curtain made of four-inch (10.2 cm) plastic strips in addition to a door. These curtains conserve energy and prevent accidents because workers can easily enter and exit coolers without having to open or close doors. Reach-in refrigerators are short-term storage units, often placed near cooking stations and stocked with food products needed during the meal period. Refrigerated drawers are an alternative to reach-in refrigerators and are also located near the cooking station. Roll-in refrigerators are specifically designed to accommodate carts. A dual-temperature unit (sometimes called a refrigerator-freezer) can be converted from a freezer to a refrigerator, or vice versa, at the flip of a switch.

Sanitation management is often more critical in refrigerated areas than in dry storage areas. Fortunately, refrigerators are relatively easy to clean and maintain if spills are wiped up promptly. Exterior surfaces should be cleaned daily with a hot water-detergent solution, rinsed, and dried with a clean cloth. The floors of walk-in units should be mopped daily. These floors are easier to maintain if they are made of ceramic quarry tile. On a weekly basis, or more frequently if necessary, the contents of each refrigerator should be transferred to another unit. All shelves should be removed, and the inner walls of the compartment washed, rinsed, and dried. A mild sanitizing solution (180–220 mg/L QUATS) should be applied to the interior surfaces to minimize mold and bacterial growth. Refrigerator shelves should also be washed, rinsed, and dried, and plastic thermal curtains should be cleaned with glass cleaner. (See Chapter 9.)

Once a month, the accumulation of dust and grease on the refrigerator's condenser and evaporator units should be cleaned away. Any water condensation should also be removed before the refrigerator is reassembled. The fans and motors inside and outside the refrigerator should be cleaned and checked every three months. Hinges and latches require oiling every six months. All refrigeration units must have thermometers, and they should be checked for accuracy ($\pm 3°F/\pm 2°C$) periodically.

Zinc- and chrome-coated wire shelving is usually a problem in high-moisture areas because it tends to rust and is difficult to keep clean. Any rusted shelving should be replaced. Only epoxy-coated or stainless steel open wire shelving on wheels should be used in refrigerators and freezers.

Frozen Storage. The maximum temperature in frozen storage areas is $0°F$ ($-18°C$). Like refrigeration units, storage freezers should have visible thermometers which should be checked four times each day. Unsafe temperatures or faulty thermometers should be reported to the food production supervisor immediately. As previously discussed, most freezers in food service operations are designed to keep already-frozen foods frozen—not to freeze foods.

Freezers are available in many forms, including walk-in, reach-in, countertop, and drawer models. Freezers should be defrosted and cleaned at least monthly; follow the same procedure as for cleaning refrigerators, avoiding harsh cleaners and abrasives. The contents should be temporarily transferred to another freezer to prevent thawing. This process is easier if freezer shelves are already on wheels. Condensers, evaporators, and other machinery should be checked monthly.

It is important to guard against loss of quality during freezer storage. Carefully wrapping food products in moisture- and air-resistant wrapping deters dehydration (freezer burn) and other forms of deterioration. The food production supervisor should personally inspect each storage area on a daily basis to be sure the operation's food and beverage assets are being protected.

Some foods freeze better than others. Those that do not freeze well include high-water-content fruits and vegetables such as cucumbers, lettuce, watermelon, and plums. Unblanched vegetables also do not freeze well, and most untreated fruits become mushy when frozen. Dairy products such as yogurt, cream (light and sour), cottage and ricotta cheese, and cream cheese do not freeze well. Some sauces and gravies separate when frozen and thawed. Desserts with dairy products or eggs, such as meringues, custard pies, and puddings, as well as gelatin-based desserts, do not maintain their appearance or consistency when thawed after freezing.

Potentially hazardous foods should never be frozen or thawed and refrozen in the food service operation. All thawing is safer and more efficient under refrigeration: foods thaw under carefully controlled conditions and enable the refrigerator to use less power. A thorough discussion of thawing appears in Chapter 4.

Violations of the food storage section of the FDA's Food Code occur regularly in food establishments. Some operations store food products uncovered and unlabeled or in non-food-grade plastic bags. In many establishments, storage areas are not designed to keep food products away from walls and floors. Some storage facilities are not equipped with accurate thermometers. In other operations, no one checks storage temperatures regularly. Such violations, although common, greatly increase the risks of running a food establishment. The operator who avoids such violations will ultimately enjoy greater success.

Storing and Change

A change in storing procedures is necessary when any of the other three control points which precede it are altered. For example, storage area requirements may change drastically if an operation changes from all-scratch preparation methods to the use of convenience foods. More refrigerated and frozen storage areas may be necessary, particularly in an older establishment. Management must consider the resources of the storing control point before making such operational changes.

Storing and the SRM Program

Storing is an important activity to monitor in a food establishment for two reasons: food products rarely improve in quality while in storage, and the risk of food contamination is increased by improper storage temperatures or times. All food products must be dated, labeled, and covered before being placed in storage. These controls encourage the use of the FIFO inventory system and minimize the risks of potential contamination. They also help prevent waste which occurs when stored products cannot be identified or when they absorb odors or flavors from other food products.

Temperatures and times must be closely monitored in dry, refrigerated, and frozen storage. Products must also be regularly checked with sensory tests to minimize the chances of serving spoiled products. Staff members at the storing control point should be trained to conduct inspections, prevent waste, identify and dispose of spoiled food products, and reduce risks.

Equipment and facilities must be regularly cleaned, sanitized, and maintained. Written schedules which include detailed staff responsibilities help ensure that these important duties are performed regularly. Such control measures at the storing control point reduce the risks for guests, staff members, and owners of a food establishment.

The Issuing Control Point

The objective of the issuing control point is to ensure proper authorization for the transfer of food products from storage to the production departments of the operation. The issuing function should be designed to guarantee that only authorized staff members order and receive products from the facility's storage areas. A properly designed issuing system also facilitates calculation of the daily food cost. In addition, issuing is an important component of the sanitation risk management program: potentially hazardous foods can be exposed to the TDZ at this control point, and additional handling may contaminate food products.

In small operations, formal issuing may be eliminated entirely. In such cases, all purchases are regarded as direct purchases: supplies are charged directly to the department or unit in which they are used. The direct purchase system eliminates the need for a formal requisition. Department staff members simply obtain supplies from a central storage area. These individuals must therefore inform the operation's purchasing agent of shortages or stockouts. Although this system is simple and less time-consuming, it does not provide as much control as a formal system. The informal system also leaves storage areas with no one specifically responsible for them, and thus the operation's issuing control point is at risk.

Issuing and Inventory

A **requisition** is a form for requesting inventory. It is an internal communication tool that shows which department needs which items. A department must provide a written and authorized requisition before being issued any products. Requisition forms may be sequentially numbered and/or color-coded by department for control purposes. A sample food requisition form is shown in Exhibit 6.9.

Written requisitions provide documentation and, therefore, greater control. Documentation is important whenever a product is transferred from one area of responsibility to another (in this case, from storage to production). A supply of products sufficient for one day or one meal period is usually issued to each department.

The costs of issues should be properly recorded on the requisition form, a process made easier when products are marked with the price during receiving. Costing issues facilitates the calculation of daily food cost and reminds staff members to think of inventory as money. Requisitions must be subtracted from perpetual inventory records to maintain accuracy. Tracking daily issues helps establish usage rates and reorder points.

Issuing should be done on an FIFO basis. This is easier if products are dated before storing. Proper stock rotation minimizes spoilage, contamination, and loss of product quality. The order in which products are assembled for issuing is the reverse of the order in which they are stored. That is, the least perishable items are taken from storage first and the most perishable products last. This minimizes possible contamination and maintains product temperature control.

The food production manager (chef or assistant manager) should be notified if perishable products are nearing the end of their shelf life. Issues should be checked for acceptable odor, feel, and appearance. In addition, a random temperature check should be made with the metal-stemmed product probe thermometer. Remember to always clean and sanitize the metal-stemmed product probe thermometer between changed uses to avoid cross-contamination.

Issuing and People

The person in charge of the storeroom ensures that each order has been properly authorized, removes product storage tags, and fills orders. The storeroom person then costs out each item ordered and totals the costs. He or she sends a copy of the completed requisition to the operation's accounting office along with any storage tags. This system helps prevent theft, pilferage, and unauthorized issues.

While assembling orders, the storeroom person should note any items in short supply and direct this information to the operation's buyer. Accuracy and careful inspection

Exhibit 6.9 Food Requisition Form

					Employee Initials	
Item	**Purchase Unit**	**No. of Units**	**Unit Price**	**Total Cost**	**Received By**	**Withdrawn By**
Col. 1	Col. 2	Col. 3	Col. 4	Col. 5	Col. 6	Col. 7
Tomato Paste	CS-6 #10	2 ½	$28.50	$71.25	JC	Ken
Green Beans	CS-6 #10	1 ½	22.75	34.13	JC	Ken
				Total	$596.17	

Food Requisition

Storage Type (check one):
Refrigerated_____
Frozen _____
Dry _____✓_____

Date: _____

Work Unit: _____

Approved for Withdrawal: _____

Source: Jack D. Ninemeier, *Planning and Control for Food and Beverage Operations*, 3d ed. (East Lansing, Mich.: Educational Institute of the American Hotel & Motel Association, 1991), p. 173.

of written requests for inventory items are important during product issuing. In some establishments, the storeroom person also delivers orders to the production departments. Specified issuing times for each department can eliminate confusion and enable the storeroom person to work more efficiently.

Issuing and Equipment

Generally, the same kinds of equipment are used during the receiving and issuing of inventory. Products issued by weight should be weighed before they are released to the production department. A thermometer is used to check internal product temperatures. Calculators are useful in determining the dollar amount of each department's order and the total of all issues for the day. Handcarts and dollies are used to transport products from storage facilities to production areas.

Issuing and Facilities

Storeroom facilities must be attended to if the issuing control system is to remain intact. For maximum security, storeroom facilities should be kept locked with access limited to the storeroom person and the manager. Prohibiting unauthorized access to storage areas helps eliminate theft and pilferage. The facilities used for issuing must be maintained to reduce the risk of product contamination.

Issuing and Change

Issuing, like all of the control points, is affected by changes that occur in the food service system. Existing policies and standards are based on the present system; if a component of the system is modified in the future, it may also be necessary to alter issuing procedures and standards.

Although the requisition form is an important control tool, food establishments with relatively low business volumes are likely to follow an informal set of issuing guidelines. In such operations, production staff members often retrieve food products from an unlocked storage area whenever they need them. However, if the volume of business increases, the operation should implement a formal issuing system. The formal system, complete with storeroom personnel and written requisition forms, will help the operation achieve more control over sanitation, cost, and quality—factors that ultimately have a dramatic effect on guest satisfaction.

Issuing and the SRM Program

Whenever food products change departments, the responsibility for those products changes departments and risks are increased. Therefore, a written and authorized requisition form is essential at the issuing control point. This tool helps reduce risks because it clearly indicates who receives each food product.

Food products should be checked at issuing with sensory tests. This inspection reduces the risks of a contaminated or spoiled product entering the production control points. Equipment and facilities used during issuing must be regularly cleaned, sanitized, and maintained to prevent cross-contamination and help ensure the safety of finished menu items.

Summary

Receiving is an important control point because the ownership of food products is transferred from the supplier to the establishment. Invoice errors become the operation's errors once the invoice is signed by the receiver. Only those products which meet the operation's sanitation, quality, and cost standards should be accepted.

The storing control point protects the establishment's inventory from risks, spoilage, contamination, pilferage, and theft. A physical inventory is an actual count of what is on the shelves at a certain point in time. It is used to calculate inventory turnover and the food cost percentage. A perpetual inventory is a running total of the inventory. It is used for the control of high-ticket and perishable raw ingredients. All stock should be rotated so the first items in are also the first items out.

Requisition forms are used to control the issuing function. Inventory items can only be issued to staff members with properly authorized requisition forms. At this control point, products are changing departments, and maintaining documentation for cost control and risk management is critical.

Key Terms

A-B-C-D scheme • credit memo • daily receiving report • food cost percentage • inventory turnover • invoice • perpetual inventory • physical inventory • requisition • storage area condition report • time-temperature monitor

Discussion Questions

1. What inventory controls, standards, and procedures are important at the receiving control point?

2. A staff member performing the receiving function should have what types of qualifications?

3. What equipment items are used at the receiving control point, and why are they important?

4. What are the elements of proper receiving facilities?

5. Why is it important to maintain an optimum inventory?

6. What is the A-B-C-D scheme of inventory classification?

7. How does a perpetual inventory differ from a physical inventory?

8. What are the major responsibilities of the storeroom person?

9. What equipment and facilities considerations are important at the storing control point?

10. What should food service managers know about the issuing control point?

Checklist for Receiving

Inventory

_____ Inventory items are checked for applicable quality, cleanliness, and labeling specifications.

_____ The internal temperatures and sensory-tested qualities of products are evaluated.

_____ Deliveries are verified against the operation's purchase specifications and purchase orders.

_____ The supplier's invoice is checked for accuracy in quality descriptions, quantities, and prices.

_____ All products billed by weight are weighed before the invoice is signed.

_____ Different meat items are weighed separately.

_____ All products billed by count are counted before the invoice is signed.

_____ Products are dated immediately with a marking pen either on the outside container or the individual packages.

_____ Prices may be marked on each product unit.

_____ Where appropriate, product storage tags are used.

_____ All deliveries are recorded on the daily receiving report.

_____ Products are moved to storage in the following order:

   _____ most perishable products (frozen foods)

   _____ moderately perishable products (refrigerated foods)

   _____ least perishable products (dry and non-food items)

_____ A credit memo is requested when products are spoiled, when they do not meet the operation's specifications, or when the wrong amount has been delivered.

People

_____ A member of the management team or a trained staff member performs the receiving function.

_____ The receiver possesses product knowledge, technical skills, and a commitment to the organization.

_____ The receiver judges the quality, quantity, and sanitary condition of products.

_____ The receiver is in good health and practices good personal hygiene and cleanliness.

_____ The receiver understands how to accurately use all required equipment, facilities, and forms.

_____ The receiver knows what to do when there is a problem with product deliveries.

_____ The receiver is able to read and write, and demonstrates honesty and attention to detail.

_____ The receiver uses the purchasing specifications for all items ordered.

_____ Delivery hours are posted on the receiving door. Delivery times are staggered whenever possible, and do not include mealtime rush periods.

_____ The receiver has been trained to perform his or her duties effectively and efficiently, in cooperation with other departments in the food establishment or hotel.

Equipment

_____ An accurate scale is used during receiving to verify product weights.

_____ Product net weights are recorded and checked against the supplier's invoice.

_____ Metal-stemmed product probe thermometers are used during receiving to check the internal temperatures of refrigerated and frozen products.

_____ Refrigerated products are at 41°F (5°C) or less and frozen products are at 0°F (–18°C) or less when delivered.

_____ Tools for opening containers and boxes are available and used properly.

_____ The date of the delivery and the AP price are recorded directly on product packages with a marking pen.

_____ Other tools (including rulers, calculators, transport trucks, dollies, and other equipment to move products) are readily available and used properly.

Facilities

_____ The loading dock and receiving areas are cleaned daily and maintained regularly.

_____ The supplier's truck is periodically inspected for contamination.

_____ Debris or food particles are not allowed to accumulate in receiving areas.

_____ Garbage and trash areas are physically separated from the receiving area, if possible.

_____ The receiving area is well-lit and equipped with the necessary tools and work tables.

SRM Program

_____ Potentially hazardous foods are carefully inspected during receiving.

_____ If acceptable, products are moved to storage as quickly as possible.

_____ Food handlers are trained to maintain standards and reduce risks during receiving.

_____ Adequate equipment and facilities are present, used, and cleaned, sanitized, and maintained frequently to reduce the risks during receiving.

Checklist for Storing

Inventory

_____ Food products are stored on shelves at least six inches (15.2 cm) off the floor and two inches (5.1 cm) away from the walls.

_____ Storage temperatures and relative humidities are maintained as follows:

_____ Dry storage: 50° to 70°F (10° to 21°C); 50 to 60% relative humidity

_____ Refrigerated storage: 41°F (5°C) or less; 80 to 90% relative humidity

_____ Freezer storage: 0°F (–18°C) or less

_____ New inventory is placed behind old inventory as part of the FIFO system.

_____ Bulky and heavy items are stored on lower shelves.

_____ High-use items are stored near the entrance.

_____ A specific place is assigned to each type of item in inventory.

_____ Storage time-temperature combinations are closely monitored.

_____ Refrigerated leftovers are marked with the date they are first stored.

_____ Perishable and potentially hazardous leftovers are stored refrigerated in pans no more than four inches (10.2 cm) deep, and served or discarded within 24 hours.

_____ Inventory items are stored so as to prevent cross-contamination.

_____ Packaged food is not stored in contact with water or undrained ice.

_____ Toxic chemicals (cleaners, sanitizers, and pesticides) are stored away from food products, in physically separate, locked areas.

_____ All damaged products and those with abnormal odors or colors are discarded.

_____ Records of all spoiled food are maintained. Problem areas are identified and deficiencies are corrected.

_____ The A-B-C-D inventory classification is used where applicable.

_____ Perpetual and/or physical inventory systems are used to control inventory.

_____ Inventory turnover is calculated and monitored.

_____ Sensory tests (such as smell, appearance, and feel) are used during storing to monitor product quality.

_____ Potentially hazardous foods are not stored in contact with other foods.

_____ Cooked foods are stored above raw foods.

_____ All foods in storage are dated and wrapped or covered.

_____ Food service freezers are used to store already-frozen foods, not to freeze or refreeze them.

People

_____ Storage area staff members are aware of standards for reducing inventory contamination, spoilage, and quality losses.

_____ Storage area staff members realize that inventory represents an investment that does not earn interest.

_____ A specific person is in charge of accurate and careful inspection of storage areas on a daily basis.

_____ Storage area staff members control the quality, sanitary condition, and costs of inventory.

_____ Storage area staff members monitor the usage rates of inventory items.

_____ Storage area staff members help establish par stocks and reorder points to minimize stockouts and spoilage.

_____ The controller and storage area staff members record inventory dollar amounts.

_____ Storage area staff members are trained to maintain the operation's standards.

Equipment

_____ All storage areas have thermometers accurate to ±3°F (±2°C).

_____ Storage area temperatures are checked several times each day.

_____ Internal product temperatures are measured with metal-stemmed product probe thermometers accurate to ±2°F (±1°C).

_____ Cleaned and sanitized equipment and utensils are stored in a clean and dry location, in a self-draining position, and covered or inverted.

_____ Cleaned and sanitized equipment and utensils are stored at least six inches (15.2 cm) off the floor and protected from splash and dust.

_____ Equipment and utensils are not stored under exposed sewer or water lines.

_____ Equipment, utensils, or single-service items are not stored in toilet rooms or vestibules.

_____ Only food-grade containers and bags are used to store food products.

_____ Utensils are stored on utensil racks or hung overhead, not in cluttered drawers.

_____ Knives and special tools are stored on trays.

_____ Cutting boards are stored vertically under counters in a cutting board rack.

_____ Self-leveling dispensers are used to store tableware, including dishes, bowls, platters, and plates.

Facilities

_____ Storage areas are kept clean, orderly, and well-ventilated.

_____ Dry storage areas do not house motors, machinery, water and heating pipes, and other utility structures.

_____ Walls and floors are constructed of easy-to-clean materials.

_____ Insect and rodent controls are checked regularly in all storage areas.

_____ Key and lock controls are used to maintain security in storage areas.

_____ Storage areas have adequate lighting, and bulbs and tubes are shielded for protection.

_____ The door of each refrigerator and freezer is marked with the contents of the unit.

_____ Refrigeration and frozen storage units are not overloaded with inventory.

_____ Stainless steel or epoxy-coated open wire shelving on wheels is used in walk-in refrigerators and freezers and in dry storage areas.

_____ A system of regular cleaning and maintenance is followed.

_____ A storage area temperature-recording form is used.

SRM Program

_____ Potentially hazardous foods are stored carefully and safely.

_____ Food handlers are trained to maintain standards and reduce risks during storing.

_____ Adequate facilities and equipment are present, used, and are frequently cleaned, sanitized, and maintained to reduce the risks during storing.

Checklist for Issuing

Inventory

_____ Requisition forms are sequentially numbered or color-coded to facilitate recordkeeping.

_____ Each department is issued sufficient product quantities to last for one meal period or one day.

_____ Proper stock rotation (the FIFO system) is used to minimize contamination, spoilage, and product quality loss.

_____ Issues are costed accurately so that the total value of requisitions can be calculated on a daily basis.

_____ Sensory tests (such as odor, feel, appearance) are used to check inventory during issuing.

_____ Temperatures are checked with a cleaned and sanitized metal-stemmed product probe thermometer.

People

_____ The issuer releases products only with a written requisition.

_____ The issuer checks to see that the requisition is properly authorized.

_____ The issuer costs the items and extends the figures on the requisition.

_____ The issuer removes storage tags from products and attaches them to the requisition.

_____ The issuer removes products from storage in the following order:

_____ least perishable products (dry and non-food items)

_____ moderately perishable products (refrigerated foods)

_____ most perishable products (frozen foods)

_____ The issuer has been trained to maintain the operation's standards.

Equipment

_____ Products issued by weight are weighed before release to the production department.

_____ Calculators, handcarts, and other tools are used when necessary.

_____ A metal-stemmed product probe thermometer is used to check the internal product temperature during issuing.

Facilities

_____ Storeroom facilities are locked when unattended.

_____ Storeroom facilities are only accessible to authorized staff members.

_____ Facilities used for issuing are cleaned and maintained regularly to reduce the risk of product contamination.

SRM Program

_____ Potentially hazardous foods are issued carefully and safely.

_____ Food handlers are trained to maintain standards and reduce risks during issuing.

_____ Adequate facilities and equipment are present, used, and are frequently cleaned, sanitized, and maintained to reduce the risks during issuing.

Case Study

Using the menu item that you selected in Chapter 5, continue with the control points covered in this chapter. Describe standards and specifications for the main ingredient inventory item. Describe what you would expect to find on the invoice and detail the product inspection techniques that you would use during receiving.

If you decide to use a product storage tag, complete the information in Exhibit 6.2. Fill in the information required for the inventory item on the daily receiving report found in Exhibit 6.3. Complete Exhibit 6.3 for all potentially hazardous ingredients in your menu item.

Describe the qualifications for receiving staff members in your operation. Specify the equipment and facilities needed to properly receive your main ingredient.

Next, follow your main ingredient through the storing control point. Discuss the problems associated with excessively large inventories. Classify your main ingredient using the A-B-C-D scheme and explain your decision. Develop a way to ensure the FIFO inventory system is used with ingredients in your menu item.

Describe the sensory tests that you will use to monitor your product's quality during storage. List any additional standards for your main ingredient. Describe a system for storing toxic and poisonous materials in a food establishment.

Outline the functions of the storeroom person. Describe the equipment that will be used to help control the storing activity for your menu item. Define ways to properly store equipment and utensils. Specify the proper storage containers for your main ingredient. Develop a system to safely store equipment, utensils, knives, special tools, cutting boards, and tableware.

Describe the standards for dry, refrigerated, and frozen storage facilities. Include temperature, relative humidity, location, shelving, lighting, and other relevant factors in your description.

Finally, turn your attention to the issuing control point. Describe relevant standards for the inventory, people, equipment, and facilities resources. Fill in the information required to requisition all ingredients in your menu item on Exhibit 6.9. Outline your approach using the checklists.

Your development of this case study will, in part, depend on the menu item you select. Nevertheless, the basic principles of the receiving, storing, and issuing control points can be analyzed even without applying them to an actual food establishment. If you are currently employed in a food establishment, you may wish to choose a menu item that is currently being offered or one that is under consideration for addition to the menu.

An SRM Program Example: Whitefish and the Receiving, Storing, and Issuing Control Points

The receiver will inspect the fresh whitefish upon delivery for proper temperature, freshness, wholesomeness, integrity, and case condition, that is, that the fish is commercially and legally caught. When received, the fish should be in the temperature range of 32° to 38°F (0° to 3°C); the receiver checks the temperature with a product probe thermometer. The receiver checks the cases; if any of the cases are damaged, the receiver opens them and inspects the contents. The ice should be clean and crushed. Ten 10- to 12-oz (280 to 336 g) fillets should be packed in each case; the receiver will randomly check the weight of the fillets.

Freshness and wholesomeness are indicators of quality. Quality fresh whitefish fillets have shiny skin with no scales. The flesh should be firm and have a mild, sweet odor. The product should be in sound condition—free from spoilage, filth, or other contamination. The receiver will randomly check for the presence of parasites. If any of the freshness and wholesomeness test results are unacceptable, the fish will be rejected. The fish must come from Lake Superior and match all factors specified on the standard purchase specification.

The receiver has been properly trained to maintain personal hygiene and cleanliness standards, use the necessary equipment and forms, and determine acceptable product quality characteristics based on the establishment's standard purchase specifications. The receiver has copies of the specifications, along with copies of all purchase orders. The receiver is honest, pays attention to details, and is committed to protecting the interests of the operation by cooperating with all other departments.

Equipment used during receipt of the whitefish includes a scale, a thermometer, and a calculator. The receiver uses the calculator to quickly verify the accuracy of the invoice. The receiver marks the date and price on the outside of the containers and transports them to storage using a handcart.

The receiving facilities are clean, with no buildup of debris, food particles, or empty shipping containers. An outdoor disposal area is located away from the receiving dock and is surrounded by a fence to block the view from the parking lot. The whitefish is stored at 28° to 32°F (-2° to 0°C) on clean crushed ice. The ice is changed daily, and drip pans are used to allow for drainage of melted ice. The containers are dated, labeled, covered, and stored below cooked foods in a refrigerator that is used exclusively for fish and shellfish. The storage time for the fresh whitefish is 1 to 2 days.

The fresh fish is a Class A inventory item, high in perishability and cost per serving. The whitefish is checked daily for acceptable odor, appearance, and feel. The FIFO inventory system is used for the whitefish, and it is monitored with a physical (but not perpetual) inventory system in the kitchen.

The people involved in storing the fresh whitefish have been properly trained to conduct inspections, prevent waste, discard unacceptable fish, and reduce risks. The storeroom person realizes the value of waste prevention and risk reduction. Whitefish usage rates are monitored closely so that in-stock inventory is always at its freshest and highest quality.

The walk-in refrigerator used to store the whitefish has a built-in thermometer accurate to ±3°F (±2°C), and the temperature in the refrigerator is set at 28°F (-2°C). The fish is stored at least six inches (15.2 cm) off the floor and two inches (5.1 cm) away from walls. The contents of the refrigeration unit are posted on the door, along with a storage area condition report. Floors are cleaned at least twice a day, and the walls, ceiling, and shelves are cleaned every two weeks.

The whitefish will be requisitioned using a written form. The FIFO inventory system will be followed, and the fish will be issued after the dry and other refrigerated items are issued. The storeroom person will check the order, fill the order, and send the requisition to the accounting office. He or she will check the whitefish for acceptable odor, appearance, and feel, as well as count the fillets and perform a temperature check.

The storage facilities are staffed by a full-time storeroom person who is responsible for security, cleanliness, and maintenance of the facilities up to the standards defined by management.

References

Baird, Patricia. "Frozen Assets." *Restaurant Business,* May 20, 1989, pp. 94, 96.

Blynn, L. C. "Inventory Control." *Lodging,* September 1982, pp. 75–77.

Bohan, G. T. "Food Receiving." *Lodging,* July 1982, pp. 53–56.

Cichy, Ronald F. "Kitchen Sanitation." *Hotel & Resort Industry,* February 1989, pp. 80–84, 86, 87.

———. "The Role of the Executive Chef in Inventory Control." *Rocky Mountain Chefs Magazine,* March 1983, p. 8.

Cichy, R. F., and R. P. Krump. "Cost Controls Part III: Receiving, Storing, and Issuing." *Rocky Mountain Chefs Magazine,* May 1985, p. 6.

Cichy, R. F., and J. M. Steuck. "Inventory Control: Guidelines for Success." *Insite,* 1984, pp. 26–27, 54.

Curran, George. "Caddy System Alleviates Dish-struction Problem." *Restaurants & Institutions,* June 24, 1987, p. 146.

———. "Chilling Prospects for Food." *Restaurants & Institutions,* June 24, 1987, pp. 144–145.

Ellis, Ray C. "How to Control Internal Theft." *Lodging,* November 1980, p. 21.

Kornblum, K. "New Monitor May Keep Tabs on Perishables." *NRA News,* March 1983, pp. 8–9.

Kosusnik, Ed. "Maximize Your Restaurant Storage Space." *Cooking for Profit,* January 15–February 14, 1988, pp. 14–15.

Main, Bill. "Inventory Technique Cuts Costs." *Restaurant Business,* May 1, 1987, pp. 106, 108.

McKennon, J. E. "How to Control Rising Food Costs, Part III: Daily and Semi-Monthly Food Cost Analysis." *Lodging,* July 1980, pp. 36–39.

Ninemeier, Jack D. *Planning and Control for Food and Beverage Operations,* 3d ed. East Lansing, Mich.: Educational Institute of the American Hotel & Motel Association, 1991.

Pinkowski, C. G. "Food Storing." *Lodging,* August 1982, pp. 69–73.

Preston, J. J. "Food Purchasing." *Lodging,* May 1982, pp. 45–48.

Smith, D. "Food Issuing." *Lodging,* October 1982, pp. 39–42.

Zaccarelli, Herman. "Receiving Check List." *Cooking for Profit,* 15 May 1983, p. 8.

REVIEW QUIZ

When you feel you have covered all of the material in this chapter, answer these questions. Choose the *best* answer. Check your answers with the correct ones found on the Review Quiz Answer Key at the end of this book.

1.   After inspecting and accepting a shipment, the receiver should:

   a. check the products against the supplier's invoice.
   b. record the shipment on the daily receiving report.
   c. put the most perishable items into the appropriate storage facilities.
   d. tag the products received.

2.   A receiver for a food establishment should have _____ experience.

   a. food production
   b. food service
   c. maintenance
   d. all of the above

3.   Receiving facilities typically include:

   a. the outside area surrounding the loading dock.
   b. refuse bins for shipping containers.
   c. storage areas for non-food items.
   d. none of the above.

4.   The problems associated with a large inventory include:

   a. stockouts.
   b. increased pilferage.
   c. frequent foodborne illness outbreaks.
   d. all of the above.

5.   Inventory items that are relatively low in cost per serving but high in perishability are those in:

   a. Class A.
   b. Class B.
   c. Class C.
   d. Class D.

6.   The purpose of inspections by storeroom staff is to ensure:

   a. that food quality standards are being maintained.
   b. that safety standards are being met.
   c. both a and b.
   d. neither a nor b.

7. In what part of storage areas should a thermometer be placed?

    a. the warmest part
    b. the coldest part
    c. the coldest part of dry storage areas and the warmest part of refrigerated and frozen storage areas
    d. the warmest part of dry storage areas and the coldest part of refrigerated and frozen storage areas

8. How should leftover foods be stored?

    a. They should be immediately placed in an airtight container and refrigerated.
    b. They should be refrigerated immediately in a non-airtight container.
    c. They should be chilled to 41°F (5°C), placed in an airtight container and refrigerated.
    d. They should be chilled to 41°F (5°C), placed in a non-airtight container and frozen.

9. Potentially hazardous leftovers should be used within _____ hours of refrigerated storage or thrown out.

    a. 8
    b. 24
    c. 36
    d. 48

10. When products are assembled for issuing, which items are taken from storage first?

    a. the least perishable
    b. the most perishable
    c. the least expensive
    d. the most expensive

Chapter Outline

The Preparing Control Point
    Preparing and Inventory
    Preparing and People
    Preparing and Equipment
    Preparing and Facilities
    Preparing and Change
    Preparing and the SRM Program
The Cooking Control Point
    Cooking and Inventory
    Cooking and People
    Cooking and Equipment
    Cooking and Facilities
    Cooking and Change
    Cooking and the SRM Program
The Holding Control Point
    Holding and Inventory
    Holding and People
    Holding and Equipment
    Holding and Facilities
    Holding and Change
    Holding and the SRM Program
Summary

Learning Objectives

1. List the special sanitation concerns, the riskiest food products, and measures for reducing risks at the preparing control point. (pp. 251–256)

2. Describe personal hygiene standards for preparation staff, and explain the role of the master food production planning worksheet. (pp. 256–257)

3. Identify the equipment used at the preparing control point, and describe its proper care and installation. (pp. 257–263)

4. Outline the three objectives of cooking, and identify measures for reducing risks at this control point. (pp. 266–270)

5. Describe the use and care of equipment used to heat food. (pp. 270–274)

6. Describe the use and care of miscellaneous food service equipment. (pp. 274–275)

7. Describe measures for protecting inventory at the holding control point. (pp. 277–279)

8. Describe equipment used at the holding control point. (pp. 279–283)

7

The Preparing, Cooking, and Holding Control Points

The integration of subsystems and management resources continues in this chapter with a discussion of the preparing, cooking, and holding control points. Collectively, these three activities are known as **production.** The emphasis on each of the control points varies with the food service operation's menu. Certain menu items might not pass through all three control points. For example, some foods are served raw and chilled. Convenience foods undergo little preparation in the kitchen. And cooked-to-order menu items are seldom held for more than a few minutes before service. Regardless of the menu, the three production control points are critical to an operation's sanitation risk management (SRM) program.

The Preparing Control Point

The preparing control point includes all activities performed on foods before they are cooked or served raw. Preparation is a critical sanitation control point for several reasons. First, when food products are removed from storage and unwrapped, they are unavoidably exposed to many potential sources of contamination. Second, the preparing function takes place at room temperature and therefore in the temperature danger zone (TDZ). Third, since people handle the food products at this control point, coughs, sneezes, and direct contact can introduce additional contamination. Finally, some foods—such as salads, fresh fruits and vegetables, unbaked frozen desserts, and dairy products—move directly from preparation to service. The sanitary handling of these products is especially important because there is no opportunity to destroy harmful microorganisms with heat. The enforcement of sanitation standards at the preparing control point enhances food safety and thus benefits both the operation and its guests.

The preparing function in a food service operation is also crucial to quality and cost control. Preparation begins the process of converting raw ingredients to finished menu items. Food preparation mistakes may be irreversible and costly. If an operation serves poorly prepared items, its guests will not be satisfied. Discarding such items adds to the operation's food cost.

It is difficult to prescribe hard and fast rules for the preparing control point because there are many different types of food service businesses, each with different menus, procedures, and objectives. Therefore, the following sections present general principles that are applicable to most operations.

Preparing and Inventory

Preparation and cooking alter foods physically and/or chemically. The objective of these activities is to enhance food quality while protecting the safety of the food and controlling waste. Preparing and cooking must be done properly to ensure safe products and maximum yields.

Some inventory items are riskier than others during the preparing control point. These items include:

- Potentially hazardous foods

- Foods that possess natural contaminants (such as soil-grown vegetables and fresh fish)

- Foods that are handled a great deal and thus susceptible to cross-contamination

- Foods that have multiple preparation steps

- Foods that are exposed to kitchen temperatures (TDZ) for long periods of time

- Foods that have gone through a number of temperature changes

- Foods that are prepared in large quantities

All of these foods must be handled very carefully. Staff members should be aware of the risks and know the procedures for reducing risks when handling these foods.

Federal and state codes address potentially hazardous foods that will not receive further cooking. The ingredients must be chilled. Potentially hazardous foods that are reconstituted or fortified during preparing must be held at 41°F (5°C) or below. Raw fruits and vegetables must be washed in potable water before preparation.

The FDA states:

3-302.15   Washing Fruits and Vegetables.

(A) Raw fruits and vegetables shall be thoroughly washed in water to remove soil and other contaminants before being cut, combined with other ingredients, cooked, served, or offered for human consumption in ready-to-eat form *except that whole, raw fruits and vegetables that are intended for washing by the consumer before consumption need not be washed before they are sold.*

(B) Fruits and vegetables may be washed by using chemicals as specified under § 7-204.12.

3-302.14   Protection from Unapproved Additives.*

(A) Food shall be protected from contamination that may result from the addition of, as specified under § 3-202.12:

(1)   Unsafe or unapproved food or color additives; and

(2)   Unsafe or unapproved levels of approved food and color additives.

(B) A food employee may not:

(1)   Apply sulfiting agents to fresh fruits and vegetables intended for raw consumption or to a food considered to be a good source of vitamin B_1; or

(2)   Serve or sell food specified in Subparagraph B(1) of this section that is treated with sulfiting agents before receipt by the establishment, except that grapes need not meet this subparagraph.

Source: FDA 1993 *Food Code.*

All ingredients should be assembled in the work area before preparation begins. This pre-preparation, known as *mise en place* ("put in place"), reduces errors and speeds up the actual preparation process. In addition, *mise en place* reduces the food handling time and exposure to the TDZ.

Preparation activities include washing, peeling, trimming, dicing, chopping, and cutting. When surfaces of cutting boards can no longer be effectively cleaned and sanitized, they should be discarded.

The FDA states:

4-501.12   Cutting Surfaces.

Surfaces such as cutting blocks and boards that are subject to scratching and scoring shall be resurfaced if they can no longer be effectively cleaned and sanitized, or discarded if they are not capable of being resurfaced.

Source: FDA 1993 *Food Code.*

Some food establishments butcher their own meats from wholesale cuts. In-house meatcutting procedures must be sanitary since these products are potentially hazardous foods. The skill levels of preparation personnel, the establishment's menu, and the facilities should be considered when deciding whether to butcher meats in-house.

Standard Recipes. A **standard recipe** is a written procedure for the production of a given food item. It lists the exact quantity of each ingredient to be used, the sequential order in which ingredients are put together, cooking times and temperatures, and the equipment necessary to produce the finished product. Standard recipes are essential if an operation is to achieve consistency in product quality, sanitation, and cost. A sample standard recipe form is illustrated in Exhibit 7.1.

Standard recipes allow the operator to precisely determine the cost per portion, or **standard recipe cost,** of finished menu items. This information is necessary for pricing menu items accurately. A **product cost analysis form** is used to calculate the cost per portion. A sample of this form is shown in Exhibit 7.2. The standard recipe cost is calculated by adding the costs of all ingredients in a recipe (total product cost) and dividing by the yield (number of servings).

For these calculations to be accurate, the operation must have and use **standard portion sizes.** Standard portion sizes help the operation deliver its products consistently without cheating itself or its guests. To help maintain consistent portion sizes, an operation should:

• Follow standard recipes exactly to obtain intended yields

• Use scales and other measuring devices during preparation, cooking, and portioning for service

Exhibit 7.1 Sample Standard Recipe Form

Standard Recipe No.: 696	Yield (No. of Servings): 32
Product Name: Cream of Lettuce Soup	Portion Size: 5 oz. (147.87 ml)
Pan Size: Sauté Pan/Stock Pot	Portion Utensil: Ladle
Temperature: Simmer	Special Directions: Follow Chef Kosec's garnish instructions.
Cooking Time: 20 minutes	

Ingredients	Quantity	Method
L. J. Minor Supreme Sauce Mix Warm water	1 14 oz. (396.90 g) package 4 qts. (3.79 l)	1. Blend water and sauce mix. Heat slowly and stir to dissolve lumps. Simmer for 10 minutes and hold hot for the next step.
Butter or margarine Head lettuce, cut in julienne strips, 2 inches long (5.08 cm)	2 Tbsp. (28.35 g) 22 oz. (623.69 g)	2. Melt butter in the sauté pan. Add lettuce and sauté for 1 minute. Add to step one ingredients.
Half and half or milk, warm Cooked bacon strips	1 qt. (0.95 l) 4 oz. (113.4 g)	3. Add warm milk or half and half to other ingredients. Blend in the bacon strips. Keep hot (140°F [60°C]) for service.

Special Equipment Needed: Metal-stemmed product probe thermometer

Source: Adapted from Lewis J. Minor and Ronald F. Cichy, *Foodservice Systems Management*, 1984.

- Purchase pre-portioned goods when available and portion as many items as possible during preparation

Standard recipes should be changed as necessary to compensate for changing resources or other operational changes. The production manager or staff members may be able to improve standard recipes. New recipes copied from magazines or supplied by other establishments should be adapted to the needs of the operation, its staff members, and its guests.

Convenience Foods. Some food service managers have a hard time deciding whether to use convenience foods. These products are delivered to the facility in a ready-to-cook or ready-to-eat form and therefore require less in-house labor to prepare for service.

The FDA states:

Ready-to-Eat Food.

Exhibit 7.2 Sample Product Cost Analysis Form

Product Name: Cream of Lettuce Soup		Standard Recipe No.: 696	
Date Revised: 6/23/00		Yield: 32 Servings (5 qts 4.73 l)	
Ingredient	Unit Price	Amount Used	Ingredient Cost
Supreme Sauce	$3.58/14 oz (396.90 g)	14 oz (396.90 g)	$3.58
Water	—	4 qts. (3.79 l)	—
Margarine	.90/lb (453.6 g)	2 Tbsp (56.70 g)	.11
Head Lettuce	.75/lb (453.6 g)	22 oz (623.69 g)	1.03
Half and Half	1.48/qt (0.95 l)	1 qt (0.95 l)	1.48
Bacon	1.60/lb (453.6 g)	4 oz (113.4 g)	.40
Total Product Cost			$6.60

$$\text{Standard Recipe Cost} = \frac{\text{Total Product Cost: \$6.60}}{\text{Yield: 32 portions}} = 20.6\text{¢/serving}$$

Source: Adapted from Lewis J. Minor and Ronald F. Cichy, *Foodservice Systems Management*, 1984.

(a) **"Ready-to-eat food"** means food that is in a form that is edible without washing, cooking, or additional preparation by the food establishment or the consumer and that is reasonably expected to be consumed in that form.

(b) **"Ready-to-eat food"** includes:

(i)   Unpackaged potentially hazardous food that is cooked to the temperature and time required for the specific food under Subpart 3-401;

(ii)   Raw, washed, cut fruits and vegetables;

(iii) Whole, raw, fruits and vegetables that are presented for consumption without the need for further washing, such as at a buffet; and

(iv) Other food presented for consumption for which further washing or cooking is not required and from which rinds, peels, husks, or shells are removed.

Source: FDA 1993 *Food Code*.

Convenience foods give kitchen staff more time for other work. For example, an executive chef who uses natural convenience food bases can devote more time to management responsibilities.

Convenience products offer several advantages to a food service operation. First, they are characterized by a consistency that is often difficult to achieve in products prepared on-site. Second, because convenience foods produce a specific yield, they have an easy-to-calculate portion cost and make it easier to control portions. Many convenience foods come pre-portioned or with a certain number of portions in the case or container. Third, convenience products can reduce waste by making it easier to use only the amount needed; for example, the chef need not prepare an entire pot of stock for a recipe that only calls for two cups. Fourth, convenience foods facilitate menu expansion. Combining high-quality convenience products with signature ingredients is a relatively easy way to add new items to the menu.

Convenience foods can reduce *or* increase handling and storage costs, depending on the existing facilities and the type of storage each product requires. Therefore, each product must be judged individually. Management should also evaluate the quality of each product carefully. Convenience foods should be of equal or higher quality than similar products prepared on-site.

Preparing and People

Federal and state standards regarding personal hygiene (see Chapter 3) apply to every staff member in a food establishment. Because these standards are especially important for food handlers, we will review them here briefly.

All production staff members should wear uniforms and preferably change into them when they report for work. Street clothes or uniforms worn outside the establishment can introduce contamination at the preparing control point. Preparation staff members must also wear hair restraints such as caps, chef's hats, or hair nets. Hair in food not only is distasteful to guests, but also is a source of pathogenic organisms.

Smoking must be prohibited in food preparation areas because food can be contaminated by tobacco, ashes, or saliva. Staff members should also not eat in food preparation areas. Given that the cook or chef must periodically taste food products, sampling procedures must be sanitary. Utensils used for tasting should never be re-introduced to food products, and no one should use his or her fingers to sample food.

Handwashing is critical before, during, and after food preparation activities. Production staff members may wear single-use gloves for limited activities such as portioning meatballs and forming meat loaf. Single-use gloves are not designed to be used in place of proper handwashing or other sanitary procedures.

Finally, the operation should not allow unauthorized people in the food preparation area. In addition to bringing in contaminants, they present a security risk.

The FDA states:

3-301.11   Preventing Contamination from Hands.*

(A) Food employees shall wash their hands as specified under §§ 2-301.12 and 2-301.13.

(B) Except when washing fruits and vegetables as specified under § 3-302.15, food employees may not contact exposed, ready-to-eat food with their bare hands and shall use suitable utensils such as deli tissue, spatulas, tongs, or single-use gloves.

Source: FDA 1993 *Food Code.*

It is important that food preparation staff members do their work accurately. Accuracy reduces waste and losses resulting from improper ingredient handling, weighing, and measuring. It also ensures a high-quality end product. Some operations have an ingredient room adjacent to the storeroom. Personnel in the ingredient room carefully measure and weigh raw ingredients before issuing them to the kitchen. This arrangement reduces waste and helps ensure that the proper quantities are used in recipe preparation.

The preparation function in large operations is easier to control with a **master food production planning worksheet.** A sample is presented in Exhibit 7.3. The worksheet provides a format for planning both people and product utilization for each meal or special function. The worksheet informs production staff members exactly what and how much to prepare: it lists each menu item, the standard portion size, and the forecasted number of portions. The form provides a guide for requisitioning and issuing raw materials. It also has a place for both the number of portions served and the number of portions left over. Because the worksheet serves as an overall food plan for a meal or special function, it can also be used to schedule production staff members.

Preparing and Equipment

A variety of equipment is used at the preparing control point. Because most preparation equipment is in direct contact with food, it is important to clean, sanitize, and maintain these items properly in order to avoid cross-contamination.

Food mixers are used to incorporate solids into liquids, liquids into solids, liquids into liquids, and gases into liquids and solids. Several attachments are available that grind, grate, whip, beat, knead, slice, emulsify, chop, and mix. Food mixers are highly versatile and are available in both countertop and floor models. Since mixers are powered by electricity, they should bear the UL seal of approval. Mixer capacities range from 5 quarts (4.7 liters) to 100 gallons (378.5 liters).

Food mixers are easy to clean. The bowl and beaters can be cleaned, rinsed, and sanitized in the pot and pan station. The exterior of the mixer should be wiped after each use with a hot water–detergent solution, rinsed, and dried with a soft cloth. Lubricating movable parts once each month keeps the mixer in good working condition. Use a food-grade lubricant, as it might come into contact with unprotected food.

Food processors, slicers, choppers, blenders, and grinders save time and reduce the number of monotonous kitchen tasks. The heavy-duty construction of a quantity kitchen food processor makes it highly versatile. This specialized equipment should be cleaned and maintained according to the manufacturer's recommendations. If not properly cleaned and maintained, such equipment can spread contamination through countless batches of food, much of which will not be cooked or heated before service.

Kitchenware—including knives, scoops, funnels, whips, spoons, spatulas, sifters, strainers, sieves, ladles, graters, slicers, peelers, forks, and other hand tools—must be

Exhibit 7.3 Master Food Production Planning Worksheet

		Forecasted Portions				Requisitioning Guide Data				
Items	Standard Portion Size	Guests	Officers*	Total Forecast	Adjusted Forecast	Raw Materials Requested	State of Preparation	Remarks	Number of Portions Left Over	Actual Number Served
Appetizers										
Shrimp Cocktail	5 ea	48	—	48	51	12 lbs of 21-25 count	R T C		—	53
Fruit Cup	5 oz	18	1	19	20	See Recipe for 20 Portions			—	19
Marinated Herring	2½ oz	15	1	16	16	2½ lbs	R T E		—	14
Half Grapefruit	½ ea	8	—	8	8	4 Grapefruit			—	9
Soup	6 oz	30	3	33	36	Prepare 2 Gallons			5	32
Entrees										
Sirloin Steak	14 oz	28	—	28	29	29 Sirloin Steaks (Btchr.)	R T C		—	28
Prime Ribs	9 oz	61	1	62	64	3 Ribs of Beef	R T C	Use Re-heat if necessary	out at 10:45 p.m.	62
Lobster	1½ lb	26	—	26	28	28 Lobsters (check stock)				26
Ragout of Lamb	4 oz	24	2	26	26	12 lbs lamb fore (¾" pcs.)		Recipe No. E.402	1 +	25
Half Chicken	½ ea	34	2	36	38	38 halves (check stock)			—	39
Vegetables & Salads										
Whipped Potatoes	3 oz	55	1	56	58	13 lbs	A P		2-3	56
Baked Potatoes	1 ea	112	3	115	120	120 Idahos			out at 11:10 p.m.	120
Asparagus Spears	3 ea	108	—	108	113	8 No. 2 cans			2	110
Half Tomato	½ ea	48	4	52	54	27 Tomatoes			2	52
Tossed Salad	2½ oz	105	3	108	112	See Recipe No. S.302			—	114
Hearts of Lettuce	¼ hd	63	2	65	67	18 heads			—	69
Desserts										
Brownie w/ice cream	1 sq./1½ oz	21	2	23	26	1 pan brownies			—	24
Fresh Fruits	3 oz	10	—	10	11	See Recipe No. D.113			—	10
Ice Cream	2½ oz	35	3	38	40	Check stock			—	43
Apple Pie	½ cut	21	—	21	21	3 Pies			out at 10:50 p.m.	21
Devils Food Cake	⅛ cut	8	—	8	8	1 cake			1	7
Total No. of Persons		173	5	178	185					180

Day Tuesday   Date 8/1/00   Master Food Production Planning Worksheet   Local Weather Forecast: Cloudy & mild   Special Plans: Party of 15 — steaks

Abbreviations: A P – as purchased; R T C – ready-to-cook; R T E – ready-to-eat.

*Officers are management staff permitted free meals from menus.

Source: Jack D. Ninemeier, *Planning and Control for Food and Beverage Operations,* 3d ed. (East Lansing, Mich.: Educational Institute of the American Hotel & Motel Association, 1991), p. 187.

cleaned and sanitized, either manually or mechanically, after each changed use. Sanitized kitchenware should be stored to prevent contamination. In-use kitchenware of any kind (including single-use gloves) must be handled carefully to avoid cross-contamination.

The FDA states:

"Kitchenware" means food preparation and storage utensils.

3-304.12   In-Use Utensils, Between-Use Storage.

During pauses in food preparation or dispensing, food preparation and dispensing utensils shall be stored:

(A)   In the food with their handles above the top of the food and the container;

(B)   On a clean portion of the food preparation table or cooking equipment and shall be cleaned and sanitized at a frequency specified under §§ 4-602.11 and 4-702.11;

(C)   In running water of sufficient velocity to flush particulates to the drain, if used with moist food such as ice cream or mashed potatoes; or

(D)   In a clean, protected location if the utensils, such as ice scoops, are used only with a food that is not potentially hazardous.

3-304.14   Single-Use Gloves, Used for One Purpose and Discarded.*

If used, single-use gloves shall be used for only one task such as working with ready-to-eat food or with raw animal food, used for no other purpose, and discarded when damaged or soiled, or when interruptions occur in the operation.

4-502.15   Slash-Resistant Gloves, Use Limitation.

Slash-resistant gloves that are used to protect hands during operations requiring cutting may be used in direct contact only with food that is subsequently cooked as specified in Part 3-4 such as frozen food or a primal cut of meat.

Source: FDA 1993 *Food Code.*

Kitchenware can sometimes be used and set aside for short periods of time. It should be placed flat on a clean food preparation surface. However, if a substantial amount of time elapses, kitchenware should be cleaned and sanitized before re-using, especially if it is being used to prepare potentially hazardous foods. Never place kitchenware in the space between preparation tables, between the wall and preparation tables, or in your pocket.

Work tables should be cleaned frequently—at least every time a change in use occurs. It is important to remove food and utensils from the surface before cleaning work tables with a hot water-detergent solution. Cleaning should be followed by sanitizing with a chlorine (100 mg/L) solution. Drawers under work tables are more useful if they are cleaned out once a week. It is even more efficient to eliminate all storage drawers from the kitchen and store utensils on stainless steel open wire shelving.

Cutting boards and blocks, like work tables, must be cleaned and sanitized after each changed use. Many public health departments do not allow wooden cutting boards because they are difficult to keep clean, particularly as they become scored with use. These regulatory agencies specify cutting boards made of rubber or plastic materials that meet National Sanitation Foundation standards. Rubber or plastic boards are not as easily scored as wooden boards. Once boards are scored to the point where they can no longer be cleaned and sanitized, they should be thrown out.

Cutting boards and blocks should be washed by hand in a hot water–detergent solution, as mechanical dishwashers can warp them. Boards are sanitized by dipping them in a dilute chlorine bleach (50 mg/L) solution. They should then be rinsed and allowed to air dry.

Equipment Installation. Preparation equipment, if properly installed and used, can raise productivity and efficiency at this control point. Equipment must be installed and located to prevent the contamination of food and food-contact surfaces. Installation must also allow for easy cleaning and sanitizing of equipment and adjacent surfaces. Equipment, whether fixed or mobile, may not be installed under exposed or unprotected sewer lines or any other potential sources of contamination, such as stairs. This requirement may be extended to include water lines, if condensation is a problem.

Exhibit 7.4 Floor- and Pedestal-Mounted Equipment Installations

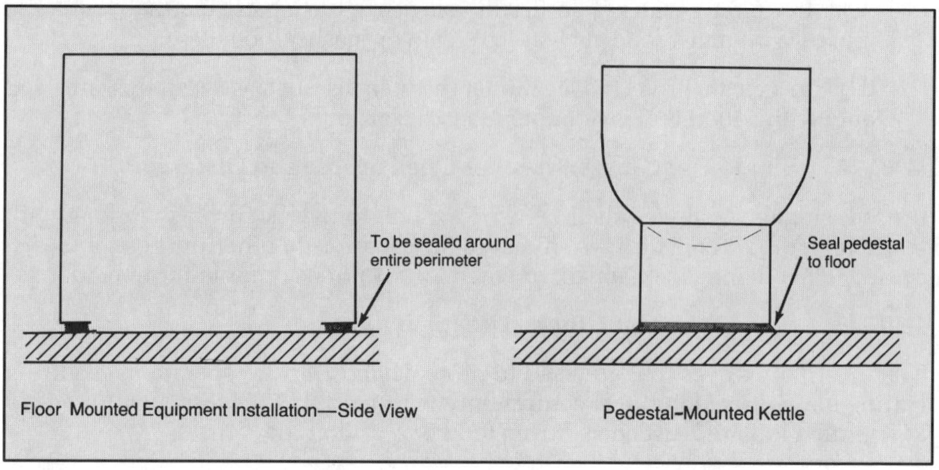

Source: National Sanitation Foundation, *Sanitation Aspects of Food Service Facility Plan Preparation and Review,* 1978, p. 73.

Mobile equipment—equipment on wheels or casters—is easier to clean and sanitize. Mobile equipment costs more than fixed equipment and has additional parts that might need maintenance. Utility connections should be flexible or fitted with quick-disconnects.

Fixed equipment should allow for easy cleaning and sanitizing of adjacent areas; otherwise, there should be no more than one thirty-second of an inch (.8 mm) of space between the equipment and walls or ceilings. Floor-mounted equipment with legs should be at least six inches (15.2 cm) from the floor. The base of equipment without legs should be sealed as illustrated in Exhibit 7.4. Heavy equipment may be installed on a masonry base, which eliminates the need for cleaning below the equipment. Such equipment should be installed as illustrated in Exhibit 7.5. All openings to hollow spaces beneath the equipment and between the masonry base and equipment must be sealed to prevent the entrance of insects or rodents. Once heavy equipment is sealed to a masonry base, it is extremely expensive to remove, so installations should be carefully considered in advance.

Some equipment is **cantilevered**—that is, wall-mounted with a horizontal support. For example, some models of steam-jacketed kettles are cantilevered. These items should be installed so that debris and liquid waste do not collect between the equipment and the wall or under the equipment. A proper installation of cantilevered equipment is illustrated in Exhibit 7.6.

Table-mounted equipment with legs should have a minimum clearance of four inches (10.2 cm) between the bottom of the equipment and the table. Portable equipment on a countertop must be easily movable by one person and must have quick-disconnects or flexible utility lines. Fixed counter equipment without legs should be sealed to the counter around the entire base.

All aisles and working spaces between equipment and walls must be unobstructed. They should be large enough to allow personnel to perform their duties without contaminating food or food-contact surfaces. Equipment can be a source of food contamination, so in all installations the prevention of potential contamination is an important consideration.

Exhibit 7.5 Solid Masonry Base Installation—Side View

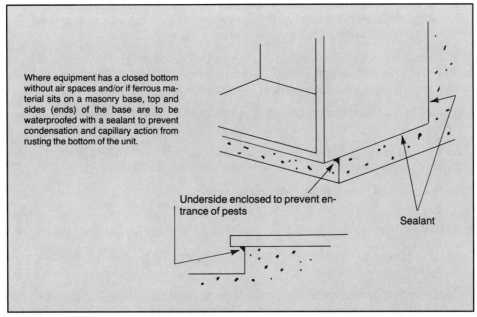

Where equipment has a closed bottom without air spaces and/or if ferrous material sits on a masonry base, top and sides (ends) of the base are to be waterproofed with a sealant to prevent condensation and capillary action from rusting the bottom of the unit.

Underside enclosed to prevent entrance of pests

Sealant

Source: National Sanitation Foundation, *Sanitation Aspects of Food Service Facility Plan Preparation and Review,* 1978, p. 74.

Exhibit 7.6 Installation of Cantilevered Equipment

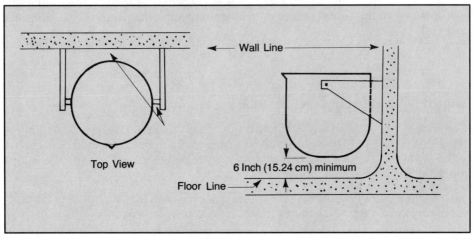

Wall Line

Top View

6 Inch (15.24 cm) minimum

Floor Line

Source: National Sanitation Foundation, *Sanitation Aspects of Food Service Facility Plan Preparation and Review,* 1978, p. 75.

The FDA states:

"Easily movable" means:

(a) Weighing 14 kg (30 pounds) or less; mounted on casters, gliders, or rollers; or provided with a mechanical means requiring no more than 14 kg (30 pounds) of force to safely tilt a unit of equipment for cleaning; and

(b) Having no utility connection, a utility connection that disconnects quickly, or a flexible utility connection line of sufficient length to allow the equipment to be moved for cleaning of the equipment and adjacent area.

"Sealed" means free of cracks or other openings that allow the entry or passage of moisture.

"Table-mounted equipment" means equipment that is not portable and is designed to be mounted off the floor on a table, counter, or shelf.

4-402.11   Fixed Equipment, Spacing or Sealing.

(A) A unit of equipment that is fixed because it is not easily movable shall be installed so that it is:

(1)   Spaced to allow access for cleaning along the sides, behind, and above the unit;

(2)   Spaced from adjoining equipment, walls, and ceilings a distance of not more than 1 millimeter or one thirty-second inch; or

(3)   Sealed to adjoining equipment or walls, if the unit is exposed to spillage or seepage.

(B) Table-mounted equipment that is not easily movable shall be installed to allow cleaning of the equipment and areas underneath and around the equipment by being:

(1)   Sealed to the table; or

(2)   Elevated on legs as specified under ¶ 4-402.12(D).

4-402.12   Fixed Equipment, Elevation or Sealing.

(A) Except as specified in ¶¶ (B) and (C) of this section, floor-mounted equipment that is not easily movable shall be sealed to the floor or elevated on legs that provide at least a 15 centimeter (6 inch) clearance between the floor and the equipment.

(B) *If no part of the floor under the floor-mounted equipment is more than 15 centimeters (6 inches) from the point of cleaning access, the clearance space may be only 10 centimeters (4 inches).*

(C) *This section does not apply to display shelving units, display refrigeration units, and display freezer units located in the consumer shopping areas of a retail food store, if the floor under the units is maintained clean.*

(D) Except as specified in ¶ (E) of this section, table-mounted equipment that is not easily movable shall be elevated on legs that provide at least a 10 centimeter (4 inch) clearance between the table and the equipment.

(E) *The clearance space between the table and table-mounted equipment may be:*

(1) *7.5 centimeters (3 inches) if the horizontal distance of the table top under the equipment is no more than 50 centimeters (20 inches) from the point of access for cleaning; or*

(2) *5 centimeters (2 inches) if the horizontal distance of the table top under the equipment is no more than 7.5 centimeters (3 inches) from the point of access for cleaning.*

Source: FDA 1993 *Food Code.*

Equipment needed for preparation is based on the menu. If a menu change is anticipated, additional preparation or cooking equipment may have to be purchased. If a new menu item will require a specialized piece of equipment, the cost of adding the equipment must be weighed against the profits the new item is expected to generate. Other factors such as operating skills required, risk management, monthly utility charges, and maintenance of the establishment's quality standards also must be considered.

It is a good idea to submit an **equipment schedule** (Exhibit 7.7) and **equipment installation information** (Exhibit 7.8) to health officials before purchasing or installing equipment. Health authorities can use these two documents to identify potential sanitation hazards. This may help the operation avoid unwise equipment purchases that add to the sanitation risks of running a food establishment.

Preparing and Facilities

Preparation facilities vary in size and layout with the type of operation and its menu. However, every kitchen is divided into a series of work centers for preparing related products. In small kitchens, the arrangement of equipment in a single room serves to divide work centers, while in larger kitchens some work centers are in separate rooms. For example, in a large operation the *garde-manger*—a cold food preparation department responsible for such dishes as aspic, pâté, mousse, salads and dressings, and sauces—may be located in a chilled pantry room; in a small establishment the *garde-manger* may consist of an area of the kitchen with chilled preparation surfaces. (The term *garde-manger* is also applied to a chef who specializes in the production of cold dishes.)

The layout of facilities is especially important in smaller operations, where every inch of space must be used efficiently. Careful planning can help management get the most out of an operation's facilities. For example, suppose management is considering the preparation of fresh fruits and vegetables. One important planning consideration might be the location of preparation activities: will all preparation take place in one area, or will items be washed, peeled, and trimmed in one area and cut and weighed in another? Management must also decide which staff members will perform which preparing functions. These decisions, in turn, will influence the layout of preparation facilities.

Preparation facilities should be designed to move products from the issuing control point to the cooking control point quickly and easily. Minimum handling also reduces sanitation risks. Adequate equipment, work tables, lighting, and ventilation are necessary for efficient preparation. Concentrating food preparation in a few areas may raise staff productivity.

Exhibit 7.7 Equipment Schedule

Item No.[1]	Quantity	List of Equipment	Description & Model Nos.[2,3,4]

Source: National Sanitation Foundation, *Sanitation Aspects of Food Service Facility Plan Preparation and Review*, 1978, p. 27.

Footnotes:

[1]Key to Floor Plan.
[2]Indicate Custom Fabricated (C.F.).
[3]Indicate Listings (UL, NSF, AGA), etc.
[4]If narrative description is required, use back of this sheet.

Preparation facilities should comply with local, state, and federal regulatory agency requirements. Facilities should be designed to minimize contamination risks and physical hazards, and should be cleaned and sanitized regularly.

Preparing and Change

Changes occur daily in the food service industry as a result of evolving guest demands and modifications in the food processing, manufacturing, and distribution systems. Many of these changes force food service managers to re-evaluate their preparing functions. Preparation activities that were once part of every food service business are often no longer necessary; for example, many operations now purchase cleaned, peeled, and trimmed fresh vegetables. Likewise, most operations now buy pre-portioned meat products, and some purchase fully cooked, ready-to-slice roasts for sandwiches and other menu items. The availability of high-quality frozen convenience doughs and bread products allows many establishments to offer freshly prepared bakery items with relatively limited equipment and facilities. The availability of several high-quality natural

Exhibit 7.8 Equipment Installation Information

Item No.	Accessories	Plumbing									Remarks	Electrical											Installation Information
		Water[1]			Waste			Faucets															
		Cold	140° F	180° F	Size	Type	Height	Type	By														

Source: National Sanitation Foundation, *Sanitation Aspects of Food Service Facility Plan Preparation and Review*, 1978, p. 28.

Footnotes:

[1]If water at other temperatures is required, indicate as a remark and supply information separately.

food bases has virtually eliminated the need for a simmering stockpot. These convenience products reduce waste, spoilage, and sanitation risks.

Because the preparing control point is subject to frequent changes, flexible equipment is a good investment for most operations. Multi-use equipment (discussed later in this chapter) enhances menu flexibility and efficient use of kitchen space.

Preparing and the SRM Program

Standards at the preparing control point, the initial production activity, are necessary to reduce risks throughout production. The standard recipe is one of the most important controls. Standard recipes allow the operation to prepare a specific quantity of each food item and to produce finished products of consistent quality. Some standard recipes can be modified to reduce risks; for example, the pH of a finished product can be lowered by adding high-acid ingredients, or the amount of a potentially hazardous ingredient can be decreased. Standard recipes should only be modified, however, if the changes do not negatively affect the quality of the menu item or guest satisfaction.

Raw products served uncooked must be carefully washed and handled during preparation. Sensory tests should be used repeatedly to evaluate the quality of all food products. Preparation staff members can help reduce risks by adhering to rules of personal cleanliness and hygiene, including frequent handwashing, and by wearing clean uniforms and proper hair restraints. Sanitary food-tasting procedures are essential. Equipment and facilities must be properly cleaned, sanitized, and maintained. All of these strategies are designed to reduce risks during preparation.

The Cooking Control Point

The heat added to food during cooking causes a number of physical and chemical changes to food products. The cooking control point should be designed to achieve three objectives: to destroy harmful microorganisms; to increase the digestibility of food; and to alter its form, flavor, color, texture, and appearance.

Cooking can destroy or inactivate some pathogens. The success of inactivation or destruction depends on the temperature, time, cooking method, characteristics of the food product, and type and quantity of organisms present. Recall that toxins and organisms that form spores are generally heat-stable. For example, spores of *Clostridium perfringens* are not destroyed by normal cooking procedures. The toxin of *Staphylococcus aureus* is also stable at normal cooking temperatures.

Cooking is necessary to increase the digestibility of many food products. Heat makes many proteins, fats, and carbohydrates easier to digest. Unfortunately, cooking can also reduce the nutritional value of food products by destroying some of the vitamins they contain. In general, shorter cooking times minimize vitamin loss.

Cooking alters the form, flavor, color, texture, and appearance of food products. These chemical and physical changes increase the palatability of food products. Strict time-temperature controls, combined with standardized production techniques, can enhance food quality and, therefore, guest satisfaction.

Cooking and Inventory

Cooking involves combining the appropriate amounts of ingredients according to standard recipes and heating at the proper temperature for a designated period of time. The product resulting from the cooking process often bears little resemblance to the raw ingredients from which it was produced.

One of the primary objectives of the FDA's guidelines for food preparation is the prevention of cross-contamination. Equipment and kitchenware must be cleaned and sanitized after each changed use. For example, if a food slicer is used to slice raw boneless beef loins into eight-ounce New York strip steaks, it must be cleaned and sanitized before it is used to slice any item other than raw beef loins. Food-contact surfaces on equipment must also be cleaned and sanitized if an interruption in operations has occurred. For example, suppose a slicer is used to slice cooked boneless prime rib for a banquet. After all of the prime rib is sliced and plated, it is placed in a food warmer and held at 130°F (54°C) or above. Forty minutes later, when the prime rib is served, the banquet workers discover that they still need 23 orders of prime rib. The slicer must be cleaned and sanitized before additional prime rib can be portioned. Any kitchenware used to handle the prime rib must also be cleaned and sanitized before re-use.

Potentially hazardous foods must be heated to a minimum internal temperature of 145°F (63°C) for 15 seconds during cooking. The exceptions to this rule are pork and game animals, comminuted fish and meats, injected meats, and eggs (155°F [68°C] for

15 seconds); field-dressed wild game animals, poultry, stuffed fish, stuffed meat, stuffed pasta, stuffed poultry, or stuffing containing fish, meat, or poultry (165°F [74°C] or above for at least 15 seconds); and beef roasts.

Beef roasts should be cooked in a preheated oven. Table A, below, shows the oven parameters required to destroy pathogens on the surface of beef roasts and corned beef. The minimum holding times required at specified temperatures are shown in Table B.

Table A

| Oven Type | Oven Temperature | |
| | Roast Weight | |
	Less than or equal to 4.5 kg (10 lbs)	Greater than 4.5 kg (10 lbs)
Still Dry	177°C (350°F)	121°C (250°F)
Convection	163°C (325°F)	163°C (325°F)
High Humidity[1]	less than 121°C (250°F)	less than 121°C (250°F)

[1]Relative humidity greater than 90% for at least 1 hour as measured in the cooking chamber or exit of the oven; or in a moisture-impermeable bag that provides 100% humidity.

Table B

Temperature °C (°F)	Time[1]	Temperature °C (°F)	Time[1]	Temperature °C (°F)	Time[1]
54 (130)	121 minutes	58 (136)	32 minutes	61 (142)	8 minutes
56 (132)	77 minutes	59 (138)	19 minutes	62 (144)	5 minutes
57 (134)	47 minutes	60 (140)	12 minutes	63 (145)	3 minutes

[1]Holding time may include postoven heat rise.

Foods cooked in a microwave oven must reach temperatures 25°F (14°C) higher than temperatures specified for the same foods cooked in conventional ovens. In addition, items cooked in a microwave oven must be allowed to remain covered for two minutes after they are cooked to obtain temperature equilibrium.

Microwave ovens might cook some foods unevenly. For example, microwaves heat and cook the outside layers of thick foods (such as roasts), while the interior is cooked by conduction, a slower heating process. Because of the uneven distribution of microwaves and the variations in the distribution of water in food products, foods such as beef roasts should be cooked to 155°F (68°C) and pork to at least 180°F (82°C) in a microwave oven. This will minimize the effect of bone in meat and meat with cold pockets. Stuffed fish should be cooked to a minimum internal temperature of 190°F (88°C) in a microwave oven.

Food establishments can still serve steak tartare, sushi, and soft-cooked eggs. However, establishments must provide consumers with information stating that food safety requires that these foods be cooked thoroughly. Alternatively, the establishment may be granted a variance by reason of its having an approved HACCP plan in place. A variance requires the adoption of a HACCP plan that is approved *in advance* by the regulatory authority.

Food products should never be reheated on a steam table. This equipment is not designed to produce sufficient internal temperatures in food products.

The FDA states:

3-401.11   Raw Animal Foods.*

(A) Except as specified in ¶ (B) and under ¶ (C) of this section and under § 3-302.13, raw animal foods such as eggs, fish, poultry, meat, and foods containing these raw animal foods, shall be cooked to heat all parts of the food to a temperature and for a time that are at least:

(1)   63°C (145°F) or above for 15 seconds for:

(a)   Shell eggs that are broken and prepared in response to a consumer's order and for immediate service, and

(b)   Fish and meat that are not specified in ¶ (A)(2) of this section;

(2)   For pork and game animals, comminuted fish and meats, injected meats, and eggs that are not prepared as specified in Subparagraph (A)(1)(a) of this section, 68°C (155°F) for 15 seconds or the temperature specified in § 3-401.12 that corresponds to the cooking time;

(3)   As specified in § 3-401.14 for roasts of beef and corned beef; or

(4)   74°C (165°F) or above for 15 seconds for field-dressed wild game animals as specified in Subparagraph 3-201.17(B)(2), poultry, stuffed fish, stuffed meat, stuffed pasta, stuffed poultry, or stuffing containing fish, meat, or poultry.

(B) *Paragraph (A) of this section does not apply if:*

(1)   *Except for establishments serving a highly susceptible population, the food is a raw animal food such as raw, marinated fish; raw molluscan shellfish; steak tartare; or a partially cooked food such as lightly cooked fish, rare meat, and soft cooked eggs that is served or offered for sale in a ready-to-eat form, and the consumer is informed as specified under § 3-603.11 that to assure its safety, the food should be cooked as specified under ¶ (A) of this section; or*

(2)   *The regulatory authority grants a variance from ¶ (A) of this section as specified in § 8-103.10 based on a HACCP plan that:*

(a)   *Is submitted by the permit holder and approved by the regulatory authority as specified under § 8-103.11,*

(b)   *Documents scientific data or other information that shows that a lesser time and temperature regimen results in a safe food, and*

(c)   *Verifies that equipment and procedures for food preparation and training of food employees at the establishment meet the conditions of the variance.*

(C) Beef roasts shall be cooked:

(1) In an oven that is preheated to the temperature specified for their weight in § 3-401.13 and that is held at or above that temperature; and

(2) To a food temperature as specified in § 3-401.14 and held for the corresponding amount of time specified in § 3-401.14 for that temperature.

3-401.12 Minimum Food Temperature and Holding Time Required Under Subparagraph 3-401.11(A)(2) for Cooking All Parts of Pork and Game Animals, Comminuted Fish and Meats, and Injected Meats.*

Minimum	
Temperature °C (°F)	Time
63 (145)	3 minutes
66 (150)	1 minute

3-401.13 Oven Parameters Required for Destruction of Pathogens on the Surface of Roasts of Beef and Corned Beef.*

	Oven Temperature	
	Roast Weight	
Oven Type	Less than or equal to 4.5 kg (10 lbs)	Greater than 4.5 kg (10 lbs)
Still Dry	177°C (350°F)	121°C (250°F)
Convection	163°C (325°F)	163°C (325°F)
High Humidity[1]	less than 121°C (250°F)	less than 121°C (250°F)

[1]Relative humidity greater than 90% for at least 1 hour as measured in the cooking chamber or exit of the oven; or in a moisture-impermeable bag that provides 100% humidity.

3-401.14 Minimum Holding Times Required at Specified Temperatures for Cooking All Parts of Roasts of Beef and Corned Beef.*

Temperature °C (°F)	Time[1]	Temperature °C (°F)	Time[1]	Temperature °C (°F)	Time[1]
54 (130)	121 minutes	58 (136)	32 minutes	61 (142)	8 minutes
56 (132)	77 minutes	59 (138)	19 minutes	62 (144)	5 minutes
57 (134)	47 minutes	60 (140)	12 minutes	63 (145)	3 minutes

[1]Holding time may include postoven heat rise.

3-401.15   Microwave Cooking.*

Raw animal foods cooked in a microwave oven shall be:

(A)   Rotated or stirred throughout or midway during cooking to compensate for uneven distribution of heat;

(B)   Covered to retain surface moisture;

(C)   Heated an additional 14°C (25°F) above the temperature specified in Subparagraphs 3-401.11(A)(1), (2), and (4) to compensate for shorter cooking times; and

(D)   Allowed to stand covered for 2 minutes after cooking to obtain temperature equilibrium.

Source: FDA 1993 *Food Code.*

Food is exposed to many sources of contamination during the cooking process. Some products must be manipulated and formed by hand, which heightens the risks. The dangers inherent in the cooking control point can be reduced by following state and local codes to the letter.

Cooking and People

Staff members at the cooking control point are responsible for cooked-to-order appetizers, entrées, side dishes, and desserts. The number of people involved in the cooking control point depends on the extent of the menu and the operation's volume of business.

Accuracy is essential at the cooking control point. Cooks and chefs are expected to follow the operation's production standards. The master food production planning worksheet outlines what to requisition and cook for each meal period. Standard recipes should be followed exactly.

Personal hygiene and cleanliness standards are especially important for staff members who cook. These standards reduce the opportunities for product contamination both before and after cooking.

In some food establishments, production and service personnel have an antagonistic relationship. This creates an atmosphere of hostility, which is not conducive to achieving the goals of the operation. Management must care enough to take an active role in improving the situation by encouraging production and service staff to work together cooperatively. Some managers have servers and kitchen staff members trade jobs one day each week or month. This strategy helps each person appreciate the complexities of the other person's job and may lead to better cooperation.

Cooking and Equipment

Cooking equipment is an investment; it must be regularly cleaned and maintained to prolong its useful life, minimize repair and energy costs, reduce risks, and protect food products. For these reasons, the discussion that follows includes requirements for cleaning and sanitizing. Equipment manufacturers' instructions should be followed if they are available. Information on equipment cleaning procedures is also available from several manufacturers of cleaning and sanitization compounds.

Equipment Used to Add Heat to Food. A quantity production kitchen uses several types of equipment to add heat to food. Broilers, fryers, griddles, grills, ovens, ranges, steam-powered equipment, tilting braising pans, food warmers, coffee urns, and toasters add heat to food by conduction (heat transfer through direct contact), convection (heat transfer through circulating air or fluid), radiation (heat transfer through wave energy), or a combination of these.

Broilers cook food with dry heat generated from an intense heat source. Broilers are fast and versatile, and a variety of models and designs are available. An overhead fired broiler cooks food from the top. The rate of cooking is controlled by raising and lowering the grate that holds the food. A salamander is a small overhead fired broiler used to glaze or finish food products immediately before service. A ceramic overhead broiler uses a series of ceramic plates to distribute heat evenly. An infrared overhead broiler offers the advantage of fast temperature recovery and is well suited to high-volume food service operations.

Char-broilers cook food on a grate from a heat source located below the food. Char-broilers may be powered by gas or electricity or may burn wood or charcoal. Char-broilers using mesquite or hardwood fuels have been used to prepare fresh fish and seafood. However, this relatively slow broiler uses energy inefficiently and results in a great deal of product shrinkage. Many fast-food chains use conveyorized broilers because they cook rapidly. Rotisserie broilers cook food while it is displayed to guests; the food rotates on a shaft or skewer while cooking. The meat used in the popular Greek sandwich called a *gyro* is usually cooked on and then sliced from a rotisserie broiler.

In general, a broiler should be cleaned and sanitized according to the manufacturer's instructions. The grease drip pans should be emptied, washed, and dried daily. The grates and drip shield should be washed and dried at least once each day or at the end of each shift. The broiler chamber and the exterior of the broiler should be cleaned with hot water and detergent and wiped dry with a clean cloth. It is also a good practice to degrease the broiler and clean the burners at least once a month. Representatives of the local public utility should periodically recalibrate the controls on broilers and all cooking equipment.

Fryers cook food products by convection in hot fat or oil. Fryers are either gas-powered or electric. Most fryers are very energy-efficient because they have automatic temperature controls. Pressure fryers decrease smoke and other vapors while reducing the amount of oil foods absorb. Pressure fryers are extremely energy-efficient and cook more quickly and evenly than regular fryers.

Most frying oil is chemically modified to extend its useful life. Only high-quality oil should be used for frying, as poor quality fat or oil may become rancid quickly (see Chapter 4). Rancidity reactions occur more rapidly in the presence of heavy metals, salt, moisture, and loose food particles. Therefore, foods to be fried should be as free as possible from moisture and crumbs and should never be salted directly over the frying oil. Filtering oil daily removes most of the food particles in the frying medium and thus helps prevent rancidity. It is important to keep the fryer covered when it is not being used.

Certain recommended cleaning techniques apply to most fryers. First, the outer surface of fryers should be wiped every day with a clean, moist cloth. Fryers should be emptied and cleaned at least once each week. If the operation does a great deal of frying, daily cleaning may be necessary. The following procedure should be used to clean fryers:

1. Remove the frying oil and filter or discard it, depending on its condition.

2. Fill the frying chamber with water and a cleaning compound, and boil this solution for 10 to 15 minutes.

3. Drain the solution from the fryer.

4. Clean the inside of the fryer with a specially designed fryer brush to remove any remaining food particles.

5. Rinse the fryer with a vinegar and water solution, followed by a clean water rinse.

6. Dry the fryer.

7. Fill the clean fryer either with the filtered frying oil or with fresh oil.

8. Cover the fryer until its next use.

Grease filters used to strain frying oil are single-service articles and should never be re-used. Filtering equipment should be handled in the same way as food-contact equipment. It should be stored covered.

A griddle cooks food on a metal surface heated from below by either gas or electricity. (The term "grill" is frequently used incorrectly to refer to a griddle; a grill is actually a broiler.) The surface temperature of a griddle is controlled by an automatic thermostat. A grooved griddle is used to cook steaks and hamburgers. Its grooves or ribs create a pattern on the surface of food similar to markings from broiler grates. Griddles are not very energy-efficient because of their large exposed heating surface. Dirty griddles use more energy than clean ones.

Griddles must be cleaned in two ways. Each time a griddle is used, excess food should be scraped off with a sharp-edged metal scraper. The griddle should also be cleaned thoroughly once each day. Rub the hot surface of the griddle with a liquid frying compound or unsalted shortening to soften burned-on food particles. A griddle pad or brick can be used to remove cooked-on food. Then wash the griddle surface with a solution of detergent in hot water. The surface of the griddle should then be rinsed, dried, and rubbed with the liquid frying compound or shortening to protect the cooking surface.

Other parts of the griddle should also be cleaned daily. A small amount of water can be carefully poured on the back of the griddle's cooking surface to steam off cooked-on food. (Be careful to avoid steam burns.) The drip pans should be removed, emptied, washed, and dried. Clean, rinse, and dry the exterior of the griddle as well.

An oven is simply a heated chamber for cooking food. A conventional or deck oven cooks food by a combination of conduction, convection, and radiation. Conventional ovens powered by gas or electricity are often used for baking and roasting.

Convection ovens use a fan to force hot air into direct contact with the food. As a result, convection ovens cook food much faster than conventional ovens at the same temperature. Products cooked in a convection oven also exhibit less shrinkage, retain more moisture, and develop better crust color than foods prepared in a conventional oven, provided that both temperature and time are strictly controlled. It is best to follow the manufacturer's time and temperature combinations.

Microwave ovens convert alternating electric current to electromagnetic energy. Microwaves cause the water molecules in food to vibrate rapidly. This vibration generates heat, which cooks the food. Metal dishes and utensils are generally not used in microwave ovens because they reflect microwaves. Follow the manufacturer's operating and cleaning instructions for microwave ovens.

Combination ovens combine the best features of convection ovens and steamers. They are capable of providing pressureless steam, convection heat, or both in a compact unit that takes up relatively little floor space. Combination ovens are frequently electrically powered, although gas models are available. Controls are electro-mechanical or solid state, and some models are capable of automated cooking. In areas with hard water (water with a high mineral content), combination ovens may need to be equipped with a water treatment system.

Careful cleaning of all ovens is important. All oven spills should be wiped up promptly. Conventional or convection ovens should be cooled before daily cleaning. Remove baked-on spills with a scraper. Brush the deck and wipe the chamber with a detergent-water solution. Never pour water directly on the oven; this can warp the deck if it is hot. Do not use caustic (highly alkaline) solutions on the oven's interior or exterior because they will damage the finish. Oven burners should be cleaned monthly. Controls should be calibrated periodically by a public utility representative.

Convection oven racks can be removed, washed, rinsed, and dried. These ovens should be cleaned at least monthly, or more often if they are used heavily. Each month, the fan in a convection oven should also be disassembled and cleaned. Microwave ovens can be washed inside and out with a detergent-water solution as needed. Remove bits of food from inside drains when cleaning combination ovens.

Along with ovens, ranges are the most frequently used type of cooking equipment in a food service kitchen. Ranges provide heated surfaces for cooking food in pots and pans. Ranges generally use energy inefficiently because a large amount of the cooking surface is exposed. Open-top ranges cook food directly over open burners. These ranges are well suited to menus with many cooked-to-order items because they heat up almost instantly. Hot-top ranges have a smooth surface made from a large metal plate or a series of concentric rings. The center ring is the hottest part of the surface. Placement of the pots and pans in relation to the center ring determines the amount of heat applied to food. Hot-top ranges require more preheating time than open-top ranges. Some ranges are designed with a combination of cooking surfaces.

All spills on ranges should be wiped up immediately. On an open-top range, grates, burner bowls, and spillover trays should be cleaned daily. Each month, the range should be degreased and the gas burners unclogged with a stiff wire brush. The surface of a hot-top range should be cleaned when slightly warm. A blunt scraper is used to remove stubborn food spills. After it has cooled, the top section can be removed, washed, and dried. All soil under rings and plates must be removed. The exterior surfaces of all ranges should be washed, dried, and wiped with a soft cloth daily.

Steam-powered equipment is becoming popular in quantity production kitchens because it is so energy-efficient. A steam-jacketed kettle consists of a stainless steel kettle within a larger kettle. Steam in the enclosed space between the two kettles cooks food very rapidly. This item is often used to cook liquid foods such as soups and sauces. Steam-jacketed kettles are available with capacities ranging from 1 quart (.95 liter) to 200 gallons (757 liters) or more. They are powered by electricity, gas, or pressurized steam from another source.

Steam-jacketed kettles should be cleaned after each use. Presoaking may be necessary if food is crusted on the inside of the kettle. Scrub the inside of the kettle with a clean soft-bristle brush. Then rinse the kettle and remove and clean the drain valve. The draw-off line and strainer should also be cleaned. The outside of the kettle should be washed with a hot water–detergent solution, rinsed, and wiped dry. The steam trap should be checked weekly, and mineral scale should be removed from the boiler at least every six months. In areas with hard water, the boiler may need to be descaled more frequently.

Compartment steamers cook foods by exposing them directly to steam. These devices are also rapid and energy-efficient, and preserve much of a product's original nutrients, texture, taste, appearance, and color. Compartment steamers cook at a constant temperature, so time must be carefully controlled to avoid overcooking. Compartment steamers may operate with steam pressure ranging from 0 to 15 pounds per square inch.

Compartment steamers are basically self-cleaning except for their interior racks, which can be cleaned in a mechanical dishwasher. The interior of a compartment steamer should be wiped dry after each use, and any food debris should be removed. In addition, the water line should be drained once each week. The boiler should be descaled once every six months, or more frequently in hard-water areas.

A tilting braising pan is a highly versatile unit. It can be used to fry, braise, simmer, or reheat a variety of food products. Food cooked in a tilting braising pan exhibits little shrinkage and retains its moisture. A tilting braising pan may be powered by gas or electricity. This equipment is also labor-efficient because it cooks a large volume of food with one person operating it.

A tilting braising pan should be cleaned after each use. Fill the pan with a detergent-water solution and close the cover to steam off food debris. Use a clean non-abrasive brush to remove remaining food particles, tilt the pan to remove the water, and rinse and dry the unit. Grease on the outside surfaces can be removed easily with an ammonia-water solution. However, this solution should never be poured on hot surfaces because toxic ammonia gas will be released. The tilting mechanism of the braising pan should be lubricated at least once each month.

Coffee urns should be cleaned after each use; accumulated oils and deposits can spoil even the most expensive coffee. After each brew, empty the leftover coffee out of the urn and discard the coffee grounds. Rinse the basket with clean cold water. Never use soap or detergent in a coffee urn. The inside of the urn should be rinsed with fresh water and then cleaned with an urn brush and a chemical specifically formulated for cleaning coffee makers. After cleaning, the cleaner should be thoroughly rinsed out by filling the urn with fresh water and emptying it twice. Leave one or two gallons of fresh water in the urn until it is used again, but discard this water before brewing. The exterior of the urn, including gauges and faucets, should be wiped down daily.

Toasters must be cleaned daily. Like all electric appliances, toasters should be unplugged before cleaning. Crumbs on the moving parts and in the collection tray can be removed with a soft brush. Trays and other moving parts are removable in some models. The outside of a toaster can be cleaned with a mild detergent-hot water solution, rinsed, and wiped dry.

Miscellaneous Food Service Equipment. Equipment not used for cooking is common in food service kitchens and must be cleaned regularly to minimize contamination risks. (Cleaning and sanitizing equipment is covered in Chapter 9.)

Ice used as a food or cooling medium should be made from drinking water. Ice machines may not be used for chilled storage of other food products. It is important to store the scoop on a clean surface or in the ice, with the handle extended out of the ice. The scoop should be washed in a hot water-detergent solution, rinsed, sanitized, and air-dried daily. The exterior of the ice machine should be similarly cleaned on a daily basis. Once a month, all ice should be removed from the ice machine, the machine should be shut down, and the inside of the machine should be washed, rinsed, sanitized, and dried. Evaporator and condenser motors should be checked, and any necessary maintenance performed at that time. Follow the manufacturer's recommendations for cleaning and descaling the interior of the unit. While the machine is shut down, check and replace the water filter if necessary.

The FDA states:

3-202.17   Ice.*

Ice for use as a food or a cooling medium shall be made from drinking water.

3-303.11   Ice Used as Exterior Coolant, Prohibited as Ingredient.

After use as a medium for cooling the exterior surfaces of food such as melons or fish, packaged foods such as canned beverages, or cooling coils and tubes of equipment, ice may not be used as food.

3-303.12   Storage or Display of Food in Contact with Water or Ice.

(A) Packaged food may not be stored in direct contact with ice or water if the food is subject to the entry of water because of the nature of its packaging, wrapping, or container or its positioning in the ice or water.

(B) Except as specified in ¶ ¶ (C) and (D) of this section, unpackaged food may only be stored in direct contact with drained ice.

(C) *Whole, raw fruits or vegetables; cut, raw vegetables such as celery or carrot sticks or cut potatoes; and tofu may be immersed in ice or water.*

(D) *Raw chicken and raw fish that are received immersed in ice in shipping containers may remain in that condition while in storage awaiting preparation, display, service, or sale.*

4-204.17   Ice Units, Separation of Drains.

Liquid waste drain lines may not pass through an ice machine or ice storage bin.

Source: FDA 1993 *Food Code.*

Can openers must be cleaned daily. It is important to scrub the blade to remove accumulations of food that may dull the blade. A dull can opener blade can cause dangerous metal splinters to drop into food. The outside of the can opener should also be washed, rinsed, and dried.

Exhaust hoods are designed to remove grease, heat, moisture, and odors from the kitchen. The outside of all hoods should be cleaned and polished weekly. Inside filters should be removed for steam-cleaning at least once a week, and more often if the hoods are located near heavily used fryers. This may be done in-house or by a contract service. Gutters or pans that catch grease can be cleaned, rinsed, and dried while the filters are out.

Cooking and Facilities

Careful planning of production facilities reduces safety hazards and sanitation risks while creating a more efficient operation. Facilities planning begins with the menu, because it determines what is to be cooked and therefore the types of facilities needed. The number of meals to be served also has an impact on the facilities design. The kind and amount of food prepared determines the allocation of work areas and storage space.

Distances between work stations are an important consideration. There must be ample space in the kitchen to avoid traffic jams of people and products. On the other hand, large distances between work areas may not result in the most efficient use of space. An operation must try to reach a balance in order to maximize return on the investment in facilities. Management must review national, state, and local codes and ordinances before making any decisions about facilities design. These codes cover lighting, ventilation, sanitation, and construction requirements.

Energy usage is another important consideration in facilities design. Well-planned facilities equipped with energy-efficient equipment can reduce energy bills and result in substantial savings. Proposed menu changes provide a good opportunity for considering how the facilities and equipment can be made more cost-effective. One strategy is to install flexible equipment such as the combination oven.

Equipment and facilities do not last forever, but cleaning and preventive maintenance will prolong their useful life. Ease of cleaning and maintenance are important considerations in selecting wall, floor, and ceiling materials for the food production work centers. (More information on these materials is presented in Chapter 9.)

Cooking and Change

Change affects the cooking control point in much the same way that it affects the other basic operating activities: standards for cooking may need to be re-evaluated if conditions change. For example, if the operation begins to use more convenience food products, cooking procedures will change. The addition of ethnic food items to the menu is another example of change at the cooking control point. Production staff members may require special training to prepare the new items. Steam equipment is often used to cook ethnic foods, and some menu items may require specialty equipment such as woks, Chinese barbecue ranges, taco ranges, and semi-automatic pasta cookers. Managers should evaluate the effects of a change on the operation's control points and on its overall SRM program *before* the change is implemented. The state or local regulatory agency must be notified prior to the installation of new equipment.

Cooking and the SRM Program

At the cooking control point, food products are exposed to physical and chemical changes that can increase risks. Standard recipes must be closely followed, especially time and temperature combinations. Cooking times and internal product temperatures are designed to produce a satisfactory finished menu item and to destroy or inactivate pathogens.

Proper training of staff members at the cooking control point is the best way to reduce risks. Training should include the use of standard recipes, time-temperature combinations, sensory tests, personal cleanliness and hygiene, sanitary food handling, and the proper use of equipment and facilities.

It is critical to regularly clean, sanitize, and maintain all equipment, facilities, and utensils used at the cooking control point, including the metal-stemmed product probe thermometer. This important piece of equipment must be cleaned and sanitized after each changed use.

The Holding Control Point

In many establishments, it is not feasible to cook all foods to order during rush periods or for large groups. Some menu items are prepared in advance and held for later service. Thus, for many food service operations, holding is a critical control point. Some menu items are held hot, some cold. To maintain product quality and minimize microbiological hazards, the holding time must be as short as possible and strict temperature controls must be observed. Holding is also critical for products removed from storage but not served; these should be promptly returned to storage for later use.

Ideally, food should be served immediately after cooking, thus avoiding the holding step altogether. However, since most operations do not always have this option, the resources under the holding control point must be standardized using the SRM program.

Holding and Inventory

Product holding aims to maintain the sanitary and culinary quality of food items until they are needed for service. Hot foods must not be allowed to cool between production and service. Hot food can be held safely with hot-holding equipment designed to operate at temperatures in excess of 140°F (60°C). Different hot foods have their own holding temperature requirements. Entrées and meat dishes are generally held at 140°F (60°C). Sauces, gravies, and thick soups are usually held between 140°F (60°C) and 180°F (82°C). Thin soups and hot beverages should be held in the range of 180°F (82°C) to 190°F (88°C).

When batches of food are held for service, there is often food left over. Cooked potentially hazardous foods should be cooled from 140°F (60°C) to 70°F (21°C) within two hours, and from 70°F (21°C) to 41°F (5°C) or below within four hours. If prepared from ingredients at ambient (kitchen) temperature, such as canned tuna, potentially hazardous foods should be cooled to 41°F (5°C) or below within four hours. Highly perishable potentially hazardous leftovers—like puddings, hollandaise sauce, and custards—should be discarded after holding.

Other leftover foods should be quick-chilled to 41°F (5°C) or less in pans that are no more than four inches (10.2 cm) deep. The size of the pan is important because it affects the **heat transfer** rate—in this case, the rate at which heat leaves the food. Large masses of food—such as soup in a stockpot—cool very slowly. Leftovers that must be stored in containers, such as soups and sauces, should be divided into small batches and chilled in shallow pans. Large pieces of food, like roasts, can be chilled quickly by cutting them into smaller or thinner pieces. Removing meat from the bone speeds the cooling process.

Slow cooling negatively affects the quality, nutritional value, and safety of food products. Leftovers should be chilled to 70°F (21°C) or less within two hours and to 41°F (5°C) or less within four hours. Placing products in a freezer or refrigeration unit with forced air circulation for 30 minutes will lower the temperature quickly. If containers of leftovers can be sealed, they can be submerged in ice water or exposed to cold running water for quick-chilling. Liquid foods can be quick-chilled by agitating them in containers exposed to ice or ice water. In some liquid foods, ice may be added as an ingredient to hasten cooling.

Leftovers should be covered, labeled, and dated before refrigeration. Airtight containers can create favorable conditions for the growth of anaerobic microbes during cooling, so covers should be loose-fitting or left slightly ajar until the product temperature is below 41°F (5°C). Remember, the temperature danger zone may be different in your area. Leftover food products should never be refrozen.

The FDA states:

3-501.14   Cooling.*

(A) Cooked potentially hazardous food shall be cooled:

(1)   From 60°C (140°F) to 21°C (70°F) within 2 hours; and

(2)   From 21°C (70°F) to 5°C (41°F), or below, within 4 hours.

(B) Potentially hazardous food shall be cooled to 5°C (41°F) or below within 4 hours if prepared from ingredients at ambient temperature, such as reconstituted foods and canned tuna.

3-501.15   Cooling Methods.

(A) Cooling shall be accomplished in accordance with the time and temperature criteria specified under § 3-501.14 by using one or more of the following methods based on the type of food being cooled:

(1)   Placing the food in shallow pans;

(2)   Separating the food into smaller or thinner portions;

(3)   Using rapid cooling equipment;

(4)   Stirring the food in a container placed in an ice water bath;

(5)   Using containers that facilitate heat transfer;

(6)   Adding ice as an ingredient; or

(7)   Other effective methods.

(B) When placed in cooling or cold holding equipment, food containers in which food is being cooled shall be:

(1)   Arranged in the equipment to provide maximum heat transfer through the container walls; and

(2)   Loosely covered, or uncovered if protected from overhead contamination as specified under Subparagraph 3-305.11 (A)(2), during the cooling period to facilitate heat transfer from the surface of the food.

Source: FDA 1993 *Food Code.*

Improper food cooling is a major cause of foodborne illness. To manage the risks, always cool foods properly. Remember that acidic foods such as chili and tomato sauce contain volatile organic acids which may negatively affect the equipment and the refrigeration process.

When potentially hazardous foods are reheated for hot holding, all parts of the food must reach a minimum internal temperature of 165°F (74°C) for 15 seconds. Recall that temperatures in a microwave oven should reach 190°F (88°C) for reheating, 25°F (14°C) higher than in a conventional oven. The minimum temperatures should be reached within two hours.

The FDA states:

3-403.11   Reheating for Hot Holding.*

(A) Except as specified under ¶¶ (B) and (C) of this section, potentially hazardous food that is cooked, cooled, and reheated for hot holding shall be reheated so that all parts of the food reach a temperature of at least 74°C (165°F) for 15 seconds.

(B) Food reheated in a microwave oven shall be covered; rotated or stirred throughout or midway during cooking or according to label instructions during heating; heated to a temperature of at least 88°C (190°F); and allowed to stand covered 2 minutes after reheating.

(C) Ready-to-eat food taken from a commercially processed, hermetically sealed container, or from an intact package from a food processing plant that is inspected by the food regulatory authority that has jurisdiction over the plant, shall be heated to a temperature of at least 60°C (140°F) for hot holding.

(D) Reheating shall be done rapidly and the minimum temperature specified under ¶ (A) of this section shall be reached within 2 hours.

Source: FDA 1993 *Food Code.*

Sensory tests are frequently used during holding. While they are important, it is even more important to regularly check the temperature of food products and holding equipment. This combination will help lower risks.

Holding and People

Food production staff members should be aware of the potential for contamination and quality deterioration in menu items held for later service. Ideally, products would be prepared, cooked, and served immediately. However, limited resources (people, equipment, and facilities) make it difficult for food service operations to approximate this ideal flow. Peaks and valleys in guest demand for menu items also make holding necessary.

Time-temperature control during holding is essential to maintain the sanitary and culinary quality of food products. Foods held hot must maintain internal temperatures of 140°F (60°C) or higher. Internal temperatures should be checked frequently with a metal-stemmed product probe thermometer. The critical temperatures chart presented in Exhibit 7.9 can be used to train and remind food service staff members of the temperatures required for safe hot and cold food holding. This chart includes temperatures that are significant for some of the other control points as well.

Staff members responsible for product holding must practice good personal hygiene. Once products are cooked and pathogens killed or inactivated, food can be recontaminated by staff members who do not maintain high standards of personal cleanliness.

Holding and Equipment

The amount of hot-holding equipment an operation needs depends on peak demand for the equipment. Generally, production staff should restock hot-holding equipment every 15 to 30 minutes in order to maintain product quality. Small batch production methods help to minimize excess holding. Hot-holding equipment is designed to facilitate rapid service with minimum effort. It is not, however, designed to

Exhibit 7.9 Critical Temperatures for Food Service

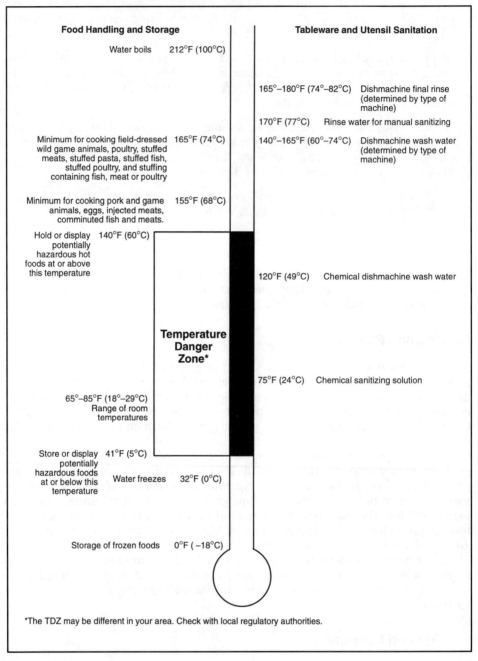

Food Handling and Storage		Tableware and Utensil Sanitation
Water boils	212°F (100°C)	
	165°–180°F (74°–82°C)	Dishmachine final rinse (determined by type of machine)
	170°F (77°C)	Rinse water for manual sanitizing
Minimum for cooking field-dressed wild game animals, poultry, stuffed meats, stuffed pasta, stuffed fish, stuffed poultry, and stuffing containing fish, meat or poultry	165°F (74°C)	140°–165°F (60°–74°C) Dishmachine wash water (determined by type of machine)
Minimum for cooking pork and game animals, eggs, injected meats, comminuted fish and meats.	155°F (68°C)	
Hold or display potentially hazardous hot foods at or above this temperature	140°F (60°C)	
		120°F (49°C) Chemical dishmachine wash water
Temperature Danger Zone*		
		75°F (24°C) Chemical sanitizing solution
65°–85°F (18°–29°C) Range of room temperatures		
Store or display potentially hazardous foods at or below this temperature	41°F (5°C)	
Water freezes	32°F (0°C)	
Storage of frozen foods	0°F (–18°C)	

*The TDZ may be different in your area. Check with local regulatory authorities.

heat food. Food products must be heated to proper temperatures before being placed in hot-holding equipment.

A variety of equipment is used to maintain the temperatures of ready-to-serve foods. Steam tables and bains-marie use steam and hot water, respectively, to keep food in containers hot. There are ovens that cook meats at low temperatures and then hold them with little additional cooking or shrinkage.

Warming drawers are typically used to hold bread and rolls near the food pickup point so that servers can plate these items immediately before service. Infrared warmers are usually mounted above the food pickup counter to keep plated foods hot; warming lamps serve the same purpose. Other equipment includes heated cabinets and pass-through holding units—units with doors on two sides, situated between preparation and service areas. Some operations use electrically powered plate warmers to heat plates before service.

Hot-holding equipment should be able to withstand the rigors of intense rush periods. If mobile equipment is purchased, the necessary utility connections must be available. Mobile units should be loaded from the bottom up to prevent them from becoming top-heavy and unstable. Heated cabinets should be purchased with insulation to reduce energy costs.

Cold-holding is designed to facilitate rapid server pickup. Pass-through refrigerators hold food between preparation and service areas. Countertop units with glass doors can be used to display food during holding. Refrigerators, freezers, and mobile refrigeration units are also used to maintain cold food products at proper storage temperatures. The temperature of refrigerated foods should not exceed 41°F (5°C). Some food items, such as frozen desserts, require lower temperatures. Frozen menu items should not exceed 0°F (–18°C). Appetizers, salads, cold meats and seafood, and desserts are often held cold before service.

Cold-holding equipment is more versatile if the temperature is adjustable. Mobile equipment allows staff members to move equipment as necessary. Cold-holding equipment should be insulated to maximize energy usage.

The one piece of equipment that is absolutely essential at the holding control point is a metal-stemmed product probe thermometer. The best model for monitoring the internal temperatures of most products is the dial face, metal probe thermometer (see Exhibit 7.10). It is accurate to ±2°F (±1°C), has a range from 0° to 220°F (–18° to 104°C), and is easy to use. To measure temperatures, insert a clean, sanitized thermometer into the geometric center of the food product. The thermometer may take time to stabilize, so the reading should only be taken when the indicated temperature is no longer changing. The manufacturer's instructions may provide other recommendations. Thermometers should be cleaned and sanitized after each use so that they do not become a source of food contamination. Thermometers should also be calibrated periodically by either the ice point method, the boiling point method, or the screening method (see Exhibit 7.11).

Alternatives to probe thermometers include battery-powered or rechargeable electronic digital testing thermometers. These products are more appropriate when measuring the temperatures of small portions or thin inventory items such as fish fillets or hamburger. Like probe thermometers, they should be cleaned and sanitized after each changed use.

Holding equipment must also be equipped with temperature sensing devices accurate to ±3°F (±2°C). Equipment thermometers should indicate the temperature in the coolest part of hot-holding equipment and the warmest part of cold-holding equipment. Temperature readings can be checked against a portable thermometer.

A variety of containers are designed to hold cooked food for service. Containers must be made of food-grade materials and be cleaned and sanitized after each changed use. Galvanized containers should not be used for holding food products, particularly those high in organic acids such as tomato products and lemon juice.

Exhibit 7.10 Information for Selecting Product Temperatures

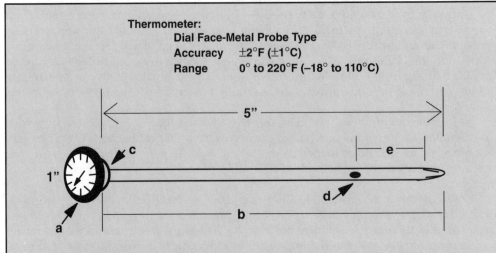

Thermometer:
Dial Face-Metal Probe Type
Accuracy   ±2°F (±1°C)
Range   0° to 220°F (−18° to 110°C)

A.   Dial face diameter should be a minimum of 1 inch (25.4 mm) with 2°F (1°C) increments. A range of 0° to 220°F (−17.8 to 104.4°C) is satisfactory for most applications. More specific ranges may be desirable in some instances. If the thermometer is not to be used as a "pocket" instrument, a larger dial face is desirable to improve readability.

B.   For most evaluations, a minimum stem length of 5 inches (127 mm) is sufficient. Some applications require a longer stem.

C.   Some instruments are available with a "calibration nut," immediately behind the dial, for adjusting the indicating needle during calibration.

D.   The immersion point on most product thermometers is about 2 inches (5 cm) up the stem. The immersion point varies for different makes, so be sure to read the manufacturer's instructions for specifics.

E.   In practice, the temperature on the dial is an approximate average of temperatures being sensed between the immersion point and immediately behind the tip.

Warning: Glass, liquid-filled instruments are **not permitted** for taking temperatures directly in food product because of the danger of breakage and mercury poisoning.

Source: National Sanitation Foundation, *Product Temperature Management.*

Portioning equipment and utensils must be used carefully to prevent cross-contamination. In a kitchen where there is an interruption in service, such as in a kitchen preparing cooked-to-order items for a hotel dining room, kitchenware must be stored in a safe and sanitary way. Plastic gloves used to portion foods during holding should not be re-used because they are single-use items.

Proper use of equipment and utensils is also important when food is portioned at the holding control point. Scoops and ladles must be used properly to ensure standard portion sizes. Scalloped dishes, vegetables, and pot pies are frequently held (and served) in individual casseroles. Such practices aid the operation's cost control program and help ensure guest satisfaction.

Exhibit 7.11 Field Checking (Calibration)

In general, the calibration shift of a thermometer will be consistent throughout its range, except when the instrument has been physically damaged, in which case it should be discarded. There are three ways to check the calibration of a thermometer.

Ice Point Method
This is the best method for checking the accuracy of any thermometer except maximum-registering thermometers. Fill an insulated container, such as a wide mouth "thermos" bottle, with a mixture of potable crushed ice and water. The container must have crushed ice throughout to provide an environment of 32°F (0°C), so you may have to pack more ice into the container during the process. When the mixture of ice and water has stabilized (after four to five minutes), insert the thermometer to the appropriate immersion depth. Be sure to hold the stem of the instrument away from the bottom and sides of the container (preferably one inch) to avoid error. The ice point method permits calibration to within 0.1°F.

Boiling Point Method
This method, accurate to within 1°F (0.6°C) of the true temperature, is not as accurate as the ice point method. But it is the only method that can be used with maximum-registering thermometers. It is also useful to verify suspicion of a damaged instrument.

Place a container of potable water on a heating element. After the water in the container has reached a complete "rolling" boil, insert the instrument to the appropriate immersion depth. Immerse maximum-registering thermometers completely. Be sure there is at least a 2-inch clearance between the stem or sensing element and the bottom and sides of the container.

In the boiling point method, you must take into account your elevation above sea level. Use this rule of thumb: for each 550 feet above sea level, the boiling point of water is lowered 1°F (0.6°C). For example, if you are at an elevation of 5000 feet, the boiling point of water is approximately 203°F (95°C) (5000/550 = 9.09, and 212°F − 9.09°F = 203°F).

Screening (checking)
The screening method, accurate to within 1°F to 2°F, can be effective for field purposes. To check fixed units, thermostats, and recording thermometers, place a portable or testing thermometer near the sensing element of the fixed unit (within 1/4 to 1/2 inch). Allow the testing thermometer to reach equilibrium, and then compare readings.

**ALWAYS KNOW THE CHARACTERISTICS OF THE
THERMOMETERS YOU ARE USING!**

Source: National Sanitation Foundation, *Product Temperature Management.*

Holding and Facilities

The facilities resource considerations during the holding control point mirror the considerations under the other two production control points: preparing and cooling. Facilities must be designed, installed, cleaned, and maintained to meet the minimum standards described in the FDA's codes. It is essential to check with local regulatory agencies to determine additional local and state requirements.

Holding and Change

Product holding requirements change with the menu and often with the day of the week and the meal period. For example, a hotel with multiple food service outlets has a variety of hot- and cold-holding needs. In the hotel coffee shop, fruits may be prepared for breakfast and held refrigerated, while hot breakfast items are probably cooked to order and served immediately. Lunch and dinner in the main dining room may involve a combination of menu items held hot, held cold, and cooked to order. For large banquets, all salads, entrées, side dishes, and desserts are held either hot or cold, depending on the nature of the product. Room service products are held hot or cold during transportation to guestrooms. Managers must constantly re-evaluate food product holding requirements based on changing needs.

Holding and the SRM Program

Holding is the most critical of the production control points because the opportunity to expose potentially hazardous foods to the temperature danger zone is greatest. Excessive holding times raise risks and also lower product quality. Internal product temperatures, as well as holding times, must be closely monitored. It is also important to clean and sanitize probe thermometers after each changed use to avoid cross-contaminating food products.

Personal cleanliness and hygiene is also important at the holding control point. Leftover foods must be handled carefully and chilled quickly, if appropriate. Potentially hazardous leftovers should be used within 24 hours or discarded.

Equipment, utensils, and facilities used for holding food products must be regularly cleaned, sanitized, and maintained. Staff members trained to follow proper procedures and maintain standards are the key to monitoring the SRM program, and thus reducing risks, at the holding control point.

Summary

The preparing, cooking, and holding control points together make up the production function in a food establishment. The preparing control point includes all activities performed on food products before they are cooked or served. Because most preparing takes place in the temperature danger zone and involves handling food, food is exposed to many potential sources of contamination at this control point. Food is also exposed to contamination when it is removed from storage. Some foods—such as salads, fresh fruits and vegetables, unbaked frozen desserts, and dairy products—move directly from preparation to service. The sanitary handling of these products is especially important because there is no opportunity to destroy harmful microorganisms with heat. Sanitation standards at the preparing control point serve to protect food safety.

Cooking destroys or inactivates pathogens, renders food more digestible, and changes its form, flavor, color, texture, and appearance. The effects of cooking on pathogens depend on the temperature, time, cooking method, characteristics of the food product, and type and quantity of organisms present. Sanitation standards at the cooking control point include heating potentially hazardous foods to the proper internal temperature, as well as guarding against cross-contamination. Staff members' personal hygiene is important at this control point, as is the proper use and care of kitchen equipment.

Holding is a critical control point. Strict time and temperature controls are necessary at this control point to maintain product quality and minimize microbiological hazards. Products removed from storage but not served should be promptly returned to storage for later use. Leftovers must be chilled rapidly to preserve food safety. The proper use and care of holding equipment, including product thermometers, will help prevent food contamination and quality loss during holding.

Key Terms

cantilevered • equipment installation information • equipment schedule • *garde-manger* • heat transfer • master food production planning worksheet • *mise en place* • production • product cost analysis form • standard portion sizes • standard recipe • standard recipe cost

Discussion Questions

1. What are the special sanitation concerns, the riskiest food products, and measures for reducing risks at the preparing control point?

2. What are the roles of standard recipes and convenience foods at each production control point?

3. Why are personal hygiene standards at the production control points important?

4. How is the master food production planning worksheet used?

5. What types of equipment are used at the preparing control point? Describe proper care and installation procedures.

6. What are the three objectives of cooking, and how are risks reduced at the cooking control point?

7. Equipment used to add heat to food requires special use and care procedures. What are they?

8. What items are included in the miscellaneous food service equipment category?

9. How is inventory protected at the holding control point?

10. What types of equipment does the holding control point require?

Checklist for Preparing

Inventory

_____ Products are protected from sanitation risks, quality deterioration, and waste.

_____ Standard (written) recipes are used to maintain consistency in quality, sanitation, and cost.

_____ Standard portion sizes are used to maintain consistency.

_____ A product cost analysis form is used and updated when market prices change.

_____ The on-site versus convenience decision is evaluated regularly.

_____ The following are treated as high-risk inventory items:

    _____ potentially hazardous foods

_____   foods that possess natural contaminants

_____   foods that are handled a great deal and could be cross-contaminated

_____   foods that have multiple preparation steps

_____   foods that are exposed to kitchen temperatures (TDZ) for long periods of time

_____   foods that have gone through a number of temperature changes

_____   foods that are prepared in large quantities

_____ Sensory tests are used to evaluate inventory items.

_____ All necessary ingredients and equipment are gathered before beginning preparation.

_____ Standard recipes are revised, if possible, to make them less risky.

People

_____ Rules of personal hygiene and cleanliness are strictly enforced.

_____ Handwashing takes place before, during, and after preparation activities.

_____ All food service staff members wear clean outer clothing.

_____ Effective hair restraints are used to prevent contamination of food and food-contact surfaces.

_____ Staff members consume food only in designated staff dining areas.

_____ Staff members use tobacco only in designated areas.

_____ Staff members handle soiled tableware in a way that minimizes contamination of their hands.

_____ Preparation staff members accurately weigh and measure ingredients.

_____ A master food production planning worksheet is used.

_____ Preparation staff members are trained to maintain the establishment's standards.

Equipment

_____ Equipment is installed and operated properly to prevent contamination of all surfaces.

____ Whenever possible, mobile equipment is purchased to facilitate cleaning.

____ Equipment is installed away from potential sources of contamination.

____ All openings to hollow spaces beneath and between equipment are sealed.

____ Aisles and working spaces between equipment and walls are unobstructed.

____ The list of proposed equipment purchases and equipment installation plans are submitted to health department officials before purchasing or installing equipment.

____ Kitchenware is cleaned and sanitized after each changed use.

____ In-use preparation equipment and utensils are handled and stored properly to reduce risks.

Facilities

____ Facilities are designed to efficiently move products from issuing to preparation areas.

____ Preparation areas have adequate equipment, work tables, lighting, and ventilation.

____ Essential equipment is added and unnecessary equipment is removed.

____ Preparation facilities comply with local, state, and federal regulatory requirements.

____ The layout of facilities is designed to reduce contamination risks and facilitate the use of equipment.

____ Facilities are cleaned, sanitized, and maintained regularly.

SRM Program

____ Inventory is handled carefully and prepared safely.

____ Food service staff members are trained to maintain standards and reduce the risks during preparing.

____ Adequate facilities and equipment are present and used, and they are cleaned, sanitized, and maintained frequently to reduce the risks during preparing.

Checklist for Cooking

Inventory

____ Food is cooked with as little manual contact as possible, and the correct utensils are used to handle food.

_____ Surfaces are cleaned and sanitized before use to avoid cross-contamination of food products.

_____ Potentially hazardous foods are cooked to a minimum internal temperature of 145°F (63°C) for 15 seconds *except:*

  _____ Field-dressed wild game animals, poultry, stuffed fish, stuffed meats, stuffed pasta, stuffed poultry, and stuffing containing fish, meat, or poultry are cooked to a minimum of 165°F (74°C).

  _____ Pork and game animals, comminuted meats and fish, injected meats, and eggs are cooked to a minimum of 155°F (68°C) for 15 seconds.

  _____ All products are cooked 25°F (14°C) higher in a microwave oven and allowed to stand covered for 2 minutes after cooking.

_____ Potentially hazardous foods are reheated to an internal temperature of 165°F (74°C) for 15 seconds.

_____ Internal temperatures are monitored with metal-stemmed product probe thermometers accurate to ±2°F (±1°C).

_____ Potentially hazardous foods are thawed safely.

_____ Sensory tests are used in combination with temperature checks.

People

_____ All staff members practice good personal hygiene and cleanliness.

_____ Staff members work accurately.

_____ Standard recipes are used to maintain consistency in quality, sanitation, and costs.

_____ Ingredient amounts, cooking times, and cooking temperatures are followed precisely.

_____ Finished products are sampled in a sanitary way.

_____ Production staff members work closely and in cooperation with service staff members.

_____ Production staff members are trained to maintain the operation's standards.

Equipment

_____ Staff members treat equipment as an investment that must be regularly cleaned and maintained.

_____ The manufacturer's instructions for cleaning, sanitizing, maintaining, and operating equipment are followed.

_____ Supervisors inspect equipment daily to determine that the establishment's standards for cleaning, sanitizing, maintenance, and operation of the equipment are being followed.

_____ Staff members are trained to clean and sanitize equipment as soon as they finish using it.

_____ A cleaning schedule is developed, including instructions for cleaning and maintenance for each piece of equipment and work area.

_____ Equipment is selected on the basis of initial costs, availability of energy sources, operating costs, maintenance costs, and personnel skill levels.

Facilities

_____ Facility requirements are based on the menu.

_____ Distances between work stations are designed for efficient movement of people and products.

_____ Cleaning and preventive maintenance are high priorities.

_____ Walls, ceilings, floors, and equipment are easy to clean and maintain.

_____ When possible, flexible equipment is installed in facilities.

SRM Program

_____ Inventory is handled carefully and cooked safely.

_____ Staff members are trained to maintain standards and reduce risks during cooking.

_____ Adequate equipment and facilities are present and used, and they are cleaned, sanitized, and maintained regularly to reduce the risks during cooking.

Checklist for Holding

Inventory

_____ When leftovers remain after the meal period, they are cooled quickly and safely in small batches; leftover egg- and cream-based potentially hazardous foods are discarded immediately after the meal period.

_____ Leftovers are cooled to 70°F (21°C) or less within two hours and 41°F (5°C) or less within four hours.

_____ Leftovers are covered, labeled, and dated before refrigerating.

_____ Leftovers are not refrozen.

_____ Sensory tests are used in combination with temperature checks.

People

_____ Staff members are aware of the potential for quality deterioration and sanitation risks during holding.

_____ Staff members maintain strict time-temperature controls.

_____ Staff members monitor internal temperatures of products and keep them at 140°F (60°C) or above.

_____ Staff members are aware of the critical temperatures for food holding.

_____ Staff members are trained to maintain the operation's standards.

_____ Staff members practice good personal hygiene and cleanliness.

Equipment

_____ The quantity of hot-holding equipment available is based on peak demand estimates.

_____ Small batch production is used whenever possible.

_____ Food holding equipment is used correctly and carefully.

_____ A metal-stemmed product probe thermometer is used to monitor internal product temperatures.

_____ The thermometer is cleaned and sanitized after each use.

_____ The temperature is read after inserting the thermometer into the geometric center of the food product.

_____ The thermometer is given time to stabilize.

_____ The manufacturer's instructions are reviewed and followed.

_____ Holding equipment has built-in thermometers accurate to ±3°F (±2°C).

_____ Containers made out of food-grade materials are used to hold food and are cleaned and sanitized after each changed use.

_____ Portion equipment and utensils are used carefully to prevent cross-contamination.

Facilities

_____ Facilities are designed, installed, cleaned, and maintained to meet local health and sanitation standards.

SRM Program

_____ Inventory is handled carefully and held safely.

_____ Staff members are trained to maintain standards and reduce risks during holding.

_____ Adequate equipment and facilities are present and used, and they are cleaned, sanitized, and maintained frequently to reduce the risks during holding.

Case Study

Apply the principles of the three control points that you learned in this chapter to the menu item you selected in Chapter 5.

Determine whether your main ingredient will be a convenience food item, based on the discussion in the text and your evaluation of the advantages of convenience foods. Next, determine how many of the risk characteristics described in "Preparing and Inventory" apply to your menu item. Using the standard recipe form (Exhibit 7.1), try to revise your recipe to make it safer (see the whitefish example near the end of this chapter) but still acceptable to guests. Describe the standard portion size of the menu item. As an optional activity, contact a local supplier or grocery store and complete the product cost analysis form (Exhibit 7.2).

Describe the sensory tests that you will use to evaluate your main ingredient during preparing. List standards of personal hygiene and cleanliness for preparation staff members. Using the concept of *mise en place,* describe the ingredients that must be assembled before preparation begins. Select the equipment and utensils necessary to prepare your menu item. Explain how you will guard against cross-contamination. Describe the facility requirements for your menu items.

Specify the internal product temperatures of your menu item for cooking, microwave cooking, and reheating. Describe rules of personal hygiene and cleanliness for staff members. Suggest ways to reduce conflict between production staff members and servers.

List the equipment used to cook your menu item, and explain the procedures for cleaning and sanitization of equipment and utensils after cooking. Consider miscellaneous food service equipment and additional kitchenware necessary to cook your menu item. Explain, in general, how to clean, sanitize, and store these resources. Describe the facilities necessary to cook your menu item.

Specify holding temperatures and times for your menu item, assuming banquet service. If the item becomes a leftover, describe how to handle it safely. Describe the holding equipment required for banquet service and for plate service in a hotel's dining room. Discuss the thermometers you will need. Describe the containers necessary to hold your menu item, as well as the portion equipment and utensils.

Your development of this case study will, in part, be dependent on the menu item that you select. Nevertheless, the basic principles of the preparing, cooking, and holding control points can be analyzed even without applying them to an actual food establishment. If you are currently employed in a food establishment, you may wish to choose a menu item that is currently being offered or one that is under consideration for addition to the menu.

Exhibit 7.12 Standard Recipe for Baked Whitefish Florentine (Revised)

Standard Recipe No.: 4135	**Yield (No. of Servings):** 25
Product Name: Baked Whitefish Florentine	**Portion Size:** 2 fillets, stuffed
Pan Size: Large Sheet Pan	**Portion Utensil:** Spatula; stainless spoon
Temperature: 350°F (176°C)	**Special Directions:** May be served with a
Cooking Time: 35 minutes	fish velouté sauce on the side.

Ingredients	Quantity	Method
Whitefish, fresh	50 6-oz (170 g) fillets	1. Select the tail sections of the fillets, no thicker than $1/2$" (1.3 cm).
Spinach	3 lb (1,361 g)	2. Clean the spinach and remove the stems. Blanch the spinach, drain, squeeze dry, and finely chop. Alternatively, use a $2^1/2$ lb (1,134 g) box of frozen chopped spinach.
Bread crumbs Butter, melted	20 oz (567 g) 2 oz (57 g)	3. Mix the spinach, crumbs, and butter with a fork.
Parsley, chopped Eggs, beaten Lemon Juice Sorrel leaves, fresh, chopped Thyme, fresh, chopped Tarragon, fresh, chopped Lemon zest, grated Pepper, white, ground	8 oz (227 g) 2 6 oz (170 g) 8 oz (227 g) 2 T (28 g) 2 T (28 g) 1 T (14 g) 1 T (14 g)	4. Add the remaining ingredients and mix well.
Oil	4 oz (113 g)	5. Oil the sheet pans. Place 25 fillets on the pans, skin side down. 6. Top each fillet with $1^1/2$ oz (42 g) of stuffing. Shape the stuffing to fit the shape of the fish. Place the second fillet on top and press down lightly.
White wine, dry	8 oz (240 ml)	7. Sprinkle the fish with wine. 8. Bake at 350°F (176°C) until the internal product temperature is 165°F (74°C), about 35 minutes. Check with a product probe thermometer.
Lemon crowns Vegetable du jour	25 25 portions	9. Serve with lemon crown and vegetable garnish.

Special Equipment Needed: Metal-stemmed product probe thermometer.

An SRM Program Example: Whitefish and the Preparing, Cooking, and Holding Control Points

Sensory tests are used to evaluate inventory during preparation. Whitefish should have bright, shiny skin with no scales. It should smell sweet and fresh. Slippery or sticky fish is a sign of deterioration. The number of portions to be prepared will be indicated by the day's food production planning worksheet.

The standard recipe (see Exhibit 7.12) for baked whitefish Florentine has been revised. The revised recipe calls for two eggs instead of three and two ounces (57 g) of butter instead of six. (Refer to Chapter 5 for the original recipe.) This change lowers the fat and cholesterol content of the finished product. It also lowers the pH, since whole eggs have a pH of 7.5 to 8.2 (see Chapter 4). Lemon juice will be added to the spinach stuffing to replace some of the lost liquid and, because it has a pH of 2.2 to 2.4, will further lower the pH of the baked whitefish. The fish will also be baked in dry white wine, with a pH of 2.8 to 3.8. The net effect of these changes is a finished product with a lower pH than the dish produced from the original recipe. Although the baked fish probably does not have a pH below 4.8 (the pH that slows pathogenic growth), these changes at the preparing control point do reduce the risks.

The whitefish will be cooked to a minimum internal temperature of 165°F (74°C) in a conventional oven. Before, during, and after cooking, the whitefish will be carefully protected against cross-contamination and will be exposed to the TDZ for a minimum amount of time.

Staff members responsible for cooking have been properly trained. They know how to correctly use the equipment, utensils, forms (such as standard recipes), and inventory to cook an item that meets or exceeds guests' expectations. Staff members responsible for cooking maintain high standards of personal hygiene and cleanliness.

Equipment used to cook the whitefish includes sheet pans and an oven. The sheet pans are cleaned and sanitized between changed uses. The oven is cleaned and maintained at least monthly, in accordance with the manufacturer's recommendations. The product thermometer used to check the fish's internal temperature is cleaned and sanitized after each changed use. Spatulas and other kitchenware used to place the fish on the pans prior to cooking or remove the fish after cooking are similarly cleaned and sanitized after each changed use.

Facilities used to prepare and cook the whitefish have been carefully planned to reduce safety hazards and sanitation risks. The local regulatory agency reviewed and approved plans before building. Management is in compliance with all relevant local, state, and national codes. A systematic approach is used to regularly clean and maintain facilities.

Individual whitefish entrées will be cooked to order for the hotel dining room. The fish will be served minutes after cooking. For banquet service the whitefish will be held, with the vegetable du jour and garnish, on covered, heated plates in a hot-holding cabinet designed to maintain a product temperature of 165°F (74°C) or above. Food handlers will wear disposable plastic gloves. The fish will not be held hot for over 30 minutes. All leftover fish is thrown out. It is never re-served, refrigerated, or refrozen.

Staff members will check the product temperature every 15 minutes with a probe thermometer. If the temperature dips below 140°F (60°C), the fish will not be served until reheated to 165°F (74°C).

References

Avery, A. C. *A Modern Guide to Foodservice Equipment.* Boston, Mass.: CBI, 1980.

Beer, Ira B. "Kitchens That Work—Efficiency + Productivity = Profit." *Restaurant Business,* November 1, 1987, pp. 145–150, 152, 154, 160.

Bertagnoli, Lisa. "Lamps, Drawers and Tables Keep Food Hot." *Restaurants & Institutions,* March 4, 1987, pp. 168–169.

Caprione, C. "13 Tips for Planning an Efficient Kitchen." *NRA News,* April 1983, pp. 23–26.

Cichy, Ronald F. "Control Waste and Increase Sales." *Michigan Hospitality Magazine,* July/August 1982, p. 21.

———. "Kitchen Sanitation." *Hotel & Resort Industry,* February 1989, pp. 80–84, 86–87.

———. "Nutrient Retention in Foodservice Operations." *The Consultant,* January 1982, pp. 43–48.

———. "The Role of the Professional Chef in a Foodservice Firm." *The National Culinary Review,* January 1983, pp. 12–13.

———. "Sanitation Control Points." *Cooking for Profit,* November 15, 1984, p. 4.

———. "Sanitation Management and Your Kitchen: Cooking." *The National Culinary Review,* July 1987, pp. 18, 21–22. Also published in *Rocky Mountain Chefs Magazine,* February 1988, pp. 17, 19–20.

———. "Sanitation Management and Your Kitchen: Holding." *The National Culinary Review,* August 1987, pp. 13–14, 17. Also published in *Rocky Mountain Chefs Magazine,* March 1988, pp. 20–22.

———. "Sanitation Management and Your Kitchen: Preparing." *The National Culinary Review,* June 1987, pp. 17–18. Also published in *Rocky Mountain Chefs Magazine,* January 1988, pp. 10–11.

———. "Sanitation Tips." *Restaurant Business,* December 10, 1984, p. 2.

Cichy, R. F., and J. Kosec. "Taking Stock: How Soups Can Become the Most Profitable Part of Your Menu." *Cooking for Profit,* December 15, 1983, pp. 12–15.

Cichy, R. F., and R. P. Krump. "Cost Controls Part IV: Production." *Rocky Mountain Chefs Magazine,* June 1985, pp. 5, 9.

———. "Cost Controls Part V: Quality Control." *Rocky Mountain Chefs Magazine,* July 1985, pp. 9, 13, 21.

"Cleaning Scheduled by Equipment." *Institutions/Volume Feeding,* October 15, 1974, p. 137.

Correll, J. D., and H. D. Wells. *Applied Cooking Technology for the Food Service Operator.* Fenton, Md.: Black Body Corporation, 1979.

Durocher, Joseph. "The Cold Truth." *Restaurant Business,* November 20, 1987, pp. 188, 190.

———. "Griddles and Grills." *Restaurant Business,* January 20, 1988, pp. 156, 158.

———. "Ice Machines." *Restaurant Business,* September 1, 1987, pp. 204, 206, 208.

———. "Ice-Making Equipment." *Restaurant Business,* March 20, 1988, pp. 200, 202.

———. "Processing Food." *Restaurant Business,* July 1, 1989, pp. 132, 134.

———. "Refrigeration." *Restaurant Business,* June 10, 1989, pp. 206, 208.

———. "Storage and Warming Cabinets." *Restaurant Business,* February 10, 1988, pp. 236, 238.

"Easy Menu Expansion." *Restaurants & Institutions,* March 18, 1987, pp. 198–200.

Eaton, W. V. "What You Should Know About Hot Food Holding." *Food Service Marketing,* December 1979, p. 23.

Food and Drug Administration, Center for Food Safety and Applied Nutrition, Retail Food Protection Branch. *Interpretation: Food Preparation—Between-Use Storage of Food Preparation Utensils,* May 14, 1984.

———. *Interpretation: Food Preparation—Product Temperature Criteria for Microwave Cooking of Pork, Pork Products and Beef Roasts,* May 3, 1984.

———. *Interpretation: Food Preparation—Raw, Marinated or Partially Cooked Fishery Products,* August 21, 1987.

Graves, Nancy. "Combination Ovens." *Cooking for Profit,* October 15 to November 14, 1987, pp. 15–16.

Kooser, R. "Sanitation and Facility Design." *Restaurant Hospitality,* December 1981, p. 74.

Lancaster, D. L. *Product Temperature Management.* Ann Arbor, Mich: National Sanitation Foundation, n.d.

Main, Bill. "Kitchen Size and Prime Costs." *Restaurant Business,* July 20, 1988, pp. 88, 90.

McKennon, J. E. "How to Control Rising Food Costs Part IV: Recipes, Sales Records, and Portions." *Lodging,* September 1980, pp. 62–64.

Minor, Lewis J., and Ronald F. Cichy. *Foodservice Systems Management.* Westport, Conn.: AVI, 1984.

Patterson, Patt. "Counter Equipment Shifts Food Prep to a Front-of-the-House Operation." *Nation's Restaurant News,* July 10, 1989, p. 23.

———. "Portion Control Is the Bottom Line for Profit and Loss in Any Business." *Nation's Restaurant News,* June 12, 1989, p. 19.

———. "Temperature Flexibility Is the Key in Refrigeration Systems." *Nation's Restaurant News,* May 23, 1988, p. 12.

Sanitation Aspects of Food Service Facility Plan Preparation and Review-Reference Guide. Ann Arbor, Mich.: National Sanitation Foundation, 1978.

"Sanitation Checklists for Management." *Cooking for Profit,* June 1978, pp. 24–26.

"Sanitation Means More Than Looking Clean." *Institutions/Volume Feeding,* August 1, 1975, p. 33.

"Serving Hot Food Hot." *Institutions,* July 1, 1980, pp. 37–40.

Sherer, Michael. "Compact Two-in-One Takes Lead Role." *Restaurants & Institutions,* June 12, 1989, pp. 107–108.

Standard No. 2 for Food Service Equipment. Ann Arbor, Mich.: National Sanitation Foundation, 1976.

Swift, L. "Kitchen Cleaning Starts with Planning." *Cooking for Profit,* July-August 1980, p. 12.

Wolson, Shelley. "Importance of Planning." *Restaurant & Institutions,* October 29, 1986, p. 191.

———. "Utensils Whip Up Efficiency." *Restaurants & Institutions,* November 12, 1986, pp. 214–215.

REVIEW QUIZ

When you feel you have covered all of the material in this chapter, answer these questions. Choose the *best* answer. Check your answers with the correct ones found on the Review Quiz Answer Key at the end of this book.

1.   Which of the following are especially risky at the preparing control point?

   a.   foods that have gone through a number of temperature changes
   b.   foods that are prepared in small quantities
   c.   foods that have only one preparation step
   d.   foods that have been in dry storage for more than a week

2.   A master food production planning worksheet can be used to plan:

   a.   labor needs.
   b.   product use.
   c.   leftover storage needs.
   d.   all of the above.

3.   Openings to hollow spaces beneath fixed equipment and between the masonry base and equipment should be:

   a.   sealed to prevent the entrance of insects and rodents.
   b.   used for utility connections.
   c.   at least six inches in diameter to facilitate cleaning.
   d.   none of the above.

4.   In general, table-mounted equipment with legs should have a minimum clearance of _____ inches between the equipment and the table.

   a.   two
   b.   four
   c.   six
   d.   ten

5.   Why should food products *not* be reheated on a steam table?

   a.   A steam table is not designed to heat food to sufficient internal temperatures.
   b.   Reheating food on a steam table lowers the overall quality of the food.
   c.   Food reheated on a steam table cannot be held safely for as long as food reheated by other methods.
   d.   all of the above

6. Frying food with a pressure fryer decreases the:

    a. nutritional value of the food.
    b. number of preparation steps required.
    c. amount of vapors produced.
    d. amount of salt required in the frying oil.

7. What is the first step in cleaning a tilting braising pan?

    a. Rub the inside with a liquid frying compound or unsalted shortening.
    b. Scrape excess food off with a metal scraper.
    c. Fill the pan with a detergent-water solution and close the cover.
    d. Use a clean, non-abrasive brush to remove food particles.

8. How should an ice scoop be cleaned?

    a. by rinsing with hot water and towel drying
    b. by sanitizing, rinsing with hot water, and air drying
    c. by washing in a detergent-water solution, rinsing with a vinegar-water solution then with clean water, and air drying
    d. by washing in a hot water–detergent solution, rinsing with clean water, sanitizing, and air drying

9. Most leftovers should be chilled to 70°F (21°C) or less within _____ and 41°F (5°C) or less within _____.

    a. 30 minutes; 2 hours
    b. 1 hour; 2 hours
    c. 2 hours; 4 hours
    d. 2 hours; 6 hours

10. How should mobile hot-holding units be loaded?

    a. from the bottom up
    b. from the top down
    c. alternating sides, working toward the center
    d. any of the above, depending on the food being served

Chapter Outline

Learning Objectives

8

The Serving Control Point

When asked to rank the internal attributes which influence their selection of a restaurant, respondents in a survey of over 1,500 fast-food and full-service restaurant guests placed "service" second only to "good quality food."[1] Almost half of the respondents said that service was "most important" or "very important" when selecting a restaurant. A majority of respondents also said that if they had a negative service experience at one restaurant in a chain, it would affect their decision to visit another restaurant within the same chain. As these results indicate, service is an essential component of the guest's overall hospitality experience. Service that meets or exceeds guest expectations generates repeat business and increases revenues.

Like the other control points, serving requires sanitation, quality, and cost controls. Quality is especially important at this control point—both in the products served and the service itself. Many factors affect the quality of service in a food service operation. They include the communication and cooperation between kitchen and dining room staff members, the flow of products, the menu, the design and layout of the kitchen and dining room, and the style of service. Service standards vary greatly among operations. However, no matter what type of service an operation offers, management is responsible for standardizing ordering procedures and abbreviations, serving procedures, sanitation practices, staff requirements, and risk reduction. Sanitation risk management (SRM) is an essential component of the service strategy. Guests expect safe food and sanitary serving techniques.

Food service assumes many forms today, and each type of service requires slightly different standards. For example, outdoor food service is limited by unique sanitation considerations. Catering service calls for specialized transportation equipment that can protect food safety. This chapter presents standards for traditional table service and its variations, followed by a brief discussion of other types of service.

Traditional Table Service

There are several variations of traditional table service. Most operations, with the exception of fast-food restaurants, offer one or more of these types of service. **Plate service** is a basic service style in which fully cooked menu items are individually portioned, plated (put on plates) in the kitchen, and carried to each guest directly. **Cart service** is used for menu items prepared by the server beside the guest's table in the dining room; menu items are cooked, and sometimes flambéed, in front of the guest. **Family-style service** requires food to be placed on large platters or in large bowls, which are taken to the tables by servers. Guests pass the food around their table and serve themselves. Self-service salad, soup, and dessert bars are popular variations of family-style service. In **platter service,** servers bring platters of fully cooked food to the dining room, present them to the guest for approval, and then serve the food.

Each service style has slightly different sanitation considerations. In plate service, foods are heated to proper serving temperatures in the kitchen and delivered to the guest quickly to maintain their proper temperature and quality. Cart service eliminates the transportation of cooked menu items from the kitchen to the dining room, but it requires servers to be certain that products cooked at tableside reach adequate internal temperatures. In addition, the ventilation system should be capable of removing heat, odors, and smoke from the dining room. For example, Japanese-style food establishments feature cooking performed at guest tables equipped with drop-in stainless steel or nickel-plated top griddles. Local health officials may require a ventilation hood above the griddle to remove cooling vapors and products of combustion. In addition, makeup air capacity needs to be carefully considered. It is always a good idea to check with local or state health officials before installing this equipment. Servers should be especially careful when preparing and presenting flambéed items.

Platter service, like plate service, aids sanitation because food products cooked in the kitchen are likelier to reach adequate internal temperatures. However, as with plate service, product temperatures are difficult to maintain as the items are carried from the kitchen to the dining room. The temperature of hot food items continues to drop as the server presents the platter for approval and transfers the food from the platter to the plates. Whether food is plated in the kitchen or the dining room, serving techniques must be sanitary.

Family-style service is appropriate for banquets because it facilitates the delivery of menu items to large groups of people. However, product temperatures are often difficult to maintain as food is passed around the table. Food may also be contaminated if a guest coughs or sneezes while passing a bowl or platter of food. Leftover portions of food may not be served again, except that packaged non-potentially hazardous food that is still packaged and is still in sound condition may be re-served. The size of the serving container and the amount of food placed at each table should be carefully considered to reduce waste. After use at a table, the serving containers and utensils must be washed, rinsed, and sanitized before the containers are refilled.

Self-service food bars also present sanitation problems. Many food service operators are discovering that salad bars can present high risks. Some fast-food chains have opted for pre-packaged salads to avoid these risks. Salad bars, if not properly maintained, can be perceived as messy and unsanitary. Some outbreaks of foodborne illness have been traced to salad bars.

However, certain procedures can help control the salad bar and reduce risks. The condition and temperature of the food and the salad bar should be checked every 10 to 15 minutes. Spills should be wiped up and utensils replaced when necessary. To ensure freshness and quality, foods should be placed in relatively small containers, replaced frequently, displayed on crushed ice or in cold inserts, and be protected by properly designed sneeze guards (food shields). These safety devices should extend the length and width of the bar and be positioned 10 to 12 inches (25.4 to 30.5 cm) above the food. Display stands for unwrapped food must be effectively shielded to intercept the direct line between the average guest's mouth and the food being displayed.

Soup and dessert bars call for similar procedures. Equipment should be able to maintain product temperatures. Covers, but not food shields, are required for self-service soup containers. The covers do not have to be hinged or self-closing. It is a good idea to display small amounts and replace them frequently. Constant supervision of all types of food bars is crucial to risk reduction and should be part of every server's responsibilities.

Serving and Inventory

Inventory items prepared by the production department are delivered to guests during service. The FDA's Food Code specifies requirements for safe food display and service. These regulations apply not only to food served from the kitchen but also to items set up for guest self-service at soup and salad bars, buffet tables, sandwich bars, and dessert bars. These guidelines can help the operation control its investment in inventory and reduce its risks at the serving control point.

Potentially hazardous foods must be kept out of the TDZ at the serving control point. Hot food should be served on heated plates, and cold food should be served on chilled plates. This practice helps to keep product temperatures outside the TDZ and enhances product quality.

Foods on display must be protected from contamination through the use of packaging; counter, service line, or salad bar food guards; display cases; or other effective means. Molluscan shellfish life-support system display tanks may be used to store and display shellfish offered for human consumption if there is an approved HACCP plan and additional controls.

When second portions and refills are offered, clean tableware, including single-service articles, must be used. Utensils or effective dispensing methods that protect food from contamination are required in self-service. Self-service buffets and salad bars shall be monitored by a staff member trained in safe operating procedures. This is an excellent procedure in all control points.

Once served, potentially hazardous foods must be discarded and not re-served. Food dispensing utensils must be available for each container displayed at a consumer self-service buffet or salad bar.

Milk and milk products served as beverages should be served in unopened, commercially filled packages of one pint (.47 liter) or less or drawn from a commercial milk dispenser into a cleaned and sanitized glass. Dairy or non-dairy coffee creamers should be individually packaged, drawn from a refrigerated dispenser, or poured from a covered pitcher. If stored at the sidestand, milk or cream must be refrigerated. Individually portioned coffee creamer that has been ultra-high-temperature pasteurized, aseptically filled, and hermetically sealed is the only liquid dairy or non-dairy coffee cream exempted from refrigeration requirements. It is exempt because it has a shelf life of 120 days at room temperature.

Dressings, seasonings, and condiments (flavor enhancers such as chutney, mustard, and relish) on tables or self-service stands must be presented in covered containers, dispensers, or single-serving packages. Catsup and other sauces may be served in their original containers or in pour-type dispensers. Generally, the refilling of original containers is prohibited. Sugar on tables should be in either individual packets or pour-type dispensers.

Ice for guest consumption should be handled with ice-dispensing utensils (scoops or tongs) or dispensed by an automatic ice machine. Guests should serve themselves only from automatic dispensers. Ice-dispensing utensils should be stored in a sanitary manner between uses.

Dispensing utensils or gloves should be used for all food serving. In-use dispensing utensils can be stored in the food with the handles extended, or under running water, or clean and dry. Production staff or servers should never dispense food with their hands unless wearing single-use gloves; likewise, guests should use utensils and not their hands for serving themselves.

Leftover food returned to the kitchen must not be re-served. For example, crocks of cheese and ramekins of butter should be served only once. The exception to this rule is packaged, non-potentially hazardous food in sound condition. Self-service guests should not re-use tableware when they return to the service area for additional food; however, they may re-use beverage glasses and cups. Unpackaged food on display should be protected from guest contamination by easily cleanable sneeze guards.

The FDA states:

3-306.11   Food Display.

Except for nuts in the shell and whole, raw fruits and vegetables that are intended for hulling, peeling, or washing by the consumer before consumption, food on display shall be protected from contamination by the use of packaging; counter, service line, or salad bar food guards; display cases; or other effective means.

4-204.110   Molluscan Shellfish Tanks.

(A) Except as specified under ¶ (B) of this section, molluscan shellfish life support system display tanks may only be used to display shellfish that are not offered for human consumption and shall be conspicuously marked so that it is obvious to the consumer that the shellfish are for display only.

(B) Molluscan shellfish life-support system display tanks that are used to store and display shellfish that are offered for human consumption shall be operated and maintained in accordance with a variance granted by the regulatory authority as specified in § 8-103.10 and a HACCP plan that:

(1)   Is submitted by the permit holder and approved by the regulatory authority as specified under § 8-103.11; and

(2)   Assures that:

(a)   Water used with fish other than molluscan shellfish does not flow into the molluscan tank,

(b)   The safety and quality of the shellfish as they were received are not compromised by use of the tank, and

(c)   The identity of the source of the shellstock is retained as specified under § 3-203.12.

3-304.15   Consumer Self-Service, Using Clean Tableware When Obtaining Second Portions and Refills.

(A) Except as specified in ¶ (B) of this section, self-service consumers may not be allowed to use soiled tableware, including single-service articles, to obtain additional food from the display and serving equipment.

(B) *Cups and glasses may be reused by self-service consumers if refilling is a contamination-free process as specified under ¶¶ 4-204.13(A), (B), and (D).*

3-306.13   Consumer Self-Service Operations.*

(A) Exposed, raw animal food, such as beef, lamb, pork, poultry, and fish may not be offered for consumer self-service. *This paragraph does not apply to consumer self-service of exposed ready-to-eat foods at buffets or salad bars that serve foods such as sushi or raw shellfish, or to ready-to-cook individual portions for immediate cooking and consumption on the premises such as consumer-cooked meats or consumer-selected ingredients for Mongolian barbecue.*

(B) Consumer self-service operations for ready-to-eat foods shall be provided with suitable utensils or effective dispensing methods that protect the food from contamination. [N]

(C) Consumer self-service operations such as buffets and salad bars shall be monitored by food employees trained in safe operating procedures. [N]

3-306.14   Reservice.*

(A) Except as specified in ¶ (B) of this section, after being served to a consumer, food that is unused by the consumer shall be discarded.

(B) *Food that is not potentially hazardous, such as crackers and condiments, is in an unopened original package, and is maintained in sound condition may be served again if it is served in a food establishment that does not serve a highly susceptible population.*

4-302.11   Utensils, Consumer Self-Service.

A food dispensing utensil shall be available for each container displayed at a consumer self-service unit such as a buffet or salad bar.

Source: FDA 1993 *Food Code.*

Servers should be trained to recognize acceptable quality because they perform the final quality control check of menu items before the items are served. Food quality can be judged by appearance, texture and consistency, temperature, and flavor.

Appearance is an important aspect of product quality. Guests evaluate food appearance based on color, spacing, neatness, and garnish. The appearance of foods should always match the pictures of the items on the menu.

Color is an important quality consideration. For example, bright yellow, artificial-looking chicken gravy is unappealing to most guests. Golden-brown bakery products, on the other hand, appeal to the eye. Casseroles are attractive when they are evenly browned. Fruits, vegetables, seafood, meats, and poultry products should have natural colors.

The size and shape of foods also contribute to their appearance. Broken, misshapen, or ragged vegetables can destroy the appearance of an entire plate of food. Food items should not be crowded on the plate or hanging over the edge. The neatness of the food presentation also makes a statement about the establishment's standards. Liquid foods should not spill or run over the edges of tableware. If two foods with sauces are to be served at the same time, one should be served in a side dish. Similarly, if a menu item is served with a thin sauce, it should be served in a side dish.

Garnishes are artistic touches that complete the image a plate of food presents. Some garnishes (such as parsley, spiced apple rings, and orange wedges) are so commonly used that guests ignore them. Some upscale establishments use a variety of in-season fresh fruit garnishes that are relatively inexpensive to buy and prepare. Melon wedges, strawberries, kiwi fruit, and mango slices are interesting garnish alternatives. Other operations use edible flowers (such as pansies) as garnishes.

The texture and consistency of food products are also important components of quality. Dried-out bakery products, broken breadsticks and crackers, wilted salads, lumpy gravies and puddings, and runny custards are examples of poor food quality. Some operations display photographs of standard food presentations in the pickup area of the kitchen so servers and production staff can easily compare them with finished items before service.

Product temperature contributes to the overall quality of food products. Internal product temperatures should be checked with a probe thermometer. As previously noted, hot foods should be served on heated tableware and cold foods should be served on chilled tableware. When assembling orders, the server should gather room temperature products first, then chilled foods, and finally hot foods.

Food flavor—a combination of taste and odor—is probably the most important quality indicator. Servers should sample menu items regularly at staff meetings so they will be able to describe menu items from experience and answer guest questions accurately.

Serving and People

The term "server" may be used to refer to any person directly involved in the service of food or beverages. The image and size of the establishment generally determine whether other positions are included in the serving function. A host may greet and seat guests and supervise dining room staff. In some large or formal dining rooms, a maître d'hôtel may supervise service and be assisted by a captain. Buspersons assist servers by clearing and setting up tables. A cashier is frequently assigned the responsibility of handling all guest payments. In some establishments, certain positions are combined. For example, one staff member serves as cashier and host. Servers sometimes clear and set up tables.

Servers, like all food service staff members, must practice good personal hygiene and cleanliness. (See Chapter 3 for a complete discussion of staff hygiene.) Standards of personal hygiene should be adapted to the individual operation and presented to all staff members during orientation and training.

Proper handwashing is extremely important. Servers should wash their hands before starting work and frequently throughout the shift. It is also important that they wash their hands immediately after any of the following activities: touching hair or skin, sneezing, coughing, using a handkerchief, smoking, visiting the restroom, handling raw food products, or handling soiled containers or tableware. (See Chapter 3 for a review of proper handwashing techniques.)

In addition to proper handwashing, the following standards apply to all servers:

- Do not smoke, chew gum, or eat in the dining room or kitchen.

- Never serve food that has left the plate or fallen to the floor.

- Replace dropped tableware with clean items.

- Avoid touching food with your hands. Use recommended utensils, and store the utensils in a sanitary manner when not in use.

- Do not touch parts of tableware which come into contact with food or with the guest's mouth.

- Never carry a service towel or napkin over your shoulder or under your arm.

- Be certain the bottom of tableware is clean before placing it on the table. Remove all soiled tableware and return it to the dirty dish station to prevent its re-use.

- Keep the tops, bottoms, and sides of serving trays clean to prevent unnecessary soiling of uniforms, tableware, and tablecloths.

- Maintain a clean and professional appearance.

- Work carefully, keeping standards of cleanliness in mind.

Guests expect their dining experiences to be both safe and pleasant. If servers violate the standards of personal hygiene or cleanliness with unsanitary practices, disease agents may be transmitted to guests. In addition, physical foodborne contaminants, such as hair or glass fragments, can result in an unpleasant dining experience or a guest injury.

When placing orders in the kitchen, the server's timing is critical to the rapid flow of products to the dining room. Properly timed orders are plated and served almost simultaneously, thus maintaining product temperatures and reducing sanitation risks. In some operations, an **expediter** acts as a communication link between the kitchen staff and servers. Servers give their orders to the expediter, who calls the orders to the appropriate kitchen stations. The expediter must know cooking times, coordinate them to sequentially deliver cooked foods for pickup, and provide leadership during hectic rush periods. He or she should be a member of the management team.

Once orders are prepared, they must be served promptly. Cooked food held hot under infrared units or heat lamps may lose some of its quality. In order to deliver cooked menu items to guests as soon as the food is ready, some operations follow a procedure known as the **flying food show.** Under this procedure, the first server to arrive at the pickup point delivers whichever menu items are ready for service. This procedure can only be implemented if order tickets show which table and guest is to receive each order.

In some operations, servers are responsible for some production and portioning. Servers might be responsible for portioning beverages, soups, or desserts, adding dressings to salads, garnishing plates, and obtaining food accompaniments such as sauces. In all cases, servers must follow the establishment's sanitation and portioning standards. Servers should also load serving trays carefully to reduce the likelihood of accidents.

Once food is served, servers should return frequently to the table to remove dirty dishes, refill water glasses, and empty ashtrays. After guests leave, the table should be cleared and reset with clean items. Whoever performs this duty—a server or a busperson—should wash his or her hands after handling soiled tableware and before resetting the table with clean items. After the table is reset, the server should make sure that the chairs are clean and properly arranged for the next guest.

Servers need not wash their hands every time they handle money. Although money is often thought of as "dirty," the FDA has determined that currency does not support enough microorganisms to be a source of contamination. However, guests generally do not like to see servers handle money and then serve food.

Serving and Equipment

Servers work with a variety of equipment. Serving equipment must be cleaned, sanitized, stored, and handled in a manner that prevents subsequent contamination.

Dishes, cups, glasses, and flatware should only be handled in places that will not come into contact with food or with the guest's mouth. Dishes should be held with four fingers on the bottom and the thumb on the edge, not touching the food. Cups and flatware should be touched only on the handles. Glasses should be grasped at the base and placed on the table without touching the rim. Ice placed in glasses and bread and rolls placed in bread baskets should only be handled with scoops or tongs designed for these purposes.

Pre-set tableware must be wrapped, covered, or inverted. Pre-setting should not be a substitute for proper utensil storage. Extra settings of tableware should be removed from the table when guests are seated. This not only helps protect the sanitary quality of tableware, but also prevents needless washing, rinsing, and sanitizing of clean tableware. Sneeze guards and proper serving utensils are required on self-service food bars in the dining room.

In some operations, a busperson clears soiled tableware and resets tables. In other operations, servers perform these duties. In both cases, care must be taken when clean and sanitized tableware is handled after touching soiled tableware. After handling soiled tableware or wiping cloths, staff members should wash their hands before touching cleaned and sanitized tableware. This minimizes the potential for cross-contamination.

The FDA states:

"Tableware" means eating, drinking, and serving utensils for table use such as flatware including forks, knives, and spoons; hollowware including bowls, cups, serving dishes, tumblers; and plates.

4-904.11   Kitchenware and Tableware.

(A) Single-service and single-use articles and cleaned and sanitized utensils shall be handled, displayed, and dispensed so that contamination of food- and lip-contact surfaces is prevented.

(B) Knives, forks, and spoons that are not prewrapped shall be presented so that only the handles are touched by employees and by consumers if consumer self-service is provided.

(C) Except as specified under ¶ (B) of this section, single-service articles that are intended for food- or lip-contact shall be furnished for consumer self-service with the original individual wrapper intact or from an approved dispenser.

4-904.12   Soiled and Clean Tableware.

Soiled tableware shall be removed from consumer eating and drinking areas and handled so that clean tableware is not contaminated.

4-904.13   Preset Tableware.

Tableware may be preset if:

(A) It is protected from contamination by being wrapped, covered, or inverted;

(B)   It is exposed and unused settings are removed when a consumer is seated; or

(C)   It is exposed and unused settings are not removed when a consumer is seated, and are cleaned and sanitized before further use.

Source: FDA 1993 *Food Code.*

Two or more servers often share a **sidestand,** which holds supplies of tableware, ice, condiments, dairy products, and some beverages for easy access. Two sanitation considerations are important at the sidestand. First, all equipment and food products must be stored to minimize contamination. No soiled napkins, tableware, or equipment should be placed on the sidestand. These items can contaminate clean food and utensils. Second, the temperatures of food products stored on the sidestand must be kept out of the TDZ. This is particularly important for dairy products (such as butter and coffee cream) and any other potentially hazardous foods. These items must be refrigerated. It is helpful to stock the sidestand with enough cups, saucers, bread and butter plates, serving trays, tray stands, and other necessary items to last through a whole shift. Supplies should be stocked in a neat, orderly, and convenient way before customers arrive. A busperson may help keep the station neat, clean, and stocked.

Tables and chairs should be dusted or wiped to remove food debris before the establishment opens each day. Servers should inspect them frequently throughout their shifts for cleanliness and proper setup. Floors should be checked for spilled food. If the dining room has windows, the ledges should be dusted at least once each day.

Equipment placed on tables must be kept clean. This is often a part of the server's side work. Sugar dispensers and salt and pepper shakers should be wiped clean at least once a day. If glass dispensers or shakers are used, they should be periodically emptied, washed, rinsed, dried, and refilled. The volume of business affects the amount of sugar, salt, and pepper used at each table and, therefore, the frequency of refilling. Some operations now use disposable dispensers and shakers to reduce the labor costs associated with maintaining these items.

If syrup or condiments such as catsup, mustard, and steak sauce are placed on tables, the exterior of the containers should be cleaned regularly. They can be wiped with a damp cloth to remove fingerprints and drips. Original condiment containers designed for dispensing (like catsup bottles) should not be washed and refilled. Wide-mouth condiment or syrup bottles can easily become contaminated and should not be used in the dining room. Individual packages or portions may be the most sanitary.

The FDA states:

3-306.12   Condiments, Protection.

(A) Condiments shall be protected from contamination by being kept in dispensers that are designed to provide protection, protected food displays provided with the proper utensils, original containers designed for dispensing, or individual packages or portions.

(B)   Condiments at a vending machine location shall be in individual packages or provided in dispensers that are filled at a location that is approved by the regulatory authority, such as the food establishment that provides food to the vending machine location, a food processing plant that is regulated by the agency that has jurisdiction over the operation, or a properly equipped facility that is located on the site of the vending machine location.

Source: FDA 1993 *Food Code.*

Napkins are usually folded before service. They should be stored so as to prevent soiling. Paper napkins should be discarded from tables after service, even if they look clean. Cloth napkins must be properly laundered after each use and should never be used to wipe flatware, glasses, cups, or ashtrays. Ashtrays should be clean and stocked with matches. Servers should check their trays before beginning work. The bottom, top, and sides of a tray should be free from grease, food, and other debris.

One item frequently neglected during side work is flatware. Soiled, spotted eating utensils are both unsightly and unsanitary. Soiled flatware may require soaking before it is washed in the dish machine. After washing, it should be checked to ensure that soil and spots have been removed.

Plate and platter covers allow servers to carry more orders on each tray. They also help maintain a menu item's serving temperature if the item is placed on a heated or chilled plate in the kitchen. Covers also help guard against contamination during transportation from the kitchen to the guest. Plate and platter covers must be regularly cleaned and sanitized and stored in such a manner as to prevent contamination before their next use.

Take-out service requires additional equipment to hold packaged foods hot or cold. Some holding units have clear covers or doors to display the selection of hot and cold menu items to guests. Equipment selection is based on the menu items offered for take-out. Holding equipment should be able to maintain the proper temperatures and relative humidities. It should be cleaned and sanitized regularly.

Care should be exercised in handling all equipment used for serving. Waste and breakage can harm the establishment's competitive position. Each time a server carelessly soils linen, wastes supplies, or throws away or breaks tableware, the operation's costs increase. If fragments of glass find their way into guests' food or beverage products, the operation's revenues decrease. The net effect of such carelessness is generally poor bottom-line results.

Serving and Facilities

The cleaning, repair, and maintenance of the operation's facilities are essential at all control points. These activities are particularly important at the serving control point because the dining room environment directly affects guest satisfaction. A clean and pleasant dining room enhances the operation's image and makes a positive first impression on guests.

The dining room supervisor should inspect the facilities with all the lights turned on before service begins. This daily inspection is part of the overall preparation for service. The supervisor should check floors, walls, and ceilings to see if maintenance or repairs are necessary. In addition, tables, chairs, and booths should be inspected for cleanliness. Menus should be inspected to ensure that daily specials are attached. Dirty or damaged menus should be removed from circulation. The inspection should include food displays and sidestands. Equipment should be functioning properly to maintain product temperatures.

After the inspection, the dining room supervisor should adjust the lighting levels to create the proper ambiance. The ventilation system should be designed so that the dining room does not become stuffy or smoky while guests are dining.

While wood is sometimes used to create a cozy dining atmosphere, untreated wood is subject to decay caused by bacteria and fungi. This process is accelerated by alternating periods of moisture and dryness. Wood for holding and displaying fresh fruits, fresh vegetables, and nuts in the shell may be treated with a preservative approved for such use.

One additional consideration is important for the serving facilities: animals. Although there are some exceptions, specifically with support animals, animals are not generally allowed in food establishments.

The FDA states:

"Support animal" means a trained animal such as a Seeing Eye dog that accompanies a person with a disability to assist in managing the disability and enables the person to perform functions that the person would otherwise be unable to perform.

2-403.11   Handling Prohibition.*

(A) Except as specified in ¶ (B) of this section, food employees may not care for or handle animals that may be present such as patrol dogs, support animals, or pets that are allowed under Subparagraphs 6-501.115(B)(2)–(4).

(B) *Food employees with support animals may care for their support animals if they wash their hands as specified under § 2-301.13 before working with exposed food; clean equipment, utensils, and linens; or unwrapped single-service and single-use articles.*

6-501.115   Prohibiting Animals.*

(A) Except as specified in ¶¶ (B) and (C) of this section, live animals may not be allowed on the premises of a food establishment.

(B) *Live animals may be allowed in the following situations if the contamination of food; clean equipment, utensils, and linens; and unwrapped single-service and single-use articles can not result:*

(1)   *Edible fish or decorative fish in aquariums, shellfish or crustacea on ice or under refrigeration, and shellfish and crustacea in display tank systems;*

(2)   *Patrol dogs accompanying police or security officers in offices and dining, sales, and storage areas, and sentry dogs running loose in outside fenced areas;*

(3)   *In areas such as dining and sales areas, support animals such as guide dogs that are trained to assist an employee or other person who is handicapped, are controlled by the handicapped employee or person, and are not allowed to be on seats or tables; and*

> *(4)   Pets in the common dining areas of group residences at times other than during meals if:*
>
> > *(a)   Effective partitioning and self-closing doors separate the common dining areas from food storage or food preparation areas,*
> >
> > *(b)   Condiments, equipment, and utensils are stored in enclosed cabinets or removed from the common dining areas when pets are present, and*
> >
> > *(c)   Dining areas including tables, countertops, and similar surfaces are effectively cleaned before the next meal service.*
>
> (C) Live or dead fish bait shall be stored so that contamination of food; clean equipment, utensils, and linens; and unwrapped single-service and single-use articles can not result.

Source: FDA 1993 *Food Code.*

Other Types of Food Service

Temporary Food Service

Temporary food establishments are granted a license to serve food for a limited period of time, often at fairs, sporting events, and concerts. Some food service and lodging establishments also set up temporary service facilities for special outdoor events such as luaus, barbecues, and weddings.

> The FDA states:
>
> **"Temporary food establishment"** means a food establishment that operates for a period of no more than 14 consecutive days in conjunction with a single event or celebration.

Source: FDA 1993 *Food Code.*

The FDA's Food Code clearly spells out the sanitation requirements for temporary food establishments. Always check state and local codes. Temporary food service requirements in your area may be more restrictive. Potentially hazardous foods may be served from such units provided that the food requires a limited amount of preparation and cooking (as, for example, frankfurters and hamburgers). Other potentially hazardous foods are strictly prohibited. Some potentially hazardous foods, such as ice cream and potato salad, may be served in individual portions if they are prepared under sanitary conditions and are not stored in the TDZ before sale.

All the general food handling requirements previously discussed apply to temporary units. Ice should be dispensed by staff members using proper utensils. Equipment in a temporary unit should be installed so that it is easy to clean. If there are no facilities for cleaning and sanitizing tableware, the operation should provide only single-service tableware. Potable water in adequate quantities is necessary for food preparation, equipment and utensil cleaning, and handwashing. Food should not be stored in contact with water or undrained ice. Waste and sewage must be disposed of according to applicable laws. Handwashing facilities are required in a temporary food service unit.

Floors should be constructed of materials that are easy to clean. Ceilings may be constructed of canvas, wood, or other material that adequately protects food preparation areas. Walls, ceilings, and doors should prevent the entry of insects. Counter service areas should have tight-fitting solid or screened windows or doors which are kept closed when not in use. Check with your local health authorities for additional regulations.

Banquet and Buffet Service

Many food service and lodging operations provide some form of banquet service. The nature of the banquet function may vary from a simple coffee break with fresh fruits and specialty pastries to a formal dinner with multiple courses. In any case, menu items should be chosen with ease and speed of service in mind since all guests should be served at about the same time.

Banquet service can be highly profitable if planned carefully. From a control standpoint, banquet service has two advantages: both the menu and the number of people to be served are established well in advance of service. This information facilitates planning and allocation of the operation's resources. Many operations use a part-time staff to supplement their regular production and service staff during banquet service.

On the other hand, an inadequately planned banquet can be a disaster. The pressures inherent in the food service business are greater when large numbers of people must be served in a relatively short period of time. Under these circumstances, mistakes can happen easily. The problems are compounded when proper time-temperature controls are not in place.

Because banquets are served so quickly, station setup is important. Equipment requirements vary with the type of banquet and the menu. General service standards apply, although they may be simplified to facilitate serving large numbers of people.

In banquet service, time-temperature control is critical. It is virtually impossible to prepare dozens, hundreds, or thousands of individual plates as service progresses. Therefore, foods are usually pre-plated for large banquets and held hot or cold in holding cabinets. Refrigerated mobile storage units must maintain internal product temperatures of $41°F$ ($5°C$) or less. Mobile hot storage cabinets must maintain a minimum internal product temperature of $140°F$ ($60°C$). Recall that the temperature danger zone may be defined differently in your area. Check with local and state health authorities.

Buffet service is popular in many food service and lodging establishments. Some use buffet service in combination with banquet service, serving, for example, appetizers buffet-style during the cocktail hour, and the rest of the meal banquet-style. Other special functions use buffet service exclusively. By attractively arranging a seemingly endless array of food products, establishments using this service exceed the expectations of guests, who enjoy being able to choose whatever they like in unlimited quantities. Buffet service also provides the opportunity to create food displays and showpieces.

Some buffets feature a carver who slices meats or poultry at the buffet table in the dining room. Servers sometimes portion some or all of the food products and assist guests. At most buffets, servers deliver beverages, bread and butter, and desserts directly to guest tables. Other buffets are completely self-serve.

Time-temperature control in buffet service is very important. Whenever large quantities of food are displayed, special equipment is necessary to keep product temperatures outside the TDZ. For cold products, ice is usually an acceptable means of maintaining chilled temperatures. However, food products must not be directly exposed to ice or melted water; food must be held in bowls and containers. Small containers that are refilled frequently not only enhance the attractiveness of the buffet table, but also help to maintain proper temperatures.

Hot buffet food can be held at or above 140°F (60°C) in a number of ways. Chafing dishes powered by electricity or canned heat are usually used to hold hot foods on a buffet table. Large roasts, hams, and turkeys to be carved in the dining room should be displayed under infrared heat lamps. Care should be taken to control time-temperature combinations, particularly when buffets are set up outdoors.

Adequate space for display tables and guest tables is an important facilities consideration for buffets and banquets. Crowded, hot, smoke-filled rooms make for an unpleasant dining experience. Adequate space also allows for more efficient movement of inventory and people.

Outdoor service presents unique concerns. The most important consideration is that food be protected from dust and contamination. The operation may need to use special coverings for food and beverage products to protect them between production and service. Outdoor food preparation may involve other special regulations enforced by local health department officials. It is a good idea to check with state or local authorities for laws governing outdoor cooking and dining areas before planning such functions.

Off-Premises Catering

In an effort to use resources more efficiently and to generate increased revenue, many food service and lodging businesses offer catering services off the premises. Some fast-food operations have also added catering services to strengthen their bottom lines. Some companies contract their catering services to specific locations such as airports.

Special holding equipment and transportation vehicles are necessary for off-premises catering. This equipment is designed to consistently maintain specified product temperatures. Because improper transportation of food products heightens the sanitation risks, special attention must be given to this aspect of off-premises catering in order to protect the health of guests. Operations that cater off-premises should consider transportation as an additional control point.

General serving standards apply to catering service. Time-temperature combinations, personal hygiene and cleanliness, and clean, sanitized, properly maintained equipment and facilities are important.

Room Service

Room service varies greatly from one lodging property to the next, but there are some basic procedures. Most room service orders are called in to the room service operator, who relays the order to the kitchen and the room server. Operators should be well informed about menu item ingredients and production techniques. While the order is being produced, the server covers a rolling table or service tray with a clean cloth or napkin. The server then assembles all tableware, cold beverages, condiments, and spices, followed by other cold food items. When these items have been placed on the table or tray, the server adds coffee or other hot beverages. When cooking is completed, the hot food is plated and covered, placed on the tray, table, or in a food warmer, and delivered to the guest.

Hot foods should be left in warmers for the guest's self-service unless he or she indicates otherwise. Before leaving, the server should ask the guest when the tray or table should be removed. Dirty dishes should be collected from rooms and hallways as soon as possible.

Transportation is a critical control point in room service, and is important to product quality and safety. Hot food should be hot; cold food should be cold. Both should be tasty and delivered promptly. Time and temperature are the most important elements, because as product holding times increase so does the likelihood of contamination. Some properties offer **split service**—that is, servers deliver courses separately. Split service helps maintain food quality and safety; each course can be portioned and served when it is ready, eliminating short-term holding in the kitchen.

For most room service operations, breakfast is the easiest meal to sell and the most difficult to deliver properly. Many breakfast combinations featuring eggs simply do not maintain product temperatures during transportation. It is also difficult to deliver toast to guestrooms at proper temperatures. A limited menu consisting of products that will survive the trip from the kitchen to the guestroom may be a good alternative. Specialty pastries, for example, may be offered instead of toast on room service menus. Scrambled eggs may be preferable to eggs Benedict because hollandaise sauce is highly perishable.

Room service is undergoing dramatic changes at some hotel properties. Because it is a costly amenity in a time when labor is short and maintenance and overhead costs are high, some hotels are opting for lower-cost alternatives. Many properties in the economy and all-suite segments have added food to guestroom mini-bars, placed microwave ovens in guestroom kitchens, added pizza delivery service, and entered joint agreements with nearby fast-food restaurants to avoid in-house food service. Regardless of which room service option a property chooses, it should be controlled by the SRM program.

Mobile Food Service

Mobile food units are those that do not necessarily operate in a fixed location. Examples of mobile units are pushcarts, catering trucks designed to sell food at a number of locations, and ice cream and snack food trucks. Generally, the serving standards already discussed apply to mobile food service units. Some local health departments do not allow the sale of potentially hazardous foods from mobile units. It is a good idea to check with state or local regulatory authorities when applying for a permit or license.

Mobile units should have a source of potable water. The water system has to be under pressure and of sufficient capacity to furnish enough cold and hot water for handwashing, equipment and utensil cleaning, and food preparation. Any liquid waste resulting from the operation of the mobile unit must be stored in a tank that is at least 15% larger in capacity than the water supply tank. Connections to the water supply tank must be of a different size or type than the connections to the waste tank.

Mobile units must operate from a **commissary** and report daily for cleaning, servicing, and restocking. The commissary must operate according to all requirements for food service operations. The commissary must have a servicing area for the mobile units. Servicing includes the emptying of liquid waste in a safe and sanitary manner. Overhead protection is required in the various areas where mobile units are supplied, cleaned, and serviced.

If a mobile food unit sells only prepared food packaged in individual servings, requirements for water and sewage systems do not apply. Cleaning and sanitizing equipment is not necessary in a mobile unit if the necessary equipment is provided and used at the unit's commissary. Frankfurters may be prepared in mobile units. Only single-service articles may be provided to the unit's guests.

The FDA states:

5-301.11   Approved.

Materials that are used in the construction of a mobile water tank, mobile food establishment water tank, and appurtenances shall meet the requirements specified under ¶¶ 4-101.11(A), (B), and (D).

5-302.11   Enclosed System, Inspection Port.

A mobile water tank shall be:

(A)   Enclosed from the filling inlet to the discharge outlet; and

(B)   Sloped to an outlet that allows complete drainage of the tank.

5-302.12   Inspection and Cleaning Port, Protected and Secured.

If a water tank is designed with an access port for inspection and cleaning, the opening shall be in the top of the tank and:

(A)   Flanged upward at least 13 mm (one-half inch); and

(B)   Equipped with a port cover assembly that is:

(1)   Provided with a gasket and a device for securing the cover in place, and

(2)   Flanged to overlap the opening and sloped to drain.

5-302.13   "V" Type Threads, Use Limitation.

A fitting with "v" type threads on a water tank inlet or outlet may be allowed only when a hose is permanently attached.

5-302.14   Tank Vent, Protected.

If provided, a water tank vent shall terminate in a downward direction and shall be covered with:

(A)   16 mesh to 25.4 mm (16 mesh to 1 inch) screen or equivalent when the vent is in a protected area; or

(B)   A protective filter when the vent is in an area that is not protected from windblown dirt and debris.

5-302.15   Inlet and Outlet, Sloped to Drain.

(A) A water tank and its inlet and outlet shall be sloped to drain.

(B) A water tank inlet shall be positioned so that it is protected from contaminants such as waste discharge, road dust, oil, or grease.

5-302.16   Hose, Construction and Identification.

A hose used for conveying drinking water from a water tank shall have a smooth interior surface and, if not permanently attached, shall be clearly and durably identified as to its use.

5-303.11 Filter, Compressed Air.

A filter that does not pass oil or oil vapors shall be installed in the air supply line between the compressor and drinking water system when compressed air is used to pressurize the water tank system.

5-303.12 Protective Equipment or Device.

A cap and keeper chain, closed cabinet, closed storage tube, or other approved protective equipment or device shall be provided for a water inlet, outlet, and hose.

5-303.13 Mobile Food Establishment Tank Inlet.

A mobile food establishment's water tank inlet shall be:

(A) 19.1 mm (three-fourths inch) in inner diameter or less; and

(B) Provided with a hose connection of a size or type that will prevent its use for any other service.

5-304.11 System Flushing and Disinfection.*

A water tank, pump, and hoses shall be flushed and sanitized before being placed in service after construction, repair, modification, and periods of nonuse.

5-304.12 Using a Pump and Hoses, Backflow Prevention.

A person shall operate a water tank, pump, and hoses so that backflow and other contamination of the water supply is prevented.

5-304.13 Protecting Inlet, Outlet, and Hose Fitting.

If not in use, a water tank and hose inlet and outlet fitting shall be protected as specified under § 5-303.12.

5-304.14 Tank, Pump, and Hoses, Dedication.

(A) Except as specified in ¶ (B) of this section, a water tank, pump, and hoses used for conveying drinking water shall be used for no other purpose.

(B) *Water tanks, pumps, and hoses approved for liquid foods may be used for conveying drinking water if they are cleaned and sanitized after each use.*

5-401.11 Capacity and Drainage.

A sewage holding tank in a mobile food establishment shall be:

(A) Sized 15 percent larger in capacity than the water supply tank; and

(B) Sloped to a drain that is 25 mm (1 inch) in inner diameter or greater, equipped with a shut-off valve.

Source: FDA 1993 *Food Code.*

Serving and Change

Changes in any of the control points before serving can necessitate changes at the serving control point. An addition to the menu changes the information that servers need to adequately answer guest questions. A new menu item may also require servers to learn new serving techniques.

Self-service options—such as a salad bar—change the work that servers perform. They also present special sanitation concerns, including protecting food products from contamination and exposure to the TDZ. Likewise, service styles other than traditional table service—such as banquet service, room service, and catering—have their own special sanitation considerations. For example, a manager must decide if the operation has sufficient staff to offer room service and which menu items can be served safely. Managers must consider the sanitation impact on the serving control point when planning other changes in the operation.

Serving and the SRM Program

Serving is a critical control point because food products must be delivered from the kitchen to the guest, which increases the risks. Serving all hot foods on heated plates and cold foods on chilled plates helps maintain proper product temperatures and enhances guest satisfaction. Servers, like other staff members, should adhere closely to rules of personal cleanliness and hygiene. They must also handle all food products carefully.

All equipment, utensils, and facilities used at the serving control point must be regularly cleaned, sanitized, and maintained. In addition to contributing to the establishment's image, these items help the operation control risks. The SRM program during serving helps ensure product safety, risk reduction, and guest satisfaction.

Summary

The purpose of the serving control point is to deliver safe, quality food products from the production department to the guest. Product quality should be assessed immediately before service. Serving and food display functions should be designed to prevent food contamination. The equipment used during service should be cleaned, maintained, and stored so as to prevent contamination. Facilities must also be clean and maintained in good repair, because a pleasant environment enhances the guest's enjoyment of the entire dining experience.

Several styles of service are used to deliver food to guests. Table service includes plate service, cart service, family-style service, and platter service. Each style has sanitation advantages and disadvantages. Other types of service include temporary food service, banquets and buffets, off-premises catering, room service, and mobile food service. Regardless of the type of service, risk reduction and guest satisfaction are of primary importance.

Endnotes

1. Steven Leipsner and Joan Vieweger, "Measuring the Service in Foodservice—Full Service," a presentation at the International Foodservice Manufacturers Association Chain Operators Exchange, 1988.

Key Terms

cart service • commissary • expediter • family-style service • flying food show • mobile food unit • plate service • platter service • sidestand • split service • temporary food establishment

Discussion Questions

1. What are the basic types of table service and what special sanitation considerations does each type entail?

2. What kinds of control measures are effective for salad bars and other self-service food bars?

3. How is food inventory protected at the serving control point?

4. What sanitation procedures and personal hygiene habits are food servers required to practice?

5. How should dishes, cups, glasses, and flatware be handled? What other procedures are required for the use and care of equipment at the serving control point?

6. Why are dining room inspections necessary? What does the supervisor/inspector look for?

7. What are the special sanitation requirements for temporary food establishments?

8. What control procedures are important for banquet and buffet service?

9. Off-premises catering and room service present what types of sanitation and quality risks?

10. What are mobile food units? What sanitation and serving standards do they require?

Checklist for Serving

Inventory

_____ Potentially hazardous foods are not exposed to the TDZ during display and service.

_____ Ice is dispensed with ice-dispensing utensils or automatic ice machines; guests should use only automatic dispensing machines.

_____ Only single-serving packages or approved self-service containers are used for condiments, seasonings, and dressings.

_____ Dispensing utensils are stored in a safe and sanitary manner before and during service.

_____ Only those foods that are not potentially hazardous and are still packaged and in sound condition are re-served.

_____ Food on display is protected from contamination and contact with the temperature danger zone.

_____ Self-service guests do not re-use tableware (except beverage cups and glasses).

_____ Servers know acceptable quality levels defined in terms of appearance, texture, color, temperature, and flavor, and check all menu items before serving the guest.

People

_____ Servers understand the operation's quality, cost, and sanitation standards.

_____ Staffing decisions are based on the menu, personnel skill levels, hours of service, the size of the operation and its sales volume, and guest expectations.

_____ Servers prepare themselves and their stations for service before the shift begins.

_____ Servers restock their stations and complete closing duties before leaving.

_____ Servers adhere to standards of personal hygiene and cleanliness.

_____ Dining room supervisors conduct a staff member line-up meeting and inspection of the facilities immediately before the meal period begins.

_____ Servers place orders with the kitchen using standard ordering procedures.

_____ Servers load their trays carefully.

_____ If an expediter is used, that individual is a selected and trained member of the management team.

_____ Servers and managers check food bars regularly for cleanliness and orderliness.

Equipment

_____ Staff members regularly clean and sanitize equipment and utensils used in the service of food and beverage products.

_____ Clean and sanitized utensils and equipment are stored in a way that prevents recontamination.

_____ Tableware is handled so as to prevent contamination.

_____ Stations and sidestands are kept stocked with adequate supplies of tableware and other necessities.

_____ Food products at stations and sidestands are kept out of the temperature danger zone.

_____ Tables, chairs, floors, and windows are cleaned and maintained regularly.

_____ Condiment and spice containers are cleaned regularly.

_____ Staff members are careful when handling all equipment used in service.

_____ Plate and platter covers are used to protect menu items and help maintain product temperatures as they are transported from the kitchen to the guest.

_____ Take-out operations are evaluated carefully before implementation.

Facilities

_____ Facilities are routinely cleaned, maintained, and repaired.

_____ Restrooms are inspected and cleaned regularly.

_____ Facilities are kept clean, dry, and odor-free.

_____ Adequate lighting levels are maintained.

_____ The supervisor conducts a facility inspection immediately before the meal period.

_____ Menus are inspected and all dirty or damaged menus are removed from circulation.

_____ Pets are not allowed in the facilities.

SRM Program

_____ Potentially hazardous foods are served carefully and safely.

_____ Food servers are trained to maintain standards and reduce risks during serving.

_____ Adequate facilities and equipment are present and used, and are cleaned, sanitized, and maintained frequently to reduce the risks during serving.

Temporary Food Establishments

_____ Local health codes regarding potentially hazardous foods are observed.

_____ Ice is stored in single-use wet strength paper or plastic bags and proper dispensing utensils are used.

_____ Equipment is installed, cleaned, sanitized, and maintained properly.

_____ Only single-service articles are used if no facilities are available for tableware cleaning and sanitizing.

_____ Potable water is available for food preparation, handwashing, and equipment and utensil cleaning.

_____ Food is not stored in contact with undrained ice or water.

_____ Sewage and waste are disposed of according to law.

_____ Handwashing facilities are available.

_____ Walls, ceilings, floors, and doors prevent the entry of pests.

Banquet and Buffet Service

_____ Correct time-temperature controls are observed.

_____ Station setup is checked before service begins.

_____ Menu items are chosen with ease, safety, and speed of service in mind.

_____ The necessary equipment and utensils to maintain product temperatures are available.

_____ Adequate spacing is provided for display tables and guest tables.

Off-Premises Catering

_____ A sufficient quantity of special equipment and transportation vehicles is available.

_____ Product time-temperature controls are closely monitored.

_____ Food is protected during storage and transportation.

Room Service

_____ Product quality and time-temperature controls are assessed.

_____ The menu is limited to those items that the operation can successfully prepare and deliver to the guestrooms.

_____ Soiled tableware, linen, and equipment are removed from the guestrooms or hallways promptly.

_____ Room service is evaluated regularly and changed if necessary.

Mobile Food Service

_____ Local health department requirements are investigated and followed.

_____ Equipment is cleaned, sanitized, and maintained regularly.

_____ Only those food products permitted by the local health authority are prepared and served.

_____ Only single-service articles are provided to guests.

_____ The water and waste retention systems conform to local health codes.

_____ Mobile food units report daily to the commissary for cleaning, servicing, and restocking of food and beverage inventory.

_____ The commissary is operated under the requirements of the local health authorities.

Case Study

Using the menu item you selected in Chapter 5, continue with the control point covered in this chapter.

Describe the type of table service used for your menu item. Assume that your operation also has a salad bar. What are the potential problems of a salad bar and how will you control these problems?

Indicate the sanitation considerations for serving your menu item, including ways to keep the item out of the TDZ. Next, define the quality characteristics of your menu item, specifying the appearance (including color, spacing, neatness, and garnish), texture and consistency, product temperature, and flavor.

Briefly describe the positions required in your dining room. Discuss the standards of personal hygiene and cleanliness for all staff members and work-specific standards for servers. Explain how an expediter can act as a communication link between kitchen staff and servers and discuss the requirements and skills necessary in the expediter.

List the equipment used in serving your item, along with proper methods for handling that equipment. Explain how to store in-service utensils and how to handle, remove, and set tableware. Discuss two sanitation standards for the sidestand. Describe the cleaning and maintenance schedule for dining room equipment. If your item is adaptable to take-out, describe how it will be displayed, served, and packaged.

Explain the facilities inspection procedure and identify who is responsible for inspections. Describe any special precautions for facilities, including the presence of pets. If your operation also serves your menu item at banquets and buffets, describe the standards of service. Develop an additional set of standards if your operation caters the item off-premises or offers it for room service.

Your development of this case study will, in part, depend on the menu item you select. Nevertheless, the basic principles of the serving control point can be analyzed even without applying them to an actual food establishment. If you are currently employed in a food establishment, you may wish to choose a menu item that is currently offered or one that is under consideration for addition to the menu.

An SRM Program Example: Whitefish and the Serving Control Point

The baked whitefish Florentine is presented to guests using plate service in the hotel's main dining room and at banquets. A salad bar accompanies all entrées in the main dining room. The salad bar is clean, regularly maintained, and one of the focal points of the dining room. Because the fish must be kept out of the temperature danger zone, it is served on heated plates. Leftover portions returned from the dining room are thrown out.

The whitefish, lemon garnish, and vegetable du jour are arranged attractively on the plate. The expediter judges the appearance, texture and consistency, color, size, and shape of each item on finished plates. The expediter also randomly checks product temperatures using a clean and sanitized product probe thermometer. When the expediter is not working, servers perform these checks.

Servers taste all menu items periodically, including the whitefish, at staff meetings. These samplings give servers first-hand knowledge of the menu items, enabling them to better answer guest questions. Servers practice good personal hygiene and cleanliness and are trained to uphold the operation's sanitation standards.

Equipment used to serve the whitefish, including all tableware and serving utensils, is cleaned and sanitized regularly and stored in such a way as to prevent contamination. The sidestand is kept clean and orderly. Potentially hazardous foods stored on the sidestand are refrigerated.

Tables and chairs in the dining room are cleaned regularly as part of the server's side work. Napkins are properly laundered, folded, and placed on the tables. Serving trays are checked for cleanliness before and during service. A clean and sanitized plate cover is used to cover the fish entrée after it is loaded on the server's tray.

The whitefish entrée is served in facilities that are regularly cleaned and maintained. Managers and staff members monitor the decor and cleanliness of the facilities closely. Regular inspections help control the facilities resource at the serving control point.

References

Albrecht, Karl. "The Service Imperative." *Restaurant Business,* May 20, 1988, pp. 156–157.

Alva, Marilyn. "The Death of the Salad Bar." *Nation's Restaurant News,* April 25, 1988, pp. F7–F8.

Bain, Laurie. "Salad Bar Safety." *Restaurant Business,* August 10, 1987, p. 98.

Bernstein, Charles. "The Room-Service Nightmare." *Nation's Restaurant News,* March 13, 1989, p. F3.

Boyle, Kathy. "Expediters." *Restaurants USA,* January 1988, pp. 19–21.

Cichy, Ronald F. "Control Waste and Increase Sales." *Michigan Hospitality Magazine,* July/August 1982, p. 21.

———. "Kitchen Sanitation." *Hotel and Resort Industry,* February 1989, pp. 80, 81–84, 86–87.

———. "The Role of the Professional Chef in a Foodservice Firm." *The National Culinary Review,* January 1983, pp. 12–13.

Dinibeit, Ron. "An Evaluation of Service Requirements." A presentation at the International Foodservice Manufacturers Association Chain Operators Exchange, 1985.

Durocher, Joseph. "Take-Out and Display Cases." *Restaurant Business,* June 10, 1988, pp. 211–212.

Faulkner, E. "Room for Growth: Room Service Gains in Popularity, Elegance." *Restaurants and Institutions,* June 1, 1983, p. 123.

Finley, M. "Cashing in on the Sun—Prospering With a Patio." *Host Magazine,* June 1983, pp. 16–17.

Food and Drug Administration, Center for Food Safety and Applied Nutrition, Retail Food Protection Branch. *Interpretation: Materials—Use of Chemically Treated Wood,* March 21, 1984.

———. *Interpretation: Personal Cleanliness—Coins and Currencies as Fomites,* July 16, 1984.

Frankin, Paul. "Operator Solutions." *Restaurant Business,* May 20, 1988, pp. 141–145.

Gebhardt, Dennis. "Conducting Operational Audits from the Guest's Point of View." *Hotel & Resort Industry,* January 1989, pp. 42–43.

Goodman, Raymond J. *The Management of Service for the Professional Restaurant Manager.* Dubuque, Iowa: Brown, 1979.

Knutson, Bonnie J. "Ten Laws of Customer Satisfaction." *The Cornell H.R.A. Quarterly,* November 1988, pp. 14–17.

LaGreca, Gen. "Improving Hospitality." *Restaurant Business,* January 20, 1988, p. 80.

LaHue, Polly M. "Hotel Roomservice Making Dramatic Changes." *Hotel & Motel Management,* February 27, 1989, pp. 28, 30.

Leipsner, Steven, and Vieweger, Joan. "Measuring the Service in Foodservice—Full Service." A presentation to the International Foodservice Manufacturers Association Chain Operators Exchange, 1988.

Lydecker, Toni. "The Crisis in Service." *NRA News,* March 1986, pp. 13–16.

Riell, Howard. "Commitment: Stocking the Sanitation Arsenal." *Nation's Restaurant News,* March 3, 1986, pp. F1, F3–F4.

Roberts, Michael. "Secret Ingredients." *Restaurants USA,* February 10, 1989, p. 88.

Schlesinger, Leonard. "Service Fundamentals." *Restaurant Business,* May 10, 1988, pp. 154–155.

Stone, Martha. "The Science of Flavor." *Restaurant Business,* February 10, 1989, p. 88.

U.S. Department of Health, Education, and Welfare. *Training Food Service Personnel for the Hospitality Industry.* Washington, D.C.: U.S. Government Printing Office, 1969.

Waskey, F.H. "Ted." "Banquets: Big Profit Producers." *Hotel & Resort Industry,* September 1988, pp. 32–34, 36, 38.

Wellins, Richard S. and Weaver, Patterson S. "Ten Myths of Customer Service." *Training,* July 1989, pp. 45–49.

REVIEW QUIZ

When you feel you have covered all of the material in this chapter, answer these questions. Choose the *best* answer. Check your answers with the correct ones found on the Review Quiz Answer Key at the end of this book.

1. The condition and temperature of the food on food bars should be checked:

    a. constantly.
    b. every 5 to 10 minutes.
    c. every 10 to 15 minutes.
    d. every 15 to 20 minutes.

2. Generally, food establishments are permitted to serve sauces such as catsup in:

    a. pour-type dispensers.
    b. refilled original containers.
    c. open single-serving containers.
    d. all of the above.

3. Which of the following is *not* a factor in judging food quality from a server's perspective?

    a. appearance
    b. consistency
    c. temperature
    d. price

4. Which of the following is acceptable according to sanitation standards?

    a. chewing gum or eating in the kitchen
    b. carrying a napkin over the shoulder
    c. handling flatware by the handles
    d. picking up glassware by the rims of the glasses

5. Sugar dispensers, salt and pepper shakers, and other table-top equipment items should be wiped clean at least once every:

    a. hour.
    b. two hours.
    c. meal period.
    d. day.

6. A temporary food establishment that does *not* have facilities for cleaning and sanitizing eating utensils should:

   a. *not* serve potentially hazardous foods.
   b. serve only prepackaged individual portions of food.
   c. provide only single-service tableware.
   d. all of the above

7. From a control standpoint, which of the following is an advantage of banquet service?

   a. The number of people to be served is established well in advance.
   b. All guests will be served at about the same time.
   c. A limited number of food items are prepared in large quantities.
   d. all of the above

8. Transportation is a critical control point for:

   a. off-premises catering.
   b. room service.
   c. both a and b.
   d. a and sometimes b.

9. Split service is a room service option in which:

   a. some food items are cooked in the kitchen and some are prepared by the server in the guestroom.
   b. special holding/transportation equipment is used to keep hot foods hot and cold foods cold.
   c. courses are delivered to the guestroom separately.
   d. none of the above

10. Mobile food units should have:

   a. a source of pressurized potable water.
   b. restroom facilities.
   c. refrigeration and hot holding facilities.
   d. all of the above.

Chapter Outline

Learning Objectives

1. Identify the types of soil found in food service operations, and define cleaning and sanitization. (p. 323)

2. Describe types and uses of cleaning agents. (pp. 323–324)

3. Identify and describe the uses of five types of sanitizers. (pp. 324–326)

4. Describe guidelines for using cleaners and sanitizers. (pp. 326–331)

5. Briefly explain manual cleaning and sanitizing procedures. (pp. 332–335)

6. Briefly explain mechanical cleaning and sanitizing procedures. (pp. 335–350)

7. Summarize the physical and behavioral characteristics of flies and cockroaches, and describe their preferred environments. (pp. 350–352)

8. Summarize the physical and behavioral characteristics of rats and mice, and describe their preferred environments. (pp. 352–353)

9. Identify guidelines for a food service pest control program, including basic environmental sanitation and chemical control. (pp. 353–356)

9

The Cleaning and Maintenance Control Point

Although the cleaning and maintenance function is presented last in the sequence of basic operating activities, it is the cornerstone of the sanitation risk management (SRM) program. Success at this control point is crucial to an operation's overall SRM program.

The cleaning and maintenance control point encompasses many facets of day-to-day food service operations. Because this control point is so comprehensive, our discussion of it is divided into two chapters. This chapter focuses on the first three of the four resources under a manager's control at the cleaning and maintenance control point: inventory, people, and equipment. The fourth resource, the facilities, is the subject of Chapter 10.

Cleaning, Maintenance, and Inventory

Many cleaning and sanitization agents are toxic chemicals. However, they are essential for the normal operation of a food service business. Cleaners and sanitizers are used to maintain safe facilities, equipment, and utensils by removing soil and killing harmful pathogens.

Throughout this chapter, the term "soil" refers to a substance which is in the wrong place. For example, cooking oil is necessary for the proper operation of a fryer, but cooking oil on tableware is considered soil. Food products are organic soil. Organic soil is produced by cooking equipment and is deposited on ceilings, walls, and exhaust hoods. Food production equipment, utensils, and tableware are also subject to organic soiling in the course of normal use.

Inorganic soil includes airborne and bonded dust. Airborne dust is free-floating, while bonded dust adheres to surfaces. Chemical deposits, which include detergent residues and mineral scale, are also considered inorganic soil. These deposits may build up on tableware, utensils, and equipment.

Cleaning is the removal of soil. The cleaning process can prevent the accumulation of food residues and the growth of microorganisms, thereby reducing spoilage. **Sanitization** is the destruction of pathogens that survive the cleaning process. Sanitization is necessary because items that look clean are not necessarily sanitary. Likewise, cleaning is necessary because it is nearly impossible to sanitize a soiled item.

Cleaning Agents

There are many types of cleaning agents used in a food establishment. Any of these products may be called a "detergent." However, this term usually refers to synthetic detergents, which are more alkaline than soaps. Soap is an alkaline salt of organic acid.

Cleaning agents dissolve or disperse soils and hold them in suspension (usually in water).

Soaps are used primarily for handwashing because they do not irritate the skin as detergents do. Although there has been some concern that bar soap may be a fomite (an inanimate object capable of transmitting infectious microorganisms), the FDA has determined that bar soap is not likely to support the growth of microorganisms. The major disadvantage of soap as a cleaning agent is that it produces a residue (soap scum) when combined with hard water.

Detergents are relatively unaffected by hard water and are therefore used for most cleaning purposes other than handwashing. They are especially effective in removing fats and oils. Some detergents soften water, and some have a germicidal effect. (Such detergents do not replace sanitization, however.) Important factors to consider when selecting a detergent include the surface to be cleaned, the type of soil, and the cleaning process.

Dishwashing detergents must be measured carefully to ensure the best results. Dishwashing machines usually use powdered detergents and are often equipped with automatic dispensing devices. Liquid detergents are usually used for manual dishwashing. Some highly alkaline detergents may irritate skin and should be used with rubber gloves.

Abrasive cleaners are used to scour off rust, grease, and heavy soil. Because they contain abrasive substances, they can permanently scratch stainless steel and porcelain surfaces. Therefore, staff members should use them with caution and only after proper training.

Acid cleaners vary in strength. Weak citric acid is used to wipe stainless steel. Hydrochloric acid (muriatic or plumber's acid) is used to remove hard water mineral deposits. Acid cleaners must be used with extreme caution and only by trained staff. Drain cleaners, many of which are acid-based, must also be used carefully to avoid skin irritation and food contamination.

Degreasers are highly alkaline and are usually skin irritants. Degreasers may be alkali-, chlorine-, or hydrocarbon solvent-based. Some are water-soluble or used as vapors. Degreasers in the form of vapors are used in cleaning kitchen exhaust ducts. Solvent cleaners are produced from emulsifiers and hydrocarbons. These heavy-duty degreasers are used to remove grease from exterior surfaces, driveways, and vehicles.

Metal cleaners and polishes are oils or oil emulsions that remove both soil and oxidation from pots and pans. If not rinsed away thoroughly, they may leave behind a white film which contaminates food and equipment.

Deodorizers are used to remove unpleasant, lingering odors in restrooms. They may leave a residue on surfaces if used improperly. Deodorizers should never be used in place of proper cleaning.

Sanitizers

Sanitizers are chemical compounds that destroy pathogens. There are five types of sanitizers in general use: chlorine-based sanitizers, iodine-based sanitizers, quaternary ammonium compounds, acid-anionic surfactants, and phenolic sanitizers. Exhibit 9.1 shows the characteristics of several sanitizers and their effectiveness for various applications. The type of sanitizer an operation uses for a particular application depends on the method of warewashing (manual or mechanical) and the type of item being sanitized.

Chlorine-based sanitizers are inexpensive and popular. These sanitizers are active against all microorganisms and spores if used in a concentration of 25 mg/L (milligrams/

Exhibit 9.1 Characteristics of Common Sanitizers

Column groups: Columns 1–3 = BY APPLICATION – MECHANICAL; Columns 4–7 = BY APPLICATION – MANUAL; Columns 8–19 = BY CHARACTERISTICS.

(NR) Not Recommended

TYPE OF SANITIZER — E.P.A. Registered	Low Temperature Dishmachine	Cold Water Rinse Bar Glass Washer	Third Tank Manual Bar Glasses	Utensils Pots Pans	Hard Surface Sanitation (Light Soil)	Hard Surface Cleaning and Sanitization	Soft Ice Cream Machines	Odor in Solution	Foam – Nonfoam	Wetting Ability	Hard Water Lime Deposits	Residual Bacteriostatic Effect	Heat Stability	Mildness to Hands in Dilution	Deodorizing Ability	Color Indication	Corrosiveness to Metals	Dilution for Use	Test Papers and Kits
CHLORINE (L)	Excellent (50 ppm)	Good	Good	Fair	NR	NR	NR	Chlorine	None	No	No	No	Moderate	No	No	No	Yes	2 oz /5 gal (200 ppm) Low temp (50 ppm)	Chlorine Test Paper
CHLORINE (P)	NR	NR	NR																
IODINE (L.F.)	NR	Excellent	Good	Very Good	NR	NR	NR	Slight Odor of Iodine	Low Foam	Yes	No	No	Not Recommended for use over 120° F.	Moderate	Minimal	Yes, Light Brown Color	Yes	1 oz /5 gal (100 ppm)	Iodine Test Kit
ACID	NR	Good	Very Good	NR	NR	NR	None	None	Foam	Yes (Best)	No	Stable	Stable	Yes	Minimal	Safe on Stainless Steel and Aluminum	Safe on Stainless Steel and Aluminum	½ oz /1 gal (200 ppm) pH 4-5	Short Range pH Paper 3-5.5
QUATERNARY (Blue)	Very Good	Excellent	Excellent	Excellent	Excellent	Good	NR	None	Foam	Yes	Yes	Yes	Stable	Yes	Minimal	Safe on Stainless Steel and Aluminum	Safe on Stainless Steel and Aluminum	1 oz /4 gal (200 ppm)	QT 0-10 Paper
10% (Clear)	Good	Good	NR	Good	Excellent	Excellent	No	None	Foam	No	Yes	Yes	Stable	Yes	Minimal	Safe on Stainless Steel and Aluminum	Safe on Stainless Steel and Aluminum	1 oz /2 gal (200 ppm)	0-10 Paper
DETERGENT QUAT (Red)	NR	NR	NR	Excellent	Excellent	Excellent	No	Spearmint	Foam	No	Yes	Yes	Stable	Excellent	Excellent	Safe on Stainless Steel and Aluminum	Safe on Stainless Steel and Aluminum	2 oz /2 gal (200 ppm)	QT 0-10 Paper
DETERGENT QUAT (Clear)	NR	NR	NR	Excellent	Excellent	Excellent	No	None	Foam	No	Yes	Yes	Moderate	Excellent	Excellent	Safe on Stainless Steel and Aluminum	Safe on Stainless Steel and Aluminum	1 oz /3.5 gal (200 ppm)	0-10 Paper
PHENOLIC	NR	NR	NR	Sanitation Only	NR	NR	NR	Pleasant and Fresh	None	None	Yes	Yes	Not Applicable	Excellent	No	No	No	Spray	None Needed

Source: Edwin B. Feldman, ed. *Programmed Cleaning Guide for the Environmental Sanitarian* (New York: The Soap and Detergent Association, 1984).

liter) at pH 10 or less and a temperature of 120°F (49°C); 50 mg/L at pH 10 or less and a temperature of 100°F (38°C); or 100 mg/L at pH 10 or less and a temperature of 55°F (13°C). Higher concentrations do not increase effectiveness. (The concentration of chlorine sanitizers can be easily determined with a field test kit.) Chlorine compounds are unaffected by hard water and do not leave a residue. However, they do possess a characteristic chlorine odor and have a relatively short shelf life. Other disadvantages include decreased effectiveness as the pH increases above 8.0, possible skin irritation, corrosion of some metals, and rapid break-up from some solutions. Chlorine sanitizers are usually applied for one minute or more at temperatures of 75°F (24°C) or above.

Iodine-based sanitizers (iodophors) are stable (do not deteriorate easily), have a long shelf life, and will destroy most bacterial cells (but not spores). Iodophors are effective in hard water and are non-corrosive. They do not leave a residue or irritate skin. Because iodophors have a brown or amber color, their concentration is easily measured visually. Iodophors work somewhat slowly at a pH of 5.0 or above (for example, when used with an alkaline detergent). They may also stain some surfaces. Iodophors are more expensive than some other sanitizers. They should be applied in a concentration of 12.5 to 25 mg/L for one minute or more at temperatures of 75° to 120°F (24° to 49°C) and a pH of 5.0 or less. They should not be used at temperatures above 120°F (49°C).

Quaternary ammonium compounds (QUATS) are stable, have a long shelf life, and are active against most microorganisms. They work best at a pH of 9 to 10 and leave behind a film that controls bacterial growth. QUATS are non-corrosive and non-irritating and both eliminate and prevent odors. However, QUATS destroy some microorganisms slowly and are incompatible with common detergents. They are also expensive. Their residue makes these sanitizers impractical for many uses (such as cleaning tableware); however, the residue is desirable on some surfaces (such as refrigerator interiors) to control bacterial activity. QUATS are usually applied in concentrations of 180 to 220 mg/L for one minute or longer at temperatures of 75°F (24°C) and above.

Acid-anionic surfactants are stable, have a long shelf life, and are active against most microorganisms. They are odorless, non-staining, and effective in hard water. They have a low toxicity when left as a residual antibacterial film. Acid-anionic surfactants are only effective at relatively low pHs (1.9 to 3.0). They are corrosive to metal surfaces other than stainless steel and aluminum and do not destroy most bacterial spores. Acid-anionic surfactants should be applied in concentrations of 100 to 200 mg/L for at least one minute at temperatures of 75° to 110°F (24° to 43°C).

Phenolic sanitizers work well at pH levels between 6 and 7. They become more stable when combined with synthetic anionics. Phenolic compounds act as deodorizers but have limited applications. They should not be used to sanitize food-handling equipment.

Proper Handling of Cleaners and Sanitizers

The chemistry of cleaner and sanitizer formulation is an exact science. It is a dangerous practice to mix cleaning or sanitizing compounds in-house. It would be wrong, for example, to assume that, because bleach is an effective sanitizer and ammonia is a good cleaner, the two combined might be an inexpensive all-purpose cleaner. These two chemicals produce a deadly gas when combined. Similarly, if QUATS are mixed with chlorine compounds, the mixture releases a great deal of heat. *Never mix your own cleaners or sanitizers.*

It is also important to follow the manufacturer's recommendations for the proper mixture and application of cleaners and sanitizers. Improper concentrations are ineffective if too low and wasteful, sometimes harmful, if too high. Staff members should be trained to measure and use cleaners and sanitizers carefully. Managers must ensure that these procedures are followed even at the busiest times.

Because many cleaners and sanitizers are toxic chemicals, these substances must be clearly labeled and stored in a locked area used for no other purpose. Toxic chemicals should never be stored with food products. They should be stored in their original containers. Only those chemicals necessary for maintaining the operation's sanitary environment can be stored on the premises. Whenever possible, toxic substances should have distinctive colors and packaging so they will not be confused with food products. Recall that chemicals to be used in dilute solution (for example, detergents and sanitizers) may be safely stored in their original containers on shelves above or below work areas. Chemicals used without dilution (such as oven cleaners and silver polishes) should not be stored in work areas.

The FDA states:

POISONOUS/TOXIC MATERIALS

7-101.11   Identifying Information, Prominence.*

Containers of poisonous or toxic materials and personal care items shall bear a legible manufacturer's label.

7-102.11   Common Name.*

Working containers used for storing poisonous or toxic materials such as cleaners and sanitizers taken from bulk supplies shall be clearly and individually identified with the common name of the material.

7-201.11   Separation.*

Poisonous or toxic materials shall be stored so they may not contaminate food, equipment, utensils, linens, and single-service and single-use articles by:

(A)   Separating the poisonous or toxic materials by spacing or partitioning;[S] and

(B)   Locating the poisonous or toxic materials in an area that is not above food, equipment, utensils, linens, and single-service or single-use articles. *This paragraph does not apply to equipment and utensil cleaners and sanitizers that are stored in warewashing areas for availability and convenience if the materials are stored to prevent contamination of food, equipment, utensils, linens, and single-service and single-use articles.*

7-202.11   Restriction.*

(A) Only those poisonous or toxic materials that are required for the operation and maintenance of a food establishment, such as for the cleaning and sanitizing of equipment and utensils and the control of insects and rodents, shall be allowed in a food establishment.[S]

(B)   ¶ *(A) of this section does not apply to packaged poisonous or toxic materials that are for retail sale.*

7-202.12   Conditions of Use.*

Poisonous or toxic materials shall be:

    (A) Used according to:

        (1)   Law and this Code,

        (2)   The manufacturers' use directions included in the labeling,

        (3)   The conditions of certification, if certification is required, for use of the pest control materials, and

        (4)   Additional conditions that may be established by the regulatory authority; and

    (B) Applied so that:

        (1)   Contamination including toxic residues due to spray, drip, drain, or splash on food, equipment, utensils, linens, and single-service and single-use articles is prevented, and

        (2)   A hazard to employees or other persons is not constituted.

7-203.11   Food Containers.*

A food container may not be used to store, transport, or dispense poisonous or toxic materials.

7-203.12   Poisonous or Toxic Material Containers.*

A container previously used to store poisonous or toxic materials may not be used to store, transport, or dispense food.

7-204.11   Sanitizers, Criteria.*

Chemical sanitizers shall meet the requirements specified in 21 CFR 178.1010 Sanitizing solutions.

7-204.12   Chemicals for Washing Fruits and Vegetables, Criteria.*

Chemicals used to wash or peel raw, whole fruits and vegetables shall meet the requirements specified in 21 CFR 173.315 Chemicals used in washing or to assist in the lye peeling of fruits and vegetables.

7-204.13   Boiler Water Additives, Criteria.*

Chemicals used as boiler water additives shall meet the requirements specified in 21 CFR 173.310 Boiler water additives.

7-204.14   Drying Agents, Criteria.*

Drying agents used in conjunction with sanitization shall:

    (A) For use with hot water:

(1)   Contain only components that are generally recognized as safe as specified in 21 CFR 182—Substances Generally Recognized As Safe, 21 CFR 184—Direct Food Substances Affirmed As Generally Recognized As Safe, or 21 CFR 186—Indirect Food Substances Affirmed as Generally Recognized As Safe, or

(2)   Be specifically reviewed according to procedures specified in 21 CFR 171—Food Additive Petitions and accepted as an indirect food additive before being used; or

(B)   For use with chemicals, contain only components that are approved under a prior sanction as specified in 21 CFR 181—Prior-Sanctioned Food Ingredients or are generally recognized as safe as specified in 21 CFR 182—Substances Generally Recognized As Safe.

7-205.11   Incidental Food Contact, Criteria.*

Lubricants shall meet the requirements specified in 21 CFR 178.3570 Lubricants with incidental food contact, if they are used on food-contact surfaces, on bearings and gears located on or within food-contact surfaces, or on bearings and gears that are located so that lubricants may leak, drip, or be forced into food or onto food-contact surfaces.

7-206.11   (Pesticides) Application.*

(A) A pesticide shall be applied in a food establishment only by a certified applicator *except that the manual or automatic spraying of a general use insecticide that only contains pyrethrins, piperonyl butoxide, and N-octyl bicycloheptene dicarboximide need not be done by a certified applicator.*

(B) A pesticide shall be applied so that direct or indirect contact with food, equipment, utensils, linens, and single-service and single-use articles is prevented by protecting those items from toxic residues due to spray, drip, drain, or splash and:

(1)   From application of a restricted use pesticide by:

(a)   Removing the items;

(b)   Covering the items with impermeable covers; or

(c)   Taking other appropriate preventive actions; and

(2)   Cleaning and sanitizing equipment and utensils after the application.

7-206.12   Bait Stations.

Bait shall be contained in a covered bait station.

7-206.13   Tracking Powders.*

Tracking powders may not be used in a food establishment.

7-207.11 Restriction and Storage.*

(A) Only those medicines that are necessary for the health of employees shall be allowed in a food establishment. *This section does not apply to medicines that are stored or displayed for retail sale.*

(B) Medicines that are in a food establishment for the employees' use shall be labeled as specified under § 7-101.11 and located to prevent the contamination of food, equipment, utensils, linens, and single-service and single-use articles.

7-207.12 Refrigerated Medicines, Storage.*

Medicines belonging to employees or to children in a day care center that require refrigeration and are stored in a food refrigerator shall be:

(A) Stored in a package or container and kept inside a covered, leakproof container that is identified as a container for the storage of employees' medicines; and

(B) Located on the lowest shelf.

7-208.11 (First Aid Supplies) Storage.*

First aid supplies that are in a food establishment for the employees' use shall be:

(A) Labeled as specified under § 7-101.11;^S and

(B) Stored in a kit or a container that is located to prevent the contamination of food, equipment, utensils, and linens, and single-service and single-use articles.^S

7-209.11 (Other Personal Care Items) Storage.

Employees shall store their other personal care items as specified under ¶ 6-305.11(B).

Personal Care Items.

(a) **"Personal care items"** means items or substances that may be poisonous, toxic, or a source of contamination and are used to maintain or enhance a person's health, hygiene, or appearance.

(b) **"Personal care items"** include items such as medicines; first aid supplies; and other items such as cosmetics, and toiletries such as toothpaste and mouthwash.

Source: FDA 1993 *Food Code.*

Some examples will illustrate the importance of these safety precautions. One operation used liquid chlorine bleach as a kitchen sanitizer. One of the staff members transferred some bleach from its large original container into a smaller, empty vinegar bottle. The next morning, the breakfast cook used the bleach in the vinegar bottle to mix a solution for poaching eggs. In another incident, the kitchen manager of a food service commissary encountered some strange-tasting soup in her operation. In the course of questioning the cook about each item in the standard recipe, the manager discovered that the cook had used soap flakes (stored in an unmarked container) in place of salt.

The objective of safe chemical storage is to prevent food and equipment contamination and to protect staff members and guests. Following the FDA's code and state and local ordinances can help managers significantly reduce the risks that toxic chemicals pose.

Cleaning, Maintenance, and People

The success of the operation's sanitation risk management program depends greatly on people. The success of the cleaning and maintenance control point is particularly dependent on the operation's systematic approach to this resource.

In some cases, outside personnel are brought in to help with cleaning and maintenance. Outside contractors may be employed for monthly, quarterly, or semi-annual heavy cleaning and maintenance jobs. They may strip and reseal floors or clean exhaust hoods and ventilation ducts in the kitchen. In most establishments, an outside contractor regularly provides pest control services.

Routine cleaning is usually the responsibility of in-house staff. All staff members should understand the proper procedures for cleaning and maintaining the equipment and facilities in their work areas. Each person in the operation is responsible, to some extent, for the cleaning and maintenance function. When production or service staff members are not busy with other duties, they should be cleaning.

To be successful, the operation's cleaning program must be formalized. Written cleaning procedures are important. Management should establish written cleaning procedures for each area and piece of equipment in the operation. Each procedure should briefly describe the task, list the steps in the task, and indicate the materials and tools necessary.

It is a good idea to post cleaning procedures near the equipment they pertain to so staff members can refer to them easily. Written procedures are also useful for on-the-job training and for management evaluation of the cleaning program. Each manager should monitor cleaning procedures in his or her department. This follow-up demonstrates to staff members that management cares about maintaining a clean environment.

Staff members are more likely to follow cleaning and maintenance procedures if they understand the importance of these routine functions. Training in cleaning procedures must be systematic to be effective. Training should cover cleanliness standards and recommended methods, products, and equipment used for cleaning and maintenance. Only after proper training can staff members be assigned regular cleaning and maintenance duties. For example, a preparation cook should not be responsible for operating and cleaning a meat slicer until he or she has been properly trained. Proper training reduces risks at this control point.

A written cleaning schedule further systematizes this important activity by indicating who is responsible for each cleaning task and how often the task should be performed. The schedule should be based on a survey of cleaning needs. If a survey has never been done, managers, supervisors, and staff members should work together to identify cleaning needs for each area in the food service operation. Questions to answer during the survey include:

- What is to be cleaned or maintained?
- Who is responsible for the cleaning or maintenance?
- When is the area or equipment to be cleaned or maintained?

- What are the safety and sanitation precautions associated with this cleaning or maintenance procedure?

- How should the cleaned item be stored to prevent recontamination?

- Who is responsible for supervising and checking the cleaning or maintenance effort?

- What must be done to reduce risks during cleaning and maintenance?

Areas which might be covered by the survey include entrance, exit, kitchen, dining, garbage, storage, and restroom areas. Once the survey is completed, a cleaning schedule can be developed. A sample cleaning schedule is presented in Exhibit 9.2.

Cleaning, Maintenance, and Equipment

Kitchen equipment and utensils must be cleaned and sanitized to prevent cross-contamination. Cleaning and sanitizing tasks can be accomplished manually or mechanically. Manual cleaning and sanitizing is usually used for in-place equipment such as ovens, broilers, griddles, and steam-powered equipment (covered in Chapter 7). Most food service businesses also clean and sanitize pots, pans, and utensils (such as mixing bowls, wire whips, and knives) manually. On the other hand, tableware is usually washed and sanitized in a dishwashing machine.

Manual Systems

Manual cleaning and sanitization of pots, pans, and utensils requires a three-compartment sink large enough to submerse the largest item to be washed, rinsed, and sanitized. The sink area should include adequate space for soiled holding—the accumulation of soiled equipment and utensils. The soiled holding area should be far enough from clean items to prevent cross-contamination. Also, staff members must wash their hands after handling soiled items. If hot water is used for sanitization, the sanitizing compartment of the sink shall be designed with an integral heating device to maintain water temperatures of at least 171°F (77°C) and provided with a basket to allow complete immersion of equipment and utensils into the hot water.

Equipment and utensils should be scraped and pre-soaked before washing to remove large food particles. Washing takes place in the first compartment of the sink. A hot detergent solution (110°F/43°C minimum) is essential for this step. The proper concentration of detergent is economical and protects guests from detergent residue on food-contact surfaces.

Items are rinsed in the second compartment of the sink. Rinsing removes detergent and food particles. Rinse water must be clean and at the proper temperature.

Once the item is washed and rinsed, it is sanitized in the third compartment. There are several methods of manual sanitization. The equipment or utensil can be placed in 170°F (77°C) water for at least 30 seconds. The item may also be exposed to a 50 mg/L chlorine and water solution at 75°F (24°C) or above for at least one minute. Exposing the item to an iodine and water solution of 12.5 mg/L at a temperature of at least 75°F (24°C) for one minute or longer is also an acceptable sanitization method.

The water used for washing, rinsing, and sanitizing should be changed regularly. Water temperatures must also be monitored with an accurate thermometer. Sanitizer concentrations should be checked with a test kit.

Exhibit 9.2 Sample Cleaning Schedule

Equipment or Area to be Cleaned	Person Responsible	Cleaning Frequency	Cleaning Manual Page Reference*
Can Opener	Dishwasher	Daily	
Ceilings	Maintenance Staff	Monthly	
Char-Broiler	Station Cook	Daily Weekly	
Coffee Urn	Server	After Each Brew Daily	
Compartment Steamer	Station Cook Dishwasher	Daily Weekly	
Convection Oven	Station Cook	Daily Weekly	
Conventional Oven	Station Cook	Daily Weekly	
Cutting Boards	Station Cook Pot and Pan Washer	After Each Use Daily	
Dishwashing Machine	Dishwasher	After Each Shift Daily	
Floors	Dishwasher Pot and Pan Washer	As Needed Daily	
Fryer	Station Cook	Daily Weekly	
Griddle	Station Cook	As Needed Daily Weekly	
Grinder	Station Cook Pot and Pan Washer	After Each Use Daily	
Hood/Filters	Pot and Pan Washer Dishwasher	Weekly	
Hot Top Range	Station Cook Pot and Pan Washer	Daily Weekly	
Ice Machine Interior Deliming	Pot and Pan Washer Maintenance Staff	Daily Weekly Per Manufacturer's Recommendations	
Microwave Oven	Station Cook	Daily Weekly	
Mixer	Station Cook	After Each Use Daily	
Mobile Food Warmer	Pot and Pan Washer	After Each Use Weekly	
Mobile Refrigeration Unit	Pot and Pan Washer	After Each Use Weekly	

(continued)

Exhibit 9.2 *(continued)*

Equipment or Area to be Cleaned	Person Responsible	Cleaning Frequency	Cleaning Manual Page Reference*
Open Top Range	Station Cook Pot and Pan Washer	Daily Weekly	
Overhead-Fired Broiler	Station Cook	Daily Weekly	
Plate Warmer	Dishwasher	Daily Weekly	
Pot and Pan Sink	Pot and Pan Washer	After Each Shift Daily	
Reach-in Freezer	Station Cook Sous Chef Maintenance Staff	Daily Weekly Monthly	
Reach-in Refrigerator	Station Cook Sous Chef Maintenance Staff	Daily Weekly Monthly	
Refrigerated Drawer	Station Cook Sous Chef Maintenance Staff	Daily Weekly Monthly	
Salamander	Station Cook	Daily Weekly Monthly	
Slicer	Station Cook Pot and Pan Washer	After Each Use Weekly	
Steam-Jacketed Kettle	Station Cook Pot and Pan Washer	Daily Weekly	
Steam Table	Station Cook	After Each Shift Daily	
Tilting Braising Pan	Station Cook	After Each Shift Daily	
Toaster	Server	Daily	
Walk-In Freezer	Sous Chef Maintenance Staff	Daily Weekly Monthly	
Walk-In Refrigerator	Sous Chef Maintenance Staff	Daily Weekly Monthly	
Walls	Dishwasher Pot and Pan Washer Maintenance Staff	Daily Weekly Monthly	
Work Tables	Station Cook	As Needed Daily	

*References are intended to be page numbers in the operation's cleaning manual.

Exhibit 9.3 Sample Chemical Supplier's Recommended Cleaning Procedures

Equipment Required:
Double compartment plastic pail
Cellulose sponges

Product Recommendation:
_____
_____

Procedure:

1. Immediately after use, take all removable parts to pot-sink for washing and sanitizing according to manual pot-washing instructions.
2. Fill both compartments of pail with warm water. To the wash compartment, add _____ in the ratio of _____ per gallon of water.
   Use separate sponges for wash and rinse compartments.
3. Unplug slicer.
   Besides the electrical hazard, serious injury could result if motor were to start while working near blade.

4. Use wash solution and cellulose sponge to scrub all stationary parts of slicer. Pay particular attention to corners, handles, and hard to get at places.
5. Sanitize, using clean sponge dipped in rinse solution and squeezed nearly dry.
   Dip and wring sponge frequently to be sure sanitizer contacts all surfaces.
6. Reassemble slicer.
7. Replace plug.
8. Return cleaning equipment to proper storage.

Source: DuBois Chemicals, *Sanitation Procedures Manual* (Undated), p. D-41.

All equipment and utensils should be air-dried after sanitizing. Once dry, equipment and utensils should be handled carefully to prevent recontamination of food-contact surfaces. Safe storage of clean, sanitized equipment and utensils is also essential.

Equipment cleaning procedures are often available from manufacturers of cleaning and sanitizing compounds. Exhibit 9.3 is an example of one company's recommended procedures for cleaning a food slicer.

Mechanical Systems

Most glasses, dishes, and flatware are cleaned and sanitized in a dishwashing machine. There are several types of dishwashing machines. Single-tank, stationary rack machines wash one rack of dishes at a time; each rack is loaded manually. Single-tank machines operate either at single or dual temperatures for wash and rinse cycles. Conveyor machines may have one or more tanks. The conveyor moves dish racks through the machine automatically. A typical warewashing station with a conveyor machine is shown in Exhibit 9.4.

Flight-type machines also use a conveyor belt. The dishes are loaded directly on the conveyor belt's plastic pegs or bars (Exhibit 9.4). Flatware is loaded in racks. This type of machine operates continuously (with a person stationed at each end) and is ideal for high-volume operations. Carousel-type machines have a circular conveyor belt. Immersion dishwashers clean racked dishes by a process similar to the manual dishwashing system.

It is important to operate dish machines properly. Each staff member responsible for operating the machine should read the manual carefully. Most machines also have exterior data plates which provide basic operating information. Management should

Exhibit 9.4   Typical Warewashing Station—Conveyor Machine

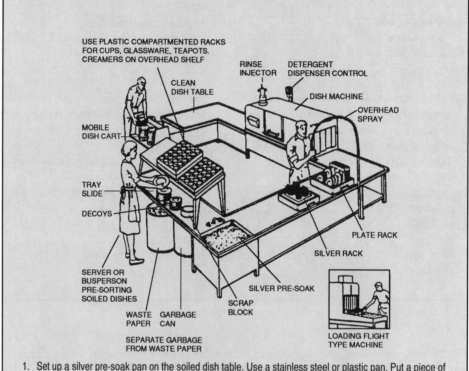

1. Set up a silver pre-soak pan on the soiled dish table. Use a stainless steel or plastic pan. Put a piece of aluminum foil in the bottom, add hot water and use a silver soak product. Change the solution when it becomes dirty.

2. Place glass, cup and bowl racks on the overhead shelf. Make sure that these items are placed in each compartment upside down.

3. Set out decoys on the table so that the buspersons can place dishes all of one kind together.

4. Always knock off excess food soil and paper before racking dishes so that food particles do not enter the wash tank.

5. Rack dishes, all of one kind, together. Then rinse with overhead spray to knock off any remaining heavy food soil.

6. Rack silver in holders with eating end up. Do not place same kind together or they will nest and not wash thoroughly.

FOLLOW LABEL INSTRUCTIONS ON PRODUCT USE AND CONCENTRATION

Source: Adapted from Edwin B. Feldman, ed. *Programmed Cleaning Guide for the Environmental Sanitarian* (New York: The Soap and Detergent Association, 1984), p. 89.

establish a cleaning and maintenance schedule based on the manufacturer's recommendations. Regular cleaning and maintenance will ensure optimal performance and minimize time-consuming and costly repairs in the long run.

The basic mechanical warewashing procedure requires ten steps. The following times and temperatures are based on the National Sanitation Foundation's recommendations for a multi-tank conveyor machine.

1. Scrape soiled dishes and pre-soak flatware.

2. Pre-rinse to remove all visible soil.

3. Rack dishes and flatware so water will spray evenly on all surfaces.

4. Wash dishes and flatware in a detergent-water solution at 150°F (66°C) for at least seven seconds.

5. Rinse dishes and flatware in clean water at 160°F (71°C) to 180°F (82°C) for at least seven seconds.

6. Final-rinse dishes and flatware in a sanitizer-water solution at 180°F (82°C) with a maximum conveyor speed of 15 feet (4.6 m) per minute.

7. Air-dry dishes and flatware.

8. Stack clean and sanitary items, being careful not to touch surfaces that will come into contact with food or the guest's mouth.

9. Store dishes and flatware in a clean, dry area.

10. Clean the machine, including the spray arms, trays, tanks, and tables.

As with manual systems, there must be sufficient counter space for the accumulation of soiled tableware. These soiled items must not touch clean and sanitary items. Large food particles should be scraped into a disposal or garbage can with a rubber scraper. Abrasive cleaning pads should not be used for scraping because they can leave behind unsightly scratches that may harbor microorganisms. Decoys (setups of one piece of each type of tableware) make it easier for staff members to pre-sort and rack soiled tableware according to type.

Some operators pre-soak only flatware in order to reduce dish handling and breakage. However, some items, such as glasses used to serve fruit juices, are difficult to clean without pre-soaking. Dishes soiled with eggs, cheese, or sauces are also hard to clean; they may need pre-soaking and, like all tableware, they should be washed as soon as possible after soiling.

Pre-rinsing removes any remaining visible soil. A pressure sprayer located over a garbage disposal can simplify this step. Next, items are racked according to type. Glasses are racked bottom-up, dishes are racked on edge, and flatware is placed in baskets. Specialized racks make the process more efficient. Tableware should be arranged in racks so that the spray can reach all surfaces. Dishes should not be stacked or crowded into the machine. This increases breakage and prevents proper cleaning and sanitization.

Time and temperature requirements for mechanical wash and rinse cycles vary according to the type of machine (see Exhibit 9.5). If the machine sanitizes with hot water alone, the final rinse water must be at least 180°F (82°C).

Items should be air-dried for at least one minute. A drying agent can be used to minimize water spots. It is important to allow cleaned and sanitized dishes to air-dry thoroughly. Moisture can damage dishes by causing them to stick together. Humidity in the dishroom must be controlled to help speed drying.

After air-drying, the items should be sorted and stacked for storage. Chipped or cracked dishes should be discarded; they are unsanitary and unsafe. Staff members who scrape, pre-rinse, and rack soiled tableware should wash their hands before handling clean tableware. Glasses, cups, and flatware may be left in dishwashing racks as long as they are stored in a way that prevents contamination. Tableware should be stored in a clean, dry area.

Exhibit 9.5 NSF Time-Temperature Requirements for Commercial Warewashing Machines

SINGLE TANK STATIONARY RACK TYPES:			
WASH		**FINAL RINSE**	
Minimum Exposure	Minimum Temperature	Minimum Exposure	Minimum Temperature
DUAL TEMPERATURE: 40 sec.	150°F (tank) (66°C)	10 sec.	180°F (manifold) (82°C)
			15 to 25 psi flow pressure
SINGLE TEMPERATURE: 40 sec.	165°F (tank) (74°C)	30 sec.	165°F (tank) (74°C)
	Discharge to waste		Discharge to waste
CHEMICAL SANITIZING: 50 sec.	120°F (tank) (49°C)	20 sec.	120°F (tank) (49°C)
	Discharge to waste		50 mg/L chlorine or other acceptable sanitizing solution

CONVEYOR TYPES					
WASH		**PUMPED RINSE**		**FINAL RINSE**	
Minimum Exposure	Minimum Temperature	Minimum Exposure	Minimum Temperature	Minimum Exposure	Minimum Temperature
					15 to 25 psi flow pressure
SINGLE TANK: 15 sec.	160°F (tank) (71°C)	NOT APPLICABLE		Maximum Conveyor Speed, 7 ft/min.	180°F (manifold) (82°C)
				6 in. wide spray, 5 in. above conveyor	
MULTIPLE TANK: 7 sec.	150°F (tank) (66°C)	7 sec.	160°F (71°C)	Maximum Conveyor Speed, 15 ft/min.	180°F (manifold) (82°C)
				3 in. wide spray, 5 in. above conveyor	

NSF Specifications for Various Types of Warewashing Machines

The accompanying chart summarizes the requirements detailed in NSF Standard No. 3 for commercial dishwashing machines[1]. Special equipment differing in design or principle of operation from the machines listed on the chart may not meet the requirements cited there. However, these machines are tested as specials and meet the requirements for soil removal and sanitization of utensils.

1. The figures on the table represent minimum requirements. NSF tests the final rinse flow pressure at 20 psi as an optimum pressure, but allowable flow pressures range from 15 to 25 psi.

2. If the manufacturer's data plate indicates a flow pressure, the machine must carry a gauge valve to measure it. If the data plate does not state a flow pressure, the machine is not required to carry a gauge valve.

3. Temperatures stated on the dish machine data plate are minimums. Except for chemical sanitizing machines, the machine should not heat to more than 15 degrees F. above its minimum temperatures.

[1]For specific machine information, consult the current NSF Food Service Equipment List.

Source: Adapted from National Sanitation Foundation, *Standard No. 3 for Spray-Type Dishwashing Machines.*

At the end of each shift, or more frequently if necessary, the dishwashing machine should be disassembled and cleaned. Spray arms and scrap collection trays should be removed and cleaned. Curtains between wash and rinse compartments should be washed, rinsed, sanitized, and dried. Tanks should be drained and the tables and exterior surfaces of the machine should be wiped down. Finally, the detergent and sanitizer dispensers should be refilled as needed.

It is important that food service managers test the operation of commercial dishwashers daily. Some common performance problems and suggested solutions are listed in Exhibit 9.6. A test kit or other device is needed to accurately measure the mg/L concentration of sanitizing solutions. Regular maintenance is also important. Dishwasher drains, valves, and pumps should be regularly checked for leaks. Nozzles and pipes should be examined for wear and mineral deposits. Detergent concentrations should be checked with a test kit. Temperature measuring devices should be tested for accuracy by running a thermometer through the machine and checking it at each cycle. If the machine is gas powered, the flame should be checked for proper burning color and height. Chains and drive wheels on machines with movable conveyors should be regularly lubricated. Some machine and chemical suppliers provide dish machine service on a contractual basis.

Rising energy costs have prompted many operators to purchase chemical sanitizing machines. Many models are approved by the NSF and other regulatory authorities. Chemical sanitizing machines use lower temperatures, higher water pressure, and longer cycle times than conventional dish machines. Although the final rinse temperature is only 120°F (49°C), tableware is sanitized chemically in the last cycle, usually with iodophors or chlorine solutions. Operations using these low-temperature machines have reported energy savings of as high as 35 to 40%. Convertible high-temperature/low-temperature dish machines are also available. When the high-temperature option is selected, a booster heater provides water at the proper temperature.

Other mechanical warewashing equipment includes pot washers, glass washers (used in bar operations), and under-counter dish machines for room service pantry areas and concierge floors in hotels.

The FDA states:

"**Warewashing**" means the cleaning and sanitizing of food-contact surfaces of equipment and utensils.

4-302.13   Temperature Measuring Devices, Manual Warewashing.

In manual warewashing operations, a temperature measuring device shall be provided and readily accessible for frequently measuring the washing and sanitizing temperatures.

4-302.14   Sanitizing Solutions, Testing Devices.

A test kit or other device that accurately measures the concentration in mg/L of sanitizing solutions shall be provided.

4-301.12   Manual Warewashing, Sink Compartment Requirements.

(A) Except as specified in ¶ (C) of this section, a sink with at least 3 compartments shall be provided for manually washing, rinsing, and sanitizing equipment and utensils.

Exhibit 9.6 Common Warewashing Problems

Symptom	Possible Cause	Suggested Solution
Dishes Soiled	Insufficient detergents	Use enough detergent in wash water to ensure complete soil suspension.
	Wash water temperature too low	Keep water temperature within recommended ranges to dissolve food residues and to further facilitate heat accumulation (for sanitization).
	Inadequate wash and rinse times	Allow sufficient time for wash and rinse operations to be effective. (Time should be automatically controlled by timer or by conveyor speed. The timer may need to be reset or the conveyor speed adjusted.)
	Insufficient prescraping	Do a better job of water-scraping dishes prior to washing
	Improper racking or placings	Rack dishes according to size and type in appropriate rack
Films	Water hardness	Use an external softening process. Use more detergent to provide internal conditioning. Use a chlorinated cleaner. Check temperature of wash and rinse water. Water maintained above recommended ranges may cause filming.
	Detergent carryover	Maintain adequate pressure and volume of rinse water.
	Improperly cleaned or rinsed equipment	Prevent scale buildup in equipment by adopting frequent and adequate cleaning practices. Maintain adequate water pressure and volume.
Greasy Films	Low pH Insufficient detergent Low water temperatures	Maintain adequate alkalinity to saponify greases. Check amount of detergent, water temperature.
	Improperly cleaned	Unclog all wash and rinse nozzles to provide proper equipment spray action. Clogged rinse nozzles may also interfere with wash tank overflow.
Streaking	Alkalinity in the water	Use an external treatment method to reduce alkalinity
Spotting	Rinse water hardness	Provide external or internal softening.
	Rinse water temperature too high or too low	Check rinse water temperature. Dishes may be flash drying, or water may be drying on dishes rather than drying off.
	Inadequate time between rinsing and storage	Allow sufficient time for air drying.
Foaming	Detergent	Change to a low sudsing product.
	Water too soft or too hard	Use an appropriate treatment method to adjust the condition of the water.
	Food soil	Adequately remove gross soil before washing. The decomposition of carbohydrates, proteins, or fats may cause foaming during the wash cycle.
	Wash temperature too low.	Increase wash temperature.

[1]"Food Service Sanitation Manual. Including a Model Food Service Sanitation Ordinance (1976 revision) USDHEW, PHS, FDA," a DHEW publication, No. (FDA) 78-2081. All NSF standards are compatible with those of the Food and Drug Administration.
[2]"National Sanitation Foundation Standard No. 3 For Commercial Spray Type Dishwashing Machines" (amended November 1979), prepared by the NSF Joint Committee on Food Equipment Standards.
[3]"Listing of Food Service Equipment, Standard No. 3," prepared by the National Sanitation Foundation.

Source: National Sanitation Foundation, *Cleaning and Sanitizing Workbook.*

(B) Sink compartments shall be large enough to accommodate immersion of the largest equipment and utensils. If equipment or utensils are too large for the warewashing sink, a warewashing machine or alternative equipment as specified in ¶ (C) of this section shall be used.

(C) *Alternative manual warewashing equipment may be used when there are special cleaning needs or constraints and the regulatory authority has approved the use of the alternative equipment. Alternative manual warewashing equipment may include:*

  (1)   High-pressure detergent sprayers;

  (2)   Low- or line-pressure spray detergent foamers;

  (3)   Other task-specific cleaning equipment;

  (4)   Brushes or other implements;

  (5)   2-compartment sinks as specified under ¶ (D) of this section; or

  (6)   Receptacles that substitute for the compartments of a multicompartment sink.

(D) A 2-compartment sink may be used only if:

  (1)   Its use is approved by the regulatory authority; and

  (2)   The nature of warewashing is limited to batch operations such as between cutting one type of raw meat and another or cleanup at the end of a shift, where the number of items cleaned is limited, and where the cleaning and sanitizing solutions are made up immediately before use and drained immediately after use. A 2-compartment sink may not be used for warewashing operations such as where cleaning and sanitizing solutions are used for a continuous or intermittent flow of kitchenware or tableware in an ongoing warewashing process.

4-301.13   Drainboards.

Drainboards, utensil racks, or tables large enough to accommodate all soiled and cleaned items that may accumulate during hours of operation shall be provided for necessary utensil holding before cleaning and after sanitizing.

4-501.14   Warewashing Equipment, Cleaning Frequency.

A warewashing machine; the compartments of sinks, basins, or other receptacles used for washing and rinsing equipment, utensils, or raw foods, or laundering wiping cloths; and drainboards or other equipment used to substitute for drainboards as specified in § 4-301.13 shall be cleaned:

  (A)   Before use;

  (B)   Throughout the day at a frequency necessary to prevent recontamination of equipment and utensils and to assure that the equipment performs its intended function; and

  (C)   If used, at least every 24 hours.

4-501.15   Warewashing Machines, Manufacturers' Operating Instructions.

(A) A warewashing machine and its auxiliary components shall be operated in accordance with the machine's data plate and other manufacturer's instructions.

(B) A warewashing machine's conveyor speed or automatic cycle times shall be maintained accurately timed in accordance with manufacturer's specifications.

4-501.16   Warewashing Sinks, Alternative Uses.

A warewashing sink may be used to wash wiping cloths, wash produce, or thaw food if the sink is cleaned as specified under § 4-501.14 before and after each time it is used to wash wiping cloths or wash produce or thaw food. Sinks used to wash or thaw food shall be sanitized as specified under Part 4-7 before and after using the sink to wash produce or thaw food.

4-501.17   Warewashing Equipment, Cleaning Agents.

The wash compartment of a sink, mechanical warewasher, or wash receptacle of alternative manual warewashing equipment as specified in ¶ 4-301.12(C), shall, when used for warewashing, contain a wash solution of soap, detergent, acid cleaner, alkaline cleaner, degreaser, abrasive cleaner, or other cleaning agent according to the cleaning agent manufacturer's label instructions.

4-501.18   Warewashing Equipment, Clean Solutions.

The wash, rinse, and sanitize solutions shall be maintained clean.

4-501.19   Manual Warewashing Equipment, Wash Solution Temperature.

The temperature of the wash solution shall be maintained at not less than 43°C (110°F) unless a different temperature is specified on the cleaning agent manufacturer's label instructions.

4-501.110   Mechanical Warewashing Equipment, Wash Solution Temperature.

(A) The temperature of the wash solution in spray type warewashers that use hot water to sanitize may not be less than:

   (1)   For a single tank, stationary rack, single temperature machine, 74°C (165°F);

   (2)   For a single tank, conveyor, dual temperature machine, 71°C (160°F);

   (3)   For a single tank, stationary rack, dual temperature machine, 66°C (150°F); or

   (4)   For a multitank, conveyor, multitemperature machine, 66°C (150°F).

(B) The temperature of the wash solution in spray-type warewashers that use chemicals to sanitize may not be less than 49°C (120°F).

4-501.111   Manual Warewashing Equipment, Hot Water Sanitization Temperatures.*

If immersion in hot water is used for sanitizing in a manual operation, the temperature of the water shall be maintained at 77°C (170°F) or above.

4-501.112   Mechanical Warewashing Equipment, Hot Water Sanitization Temperatures.

In a mechanical operation, the temperature of the fresh hot water sanitizing rinse as it enters the manifold may not be less than:

(A)   For a single tank, stationary rack, single temperature machine, 74°C (165°F); or

(B)   For all other machines, 82°C (180°F).

4-501.113   Mechanical Warewashing Equipment, Sanitization Pressure.

The flow pressure of the fresh hot water sanitizing rinse in a warewashing machine may not be less than 100 kilopascals (15 pounds per square inch) or more than 170 kilopascals (25 pounds per square inch) as measured in the water line immediately upstream from the fresh hot water sanitizing rinse control valve.

4-501.114   Manual and Mechanical Warewashing Equipment, Chemical Sanitization—Temperature, pH, Concentration, and Hardness.*

A chemical sanitizer used in a sanitizing solution for a manual or mechanical operation at exposure times specified in ¶ 4-703.11(C) shall be listed in 21 CFR 178.1010 Sanitizing solutions, shall be used in accordance with the EPA-approved manufacturer's label use instructions, and shall be used as follows:

(A)   A chlorine solution shall have a minimum temperature based on the concentration and pH of the solution as listed in the following chart;

Minimum Concentration	Minimum Temperature	
mg/L	pH 10 or less °C (°F)	pH 8 or less °C (°F)
25	49 (120)	49 (120)
50	38 (100)	24 (75)
100	13 (55)	13 (55)

(B)   An iodine solution shall have a:

(1)   Minimum temperature of 24°C (75°F),

(2)   pH of 5.0 or less, unless the manufacturer's use directions included in the labeling specify a higher pH limit of effectiveness, and

(3)   Concentration between 12.5 mg/L and 25 mg/L;

(C)   A quaternary ammonium compound solution shall:

   (1)   Have a minimum temperature of 24°C (75°F),

   (2)   Have a concentration as specified under § 7-204.11 and as indicated by the manufacturer's use directions included in the labeling, and

   (3)   Be used only in water with 500 mg/L hardness or less;

(D)   Other solutions of the chemicals specified in ¶¶ (A)–(C) of this section may be used if demonstrated to the regulatory authority to achieve sanitization and approved by the regulatory authority; or

(E)   Other chemical sanitizers may be used if they are applied in accordance with the manufacturer's use directions included in the labeling.

4-501.115   Manual Warewashing Equipment, Chemical Sanitization Using Detergent-Sanitizers.

If a detergent-sanitizer is used to sanitize in a cleaning and sanitizing procedure where there is no distinct water rinse between the washing and sanitizing steps, the agent applied in the cleaning step shall be the same detergent-sanitizer.

4-501.116   Warewashing Equipment, Determining Chemical Sanitizer Concentration.

Concentration of the sanitizing solution shall be accurately determined by using a test kit or other device.

4-204.113   Warewashing Machine, Data Plate Operating Specifications.

A warewashing machine shall be provided with an easily accessible and readable data plate affixed to the machine by the manufacturer that indicates the machine's design and operating specifications including the:

(A)   Temperatures required for washing, rinsing, and sanitizing;

(B)   Pressure required for the fresh water sanitizing rinse *unless the machine is designed to use only a pumped sanitizing rinse;* and

(C)   Conveyor speed for conveyor machines or cycle time for stationary rack machines.

4-204.114   Warewashing Machines, Internal Baffles.

Warewashing machine wash and rinse tanks shall be equipped with baffles, curtains, or other means to minimize internal cross contamination of the solutions in wash and rinse tanks.

4-204.115   Warewashing Machines, Temperature Measuring Devices.

A warewashing machine shall be equipped with a temperature measuring device that indicates the temperature of the water:

(A)   In each wash and rinse tank; and

(B)   As the water enters the hot water sanitizing final rinse manifold or in the chemical sanitizing solution tank.

4-204.116   Manual Warewashing Equipment, Heaters and Baskets.

If hot water is used for sanitization in manual warewashing operations, the sanitizing compartment of the sink shall be:

(A)   Designed with an integral heating device that is capable of maintaining water at a temperature not less than 77°C (171°F); and

(B)   Provided with a rack or basket to allow complete immersion of equipment and utensils into the hot water.

4-204.117   Warewashing Machines, Flow Pressure Valve.

A 6.4 millimeter or one-fourth inch Iron Pipe Size (IPS) valve shall be provided immediately upstream from the fresh hot water sanitizing rinse control valve of a warewashing machine to permit checking the flow pressure of the sanitizing rinse. *This section does not apply to a machine that uses only a pumped sanitizing rinse.*

4-204.118   Warewashing Sinks and Drainboards, Self-Draining.

Sinks and drainboards of warewashing sinks and machines shall be self-draining.

4-204.119   Equipment Compartments, Drainage.

Equipment compartments that are subject to accumulation of moisture due to conditions such as condensation, food or beverage drip, or water from melting ice shall be sloped to an outlet that allows complete draining.

4-501.11   (Equipment) Good Repair and Proper Adjustment.

(A) Equipment shall be maintained in a state of repair and condition that meets the requirements specified in Parts 4-1 and 4-2.

(B) Equipment components such as doors, seals, hinges, fasteners, and kick plates shall be kept intact, tight, and adjusted in accordance with manufacturers' specifications.

6-501.11   (Premises, Buildings, Systems, Rooms, Fixtures, Equipment, Devices, and Materials) Repairing.

The physical facilities shall be maintained in good repair.

6-501.12   Cleaning, Frequency and Restrictions.

(A) The physical facilities shall be cleaned as often as necessary to keep them clean.

(B) Cleaning shall be done during periods when the least amount of food is exposed such as after closing. *This requirement does not apply to cleaning that is necessary due to a spill or other accident.*

4-602.12   Cooking Equipment.

(A) The food-contact surfaces of cooking equipment shall be cleaned at least every 24 hours. *This section does not apply to hot oil cooking and filtering equipment if it is cleaned as specified under Subparagraph 4-602.11(D)(5).*

(B) The cavities and door seals of microwave ovens shall be cleaned at least every 24 hours by using the manufacturer's recommended cleaning procedure.

4-602.13   Nonfood-Contact Surfaces.

Nonfood-contact surfaces of equipment shall be cleaned at a frequency necessary to preclude accumulation of soil residues.

4-603.11   Dry Cleaning.

(A) If used, dry cleaning methods such as brushing, scraping, and vacuuming shall contact only surfaces that are soiled with dry food residues that are not potentially hazardous.

(B) Cleaning equipment used in dry cleaning food-contact surfaces may not be used for any other purpose.

4-603.12   Precleaning.

(A) Food debris on equipment and utensils shall be scraped over a waste disposal unit, scupper, or garbage receptacle or shall be removed in a warewashing machine with a prewash cycle.

(B) If necessary for effective cleaning, utensils and equipment shall be preflushed, scrubbed with abrasives, or presoaked.

4-603.13   Loading of Soiled Items, Warewashing Machines.

Soiled items to be cleaned in a warewashing machine shall be loaded into racks, trays, or baskets or onto conveyors in a position that:

(A)   Exposes the items to the unobstructed spray from all cycles; and

(B)   Allows the items to drain.

4-603.14   Wet Cleaning.

(A) Equipment food-contact surfaces and utensils shall be effectively washed to remove or completely loosen soils by using the manual or mechanical means necessary such as the application of detergents containing wetting agents and emulsifiers; acid, alkaline, or abrasive cleaners; hot water; brushes; scouring pads; or high-pressure sprays.

(B) The washing procedures selected shall be based on the type and purpose of the equipment or utensil, and on the type of soil to be removed.

4-603.15   Washing, Alternative Manual Warewashing Equipment.

If washing in sink compartments or a warewashing machine is impractical such as when the equipment is fixed or the utensils are too large, washing shall be done by using alternative manual warewashing equipment as specified in ¶ 4-301.12(C) in accordance with the following procedures:

(A) Equipment shall be disassembled as necessary to allow access of the detergent solution to all parts;

(B) Equipment components and utensils shall be scraped or rough cleaned to remove food particle accumulation; and

(C) Equipment and utensils shall be washed as specified under ¶ 4-603.14(A).

4-603.16   Rinsing Procedures.

Except as specified under ¶ (B) of this section, washed utensils and equipment shall be rinsed so that abrasives are removed and cleaning chemicals are removed or diluted through the use of water or a detergent-sanitizer solution by using one of the following procedures:

(A) Use of a distinct, separate water rinse after washing and before sanitizing if using:

(1) A 3-compartment sink,

(2) Alternative manual warewashing equipment equivalent to a 3-compartment sink as specified under Subparagraph 4-301.12(C)(1), or

(3) A 3-step washing, rinsing, and sanitizing procedure in a warewashing system for CIP equipment;

(B) Use of a detergent-sanitizer as specified under § 4-501.115 if using:

(1) Alternative warewashing equipment as specified under ¶ 4-301.12(C) that is approved for use with a detergent-sanitizer, or

(2) A warewashing system for CIP equipment;

(C) Use of a nondistinct water rinse that is integrated in the hot water sanitization immersion step of a 2-compartment sink operation;

(D) If using a warewashing machine that does not recycle the sanitizing solution as specified in ¶ (E) of this section, or alternative manual warewashing equipment such as sprayers, use of a nondistinct water rinse that is:

(1) Integrated in the application of the sanitizing solution, and

(2) Wasted immediately after each application; or

(E) If using a warewashing machine that recycles the sanitizing solution for use in the next wash cycle, use of a nondistinct water rinse that is integrated in the application of the sanitizing solution.

4-701.11   Food-Contact Surfaces and Utensils.*

Equipment food-contact surfaces and utensils shall be sanitized.

4-702.11   Before Use After Cleaning.

Utensils and food-contact surfaces of equipment shall be sanitized before use after cleaning.

4-703.11   Hot Water and Chemical.*

After being cleaned, equipment food-contact surfaces and utensils shall be sanitized in:

(A)   Hot water manual operations by immersion for at least 30 seconds as specified under § 4-501.111;

(B)   Hot water mechanical operations by being cycled through equipment that is set up as specified under §§ 4-501.15 and 4-501.112–.113 and achieving a utensil surface temperature of 71°C (160°F) as measured by an irreversible registering temperature indicator; or

(C)   Chemical manual or mechanical operations, including the application of sanitizing chemicals by immersion, manual swabbing, brushing, or pressure spraying methods, using a solution as specified under § 4-501.114 by providing:

(1)   An exposure time of at least 10 seconds for a chlorine solution,

(2)   An exposure time of at least 30 seconds for other chemical sanitizer solutions, or

(3)   An exposure time used in relationship with a combination of temperature, concentration, and pH that, when evaluated for efficacy, yields sanitization as defined in Subparagraph 1-201.10(B)(69).

4-901.11   Equipment and Utensils, Air-Drying Required.

(A) Except as specified in ¶ (C) of this section, after cleaning and sanitizing, equipment and utensils may not be cloth-dried.

(B) Equipment and utensils may be air-dried or used after adequate draining as specified in ¶ (a) of 21 CFR 178.1010 Sanitizing solutions, before contact with food.

(C) *Utensils that have been air-dried may be polished with cloths that are maintained clean and dry.*

4-903.11   (Storing) Equipment, Utensils, Linens, and Single-Service and Single-Use Articles.

(A) Except as specified in ¶ (D) of this section, cleaned equipment and utensils, laundered linens, and single-service and single-use articles shall be stored:

(1)   In a clean, dry location;

(2)   Where they are not exposed to splash, dust, or other contamination; and

(3)   At least 15 cm (6 inches) above the floor.

(B) Clean equipment and utensils shall be stored as specified under ¶ (A) of this section and shall be stored:

    (1)   In a self-draining position; and

    (2)   Covered or inverted.

(C) Single-service and single-use articles shall be stored as specified under ¶ (A) of this section and shall be kept in the original protective package or stored by using other means that afford protection from contamination until used.

(D) *Items that are kept in closed packages may be stored less than 15 cm (6 inches) above the floor on dollies, pallets, racks, and skids that are designed as provided under §4-204.121.*

4-903.12   Prohibitions.

(A) Except as specified in ¶ (B) of this section, cleaned and sanitized equipment, utensils, laundered linens, and single-service and single-use articles may not be stored:

    (1)   In locker rooms;

    (2)   In toilet rooms;

    (3)   In garbage rooms;

    (4)   In mechanical rooms;

    (5)   Under sewer lines that are not shielded to intercept potential drips;

    (6)   Under leaking water lines including leaking automatic fire sprinkler heads or under lines on which water has condensed;

    (7)   Under open stairwells; or

    (8)   Under other sources of contamination.

(B) *Laundered linens and single-service and single-use articles that are packaged or in a facility such as a cabinet may be stored in a locker room.*

Source: FDA 1993 *Food Code.*

Staff members who operate dishwashing machines should be well trained. Supervision of the warewashing function is important; a dish machine is expensive to purchase and operate. Dish machine and chemical manufacturers usually provide free materials and technical assistance to help train dishwashing staff.

Cleaning and maintenance tools other than warewashing equipment (such as mops and buckets) must be stored so that they are easily accessible and do not contaminate food, utensils, or linens. Such equipment may not be cleaned in food production, hand-washing, or warewashing sinks.

Preventive maintenance of all equipment is essential to reduce risks and control long-term costs. Like cleaning activities, maintenance should be based on a survey of

Exhibit 9.7 Life Cycle of the Common Housefly

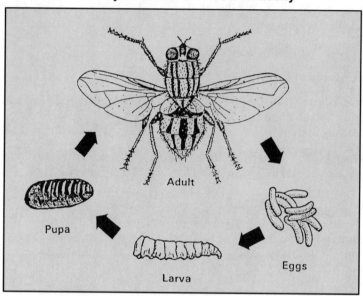

Source: H. D. Pratt, K. S. Littig, and H. G. Scott, *Flies of Public Health Importance and Their Control,* 1975, p. 5.

needs and performed according to a schedule. The schedule should indicate all services and equipment item needs. Equipment maintenance should always be performed according to the manufacturer's recommendations. Maintenance operations should be recorded in a maintenance log, which should list the service, date, and replacement parts, if appropriate. Assigning responsibility for all equipment maintenance to one individual or position is a good control measure. If this is impossible, consider hiring a contract service firm to maintain all equipment.

Pest Control

Insects and rodents are disease-carrying pests that contaminate food products. Some pests contaminate foods with disease agents; a housefly, for example, can carry over six million microbes on its body and many more internally. Other pests (**stored-food insects**) render food products unfit for human consumption. The pests of public health significance are flies, cockroaches, rats, mice, small beetles, and moths.

Insects

The common housefly (*Musca domestica*) has been known to carry typhoid fever, leprosy, amoebic dysentery, tuberculosis, and bubonic plague. Flies eat many of the same foods that humans eat.

The female fly lays about 100 to 120 eggs at a time. In warm, moist, decaying environments, the eggs hatch in as little as eight hours. Within a week or two, the larvae become adult flies. A single fly can produce as many as 14 generations in a single summer season. Exhibit 9.7 shows the life cycle of a common housefly.

Exhibit 9.8 Common Species of Cockroaches in the United States (Females)

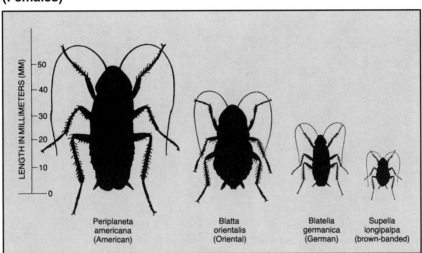

Periplaneta americana (American)   Blatta orientalis (Oriental)   Blatella germanica (German)   Supella longipalpa (brown-banded)

Source: H. D. Pratt, K. S. Littig, and H. G. Scott, *Household and Stored-Food Insects of Public Health Importance and Their Significance*, 1979, pp. 7–8.

Flies have six legs, each with a claw and a sticky pad. The claws enable flies to cling to rough surfaces, while the sticky pads allow them to walk on smooth surfaces at any angle. Each foot pad is a germ-laden surface that can contaminate food.

A fly can only consume fluids. It draws liquid foods through its proboscis, a fleshy sucking tube at the bottom of its face. In order to eat solid food, a fly must first dissolve the solids by regurgitating some of its stomach fluids. This process can contaminate food products with pathogens.

Cockroaches are ubiquitous and troublesome pests. Four species account for most cockroach problems in American food establishments. These four species are shown in Exhibit 9.8.

The German cockroach (*Blatella germanica*) is the commonest species and is found primarily in the northern United States. It is gray and approximately ¾ of an inch (19 mm) long. It prefers warm, dry areas with ready access to water (such as kitchens, storerooms, and bathrooms). The German cockroach is resistant to most chemical killers.

The brown-banded cockroach (*Supella longipalpa*) is approximately ½ of an inch (13 mm) long and has two brown or yellow bands on its wings. The brown-banded cockroach is found in most parts of the United States and Canada. It prefers warm, dark places and often hides in electric clocks, radios, television sets, and under booth seats.

The Oriental cockroach (*Blatta orientalis*) is black and approximately ¾ to 1½ inches (19 to 38 mm) long. The Oriental cockroach usually lives in sewers, in cool, damp basements, and under sinks and refrigerators. It has a strong repulsive odor.

The American cockroach (*Periplaneta americana*) is red to dark brown and about 1½ to 2 inches (38 to 51 mm) long. The American cockroach can be found in warm, humid environments such as boiler rooms, warm basements, kitchens, and garbage areas. This species consumes sweets and beer, so it may also be attracted to empty beverage bottles and cans.

Exhibit 9.9 Common Rodent Pests

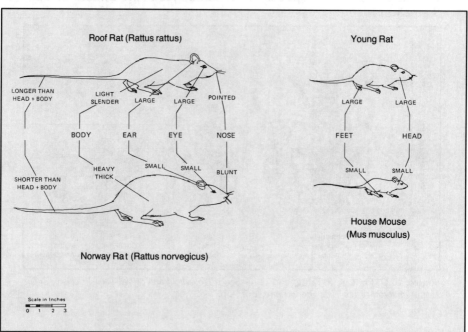

Source: H. D. Pratt and R. Z. Brown, *Biological Factors in Domestic Rodent Control*, 1977, p. 4.

Beetles and moths are classified as stored food insects because they destroy stored food products. Some species of beetles attack leather products, woolens, and food products such as flour, spices, cookies, and dried fruits. Other beetles prefer dry grains and vegetables such as corn, rice, peas, beans, and wheat. Moths, commonly known to eat wool, may also damage food; some species destroy wheat, corn, and other grains.

Rodents

Rats and mice carry pathogenic microbes and destroy food products in storage. The roof rat, the Norway rat, and the house mouse are responsible for most rodent problems in food establishments in the United States. These three rodents are illustrated in Exhibit 9.9.

The roof rat (*Rattus rattus*) is either black or brown with a pointed nose and a slender body. The roof rat weighs from 4 to 12 ounces (112 to 336 g) and is 14 to 18 inches (35.6 to 45.7 cm) long, including the tail. It is found in the southeastern and western United States.

The Norway rat (*Rattus norvegicus*) has a blunt nose, a thick, heavy body, and has red to gray-brown fur. It weighs from 10 to 17 ounces (280 to 476 g) and measures 13 to 18 inches (33 to 45.7 cm) in length. The Norway rat is found throughout most of North America.

The house mouse (*Mus musculus*) ranges in color from gray to brown. It has a pointed nose and a small body weighing from $1/2$ to $3/4$ of an ounce (14 to 21 g) and measuring 6 to 7 $1/2$ inches (15.2 to 19.1 cm) in length. The house mouse is more widely distributed in the environment than the other two rodents.

Rodents tend to nest in safe areas near food and water. They prefer quiet places like basements. All three of these rodents can climb and jump well and are exceptional swimmers, especially the rats. Their front teeth (incisors), used for gnawing, grow continuously. Rodents gnaw wood, cinder block, aluminum, paperboard, cloth sacks, and even lead pipes to keep their teeth short. If not controlled, these rodents will consume a wide variety of foods. They have been known to eat grain, meat, eggs, potatoes, and even citrus fruits. They often forage for food in garbage.

Rodents have been linked to a variety of human diseases. Salmonellosis can be transmitted through food contaminated by rat or mouse droppings. Rat-bite fever is caused by a pathogenic species of *Streptobacillus* present in rats. All three rodents can carry leptospirosis (Weil's disease) and spread trichinosis by contaminating hog feed. Rats can transmit murine typhus fever to humans, and the house mouse may transmit rickettsial pox.

Control Measures

A successful pest control program has two parts: basic environmental sanitation and effective chemical control. **Basic environmental sanitation** includes methods of keeping rodents and insects out of the food establishment. All materials that serve as food or shelter for pests should either be made pest-resistant or removed from the facility and its immediate vicinity.

Prompt refuse removal—at least twice each week—is critical. Refuse storage areas must be kept clean. Prompt cleanup of spilled food in storage and production areas also minimizes problems. All staff members should be trained to clean as they complete a job.

Doors should be screened and fitted with self-closing devices. Windows should also be screened, and screens should be maintained in a good state of repair. Toilet and lavatory facilities should be kept clean.

Food storage areas must be kept clean as well. Shelves in storage areas should be cleaned at least twice each week. All deliveries should be examined for signs of infestation. Stock rotation (FIFO) also reduces problems. Opened packages should either be used immediately or their contents stored in covered, dated, and labeled containers. Regular inspections can identify problems before food products become unusable.

Cool, dry storage conditions inhibit insect and rodent breeding. Food products in storage areas should be at least two inches (5.1 cm) from walls and six inches (15.2 cm) from the floor. This reduces harborage areas and improves ventilation. Aisles at least two feet (.6 m) wide also reduce harborage areas and allow for easy cleaning. Floor areas in food storage rooms are to be swept and mopped at least twice daily.

Facilities can be made rodent-resistant by closing small openings. A rat, for example, can crawl through a $1/2$-inch (1.3 cm) opening, while a mouse can penetrate an opening as small as $1/4$ of an inch (.6 cm). Openings around fans, doors, windows, pipes, floor drains, and foundations can be effectively blocked with a combination of brick, mortar, concrete, and galvanized hardware cloth.

Rodent traps are preferable to rodenticides. Snap traps kill or injure mice and rats, while live traps capture and hold live animals for later disposal. Traps can effectively deter expanding rodent populations. Rodent traps should be checked frequently (at least once every 24 hours). Cockroach traps are effective for slight infestations. They can help locate problem areas within the facility.

In addition to basic environmental sanitation, food service operations can control pests with chemicals. Always remember that pesticides are toxic chemicals. If improperly applied, they can be harmful to humans. It is therefore easier and safer to prevent infestation than to try to eliminate pests after they have reproduced unchecked. Pesticides can only be used safely in food establishments by following instructions exactly.

Automatic insecticide dispensers, which spray pesticides at regular intervals, should be installed according to the manufacturer's recommendations. Federal, state, and local authorities approve only certain chemicals for use in these dispensers.

Devices that electrocute flying insects are effective; however, they may only be used if they are positioned so that dead insects do not contaminate food, food-contact surfaces, or clean equipment and utensils. These devices must be fitted with an "escape-resistant" tray which is emptied at least weekly. These devices cannot be used in food storage, preparation, or service areas. There is little scientific data available to support the effectiveness of ultrasonic pest control devices. Most regulatory authorities do not recommend the use of this equipment.

The FDA states:

"General use pesticide" means a pesticide that is not classified by EPA for restricted use as specified in 40 CFR 152.175.

"Restricted use pesticide" means a pesticide product that contains the active ingredients specified in 40 CFR 152.175 Pesticides classified for restricted use, and that is limited to use by or under the direct supervision of a certified applicator.

6-501.111   Controlling Pests.*

(A) Insects, rodents, and other pests shall be controlled as specified in ¶ (B) of this section to minimize their presence:

(1)   Within the physical facility and its contents; and

(2)   On the contiguous land or property under the control of the permit holder.[N]

(B) The presence of insects, rodents, and other pests shall be controlled by:

(1)   Routinely inspecting the premises for evidence of pests;[N]

(2)   Using methods, if pests are found, such as trapping devices or extermination as specified under §§ 7-206.11–7-206.13;[N] and

(3)   Eliminating harborage conditions.[N]

6-501.112   Removing Trapped or Dead Birds, Insects, Rodents, and Other Pests.

Trapped or dead birds, insects, rodents, and other pests shall be removed from control devices and the premises at a frequency that prevents their accumulation, decomposition, or the attraction of pests.

6-202.13   Insect Control Devices, Design and Installation.

(A) Devices that are used to electrocute flying insects and that may impel insects or insect fragments shall be:

(1)   Designed to have "escape-resistant" trays; and

(2)   Installed so that:

(a)   The devices are not located over a food preparation area, and

(b)   Dead insects and insect fragments are prevented from falling on or being impelled onto exposed food; clean equipment, utensils, and linens; and unwrapped single-service and single-use articles.

(B)   Devices used to trap insects by adherence may not be installed above exposed food; clean equipment, utensils, and linens; or unwrapped single-service and single-use articles.

Source: FDA 1993 *Food Code.*

All pesticides used in a food service operation must be clearly labeled and stored in a locked area away from food products and other non-pesticide chemicals (detergents, sanitizers, oven cleaners, and silver polishes, for example). The label must show the product has been registered with the Environmental Protection Agency; the chemical manufacturer is responsible for this registration. The EPA only approves pesticides that are, if used properly, harmless to humans, plants, livestock, wildlife, and the environment.

Some pesticides (restricted-use) can be applied only by certified applicators. General use residual pesticides may be applied to ceilings, floors, and walls. They are not allowed in food storage, production, or service areas. Spot residual pesticides are applied in an area not to exceed two square feet (.19 sq m) to walls, ceilings, floors, and the undersides of equipment. They are also prohibited near food and for use on utensils and food-contact surfaces. Some pesticides are applied into cracks and crevices with a special nozzle. In all cases, the exterminator must guard against contaminating food, equipment, or utensils with the pesticide.

An in-house chemical pest control program requires properly trained staff members. It is safer and easier to contract a commercial exterminator who is specially trained to handle toxic chemicals. A professional exterminator can be scheduled for monthly visits or more frequent applications if there is evidence of infestation. Of course, a pest control professional is a waste of money if pests can easily enter, nest, and obtain food in the food establishment. Food establishments should therefore concentrate their efforts on basic environmental sanitation.

Pest control companies fall into one of two general categories: application companies and integrated pest management companies. Both types must be licensed. The integrated pest management company usually works with management on a long-term approach to pest control.[1]

The integrated pest management company usually conducts an audit of the pest population. This audit identifies the pests present, their distribution throughout the facilities, and the factors that contribute to existing and potential problems. The company then presents management with an outline of what is to be done and why it is necessary, including the pesticides to be used and the application time and methods.

The company then applies the selected pesticide and uses a pest monitoring system to measure results, periodically reporting the results to management. These reports help management and the company evaluate the program's effectiveness.

There are several factors to consider when selecting a pest control company. Check with your local health department and area food service operators for references. Find out if all staff members are licensed and bonded, how often the company will visit your operation, the extent of chemical application, and the follow-up schedule. It is a good idea to sign a contract that states exactly which services will be performed and how much they will cost. Follow-up inspections should be scheduled at least monthly.

Cleaning, Maintenance, and Change

Cleaning and maintenance technology is evolving rapidly. Technological developments include low-temperature dishwashing machines, new cleaners and sanitizers, and new materials. These advances demand a periodic re-evaluation of the cleaning and maintenance program in a food service business. Managers can keep abreast of changes in cleaning and maintenance technology by reading trade publications, attending trade shows and seminars, and communicating with suppliers.

Other changes include the passage of federal and state "right-to-know" legislation requiring employers to inform their staff members about hazardous chemicals they may need to handle. Many cleaners and sanitizers are included in this category.

Cleaning, Maintenance, and the SRM Program

The final control point, cleaning and maintenance, can add to or reduce the risks of running a food establishment. Unsafe chemical handling, storage, and usage can add unnecessary risks.

Staff members are largely responsible for reducing the risks of cleaning and maintaining equipment and inventory. Staff orientation and initial training, followed by ongoing training programs to reinforce critical items, is the key to reducing risks. Standards established by a cooperative effort between management and staff members help ensure risk reduction. Equipment must be frequently cleaned, sanitized, and maintained. Equipment must also be used correctly in day-to-day operations. The SRM program applied to this control point reduces risks to owners, guests, and staff members alike.

Summary

The cleaning and maintenance control point is an important component of food protection and risk management. Cleaning and maintenance needs should be carefully determined. Staff members can then be assigned regularly scheduled cleaning jobs.

Cleaners and sanitizers are toxic chemicals that must be stored and used safely. These chemicals, as well as cleaning equipment, must be used properly to achieve the best results. Equipment must be maintained in good repair.

A variety of disease-carrying insects and rodents can invade a food service facility. Pest control requires both basic environmental sanitation and effective chemical control. Prevention is the best approach to pest management. It is always easier to prevent the entry of pests than it is to destroy a population that has taken up residence in the building.

Endnotes

1. This information is based on a discussion with Louis Keenan, RPE, President, Metro Pest Management Consultants, Denver, Colorado.

Key Terms

acid-anionic surfactant • basic environmental sanitation • chlorine-based sanitizer • cleaning • iodine-based sanitizer (iodophor) • phenolic sanitizer • quaternary ammonium compounds (QUATS) • sanitization • sanitizers • stored-food insects

Discussion Questions

1. What are some of the common types of cleaning agents used in food establishments?

2. How does sanitization differ from cleaning? Can you identify five types of sanitizers?

3. What are the major safety precautions that must be taken in handling cleaners and sanitizers?

4. Why are written cleaning procedures important?

5. How are pots, pans, and utensils typically cleaned and sanitized?

6. How often should the operation of commercial dishwashers be tested? What types of regular maintenance are required?

7. What are the advantages of using chemical sanitizing machines?

8. What are some of the physical and behavioral characteristics of common pests? What are their preferred environments?

9. A pest control program for food establishments involves what two parts?

10. What are the advantages of contracting with an integrated pest management company?

Checklist for Cleaning and Maintenance

Inventory

_____ Staff members responsible for cleaning and sanitization are trained to understand the major types of cleaners and sanitizers.

_____ Cleaners and sanitizers are not mixed in-house.

_____ Cleaning and sanitizing chemicals are always used in the concentrations recommended by the manufacturer.

____ Cleaners and sanitizers are clearly labeled and stored in a locked area used for no other purpose.

People

____ All food service staff members are trained to understand their cleaning and maintenance responsibilities.

____ All food service staff members understand and follow proper cleaning and maintenance procedures.

____ Supervisors ask staff members to help identify cleaning and maintenance needs and develop schedules.

____ Staff members receive initial and ongoing training in upholding the operation's cleaning and maintenance standards.

Equipment

____ Equipment, utensils, and tableware are cleaned, sanitized, stored, and used so as to prevent cross-contamination.

____ Manual cleaning and sanitization of equipment and utensils are done in a three-compartment sink.

____ The manual warewashing area is designed to facilitate holding, scraping and pre-soaking, washing, rinsing, and sanitizing.

____ Equipment, utensils, and tableware are air-dried before storage.

____ Equipment, utensils, and tableware are stored in self-draining positions at least six inches (15.2 cm) from the floor.

____ Staff members understand cleaning procedures for equipment, utensils, and tableware.

____ Mechanical warewashing equipment is regularly serviced by a qualified person.

____ Washing, rinsing, and sanitizing times and temperatures are monitored regularly.

____ All mechanical warewashing equipment (such as pot washers, glass washers, under-counter dish machines) are regularly cleaned and maintained.

____ Preventive maintenance programs (including schedules) are established and routinely followed.

____ A separate storage area is maintained for cleaning equipment.

Pest Control

____ Basic environmental sanitation is used to keep insects and rodents out of the facility.

_____ Effective chemical control is used to rid the facility of insects and rodents.

_____ The pest control company is selected after checking references with the local health department and food service operators.

_____ Contracted chemical control companies are scheduled for follow-up inspections at least monthly.

SRM Program

_____ Chemicals are carefully handled, stored, and used.

_____ Food service staff members are trained to maintain standards and reduce risks during cleaning and maintenance.

_____ Adequate facilities and equipment are present and used, and are frequently cleaned, sanitized, and maintained to reduce risks at the cleaning and maintenance control point.

Case Study

Using the menu item you selected in Chapter 5, continue with the cleaning and maintenance control point. Present the procedures for manually or mechanically cleaning and sanitizing the equipment and utensils used to store, prepare, cook, and serve your menu item.

Your development of this case study will, in part, depend on the menu item that you selected and developed in the previous cases. If you are presently employed in a food establishment, you may wish to choose a current menu item or one that is under consideration for addition to the menu.

An SRM Program Example: Whitefish and the Cleaning and Maintenance Control Point

People involved in the cleaning and maintenance of equipment and utensils used to store, prepare, cook, and serve the whitefish have been trained in cleaning procedures, including the proper use of chemicals. Equipment is maintained regularly. The cooking and serving utensils are cleaned and sanitized in a mechanical dish machine. Other equipment is cleaned and sanitized manually. Insects and rodents are controlled by basic environmental sanitation and by a pest control company on a contract basis.

References

Avery, Arthur C. "Dishwashing, Clean and Simple." *Cooking for Profit,* January 15, 1989, pp. 4–5.

Beer, Ira B. "Warewashing—Choosing the Right Features." *Cooking for Profit,* May 15, 1986, pp. 15–17.

Bernstein, Charles. "Garbage Crisis: Operators Must Act Now." *Nation's Restaurant News,* June 26, 1989, p. F-3.

Bertgnoli, Lisa. "Next to Godliness." *Restaurants & Institutions,* May 27, 1987, pp. 238–239.

Caprione, C. "Sparkle! It's Top Priority." *NRA News,* February 1983, pp. 26–29.

Carules, Alan. "Pest Control: Know How Much to Specify." *Restaurants & Institutions,* March 19, 1986, p. 227.

"Chemicals for Cleaning: Weigh the Advantages." *Institutions/Volume Feeding,* February 15, 1976, p. 55.

Cichy, R. F. "Chemical Cleaning Agents." *Restaurant Business,* July 1, 1987, p. 102.

———. "Choosing the Right Cleaning Agent." *Restaurant Business,* May 20, 1985, pp. 104, 108.

———. "Floor Story." *Restaurant Business,* May 1, 1989, p. 240.

D'Ambrosio, Elizabeth. "Keep It Clean." *Restaurant Business,* May 20, 1988, p. 84.

"Dishwashers and Water Heaters." *Restaurants & Institutions,* February 19, 1986, p. 247.

"Disposing of Waste Disposal Headaches." *Institutions/Volume Feeding,* September 1, 1974, pp. 31–32.

"Don't Let Maintenance Bug You." *Institutions/Volume Feeding,* April 15, 1976, p. 57.

Dunsmore, D. G. "Bacteriological Control of Food Equipment Surfaces by Cleaning Systems, Part VI: Detergent Effects." *Journal of Food Protection,* January 1981, pp. 15–20.

Durocher, Joseph. "Warewashing Systems." *Restaurant Business,* April 10, 1989, pp. 148, 150.

Eaton, W. V. "How Sanitary Conditions Affect Food Service Facility Design and Layout." *Food Service Marketing,* June 1981, p. 46.

Faulkner, E. "Ventilation: A Lot of Hot Air." *Restaurants and Institutions,* November 15, 1982, pp. 137–139.

Feldman, Edwin B. ed. *Programmed Cleaning Guide for the Environmental Sanitarian.* New York: The Soap and Detergent Association, 1984.

Finn, M. "Are Profits Going Out With the Garbage?" *Hospitality Food and Lodging,* January 1974, p. 69.

———. "Light Up for Safety—and Savings." *Hospitality Food and Lodging,* October 1975, pp. L65–L67.

Food and Drug Administration, Center for Food Safety and Applied Nutrition, Retail Food Protection Branch. *Interpretation: Equipment and Utensil Cleaning and Sanitization—pH of Iodine Sanitizing Solutions,* July 8, 1985.

———. *Interpretation: Equipment and Utensil Cleaning and Sanitization—Temperature of Chemical Sanitizing Rinse,* March 21, 1984.

———. *Interpretation: Equipment and Utensil Cleaning and Sanitization—Temperature of Chemical Sanitizing Rinse,* August 29, 1985.

———. *Interpretation: Handwashing Supplies—Bar Soaps as Fomites,* July 19, 1984.

———. *Interpretation: Insect and Rodent Control—Devices for Electrocuting Flying Insects,* August 14, 1986.

———. *Interpretation: Insect and Rodent Control—Devices for Electrocuting Flying Insects,* September 3, 1987.

———. *Interpretation: Insect and Rodent Control—Effectiveness of Ultrasonic Pest Control Devices,* March 30, 1984.

———. *Interpretation: Poisonous or Toxic Materials—Automatic Insecticide Dispensers,* April 27, 1984.

———. *Interpretation: Poisonous or Toxic Materials—Storage,* May 3, 1984.

"Foodservice Flows with Water Treatment System." *Restaurants & Institutions,* February 18, 1987, p. 149.

Food Service Recommended Field Evaluation Procedures for Spray-Type Dishwashing Machines. Ann Arbor, Mich.: National Sanitation Foundation, 1982.

Forwalter, J. "1980 Selection Guide—Cleaning and Sanitizing Compounds." *Food Processing,* February 1980, pp. 40–43.

Giampietro, F. N. "Preventive Maintenance—The Best Cure for Trouble." *Restaurant Business,* December 1977, pp. 101–102.

Gillespie, R. W. "Insect and Rodent Control in Food Establishments." *Dairy and Food Sanitation,* February 1981, pp. 58–61.

———. "Plumbing Hazards in the Food Industry." *Dairy and Food Sanitation,* January 1982, pp. 14–17.

Haverland, H. "Cleaning and Sanitizing Operations." *Dairy and Food Sanitation,* August 1981, pp. 331–335.

Kooser, R. "Sanitation and Facilities Design." *Restaurant Hospitality,* December 1981, p. 74.

Lancaster, D. L. *Cleaning and Sanitizing Workbook.* Ann Arbor, Mich.: National Sanitation Foundation, undated.

"New Exhaust Systems Save $$$ and Btu's." *Cooking for Profit,* August 1977, pp. 18–20.

Patterson, Patt. "Preventive Maintenance Cuts Equipment Costs, But Who Does It?" *Nation's Restaurant News,* July 4, 1988, p. 61.

Pratt, H. D., and R. Z. Brown. *Biological Factors in Domestic Rodent Control.* Atlanta, Ga.: Centers for Disease Control, Public Health Service, U.S. Department of Health, Education, and Welfare, 1977.

Pratt, H. D.; K. S. Littig.; and H. G. Scott. *Flies of Public Health Importance and Their Control.* Atlanta, Ga.: Centers for Disease Control, Public Health Service, U.S. Department of Health, Education, and Welfare, 1975.

———. *Household and Stored-Food Insects of Public Health Importance and Their Control.* Atlanta, Ga.: Centers for Disease Control, Public Health Service, U.S. Department of Health, Education, and Welfare, 1979.

Sanitation Aspects of Food Service Facility Plan Preparation and Review—Reference Guide. Ann Arbor, Mich.: National Sanitation Foundation, 1978.

Spray-Type Dishwashing Machines—Standard No. 3. Ann Arbor, Mich.: National Sanitation Foundation, 1976.

Stein, Gary M. "About Creepy, Crawly, Squirmy Things and How to Keep Them Out." *Restaurants USA,* August 1989, pp. 26–28.

Swientek, R. J. "Insect Control Update." *Food Processing,* February 1982, pp. 34–36.

Wareham, E. A. "Proper Lighting Helps Ambience, Energy Use." *Restaurants & Institutions,* October 1, 1986, p. 174.

Zaccarelli, Herman. "Decrease Costs with Preventive Maintenance." *Restaurants & Institutions,* January 22, 1986, p. 199.

REVIEW QUIZ

When you feel you have covered all of the material in this chapter, answer these questions. Choose the *best* answer. Check your answers with the correct ones found on the Review Quiz Answer Key at the end of this book.

1. Which of the following is an example of organic soil?

    a. food residue
    b. airborne dust
    c. mineral scale
    d. all of the above

2. Degreasers are usually:

    a. skin irritants.
    b. used to remove fats and oils from pots and pans.
    c. fomites.
    d. highly acidic.

3. One of the advantages of using quaternary ammonium compounds (QUATS) is:

    a. their low cost.
    b. their ability to eliminate and prevent odors.
    c. that they leave behind no residue.
    d. that they are compatible with most detergents.

4. Which of the following is *not* a characteristic of iodine-based sanitizers?

    a. They have a long shelf life.
    b. They do *not* deteriorate easily.
    c. They do *not* stain.
    d. They are effective in hard water.

5. Mixing ammonia with bleach produces:

    a. an effective sanitizing compound.
    b. a deadly gas.
    c. an inexpensive all-purpose cleaner.
    d. a harmless but useless mixture.

6. Manual cleaning is usually used for which of the following?

    a. flatware
    b. serving dishes
    c. pans
    d. glasses

7. Mechanical warewashing systems require:

   a. that dishes be scraped.
   b. that flatware be soaked.
   c. both a and b.
   d. neither a nor b.

8. Under ideal conditions, housefly eggs can hatch in as little as:

   a. 8 hours.
   b. 24 hours.
   c. 3 days.
   d. 1 week.

9. In what regions is the roof rat found?

   a. northeastern and midwestern United States
   b. midwestern and western United States
   c. southeastern and western United States
   d. throughout most of North America

10. To inhibit rodent and insect breeding, storage conditions should be:

    a. cool and dry.
    b. warm and humid.
    c. cool and damp.
    d. warm and dry.

Chapter Outline

Learning Objectives

1. Describe floor cleaning methods used in food service operations. (pp. 363–371)

2. Describe cleaning methods for food service walls and ceilings. (pp. 371–375)

3. Identify the most important lighting concerns and the major ventilation problem in food establishments. (pp. 376–378)

4. Explain restrictions on the uses of dressing rooms in food service operations. (p. 378)

5. Summarize major plumbing requirements and concerns in food service operations, and describe basic requirements for toilet and lavatory facilities. (pp. 380–388)

6. Describe requirements for outdoor refuse containers. (pp. 390–394)

10

Facilities Cleaning and Maintenance

The cleaning and maintenance of physical facilities is presented in its own chapter because these activities influence the overall success of the cleaning and maintenance control point. This chapter includes cleaning and maintenance procedures as well as important facilities design and construction considerations.

In general, state and local building codes dictate the construction and maintenance of physical facilities in a food establishment. The FDA, along with state and local regulatory agencies, provides additional guidelines. The National Sanitation Foundation's *Sanitation Aspects of Food Service Facility Plan Preparation and Review* also addresses the design and construction of food service facilities. The standards presented throughout this chapter are based on this publication and the FDA code.

Much of the information presented here applies to the dining room—a food establishment's "front of the house." This information is equally applicable to other front-of-the-house areas in lodging operations, such as guestrooms, public restrooms, lobbies, and banquet/meeting rooms.

This chapter also includes an overview of the role of the housekeeping department in the cleaning and maintenance of lodging facilities, followed by a brief discussion of the on-premises laundry.

Floors

There are four basic types of floors: hard floors, resilient floors, wood floors, and carpeting. The selection of floor materials for each area in an operation should be based on how the area will be used. Exhibit 10.1 presents a breakdown of materials used for hard floors and resilient floors. This exhibit also presents recommendations (not strict rules) on how the various floor materials can be used.

Hard Floors

Hard floor materials include concrete, magnesium oxychloride cement, granolith, marble, terrazzo, ceramic tile, quarry tile, slate, terra cotta, and brick.

Concrete is a mixture of gravel, sand, cement, and water. It is relatively easy and inexpensive to install and maintain. According to federal codes, it must be sealed and may also be painted. Magnesium oxychloride cement is a combination of magnesium oxychloride and various other materials. The appearance and durability of this flooring material may vary depending on the fillers used. It must be sealed to protect the surface. Granolith is a mixture of cement and granite chips. It resists abrasion better than concrete.

Marble is naturally crystallized limestone. Marble is very durable, but is also expensive and easily stained, and it can be damaged by improper care. Acids should never be

Exhibit 10.1 A Classification of Floor Materials and Their Uses

	FLOOR MATERIAL	RECOMMENDED USES
HARD FLOORS	Brick and Slate	Stair Treads
	Ceramic Tile	Bathroom Kitchen Restroom Utility Room
	Concrete	Basement Garage Laundry Mechanical Room Service Room
	Granolithic	Hallway Lobby
	Magnesite	Hallway Office Workroom
	Marble	Bathroom Lobby Restroom Shower Room Stairs
	Terrazzo	Dressing Room Hallway Kitchen Lobby Utility Room Washroom
RESILIENT FLOORS	Asphalt Tile, Linoleum, Rubber Tile, Vinyl-Asbestos Tile	Lobby Elevator Hallway Office
	Cork	Office Meeting Room
	Vinyl	Elevator Guestroom Hallway Lobby Office
CARPET	Carpet	Dining Room Elevator Guestroom Hallway Lobby Office
WOOD	Wood	Dining Room Meeting Room Elevator

used on marble. Terrazzo is a mixture of cement or synthetic plastic and marble or granite chips; it must be sealed. Terrazzo is durable and easy to clean and maintain, but it is expensive. Ceramic tile is a dense, hard material. It is durable, stain-repellent, easy to maintain, and expensive to install.

Quarry tile is usually red or brown. It is porous and requires sealing. Quarry tile is often used in high traffic areas such as kitchens. Slate, terra cotta, and brick are also common natural stone flooring materials.

In general, hard floors are relatively easy to keep clean if they are properly maintained. Most sealed hard floors require daily sweeping with a dry mop or floor brush. These floors may need to be refinished periodically.

Floor finishes provide three benefits: they provide a glossy appearance, they protect the surface of the floor, and they facilitate daily cleaning. Floor finishes should be selected according to the floor manufacturer's recommendations.

Finished floors should be stripped periodically to remove buildup of floor finishing materials. Floors may be stripped by wet or dry methods. Dry stripping combines the mechanical agitation of an abrasive scrubbing compound with a small amount of moisture. The compound is usually applied by means of a floor machine with a pad or brush. As the floor machine agitates the abrasives on the floor, the floor's finish is turned into a powder which can be vacuumed. Dry stripping is faster than wet stripping. However, the combination of agitation and abrasive compounds may damage some floors.

There are two basic methods of wet stripping. The more common method combines machine scrubbing with chemical emulsification. A chemical emulsifier applied to the floor dissolves the old finish. The floor is then machine-scrubbed and the residue removed with a wet vacuum. The emulsifiers are then neutralized and the floor is rinsed.

The other method of wet stripping involves total chemical emulsification of the old finish, eliminating the mechanical scrubbing. The stripping chemical is mopped onto the floor and allowed to completely emulsify the finish. After the finish has been dissolved, it is removed with a wet vacuum. Cleanup operations are faster and less expensive.

The costly procedures of stripping, waxing, and polishing are losing popularity. No-wax hard flooring materials save time and money. A water-dispersed, non-yellowing polymer compound is applied to the surface of the flooring material at the factory. Once installed, the no-wax floor is initially buffed to a high gloss which resists scuffing and marking. Occasional machine buffing with a cleaning/polishing compound maintains the finish and the floor's resistance to marking and scuffing. No-wax floors must be damp-mopped daily.

High-pressure cleaning is often used for irregular surfaces such as those in refuse areas, loading docks, tiled areas, and kitchen areas. The surfaces are cleaned by the force of pressurized water and a chemical added to break down and emulsify the dirt. Drainage is necessary for this method of cleaning.

Resilient Floors

Resilient floors are relatively soft in comparison with hard floors. These floors reduce both noise and staff member fatigue. The resilient category includes floors made of asphalt, linoleum, rubber, vinyl, and cork. Resilient floors usually require sealing.

Asphalt tile is inexpensive and resists moisture, but is easily dented and marked. Some types of asphalt tile contain asbestos, which is illegal in many states and must be disposed of as hazardous waste. Linoleum is a combination of ground wood or cork, binders, mineral fillers, and oxidized linseed oil bonded to burlap or felt. It is available in sheet or tile form and is moderately priced. Linoleum is durable, but it can be dented.

Rubber tile absorbs sound and provides good traction, even when wet. It is expensive, however, and is easily damaged by oils, detergents, heat, and sunlight. Rubber tile is also susceptible to dents. Vinyl floor coverings are made from a combination of mineral fillers, acetylene, hydrochloric acid, and pigments. Vinyl is an expensive but highly stain-resistant flooring material. It is also available with a no-wax finish.

Cork floors are made from ground cork and resins. This expensive material is difficult to maintain, dents easily, and is frequently damaged by oils or moisture. Cork floors must be sealed with solvent-based epoxy and urethane.

Wood Floors

Wood floors may be constructed of hard or soft woods. They are susceptible to warping if they are exposed to excessive moisture; however, they are durable if properly sealed. Wood floors are potential fire hazards and can be relatively difficult to maintain.

Carpeting

Carpeting, often used in dining and public areas, helps to reduce staff member fatigue, controls noise, and, when installed at entrances, reduces the amount of dirt tracked onto interior floors. Carpeting is made of either natural or synthetic fibers. The type of carpeting selected depends on the traffic in the area to be carpeted. Solid-color carpeting shows traffic patterns in dirt and crushed pile. Patterned carpeting is preferable for high-traffic areas.

Modular carpeting may reduce an operation's overall carpet maintenance costs. Carpet modules or squares can be rotated from high- to low-traffic areas. This rotation results in a better overall appearance and extends the useful life of the carpet.

Proper carpet care is essential to protect this expensive asset. The frequency of carpet cleaning depends on the level of traffic in the area. Carpet cleaning is a labor-intensive task; the cost of labor can be more than 80% of the total cost of carpet care. Special equipment such as wet vacuums, steam cleaning or extraction machines, or rotary floor machines might be needed.

Dry carpet cleaning uses a cleaning compound or powder to suspend the dirt so it can be removed by a vacuum. However, this method can create problems. Residue remaining in the carpet pile will attract more soil and may necessitate more frequent cleaning by another method. An advantage of the dry method is that it minimizes the amount of time the carpet is not available for use.

Wet carpet cleaning methods require more labor and more downtime; overnight drying is usually necessary. Wet cleaning that is improperly done can also oversoak carpets, leading to shrinkage, mildew, and residue build-up. All of these conditions may shorten the useful life of the carpeting.

Steam cleaning or water extraction require specialized machinery that ranges in price from $2,000 to $10,000. Some extraction equipment can be used to dry-vacuum and clean hard floors as well. Because extraction cleaning is hard on carpeting, it should normally be done only once a year.

Some carpet cleaning procedures fall between the dry and wet categories. The dry foam method involves spraying a dry foam carpet shampoo onto the carpet; rotating brushes on the bottom of the machine scrub the foam-covered carpet. After the foam dries, heavy vacuuming is required to remove the shampoo residue. Again, any remaining residue will speed resoiling. Dry foam cleaning may also be done by hand.

The bonnet spin pad method is closer to a wet method than a dry method. A rotary floor machine is fitted with a circular abrasive yarn pad. Then the machine scrubs shampoo into the carpet and, in the process, soaks up the dirt in the yarn pad. Unfortunately,

Exhibit 10.2 Recommended Floor Finishes

Food Service Area	Floor Finish			
	Commercial Grade Vinyl Asbestos Tile	Quarry Tile	Sealed Concrete	Poured Seamless
Kitchen		X		X
Dry Storage	X	X	X	X
Serving		X	X	X
Restroom	X	X		X
Bar	X	X		X
Janitor Closet		X	X	X

Source: National Sanitation Foundation, *Sanitation Aspects of Food Service Facility Plan Preparation and Review,* 1978, p. 9.

this procedure does not effectively achieve deep cleaning. Rotary shampooing—using a bristle brush instead of a pad—is more effective.

Vacuuming is the most important part of overall carpet care. Vacuuming at least once a day prolongs the life of a carpet by removing sand and other substances that can cut or shred carpet fibers. Spots should also be cleaned daily—or when they occur—to minimize staining.

Recommended Floors for Food Establishments

In general, the FDA and NSF recommend that all floor coverings be non-toxic and able to withstand normal wear. It is important that floor surfaces be maintained in good repair. A smooth, durable floor material (such as sealed concrete, terrazzo, ceramic tile, or durable plastic) is essential in most food service areas. These areas include kitchen, storage, production, and warewashing areas, as well as locker rooms, dressing rooms, and vestibules. Anti-slip floor coverings are a good safety precaution for high-traffic areas, such as those behind the production line and in warewashing stations. Recommended floor finishes are presented in Exhibit 10.2.

In most cases, red quarry tile with acid-resistant grout is the best choice for flooring material. The tile can be made less slippery by impregnating it with an abrasive material such as carborundum. Poured seamless floors are also acceptable. They must be installed by a specialized contractor, as the quality of the end product depends more on the installation process than the raw materials.

The FDA and most state and local codes prohibit the use of carpeting in floor areas exposed to large amounts of water or grease. Such areas include toilet rooms, dining room service stations, equipment and utensil washing areas, handwashing areas, and food storage and production areas. Carpeting in dining rooms or other public areas must be closely woven and properly installed. Shag carpeting is not permitted because it is difficult to clean and because servers carrying trays of food may stumble easily. Carpeting has to be easily cleanable and maintained in good repair.

If floors are cleaned with large amounts of water or if they are exposed to fluid waste from equipment, they must have properly installed floor drains with traps. Such floors may only be constructed of terrazzo, ceramic tile, sealed concrete, or other similar materials. The floor should be graded properly to ensure adequate drainage.

Floor mats and duckboards may be used in areas where staff members stand for long periods of time: behind the production line, in warewashing areas, behind the bar, and in other areas where the floor may be wet. It is essential that mats and duckboards be easily cleanable, grease-resistant, and non-absorbent. The use of duckboards as storage racks is prohibited. Duckboards may not be constructed of soft wood.

The FDA's code also specifies that the junctures between walls and floors must be covered and sealed if they are likely to get wet. In dry areas, a closed seam no more than $1/32$ of an inch (1.0 mm) is acceptable. Utility pipes and service lines must be installed so as to allow easy floor cleaning. Exposed pipes and sewer lines running horizontally on the floor are prohibited in all new and extensively remodeled food service operations. The objectives of the FDA's code are clear—to prevent the accumulation of soil and to allow easy cleaning and maintenance of all floors in food service facilities.

The FDA states:

"Smooth" means:

(a) A food-contact surface having a surface free of pits and inclusions with a cleanability equal to or exceeding that of (100 grit) number 3 stainless steel;

(b) A nonfood-contact surface of equipment having a surface equal to that of commercial grade hot-rolled steel free of visible scale; and

(c) A floor, wall, or ceiling having an even or level surface with no roughness or projections that render it difficult to clean.

6-101.11   Surface Characteristics.

(A) Except as specified in ¶ (B) of this section, materials for indoor floor, wall, and ceiling surfaces under conditions of normal use shall be:

(1)   Smooth and durable for areas where food establishment operations are conducted;

(2)   Closely woven and easily cleanable carpet for carpeted areas; and

(3)   Nonabsorbent for areas subject to moisture such as food preparation areas, walk-in refrigerators, warewashing areas, toilet rooms, mobile food establishment servicing areas, and areas subject to flushing or spray cleaning methods.

(B) *In a temporary food establishment:*

(1)   *If graded to drain, a floor may be concrete, machine-laid asphalt, or dirt or gravel if it is covered with mats, removable platforms, duckboards, or other suitable materials approved by the regulatory authority that are effectively treated to control dust and mud; and*

(2)   *Walls and ceilings may be constructed of a material that protects the interior from the weather and windblown dust and debris.*

6-102.11   Surface Characteristics.

(A) The outdoor walking and driving areas shall be surfaced with concrete, asphalt, or gravel or other materials that have been effectively treated to minimize dust, facilitate maintenance, and prevent muddy conditions.

(B) Exterior surfaces of buildings and mobile food establishments shall be of weather-resistant materials and shall comply with law.

(C) Outdoor storage areas for refuse, recyclables, or returnables shall be of materials specified under §§ 5-501.12 and 5-501.13.

6-201.11   Floors, Walls, and Ceilings.

The floors, floor coverings, walls, wall coverings, and ceilings shall be designed, constructed, and installed so they are smooth and easily cleanable, *except that antislip floor coverings or applications may be used for safety reasons.*

6-201.12   Floors, Walls, and Ceilings, Utility Lines.

(A) Utility service lines and pipes may not be unnecessarily exposed.

(B) Exposed utility service lines and pipes shall be installed so they do not obstruct or prevent cleaning of the floors, walls, or ceilings.

(C) Exposed horizontal utility service lines and pipes may not be installed on the floor.

6-201.13   Floor and Wall Junctures, Coved, and Enclosed or Sealed.

(A) In food establishments in which cleaning methods other than water flushing are used for cleaning floors, the floor and wall junctures shall be coved and closed to no larger than 1 mm (one thirty-second inch).

(B) The floors in food establishments in which water flush cleaning methods are used shall be provided with drains and graded to drain, and the floor and wall junctures shall be coved and sealed.

6-201.14   Floor Carpeting, Installation and Restrictions.

(A) Except as specified under ¶ (B) of this section, carpeting may be installed as a floor covering if it is:

(1)   Securely attached to the floor with a durable mastic, by using a stretch and tack method, or by another method; and

(2)   Installed tightly against the wall under the coving or installed away from the wall with a space between the carpet and the wall and with the edges of the carpet secured by metal stripping or some other means.

(B) Carpeting may not be installed as a floor covering in food preparation areas, food storage areas, warewashing areas, handwashing areas, toilet room areas where urinals and toilets are located, or refuse storage rooms and areas.

6-201.15   Floor Covering, Mats and Duckboards.

Mats and duckboards shall be designed to be removable and easily cleanable.

6-201.16   Wall and Ceiling Coverings and Coatings.

(A) Wall and ceiling covering materials shall be attached so that they are easily cleanable.

(B) *Except in areas used only for dry storage,* concrete, porous blocks, or bricks used for indoor wall construction shall be finished and sealed to provide a smooth, nonabsorbent, easily cleanable surface.

6-201.17   Walls and Ceilings, Attachments.

(A) Except as specified in ¶ (B) of this section, attachments to walls and ceilings such as light fixtures, mechanical room ventilation system components, vent covers, wall mounted fans, decorative items, and other attachments shall be easily cleanable.

(B) *In a consumer area, wall and ceiling surfaces and decorative items and attachments that are provided for ambiance need not meet this requirement if they are kept clean.*

6-201.18   Walls and Ceilings, Studs, Joists, and Rafters.

Studs, joists, and rafters may not be exposed in areas specified in Subparagraph 6-101.11(A)(3). *This requirement does not apply to temporary food establishments.*

6-501.13   Cleaning Floors, Dustless Methods.

(A) Except as specified in ¶ (B) of this section, only dustless methods of cleaning shall be used, such as wet cleaning, vacuum cleaning, mopping with treated dust mops, or sweeping using a broom and dust-arresting compounds.

(B) *Spills or drippage on floors that occur between normal floor cleaning times may be cleaned:*

  (1) *Without the use of dust-arresting compounds; and*

  (2) *In the case of liquid spills or drippage, with the use of a small amount of absorbent compound such as sawdust or diatomaceous earth applied immediately before spot cleaning.*

6-501.16   Drying Mops.

After use, mops shall be placed in a position that allows them to air-dry without soiling walls, equipment, or supplies.

6-501.17   Absorbent Materials on Floors, Use Limitation.

Except as specified under ¶ 6-501.13(B), sawdust, wood shavings, granular salt, baked clay, diatomaceous earth, or similar materials may not be used on floors.

Exhibit 10.3 Characteristic Problems of Each Area in a Food Establishment

	Food Service Area						
Characteristic	Kitchen Cooking	Kitchen Preparation	Dry Storage	Manual and Mechanical Warewashing	Serving	Restroom	Janitor Closet
Detergents/Chemicals				X		X	X
Dust		X					
Food Acid		X					
Food Splash		X			X		
Grease	X			X			
Heat	X			X			
Impact			X	X	X	X	
Microbial Contamination		X					
Moisture				X		X	X
Rodents/Insects			X	X		X	X
Steam	X						

Source: National Sanitation Foundation, *Sanitation Aspects of Food Service Facility Plan Preparation and Review,* 1978, p. 10.

6-501.18   Maintaining and Using Handwashing Lavatories.

Handwashing lavatories shall be kept clean and maintained and used as specified under § 5-205.11.

Source: FDA 1993 *Food Code.*

The FDA recommends only dustless floor cleaning methods for all types of floor surfaces. These include wet cleaning, vacuum cleaning, mopping with treated dust-mops, or sweeping with compounds that minimize dust. Wet cleaning equipment (such as mops) must be cleaned and rinsed in a utility sink with a floor drain. Mop water or similar liquid wastes can be disposed of only in a utility sink—not in food preparation areas, food service utensil or equipment washing areas, or lavatories. It is also unsafe and unsightly to pour liquid cleaning waste in parking lots or other exterior surfaces.

Walls and Ceilings

All wall coverings must be non-toxic and able to withstand normal wear and tear. Walls, doors, and windows should be designed for easy maintenance. Wall finishes for each area in a food establishment must be selected to withstand the abuses characteristic of that area. Some of these characteristic problems are presented in Exhibit 10.3.

The FDA and most state and local codes suggest that easily cleanable, light-colored, smooth, non-absorbent wall coverings be installed in food storage, food production,

Exhibit 10.4 Recommended Wall Finishes

Food Service Area		Wall Finish				
		Glazed Surface	Block Filled and Epoxy Paint	Drywall Taped Epoxy	Wall Panels	Stainless Steel or Aluminum
Kitchen	Cooking					X
	Food Prep.	X	X	X	X	X
Dry Storage		X	X	X	X	X
Warewashing	Manual	X	X			X
	Mechanical	X	X			X
Serving		X	X	X	X	X
Restroom		X	X	X	X	X
Janitor Closet		X	X	X	X	X

Source: National Sanitation Foundation, *Sanitation Aspects of Food Service Facility Plan Preparation and Review*, 1978, p. 10.

equipment and utensil washing, vestibule, and toilet room areas. The NSF's recommended wall finishes are presented in Exhibit 10.4. Most food service facilities have their masonry walls in these areas covered with several coats of epoxy-based paint. It is essential that all holes be filled in before painting to prevent splashed food and bonded dust from accumulating in crevices. Drywall is usually less expensive than masonry but might require more repairs. This is particularly true in high-moisture areas such as the warewashing station. Corner and bumper guards are necessary to protect drywall construction.

Modular, pre-finished wall panels are easy to install and clean. They are usually constructed of fiberglass and are self-extinguishing when exposed to flames. It is important to check local fire code requirements. Stainless steel and aluminum are ideal wall finishes, but they are expensive. Ceramic tile and concrete or pumice blocks must be glazed. The glaze provides additional protection for walls and ceilings made of these materials.

No exposed wall construction (such as rafters, joists, or studs) is permitted in walk-in refrigeration units, food production areas, equipment or utensil washing areas, vestibules, or toilet rooms. Exposed construction is permitted in other areas provided that it is surfaced or coated and easy to clean. In some food establishments, these features are part of a rustic decor.

Exposed utility service pipes and lines are permitted in some areas as long as the walls can be cleaned. Unnecessary exposure of utility lines and pipes is prohibited in food production areas, refrigerated storage areas, utensil and equipment washing areas, vestibules, and toilet rooms. Wall attachments (such as light fixtures, decorations, and fans) must be easy to clean and maintain.

Exhibit 10.5 Sample Room Finish Schedule

Room Number	Room Name	Floor Material	Base Material	Wall Finish Material				Ceiling		Remarks
				Top	Bottom	Top	Bottom	Material	Height	

Source: National Sanitation Foundation, *Sanitation Aspects of Food Service Facility Plan Preparation and Review,* 1978, p. 29.

Ceilings must be made of non-porous, easily cleanable materials. Recommended materials include plastic-coated fiberboard, epoxy-coated drywall, glazed surfaces and plastic-laminated panels. No exposed construction is permitted on the ceilings of walk-in refrigeration units, food production areas, equipment and utensil washing areas, vestibules, and toilet rooms. If utility lines and pipes are exposed on the ceiling (in other areas), the ceiling must be easily cleanable. Light fixtures, fans, and other equipment or decorations attached to the ceiling must be in good repair and easily cleanable. Noise control is important, especially in the dishwashing area. Some vinyl-clad fiberboard acoustical tiles are acceptable for use in noisy areas.

To help food establishment management prepare and review facilities plans, the NSF has developed a room finish schedule that can be used to specify construction materials. A sample room finish schedule is presented in Exhibit 10.5.

Walls should be cleaned frequently with a dust mop and washed periodically. Ceilings should be cleaned periodically by washing with a detergent designed for such applications. Walls and ceilings may be washed by hand or with a machine designed for this purpose. The proper cleaners in the right concentration are critical in either case. Thorough rinsing is necessary to remove all soil and residue. Smudges and fingerprints should be wiped off daily with an all-purpose cleaner. Painting should be done by an independent contractor if the establishment has no designated staff member.

Ceilings and walls in dining areas may be constructed or covered with a variety of materials, including wallpaper, fabric, tile, marble, and wood. Most of these materials require special care. They should be cleaned according to the manufacturer's recommendations when possible. Exhibit 10.6 presents some general guidelines for cleaning various materials.

All floors, walls, and ceilings in the facility must be kept clean and in a state of good repair. These areas should be cleaned when the least amount of food is exposed. General cleanup is permitted during non-rush periods (between meals) and after closing. In some cases, emergency cleaning is necessary; if a cook accidentally spills a gallon of beef

Exhibit 10.6 How to Care for Materials in Your Building

MATERIAL	ROUTINE CLEANING AND MAINTENANCE
Acoustical Tile	Remove loose dirt or dust with a vacuum or soft brush. A gum eraser will remove most smudges. Soft chalk can cover many stains. More thorough cleaning can be accomplished with wallpaper cleaners or mild soap cleaners. Care must be taken to avoid excessive water and abrasive rubbing action; using a soft sponge is best.
Aluminum	Wash with a mild detergent solution; avoid common alkalies which dull the finish. A fine abrasive may be used periodically; rub in one direction, not in a circle.
Asphalt Tile	Wash with a mild detergent or soap solution; rinse with clean water and dry immediately either with mops or wet/dry vacuums.
Bamboo, Crane, Reed, Wicker, Rattan	Wash with a mild soap or detergent solution; rinse with clear water, dry. Periodic shellacking maintains a natural finish.
Brass	Acidic-type brass cleaners and polishes are used for unfinished brass. Wash lacquered brass with a mild detergent solution, rinse, and wipe dry.
Bronze	Clean with a metal cleaner or polish applied with a soft cloth; work with the grain, covering one small area at a time. Rub statuary finishes periodically with lemon oil on a soft cloth. Then rub briskly with a clean, soft cloth to remove excess oil.
Carpets	All types of carpeting—wool, polyester, nylon, polypropylene, etc.—must be vacuumed regularly to extend their useful life. (Abrasives which are allowed to accumulate in the carpet fibers will actually cut the fibers at the backing.) Also, a daily spotting program ensures prompt removal of spots. Overall cleaning can be accomplished with impregnated granular cleaners, shampoos, or extraction chemicals with a dry residue to prevent rapid resoiling.
Ceramic Tile	Use neutral soap or detergent applied with a sponge, mop, or brush, depending on the stain. Remove excess cleaning solution, rinse with clean water, and thoroughly dry the surface. Avoid alkalies, salts, acids, and abrasive cleaners. These tend to break down the surfaces of glazed and vitreous tiles, and cause problems with the porous cement grout. Some soap cleaners may result in a soap film buildup.
Chromium	Avoid harsh polishes and powders. A damp cloth is usually sufficient, or a mild detergent solution may be used. Then polish with a dry cloth.
Concrete	As soon as the floor can be used, it should be swept clean and a dust seal applied. Old concrete should be thoroughly cleaned and also sealed. Concrete floors can be swept with treated mops, damp-mopped, or scrubbed with a neutral cleaner. Excess solution should be picked up with a squeegee or wet vacuum. Never use acids because concrete dissolves in acidic solutions.
Conductive Floors	These floors are found in hospitals, computer rooms, or anywhere that it is necessary to prevent the building of a static electrical charge on the floor. These floors must be kept *film-free*. This includes coatings, soap films or dust mop dressings, as they will build an insulating residue on the floors. In hospitals, clean with a disinfectant/detergent. In other areas, use a detergent recommended for conductive floors.
Copper	Wash with soap and water, rinse, and dry. Stains and corrosion may be removed with metal polishes. If acidic solutions are used, always rinse thoroughly to avoid excess tarnishing.
Cork Tile	Sweep with a treated mop and buff. Avoid excessive water. If wet cleaning is needed, a mild soap or detergent solution should be applied with a damp mop. Sealed cork floors are preferred as they protect the natural colors of the cork.
Fiberglass	For normal bathtub soils and water conditions, use a multi-purpose alkaline detergent, according to label directions. If the alkaline cleaner does not have built-in disinfectant properties, a liquid or spray disinfectant may be applied to the bath fixture after cleaning. Where hard water is a problem, and accumulated mineral deposits need to be removed, a controlled acid cleaner may be used, containing phosphoric or oxalic acid. Do not use cleaners containing hydrofluoric or hydrochloric acid since these can etch the surface. Solvents such as acetone, xylene, toluene, or turpentine can be used on fiberglass; generally for construction site soils, debris, paint, vinyl adhesives, grease, or tar. Do not allow solvent cleaners to come in contact with drain pipes. Acids and solvents are not recommended for regular cleaning of fiberglass fixtures.
Glass	Wash with a special window cleaning concentrate dissolved in clean water; apply with a window washer's brush; use a squeegee or chamois to dry glass.
Granite	Polished granite may be washed with a detergent solution or applied poultices. Treat unpolished granite with water and sand cleaning at a pressure of 50 psi or less.

Iron	Wash with a soap or detergent solution, rinse, and dry. A phosphoric acid cleaner can also be used. Rinse and dry thoroughly. Rust can be removed with steel wool soaked in mineral spirits. Surfaces that can withstand acid cleaning can be treated with a phosphoric-oxalic acid solution. Rinse thoroughly because oxalic acid is toxic.
Leather Furniture	Wash with a neutral soap or saddle soap. Leather trappings, etc., should be treated with neat's-foot oil to prevent drying and cracking.
Linoleum	Wash with a mild detergent solution; rinse with clear water. Remove water and dry as rapidly as possible. *Avoid* alkaline solutions.
Magnesite	Wash with a neutral detergent; do not use acids or alkaline cleaners. Remove solutions with a wet vacuum; avoid excess water.
Marble	Newly installed marble is best cleaned with a neutral cleaner and clean mops. Marble that has been soiled or stained through neglect has to be cleaned with the poultice method using a powdered abrasive cleaner and hot water. Only mildly alkaline detergent (never acids) should be used on seasoned marble; wash from the bottom up and rinse thoroughly. Then dry either with a chamois or soft cloth to prevent streaking.
Masonry	Steam cleaning with detergents or water and sand cleaning under low pressure may be required for brick, cement block, cinder block, stone and stucco. Interior masonry work may be vacuumed with heavy duty commercial-type machines.
Oil Paintings	Dust *lightly* with a soft dusting brush using extreme care. *Never use water or cleaners.* For badly soiled oil paintings, consult an expert.
Painted Surfaces	Immediately remove spots with a cloth wrung from a detergent solution. Washing should be performed under controlled conditions.
Pewter	Wash with a neutral detergent solution, rinse, and dry with a soft cloth. Apply a commercial silver polish to remove stains or browning.
Porcelain	Use an alkaline detergent; avoid acids, which can dissolve the surface and cause blemishes.
Rubber Tile	Use a mild detergent solution; rinse and remove water promptly.
Slate	Wash with a detergent solution; rinse and dry thoroughly. Chalkboards should *not* be washed on a regular basis; a thin film of chalk dust is best for vision and the care of the board.
Stainless Steel	Wash with a solution of soap or detergent. Rinse thoroughly; dry with a soft cloth. For heavier dirt, or deposits which require scrubbing, there are many specialty products; always rinse and dry, making sure to rub with the grain. Polish with a hydrocarbon-based stainless steel cleaner to prevent fingerprinting and resoiling.
Terra Cotta	Wash with a neutral detergent solution.
Terrazzo	Only neutral detergents should be used. Stains can be removed by the poultice method. Avoid alkaline cleaners as they cause powdering. Avoid using sweeping compounds which contain oil or wax. Acids dissolve the marble chips in terrazzo, soap tends to build up and leave a surface film; steel wool leaves splinters that rust.
Vinyl	Use a neutral detergent solution, rinse, and dry with a wet vacuum.
Wood	Wood floors must be sealed if they are to be maintained properly. Dust mopping and damp mopping sealed floors are usually all that is necessary if a regular maintenance program is followed. Polishing with a floor wax finish may be required. Some of the soft woods can be seriously damaged by strong solutions of soap or detergent and water; oils, grease, and strong alkalies are also harmful. Avoid excessive use of water and always remove water as rapidly as possible.
Vehicles	Trucks should be cleaned with a concentrated alkaline cleaner/degreaser, using high pressure and hot water equipment, to effectively remove road soils, grease, soot, etc.

Source: Adapted from the Soap and Detergent Association, *Programmed Cleaning Guide,* 1984, pp. 143–145.

stock on the kitchen floor, it must be cleaned up immediately to prevent further accidents. Staff members should be reminded during training to clean when not busy with other responsibilities.

Lighting and Ventilation

Adequate lighting is essential in all areas of a food establishment. Proper lighting facilitates cleaning and improves safety. Light intensity is measured in units called **footcandles.** One footcandle equals one lumen per square foot (a lumen is a measure of power equal to 0.0015 watt). Footcandles are measured with a light meter.

The FDA recommends at least 10 footcandles (110 lux) at a distance of 30 inches (75 cm) above the floor in all areas and rooms during cleaning. In areas where fresh produce or packaged foods are sold or offered for consumption, in areas used for handwashing, warewashing, and equipment and utensil storage, and in toilet rooms, the minimum is 20 footcandles (220 lux) at the same distance. At least 50 footcandles (540 lux) is required when staff members are working with potentially hazardous foods, or with equipment and utensils that pose safety risks. Most lighting engineers and occupational health and safety inspectors recommend up to 50 to 70 footcandles of light for kitchen work areas. The objective of these requirements is to provide adequate lighting for cleaning, food storage, food production, and service. It is easier to clean and maintain a well-lit facility. Some areas in the facility (such as walk-in refrigerators and freezers) usually need extra lighting. Adequate exterior lighting renders the establishment more visible and makes guests feel secure as they approach the entrance.

The FDA and most state and local codes also address protective shielding for lighting fixtures (see Chapter 6). The objective is to prevent broken glass from contaminating food products.

Lighting fixtures, including lamps and shades in dining areas, should be cleaned routinely by dusting or vacuuming, as dust is the primary cause of reduced light intensity. Bulbs or lamps must be replaced promptly when necessary. Small glass fixtures can be removed for cleaning. Large fixtures, including chandeliers, are usually cleaned in place. This difficult job can be performed by an outside contractor.

The FDA states:

6-303.11   (Lighting) Intensity.

The light intensity shall be:

(A)   In all areas and rooms during periods of cleaning, at least 110 lux (10 footcandles) at a distance of 75 cm (30 inches) above the floor;

(B)   In areas where fresh produce or packaged foods are sold or offered for consumption; areas used for handwashing, warewashing, and equipment and utensil storage; and in toilet rooms, at least 220 lux (20 footcandles) at a distance of 75 cm (30 inches) above the floor; and

(C)   At a surface where a food employee is working with unpackaged potentially hazardous food or with food, utensils, and equipment such as knives, slicers, grinders, or saws where employee safety is a factor, at least 540 lux (50 footcandles).

Source: FDA 1993 *Food Code.*

Ventilation equipment is designed to remove smoke, fumes, condensation, steam, heat, and unpleasant odors from food service kitchens and dining rooms. Sufficient ventilation also helps to maintain comfortable temperatures and minimizes soil buildup on walls, ceilings, and floors. State and local building codes, and, in some jurisdictions, public health officials, dictate specific ventilation requirements for each area of a food establishment.

The major ventilation problem most food service businesses face is the transfer of unpleasant odors and fumes from the kitchen to public areas such as dining, meeting, and banquet rooms. This problem usually occurs when the kitchen ventilation system is improperly designed, including an inadequate amount of tempered (approximately 70°F [20°C]) makeup air to balance the system. Ventilation in the public areas is usually recirculated through heating and/or air conditioning units. Small percentages of exhausted air are usually replaced with outside fresh air. To avoid this ventilation problem, air from the kitchen must be completely exhausted to the outside and replaced with an equal amount of tempered makeup air.

The FDA states that air exhausted from a food service facility may not create an unlawful discharge or a public health nuisance. All intake and exhaust air ducts must be well maintained to prevent the entrance of dust, dirt, and other contaminants. Regular maintenance also reduces fire hazards and keeps exhaust vents from becoming unsightly; vents dripping with grease are an unappealing sight to guests approaching the building. In new and extensively remodeled buildings, ventilation to the outside is required in all rooms where fumes or obnoxious odors are likely to be created.

The FDA states:

4-204.11   Ventilation Hood Systems, Drip Prevention.

Exhaust ventilation hood systems in food preparation and warewashing areas including components such as hoods, fans, guards, and ducting shall be designed to prevent grease or condensation from draining or dripping onto food, equipment, utensils, linens, and single-service and single-use articles.

4-301.14   Ventilation Hood Systems, Adequacy.

Ventilation hood systems and devices shall be sufficient in number and capacity to prevent grease or condensation from collecting on walls and ceilings.

6-202.12   Ventilation System, Exhaust Vents.

Heating and air conditioning systems shall be designed and installed so that vents do not cause contamination of food, food preparation surfaces, equipment, or utensils.

6-304.11   (Ventilation) Mechanical.

If necessary to keep rooms free of excessive heat, steam, condensation, vapors, obnoxious odors, smoke, and fumes, mechanical ventilation of sufficient capacity shall be provided.

6-501.14   Cleaning Ventilation Systems, Nuisance and Discharge Prohibition.

(A) Intake and exhaust air ducts shall be cleaned and filters changed so they are not a source of contamination by dust, dirt, and other materials.

(B) If vented to the outside, ventilation systems may not create a public health nuisance or unlawful discharge.

Source: FDA 1993 *Food Code.*

Dressing Rooms and Food Service Laundry Facilities

Staff members who wear their uniforms into the building may bring in many contaminants on their apparently clean clothes. Therefore, they should change into the required uniforms at the establishment immediately before they begin work, if possible. If staff members are required to change their clothes at the establishment, the facilities should include an appropriate dressing area (see Chapter 3). Dressing rooms may not be used for food storage, production, or service, or equipment and utensil washing or storage. The objective of these regulations is to reduce the likelihood of food contamination.

Even if staff members do not change into uniforms after arriving at work, the operation must provide storage facilities for personal belongings (such as coats, shoes, and purses). Locker storage areas must be adequate, secure, orderly, and clean. Lockers may be located in storage areas containing only completely packaged food or packaged single-service articles.

The FDA states:

Dressing Areas and Lockers

6-305.11   Designation.

(A) Dressing rooms or dressing areas shall be designated if employees routinely change their clothes in the establishment.

(B) Lockers or other suitable facilities shall be provided for the orderly storage of employees' clothing and other possessions.

6-501.110   Using Dressing Rooms and Lockers.

(A) Dressing rooms shall be used by employees if the employees regularly change their clothes in the establishment.

(B) Lockers or other suitable facilities shall be used for the orderly storage of employee clothing and other possessions.

6-403.11   Designated Areas.

Lockers or other suitable facilities shall be located in a designated room or area where contamination of food, equipment, utensils, linens, and single-service and single-use articles cannot occur.

Source: FDA 1993 *Food Code.*

Laundry facilities may be installed in a food establishment if they are used *only* to wash and dry aprons, uniforms, cloths, and linens needed for normal operation. Ideally, laundry facilities should be isolated. However, washers and dryers may be placed in a storage area, provided that the room contains only completely packaged foods or packaged single-service articles. Soiled laundry must be stored in washable laundry bags or non-absorbent containers, and may not be stored in cold food storage rooms. Clean linens and cloths must be stored to prevent contamination.

Cloths used for wiping up food spills cannot be used for other purposes. Dry cloths may be used for wiping food spills from tableware and carryout containers. Moist cloths should be stored in a chemical sanitizer and can be used for wiping spills from food-contact and nonfood-contact surfaces. Cloth gloves must be laundered before being used with a different type of raw animal food such as meat or fish. Once soiled, both gloves and cloths must be properly laundered and dried and stored until used again.

If laundry operations are confined to laundering wiping cloths that are used wet, clean cloths may be stored in a sanitizing solution, air-dried in an area away from food, equipment, and utensil storage areas, or stored moist in the washing machine. (Laundry operations for lodging properties are discussed in the final section of this chapter.)

The FDA states:

3-304.13   Wiping Cloths, Used for One Purpose.

(A) Cloths that are in use for wiping food spills shall be used for no other purpose.

(B) Cloths used for wiping food spills shall be:

(1)   Dry and used for wiping food spills from tableware and carry-out containers; or

(2)   Moist and cleaned as specified under ¶ 4-802.11(D), stored in a chemical sanitizer as specified under § 7-204.11, and used for wiping spills from food-contact and nonfood-contact surfaces of equipment.

(C) Dry or moist cloths that are used with raw animal foods shall be kept separate from cloths used for other purposes, and moist cloths used with raw animal foods shall be kept in a separate sanitizing solution.

4-803.13   Use of Laundry Facilities.

(A) Except as specified in ¶ (B) of this section, laundry facilities on the premises of a food establishment shall be used only for the washing and drying of items used in the operation of the establishment.

(B) *Separate laundry facilities located on the premises for the purpose of general laundering such as for institutions providing boarding and lodging may also be used for laundering food establishment items.*

4-901.12   Wiping Cloths, Air-Drying Locations.

Wiping cloths laundered in a food establishment that does not have a mechanical clothes dryer as specified in ¶ 4-301.15(B) shall be air-dried in a location and in a manner that contamination of food, equipment, utensils, linens, and single-service and single-use articles and the wiping cloths is prevented. *This section does not apply if wiping cloths are stored after laundering in a sanitizing solution as specified under § 4-501.114.*

"Linens" means fabric items such as cloth hampers, cloth napkins, table cloths, wiping cloths, and work garments including cloth gloves.

4-801.11   Clean Linens.

Clean linens shall be free from food residues and other soiling matter.

4-802.11   Specifications.

(A) Linens that do not come in direct contact with food shall be laundered between operations if they become wet, sticky, or visibly soiled.

(B) Cloth gloves specified in ¶ 4-101.16(C) shall be laundered before being used with a different type of raw animal food such as beef, lamb, pork, and fish.

(C) Linens that are used as specified in ¶ 4-101.16(B) and cloth napkins shall be laundered between each use.

(D) Wet wiping cloths shall be laundered before being used with a fresh solution of cleanser or sanitizer.

(E) Dry wiping cloths shall be laundered as necessary to prevent contamination of food and clean serving utensils.

4-803.11   Storage of Soiled Linens.

Soiled linens shall be kept in clean, nonabsorbent receptacles or clean, washable laundry bags and stored and transported to prevent contamination of food, clean equipment, clean utensils, and single-service and single-use articles.

4-803.12   Mechanical Washing.

(A) Except as specified in ¶ (B) of this section, linens shall be mechanically washed.

(B) *In food establishments in which only wiping cloths are laundered as specified in ¶ 4-301.15(B), the wiping cloths may be laundered in a mechanical washer, a sink designated only for laundering wiping cloths, or a warewashing or food preparation sink that is cleaned as specified under § 4-501.14.*

Drinking Water.

(a) **"Drinking water"** means water that meets 40 CFR Part 141 National Primary Drinking Water Regulations.

(b) **"Drinking water"** is traditionally known as "potable water."

(c) **"Drinking water"** includes the term "water" except where the term used connotes that the water is not potable, such as "boiler water," "mop water," "rainwater," "wastewater," and "nondrinking" water.

"Plumbing fixture" means a receptacle or device that:

(a) Is permanently or temporarily connected to the water distribution system of the premises and demands a supply of water from the system; or

(b) Discharges used water, waste materials, or sewage directly or indirectly to the drainage system of the premises.

"Plumbing system" means the water supply and distribution pipes; plumbing fixtures and traps; soil, waste, and vent pipes; sanitary and storm sewers and building drains, including their respective connections, devices, and appurtenances within the premises; and water-treating equipment.

5-101.11   Approved System.*

Drinking water shall be obtained from an approved source that is:

(A)   A public water system; or

(B)   A private water system that is constructed, maintained, and operated according to law.

5-101.12   System Flushing and Disinfection.*

A drinking water system shall be flushed and disinfected before being placed in service after construction, repair, or modification and after an emergency situation, such as a flood, that may introduce contaminants to the system.

5-101.13   Bottled Drinking Water.*

Bottled drinking water used or sold in a food establishment shall be obtained from approved sources in accordance with 21 CFR 129—Processing and Bottling of Bottled Drinking Water.

Quality

5-102.11   Standards.*

Except as specified under § 5-102.12:

(A)   Water from a public water system shall meet 40 CFR 141—National Primary Drinking Water Regulations and state drinking water quality standards; and

(B)   Water from a private water system shall meet state drinking water quality standards.

5-102.12   Nondrinking Water.*

If the use of a nondrinking water supply is approved by the regulatory authority, the supply shall be used only for purposes such as air conditioning, nonfood equipment cooling, fire protection, and irrigation, and may not be used so that the nondrinking water is allowed to contact, directly or indirectly, food, equipment, or utensils.

5-102.13   Sampling.

Except when used as specified under § 5-102.12, water from a private water system shall be sampled at least annually and sampled and tested as required by state water quality regulations.

5-102.14   Sample Report.

The most recent sample report of the private water system shall be retained on file in the establishment or the report shall be maintained as specified by state water quality regulations.

Quantity and Availability

5-103.11   Capacity.*

The water source and system shall be of sufficient capacity to meet the water demands of the food establishment.

5-103.12   Pressure.

Water under pressure shall be provided to all fixtures, equipment, and nonfood equipment that are required to use water *except that water supplied as specified in ¶¶ 5-104.12(A) and (B) to a temporary facility or in response to a temporary interruption of a water supply need not be under pressure.*

5-103.13   Hot Water.

Hot water generation and distribution systems shall be sufficient to meet the peak hot water demands throughout the food establishment.

Distribution, Delivery, and Retention

5-104.11   System.

Water shall be received from the source through the use of:

(A)   An approved public water main; or

(B)   One or more of the following that shall be constructed, maintained, and operated according to law:

　　(1)   Private water main, water pumps, pipes, hoses, connections, and other appurtenances,

　　(2)   Water transport vehicles, and

　　(3)   Water containers.

5-104.12   Alternative Water Supply.

Water meeting the requirements specified under Subparts 5-101, 5-102, and 5-103 shall be made available for a mobile facility, for a temporary facility without a permanent water supply, and for a food establishment with a temporary interruption of its water supply through:

(A)   A supply of containers of commercially bottled drinking water;

(B)   One or more closed portable water containers;

(C)   An enclosed vehicular water tank;

(D)   An on-premises water storage tank; or

(E)   Piping, tubing, or hoses connected to an adjacent approved source.

Materials

5-201.11   Approved.*

(A) A plumbing system and hoses conveying water shall be constructed and repaired with approved materials according to law.

(B) A water filter shall be made of safe materials.

Design, Construction, and Installation

5-202.11   Approved System and Cleanable Fixtures.*

(A) A plumbing system shall be designed, constructed, and installed according to law.

(B) A plumbing fixture such as a handwashing lavatory, toilet, or urinal shall be easily cleanable.[N]

5-202.13   Backflow Prevention, Air Gap.*

An air gap between the water supply inlet and the flood level rim of the plumbing fixture, equipment, or nonfood equipment shall be at least twice the diameter of the water supply inlet and may not be less than 25 mm (1 inch).

5-202.14   Backflow Prevention Device, Design Standard.

A backflow or backsiphonage prevention device installed on a water supply system shall meet American Society of Sanitary Engineers (A.S.S.E.) standards for construction, installation, maintenance, inspection, and testing for that specific application and type of device.

5-202.15   Conditioning Device, Design.

A water filter, screen, and other water conditioning device installed on water lines shall be designed to facilitate disassembly for periodic servicing and cleaning. A water filter element shall be of the replaceable type.

"Sewage" means liquid waste containing animal or vegetable matter in suspension or solution and may include liquids containing chemicals in solution.

Retention, Drainage, and Delivery

5-402.11   Establishment Drainage System.

Food establishment drainage systems, including grease traps, that convey sewage shall be sized and installed as specified under ¶ 5-202.11(A).

5-402.12   Backflow Prevention.*

(A) Except as specified in ¶¶ (B) and (C) of this section, a direct connection may not exist between the sewage system and a drain originating from equipment in which food, portable equipment, or utensils are placed.

(B) *If allowed by law, a warewashing machine may have a direct connection between its waste outlet and a floor drain when the machine is located within 1.5 m (5 feet) of a trapped floor drain and the machine outlet is connected to the inlet side of a properly vented floor drain trap.*

(C) *If allowed by law, a warewashing or culinary sink may have a direct connection.*

5-402.13   Grease Trap.

If used, a grease trap shall be located to be easily accessible for cleaning.

5-402.14   Conveying Sewage.*

Sewage shall be conveyed to the point of disposal through an approved sanitary sewage system or other system, including use of sewage transport vehicles, waste retention tanks, pumps, pipes, hoses, and connections that are constructed, maintained, and operated according to law.

5-402.15   Removing Mobile Food Establishment Wastes.

Sewage and other liquid wastes shall be removed from a mobile food establishment at an approved waste servicing area or by a sewage transport vehicle in such a way that a public health hazard or nuisance is not created.

5-402.16   Flushing a Waste Retention Tank.

A tank for liquid waste retention shall be thoroughly flushed and drained in a sanitary manner during the servicing operation.

5-403.11   Approved Sewage Disposal System.*

Sewage shall be disposed through an approved facility that is:

(A) A public sewage treatment plant; or

(B) An individual sewage disposal system that is sized, constructed, maintained, and operated according to law.

5-403.12   Other Liquid Wastes and Rainwater.

Condensate drainage and other nonsewage liquids and rainwater shall be drained from point of discharge to disposal according to law.

Source: FDA 1993 *Food Code.*

Plumbing Systems

Hot and cold water of sufficient quantity and pressure is necessary for any food service operation. Water is used for food production, cleaning and sanitization, and handwashing. Faulty or careless water hook-ups can contaminate otherwise potable or drinking water. Contaminated water is in turn likely to contaminate food, equipment, utensils, and people.

In most places, the public water supply is closely monitored. However, some food service operations may obtain their water from a private source. If water is supplied privately, it must meet the requirements of state laws and be routinely monitored by the supplier in regard to testing (chemical and bacteriological), treatment, storage, and transport. In rare cases, water may be transported from the supplier to the operation either as bulk water or as packaged (bottled) water. Bulk water is stored in the operation's closed-water system.

The types and sizes of equipment in the food service operation dictate hot and cold water requirements. Plumbing codes provide general requirements for water pressure and usage volume for fixtures and equipment. In general, the volume of water supplied and its flow pressure must meet the anticipated peak demand and pressure requirements. Equipment lists in catalogs usually indicate usage pressures and volumes.

If steam comes into contact with food or food-contact surfaces, it must be potable steam; that is, free from harmful additives or materials. A source of drinking water must also be provided for ice-making equipment.

The FDA and state or local plumbing codes cover the installation requirements of the building's plumbing system. The basic objective of these regulations is to guard against contamination of the potable water supply. Direct cross-connections between the potable water supply and a non-potable supply are prohibited.

Plumbing systems must include devices to prevent indirect cross-connections caused by backflow and back siphonage. Backflow is a flow reversal due to a greater pressure in the system compared to the potable water supply. Backflow usually occurs with a sewage line backup in a food sink. Back siphonage can occur when the supply pressure is less than the atmospheric pressure. Usually, back siphonage is caused by a negative pressure on the water supply. This turns an outflow source into an intake source. A hose attached to a faucet with its tip submerged in contaminated water can create an indirect cross-connection subject to back siphonage. Harmful contaminants can be siphoned back into the potable water supply. An air gap between the water supply inlet and the flood level rim of the plumbing fixture, equipment, or nonfood equipment must be at least twice the diameter of the water supply inlet, and cannot be less than 1 inch (25 mm).

If grease traps are part of the plumbing system, they must be easily cleanable. Garbage grinders and disposers must be properly installed. Drains are an important component of the plumbing system. Indirect drains are essential to prevent the backup of sewage into sinks used to clean food, utensils, equipment, or tools. Strict observance of this part of the state and local plumbing codes serves to eliminate faulty plumbing installations and to provide a source of safe drinking water to the public.

Sewage and other liquid waste must be removed from the premises promptly and properly. Sewage is usually removed through a public system. In some areas, an on-site private system for the elimination of sewage and liquid waste is permitted, although some localities limit the capacity of these systems. Such systems require a permit. Care in the disposal of sewage and liquid waste will prevent the contamination of potable water, equipment, utensils, and food.

Most plumbing and sewage codes in the United States are under the jurisdiction of state and local governments. Check with authorities in your area.

Toilet and Lavatory Facilities

The installation, number, convenience, and accessibility of toilet and lavatory facilities are strictly defined in state and local plumbing codes. Toilet facilities must be available for all staff members and guests; usually, staff members should not share restroom facilities with guests if the seating capacity exceeds 50 people in the serving area. Toilet rooms should be completely enclosed and fitted with tight-fitting, self-closing doors which should be kept closed except during cleaning and to assist the handicapped. Each toilet must have a supply of toilet tissue. Fixtures should, like all areas of the facility, be clean and well maintained.

Lavatories (i.e., sinks) may be located either in or immediately adjacent to toilet rooms. Handwashing sinks may not be used for food production or equipment and utensil washing. Each lavatory must have hot and cold running water. A 15-second minimum water flow is required on all metered self-closing or slow-closing faucets.

Each lavatory must be stocked with liquid or powdered handwashing soap or detergent. Handwashing facilities must also have a continuous towel system, single-use paper towels, or heated air-drying devices. Air-drying devices are the most sanitary. If disposable paper towels are used, a waste receptacle is necessary. All equipment in the lavatory must be easy to clean and maintain.

Dispensing systems for restroom supplies (towels, tissue, and soap) can discourage waste and help control costs. Toilet tissue dispensers with the capacity for a reserve roll are best. Fully automatic paper towel dispensers control usage with a timed delay and thus minimize waste.

Liquid soap dispensers are widely used in public restrooms today. These dispensers usually hold approximately one pint (500 ml) to one quart (1 liter) of soap—enough for 1,000 to 3,000 washings. Liquid soap dispensers should be self-cleaning and checked periodically for leaks or clogs. Powdered soap dispensers are also available. Bar soaps, although acceptable for staff member handwashing stations, may be inappropriate for public restrooms because they may become mushy, brittle, or dirty. They may also leave an unsightly residue on lavatories.

The importance of adequate lavatory facilities in a food establishment is obvious: food service staff members are continually touching food and food-contact surfaces. To ensure proper handwashing, an operation must have proper facilities. (Handwashing is also discussed in Chapter 3.)

The FDA states:

5-203.12   Toilets and Urinals.*

At least 1 toilet and not fewer than the number of toilets required by law shall be provided. In accordance with law, urinals may be substituted for toilets if more than the required minimum number of toilets are provided.

5-203.13   Service Sink.

At least 1 service sink or 1 curbed cleaning facility equipped with a floor drain shall be provided and conveniently located for the cleaning of mops or similar wet floor cleaning tools and for the disposal of mop water and similar liquid waste.

5-203.14   Backflow Prevention Device, When Required.*

A plumbing system shall be installed to preclude backflow of a solid, liquid, or gas contaminant into the water supply system at each point of use at the food establishment, including on a hose bibb if a hose is attached or on a hose bibb if a hose is not attached and backflow prevention is required by law, by:

(A)   Providing an air gap as specified under § 5-202.13; or

(B)   Installing an approved backflow prevention device as specified under §
5-202.14.

5-203.15   Backflow Prevention Device, Carbonator.*

(A) If not provided with an air gap as specified under § 5-202.13, a double check
valve with an intermediate vent preceded by a screen of not less than 100 mesh to
25.4 mm (100 mesh to 1 inch) shall be installed upstream from a carbonating device and downstream from any copper in the water supply line.

(B)   *A single or double check valve attached to the carbonator need not be of the vented
type if an air gap or vented backflow prevention device has been otherwise provided as specified under ¶ (A) of this section.*

5-204.12   Backflow Prevention Device, Location.

A backflow prevention device shall be located so that it may be serviced and
maintained.

5-204.13   Conditioning Device, Location.

A water filter, screen, and other water conditioning device installed on water lines
shall be located to facilitate disassembly for periodic servicing and cleaning.

5-205.12   Prohibiting a Cross Connection.*

(A) *Except as allowed under 9 CFR 308.3(d) for firefighting,* a person may not create a
cross connection by connecting a pipe or conduit between the drinking water system and a nondrinking water system or a water system of unknown quality.

(B)   The piping of a nondrinking water system shall be durably identified so that
it is readily distinguishable from piping that carries drinking water.[N]

5-205.13   Scheduling Inspection and Service for a Water System Device.

A device such as a water treatment device or backflow preventer shall be scheduled for inspection and service, in accordance with manufacturers' instructions
and as necessary to prevent device failure based on local water conditions, and
records demonstrating inspection and service shall be maintained by the person in
charge.

6-202.14   Toilet Rooms, Enclosed.

A toilet room located on the premises shall be completely enclosed and provided
with a tight-fitting and self-closing door *except that this requirement does not apply to
a toilet room that is located outside a food establishment and does not open directly into the
food establishment such as a toilet room that is provided by the management of a shopping
mall.*

Toilets and Urinals

6-302.10   Minimum Number.

Toilets and urinals shall be provided as specified under § 5-203.12.

Exhibit 10.7 Restroom Inspection Report Form

Date	Time	Condition(s) Requiring Action	Time Action Taken	Staff Member's Initials	Supervisor's Initials

6-302.11   Toilet Tissue, Availability.

A supply of toilet tissue shall be available at each toilet.

Toilet Rooms

6-402.11   Convenience and Accessibility.

Toilet rooms shall be conveniently located and accessible to employees during all hours of operation.

6-501.19   Closing Toilet Room Doors.

Toilet room doors as specified under § 6-202.14 shall be kept closed *except during cleaning and maintenance operations.*

Source: FDA 1993 *Food Code.*

A clean and well-maintained public restroom is very important. Many people feel that the condition of the restroom reflects the general level of sanitation in a food service or lodging property. Staff members should check restrooms according to a set schedule. A form for this purpose is presented in Exhibit 10.7.

The cleanliness of guestroom and public restrooms is critical to a successful sanitation risk management program. If these facilities are not cleaned correctly, a buildup of pathogens can occur in corners, junctions, spaces between the sink and counter and floor and toilet, and hard-to-reach corners in the bathtub or shower. The pathogens can make people ill. Pathogens can be transferred to guests who place makeup, toothbrushes, or shaving equipment on counters that have not been properly cleaned.

Restroom cleaners containing detergents and quaternary ammonium compounds can be used on all restroom surfaces. A detailed restroom cleaning procedure is provided in *Housekeeping Procedures,* a book published by Ecolab, Inc. An outline of the critical steps follows:

1. Turn on all lights and the ventilating fan.
2. Flush the toilet. After it has refilled, pour cleaner-detergent into the toilet bowl.
3. Wash the tub area, tile walls, tub enclosure, and shower curtain to remove soap film and hair. Flush the tracks and guides free of soapy water and hair if there is a glass or plastic tub enclosure.
4. Clean the tub fixtures. Make certain there is no ring around the tub or marks near the drain. If the tub has a pop-up stopper, remove it and clean it thoroughly. Polish it dry.
5. Clean the lavatory. Flush soap dishes with hot water. Remove, clean, and polish pop-up stoppers.
6. Wash off counter and tile splash-areas and all fixtures.
7. With a clean damp cloth, dust light fixtures, the door (including the top of the door), all exposed piping, the top of the tub enclosure, and the shower curtain rod.
8. Clean and polish mirrors with glass cleaner.
9. Clean the toilet by swabbing the bowl thoroughly, including around and under the rim. Clean outer areas and all fixtures.
10. Rinse your hands in the lavatory and dry with a clean cloth.
11. Dry the lavatory, counter, and fixtures.
12. Replace supplies (soap, towels, paper products).
13. Clean the floor, starting at the corner of the room and finishing at the door.
14. Always clean from top to bottom so you are not resoiling surfaces already cleaned.

When used frequently and properly, this system of restroom cleaning is effective and economical; it reduces labor and eliminates a buildup of pathogenic organisms.

Cleaning and Maintaining Furniture, Glass, and Decorative Items

Many decorative items are used to enhance an operation's image and ambiance. The frequency of cleaning and maintenance depends on the item and its use.

Curtains, draperies, and upholstered furniture can add a great deal to the ambiance of a food establishment or lodging property. In most cases, careful vacuuming will prolong the life of these items. Some fabrics may be handwashed when soiled, while other fabrics must be dry-cleaned. Because of the variety of fabrics used for these items, it is best to follow the manufacturer's cleaning recommendations.

Hot solvent cleaning can be used to clean silks, crushed velvet, and other fine fabrics. This method minimizes color bleeding and shrinkage. Portable equipment is used for in-place cleaning of curtains, draperies, and upholstered furniture. The equipment resembles a miniature water extraction unit.

A dry foam soil extractor may be used to shampoo and remove spills from upholstery. The machine loosens dirt and the attached vacuum removes the soil. The equipment can also be used to clean carpeted stairs. Some upholstery fabrics can be made soil-resistant by applying a protective coating after cleaning.

Blinds and shades should be vacuumed or dusted frequently. Some metal and plastic surfaces can be washed with a mild detergent solution and rinsed with clean water. Cloth or fabric materials may require specialized cleaning chemicals and procedures.

Glass is relatively easy to clean and maintain, and the necessary equipment and supplies are relatively inexpensive. Squeegees come in a variety of sizes. Brass models with hardwood handles are more durable than aluminum models. An ammonia-water solution cleans glass effectively. Alcohol may be added to the water as an anti-freeze when cleaning windows at temperatures below freezing. Commercial glass cleaners are also effective.

Periodic, scheduled cleaning of glass surfaces is necessary to prevent excessive soil buildup. Some establishments contract their outdoor window cleaning to professional companies. This reduces the safety risks for the operation's own staff members.

Plant care programs are essential for establishments using live plants to enhance decor. A typical plant care program includes watering, periodic trimming and grooming, fertilizing, insect and disease control, and replacement of unhealthy plants.

Interior plants should be selected and placed according to the individual plant's requirements. Each species may have slightly different needs for water, air, light, humidity, nutrients, grooming, and transplanting. In most cases, light should be continuous for 12 to 14 hours daily. A minimum intensity of 50 footcandles is generally recommended. Ideal temperatures range from 70° to 75°F (21° to 24°C). Indoor plants usually come from tropical environments; therefore, they prefer humid air.

Most plants prefer soil that is barely moist throughout at all times. Potting soil is a lightweight soil that drains quickly; it is cleaner and contains more nutrients than outdoor soil. Indoor plants should be fed lightly with fertilizer about three times annually. Many properties contract their plant care to an outside company. This ensures that the plants are always healthy and attractive.

Refuse Storage and Disposal

Food contamination and pest problems can be prevented by the proper storage and disposal of refuse. Refuse is solid waste not carried through the sewage system. Refuse is often stored outdoors before removal. Containers used for this purpose must be insect- and rodent-resistant, durable, non-absorbent, leak-proof, easily cleanable, and maintained in good repair. Refuse containers should be lined with wet-strength paper or plastic bags. Bags alone should not be used for outdoor refuse storage because they are not pest-resistant. Outdoor receptacles must have tight-fitting doors or lids.

A food establishment's refuse facilities must be of adequate capacity. Refuse containers not in use should be stored outdoors on a rack or in a storage box at least 18 inches (46 cm) off the ground. Refuse containers should be cleaned regularly to prevent insect and rodent infestation. Containers can be cleaned effectively with a combination of detergent and hot water or steam.

Refuse must be removed from the premises frequently to prevent odor and pest problems. Outdoor refuse storage areas must be clean and well-maintained. Enclosures must be made of durable, easily cleanable materials. Outdoor refuse storage areas must have a smooth, non-absorbent base (such as asphalt or concrete) that is sloped to drain.

The FDA states:

"Refuse" means solid waste not carried by water through the sewage system.

5-5 REFUSE, RECYCLABLES, AND RETURNABLES

Facilities on the Premises

5-501.11 Indoor Storage Area.

If located within the food establishment, a storage area for refuse, recyclables, and returnables shall meet the requirements specified under Parts 6-1 and 6-2.

5-501.12 Outdoor Storage Surface.

An outdoor storage surface for refuse, recyclables, and returnables shall be constructed of nonabsorbent material such as concrete or asphalt and shall be smooth, durable, and sloped to drain.

5-501.13 Outdoor Enclosure.

If used, an outdoor enclosure for refuse, recyclables, and returnables shall be constructed of durable and cleanable materials.

5-501.14 Receptacles.

(A) Except as specified in ¶ (B) of this section, equipment and receptacles for refuse, recyclables, and returnables and for use with materials containing food residue shall be durable, cleanable, insect- and rodent-resistant, leakproof, and nonabsorbent.

(B) *Plastic bags and wet strength paper bags may be used to line receptacles for storage inside the food establishment, or within closed outside receptacles.*

5-501.16 Outside Receptacles.

(A) Equipment and receptacles for refuse, recyclables, and returnables used with materials containing food residue and used outside the food establishment shall be designed and constructed to have tight-fitting lids, doors, or covers.

(B) Equipment for refuse and recyclables such as an on-site compactor shall be installed so that accumulation of debris and insect and rodent attraction and harborage are minimized and effective cleaning is facilitated around and, if the equipment is not installed flush with the base pad, under the unit.

5-501.17 Storage Areas, Rooms, and Receptacles, Capacity and Availability.

(A) An inside storage room and area and outside storage area and enclosure, and receptacles shall be of sufficient capacity to hold refuse, recyclables, and returnables that accumulate.

(B) A receptacle shall be provided in each area of the establishment or premises where refuse is generated or commonly discarded, or where recyclables or returnables are placed.

(C) If disposable towels are used at handwashing lavatories, a waste receptacle shall be located at each lavatory or group of adjacent lavatories.

5-501.18 Toilet Room Receptacle, Covered.

A toilet room used by females shall be provided with a covered receptacle for sanitary napkins.

5-501.19   Cleaning Equipment and Supplies.

(A) Except as specified in ¶ (B) of this section, suitable cleaning equipment and supplies such as high pressure pumps, hot water, steam, and detergent shall be provided as necessary for effective cleaning of equipment and receptacles for refuse, recyclables, and returnables.

(B) *If approved by the regulatory authority, off-premise-based cleaning services may be used if on-premises cleaning equipment and supplies are not provided.*

5-501.110   Storage Areas, Redeeming Machines, Equipment, and Receptacles, Location.

(A) An area designated for refuse, recyclables, returnables, and, except as specified in ¶ (B) of this section, a redeeming machine for recyclables or returnables shall be located so that it is separate from food, equipment, utensils, linens, and single-service and single-use articles and a public health nuisance is not created.

(B) *A redeeming machine may be located in the packaged food storage area or consumer area of a food establishment if food, equipment, utensils, linens, and single-service and single-use articles are not subject to contamination from the machines and a public health nuisance is not created.*

(C) The location of equipment and receptacles for refuse, recyclables, and returnables may not create a public health nuisance or interfere with the cleaning of adjacent space.

5-501.111   Storing Refuse, Recyclables, and Returnables.

Refuse, recyclables, and returnables shall be stored in equipment or refuse receptacles so that they are inaccessible to insects and rodents.

5-501.112   Areas, Enclosures, and Receptacles, Good Repair.

Storage areas, enclosures, and receptacles for refuse, recyclables, and returnables shall be maintained in good repair.

5-501.113   Outside Storage Prohibitions.

(A) Except as specified in ¶ (B) of this section, refuse receptacles not meeting the requirements specified under ¶ 5-501.14(A) such as receptacles that are not rodent-resistant, unprotected plastic bags and paper bags, or baled units that contain materials with food residue may not be stored outside.

(B) *Cardboard or other packaging material that does not contain food residues and that is awaiting regularly scheduled delivery to a recycling or disposal site may be stored outside without being in a covered receptacle if it is stored so that it does not create a rodent harborage problem.*

5-501.114   Covering Receptacles.

Equipment and receptacles for refuse, recyclables, and returnables shall be kept covered:

(A)   Inside the establishment if the equipment and receptacles:

    (1)   Contain food residue and are not in continuous use; or

    (2)   After they are filled; and

(B)   With tight-fitting lids or doors if kept outside the establishment.

5-501.115   Using Drain Plugs.

Drains in equipment and receptacles for refuse, recyclables, and returnables shall have drain plugs in place.

5-501.116   Maintaining Refuse Areas and Enclosures.

A storage area and enclosure for refuse, recyclables, or returnables shall be maintained free of unnecessary items, as specified under § 6-501.114, and clean.

5-501.117   Cleaning Receptacles.

(A) Equipment and receptacles for refuse, recyclables, and returnables shall be thoroughly cleaned in a way that does not contaminate food, equipment, utensils, linens, or single-service and single-use articles, and waste water shall be disposed of as specified under § 5-402.14.

(B) Soiled equipment and receptacles for refuse, recyclables, and returnables shall be cleaned at a frequency necessary to prevent them from developing a buildup of soil or becoming attractants for insects and rodents.

Removal

5-502.11   Frequency.

Refuse, recyclables, and returnables shall be removed from the premises at a frequency that will minimize the development of objectionable odors and other conditions that attract or harbor insects and rodents.

5-502.12   Receptacles or Vehicles.

Refuse, recyclables, and returnables shall be removed from the premises by way of:

(A)   Portable receptacles that are constructed and maintained according to law; or

(B)   A transport vehicle that is constructed, maintained, and operated according to law.

Facilities for Disposal, Recycling, and Refilling

5-503.11   Community or Individual Facility.

Solid waste not disposed of through the sewage system such as through grinders and pulpers shall be recycled or disposed of in an approved public or private community recycling or refuse facility; or solid waste shall be disposed of in an individual refuse facility such as a landfill or incinerator which is sized, constructed, maintained, and operated according to law.

Refuse, Recyclables, and Returnables

6-405.10   Equipment, Receptacles, and Designated Storage Area.

Equipment, receptacles, and areas designated for storage of refuse and recyclable and returnable containers shall be located as specified under § 5-501.110.

5-503.12   Returnables, On-Site Cleaning and Refilling.

(A) Except as specified in ¶¶ (B) and (C) of this section, empty containers intended for cleaning and refilling with food shall be cleaned and refilled in a regulated food processing establishment.

(B) *A food-specific container for beverages may be refilled at a food establishment if:*

　　(1) *Only beverages that are not potentially hazardous are used;*

　　(2) *The design of the container and of the rinsing equipment and the nature of the beverage, when considered together, allow effective cleaning at home or in the establishment;*

　　(3) *Facilities for rinsing before refilling returned containers with fresh, hot water that is under pressure and not recirculated are provided as part of the dispensing system;*

　　(4) *The consumer-owned container returned to the food establishment for refilling is refilled for sale or service only to the same consumer; and*

　　(5) *The container is refilled by:*

　　　　(a) *An employee of the establishment, or*

　　　　(b) *The owner of the container if the beverage system includes a contamination-free transfer process that can not be bypassed by the container owner.*

(C) *Consumer-owned containers that are not food-specific may be filled at a water vending machine.*

Source: FDA 1993 *Food Code.*

Many large food service operations use trash compactors. Such equipment can reduce solid waste bulk by up to 75%. Some compactors automatically deodorize and apply insecticides to solid waste. Liquid waste generated by a compactor should be disposed of as sewage. Suitable facilities with hot water are also required for compactors.

Recycling has become an important consideration for some food service operators. Fast-food operations are often accused of generating large amounts of paper, plastic, and polystyrene refuse. Many chains have responded by reducing the weight and thickness of their containers or by completely changing the materials used. Recycled paper can be used for cash receipts, order pages for servers, and placemats.

Recycling will increasingly be required of food service operators. Protection from insects and rodents is critical during storage of recyclables. Recyclables must be regularly removed from the premises of a food establishment. They can be temporarily stored in portable receptacles or removed with transport vehicles. Food service operators would be wise to make a positive difference in their communities through the use of recycling.

Exterior Cleaning and Maintenance

Exterior masonry surfaces are typically brick, concrete block, stucco, stone, or a combination of these materials. These surfaces are porous and attract water, dirt, and scale. Cleaning such surfaces is difficult but important. Cleaning methods vary according to the climate, the type and condition of the masonry, and the design of the building. (Exhibit 10.6 includes cleaning procedures for some of these surfaces.)

Exterior masonry cleaners are frequently applied with spray guns and hoses. During cleaning operations, glass and aluminum exterior surfaces, as well as plants and shrubs, must be protected. Damaged masonry surfaces can be repaired and waterproofed with special chemical compounds. These applications not only enhance the exterior appearance of the building; they also prolong its life and increase its value.

Clean parking lots and sidewalks contribute to a positive first impression as guests approach the facility. These surfaces should be easy to maintain and should not cause dust problems. The type of outdoor cleaning equipment to select depends on the area to be cleaned, surface characteristics, the type of debris to be removed, the frequency of cleaning, and the financial resources available. A number of different types of sweeping machines are available. Air-recycling machines create an air blast with a fan to loosen debris. The debris is pulled up through a hose and deposited in a collection tank. Broom-vacuum machines loosen debris with a rotating broom and deposit it into a hopper. Push vacuum machines are walk-behind units used primarily to clean large outdoor surfaces. They function much like regular vacuum cleaners.

The FDA states:

6-202.15   Outer Openings, Protected.

(A) *Except in temporary food establishments,* openings to the outdoors shall be protected against the entry of insects and rodents by:

   (1)   Closed, tight-fitting windows, and

   (2)   Solid self-closing, tight-fitting doors; or

(B) Except as specified in ¶ (C) of this section, if windows or doors are kept open for ventilation or other purposes, or the food operation is conducted in a temporary food establishment that is not provided with windows and solid doors, the openings shall be protected against the entry of insects and rodents by:

   (1)   16 mesh to 25.4 mm (16 mesh to 1 inch) screens,

   (2)   Properly designed and installed air curtains, or

   (3)   Other effective means.

(C) *Paragraph (B) of this section does not apply if flying insects and other pests are absent due to the location of the establishment, the weather, or other limiting condition.*

6-202.16   Exterior Walls and Roofs, Protective Barrier.

Perimeter walls and roofs of a food establishment shall effectively protect the establishment from the weather and the entry of insects, rodents, and other animals.

6-202.17 Outdoor Food Vending Areas, Overhead Protection.

If located outside, a machine used to vend food shall be provided with overhead protection *except that machines vending canned beverages need not meet this requirement.*

6-202.18 Outdoor Servicing Areas, Overhead Protection.

Servicing areas shall be provided with overhead protection *except that areas used only for the loading of water or the discharge of sewage and other liquid waste, through the use of a closed system of hoses, need not be provided with overhead protection.*

6-202.19 Outdoor Walking and Driving Surfaces, Graded to Drain.

Exterior walking and driving surfaces shall be graded to drain.

6-202.110 Outdoor Refuse Areas, Curbed and Graded to Drain.

Outdoor refuse areas shall be constructed in accordance with law and shall be curbed and graded to drain to collect and dispose of liquid waste that results from the refuse and from cleaning the area and waste receptacles.

6-202.111 Private Homes and Living or Sleeping Quarters, Use Prohibition.

A private home, a room used as living or sleeping quarters, or an area directly opening into a room used as living or sleeping quarters may not be used for conducting food establishment operations.

6-202.112 Living or Sleeping Quarters, Separation.

Living or sleeping quarters located on the premises of a food establishment such as those provided for lodging registration clerks or resident managers shall be separated from rooms and areas used for food establishment operations by complete partitioning and solid self-closing doors.

6-501.114 Maintaining Premises, Unnecessary Items and Litter.

The premises shall be free of:

    (A)   Items that are unnecessary to the operation or maintenance of the establishment such as equipment that is nonfunctional or no longer used; and

    (B)   Litter.

Source: FDA 1993 *Food Code.*

Ice and snow melting compounds play an important role in exterior building maintenance in certain climates. These compounds are only effective if the bulk of the snow has already been removed. Snow removal can be expensive, but it is necessary for the sake of appearance and safety. Many operations contract snow removal to an outside company rather than purchasing the equipment and having a regular staff member do it.

The three major types of ice and snow melting compounds are rock salt, calcium chloride, and pre-formulated chemicals. These compounds should always be used according to the manufacturer's directions.

Rock salt is relatively abundant and inexpensive. This compound lowers the freezing point of water; however, it is ineffective at temperatures below 0°F (–18°C). Rock salt leaves behind a powdered residue which may soil carpeting near entrances. Rock salt can also be corrosive to metals containing iron.

Calcium chloride compounds create an intense heat and absorb moisture; thus they are effective at temperatures below 0°F (–18°C). However, these compounds can destroy animal and plant life, concrete, carpeting, fabrics, and metal surfaces. Calcium chloride may irritate the skin, so gloves should be worn when using this chemical. Calcium chloride compounds are more expensive than rock salt.

Pre-formulated chemicals are the most expensive ice and snow removal compounds. They are also the safest. They melt snow and ice quickly, are non-toxic, and are non-corrosive to metals and fabrics. They are also effective at temperatures below 0°F (–18°C).

The selection of ice and snow melting compounds should be based on the requirements of the individual operation. The compounds should be stored in low-moisture areas and applied with caution.

Cleaning and Maintenance in Lodging Operations

As pointed out at the beginning of this chapter, much of the discussion of the cleaning and maintenance of food service facilities applies to lodging operations as well. The rest of this chapter is devoted exclusively to special cleaning and maintenance considerations for lodging establishments. We will consider the role of the housekeeping department in the cleaning and maintenance of hotels and motels, and then briefly discuss on-premises laundry facilities.[1]

The Housekeeping Department

The housekeeping department of a modern lodging property does more than just clean; it provides a pleasant, clean, and comfortable environment in which guests can feel secure and satisfied. Housekeeping staff members should be made aware of their vital contribution to the property's overall image and their tremendous impact on guest satisfaction. By consistently exceeding guest expectations, an efficient housekeeping department encourages guests and their acquaintances to return to the property, stimulating both repeat business and positive word-of-mouth advertising.

The **executive housekeeper** is in charge of the housekeeping department of a lodging property, and is a member of the management team. Although department organization and operations vary with the size and individual needs of a property, housekeeping is a 24-hour effort in many properties.

Consider a 400-room hotel that can accommodate 900 guests. In addition to its guestrooms, the hotel has two restaurants, a large lobby area, four banquet/conference rooms, and an outdoor pool and courtyard area. The equipment requirements of this property are staggering. The housekeeping department alone requires thirty vacuum cleaners, two wet vacuums, one extractor, three carpet shampooers, several portable cleaning units for upholstery, and a floor machine. The department also needs a large inventory of cleaning chemicals, room supplies, and cleaning accessories.

The hotel also requires a large housekeeping staff. The executive housekeeper is in charge of four supervisors; each supervisor oversees 100 guestrooms. The department also includes 70 room attendants and 20 laundry operators. The on-premises laundry processes over 150,000 pounds (68,100 kg) of linens each month from the rooms and food and beverage departments—over 900 tons (816,000 kg) in an average year. The cost of supplies (cleaning chemicals, equipment, room supplies) and labor for the house-keeping department exceeds half a million dollars annually.

In some lodging properties, a room attendant cleans 15 to 18 guestrooms in an eight-hour shift. The supervisor spot-checks cleaned guestrooms. The supervisor is also usually responsible for distributing supplies and training new staff members. The housekeeping staff may also assist the food and beverage department in preparing meeting and banquet rooms.

What makes an efficient housekeeping department? Six basics of housekeeping management have been identified in progressive and successful lodging operations. These fundamentals form the core of a lodging property's housekeeping program.

1. Contact with top management on a regular basis

2. Development of supervisors' leadership skills

3. Training of supervisors and staff members

4. Motivation of supervisors and staff members

5. Providing the necessary equipment and supplies

6. Measuring the efficiency of the overall effort

The six basics of housekeeping management provide a realistic set of objectives for any lodging property.

Housekeeping tasks should be performed when business is the slowest. For example, public areas are usually cleaned late at night. Guestrooms, on the other hand, are usually cleaned by mid-afternoon because they must be ready for assignment to guests, who generally arrive in the afternoon or early evening.

Waste Collection and Disposal

One of the main functions of the housekeeping department is the collection and disposal of litter and waste. A lodging property typically uses a variety of receptacles for this purpose.

Cigarettes are usually disposed of in some type of urn. Self-closing urns are best because they are attractive and minimize fire hazards. Water-quenching urns are also effective; however, they are difficult to refill, may cause odor problems, and are subject to corrosion. Granular-filled urns, which contain stone chips or sand, are another alternative. However, if these urns tip over, the stone chips or sand may damage carpets and floors. Urns should be placed near telephones, elevators, drinking fountains, restrooms, and in landings, foyers, and lobby areas. Their contents should only be emptied into metal containers.

Waste receptacles should be located near entrances, exits, and on terraces. Outside receptacles must be covered to protect them from the elements. Guestroom wastebaskets should be conveniently located. Waste receptacles should be seamless to reduce odors and facilitate cleaning. Plastic film liners protect waste receptacles and make them easier to empty.

Waste may be collected from urns and receptacles and placed on a custodial cart or in a plastic drum on wheels. Some operations use litter vacuums that shred waste, depositing it in a collection bag. Once collected, waste must be disposed of properly. (Refuse storage and disposal are discussed in an earlier section of this chapter.)

The On-Premises Laundry

Many hospitality properties operate their own **on-premises laundry (OPL)**.[2] The OPL should be designed and operated according to the specific needs of the property. The following list suggests some important planning considerations:

- Property size and level of service
- The maximum amount of laundry (output) the OPL will be expected to handle
- The amount of space allocated to the OPL
- How much and what kind of equipment to purchase
- Valet laundry service for guests

The OPL launders primarily linens—bedding, towels, and dining room linens. Linens may be made of all-natural fabrics (such as cotton and wool) or synthetic fabrics (such as nylon and polyester). Most properties select a polyester/cotton blend since this fabric offers most of the comfort of all-natural fabrics but is easier to care for. Regardless of the fabric, linens should be laundered according to the manufacturer's instructions.

Exhibit 10.8 shows the flow of linens through a property. In a lodging property, linens are collected in guestrooms, guest bathrooms, public restrooms, and dining areas. Housekeeping staff members place soiled guestroom linens into soiled-linen bags. Buspersons or servers usually collect soiled linens in food service outlets. It is important to keep tableware out of the bags since it can stain linens permanently. Linens are transported to the OPL either by hand or on carts. Linens should never be dragged across the floor.

Once inside the OPL, linens are sorted by the color and type of fabric and degree of soiling. Cleaning rags should be washed separately because they are more heavily soiled than bed sheets. Fabric color, type, and soil will determine the washing process, washing time, water temperature, amount of agitation, and proper chemicals. Wash cycles may include as many as nine steps.

In addition to water and detergent, several chemicals are commonly used in OPLs. These include fabric brighteners, bleaches, mildewcides, fabric softeners, starches, antichlors (which remove bleach), alkalies (detergent boosters), and sours (which neutralize residual alkalinity). These chemicals are inventory resources that must be handled carefully, used according to manufacturer's recommendations, and controlled in the same way as food and beverage inventory items. (The handling of chemicals is discussed further in Chapter 9.)

Staff training is the key to success in the OPL. Training should include safety, equipment operation, and inventory handling. Regular equipment inspection should also be included. Periodic retraining for everyone helps ensure that standards are being maintained. Retraining reinforces earlier training and demonstrates the property's commitment to safety and other standards. Training materials should be presented to staff members in a language they can understand. With the rising number of non-English-speaking staff members in hospitality properties, multi-lingual training programs are becoming a necessity. Chemical and equipment suppliers can often help with training programs.

Equipment resources in an OPL are a major investment. This equipment may include washers, dryers, steam cabinets and tunnels, ironers and pressing machines, folding machines, and rolling/holding equipment. Each specialized piece of equipment must be regularly serviced as part of a preventive maintenance program.

Exhibit 10.8 The Flow of Laundry Through a Hotel and Food Service Operation

Source: *On Premises Laundry Procedures in Hotels, Motels, Healthcare Facilities, and Restaurants* (St. Paul, Minn.: Ecolab, Institutional Products Division), undated.

Facilities and the SRM Program

Facilities represent the greatest dollar investment in assets by a hospitality establishment. These assets can become liabilities if a realistic sanitation risk management (SRM) program is not developed, implemented, and monitored.

All of the activities associated with the nine control points discussed so far take place in facilities. The cleaning and maintenance of all areas of hospitality facilities must receive a high priority after the facilities are properly designed and constructed. Surfaces (such as floors, walls, and ceilings) must be regularly cleaned and maintained. The SRM program must also address lighting, ventilation, plumbing systems, and decorative lighting. Dressing rooms and laundries have unique SRM considerations, as does the exterior of the facilities.

By establishing procedures in each area of the facilities, managers can reduce risks and maximize the return on investment in relation to these assets.

Summary

The construction and maintenance of physical facilities according to guidelines provided by the National Sanitation Foundation and the FDA can reduce risks. Floors, walls, and ceilings must be designed and constructed to be easy to clean and maintain. Lighting levels are important to maintain a clean and accident-free environment. Proper ventilation removes fumes, smoke, steam, heat, and unpleasant odors. Dining room and kitchen ventilation must be coordinated.

Sanitary facilities are important for staff morale and public safety. A safe, potable water supply must be provided in all food establishments. Properly designed plumbing and sewage systems are essential components of sanitary facilities.

Refuse containers must be durable, easy to clean, pest-resistant, and maintained regularly. Exterior cleaning and maintenance help enhance the guest's first impression of the operation.

In this chapter, special concerns were presented regarding the cleaning and maintenance of lodging facilities, including the housekeeping department, on-premises laundry, and waste collection and disposal.

Remember, it is important to follow state and local health codes.

Endnotes

1. For a thorough discussion of housekeeping operations in the hospitality industry, see *Managing Housekeeping Operations* by Margaret M. Kappa, Aleta Nitschke, and Patricia B. Schappert (East Lansing, Mich: The Educational Institute of the American Hotel & Motel Association, 1990).
2. This section is based on Chapter 8 of *Managing Housekeeping Operations.*

Key Terms

executive housekeeper • footcandle • hard floor • modular carpeting • on-premises laundry • resilient floor

Discussion Questions

1. What types of floors do the FDA and NSF recommend for food establishments?

2. According to the FDA, wall coverings or finishes in food production areas should be light-colored, smooth, and non-absorbent. Why?

3. How is lighting intensity measured?

4. Ventilation serves what purposes in a food establishment? What is the major ventilation problem in most restaurants?

5. Laundry facilities may be installed in a food establishment to wash what types of items?

6. Requirements for toilet and lavatory facilities are defined by what agencies or regulations?

7. What types of care do window blinds and shades require?

8. What are the requirements for containers used for outdoor storage of refuse?

9. The selection of outdoor cleaning equipment should be based on what factors?

10. An on-premises laundry for a lodging operation requires what five planning considerations?

Checklist for Facilities Cleaning and Maintenance

General

____ Facilities are constructed and maintained in accordance with state, local, and federal codes and ordinances.

____ A room finish schedule is submitted to local health officials when renovations or new facility construction is planned.

____ Cleaning takes place when the least amount of food is exposed.

____ Staff members are trained to clean when not busy with other responsibilities.

Floors, Walls, and Ceilings

____ Floors, ceilings, and walls are properly constructed and maintained in good repair.

____ A regular cleaning and maintenance program is established for walls and ceilings.

____ Anti-slip floor coverings are used where permitted.

____ Dustless methods of floor cleaning are used.

____ Floor materials in each area are selected according to the area's planned use.

_____ Floor maintenance methods are based on the characteristics of the materials.

_____ High-pressure cleaning is used for floors with irregular surfaces.

_____ Selection of floor-cleaning chemicals is based on the floor manufacturer's recommendations.

Lighting and Ventilation

_____ Utilities are installed to minimize the likelihood of contamination and soil buildup.

_____ Adequate lighting is present in all areas of the facility, and light fixtures are cleaned and maintained regularly.

_____ Light bulbs and tubes are shielded in food storage, production, service, or display areas and in equipment and utensil cleaning and storage areas.

_____ Ventilation equipment is available and used to remove smoke, fumes, steam, condensation, excessive heat, vapors, and obnoxious odors.

_____ Ventilation systems are present and meet all regulatory authority requirements.

_____ Kitchen and serving area ventilation systems are coordinated.

Dressing Rooms and Laundry Facilities

_____ Dressing and locker rooms are not used for food storage, preparation, or service, or equipment and utensil washing or storage.

_____ Laundry facilities are installed and operated according to established standards.

Plumbing Systems

_____ Water in the proper quantity, quality, and temperature is available for normal operations.

_____ Liquid waste and sewage are removed promptly and properly.

_____ The building's plumbing system meets all applicable codes.

_____ The plumbing system is designed and maintained to prevent backflow and back siphonage.

_____ Toilet facilities and lavatories are regularly inspected, cleaned, and maintained, and meet all applicable codes.

_____ Staff members are assigned to check the condition of public restrooms frequently throughout the day.

_____ Restroom supplies are checked regularly and replaced when necessary.

Decorative Items

_____ Draperies and upholstery are vacuumed regularly to prolong their useful lives.

_____ Fabrics are cleaned according to the manufacturer's recommendations.

_____ Glass and windows are cleaned regularly.

_____ A contract service is used for exterior window cleaning.

_____ The plant care program covers watering, trimming, fertilizing, and insect and disease control.

_____ Plants are healthy, properly shaped, and attractive.

Refuse Storage and Disposal

_____ Refuse containers are durable, easy to clean, and pest-resistant.

_____ Outdoor refuse containers are kept covered.

_____ Refuse containers are cleaned and maintained at regular intervals.

_____ Refuse recycling is evaluated and implemented when appropriate.

Exterior Cleaning and Maintenance

_____ Cleaning methods selected for exterior building surfaces are suited to the climate, the type and condition of the materials, and the building design.

_____ Parking lots and sidewalks are regularly cleaned and maintained.

_____ Ice and snow melting compounds are used during the winter to maintain the attractiveness and safety of the property's sidewalks and entrance areas.

Housekeeping

_____ Housekeeping staff members are aware that they are part of the property's public relations efforts.

_____ The six basics of housekeeping management are used to evaluate the department's efficiency and effectiveness.

_____ Housekeeping activities take place when business is slowest.

_____ Chemicals used in public areas work safely and rapidly and dry quickly.

Waste Collection and Disposal

_____ Urns and waste receptacles are conveniently located and properly maintained.

_____ Urns and waste receptacles are emptied regularly and their contents disposed of properly.

On-Premises Laundry (OPL)

_____ The OPL is planned according to its expected output, space, services provided, equipment, and the size of the property.

_____ Linens are selected and maintained using manufacturer's instructions.

_____ Laundry chemicals are handled carefully and used in the proper amounts.

SRM Program

_____ All areas of the facilities are designed, constructed, cleaned, and maintained in accordance with applicable laws.

References

Almund, J. "A Look at Applications for Truck Mounted Hot Water Extraction Equipment for Carpet Care and Pressure Washing." *Cleaning Management,* February 1982, p. 22.

Ames, A. "Checklists for Preventive Maintenance." *Cleaning Management,* November 1982, pp. 13–14.

———. "Hot Solvent Cleaning for Upholstery and Delicate Fabrics." *Cleaning Management,* July 1982, p. 28.

———. Ultra High-Speed Cleaning and Polishing." *Cleaning Management,* April 1982, p. 34.

———. "Planning for Preventive Maintenance." *Cleaning Management,* July 1982, p. 28.

———. "What's New in Floor Seals?" *Cleaning Management,* June 1982, p. 12.

Arthurs, Sandra. "Mr. Clean Was Right—Everyone Does Notice." *Ontario Innkeeper,* December/January 1987, pp. 31–35.

Bondurant, J. "Caring for Interior Plants." *Cleaning Management,* December 1981, p. 6.

Borges, M. "Calculating Cleaning Costs." *Cleaning Management,* September 1982, p. 46.

"Carpet Care Economics." *Club Management,* June 1989, pp. 34–35.

Cichy, R. F. "A Clean Sweep." *Restaurant Business,* June 10, 1989, p. 244.

Curran, George. "Restrooms: Bubble, Bubble, Toilets and Trouble." *Restaurants & Institutions,* September 2, 1987, p. 160.

"Electric Hand Dryers vs. Paper Towels." *Cleaning Management,* November 1982, p. 40.

Entzminger, B. "Improving Cleaning Accessibility." *Cleaning Management,* September 1982, p. 26.

Feldman, E. B. "Waste Collection and Disposal." *Cleaning Management,* October 1981, p. 24.

———. "Universal Factors of Effective Housekeeping." *Cleaning Management,* September 1982, p. 6.

———. "Housekeeping's Role in Developing a Good Public Image." *Cleaning Management,* April 1982, pp. 56–57.

Fivecoat-Wihelm, T. "Dispensing with Restroom Servicing Problems." *Cleaning Management,* February 1982, p. 6.

―――. "Managing Your Window Washing Operation." *Cleaning Management,* May 1982, p. 6.

―――. "Selecting Ice and Snow Melting Compounds." *Cleaning Management,* November 1981, p. 32.

―――. "A Look at Hotel Housekeeping Operations." *Cleaning Management,* November 1981, p. 6.

Food and Drug Administration, Center for Food Safety and Applied Nutrition, Retail Food Protection Branch. *Interpretation: Premises—Clothes Dryers,* November 7, 1985.

Food and Drug Administration, Center for Food Safety and Applied Nutrition, Retail Food Protection Branch. *Interpretation: Premises—Storage of Soiled Linens and Clothes in Cold Rooms,* November 7, 1985.

Green, A. S. "Cleaning Exterior Masonry Surfaces." *Cleaning Management,* May 1982, p. 30.

Heiland, R. "High-Pressure Cleaning Does the Tough Jobs." *Cleaning Management,* November 1981, p. 22.

Hillyard, S. "How a Chemical Manufacturer Views Carpet Care Methods." *Cleaning Management,* December 1981, p. 28.

Kappa, Margaret M.; Aleta Nitschke; and Patricia B. Schappert. *Managing Housekeeping Operations.* East Lansing, Mich: Educational Institute of the American Hotel & Motel Association, 1990.

Koppi, J. "How to Calculate Your Return on Investment for Equipment Purchases." *Cleaning Management,* May 1982, p. 26.

Lima, Tony. "Chicago Hilton's Clean Machine." *Lodging Hospitality,* May 1989, pp. 5, 59.

"New Products Change Look—and Life—of Flooring." *Institutions/Volume Feeding,* April 1977, p. 65.

O'Dwyer, Christine. "Are Budget Bathrooms Bad News?" *Lodging,* June 1990, pp. 25–26.

"Questions About Acoustical Ceiling Cleaning." *Cleaning Management,* July 1982, p. 24.

"There's More Than One Way to Strip a Floor." *Cleaning Management,* July 1982, p. 8.

Trainor, L. "How Modular Carpeting Saves on Maintenance." *Cleaning Management,* October 1982, p. 22.

"A Uniform Approach to Restroom Care." *Cleaning Management,* February 1982, pp. 32–33.

REVIEW QUIZ

When you feel you have covered all of the material in this chapter, answer these questions. Choose the *best* answer. Check your answers with the correct ones found on the Review Quiz Answer Key at the end of this book.

1. Which of the following is often used for irregular floor surfaces such as those found in kitchen areas?

   a. high-pressure cleaning
   b. steam cleaning
   c. damp mopping with alkalis
   d. broom vacuuming

2. Mop water, or similar liquid wastes, should be disposed of in:

   a. food service equipment washing areas.
   b. parking lots.
   c. utility sinks.
   d. any of the above.

3. Which of the following floor care procedures combines the mechanical agitation of an abrasive scrubbing compound with a small amount of moisture?

   a. dry stripping
   b. broom vacuuming
   c. rotary shampooing
   d. polishing

4. Smudges and fingerprints on walls should be wiped off:

   a. weekly.
   b. daily.
   c. after every meal period.
   d. immediately.

5. Most lighting engineers and occupational health and safety inspectors recommend up to _____ footcandles of light for kitchen work areas.

   a. 10 to 20
   b. 25 to 50
   c. 50 to 70
   d. 75 to 100

6.   The major ventilation problem in most food service operations is:

   a. the transfer of odors and fumes from the kitchen to public areas.
   b. uneven distribution of cold air in the dining areas.
   c. high humidity in the dining areas from the recirculation of stale tempered air.
   d. greasy kitchen exhaust vents.

7.   The primary objective of restrictions on the use of dressing rooms in food service operations is to:

   a. reduce the likelihood of food contamination.
   b. set a minimum standard for staff working conditions.
   c. minimize the spread of contagious diseases or illnesses among the staff.
   d. maintain sanitary conditions in the dressing room.

8.   Which of the following is/are required in all lavatories?

   a. metered self-closing faucets
   b. handwashing soap or detergent
   c. heated air drying machines
   d. all of the above

9.   An air gap between the water supply inlet and the flood level rim of a plumbing fixture must be at least _____ the diameter of the water supply inlet and no less than _____ .

   a. equal to; 2 inches (50 mm)
   b. twice; 1 inch (25 mm)
   c. twice; 2 inches (50 mm)
   d. two and a half times; 4 inches (100 mm)

10.   Refuse containers should be cleaned regularly with:

   a. an all-purpose cleaner and hot water.
   b. a specially designed detergent.
   c. a detergent and hot water or steam.
   d. antichlors and clean warm water.

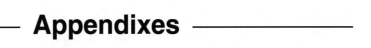 **Appendixes**

Appendix A

Agencies and Organizations

American Culinary Federation
American Culinary Federation Educational Institute
10 San Bartola Road
P.O. Box 3466
St. Augustine, FL 32084
(904) 824-4468

American Hotel & Motel Association (AH&MA)
1201 New York Avenue, NW, Suite 600
Washington, DC 20005-3931
(202) 289-3100

Centers for Disease Control and Prevention (CDC)
1600 Clifton Road, NE
Atlanta, GA 30333
(404) 639-3311

Educational Foundation of the National Restaurant Association
250 South Wacker Drive, Suite 1400
Chicago, IL 60606
(312) 782-1703

Educational Institute of the American Hotel & Motel Association
1407 South Harrison Road
P.O. Box 1240
East Lansing, MI 48826
(517) 353-5500

Environmental Protection Agency (EPA)
Office of Public Affairs (A-107)
401 M Street
Washington, DC 20460
(202) 382-4361; Safe Drinking Water Hotline: (800) 426-4791

Food and Drug Administration (FDA)
Retail Food Protection Branch
Center for Food Safety and Applied Nutrition
200 C Street, NW (HFF-342)
Washington, DC 20460
(202) 485-0140

Foodservice Consultants Society International (FCSI)
12345 30th Avenue, NE, Suite A
Seattle, WA 98125-5405
(206) 367-3274

International Association of Milk, Food and Environmental Sanitarians (IAMFES)
502 East Lincoln Way
Ames, IA 50010-6666
(515) 232-6699

International Food Service Executives Association (IFSEA)
1100 South State Road 7, Suite 103
Margate, FL 33068
(305) 977-0767

National Environmental Health Association (NEHA)
720 South Colorado Boulevard
Suite 970, South Tower
Denver, CO 80222
(303) 756-9090

National Restaurant Association (NRA)
1200 17th Street, NW
Washington, DC 20036
(202) 331-5900

National Sanitation Foundation (NSF)
NSF Building
3475 Plymouth Road
P.O. Box 1468
Ann Arbor, MI 48106
(313) 769-8010

Society for the Advancement of Foodservice Research (SAFSR)
304 West Liberty Street, Suite 301
Louisville, KY 40202
(502) 583-3783

Society for Foodservice Management (SFM)
304 West Liberty Street, Suite 301
Louisville, KY 40202
(502) 583-3783

United States Department of Agriculture (USDA)
Agricultural Marketing Service (AMS)
Information Division, Room 3510
South Agricultural Building
14th and Independence Avenue, SW
Washington, DC 20090-6456
(202) 720-2791

Appendix B

A Summary of Pathogenic Microorganisms

Name of Microorganism	Environmental and Food Sources	Incubation Time
Anisakis spp. (Ann-is-ah-kiss)	Saltwater fish (e.g., salmon, striped bass, Pacific snapper)	(Several days)[b]
Bacillus cereus (Bah-sill-us seer-ee-us)	Soil, dust, grains, vegetables, cereal products, puddings, custards, sauces, soups, meatloaf, meat products, boiled or fried rice	15 minutes to 16 hours[a] (1 to 5 hours)[b]
Campylobacter jejuni (Camp-ill-oh-back-ter jeh-june-knee)	Intestinal tract of infected cattle, swine, chickens, turkeys, and other animals. Raw or inadequately cooked or processed foods of animal origin (milk, poultry, clams, hamburger), unchlorinated water	(1 to 7 days or longer)[b]
Clostridium botulinum (Claws-trid-ee-um botch-you-line-um)	Soil, contaminated water, dust, fruits, vegetables, animal feed and manure, honey, sewage, inadequately processed or heated low-acid canned foods, inadequately processed fermented foods, and smoked fish	2 hours to 14 days[a] (12 to 36 hours)[b]
Clostridium perfringens (Claws-trid-ee-um per-frin-jens)	Soil, dust, animal manure, human feces, cooked meat and poultry, meat pies, gravies, stews, soil-grown vegetables, food cooked and cooled slowly in large quantities at room temperatures	6 to 24 hours[a] (8 to 12 hours)[b]
Diphyllobothrium latum (Die-file-oh-bo-three-um late-um)	Freshwater fish (e.g., salmon)	(3 to 6 weeks)[b]
Escherichia coli (Es-cher-ee-chee-ah coal-eye)	Feces of infected humans; air; sewage-contaminated water; cheese; shellfish; watercress, ground beef	8 to 24 hours[a] (11 hours)[b]
Listeria monocytogenes (Lis-teer-ee-ah mon-oh-site-oh-jean-ees)	Widely distributed; contaminated feces, coleslaw, domestic and imported cheeses, chickens, dry sausages, contaminated meat and meat products	(4 days to 3 weeks)[b]
Norwalk virus (Nor-walk)	Fish and shellfish harvested from contaminated waters, infected humans	(24 to 48 hours)[b]

Symptoms	Controls
Irritation of the throat and digestive tract, diarrhea, abdominal pain	1. Purchase food from approved sources. 2. Cook thoroughly. 3. Heavy salting. 4. Freeze food at –4°F (–20°C) for 168 hours.
Nausea, abdominal pain, vomiting, diarrhea	1. Hold foods out of the TDZ. 2. Chill leftover hot foods rapidly to less than 41°F (5°C). 3. Reheat all leftovers to a minimum of 165°F (74°C) for 15 seconds prior to service. (Add 25°F/14°C for micro-wave cooking.) 4. Serve and eat foods immediately after cooking.
Diarrhea, abdominal pain, fever, malaise, sometimes nausea, headache, urinary tract infection, reactive arthritis	1. Cook foods thoroughly. 2. Properly handle foods. 3. Dry or freeze food products. 4. Add acids.
High fever, dizziness, dry mouth, respiratory difficulties including paralysis, loss of reflexes	1. Destroy the toxin with correct time-temperature combinations. 2. Add acids. 3. Store foods under refrigeration. 4. Add salts during curing. 5. Destroy all bulging cans and their contents. 6. Refuse to serve home-canned foods.
Acute abdominal cramps, diarrhea, dehydration, and prostration (occasionally)	1. Thoroughly clean, cook, and chill food products. 2. Reheat all leftovers to a minimum of 165°F (74°C) for 15 seconds prior to service. (Add 25°F/14°C for micro-wave cooking.) 3. Hold foods out of the TDZ. 4. Enforce rules of good personal hygiene.
Hard to detect (sometimes anemia)	1. Purchase food from approved sources. 2. Cook thoroughly.
Abdominal pain, diarrhea, fever, chills, headache, blood in the feces, nausea, dehydration, prostration	1. Heat and chill food products rapidly. 2. Enforce rules of good personal hygiene. 3. Control flies. 4. Prepare all food products in a sanitary manner.
Mild and flu-like, headache, vomiting. More severe and possibly death in pregnant women and those with compromised immune systems.	1. Pasteurize or heat-process food products. 2. Avoid recontamination. 3. Refrigerate or freeze dairy products. 4. Properly clean and sanitize equipment.
Fever, headache, abdominal pain, diarrhea, vomiting	1. Purchase food from approved sources. 2. Cook shellfish by steaming for a minimum of 4 minutes. 3. Enforce rules of good personal hygiene and cleanliness. 4. Freeze at –4°F (–20°C) for 168 hours.

Name of Microorganism	Environmental and Food Sources	Incubation Time
Salmonella spp. (Sell-mon-ell-ah species)	Intestinal tract of humans and animals; turkeys, chickens, hogs, cattle, dogs, cats, frogs, turtles, and birds; meat products; egg and poultry products; coconut; yeast; chocolate candy; smoked fish; raw salads; fish; shellfish	5 to 72 hours[a] (12 to 48 hours)[b]
Shigella spp. (Shig-ell-ah species)	Feces of infected humans; direct contact with carriers; contaminated water; uncooked food that is diced, cut, chopped, and mixed; moist and mixed foods (tuna, shrimp, turkey, macaroni and potato salads); milk; beans; apple cider; contaminated produce	1 to 7 days[a] (less than 4 days)[b]
Staphylococcus aureus (Staff-low-cock-us or-ee-us)	In and on human nose and throat discharges, hands and skin, infected wounds and burns, pimples and acne, hair, feces; cooked ham; poultry and poultry dressing; meat products; gravies and sauces; cream-filled pastries; milk; cheese; hollandaise sauce; bread pudding; fish, potato, ham, poultry, and egg salads; high-protein leftover foods	1 to 8 hours[a] (2 to 4 hours)[b]
Trichinella spiralis (Trick-in-ell-ah spur-el-is)	Infected hogs, flesh of bear and walrus	4 to 28 days[a] (9 days)[b]
Vibrio parahaemolyticus (Vib-ree-oh para-heemo-lit-ick-us)	Marine life, sea water, raw foods of marine origin, saltwater fish, shellfish, fish products, salty foods, cucumbers	2 to 48 hours[a] (10 to 20 hours)[b]
virus of infectious hepatitis (in-feck-shus hep-a-tie-tis)	Blood, urine, and feces of human and animal carriers; water; rodents; insects; shellfish; milk; potato salad; cold cuts; frozen strawberries; orange juice; whipped cream cakes; glazed doughnuts; sandwiches	10 to 50 days[a] (30 days)[b]
Yersinia enterocolitica (Your-sin-ee-ah enter-oh-coal-it-ah-kah)	Contaminated raw pork and beef, drinking water, ice cream, raw and pasteurized milk, tofu (soy bean curd)	(3 to 7 days)[b]

[a]Range of reported incubation times.
[b]Usual, average, or most frequently reported incubation time.

Symptoms	Controls
Abdominal pain, diarrhea, fever, chills, vomiting, dehydration, headache, prostration	1. Cook food products thoroughly. 2. Rapidly chill all hot foods. 3. Guard against cross-contamination. 4. Enforce rules of good personal hygiene.
Abdominal pain, diarrhea, fever, chills, headache, blood in feces, nausea, dehydration, prostration	1. Chill and heat food products rapidly. 2. Enforce rules of good personal hygiene. 3. Control flies. 4. Prepare all food products in a sanitary manner.
Vomiting, abdominal cramps, diarrhea, nausea, dehydration, sweating, weakness, prostration	1. Remove ill staff members from food production and handling activities. 2. Enforce rules of good personal hygiene. 3. Handle food products with the utmost care. 4. Thoroughly cook and reheat foods. 5. Rapidly chill and properly refrigerate food products.
Muscle invasion and soreness, weakness, swelling of muscles	1. Heat pork to an internal temperature of 155°F (68°C) or above for 15 seconds. (Add 25°F/14°C for microwave cooking.) 2. Freezing pork will destroy the parasite. 3. Store at 5°F (−15°C) or lower for not less than 20 days.
Abdominal cramps, diarrhea, nausea, vomiting, mild fever, chills, headache, prostration	1. Cook and chill food products properly. 2. Separate raw and cooked foods. 3. Do not rinse food products with sea water.
Fever, nausea, abdominal pain, tired feeling, jaundice, liver infection	1. Purchase all food products from approved sources. 2. Enforce rules of good personal hygiene. 3. Cook foods thoroughly.
Varies with the age of the victim. Digestive upset and acute abdominal pain (children). Acute abdominal disorders, diarrhea, fever, arthritis (adults). Skin and eye infections (both groups).	1. Pasteurize or heat-process food products. 2. Avoid recontamination. 3. Practice proper personal hygiene. 4. Properly clean and sanitize equipment. 5. Obtain food from approved sources.

Appendix C

A Summary of Food Spoilage

Type of Food	Type of Spoilage/ Indicators	Causative Agents	Control Method(s)
Bakery Products	Rope – odor of ripe melons – yellow crumbs – color change – sticky crumbs – slimy thread-like material	*Bacillus* bacteria (Bah-sill-us)	1. Add acid before baking 2. Fast cooling 3. Freezing 4. Proper and prompt wrapping
	Black color change	*Rhizopus nigricans* mold (Rye-zoe-pus nie-gri-kans)	1. Add propionates before baking 2. Fast cooling 3. Proper and prompt wrapping
	Green color change	*Penicillium expansum* mold (Pen-ah-sill-ee-um ek-spans-um)	1. Add propionates before baking 2. Fast cooling 3. Proper and prompt wrapping 4. Freezing
Dairy Products	Protein breakdown	*Bacillus* bacteria (Bah-sill-us) *Clostridium* bacteria (Claws-trid-ee-um) *Pseudomonas* bacteria (Sood-oh-moan-ahs)	1. Commercially sterilize 2. Pasteurize and refrigerate 3. Dry
	Souring	*Streptococcus lactis* bacteria (Strep-toe-cock-us lack-tis) *Lactobacillus bulgaricus* bacteria (Lack-toe-bah-sill-us bul-gar-ih-kus) *Lactobacillus thermophilus* bacteria (Lack-toe-bah-sill-us therm-ah-fill-us)	1. Commercially sterilize 2. Pasteurize and refrigerate 3. Dry
Eggs	Microbial – green rot (whites) – colorless rot (whole eggs) – black rot (whole eggs)	bacteria	1. Refrigerate 2. Freeze 3. Dry
	Non-microbial – loss of moisture – addition of oxygen – thinning of albumen – weakening of yolk membrane – increase in pH from 7.6 to 9.5	environment (addition of oxygen)	1. Coat shells with colorless, odorless, tasteless mineral oil 2. Refrigerate
Fats and Oils	Autoxidation – oxidative rancidity – addition of oxygen – increased with light, heat, heavy metals, salt – off-odors and flavors	environment (addition of oxygen)	1. Add BHA and/or BHT before baking 2. Wrap properly and promptly
	Hydrolytic rancidity – flavor, odor, taste changes	lipase enzyme (Lie-pays)	1. Heat to destroy

Type of Food	Type of Spoilage/ Indicators	Causative Agents	Control Method(s)
	Flavor reversion – oxidative rancidity – unsaturated vegetable oils – linolenic fatty acid – beany, fishy, paint-like odor	environment (addition of oxygen)	1. Partially hydrogenate
Fruits and Vegetables, canned	Carbon dioxide gas spoilage – swollen cans due to gas production – frothy and slimy contents	*Micrococcus spp.* bacteria (Mike-row-cock-us) *Streptococcus thermophilus* bacteria (Strep-toe-cock-us therm-ah-fill-us)	1. Proper sealing of cans 2. Proper heating during processing
	Flat sour spoilage – flavor change	*Bacillus coagulans* bacteria (Bah-sill-us coe-ag-you-lans)	1. Sufficient time-temperature combination during processing
	Thermophilic gas spoilage – swollen cans due to gas production – flipper, springer, soft swell, hard swell	*Clostridium sporogenes* bacteria (Claws-trid-ee-um spore-ah-jen-ees) *Clostridium putrefaciens* bacteria (Claws-trid-ee-um pyut-rah-face-yens) *Clostridium thermosaccharolyticum* bacteria (Claws-trid-ee-um thermo-sack-ah-roe-lit-ah-cum)	1. Sufficient time-temperature combination during processing
Fruits and Vegetables, fresh	Black rot – color change – sour, bitter flavors – softening	Molds	1. Low temperatures (refrigeration, freezing) 2. Commercial sterilization 3. Dry 4. Use rapidly
	Blue rot – color change – sour, bitter flavors – softening	*Penicillium* mold (Pen-ah-sill-ee-um)	1. Low temperatures (refrigeration, freezing) 2. Commercial sterilization 3. Dry 4. Use rapidly
	Gray rot – color change – flavor change – softening	*Botrytis cinerea* mold (Bow-trite-is sin-er-ee-ah)	1. Low temperatures (refrigeration, freezing) 2. Commercial sterilization 3. Dry 4. Use rapidly
	Soft rot – flavor change – softening – mushy – odorous	*Pseudomonas* bacteria (Sood-oh-moan-ahs)	1. Low temperatures (refrigeration, freezing) 2. Commercial sterilization 3. Dry 4. Use rapidly
Meats	Souring – flavor change – odor change – color change	*Pseudomonas* bacteria (Sood-oh-moan-ahs)	1. Carefully handle 2. Quickly slaughter 3. Rapid chilling 4. Avoid contamination 5. Clean and sanitize equipment

Type of Food	Type of Spoilage/ Indicators	Causative Agents	Control Method(s)
	Surface color/texture changes – fuzziness – stickiness – unacceptable odor, color, taste, texture	*Penicillium* and other molds (Pen-ah-sill-ee-um)	1. Can (commercially sterilize) 2. Pasteurize and store refrigerated 3. Low temperatures (freeze and refrigerate) 4. Carefully wrap
Poultry	Chemical changes and deterioration – stickiness – sliminess – objectionable odor	*Pseudomonas* bacteria (Sood-oh-moan-ahs) *Flavobacterium* bacteria (Flave-oh-back-tear-ee-um) Enzymes Molds	1. Rapid slaughter, then wash with chlorinated water 2. Immediate chilling 3. Low temperatures (refrigerate or freeze) 4. Carefully wrap 5. Commercially sterilize 6. Add organic acids
Seafood	Ammonia-like odor	*Pseudomonas* bacteria (Sood-oh-moan-ahs) *Proteus* bacteria (Pro-tee-us)	1. Immediate chilling 2. Low temperatures (refrigerate or freeze) 3. Carefully wrap 4. Commercially sterilize
	Fruity or unpleasant sweet odor	*Acinetobacter* bacteria (Ah-seen-oh-back-ter) *Aeromonas* bacteria (Air-oh-moan-ahs)	1. Immediate chilling 2. Low temperatures (refrigerate or freeze) 3. Carefully wrap 4. Commercially sterilize

Managing and Conducting Employee Sanitation Training

The Benefits of the Manager as Trainer

Many managers do not see training as a primary part of their jobs. That is unfortunate because few people are as qualified to manage and conduct training, especially in the important area of sanitation.

Consider these benefits of the manager as trainer:

- *Expertise.* Most food service industry managers have experience with or formal training in sanitary procedures and governmental sanitation regulations. Managers also know which procedures and regulations apply to their own establishments and how to implement them in the most efficient manner possible. This knowledge will help them choose the sanitation information appropriate for employees at their own establishments.

- *Cost-effectiveness.* It is generally cheaper and less time-consuming for managers to conduct training themselves than to work with a trainer (especially one who must be hired from outside the establishment).

- *Targeted training.* Most employees who work in a food establishment already know something about sanitation. The manager is best able to pinpoint gaps in employees' knowledge and to develop training that will fill those gaps. The manager also is best able to identify those employees who are new to the food service industry and need more intensive training.

- *Understanding of employee training needs.* Managers, unlike in- or out-of-house trainers, are in constant contact with employees. Managers know, for example, how to communicate effectively with employees who are non-native speakers of English or with employees who have poor reading skills. Managers also have a feeling for how much time they can spend on a training session without employees' attention wandering. Such communication skills and insights are invaluable in planning and conducting training for employees.

- *Efficient scheduling of training.* Managers know their establishment's peak service times and can identify the best times to train, such as when employees are less busy and can concentrate on the information presented.

- *Effective follow-up.* Managers are among the first to see the results of training and can quickly correct or augment training that has not been effective.

Characteristics of Good Trainers

Managers whose training efforts have been unsuccessful are sometimes puzzled: After all, they were familiar with the information and conveyed it all to employees. What went wrong? Puzzlement sometimes turns to frustration, and this may lead managers to turn training over to others or, worse, give up on training altogether in the mistaken belief that it just does not work.

In fact, training skills do not automatically follow from knowledge and expertise. Besides knowledge and expertise, good trainers share specific qualities, including:

- *Enthusiasm for the topic.* Most employees are eager to learn new skills. Unenthusiastic trainers, however, kill that eagerness and make training a chore for themselves and the employees.

- *Ability to convey information.* Good trainers logically and clearly explain the steps needed to perform a job. In addition, they are quick to recognize when employees are not following the presentation and to provide additional explanation when necessary.

- *Patience.* Employees get nervous when trainers are tense or irritated by their mistakes. A good trainer offers encouragement and lets employees learn at their own pace.

- *A sense of humor.* Trainers who can laugh at their own mistakes help employees relax and enjoy training more.

- *Time to train.* Trainers who rush through training because they are impatient or because they have other concerns do not train effectively.

The Four-Step Training Method

Once managers make up their minds to train, they must approach the task in a logical, systematic manner. The simple four-step training method can help by providing a framework on which managers can logically and systematically build a successful training program. The four steps in the method are: preparation, presentation, practice, and follow-up.

Preparation

Preparation is essential for successful training. When managers do not prepare, their training lacks a logical sequence and they omit key details. They may also feel more anxiety about the training session.

To prepare for sanitation training, managers should:

- Work from a job list to identify which tasks employees perform that affect sanitation at the establishment. These are the tasks managers will concentrate on during training. Later, the job list can be used as a checklist to confirm tasks that have been mastered.

- Identify training objectives. Training objectives, sometimes already identified in ready-made training materials, describe in specific terms what employees should know or be able to do after training.

- Choose training methods. The training method managers choose will depend on the group of employees to be trained. For example, are employees from different departments? How much do they already know about your establishment's sanitation procedures? What do they need to get out of the training?

- Schedule training. Estimate how long the training will take and schedule it at an appropriate time.

- Select the training location. Choose a location that is as convenient as possible for the employees. Training will be more effective if it is conducted in a well-lighted, well-ventilated area, away from noise. There should be enough chairs for employees to sit in and have a good view of any materials or equipment that will be used in the training session. Employees should not be disturbed with work duties during training sessions.

- Prepare training materials and equipment. Prepare relevant training aids, such as handbooks, flip charts, and audiovisual equipment. This step is made easier if managers purchase ready-made sanitation training materials and customize them to their specific establishment's needs.

Presentation

Many experienced trainers find it helpful, if time permits, to conduct a warm-up activity—sometimes called an ice-breaker—to help employees get to know each other and to set a friendly, informal tone for the training session. It is also a good idea to tell employees how long the training session will last and, if it is lengthy, to tell employees when breaks are scheduled and where the restrooms are. Finally, employees will want to know what the training session will cover, what they will get out of it, and why it is important to them.

When presenting sanitation information, it is important to explain key principles and tasks clearly. Most professional trainers caution against using jargon or technical terms when conducting training, especially for line-level employees. That, of course, does not mean that managers should avoid the "whys" when they train. It is essential that employees understand why they must follow certain procedures so they are not tempted to cut corners. The "whys," however, can be explained in terms that novices will understand, and effective trainers can use examples to illustrate important points. Consider the following examples. Both explain why it is important to clean and sanitize utensils after each changed use, but the second example avoids technical terms and illustrates the point, and will be more effective in training:

Example #1

It is essential that food preparation staff clean and sanitize utensils after each changed use so as to prevent the spread of microorganisms, such as salmonella, which have deleterious effects on humans.

Example #2

All food preparation staff must clean and sanitize utensils after each changed use, for example, after cutting meat and before chopping lettuce with the same knife. Unless the knife is cleaned and sanitized before the lettuce is chopped, it can pick up harmful microbes from the meat and transfer them to the lettuce. Although the meat will later be cooked, thus killing the microbes, the lettuce will be served raw and the microbes will not be destroyed. The microbes on the lettuce could make guests seriously ill.

A common pitfall in the presentation step is to rush through training quickly. Managers new to training should remember that many employees are hearing the information for the first time and will need time to absorb it and think about how it applies to their jobs. In the two presentation examples provided, the second example takes more time to present, but it will be much clearer to employees.

Along with providing clear, simple explanations, managers should demonstrate points whenever possible. For example, the explanation of cleaning and sanitizing after each changed use could be followed by a demonstration of the proper way to clean and sanitize utensils. Along the way, employees should be encouraged to ask any questions they wish.

Practice

Employees will learn most effectively if they are given time after the presentation to practice what they have learned. Generally, employees should practice slowly, perhaps with a partner, explaining the steps to their partners as they practice. When employees correctly perform tasks, the manager should praise them. Practice should ideally continue until all employees have a thorough understanding of how to do the tasks.

Follow-Up

As noted earlier in this appendix, managers are among the first to see the results of training and therefore are in an ideal position to follow up with employees. This step can be done in several ways. For example, a manager can ask an employee to demonstrate a sanitation procedure, either on the job or in a review session before or after the employee's shift. Or a manager may want to unobtrusively observe employees as they perform newly learned tasks, praising when possible or tactfully correcting employees when necessary.

Managers should also measure progress by evaluating whether employees have met the training objectives. If they have not, further training and practice may be necessary.

Finally, it is important that employees have a chance to offer feedback about the training, either on an evaluation form or in informal discussions. This helps managers improve their training skills.

Tips for Training

It is important that trainers remember that employees are adults, not children. As adult learners, employees want practical information about sanitation, not theory. They want trainers to recognize the experience and knowledge they bring to the training session. And they appreciate feedback and coaching.

Training is most effective when conducted in short segments of 15 minutes to an hour. Coincidentally, short training sessions usually fit better into the schedules of most busy food service operations.

Passive training, when employees simply listen to a lecture or watch a videotape, is usually not very effective. Employees want to see the immediate relevance of sanitation information to them, and they want time to ask questions to find out how to apply it to their jobs.

Employees learn best when the training delivery style is interesting. Although some managers are better than others at public speaking, even reticent managers can become effective trainers by remembering these tips:

- Speak loudly enough for all employees to hear.

- Enunciate and use good grammar.

- Do not ad-lib from prepared materials too much, and keep employees on the topic at hand.

- Make eye contact with employees.

- Maintain good posture and use gestures. Move around if possible.

- Display a positive attitude. Smile.

- Listen to employees' questions and answer them in a friendly, helpful manner; never ridicule an employee.

Independent Study Considerations

When most managers think of training, they often think of a classroom situation attended by a group of employees. However, independent study is often a good option if appropriate materials are available for employees. Managers should think carefully about employee training needs before deciding to offer independent study. For example, if independent study involves reading a handbook or textbook, it is probably not the best approach for employees with poor reading skills or only basic English-speaking ability (unless the materials are in their native language). On the other hand, some employees enjoy independent study because they can learn at their own pace. They can also take materials home or to some other quiet place where distractions are fewer.

Once a manager has decided to use independent study, he or she does not simply hand the materials to the employee and fade out of the picture. Typically, an independent study program works like this:

1. The manager explains why he or she wants an employee to study the materials and how it will help the employee on the job. The manager gives the employee the independent study materials, usually a handbook, videotape, and/or audiotape. The manager explains how to use the materials.

2. The manager schedules training for the employee in a quiet place and provides any equipment the employee needs, such as paper, pencils, videotape player, and so on.

3. After the independent study session, the manager asks the employee if he or she has questions about the material.

When using independent study, managers should remember that:

- Someone at the establishment should serve as a resource person for employees who do not understand the material or who have questions. This can be the manager, a supervisor, a team leader, or an experienced employee.

- All employees learn at different rates. Allow employees to move at their own pace.

What Your Employees Should Know About Sanitation

All employees must understand the "big picture" with regard to sanitation; that is, they must understand the needs and expectations of guests, owners, and staff. The final outcome of sanitation training should be to reduce sanitation risks that could endanger guests, owners, and staff. The specific goals of any employee sanitation training should be:

- To emphasize to employees that they are responsible for food safety
- To help employees understand essential food safety principles
- To show employees how to use essential food safety principles in their own jobs

All employees must know the following essential food safety principles:

1. How important serving safe food is and how employees contribute to the food safety effort

2. How food becomes contaminated and how to prevent it

3. How to store food safely

4. How time and temperature affect food safety (including how and when to use a thermometer)

5. How to clean and sanitize properly and when to do so

6. What food safety warnings to be aware of and what action to take when these warnings are noticed

Besides a general knowledge of these principles, employees in all areas of the operation should understand how the principles apply to their specific jobs. To make training most efficient, it makes sense to conduct separate training sessions for employees who work in different areas of the operation. For example, employees in warewashing and employees in food production would approach the first principle very differently. If a joint training session were scheduled for employees in both job areas, warewashers might well become bored while contributions in food production were being explained, and vice versa.

Glossary

A

A-B-C-D INVENTORY CLASSIFICATION SCHEME

A technique for grouping inventory items on a relative basis according to perishability and cost per serving, with Class A items being high in both perishability and cost per serving; Class B items being relatively high in cost, but low in perishability; Class C items being relatively low in cost per serving, but relatively high in perishability; and Class D items having both the lowest perishability and the lowest cost per serving.

ACCIDENT REPORTING FORM

A document used to record and analyze pertinent information in the event of injuries to guests or staff members.

ACID-ANIONIC SURFACTANTS

Stable sanitizers that have a long shelf life and are active against most microorganisms. They are odorless, non-staining, and effective in hard water, and they have a low toxicity when left as a residual antibacterial film.

ACUTE HAZARDS

Potential health threats of a product that could affect a user immediately.

AEROBIC ORGANISMS

Microorganisms that require free oxygen.

AEROBIC SPOILAGE

Spoilage of meat tissue in an oxygen environment. Bacteria are responsible for the greatest amount of aerobic meat spoilage.

AFLATOXIN

A poisonous mycotoxin produced by the mold *Aspergillus flavus*, which is found worldwide and grows on nuts, corn, wheat, and other grains. Aflatoxin may be found in finished products like bread and peanut butter. Ingestion of aflatoxin usually only causes low grade fever in humans, but it can produce cancer in trout, rats, and ducks and has been linked to some cases of liver cancer in humans.

ANAEROBIC GLYCOLYSIS

A chemical reaction in slaughtered animals in which glycogen (a chemical form of energy stored in muscle tissue) is converted to lactic acid.

ANAEROBIC ORGANISMS

Microorganisms that reproduce best in the absence of oxygen.

ANAEROBIC SPOILAGE

The decay of meat tissue that takes place with a limited amount of oxygen.

ASEPTIC CANNING

A process used for food products that are particularly sensitive to heat; it involves the separate sterilization of containers (using hydrogen peroxide) and contents, and uses more heat for substantially shorter periods of time than conventional canning. Once sterilized, the contents are placed into the containers and hermetically sealed in a sterile environment. This process conserves nutrients, color, taste, odor, and texture but is relatively expensive.

AUTOLYSIS

The chemical breakdown of food products caused by substances (primarily enzymes) within the food.

B

BASIC ENVIRONMENTAL SANITATION

An approach to keeping rodents and insects out of a food establishment, requiring all materials that serve as food or shelter for pests to be made pest-resistant or removed from the facility and its immediate vicinity.

BLANCHING

The process of exposing a food product to either steam or hot water for a short time, setting the color of green vegetables and rendering enzymes inactive; destroys some microorganisms.

C

CANTILEVERED EQUIPMENT

Food production equipment that is wall-mounted with a horizontal support.

CARDIOPULMONARY RESUSCITATION (CPR)

A technique used to provide circulation and breathing to a victim whose heart or lungs have stopped functioning.

CART SERVICE

A variation of table service used by servers for preparing menu items beside the guest's table in the dining room. Menu items are cooked, and sometimes flambéed, in front of the guest.

CELL AGGREGATES

Long chains or groups of cells formed by some bacteria; examples are *Staphylococcus aureus* and *Streptococcus pyogenes.* Cell aggregates are more difficult to destroy than individual cells.

CHLORINE-BASED SANITIZERS

Pathogen-destroying compounds that are active against all microorganisms and spores if used in a concentration of 50 to 100 mg/L (milligrams/liter). They are inexpensive, unaffected by hard water, and do not leave a residue, but have a characteristic chlorine odor and a relatively short shelf life.

CHRONIC HAZARDS

Potential health threats of a product that could affect a user over time with repeated, long-term use.

CLASS A FIRES

The burning of ordinary combustibles such as wood, paper, and cloth; can be extinguished by the cooling action of water-based or general purpose chemicals.

CLASS B FIRES

Fires involving flammable liquids such as grease, gasoline, paints, and other oils; can be extinguished by eliminating the air supply and smothering the fire, not by using water.

CLASS C FIRES

Electrical fires, usually involving motors, switches, and wiring; can be extinguished with chemicals that do not conduct electricity; never with water.

CLEANING

The removal of soil.

CLEANING AND MAINTENANCE

The final control point; also one of the most important. It involves upkeep and sanitation associated with the other basic operating activities (i.e., purchasing, receiving, storing, issuing, preparing, cooking, holding, and serving), as well as cleaning and maintenance of equipment and facilities.

COLONY

A large number of cells that have developed from a single cell; can be seen with the naked eye and can contain more than 10 million cells.

COMMISSARY

A centralized servicing area for mobile food service units.

CONTROL POINTS

A system of basic operating activities in a food service operation. Each control point is a miniature system with its own recognizable structure and functions.

CONVENIENCE FOODS

Food products purchased in partially or fully prepared forms that enable food service operations to offer new items without buying additional raw ingredients or elaborate equipment. These products reduce in-house labor requirements, but have a higher purchase price.

COOKING

The control point at which heat is applied to food in order to change its color, odor, texture, taste, appearance, and nutritional value.

CREDIT MEMO

A form issued by a supplier to adjust an establishment's account. Issued in response to a request-for-credit memo when products are spoiled, do not meet the establishment's specifications, or are delivered in the wrong quantities. Helps ensure that the food establishment is charged only for the products that conform to its standards.

CRITICAL CONTROL POINT

A point or procedure in a specific food system where loss of control may result in an unacceptable health risk.

CRITICAL LIMIT

The maximum or minimum value to which a physical, biological, or chemical parameter must be controlled at a critical control point to minimize the risk that the identified food safety hazard may occur.

CROSS-CONTAMINATION

The process in which a food product becomes contaminated by its contact with a bacteria-carrying non-food source (knives, cutting boards, thermometers, and other equipment) or with raw food.

CROSS-UTILIZATION

A menu-planning strategy related to rationalization. Its objective: to prepare and serve as many menu items as possible from a limited number of raw ingredients.

D

DAILY RECEIVING REPORT

A record of everything a facility receives; shows what was received, the date of the delivery, the name of the supplier, the quantity, the price, and any other relevant comments. Also provides a record of delivery distribution; the form's "Food Directs" column indicates the dollar value of products to be sent directly to kitchen production areas, and the "Food Stores" column records the dollar value of products to be placed in storage.

DEATH PHASE

In bacterial growth, a reduction in the total number of living bacteria. During this phase, the bacteria population falls at a rapid rate, but if no effort is made to completely destroy the bacteria, the death rate eventually levels off and a number of organisms survive to begin the cycle again.

E

ENCAPSULATION

A process in which some bacilli-shaped bacteria form a dense, slime-like protective coating around cell walls; the coating protects the organism from chemicals and heat and increases the bacterial cell's resistance to death.

ENZYMES

Proteins that catalyze the breakdown of food products; that is, speed up the rate of autolysis.

EQUIPMENT INSTALLATION INFORMATION

Details about food production equipment that should be submitted to health officials (with an equipment schedule) to identify potential sanitation hazards.

EQUIPMENT SCHEDULE

A list of planned food production equipment; submitted to health officials before purchase or installation to identify potential sanitation hazards.

EXECUTIVE HOUSEKEEPER

The person in charge of a housekeeping department in a lodging property; a member of the management team.

EXPEDITER

A staff member who acts as a communication link between kitchen personnel and servers. Servers give their orders to the expediter, who calls the orders to the appropriate kitchen stations. The expediter must know cooking times, coordinate them to sequentially deliver cooked foods for pickup, and provide leadership during hectic rush periods; should be a member of the management team.

F

FACULTATIVELY ANAEROBIC ORGANISMS

Microorganisms that reproduce either with or without free oxygen.

FAMILY-STYLE SERVICE

A table service style in which food is placed on large platters or in large bowls which are taken to the tables by servers. Guests pass the food around their table and serve themselves.

FIRST-IN-FIRST-OUT (FIFO) INVENTORY SYSTEM

A rotation method in which products held in inventory the longest are the first to be issued to production areas; when newly received products enter storage areas, they are placed under or behind products already in storage.

FLYING FOOD SHOW

A procedure for delivering cooked menu items to guests as soon as the food is ready. The first server to arrive at the pickup point delivers the menu items that are ready for service; can only be implemented if order tickets show which guest at which table is to receive each order.

FOOD AND DRUG ADMINISTRATION (FDA)

A division of the United States Public Health Service within the Department of Health and Human Services. Its main responsibility is to enforce the Federal Food, Drug, and Cosmetic Act and to protect the public health of the nation; the FDA also develops and interprets surveillance and compliance programs, model ordinances, codes and regulations, and good manufacturing practices.

FOOD CODE

A model code published by the U.S. Food and Drug Administration (FDA) in 1993. It represents the FDA's best advice for a uniform system of regulation to ensure that food at retail is safe and properly protected and presented. Although not federal requirements, the model Food Code provisions are designed to be consistent with federal food laws and regulations, and are written for ease of legal adoption at all levels of government.

FOOD COST PERCENTAGE

A calculation that expresses food cost as a percentage of sales income.

FOOD DEHYDRATION

A dry food preservation method, thought to be the oldest; effective because it reduces the a_w of food and thus inhibits microbial activity. Four types are sun drying, mechanical drying, freeze-drying, and drying during smoking.

FOOD, DRUG, AND COSMETIC ACT

A 1938 law that provided increased consumer protection; it covered labeling requirements, standards of identity and fill, sanitary manufacturing techniques, and misbranding and mislabeling of food products. The Pesticide Chemicals Amendment (1954), the Food Additives Amendment (1958), and the Color Additives Amendment (1960) brought the 1938 act up to date with technological advances in food production. This act with its amendments continues to be the most all-encompassing law related to the food industry in the United States.

FOOD ESTABLISHMENT

The point in the food distribution chain where the consumer takes possession of the food; a commercial or institutional food service facility.

FOOD ESTABLISHMENT INSPECTION

The primary means by which food establishment management and staff members and the regulatory authority detect hazardous procedures and practices. Inspections serve as educational sessions regarding Food Code requirements as they apply to a particular establishment. They also convey new food safety information, provide opportunities to ask questions, and provide a written report to the permit-holder or person in charge, who can then bring the establishment into compliance with the Food Code.

FOOD SAMPLE DATA SHEET

A form that standardizes evaluations of products that an operation is considering for purchase; can be used to record purchasing, storing, preparing, and serving information about such products, and also to request nutritional and ingredient analysis information.

FOOTCANDLE

Unit of light intensity; measured with a light meter. One footcandle equals one lumen per square foot (a lumen is a measure of power equal to 0.0015 watt).

G

GARDE-MANGER

In a large operation, a cold food preparation department responsible for such dishes as aspic, pâté, mousse, salads and dressings, and sauces; in a small establishment, an area of the kitchen with chilled preparation surfaces; also, a chef who specializes in the production of cold dishes.

GENERATION TIME

The time it takes for one cell to undergo binary fission.

H

HACCP PLAN

A written document that delineates the formal procedures for following the Hazard Analysis Critical Control Point principles.

HARD FLOOR

A floor constructed of one of the following: concrete, magnesium oxychloride cement, granolith, marble, terrazzo, ceramic tile, quarry tile, slate, terra cotta, or brick; generally, relatively easy to keep clean if properly maintained.

HAZARD

A biological, chemical, or physical property that may cause an unacceptable consumer health risk.

HAZARD COMMUNICATION (HAZCOMM) STANDARD

Also known as OSHA's right-to-know legislation; a regulation requiring employers to inform their staff members about hazardous chemicals they may need to use on the job.

HEAT TRANSFER RATE

The rate at which heat leaves cooked food; pan size is an important factor.

HEIMLICH MANEUVER

A generally accepted technique for saving a choking victim by squeezing the trapped air out of the victim's lungs, forcing the obstruction out.

HIGH TEMPERATURE-SHORT TIME (HTST) PASTEURIZATION

The process in which a food product is heated to 161°F (72°C) for 15 seconds, then immediately cooled to 50°F (10°C) or less.

HOLD ORDER

A written notice placed by a sanitarian on food products that, for reasons specified in the notice, cannot be served; immediate destruction of the food may be ordered.

HOLDING

A critical control point in which menu items are maintained either hot or cold after cooking and in advance of service.

HOMOGENIZATION

The process that breaks up the fat globules present in whole milk so that they are permanently suspended in the whey (liquid portion of the milk); the fat globules cannot recombine and rise to the top as cream.

I

IMMINENT HEALTH HAZARD

A serious health threat that may cause a sanitarian to order food operations to cease immediately; examples are sewage backups, complete lack of refrigeration, or evidence of a communicable disease outbreak such as hepatitis.

INCUBATION TIME

The amount of time between consumption of contaminated food and the first symptoms of illness.

INFECTION

A foodborne disease caused by bacteria and viruses that are transmitted in food and later reproduce inside the body.

INTOXICATION

A foodborne disease that results from the ingestion of poisonous plants or animals or of toxin-contaminated food.

INVENTORY

The total supply of items an operation has in stock.

INVENTORY TURNOVER

The rate at which inventory is converted to revenue during a given period.

INVOICE

A supplier's statement detailing all the products being delivered to a facility and their corresponding prices; may show products that are back-ordered or not yet available for delivery.

IODINE-BASED SANITIZERS (IODOPHORS)

Pathogen-destroying compounds that are stable (do not deteriorate easily), have a long shelf life, and will destroy most bacterial cells (but not spores). They are effective in hard water, are non-corrosive, and do not leave a residue or irritate skin, but work somewhat slowly, may stain, and are expensive. They should be applied in a concentration of 12.5 to 25 mg/L for one minute or more at temperatures of 75° to 120°F (24° to 49°C).

ISSUING

The control point at which food products are released from storage; issuing controls ensure that products are only released to the production department with proper authorization.

J

JOB ANALYSIS

A study of the duties, tasks, behaviors, and responsibilities of a position or each position in an organization or organizational segment; focuses on what is expected of a staff member performing a certain job.

JOB DESCRIPTION

A summary of the duties, responsibilities, and tasks of a particular position, based on the knowledge, skills, and abilities (KSAs) needed to perform the job.

JOB INSTRUCTION TRAINING

A structured on-the-job training method in which a trainer (1) prepares the trainee; (2) presents the task or skill to the trainee; (3) tries out the trainee's performance; and (4) follows up by allowing the trainee to perform alone and provides feedback.

JOB PERFORMANCE STANDARDS

The quality and quantity requirements for each task or responsibility of a position. These standards form the basis for performance reviews.

JOB SPECIFICATION

A form that identifies the knowledge, skills, and abilities (KSAs) needed to do a job properly; a description of the type of individual needed for the position. Also called a job qualification.

L

LAG PHASE

The initial period in a normal bacterial growth curve. Living bacteria are present during this phase, but there is no increase in the number of cells.

LINE-UP MEETING

A five- to ten-minute informal training period with service staff members before each meal period; gives the chef and the manager an opportunity to explain daily specials, and gives the servers an opportunity to sample portions of new menu items and to ask questions.

LOG PHASE

The phase that follows the lag phase of bacterial growth. Having adjusted to their new environment, the bacteria reproduce rapidly. Bacterial generation time is shortest and most prolific during this stage.

M

MASTER DISTRIBUTOR

A supplier who serves as a full-line or one-stop shopping and delivery service.

MASTER FOOD PRODUCTION PLANNING WORKSHEET

An overall plan for a meal or special function that helps control the preparation function in large operations. It provides a format for planning staff and product utilization for each meal or special function; it also shows production personnel exactly what and how much to prepare—each menu item, the standard portion size, and the forecasted number of portions.

MATERIAL SAFETY DATA SHEET (MSDS)

A record of product information from a manufacturer indicating chemical identity, hazardous ingredients, physical and chemical characteristics, fire and explosion hazard data, reactivity data, health hazards, precautions for safe handling and use, control measures, and manufacturer's name, address, and telephone number.

MENU PLANNING

In the food service system, the initial control point, which influences all the remaining control points. It includes considering trends and other marketing factors, deciding what items to offer, pricing, image-projection, knowledge of preparation and production methods, inventory and equipment concerns, and guest and staff member concerns.

MESOPHILES

Microbes that prefer intermediate temperatures, generally from 68°F (20°C) to 113°F (45°C). Most pathogenic bacteria are mesophiles, so they can thrive at normal room temperatures.

MISE EN PLACE

Literally, put in place. In the production area, the assembly of raw ingredients for menu items; reduces errors, speeds up the actual preparation process, and reduces food handling time and exposure to the temperature danger zone (TDZ).

MOBILE FOOD UNIT

A moving food service operation; does not necessarily operate in a fixed location. Examples are pushcarts, catering trucks designed to sell food in a number of locations, and ice cream and snack food trucks.

MODULAR CARPETING

Carpet modules or squares that can be rotated from high- to low-traffic areas, resulting in a better overall appearance and extending the useful life of the carpet; may reduce an operation's overall carpet maintenance costs.

N

NON-PERISHABLE FOODS

Food products that resist spoilage unless they are improperly handled and stored; for example, dry grocery items such as sugar, flour, spices, and dry beans.

O

OCCUPATIONAL SAFETY AND HEALTH ADMINISTRATION (OSHA)

An independent regulatory agency in the executive branch of the U.S. government, formed in 1970 to enforce the Occupational Safety and Health Act of the same year. There are several similar agencies at the state level. OSHA develops and enforces mandatory standards and regulations related to the safety and health of workers throughout the United States.

ON-PREMISES LAUNDRY (OPL)

Washing and drying facilities housed in a hospitality operation.

ORIENTATION

A program for introducing a new staff member to the workplace after the staff member has been hired and has reported for work.

ORIENTATION CHECKLIST

A list of procedures that help make orientation more thorough and objective.

P

PARTIAL HYDROGENATION

A process that controls flavor reversion in foods by adding hydrogen gas so that the polyunsaturated linolenic fatty acid becomes saturated and the problem is eliminated.

PASTEURIZATION

A method of high-temperature food preservation in which the product is heated to 145°F (63°C) for 30 minutes or 161°F (72°C) for 15 seconds; it is then immediately cooled to 50°F (10°C) or less.

PATHOGENS

Disease-causing microorganisms; the source of many foodborne diseases.

PERISHABLE FOODS

Food products that spoil readily without special processing or preservation techniques; includes most products used daily in a food service facility: meats, poultry, fish, shellfish, eggs, dairy products, and most fruits and vegetables.

PERPETUAL INVENTORY

An ongoing record of what is in storage at any given time. As products are added to or removed from storage, the balance figure for each item is adjusted.

pH

The standard measure of acidity or alkalinity—the hydrogen ion concentration; an important influence on bacterial activity. Food products with pH values less than 7 are acidic; those with pH values greater than 7 are basic or alkaline. A pH of 7 is neutral.

PHENOLIC SANITIZERS

Pathogen-destroying compounds that act as deodorizers, but have limited applications and should not be used to sanitize food-handling equipment. They work well at pH levels between 6 and 7 and become more stable when combined with synthetic anionics.

PHYSICAL INVENTORY

An actual count of what is in storage, taken each time an income statement is prepared.

PLATE SERVICE

A variation of table service; basic service style in which fully cooked menu items are individually portioned, plated (put on plates) in the kitchen, and carried to each guest directly.

PLATTER SERVICE

A table service style in which servers carry platters of fully cooked food to the dining room, present them to the guest for approval, and then serve the food.

POISONING

A type of foodborne disease caused by ingesting (1) harmful chemicals, (2) poisonous plant or animal products, or (3) food contaminated with the poisonous waste products (toxins) of toxigenic bacteria or fungi.

POTENTIALLY HAZARDOUS FOOD

Any food or ingredient, natural or synthetic, in a form capable of supporting (1) the rapid and progressive growth of infectious or toxigenic microorganisms or (2) the slower growth of *C. botulinum*. Includes any food of animal origin, either raw or heat treated, and any food of plant origin which has been treated or which is raw seed sprouts.

PREMISES

The physical facility, its contents, and the contiguous land or property under the control of the food establishment permit-holder; or the physical facility, its contents, and the contiguous land or property and its facilities and contents that are under the control of the permit-holder that may affect food establishment personnel, facilities, or operations, if a food establishment is only one component of a larger organization such as a health care facility, hotel, motel, school, recreational camp, or prison.

PREPARING

The control point comprising the functions that must take place after food is issued and before food is cooked or otherwise readied for serving.

PRODUCT COST ANALYSIS FORM

A document used to calculate the cost per portion of standard recipes.

PRODUCTION

A combination of the preparing, cooking, and holding control points.

PSYCHROPHILES

Cold-loving microorganisms that can survive at temperatures as low as $-19°F$ $(-28°C)$, yet are able to reproduce at temperatures as high as $68°F$ $(20°C)$.

PURCHASE ORDER

A form that helps maintain purchasing control; it contains the details of an order placed with a supplier. This standard form is completed by the operation's buyer and sent to the supplier. A copy is retained to facilitate in-house recordkeeping.

PURCHASING

The control point important in maintaining the value and quality of products, minimizing the investment in inventory, and strengthening the operation's competitive position.

PUTREFACTION

Bacterial splitting of meat proteins, resulting in the formation of foul odors.

Q

QUATERNARY AMMONIUM COMPOUNDS (QUATS)

Stable sanitizers that have a long shelf life, are active against most microorganisms, work best at a pH of 9 to 10, and leave a film that controls bacterial growth. Non-corrosive and non-irritating, they eliminate and prevent odors, but destroy some microorganisms slowly and are incompatible with common detergents. They are expensive, and their residue makes them impractical for some uses. Usually applied in concentrations of 180 to 220 mg/L for one minute or longer at temperatures of 75°F (24°C) and above.

R

RATIONALIZATION

In menu planning, the creation of a simplified, balanced menu for the sake of guest satisfaction and operational efficiency; frequently results in a limited menu, but the operation can offer several menu items that use the same raw ingredients.

RECEIVING

A control point that involves checking the quality, quantity, and price of incoming purchased products; a critical control point wherein a food service operation assumes ownership of purchased products.

RECONSTITUTE

To recombine dehydrated food products with water or other liquids.

REQUISITION

A form for requesting inventory; an internal communication tool that shows which department needs which items. Required before products can be issued.

RESILIENT FLOOR

A relatively soft floor made of asphalt, linoleum, rubber, vinyl, or cork; reduces noise and staff member fatigue; usually requires sealing.

S

SANITARIAN

A representative of a regulatory agency, often called a health official or inspector, who may examine all areas of a food establishment and its records to obtain information on the purchase, receipt, and use of food supplies.

SANITIZATION

The destruction of pathogens that survive the cleaning process. It is necessary because items that look clean are not necessarily sanitary.

SANITIZERS

Chemical compounds that destroy pathogens. *See* **chlorine-based sanitizers, iodine-based sanitizers, quaternary ammonium compounds, acid-anionic surfactants,** and **phenolic sanitizers**.

SEMI-PERISHABLE FOOD

Food products that have a longer shelf life than perishable foods, but should be stored under recommended time-temperature combinations; includes nuts, apples, potatoes, and waxed vegetables such as cucumbers.

SERVING

The control point in which finished menu items are transferred from the production department to guests.

SIDESTAND

A service stand that holds supplies of tableware, ice, condiments, dairy products, and some beverages for easy access.

SOUS VIDE

Literally, under vacuum. A low-temperature food preservation method that consists of packaging food items in plastic bags or pouches, vacuum-sealing the pouches, and cooking the pouches of food while carefully controlling both moisture and temperature. The food is immediately chilled to stop the cooking, then it is stored refrigerated. The pouches may be reheated in hot water for service, or the fully cooked food may be served chilled.

SPLIT SERVICE

A food service method in which servers deliver courses separately; helps maintain food quality and safety because each course can be portioned and served when it is ready, eliminating short-term holding in the kitchen.

SPOILAGE ORGANISMS

Microorganisms that do not cause disease, but make food products unfit for human consumption by altering their color, odor, texture, taste, and appearance.

SPORES

Dormant forms assumed by some bacilli-shaped microorganisms. Spores are vegetative cells subjected to environmental conditions that are unfavorable for reproduction.

STANDARD PORTION SIZES

Consistent serving sizes; made possible by following standard recipes exactly to obtain intended yields; using scales and other measuring devices during preparation, cooking, and portioning; purchasing pre-portioned foods when available; and portioning as many items as possible during preparation.

STANDARD PURCHASE SPECIFICATIONS

Written guidelines that precisely define the quality, quantity, and other characteristics of the products an establishment buys.

STANDARD RECIPE

A written procedure for the production of a given food item; lists the exact quantity of each ingredient to be used, the sequential order in which ingredients are put together, cooking times and temperatures, and the equipment necessary to produce the finished product. Essential for consistency in product quality, sanitation, and cost.

STANDARD RECIPE COST

The cost per portion of finished menu items—information necessary for pricing menu items accurately. Calculated by adding the costs of all ingredients in a recipe (total product cost) and dividing by the yield (number of servings).

STATE OR LOCAL REGULATORY AGENCY

The public health authority that has the greatest influence over sanitation regulations in a particular food establishment.

STATIONARY PHASE

The third stage of bacterial growth. In this stage, the number of new bacterial cells equals the number of dying cells, so the total number of cells remains constant; there is no *net* increase in the bacterial population.

STERILIZATION

A process that destroys virtually all microorganisms and their spores. Heating for sterilization usually takes place in a large container which is pressurized according to the food product, its ability to withstand heat, and packaging.

STORAGE AREA CONDITION REPORT

A record of the temperatures of food storage areas, taken twice each day. Other information may also be noted.

STORED FOOD INSECTS

Pests that render stored food products unfit for human consumption.

STORING

The control point that protects valuable food products from deterioration and theft; standards for different types of storage (dry, refrigerated, and frozen) provide this protection.

T

TEMPERATURE DANGER ZONE (TDZ)

The temperature range of 41°F (5°C) to 140°F (60°C), defined by the U.S. Public Health Service as the range in which most pathogenic activity takes place and food spoilage can occur. The TDZ may vary in your locality; check with your state or local regulatory agency.

TEMPORARY FOOD ESTABLISHMENT

A food establishment that operates at a fixed location for not more than 14 consecutive days in conjunction with a single event or celebration.

THERMOPHILES

Microbes that prefer temperatures from 113°F (45°C) to 140°F (60°C), and sometimes higher.

TIME-TEMPERATURE MONITOR

A device used for perishable product inspection during receiving; it is attached to boxes or cartons of refrigerated and frozen products just before they leave the processing plant. Measures the combined effects of heat and age by changing color when a product's temperature exceeds a certain level for an excessive length of time, allowing an operation's receiver to quickly see whether a product has been thawed and then refrozen.

TRUTH-IN-MENU REGULATIONS

State and local laws requiring accurate menu descriptions of raw ingredients and finished menu items. For example, the correct quality or grade of food products must be stated; care must be exercised when USDA grades are printed on the menu. Items billed as "fresh" must truly be fresh. A product's point of origin must also be represented accurately.

V

VALUE-ADDED DISTRIBUTORS

Suppliers who offer services beyond those normally expected, including nutritional analysis, quality control testing, idea shows geared toward certain market segments, product education, computer services, and others.

VEGETATIVE CELL

An actively growing bacterial cell that can reproduce.

VELOCITY REPORT

A computer printout provided by a supplier of all the products ordered by a food establishment during a given period (such as a week, a month, or a year). The report is a management tool for analyzing loss, waste, and theft.

W

WATER ACTIVITY (a$_w$)

The amount of water available to microorganisms. The water activity value is the ratio of the water vapor pressure in the food to the vapor pressure of pure water at the same temperature.

Index

QUALITY SANITATION MANAGEMENT

REVIEW QUIZ ANSWER KEY

The numbers in parentheses refer to the learning objective addressed by the question and the page where the answer may be found.

Chapter 1	Chapter 2	Chapter 3	Chapter 4
1. b (LO1, 4)	1. b (LO1, 36)	1. d (LO2, 78)	1. b (LO1, 128)
2. a (LO2, 4)	2. c (LO2, 38)	2. c (LO3, 83)	2. c (LO2, 128)
3. b (LO3, 7)	3. d (LO3, 39)	3. d (LO4, 87-88)	3. b (LO2, 128)
4. d (LO4, 8)	4. a (LO4, 41)	4. a (LO4, 86)	4. b (LO3, 131)
5. a (LO5, 8-9)	5. d (LO5, 42)	5. d (LO4, 87)	5. c (LO3, 133)
6. d (LO6, 9)	6. b (LO6, 45)	6. a (LO5, 93)	6. c (LO4, 133)
7. c (LO7, 14)	7. c (LO7, 52)	7. c (LO6, 95)	7. b (LO5, 145)
8. a (LO8, 23)	8. d (LO8, 62)	8. a (LO7, 112)	8. c (LO5, 151)
9. a (LO9, 26, 29)	9. a (LO9, 62)	9. c (LO8, 117)	9. a (LO6, 160)
10. c (LO10, 28)	10. a (LO10, 63)	10. b (LO9, 120)	10. c (LO6, 159)

Chapter 5	Chapter 6	Chapter 7	Chapter 8
1. a (LO1, 169)	1. d (LO1, 217)	1. a (LO1, 252)	1. c (LO1, 298)
2. c (LO2, 170)	2. a (LO2, 219)	2. d (LO2, 257)	2. a (LO2, 299)
3. d (LO3, 172-173)	3. a (LO3, 221)	3. a (LO3, 260)	3. d (LO2, 301)
4. b (LO4, 174)	4. b (LO4, 223)	4. b (LO3, 260)	4. c (LO3, 302-303)
5. c (LO5, 178)	5. c (LO5, 223-224)	5. a (LO4, 268)	5. d (LO4, 305)
6. d (LO5, 177)	6. c (LO6, 228)	6. c (LO5, 271)	6. c (LO5, 308)
7. c (LO6, 179)	7. a (LO7, 228)	7. c (LO5, 274)	7. a (LO6, 309)
8. b (LO6, 182)	8. c (LO8, 233)	8. d (LO6, 274)	8. c (LO7, 310-311)
9. a (LO7, 186)	9. b (LO8, 233)	9. c (LO7, 277)	9. c (LO7, 311)
10. c (LO8, 197)	10. a (LO9, 236)	10. a (LO8, 281)	10. a (LO8, 311)

Chapter 9	Chapter 10
1. a (LO1, 323)	1. a (LO1, 365)
2. a (LO2, 324)	2. c (LO1, 371)
3. b (LO3, 326)	3. a (LO1, 365)
4. c (LO3, 326)	4. b (LO2, 373)
5. b (LO4, 326)	5. c (LO3, 376)
6. c (LO5, 332)	6. a (LO3, 377)
7. c (LO6, 336–337)	7. a (LO4, 378)
8. a (LO7, 350)	8. b (LO5, 386)
9. c (LO8, 352)	9. b (LO5, 385)
10. a (LO9, 353)	10. c (LO6, 390)